TECHNICAL WRITING
FOR SUCCESS

FOURTH EDITION

Darlene Smith-Worthington
& Sue Jefferson

CENGAGE

Australia · Brazil · Mexico · Singapore · United Kingdom · United States

Technical Writing for Success, **Fourth Edition**
Darlene Smith-Worthington & Sue Jefferson

SVP, GM Skills & Global Product Management: Jonathan Lau

Product Director: Matt Seeley

Associate Product Manager: Kelly Lischynsky

Executive Director of Development: Marah Bellegarde

Senior Product Development Manager: Larry Main

Senior Content Developer: Anne Orgren

Product Assistant: Mara Ciacelli

Vice President, Marketing Services: Jennifer Ann Baker

Marketing Manager: Scott Chrysler

Senior Content Project Manager: Nina Tucciarelli

Design Director: Jack Pendleton

Text and Cover Design: kedesign

Cover image(s): agsandrew/Shutterstock

For product information and technology assistance, contact us at
Cengage Learning Customer & Sales Support, 1-800-354-9706

For permission to use material from this text or product, submit all requests online at **www.cengage.com/permissions.**
Further permissions questions can be e-mailed to
permissionrequest@cengage.com

Library of Congress Control Number: 2017948365

ISBN: 978-1-305-94882-2

Cengage
20 Channel Street
Boston, MA 02210
USA

Cengage is a leading provider of customized learning solutions with employees residing in nearly 40 different countries and sales in more than 125 countries around the world. Find your local representative at **www.cengage.com.**

Cengage products are represented in Canada by Nelson Education, Ltd.

To learn more about Cengage platforms and services, register or access your online learning solution, or purchase materials for your course, visit **www.cengage.com.**

Notice to the Reader
Publisher does not warrant or guarantee any of the products described herein or perform any independent analysis in connection with any of the product information contained herein. Publisher does not assume, and expressly disclaims, any obligation to obtain and include information other than that provided to it by the manufacturer. The reader is expressly warned to consider and adopt all safety precautions that might be indicated by the activities described herein and to avoid all potential hazards. By following the instructions contained herein, the reader willingly assumes all risks in connection with such instructions. The publisher makes no representations or warranties of any kind, including but not limited to, the warranties of fitness for particular purpose or merchantability, nor are any such representations implied with respect to the material set forth herein, and the publisher takes no responsibility with respect to such material. The publisher shall not be liable for any special, consequential, or exemplary damages resulting, in whole or part, from the readers' use of, or reliance upon, this material.

Printed in the United States of America
Print Number: 03   Print Year: 2019

CONTENTS

AN APPLIED APPROACH TO WORKPLACE WRITING!

Welcome to the Fourth Edition of *Technical Writing for Success*. This text is lively and relevant for students, and easy to use and effective for instructors. Using a learn-by-doing approach, skills are introduced and applied so that mastering technical writing is relevant and exciting.

GETTING STARTED

GOALS are clearly defined learning objectives to guide learning.

TERMS are highlighted and defined in the chapter.

WHAT IF? questions relating to the sample documents provide students with critical-thinking opportunities.

WRITE TO LEARN activities prepare students for the chapter's detailed instruction.

FOCUS ON . . . provides questions to help students analyze the sample document on the facing page.

Real-world **SAMPLE DOCUMENTS** add relevance to the chapter.

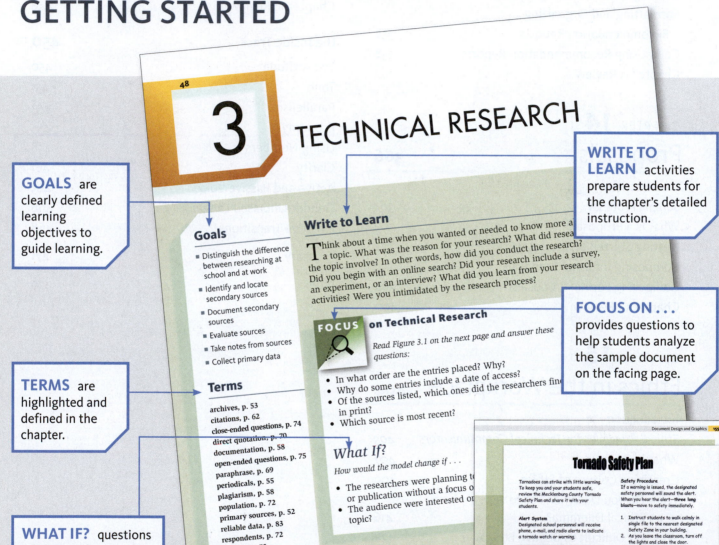

48

3 TECHNICAL RESEARCH

Goals

- Distinguish the difference between researching at school and at work
- Identify and locate secondary sources
- Document secondary sources
- Evaluate sources
- Take notes from sources
- Collect primary data

Terms

archives, p. 53
citations, p. 62
close-ended questions, p. 74
direct quotation, p. 70
documentation, p. 58
open-ended questions, p. 75
paraphrase, p. 69
periodicals, p. 55
plagiarism, p. 58
population, p. 72
primary sources, p. 52
reliable data, p. 83
respondents, p. 72
sample, p. 72
secondary sources, p. 52
summarize, p. 69
valid data, p. 82

Write to Learn

Think about a time when you wanted or needed to know more about a topic. What was the reason for your research? What did research the topic involve? In other words, how did you conduct the research? Did you begin with an online search? Did your research include a survey, an experiment, or an interview? What did you learn from your research activities? Were you intimidated by the research process?

FOCUS on Technical Research

Read Figure 3.1 on the next page and answer these questions:

- In what order are the entries placed? Why?
- Why do some entries include a date of access?
- Of the sources listed, which ones did the researchers find in print?
- Which source is most recent?

What If?

How would the model change if . . .

- The researchers were planning to or publication without a focus o
- The audience were interested on topic?

Document Design and Graphics **155**

Tornado Safety Plan

Tornadoes can strike with little warning. To keep you and your students safe, review the Mecklenburg County Tornado Safety Plan and share it with your students.

Alert System
Designated school personnel will receive phone, e-mail, and radio alerts to indicate a tornado watch or warning.

Tornado Watch
Conditions are favorable for a tornado.
Tornado Warning
A tornado has been spotted or indicated on radar.

If a tornado warning is issued, the alarm will sound—**three long blasts.**

Designated Personnel
Table 1 lists contact information for the designated safety personnel.

Personnel	Phone Numbers
Dr. C. Webber, Superintendent	704-555-0114
Dr. R. Gaskins, Principal ELS	704-555-0115
V. Romerez, Safety Officer ELS	704-555-0116
Dr. T. Mazurka, Principal EHS	704-555-0117
K. Isenhour, Safety Officer EHS	704-555-0118
Dr. C. Shaut, Principal EMS	704-555-0119
S. Cho, Safety Officer EMS	704-555-0120

Table 1. Emergency Contacts

Once a tornado warning has been issued, designated personnel will tune in to one of the local stations below and stay tuned until the danger has passed.

WKIX FM Radio 91.5
WNRT TV Channel 8

Safety Procedure
If a warning is issued, the designated safety personnel will sound the alert. When you hear the alert—**three long blasts**—move to safety immediately.

1. Instruct students to walk calmly in single file to the nearest designated Safety Zone in your building.
2. As you leave the classroom, turn off the lights and close the door. DO NOT stop to open the windows. Spend your time getting to safety.

Safety Zones
Each school has posted signs in hallways showing the location of the Safety Zones. The orange signs, like the one in Figure 1, have the words *SAFETY ZONE* and an arrow directing students to the appropriate area in their school. Become familiar with the signs and the location of designated Safety Zones.

SAFETY ZONE
This way

Figure 1 Safety Zone Sign

"Duck and Cover" Position
When students arrive at the Safety Zone, instruct them to get on their knees facing the interior walls. Students should assume the "duck and cover" position (duck and cover the head) illustrated in Figure 2.

Figure 2. "Duck and Cover" Position

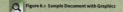 **Figure 6.1 Sample Document with Graphics**

A LOOK INTO THE REAL WORLD OF TECHNICAL WRITING

Writing @Work

Agriculture, Food & Natural Resources
Source: The Center to Advance CTE

Mark Overbay manages marketing and communications for Counter Culture Coffee, a Durham, North Carolina–based specialty coffee organization. His many responsibilities include producing product copy, white papers, advertisements, packaging copy, online content, thematic signage, and tradeshow displays.

"Marketing is a form of storytelling," says Mark, who believes that marketing copy must be "short and sweet." "You only have a few words or phrases to 'hook' your readers, whether they are journalists reading a press release or grocery shoppers glancing at the coffee bags on a shelf. Good marketing copy must tell an interesting, sometimes even romantic story, but it should never be long-winded."

Mark's biggest technical writing challenge involves presentation and style: "Developing a Counter Culture Coffee 'voice' that authentically represents our company and all that we do is the most difficult aspect of my professional writing. When I write for our online news section or blog, I can write as Mark Overbay; but most of my professional writing is in the voice of Counter Culture Coffee, which represents not just me, but more than 40 staff members and hundreds of partnering coffee farmers."

Mark relies heavily on e-mail. "E-mail, for all its limitations and sterility, is invaluable in my professional life. Not only does it allow for structured written communication and instant delivery, but it also provides a permanent record of every e-conversation."

Mark advises aspiring technical writers to hone three skills in particular: (1) work ethic to constantly improve their writing; (2) preparation and care for each assignment because "every word and detail matters. Successful communicators take the time to research their subjects thoroughly"; and (3) clarity because "successful communicators keep things simple—not dumbed down—and to the point. Be clear, concise, and confident in your message."

Think Critically

1. Search for the Counter Culture Coffee website and sample some of the writing. Does the writing tell stories, as Mark claims? Do you hear a distinctive "voice" in the writing? Explain.

2. What is a white paper? Research the origin of this term. What are some topics about which Mark might write papers?

Printed with permission of Mark Overbay

Writing in Agriculture, Food, & Natural Resources

Conservation scientists work to preserve our natural resources, such as our farmland, rivers, and forests.

As scientists, conservationists understand the rigor imposed by the scientific method and thus the necessity for objective reporting and accurate data entry using the tools of forestry. A forester, for example, may estimate tree growth using clinometers to measure tree heights or may measure forest density by using remote sensing technology. Accurate record keeping enables conservationists to make informed recommendations such as sustainable practices for harvesting timber. The records also ensure compliance with government regulations.

In addition, conservationists engage in other kinds of writing—from the practical to the political. They may negotiate terms for land use management and assist in writing contracts with land owners. Conservationists write grants, such as the $300,000 grant from the Renewable Resources Extension Act to restore Strentzel Meadow, part of the John Muir National Historic Site. They also argue for environmental responsibility with new recycling or tree conservation initiatives. Luke Wallin suggests a three-part structure for such scientific journalism: Articles should establish a bond with the reader through shared values, present new information, and then call for an action—a request for money or a letter to a senator for political support (124).

WRITING@WORK addresses the 16 Career Clusters and demonstrates various career options while showcasing people who use technical writing in their careers.

NEW: WRITING IN THE DISCIPLINES immediately follows each chapter's "Writing@Work" feature and is tied to the same career cluster that is featured in the related "Writing @ Work" profile.

Writing @Work

Education & Training
Source: The Center to Advance CTE

Sonya Parrish is a teaching associate and doctoral student in literature at Miami University in Oxford, Ohio. She has taught first-year college composition courses for three years. She researches primary and secondary sources regularly for her roles as graduate student and English teacher and incorporates technical writing in the syllabus for her composition courses.

Sonya's scholarly research includes hunting through digital archives, essays, and books by other scholars and through the literature in her field. "I rely heavily on using print sources in which I can write notes, underline important points or quotes, and make comments in the margins. I also compile notes from texts into Word documents that present the information in a more unified and organized manner."

Sonya teaches her students to evaluate sources using five criteria: authorship, objectivity, knowledge, accuracy, and relevance. When evaluating websites, Sonya helps her students see the way in which information on the Web is authored and constructed.

Different kinds of sites—such as .org and .edu sites—deliver different kinds of information to different audiences in different ways.

When scholarly research responds thoughtfully to other scholars' work, it creates a dialogue that requires proper documentation. "Writers should acknowledge others who have provided them with information on a given topic," according to Sonya. "They should also think about their audience's expectations of accuracy and honesty in writing." She uses GPS navigation instructions as a metaphor for what proper citations should do: show the reader what "path" the author took in constructing his or her argument and prove that the path is credible. Another scholar or teacher, like Sonya, can then pick up the hunt for information using the bibliographical trail left by other authors.

Think Critically

1. If Sonya were getting an advanced degree in biology or architecture, would she rely as heavily on printed source material? Why or why not?

2. Suppose Sonya is teaching a section about Maya Angelou's poetry. Give an example of a primary source and a secondary source that Sonya might use.

Printed with permission of Sonya Parrish

Writing in Education and Training

People who work in education and training usually need strong communication skills. One of their roles is to share their skills with learners, whether those learners are young people in primary or secondary schools, adults in colleges and universities, or adults in the workplace or in other areas of society. Whether a student in second grade or an engineer who requires training on a new computer-assisted drafting (CAD) program, every student should receive clear, accurate, detailed, and complete instruction in a form which he or she can easily understand. In addition, educators and trainers must engage their audiences, so they need the ability to use technology effectively to convey a clear message. Another role of education and training professionals is to advance the body of knowledge in their fields. Thus, these professionals write reports and journal articles as well as books using the style manual accepted by professionals in the given field to disseminate research findings and new ideas and interpretations. For instance, a biology professor who wants to publish an article on her most recent research results could use CBE (Council of Biology Editors) style, the manual issued by the Council of Science Editors. An art or history professor wanting to submit a manuscript for publication might use the University of Chicago's *Chicago Manual of Style*, while a Spanish or American literature researcher would likely use the Modern Language Association's *MLA Handbook for Writers of Research Papers*.

CAREER CLUSTERS

The U.S. Department of Education has grouped careers into 16 different clusters based on similar job characteristics.

The value of using these clusters is that they:

- Show the importance of writing in all careers

- Allow students to explore a wide range of career opportunities from entry level through management and professional levels

- Provide an easy solution to implementing careers into any class

SPECIAL FEATURES ENHANCE LEARNING

Discriminating readers use their critical-thinking skills to look out for information that is inaccurate, biased, sensationalized, or lacking in pertinent details.

When you use material from your reading, you have an ethical obligation to double-check its accuracy, looking for other sources that report the same findings. Publications that must be produced quickly—such as newspapers, magazines, and books on the latest technology—are prone to errors. Information published with few, if any,

editorial guidelines—for example, some articles on the Internet and stories in tabloids—cannot be trusted.

The next time you find an Internet article that promises the fountain of youth or hands you a get-rich-quick scheme, be skeptical and remember: You cannot believe everything you read.

Think Critically

What might motivate people to publish articles that are not completely factual?

Communication Dilemma

Focus on Ethics

Claudia is setting up a website for her floral business, Claudia's Creations. She is in a hurry to get the site up and running. She wants to show some of the sprays, wedding bouquets, and dish gardens she has created, but she cannot find the pictures she took of them. So she searches the Web and finds designs that she likes on two websites: Floral Fantasia and Flowers by Chenda. Claudia decides to use some of the designs from those sites on her own website until she

finds her misplaced pictures or takes new ones.

Think Critically

What might happen if Claudia's customers discover that she used flower designs from other sites?

Communication Dilemma provides real-world communication situations.

Focus on Ethics provides examples and scenarios of real-world ethical dilemmas for students to consider.

Communication Technologies

Communication Technologies contains helpful information about current workplace technologies.

Want to shore up your interview skills while you walk the dog? Help is available for both Android and Apple devices with Job Interview Questions and Answers from Career Confidential. It's an interactive video app to give you practice with "tough interview questions in an easy-to-use mock interview format." You can practice and compare your answers to suggestions supplied by a professional coach. Play Store also offers 101 HR Interview Questions from Programmerworld with 16 categories of questions.

With The SimuGator, an iTunes app with over 50 questions, users can experience various interviewing styles from different interviewers.

Think Critically

What is the benefit to using an app to help you practice your interview skills? Is there some way the app could hurt your performance during an interview?

 WARM UP 7.4 SPECIAL WEB CONTENT

Warm Up activities provide scenarios and questions to encourage students to start thinking ahead for each section of the text.

Describe your experiences with two of these situations: (1) choosing a theme for a prom, a dance, a reunion, or a holiday event; (2) keeping a journal; (3) answering the same questions over and over; (4) collaborating on a project; or (5) writing posts on Facebook.

The Web offers a new medium for established ways of communicating. The type of writing is not altogether new, but when the audience and medium change, good writers adapt. The result? New avenues of writing for existing genres. Six of these adaptations are outlined next: home page, blog, FAQ, wiki, social media, and video sharing.

Home Page

Think of your website as a theme park. Your park may have many areas—rides, a petting zoo, edutainment, restaurants, and more, or only a single nature trail. The home page of your website is like the entrance to the park. Because you want many visitors, you design an inviting entrance, one that

Stop and Think allows students to check comprehension before moving to the next section.

STOP AND THINK 7.4

Name five types of writing assignments adapted especially for the Web. Choose two and describe them in detail.

ABUNDANT END-OF-CHAPTER ASSESSMENT

The assessments found at the end of every chapter give students the opportunity to test their knowledge.

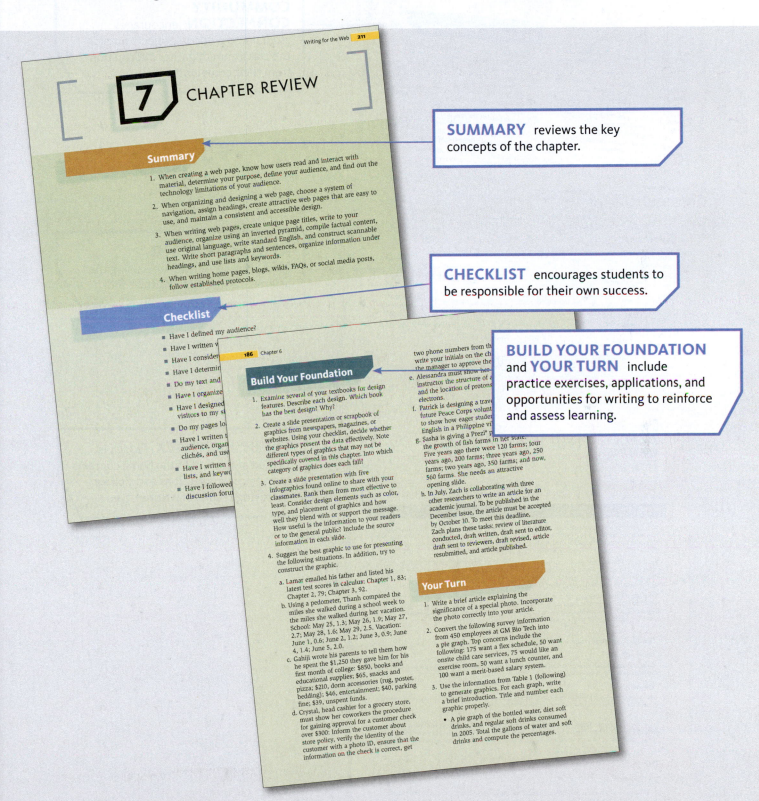

7 CHAPTER REVIEW

Summary

1. When creating a web page, know how users read and interact with material, determine your purpose, define your audience, and find out the technology limitations of your audience.

2. When organizing and designing a web page, choose a system of navigation, assign headings, create attractive web pages that are easy to use, and maintain a consistent and accessible design.

3. When writing web pages, create unique page titles, write to your audience, organize using an inverted pyramid, compile factual content, use original language, write standard English, and construct scannable text. Write short paragraphs and sentences, organize information under headings, and use lists and keywords.

4. When writing home pages, blogs, wikis, FAQs, or social media posts, follow established protocols.

SUMMARY reviews the key concepts of the chapter.

Checklist

- Have I defined my audience?
- Have I written v
- Have I consider
- Have I determin
- Do my text and
- Have I organize
- Have I designed
  visitors to my si
- Do my pages lo
- Have I written t
  audience, organ
  clichés, and use
- Have I written s
  lists, and keywo
- Have I followed
  discussion foru

CHECKLIST encourages students to be responsible for their own success.

BUILD YOUR FOUNDATION and **YOUR TURN** include practice exercises, applications, and opportunities for writing to reinforce and assess learning.

186   Chapter 6

Build Your Foundation

1. Examine several of your textbooks for design features. Describe each design. Which book has the best design? Why?

2. Create a slide presentation or scrapbook of graphics from newspapers, magazines, or websites. Using your checklist, decide whether the graphics present the data effectively. Note different types of graphics that may not be specifically covered in this chapter. Into which category of graphics does each fall?

3. Create a slide presentation with five infographics found online to share with your classmates. Rank them from most effective to least. Consider design elements such as color, type, and placement of graphics and how well they blend with or support the message. How useful is the information to your readers or to the general public? Include the source information in each slide.

4. Suggest the best graphic to use for presenting the following situations. In addition, try to construct the graphic.

   a. Lamar emailed his father and listed his latest test scores in calculus: Chapter 1, 83; Chapter 2, 79; Chapter 3, 92.

   b. Using a pedometer, Thanh compared the miles she walked during a school week to the miles she walked during her vacation. School: May 25, 1.3; May 26, 1.9; May 27, 2.7; May 28, 1.6; May 29, 2.5. Vacation: June 1, 0.6; June 2, 1.2; June 3, 0.9; June 4, 1.4; June 5, 2.0.

   c. Gahiji wrote his parents to tell them how he spent the $1,250 they gave him for his first month of college: $850, books and educational supplies; $65, snacks and pizza; $210, dorm accessories (rug, poster, bedding); $46, entertainment; $40, parking fine; $39, unspent funds.

   d. Crystal, head cashier for a grocery store, must show her coworkers the procedure for gaining approval for a customer check over $300: Inform the customer about store policy, verify the identity of the customer with a photo ID, ensure that the information on the check is correct, get

two phone numbers from the
write your initials on the ch
the manager to approve the

e. Alessandra must show her
instructor the structure of a
and the location of protons
electrons.

f. Patrick is designing a trave
future Peace Corps volunt
to show how eager studen
English in a Philippine vi

g. Sasha is giving a Prezi® p
the growth of fish farms in her state.
Five years ago there were 120 farms; four years ago, 200 farms; three years ago, 250 farms; two years ago, 350 farms; and now, 560 farms. She needs an attractive opening slide.

h. In July, Zach is collaborating with three other researchers to write an article for an academic journal. To be published in the December issue, the article must be accepted by October 10. To meet this deadline, Zach plans these tasks: review of literature conducted, draft written, draft sent to editor, draft sent to reviewers, draft revised, article resubmitted, and article published.

Your Turn

1. Write a brief article explaining the significance of a special photo. Incorporate the photo correctly into your article.

2. Convert the following survey information from 450 employees at GM Bio Tech into a pie graph. Top concerns include the following: 175 want a flex schedule, 50 want onsite child care services, 75 would like an exercise room, 50 want a lunch counter, and 100 want a merit-based salary system.

3. Use the information from Table 1 (following) to generate graphics. For each graph, write a brief introduction. Title and number each graphic properly.

   - A pie graph of the bottled water, diet soft drinks, and regular soft drinks consumed in 2005. Total the gallons of water and soft drinks and compute the percentages.

SPECIAL FEATURES ENHANCE LEARNING

3. Write an essay or a paragraph on a topic of your choice. After you complete one draft, exchange papers with at least two of your classmates. Ask them to make comments using the list of questions for copyediting in this chapter.

4. Select one of the following topics and write a one-page essay: Why people should exercise regularly, why people should stay informed about news events, or why people should recycle. Then practice writing collaboratively by dividing the topic into stages. Writer 1 will prewrite and organize three subtopics and pass the prewriting to Writer 2. Writer 2 will write the first draft and pass the draft to Writer 3. Writer 3 will revise and pass the revision to Writer 4, who will edit the revision, make changes, and submit the final draft.

5. In small groups, write a letter to the editor of your local newspaper, expressing your views on a current event (for example, a choice of a political candidate, the way your tax dollars are spent, or a community concern). Individually, brainstorm ideas, organize your ideas, and take notes. In one session, write the letter as a group. Ask one person to copyedit the final version, bringing it back to class for the group to see.

6. Think of the last time you worked on a group project. What kind of experience did you have? What were the benefits of working with this group? What were the drawbacks? What could you do differently the next time you are part of a group to make sure you have a positive experience? Write a one- to two-page analysis.

Community Connection

1. Interview a writer in your area (a reporter, technical writer, local novelist, or public relations expert) about his or her writing process. Does the writer come up with topics, or does someone else provide them? What advice, if any, does the writer have for your classmates? What technology does the writer find most helpful? Summarize the writer's process and share your findings with the class. If possible, bring to class something the writer has written. Better yet, invite the writer to class to talk about the writing process.

2. Help another person with all or part of the writing process for a writing project. You might help a family member or a member of Big Brothers Big Sisters or AmeriCorp. Coach the person through the stages of the writing process. Write a description of your experience.

3. Interview employees in your area, asking how often they work collaboratively, what kinds of projects they complete collaboratively, which technology aids they use, and how they organize tasks.

EXPLORE THE NET

Choose five boldfaced terms from the chapter. Then visit the Merriam-Webster online dictionary and use the thesaurus to find one or two synonyms for each term you chose. Do the synonyms help you remember the definitions of the terms? Explain.

COMMUNITY CONNECTION encourages students to work on projects outside the classroom to gather information from their community.

NEW: EXPLORE THE NET focuses on students using the Internet to research information.

TECH WRITING TIPS

THE INSIDE TRACK

THE INSIDE TRACK, which is located at the end of the book, contains 24 pages of suggestions and tips for improving technical writing style.

YOU ATTITUDE

With the exception of the science lab report, most technical writing should be reader-centered rather than writer-centered. A reader-centered approach, or *you* attitude, attempts to look at situations from the reader's perspective instead of the writer's perspective. The *you* attitude points out advantages to the reader and makes him or her more likely to accept what the writer says.

Use the *you* attitude to persuade your audience to think or act in a certain way. For example, you might send an e-mail to your supervisor asking for time off, a letter to a newspaper editor opposing a proposed city curfew, or a message to a dry cleaner asking for a reduction in your bill because your clothes were not clean when you picked them up.

Notice the difference between the *I* or *we* attitude and the *you* attitude in the following example. The *you* attitude sounds friendlier and more positive. The *you* attitude stresses how a customer can benefit from buying a home from Mountain View Homes. Using the *you* approach is psychologically smart as a motivator, and it makes a good sales pitch.

Manufactured Home Dealer

***I* or *we* attitude:**

Do we, at Mountain View Homes, have deals! Our 14 × 70 single-wides have been marked down 20%. And our 14 × 80s can be purchased with a rebate of $1,000!

***You* attitude:**

You can find a real deal at Mountain View Homes. You can purchase our 14 × 70 single-wides at 20% off the regular price. And you can receive a rebate of $1,000 on a brand new 14 × 80.

To use the *you* attitude, simply consider the situation from your reader's viewpoint. What is the advantage to him or her? Then, where appropriate, add more *you*'s and *your*'s to your message and take out some of the *I*'s, *we*'s, or company names. Point out the benefit of your message to your reader.

THE INSIDE TRACK: *YOUR TURN*

1. Rewrite these sentences to reflect a stronger *you* attitude. Remember, you cannot eliminate uses of *I, we,* and company names, but you can slant the writing to be more reader-centered. Add any information that will help the reader see the advantages.

   a. We will ship the rest of your order next week.

   b. Powell Insurance Company is reliable. We have been in business at the same location for more than 50 years.

ABOUT THE AUTHORS

Darlene Smith-Worthington is currently enjoying retirement after 30-plus years of teaching at Pitt Community College. Having served as Interim Director of the Developmental Studies Department, Coordinator of Developmental Reading and English, and Director of PCC Abroad, Darlene misses her colleagues and students. However, she is finding new challenges in building a house and supporting other family projects. Darlene has enjoyed diverse employment experiences, including managing a poultry farm and editing a weekly newspaper, and recreation opportunities, including world travel, scuba diving, and gardening/farming. In retirement, she hopes to cook more, travel more, and enjoy times with friends and family more. And she may even decide to teach some more!

Sue Jefferson currently chairs the English and Humanities Department at Pitt Community College, where she teaches composition, critical thinking, mythology, and literature. Early in her teaching career, she taught grades 7–12 and more recently spent seven months teaching English at the Wuxi Institute of Technology in China. In addition to teaching, Sue has managed a restaurant, edited a weekly newspaper, and directed a choir. Traveling, yoga, t'ai chi, and swimming provide balance for her busy life. Sue's best writing is done on her porch overlooking the Pamlico River.

REVIEWERS

Julie Book
Oklahoma Panhandle
State University

Michael P. Collins
Arizona State University

Lisa J. G. Karney
Fortis Institute
(Pennsylvania)

Joseph McCallus
Columbus State University
(Georgia)

Rochelle Morris
Bethune Cookman
University (Florida)

James W. Savage
Ivy Tech Community
College (Indiana)

NEW TO THIS EDITION

New Features

Writing in the Disciplines

A **new feature,** "Writing in the Disciplines," immediately follows each chapter's "Writing@Work" feature and is tied to the same career cluster discipline that is featured in the related "Writing@Work" profile.

Explore the Net

A **new end-of-chapter activity,** Explore the Net (based on previous-edition Net Bookmarks), focuses on students using the Internet to research information.

Chapter Updates

Chapter 1: What Is Technical Writing?

- Restructured chapter to include a variety of technical writing models up front
- Added new topic: following standard conventions of the genre
- Updated models and discussion to differentiate academic, technical, and imaginative writing

Chapter 2: Audience and Purpose

- Included brief segments on rhetorical situation, need for rhetorical sensitivity, and appeals to ethos, pathos, kairos, and logos
- Included segments illustrating context for traditional media (print, TV, radio) and online media (social media, web presence); new graphic illustrating how traditional and nontraditional media can complement each other
- Updated terms in the exercises

Chapter 3: Technical Research

- Updated opening Working Bibliography, including recent research on the topic, and used ACS style, appropriate to the topic of the research
- Included sections on Write the Survey Results, Write the Interview Results, Write the Observation Results, and Write the Experiment Results
- Added references, tips, and uses of newer electronic devices for research
- Updated information on research resources, such as WorldCat and Deep Web
- Updated reference materials and Communication Technologies
- Revised Communication Dilemma
- Included information on APA, CSE, and Chicago Manual of Style
- Included notetaking software and survey-generating sites
- Revised model survey for electronic delivery

- Added enhanced interviewing guides
- Updated instructions in "Build Your Foundation" to use any style guide instructor requires

Chapter 4: Writing Process

- Added new topic: analysis of rhetorical situation
- Added new topic: using Collaboration Tools section with technology focus (wikis, coauthoring software, online meetings)
- Added concept map
- Updated Communication Technologies and Communication Dilemma

Chapter 5: Brief Correspondence

- Updated opening models and added an e-mail message as a third sample
- Included electronic correspondence, such as instant messages, blogs, and e-mail
- Updated Communication Dilemma

Chapter 6: Document Design and Graphics

- Added new visual aids including horizontal bar graph, divided column graph, histogram, information graphic (infographic), and poster board presentations
- Updated bar and line graphs in Theresa's story to be more realistic
- Updated Communication Technologies and Communication Dilemma
- Updated exercises and technology discussion

Chapter 7: Writing for the Web

- Updated webpage screen shots
- Added new topic: writing script for an informative video
- Updated Communication Technologies

Chapter 8: Informative Reports

- Added a scientific technical process description and revised the mechanical technical process description
- Changed Example of a Mechanism description

Chapter 9: Investigative Reports

- Updated Example of Trip Report
- Revised Communication Dilemma and end-of-chapter activities

Chapter 10: Instructions

- Changed opening model, Sample Instructions
- Changed Instructions Using Images (Pictures) Only
- Revised Communication Technologies
- Revised and expanded information on online instructions

Chapter 11: Employment Communication

- Updated models
- Added new topic: video resume
- Added new topic: creating a web presence using ePortfolio and social media
- Added new models: About Me example and ePortfolio home page

Chapter 12: Presentations

- Changed opening model, Sample Presentation Graphics
- Updated to discuss recent presentation software

Chapter 13: Recommendation Reports

- Revised opening model, Sample Recommendation Report, to use real 2016 hybrid vehicles
- Added a brief section to include references in recommendation reports
- Revised Communication Technologies

Chapter 14: Proposals

- Updated opening model, Sample Internal Proposal, for dates and costs
- Added a brief section on collaboration
- Revised the Formal Proposal model to suggest replacing metal halide lamps with LED bulbs and fixtures (a more current and realistic discussion)

Chapter 15: Ethics in the Workplace

- Updated most accounts of unethical practice to include more current examples
- Added new topic: healthy work environment including Title VII of the Civil Rights Act
- Added new topic: ethical challenges of emerging technology, including discussions of gene therapy, electronic surveillance, and artificial intelligence

Chapter 16: Technical Reading

- Updated most reading excerpts and graphics
- Added new topic: how to read online including how to evaluate a website
  Added new topic: how to "read" a video

SUPPLEMENTAL TEACHING AND LEARNING MATERIALS

MindTap: Empower Your Students

MindTap is a platform that propels students from memorization to mastery. It gives you complete control of your course, so you can provide engaging content, challenge every learner, and build student confidence. Customize interactive syllabi to emphasize priority topics, then add your own material or notes to the eBook as desired. This outcomes-driven application gives you the tools needed to empower students and boost both understanding and performance.

Access Everything You Need in One Place

Cut down on prep with the preloaded and organized MindTap course materials. Teach more efficiently with interactive assignments, quizzes, and more. Give your students the power to read, listen, and study on their phones, so they can learn on their terms.

Empower Students to Reach Their Potential

Twelve distinct metrics give you actionable insights into student engagement. Identify topics troubling your entire class and instantly communicate with those struggling. Students can track their scores to stay motivated towards their goals. Together, you can be unstoppable.

Control Your Course—and Your Content

Get the flexibility to reorder textbook chapters, add your own notes, and embed a variety of content including Open Educational Resources (OER). Personalize course content to your students' needs. They can even read your notes, add their own, and highlight key text to aid their learning.

Get a Dedicated Team Whenever You Need Them

MindTap isn't just a tool, it's backed by a personalized team eager to support you. We can help set up your course and tailor it to your specific objectives, so you'll be ready to make an impact from day one. Know we'll be standing by to help you and your students until the final day of the term.

Instructor Companion Website

Spend less time planning and more time teaching. The instructor companion website to accompany *Technical Writing* allows you "anywhere, anytime" access to all of your resources.

- The online Instructor's Manual contains various resources for each chapter of the book, including lesson plans and solutions to core text activities.
- The Computerized Testbank makes generating tests and quizzes a snap, with many questions and different styles to choose from.
- Customizable PowerPoint® presentations focus on key points for each chapter.

To access the instructor companion site materials, go to login.cengage. com, then use your SSO (single sign on) login to access the materials.

1 WHAT IS TECHNICAL WRITING?

Goals

- Define technical writing and its importance in the workplace
- Identify the characteristics of technical writing
- Compare and contrast technical writing to other types of writing

Terms

Write to Learn

Think about the different types of writing you engage in at school, at work, at home, or online. With what kind of writing are you most comfortable? What kind of writing do you find most difficult? Explain the differences in your reactions. Do you think any of your pieces could be described as technical writing? How would you define the term *technical writing?*

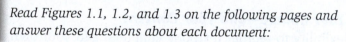

FOCUS on Technical Writing

Read Figures 1.1, 1.2, and 1.3 on the following pages and answer these questions about each document:

- What is the subject and purpose of each document?
- For whom was the document likely produced?
- How difficult is it to follow the organization of material?
- How would you describe the style of writing? Which documents are easier to read?
- Are there differences in tone in any of the documents? What role does the writer seem to adopt in each?
- Which kinds of design features does the document use (for example, boldfacing, numbering, color, visual aids)?
- Where did these documents most likely first appear?
- Are any of these types of documents familiar to you?

ABOUT *THE HEART TRUTH*®

To make women more aware of the danger of heart disease, the National Heart, Lung, and Blood Institute (NHLBI) is sponsoring a national program called *The Heart Truth*®, in partnership with many national and community organizations. The program's goal is to raise awareness about heart disease and its risk factors among women and educate and motivate them to take action to prevent the disease and control its risk factors.

National Symbol

The centerpiece of *The Heart Truth* is the *Red Dress*®, which was introduced as the national symbol for women and heart disease awareness in 2002 by the NHLBI. The *Red Dress*® reminds women of the need to protect their heart health and inspires them to take action to lower their risk for the disease.

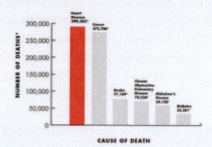

LEADING CAUSES OF DEATH FOR AMERICAN WOMEN (2010)

Of the women who died in 2010, one in four women died from heart disease. It's the #1 killer of women. It strikes at younger ages than most people think, and the risk rises in middle age.

To learn more, visit www.hearttruth.gov.
Numbers of deaths are based on the most recent data available and rounded to the nearest tenth.

National Vital Statistics System, Underlying Cause of Death on CDC Wonder Online Database

The Heart Truth, its logo and The Red Dress are registered trademarks of HHS.

Download PDF (PDF, 347 KB)
HTML

Program Objectives

Primary Objectives

1. Increase awareness that heart disease is the leading cause of death among women.

2. Increase awareness of the risk factors for heart disease.

3. Increase awareness that having risk factors can lead to heart disease, disability, and death.

4. Increase perceived susceptibility to heart disease (e.g. an individual's perception she may be at personal risk for heart disease).

5. Increase the number of women who intend to take action to prevent heart disease and/or control its risk factors.

Secondary Objective

1. Increase the frequency of conversations between women and their health care provider about risk for heart disease and importance of taking preventive action.

Figure 1.1 Heart Truth Webpage Source: National Institutes of Health, https://www.nhlbi.nih.gov/health/educational/hearttruth/about/

Million Hearts: Prevalence of Leading Cardiovascular Disease Risk Factors — United States, 2005–2012

Matthew D. Ritchey, DPT1, Hilary K. Wall, MPH1, Cathleen Gillespie, MS1, Mary G. George, MD1, Ahmed Jamal, MBBS2

Each year, approximately 1.5 million U.S. adults have a heart attack or stroke, resulting in approximately 30 deaths every hour and, for nonfatal events, often leading to long-term disability (1). Overall, an estimated 14 million survivors of heart attacks and strokes are living in the United States (1). In 2011, the U.S. Department of Health and Human Services, in collaboration with nonprofit and private organizations, launched Million Hearts (http://www.millionhearts.hhs.gov), an initiative focused on implementing clinical and community-level evidence-based strategies to reduce cardiovascular disease (CVD) risk factors and prevent a total of 1 million heart attacks and strokes during the 5-year period 2012–2016 (2,3). . . .

ABCS [for aspirin, blood pressure, cholesterol, smoking] Clinical Measures

In 2009–2010, prevalence of recommended aspirin use was greater among men (58.5%) than women (48.0%) and greater among non-Hispanic whites (55.7%) compared with Hispanics (43.6%) (Table 1). The prevalence of blood pressure control improved from 43.4% in 2005–2006 to 51.9% in 2011–2012 (Figure 1); in 2011–2012, the prevalence was greater among women (54.6%) than men (48.9%) and greater among adults aged 45–64 years (56.3%) compared with those aged 18–44 (42.2%) and ≥75 years (41.7%).

The prevalence of cholesterol management increased from 33.0% in 2009–2010 to 42.8% in 2011–2012 (Figure 1); in 2011–2012, the prevalence was greater among adults aged 65–74 years (59.6%) and lower among those aged 20–44 (11.6%) compared with those aged 45–64 years (44.1%) (Table 1). . . .

Community-Level Risk Factor Measures

Current tobacco product (cigarettes, cigars, or a pipe) smoking prevalence decreased from 28.2% in 2005–2006 to 25.1% in 2011–2012 (Figure 2). This 11% decline corresponded with a decrease of 11% in current cigarette smoking prevalence from 20.9% in 2005–2006 to 18.5% in 2011–2012, measured using National Health Interview Survey data.††† In 2011–2012, current tobacco product smoking was greater among men (30.3%) than women (20.4%), adults aged 18–44 years (30.5%) compared with those aged 45–64 (24.6%) or ≥65 years (11.4%), and non-Hispanic whites (27.1%) compared with non-Hispanic blacks (26.2%) and Hispanics (18.1%) (Table 2). . . .

References

1. Go AS, Mozaffarian D, Roger VL, et al. Heart disease and stroke statistics—2014 update: a report from the American Heart Association. Circulation 2014;129:e28–292.

2. Frieden TR, Berwick DM. The "Million Hearts" initiative—preventing heart attacks and strokes. N Engl J Med 2011;365:e27.

3. CDC. CDC Grand Rounds: the Million Hearts initiative. MMWR 2012;61:1017–21. . . .

Figure 1.2   Million Hearts Medical Report Source: Centers for Disease Control and Prevention, https://www.cdc.gov/mmwr/preview /mmwrhtml/mm6321a3.htm

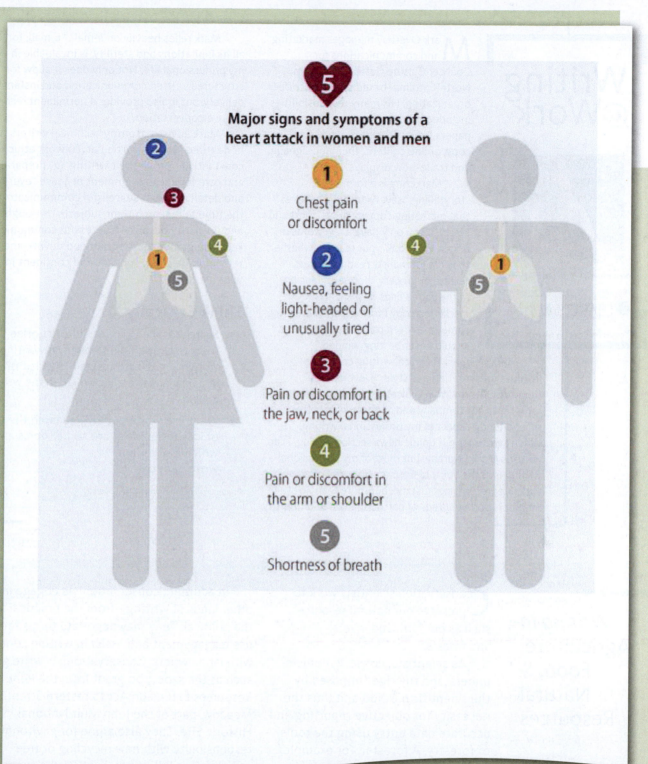

Figure 1.3 Heart Truth Web Page Source: https://www.cdc.gov/heartdisease/images/quiz_4.jpg

Writing @Work

Courtesy of Mark Overbay

CareerClusters
PATHWAYS TO COLLEGE & CAREER READINESS
Agriculture, Food & Natural Resources

Source: The Center to Advance CTE

Mark Overbay manages marketing and communications for Counter Culture Coffee, a Durham, North Carolina–based specialty coffee organization. His many responsibilities include producing product copy, white papers, advertisements, packaging copy, online content, thematic signage, and tradeshow displays.

"Marketing is a form of storytelling," says Mark, who believes that marketing copy must be "short and sweet." "You only have a few words or phrases to 'hook' your readers, whether they are journalists reading a press release or grocery shoppers glancing at the coffee bags on a shelf. Good marketing copy must tell an interesting, sometimes even romantic story, but it should never be long-winded."

Mark's biggest technical writing challenge involves presentation and style: "Developing a Counter Culture Coffee 'voice' that authentically represents our company and all that we do is the most difficult aspect of my professional writing. When I write for our online news section or blog, I can write as Mark Overbay; but most of my professional writing is in the voice of Counter Culture Coffee, which represents not just me, but more than 40 staff members and hundreds of partnering coffee farmers."

Mark relies heavily on e-mail. "E-mail, for all its limitations and sterility, is invaluable in my professional life. Not only does it allow for structured written communication and instant delivery, but it also provides a permanent record of every e-conversation."

Mark advises aspiring technical writers to hone three skills in particular: (1) work ethic to constantly improve their writing; (2) preparation and care for each assignment because "every word and detail matters. Successful communicators take the time to research their subjects thoroughly"; and (3) clarity because "successful communicators keep things simple—not dumbed down—and to the point. Be clear, concise, and confident in your message."

Think Critically

1. Search for the Counter Culture Coffee website and sample some of the writing. Does the writing tell stories, as Mark claims? Do you hear a distinctive "voice" in the writing? Explain.

2. What is a white paper? Research the origin of this term. What are some topics about which Mark might write papers?

Printed with permission of Mark Overbay

Writing in Agriculture, Food, & Natural Resources

Conservation scientists work to preserve our natural resources, such as our farmland, rivers, and forests.

As scientists, conservationists understand the rigor imposed by the scientific method and thus the necessity for objective reporting and accurate data entry using the tools of forestry. A forester, for example, may estimate tree growth using clinometers to measure tree heights or may measure forest density by using remote sensing technology. Accurate record keeping enables conservationists to make informed recommendations such as sustainable practices for harvesting timber. The records also ensure compliance with government regulations.

In addition, conservationists engage in other kinds of writing—from the practical to the political. They may negotiate terms for land use management and assist in writing contracts with land owners. Conservationists write grants, such as the $300,000 grant from the Renewable Resources Extension Act to restore Strentzel Meadow, part of the John Muir National Historic Site. They also argue for environmental responsibility with new recycling or tree conservation initiatives. Luke Wallin suggests a three-part structure for such scientific journalism: Articles should establish a bond with the reader through shared values, present new information, and then call for an action—a request for money or a letter to a senator for political support (124).

1.1 YOU ARE A TECHNICAL WRITER!

WARM UP

Think about a profession in which you are interested. What kinds of documents would you write in this profession?

Have you ever given someone written directions or drawn a map to your home? Have you ever set up an event on Facebook or told someone how to make French toast? If you answered yes to any of those questions or have had similar experiences, you have already engaged in technical communication or technical writing.

In today's business environment, readers can easily be overwhelmed by information overload, with information competing for their attention from every direction—print and electronic news sources and books, not to mention e-mail, social media, podcasts, and television, all clamoring for attention. To navigate through the maze of information, readers must be able to read documents quickly and efficiently, understand them the first time they read them, and know the reports are accurate. Writers help readers sort through information overload by assimilating material from a variety of places and then presenting what readers need—often reframing and repurposing (but *never* misrepresenting) that data to be of use to a different audience. Up-to-date information provides companies with a competitive edge, speeding critical decision making and allowing job specialization.

Definition of Technical Writing

Candace, a saxophonist in her high school band, began teaching saxophone lessons to sixth graders to earn some extra money. For the first lesson, she drew a diagram of an alto sax and created a step-by-step guide explaining how to take the instrument apart and reassemble it. When she saw how easily students could follow her instructions, she was pleased to know her words were helping them do something she enjoyed. Candace might have been surprised to learn she was using **technical communication**, or communication associated with the workplace.

© ksalt/iStockphoto.com

Technical communication, used in technical, scientific, or business fields, has a clear purpose and specific audience. Candace's purpose was to teach, to offer her students information that would enable them to do something—to play the saxophone. When she referred to the diagram and explained the procedure aloud to her students, answering their questions, she was using technical communication. When she wrote the instructions to accompany her diagram, she was using technical writing. The better Candace did her job, the better the students did theirs. Respect for Candace's teaching skills in the community grew, giving her credibility as a teacher—and, consequently, more students.

A form of technical communication, **technical writing** is also associated with the workplace, whether the workplace is an office, a construction site, or a kitchen table. Like Candace's diagram and step-by-step instructions, the writing is functional, practical, and written carefully for an identified audience for a particular purpose. Technical documents can range from a half-page memo announcing the winner of a sales competition to a 500-page research grant proposal requesting money to test a new drug for treating obesity. The term *technical writing* describes a variety of documents produced in areas such as business, science, social science, engineering, and education.

Sales catalogs, business letters, financial reports, standard operating procedures, medical research studies, lab reports—all of these and more are examples of technical writing. Technical documents are not only written but also designed to integrate visual elements to enhance the message.

Today, technical writers work at the helm of a creative, robust technological environment with many media outlets for their messages. Kurstin used paper and text to start a neighborhood fundraiser to help struggling pet owners obtain pet food. In a few weeks, some of that text was inserted into a desktop publishing template, and newsletters and flyers were circulated in the small town. Public response was positive. As a result, in a few months text from the flyer was used in a slide presentation with art and video and presented to the Chamber of Commerce. As the fundraiser gained momentum, Kurstin researched turning her charitable effort into a nonprofit and moved online with her text, photos, and video. She refined her online presence with a slogan, pet-adoption blog, pet health hyperlinks, and donation forms. Soon her website had a following and was linked to social media sites. As Kurstin's experience shows, the many possible combinations of text and media enable writers to reach an ever-widening audience.

Technical Writing Is Essential in the Workplace

Written communication is essential in the workplace. It allows readers to read and study at their convenience, pass along information to others, contribute to a body of shared knowledge, keep a permanent record for future reference, and, if done well, establish healthy working relationships.

Different careers generate different kinds of reports. Figure 1.4 shows some possibilities. Perhaps one of your career choices is represented here.

PROFESSIONALS	WRITE THIS	FOR THIS PURPOSE
Nurses	Patient charts	To continue patient care
Police officers	Accident reports	To use as evidence
Chemists/ engineers	Document procedures	To comply with government regulations
Accountants	Financial reports	To assist decision making
Sales representatives	Sales proposals	To compete in a market economy
Professors	Grant proposals	To secure funding for a research project
Claims adjusters	Incident reports	To determine fair payment
Public relations officers	Brochures, letters, speeches	To market an idea or product

Figure 1.4 Writing in Careers

When you write, you demonstrate your credibility as an employee with your ability to analyze, solve problems, and understand technical processes. For example, Matheus Cardoso, personnel director for Osgood Textile Industries, impresses his supervisor and earns his colleagues' respect when his proposal for tax-deferred retirement plans is approved. On the other hand, the drafting crew at Stillman Manufacturing is frustrated with Jeff Danelli's instructions for installing wireless computing at the industrial site. The crew must take extra time to redraft plans because Jeff's instructions are vague and incomplete. When writing is not clear, the thinking behind the writing may not be clear either.

Regardless of the career you choose, you will write in the workplace. According to "Writing: A Ticket to Work . . . Or a Ticket Out," writing is a "threshold skill," necessary to get over the "threshold," through the door, and into gainful employment. Applicants submitting poorly written letters of application do not get interviews. Employees lacking writing skills are not promoted. According to the National Commission on Writing, in corporate America,

- two-thirds of salaried employees are required to write
- over half of companies surveyed require employees to write technical or formal reports, and "communication through e-mail and PowerPoint presentations is almost universal."
- Eighty percent of companies in service industries—finance, insurance, and real estate—evaluate writing ability as part of the hiring process. (3–4)

As you can see, writing is truly your "ticket" to meaningful employment and advancement.

All careers rely on technical communication to get the job done. Technical writing is the written link—connecting technology to user, professional to client, colleague to colleague, supervisor to employee, and individual to community. No matter what career you choose, you can expect to read and compose e-mail, send accompanying attachments, explain procedures, and write short reports.

In addition to work-related writing, the responsibilities of being a community and family member require technical communication. Figure 1.5 shows how Sergeant Thomas Hardy of the Palmer City Police Department, father of two and concerned citizen, uses technical communication on the job and at home.

READER	TYPE OF COMMUNICATION
Colleagues	e-mail, collaborative incident reports
Boy Scout parents	fundraiser announcements, directions to jamboree, ad for bake sale
Victims	incident reports, investigative reports
Legislators	letter and e-mail in favor of clean-air regulations
Court officials, lawyers	depositions, testimonies, statements (possibly televised)
State FBI office	letter of application and resume
Community	safety presentation at the local high school
Employees	performance evaluations, letters of reference, training procedures
Newspaper editor	letter thanking community for help with jamboree, press release announcing purchase of state-of-the-art police car

Figure 1.5 Technical Writing on the Job and at Home

STOP AND THINK 1.1

How important is technical writing in the workplace? How can writing affect your chances for advancement? How is workplace writing impacted by technology?

WARM UP

Review the three documents at the beginning of the chapter, in Figures 1.1, 1.2, and 1.3. Have you written or read similar types of documents? If so, why? What was the situation? Which of the documents would you use to make a decision or to perform an action? Which type of document would you prefer to write? Why?

While technical writing shares some characteristics with other kinds of writing, it is also significantly different. From the factual treatment of the subject to audience considerations, technical writing is unique. A clear purpose, easy-to-follow organization, current and relevant research, concise style, objective tone, attractive and interesting design, appropriate media, and dependence on established formats all characterize the kind of writing designed for the workplace.

Clear Purpose

The subject, heart health, of the models at the beginning of this chapter is from medical science. Cardiovascular disease is one of the leading causes of death in the world and is the number one killer of American women. It is within the larger context of this medical crisis that all three of these documents were created. The situation—heart disease—prompts a variety of responses from individuals as well as organizations who want to change this statistic. While the larger context—the threat of cardiovascular disease—is the same for all the documents, the purpose is different in each because the approach to meeting the crisis is different.

© sjlocke/iStockphoto.com

Each responder in our opening models adds a voice, establishes a point of view, and develops a message with a clear purpose. The purpose of Figure 1.1, the "Heart Truth" webpage, is to announce an initiative from the National Heart, Lung, and Blood Institute to raise women's awareness of the risk factors associated with heart disease. The purpose of Figure 1.2, "Million Hearts: Prevalence of Cardiovascular Disease Risk Factors," is to summarize medical data to investigate new areas of research. Each document fulfills a need for information, but Figure 1.3, "Major Signs and Symptoms of a Heart Attack," fulfills an immediate and compelling need: saving the life of an unconscious victim. All three pieces offer information, but the red heart, simple diagrams, and color-coded numbered list in "Major Signs" propel the reader into action. In each case, the writer has answered a call for information.

Accurate and Relevant Research

Technical writers must incorporate accurate, current, and relevant research—library research, scientific observation, statistical analyses, or **field research** (research done in the field, especially through surveys, experiments, and interviews). The research required depends on the needs of the reader or the community of readers. Whether to inform or persuade, technical writing relies on data—often factual data researched by others—presented with precision and accuracy.

Figures 1.1 and 1.2, the "Heart Truth" webpage and the "Million Hearts" medical report, present research that impacts lives, research others need to fulfill their roles in preventing heart disease. The medical report cites data from other sources and includes a numbered list of references, which adds to

Communication Technologies

Technical writers must be familiar with desktop publishing software. Using programs such as Page Plus, Microsoft® Publisher, Adobe® PageMaker®, and QuarkXPress®, technical writers can apply special features (for example, boldfaced type, different fonts, bulleted lists, sidebars) to their documents. In addition, they can add visual aids such as diagrams, charts, and graphs to enhance the message.

Think Critically

Does your composing process change when you lack knowledge of software? For example, if you do not know how to insert tables or bulleted lists in a document, do you approach the writing differently? Explain.

---

the veracity of the report. Figure 1.3, "Major Signs," is written to provide an ordinary citizen with a quick guide to an emergency procedure.

If any information in these documents is out of date or inaccurate, readers may take action based on the misinformation—and do more harm than good. In this instance, the reader trusts the writer to give him sound life-saving advice. To give such advice, a writer must be trustworthy. Hence, writers have an ethical responsibility to present readers with the most up-to-date information available.

Relevant research is also timely, well-positioned research. Since heart disease is a major killer, the "Heart Truth" webpage and the "Million Hearts" report are presented through appropriate online and print media at a critical time in our medical history. The placement of the "Major Signs" visual, possibly as a larger poster, is also a factor. A school office and hospital waiting room, for example, are physical spaces where a poster is likely to be seen by ordinary citizens. When, where, and how to position relevant research are decisions you make as a technical writer.

Identified Audience

Technical writers do not write in a vacuum: They write *to* someone, either a specific reader or a group of readers, to fill a need for information. The writer of "Heart Truth" uses text, color, and symbolism to address a general audience of women. The red color is reminiscent of a red heart while the dress symbolizes a movement initiated for the benefit of women. Plus, the audience, women, is addressed directly in the first sentence.

The "Million Hearts" medical report and "Major Signs," however, are directed to a more selective group. The statistical data analysis is not written for the general audience of women but for a community of medical professionals with specialized training. The signs and symptoms graphic is directed toward the most specific audience of all—someone already experiencing a medical emergency. The statistical data in "Million Hearts" will not help the person experiencing a heart attack now but may assist professionals attempting to educate the public.

In each model, writers are conscious of the reader on the other side of the communication exchange and work hard to present information in an easy-to-follow format. In technical writing, one rule dominates: *The needs of the reader dictate every decision the writer makes.*

Clear Organization

Technical documents make their organizational plan clear to their readers from the start.

Headings separate information into easily digestible bits for a reader. They draw attention to information even before someone reads it, and they give readers an opportunity to read only what they want or need to read. In organizing technical communication, the writer should ensure there will be no surprises for the reader.

In technical writing, headings—appropriately named and set apart—help readers skim through a lot of information quickly. If you want to know mortality statistics in "Heart Truth," you can see them easily in the graph to the right where heart disease deaths have been highlighted in red. If you want to know the secondary objective of this program, it is easy to spot at the end of the document because it appears after a heading. "Million Hearts" also offers headings that separate the *risk factors studied* under Clinical Measures and *risk factors by communities* under Community-Level Risk Factor Measures.

Similarly, the "Major Signs and Symptoms" visual is designed to direct the reader's attention quickly. Numbered warning signs are color coded to correspond to specific areas of the body. Short, terse descriptions of each symptom allow readers to identify the type of discomfort quickly. Because the body drawings are light gray with few details except for the dress and pants, the eye is drawn to the numbers. At a glance, it's clear that women can experience more signs and different signs from men, and it's clear where the symptoms are felt. The most pressing information, vertically presented in the middle, tells a responder or a victim only what she needs to know. From here a person can make a decision about calling 9-1-1.

In each case the organizational pattern is not something the reader has to think about because the *writer thought about it*—and figured out the best plan *so the reader would not have to*. This way the reader gets to concentrate on the message without the distraction of figuring out where pertinent information is located.

Direct Style

The **style** of a document, the way an author uses words and sentences, usually gives the audience an idea of the type of document they are reading. To be easily understood, technical documents tend to employ a simple, concise, straightforward style. Often information is presented in lists. Sentences are relatively short, not overly complex, and the sentence order is predictable. **Jargon,** the highly specialized language of a particular discipline or technical field, is used when appropriate.

Each model opening this chapter uses a style accessible to its readers. "Heart Truth" and "Major Signs" are written in simple language for anyone to read—regardless of educational background. The most difficult word in

Isabel was recently assigned as lead technical communicator on a team that is developing a high-profile software known as SpeedQuest. She is responsible for coordinating communication between the programming team and the marketing team. Because this position is likely to result in a promotion and career advancement, Isabel is eager to do a good job.

One evening Isabel overhears the lead computer programmer tell the project manager that SpeedQuest is not as advanced as advertised in the company's marketing materials. The programmer recommends delaying the launch date, but the project manager ignores the suggestion, deciding to issue a second release after the product is complete.

The next day in the meeting to discuss SpeedQuest's marketing materials, Isabel struggles to decide whether she should include in the brochure those features still in development. She knows the new features would help sales of SpeedQuest. On the other hand, she knows if she tells the truth and decides not to publish information about the features, she may not get the promotion she is counting on. What should Isabel do?

Think Critically

What resources might Isabel use to better understand and resolve this situation?

Communication
Dilemma

"Heart Truth," "susceptibility," has been defined for the general reader. In the "Major Signs" graphic, there are no difficult words. Indeed, the terse phrases can be skimmed in a few seconds, thus removing the guess work for anyone trying to decide whether to call 9-1-1.

The style of a technical document can be more complex, however, depending on the audience's expectations and its ability to comprehend. The writers summarizing medical research for medical personnel in "Million Hearts" can use more complex sentence structures and specialized language: research terms such as "community-level evidence-based strategies" as well as abbreviations such as "CVD" for cardiovascular disease and "ABCS" for aspirin, blood pressure, cholesterol, and smoking. The style here relies heavily on the use of numbers, yet it is still clear and direct.

As you can see, technical writing is always directed *to* someone. That someone determines how complex the language and style should be.

Objective Tone

Tone refers to emotional overtones—the emotional character of a document, or the way the words make a person feel. The tone of a document also hints at the kind of document the audience is reading. Generally, a more serious topic adopts a more objective tone. The tone in technical writing is best described as objective or businesslike.

The opening models convey little, if any, emotion. "Heart Truth" announces a new program, explaining its symbol and setting up objectives. While the language is positive and the outcome is hopeful, the tone is still objective. The medical research presents its findings in the neutral, detached language of numbers. The signs and symptoms graphic does imply a sense of urgency but still bypasses emotion associated with an emergency and, instead, assists the reader in making a rational decision.

Design Elements

Technical writers use special features such as boldface, italics, capital letters, columns, underlining, and bulleted lists to draw readers' attention to certain words and to help important information stand out. Also, the use of graphics such as tables, graphs, pictures, and diagrams helps the audience grasp complex material quickly.

All the opening models use design features. "Heart Truth" uses color, a graph, two major headings, two second-level headings, and a numbered list. The logo of the red dress, though small, catches the reader's eye. The least attractive of the three models, "Million Hearts" is nonetheless set up with headings to visually separate the data. The signs and symptoms visual includes the most innovative design of the three models with less text and more carefully placed graphics.

Technical documents require more visual effort if they are to grab and hold the readers' attention. Writers use some of the following design features to make their documents more effective for the audience:

DESIGN FEATURE	THINGS TO CONSIDER
Font size, style, boldface	What size is readable for the targeted audience? How many styles are appropriate? How much boldface is effective?
Numbered or bulleted lists	Which is more appropriate? What kind of bullets should be used?
Highlights	What information should stand out? Should I boldface, underline, or italicize?
Columns and headings	What is the best way to divide the major ideas? Into two or three columns? With several boldfaced headings?
Color	Which colors? How much color? Is there already a logo with a color scheme? Should I create one?
Graphs and tables	What's the best way to present to my audience: one-, two-, or three-dimensional? Horizontal or vertical? Number of columns? Color or no color?
Photos and drawings	What is the subject of the art? What style works best? Should photos and drawings be black and white or color? Do I need permission to use the art?
Sidebars	What information deserves attention, and where should I place it?

Technical writers face a double challenge. They not only must write with clear, accurate, and specific words, but also must design the document to look inviting and attractive. Therefore, technical writers are production artists—writing with precision to locate the best word and sentence structure for the message and designing pages which combine a professional image with a user-friendly approach. To do so, writers use a tool of their trade: desktop publishing software. The software allows writers to craft documents that meet their readers' needs.

Standard Conventions

You have grown up in a multimedia world and are used to reading, seeing, and hearing messages on paper, bulletin boards, TV, radio, websites, video, online magazines, and blogs. Some of these media outlets have evolved into familiar sights. Indeed, readers today expect certain things from a website, just as they expect certain things from a map or a restaurant menu. A Facebook page, a medium now familiar worldwide, uses an online environment to reach thousands of readers. The Heart Truth page in Figure 1.6 follows **standard conventions**—expectations for content, organization, and design—which have evolved over Facebook's short life span. Readers expect to see the cover and profile photos representing the organization or person. They are used to Like, Haha, and Wow buttons; Comment, Message, and Share buttons; and the newsfeed and year-by-year or special-day history. Organizations and individuals posting on Facebook insert text and art using these already-established conventions.

Figure 1.6 Heart Truth Facebook Page Source: https://www.facebook.com/hearttruth/

Consider the established writing conventions in something as simple as a recipe. The recipe for Mom's Heart-Healthy Chili in Figure 1.7 meets the reader's expectations for recipes: a list of ingredients, directions for assembling the ingredients, and instructions for cooking or processing these ingredients.

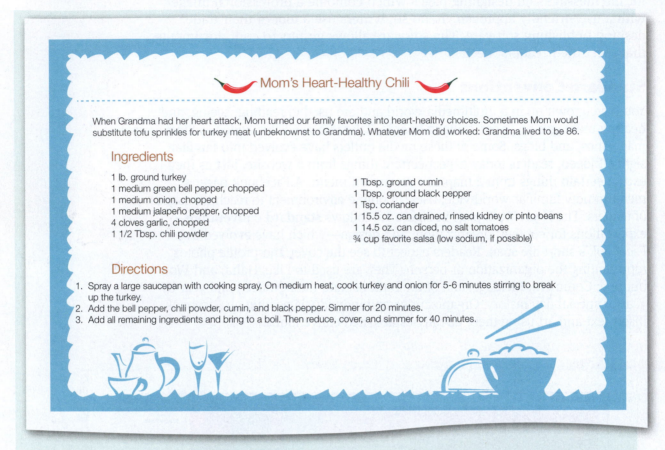

When Grandma had her heart attack, Mom turned our family favorites into heart-healthy choices. Sometimes Mom would substitute tofu sprinkles for turkey meat (unbeknownst to Grandma). Whatever Mom did worked: Grandma lived to be 86.

Ingredients

1 lb. ground turkey
1 medium green bell pepper, chopped
1 medium onion, chopped
1 medium jalapeño pepper, chopped
4 cloves garlic, chopped
1 1/2 Tbsp. chili powder

1 Tbsp. ground cumin
1 Tbsp. ground black pepper
1 Tsp. coriander
1 15.5 oz. can drained, rinsed kidney or pinto beans
1 14.5 oz. can diced, no salt tomatoes
¾ cup favorite salsa (low sodium, if possible)

Directions

1. Spray a large saucepan with cooking spray. On medium heat, cook turkey and onion for 5-6 minutes stirring to break up the turkey.
2. Add the bell pepper, chili powder, cumin, and black pepper. Simmer for 20 minutes.
3. Add all remaining ingredients and bring to a boil. Then reduce, cover, and simmer for 40 minutes.

Figure 1.7 Mom's Heart-Healthy Chili

But do all recipes look the same? No. Some include photos, some nutritional information, and some a short motivational introduction or history of the dish. Others will tell a cook how long it will take to prepare the dish, where ingredients can be found, or which ingredients can be substituted. Thus, while recipes can be different, they do have common elements, certain conventions we all expect to see in a recipe.

A good technical writer knows the established conventions of the type of document he is writing and also knows how to adjust the document to accommodate more or less or different information. A writer adjusting a recipe might take the basic format (ingredients and process) and expand it (add nutrition information), condense it (leave out the family story), or change it (write in Spanish and use metric measurements). The writer makes these decisions based on the complexity of the topic, the needs of the audience, and the limitations of the media.

Different disciplines have adopted a range of conventions for relaying a message based on the needs of the field of study. Science uses the scientific method; business adopts a problem-solving/solution approach. E-mail shares the To/From/Subject/Date formatting of the memo, and a resume calls for

Focus on Ethics

Technical communicators can face thorny issues when they provide a service for a company or an organization that may expect results a technical writer finds questionable or problematic. For instance, Joel is a technical writer working for Energy Battery Company. He is asked to write a press release announcing the plant's unexpected two-week shutdown but is told not to include information about the chemical spill which could have leaked into the local estuary. In this case the writer is torn between meeting management's expectations (and keeping his job) or serving the public good. Writers need to be thoroughly aware of their ethics and explore all possible actions and outcomes in such situations.

Think Critically

To whom does Joel hold himself accountable? Energy Battery Company? his wife and children? his readers? his conscience?

standard headings such as education and employment experience. These conventions, ranging from style to organization to content, are repeated over the course of time, standardizing them into a kind of genre. With them, there is no need to reinvent the wheel, as the saying goes. Things are already in place—an organization creating certain expectations for content. This way a writer can focus on the message without developing the form, and readers can relax into familiar texts. For a writer, familiarity with the type of document means understanding the basic conventions and adjusting them as needed. As you will see, flexibility is an asset in any rhetorical situation.

 STOP AND THINK 1.2

Drawing from the activities in this section's Warm Up, come up with your own definition of *technical writing*. Make sure you incorporate concepts from this section, such as subject, organization, audience, style, tone, and special features.

1.3 HOW TECHNICAL WRITING COMPARES TO OTHER WRITING

 WARM UP

Technical writing has much in common with the academic writing or personal writing you have experienced in school and at home. Technical writing also shares aspects of literature you have read. The differences, however, set technical writing apart from other writing with which you are familiar.

From your experience with writing, what characteristics does high-quality writing share? In other words, how would you describe an effective piece of writing?

Technical Writing and Academic Writing

Academic writing (for example, research papers, analyses, and arguments) is the **expository** (writing to explain) and **persuasive writing** (writing to convince others) produced in academic circles. It must be unified, coherent, and well organized. Technical writing also must be unified, coherent, and well organized. Style and standard usage (the spoken and written English expected in business communication) are important in academic and technical writing. Both types of writing rely on a process of thinking and writing that takes place over a few hours, a few days, or several weeks. The purpose is often the same—to inform or persuade. Figure 1.8 shows an excerpt from a typical academic research paper.

DRIVERLESS CARS?

Imagine sitting in the driver's seat texting, answering e-mail, reading the newspaper, even taking a nap while your car drives you to work. The self-driving car, says Thomas Weber, in charge of development for Mercedes-Benz Cars, "is set to become a reality much more quickly than the public thinks" and predicts Mercedez-Benz will have an autonomous vehicle by 2020 ("Mercedez Will Offer"). Tesla CEO Elon Musk claims his company will produce an autonomous car by 2018 ("Toyota Show"), while Toyota Corporation has set a goal for 2020 (Charlton). To test their prototypes, fifteen major auto companies each paid a million dollars to help build MCity, a 32-acre make-believe city at the University of Michigan. With so much interest, is a self-driving car really a good idea? Apparently, there are a number of intriguing advantages to driverless roadways.

Proponents say self-driving cars are safer. Research by the U.S. Department of Transportation attributes over 90% of cars crashes to human error. Data suggest 41% of those errors were recognition errors including inattention, internal and external distractions, and inadequate surveillance (USDOT 2). The ability of technology already installed on Chevrolet Traverse, Ford Edge, and Jeep Cherokee to warn of a forward collision or an overlooked blind-spot has the potential to lower these statistics ("Avoiding Crashes"). So if the technology currently installed in some vehicles is already making our roadways safer, can the truly driverless car be far behind?

Figure 1.8 Academic Research Paper Excerpt

The difference between academic writing and technical writing is in the presentation, audience, and approach. Academic writing includes paragraphs—usually at least one introductory paragraph with a stated thesis or argument (like the "number of advantages to driverless roadways"), paragraphs that develop the thesis or prove the argument, and a concluding paragraph or two. In many English classes, students document their research using the in-text citations required by the Modern Language Association (MLA) style guide, as illustrated in our excerpt, and provide a Works Cited page. Academic writing is written for an academic audience—an instructor, classmates, or a group of interested scholars.

Generally, the purpose of academic writing is to argue a point, expand on an idea, or make observations about human experience. For example, Francis Bacon's essay entitled "On Reading" elaborates on the benefits of reading. In "Two Views of the Mississippi," Mark Twain observes that while a close study of the river is necessary to reveal its dangers, such knowledge also takes away the river's mystery.

Like academic writing, technical writing also includes paragraphs. It, too, often begins with an introduction and closes with a conclusion. However, there is less flexibility in the subject matter, style, and tone of a technical document. Written for a specific audience, the subject is generally technical, business-related, or scientifically oriented. Often the intent is to clarify and consolidate rather than expand. Technical writing (with its headings, itemized lists, boldfaced type, and graphics) looks different from academic writing.

You might wonder: Does academic writing cross over into technical writing? The answer is yes. The writer of "Driverless Cars?" could have set up the paper with another style guide; used headings, graphs, and photos; and shifted the focus from advantages of autonomous vehicles to a technical discussion of safety or economic issues. This way, the paper would look and feel more like a technical document.

Technical Writing and Personal Writing

The expressive nature of a personal essay can display a range of emotions—sadness, excitement, irony, humor. However, the aim of research papers and technical documents is not to convey emotion. In fact, emotion can interfere with a person's understanding of an academic or technical document.

Readers of technical documents read for information, not for entertainment. They read to learn something or to take action. Some people say that technical writing is boring because of its lack of emotion. Yet, for the target audience, the person needing or wanting that information, the topic is rarely boring.

The following excerpt in Figure 1.9 could have been written by a student in an English class or by a blogger bewailing the difficulties of car ownership. As a personal essay, the tone is conversational, almost humorous. The audience is anyone who has owned a car and had a similar experience. In some ways, the writer is writing as much to herself as she is to another reader.

CAR OWNERSHIP: THE REAL DEAL

Owning a car is not all it's cracked up to be. My parents offered to make the down payment on a used Ford Mustang, but I was responsible for the monthly payments, half the insurance premium, and the cost of maintenance. Sure, a job waiting tables at Schooner's promised to cover all my expenses—that is, until the restaurant closed for repairs. And then my "maintenance-free" Ford sprang a leak when the radiator rusted out. Oil changes, inspections tickers, a headlight out, a fuse blown—I began to wish I lived in a big city with public transportation, or maybe in a very small town where my bike could get me where I wanted to go. . . .

Figure 1.9 Personal Essay Excerpt

Technical Writing and Imaginative Writing

Imaginative writing also adheres to principles of unity, coherence, and standard conventions. Imaginative writers allow their ideas to evolve over time. However, compared to technical and academic writing, imaginative writing is less academic and more artistic, with writers taking creative license with some rules for a particular effect.

Imaginative writing includes novels, short stories, drama, and poetry whose situations grow out of fantasy or imagination. Events and people are fictional, although the themes may reveal universal truths. Imaginative writing is often **ambiguous** and can be interpreted in more than one way. A single passage can mean different things to different people. Imaginative writing also requires the reader to draw **inferences,** judgments about the reading that the writer does not make for the reader.

As you read "Goodbye" in Figure 1.10, you probably have some questions. Who is the friend? Male? Female? This friend has been on stage. Is this person a musician? And then you wonder, maybe the friend is a pet, a dog or cat. In the last sentence, we learn the subject of the poem is a car, the ten-year companion the author is personifying here. While this approach is applauded in imaginative writing, it does not work in technical communication. Readers of technical communication should not be left to wonder who or what is the subject of the document under review.

GOODBYE

Today I say goodbye to an old friend.

Our adventures have taken us from Wrightsville Beach to Ocean Beach.
We've climbed the Rockies and braved Death Valley.
We've peered over the edge of the Grand Canyon.
We've found ourselves buried in snow, caked in Playa dust.
We've fallen asleep to the sound of rain on the roof.

You've been a stage for musical performances and a sanctuary for quiet conversation.
Twice you were taken from me, but you always found your way back.
For the last ten years, you've been a constant, daily presence in my life—
Not something I can say about any other person, place, or thing.

So cheers, Rhonda the Honda. May your odometer roll on.

Figure 1.10 Imaginative Writing

Technical writing should be unambiguous and direct. A work of literature may be rich because it means different things to different readers. A reader might ponder the different meanings of the old man's voyage in Hemingway's *The Old Man and the Sea*, but W. Earl Britton says "that the primary, though not the sole, characteristic of technical and scientific writing lies in the effort of the author to convey one and only one meaning in what he says" (114). The meaning of a sentence in technical writing must be clear. "Turn there," Mr. Ybarra said, and his daughter turned left when he meant for her to turn right. The word *there* can have different meanings to different people. However, "Turn right at Nottingham Road, the next paved road," has only one meaning.

Imaginative writing such as Emily Dickinson's "Because I could not stop for Death—He kindly stopped for me" often requires you to make inferences. Who is the driver of the carriage in Dickinson's poem? Why is he kind? You do not expect to make inferences about technical writing. Leaving it up to the reader to infer whether circumstances warrant a call to 9-1-1 could waste precious time.

We are not saying technical writers have all the answers. Sometimes their task is to present the known facts so readers can make their own decisions. And we are not implying technical writing is not creative. All writing is a creative act. The writer of the best-selling novel and the writer of the user-friendly manual both channel their talents to serve a purpose. One helps us reflect, to examine what it means to be human; the other helps us do things, to apply our expertise in practical and meaningful ways.

We'd like to tell you writing has distinct categories that never overlap, but we can't. Any subject can be turned into a technical document, depending on the treatment of that subject. Likewise, any subject can be turned into a personal essay or imaginative piece. When heart topics are medical, they fall under the realm of technical writing. When heart topics become emotional—such as advice for healing from a broken relationship or a poem lamenting a loss—they morph into personal or imaginative writing. When heart topics become the subject of a psychological study to determine the causes of divorce, the topic uses elements of both personal stories *and* social science research. The mark of a good writer, then, is how well he or she adjusts to the rhetorical situation at any given moment. Certainly, flexibility is key to a writer's success.

 STOP AND THINK 1.3
Compare technical writing to academic, personal, and imaginative writing.

CHAPTER REVIEW

Summary

1. You have probably used technical writing if you have given someone directions, planned an event, explained closing procedures at work, or done many other everyday activities.

2. Technical communication, whether a written document or an oral presentation, presents technical information with a specific purpose and audience and a clear, straightforward approach.

3. Required in all professions, technical writing is critical in the workplace. Recent research describes writing as a "threshold skill."

4. Technical writing exhibits the following characteristics:

   - Subject and purpose: technical factual subject, clear purpose

   - Audience: carefully considered, targeted

   - Organization: predictable, apparent

   - Style: concise, direct, specialized vocabulary

   - Tone: objective, businesslike, detached

   - Design features: visual elements—headings, boldface, color graphics

   - Standard conventions: knowledge of familiar structures, format, and content

5. Technical writing differs from academic and personal writing in its presentation, approach to subject matter, and audience, and from imaginative writing in its "one-meaning-and-one-meaning-only" intent.

Checklist

- Can I define technical writing?

- Can I list the characteristics of technical writing?

- Can I give examples of technical writing in the workplace?

- Can I explain how technical writing differs from academic, personal, and imaginative writing?

- Can I identify ways in which technical writing is similar to academic, personal, and imaginative writing?

Build Your Foundation

1. What characteristics does technical writing share with other types of writing?

2. Which of these subjects would most likely be written about in a technical style? Which of these subjects would most likely be written about in an academic style?

a sunset	homelessness	a first pet
electric circuits	graduation	a wedding
a computer screen	a close friend	flowers

3. Which of the following statements would you expect to come from a technical writing document? Which would come from personal writing or imaginative literature? How can you tell? What are your clues?

   a. My memory of her will never fade. She brought music into my life.
   b. A neutral pH range between 6.5 and 7.5 provides a healthy environment for most community fish in a freshwater aquarium.
   c. The bandwidth of a telecommunications medium is measured in Mbps, which stands for millions of bits per second or megabits per second.
   d. The mist peeked over the marshland.
   e. Once upon a time there was a princess who ruled a vast country.
   f. To meet International Building Code requirements, stair risers must measure a maximum height of 7 inches and a minimum height of 4 inches.

4. In a role you have held, such as chairperson of an organization or a committee, employee, or team member, describe the kinds of communication required of you in that role. Would you describe the communication you did as technical communication? Why or why not?

5. Find a piece of technical writing (or another kind of writing) you think is ineffective. Write a brief analysis of the writing, focusing on the characteristics that make it ineffective. Then analyze a piece of writing you believe is effective. Compare the two pieces of writing for subject, audience, organization, style, tone, and special features.

6. Read each statement and identify the audience you think the writer is targeting.

   a. As instructed by the dentist, oxygenate the patient 5 minutes for every 15 minutes of nitrous oxide exposure to prevent diffusion hypoxia.
   b. Here at the office, when nitrous oxide is used, the oxygen administered with it prevents headaches, grogginess, nausea, and that "hung-over" feeling.
   c. Make no bones about it—*City Dogs* is a gentle, funny movie that your entire family will enjoy!

d. When booking train reservations in Spain, be aware that INTERCITY is the standard day time service, while TALGOS offers more amenities and is more expensive.

e. Come and see Big Bear at Ayden Centre on Saturday morning. Have your picture taken with him and take home one of the balloon animal she makes for you.

7. Examine the information found on a box or can of your favorite packaged food or beverage. In particular, notice the nutrition information. Write an explanation of why the information on the package is considered technical communication.

Your Turn

1. What skills do you need to improve your technical writing? How can you acquire those skills?

2. Conduct an Internet search for the keywords *technical writing, technical editing,* and *technical communication.* Write a summary of your findings and share your summary with the class.

3. Find an article in a professional journal, either in print or online. Read the article to understand the organizational strategy used. Because obvious organization is one of the characteristics of technical communication, analyze the article to determine whether its organization is obvious and is easy for readers to follow. Write a report of your findings and attach a copy of the article.

4. Collect brochures or pamphlets from credible online organizations or from a local government agency such as the health department or parks and recreation office. Use the headings and subheadings to create an outline. Then compare the outline you have created to the overall message of the document. Write a brief description of how effectively (or ineffectively) the system of headings and subheadings provides emphasis for important information in the document.

5. Read an article in your favorite magazine or textbook. Choose special features of technical writing. How do those features make the writing easy to read?

6. Write a short report describing the writing skills required in three of the following careers. You may need to research some of the job titles so you know the kinds of writing the jobs require. Or choose three careers that interest you and write a short report describing the writing skills those careers require.

physical therapist	computer network administrator	medical assistant
audiologist	agricultural extension agent	veterinary care aide
research scientist	food service manager	electrical technician
real estate broker	construction project manager	insurance adjustor

7. Search the Internet for an example of technical writing written by someone who holds a job you might like to have someday. Explain the purpose of the example and the way the author used technical writing characteristics to achieve the purpose.

8. Visit the websites of two competing organizations, such as PepsiCo and the Coca-Cola Company or AT&T and Verizon. Can you determine the audience each site targets? Why or why not? Is the site designed to reach consumers or shareholders or both? How effectively does each site use the principles of technical communication?

Community Connection

1. Interview a business person about technical writing on the job. What types of documents does this person write most often? Ask if you may bring a sample of the writing to class.

2. Ask a technician or scientist about technical writing on the job. Ask what mistakes may have been made as a result of imprecise reporting.

EXPLORE THE NET

Visit the U.S. Department of Labor, Bureau of Labor Statistics website to research employment opportunities over the next 10 years for technical writers. Write an ad for a technical writer based on your findings.

Works Cited

Britton, W. Earl. "What Is Technical Writing?" *College Composition and Communication*. May 1965: 113–116.

The National Commission on Writing for America's Families, Schools, and Colleges. *Writing: A Ticket to Work . . . Or a Ticket Out: A Survey of Business Leaders*. September 2014: 3–4.

Wallin, Luke. *Conservation Writing: Essays at the Crossroads of Nature and Culture*. Center of Policy Analysis, University of Massachusetts–Dartmouth. 2006.

2

AUDIENCE AND PURPOSE

Goals

- Determine how to meet the needs of a specific audience and a multiple audience
- Plan a document's purpose, scope, and medium

Terms

Write to Learn

Think of something you did recently about which you told a number of people. Consider how your description of the incident changed depending on whom you talked to. In one page, explain how you described this incident to (1) authority figures (for example, parents, instructors, or employers) and (2) close friends (who may include sisters and brothers). Did the purpose of your conversation change when you switched audiences? If so, how? How did each audience affect your tone, your body language, your choice of words, and the information you chose to include or omit?

 FOCUS **on Audience and Purpose**

Read Figure 2.1 on the next page and answer these questions:

- Who is the audience for this web page?
- Who is the writer, and what does the writer want the reader to do?
- What has the writer done to show an understanding of this reader?
- What kind of information has the writer provided to convince the reader to give blood? Do you think the writer has done a good job? Explain.

What If?

How might the model change if . . .

- The reader did not have access to the Internet?
- The reader is a regular donor, but he does not have transportation to the Blood Mobile site?
- The reader is a willing first-time donor but wonders if it is all right to give blood on her way home after lifting weights at the gym?
- The reader might be willing to donate but is legally blind?

Top 10 Reasons People Don't Give Blood

1. I don't like needles / I am scared of needles / I am afraid to give blood
   Nearly everyone feels that way at first. However, most donors will tell you that you feel only a slight initial pinch, and 7–10 minutes later, you are finished and headed for the canteen. If you take the time (and courage) to make one donation, you'll wonder why you ever hesitated.

2. I am too busy
   The entire process takes about an hour, and the actual blood donation time is only 7–10 minutes. If you stop to think that an hour of your time could mean a lifetime for a premature baby, someone with cancer undergoing chemotherapy, or someone who's had an accident, you might decide that you can make the time to give the gift of life.

3. No-one ever asked me . . . I didn't realize my blood was needed
   Consider yourself asked! There is simply no other way to supply the blood needs of hospital patients but for the generous donations of people like you. Every two seconds someone in America needs blood. More than 38,000 donations are needed every day in communities across the U.S.

4. I already gave this year
   You can give every 56 days. Many donors give 5 times a year!

5. I am afraid I'll get AIDS
   It is not possible to get AIDS by donating blood to the American Red Cross. A new sterile needle is used for each donor and discarded afterwards.

6. My blood isn't the right type
   Every type of blood is needed daily to meet patient needs. If you have a common blood type, there are many patients who need it, so it is in high demand. If you have a less common blood type, there are fewer donors available to give it, so it is in short supply.

7. I don't have any blood to spare
   The average adult body has 10–12 pints of blood. Doctors say that healthy adults may give regularly because the body quickly replaces the blood you donate.

8. I don't want to feel weak afterward
   Donating blood should not affect adversely a healthy adult because your body has plenty of blood. You will donate less than one pint, and your body, which constantly makes new blood, will replace the donated volume within 24 hours. Most people continue their usual activities after donating.

9. They won't want my blood (I am too old / I've had an illness)
   If you have doubts, check with your physician. The qualified staff on duty at a blood drive or donor center will also review your medical history with you. There is no upper age limit to donate blood with the American Red Cross, and a great many medical conditions do not prevent you from donating blood, or may have done so only temporarily in the past.

10. I have a rare blood type, so I'll wait until there is a special need
    Blood that is rare or special is almost always in short supply. There is a constant need for these blood types in order to avoid having to recruit specific blood types in a crisis.

Figure 2.1 Document Written for a Specific Audience Source: www.givelife.org/donor/top10excuses.asp

Writing @Work

Courtesy of Christopher Blackwell

CareerClusters®
PATHWAYS TO COLLEGE & CAREER READINESS
Human Services

Source: The Center to Advance CTE

Dr. Christopher Blackwell is an assistant professor at the University of Central Florida's College of Nursing. He teaches graduate-level nursing courses, serves on several faculty committees, and researches health and social disparities in vulnerable patient populations.

When Christopher needs to persuade fellow faculty members to make a change to their graduate program, he knows that he has to do more than simply speak up: He must produce documented evidence to support his case. "Verbally, I am able to communicate my opinion to my colleagues, but when I present effectively written documentation based on research, my points of view are validated by others."

Christopher's gift for speaking comes in handy in the classroom, where he has a different audience: nursing students. "To help students remember essential information," he says, "I use real clinical scenarios that I have experienced and also tell jokes. Students appreciate these types of communication." In addition to instructive anecdotes and humor, Christopher believes that body language, or nonverbal cues, is important to effective classroom communication.

While he teaches for a student audience, he researches and publishes writing for a professional scholarly audience. Christopher strongly believes that "the one thing that is most essential when preparing formal writing is focus." To focus his writing for an academic audience, Christopher writes an article's abstract—or a summary of the article—first and then uses this synopsis as an outline for the longer piece.

Think Critically

1. The profile describes three types of communication in which Christopher engages. What are they? How are they different? How are they similar? How does Christopher prepare to communicate effectively in each situation?

2. Are you surprised to read that a nursing professor tells jokes in class? Why does Christopher use humor?

Printed with permission of Dr. Christopher Blackwell

Writing in Human Services

Employed in every state and county in schools, hospitals, and service-related agencies, social workers match clients' needs with services such as foster care, food stamps, counseling, and healthcare. They serve as protectors of at-risk populations including the elderly and children. As social scientists, case workers not only observe human behavior but also employ the objectivity of scientific analysis. Writing consists mainly of factsheets, intake interviews, and invoices. Letters and e-mails to providers and clients help set up and track services. Sometimes a social worker is required to testify in court.

The intake interview forms the basis of any case. A case worker investigates the *who*, *what*, *why*, and *how* of an allegation and writes a narrative of the findings. Accurate and thorough documentation is imperative, for it is used to justify critical-care services such as the referral of a surgical patient to a rehabilitation facility or a military veteran to counseling. Information must be clear, concise, and organized for other readers, who may be another social worker assigned to the case, a supervisor making a referral, or a judge mandating a child to foster care. Most items on an intake form are prescriptive and routine, for example, "What brought you here today?" and "Tell me about your family." However, a perceptive case worker might add information regarding a client's mental state.

An interviewer's approach should be neutral, objective, sympathetic, and sensitive to cultural differences in communication styles. A Hispanic family may resist eye contact, for example, or a family from a large city may be more direct.

2.1 MEETING THE AUDIENCE'S NEEDS

Audience, reader, and *viewer* are nearly interchangeable terms. As technical communication channels expand to include a host of multimedia, *audience* has a broader meaning. Sometimes the audience is not a reader but a listener or an observer. On the Web, the reader is also an active participant. In any case, technical writers must know who the members of their audience are and what those readers, viewers, and listeners need or want to know.

In Figure 2.1, the writer knows who the audience is—potential blood donors. The focus is on the reader, and the writing shows an understanding of the reader's point of view. The Red Cross knows this reader well, obviously having heard these reasons many times. After identifying this audience, the writer systematically counters any objections with objective, precise, factual information.

Technical writing is written for both internal and external audiences. When Roweena, a dispatcher, composes an e-mail announcing pay increases to the police officers in her district, she is writing to the members of her organization—an internal audience. The author of "Top 10 Reasons People Don't Give Blood" is writing for an external audience—people outside the organization.

An expression of personal, social, or professional culture, a communication **artifact** can be a document, video, tool, painting, sculpture, or any item representing a message created by and for human beings. A **rhetorical act**, or communication process designed to influence another's point of view, requires a speaker or writer to think through the **rhetorical situation**, the real-life event prompting the need for some kind of response. To examine the situation, a writer considers who's involved (the audience), the purpose (the reason for the message), and any constraints—what circumstances (time, money, attitude, knowledge) affect the way a message is delivered. Aristotle, a Greek philosopher in the 4th century BCE, declared a good writer's task is to ascertain "in any given case, the available means of persuasion." He claimed communicators have four means of persuasion, or four ways to appeal to an audience:

■ **Logos:** appeal to logic; use of evidence and a well-reasoned argument

■ **Ethos:** appeal to ethics; use of the speaker's or writer's credibility and good character

■ **Pathos:** appeal to emotion; identification with or sympathy for an audience or cause

■ **Kairos:** appeal to the opportune moment, the best time to deliver a message.

Any communication artifact has the potential to include all four of Aristotle's appeals. Nonetheless, as you saw in Chapter 1, technical and academic communication is primarily an appeal to logos, ethos, and kairos: logical arguments, credible authorship, and a message offered when and where it will do the most good. Personal and imaginative writing are more suitable venues for pathos. As also suggested in Chapter 1, it is important not to compartmentalize communication: A good advertising campaign employs logic, credibility, timeliness, *and* emotion to sell a product. The lines among different forms of discourse are often blurred, yet a given text tends to lean toward one appeal more than another.

Technical communicators work through the rhetorical situation while maintaining transparency. A technical writer is like a member of a stage crew, a behind-the-scenes operator, whose primary obligation is to satisfy the audience's desire for a memorable performance. In a good play, the audience is barely aware of the crew who is moving sets and producing sound on cue; but without the crew, the show would not go on. Similarly, good writers produce work without drawing undue attention to their role, relying on logos, ethos, pathos, and kairos to carry their message.

Types of Audiences

You may write a poem or short story without the intention of sharing it with anyone. However, technical writing implies an audience, often a very specific audience, and sometimes a more varied audience. Your readers may be customers, coworkers, managers, subordinates, or the general public. Usually, your relationship to your readers determines how you write your document—the tone you use, the formality of the language, and its medium. A memo to the chief executive officer (CEO), for example, would be more formal than a memo to a coworker.

As you are planning your document, consider whether your readers fall into one of these categories:

- **Lay reader:** a general reader without expert knowledge but with an interest in a subject. Readers of newspapers and magazines such as *Psychology Today* and *Popular Science* are lay readers.

Communication
Technologies

The BBC, the British Broadcasting Corporation, has two versions of the news on its website, a United Kingdom version and an international version. Users logging on are automatically taken to the broadcast deemed most relevant based on their geographic locations. Thus, a person from the Middle East will see news from the Middle East; a person from South Asia will see news from South Asia. Other news websites including Voice of America (VOA) and

Google News offer news in similar formats. As you can see, these organizations have designed websites to reach out to many different audiences.

Think Critically

How might news about an event reported in India be different from the news about the same event reported in the United States?

- **Technician:** a person with skilled training who implements the ideas or plans of the expert. Technicians, like lathe operators and network administrators, operate equipment, repair machinery, and train others. They read manuals, schematics, blueprints, and technical reports.

- **Expert:** an authority in a particular field who is highly skilled and professional, perhaps with an advanced degree. Leaders in their fields, they design equipment, conduct research, and create new products. Experts such as medical doctors and engineers learn from and contribute to publications such as the *Journal of the American Medical Association* and the *Journal of Applied Physics*, respectively.

- **Manager:** a person who organizes personnel and is responsible for the day-to-day operations as well as long-range planning. Upper-level managers are leaders who create a vision and move the organization forward. Depending on their level of expertise, managers may read feasibility reports, research reports, financial reports, or professional articles.

A reader can fall into more than one category. Thinking through the categories will help you make decisions about how best to communicate with your audience.

Meeting the Needs of a Specific Audience

Do you understand the following message? It is written in Morse code—letters as a series of dots and dashes transmitted as sounds, lights, or electrical pulses. Unless you are a ham radio operator or in an aeronautical field, you probably have no need to know Morse code. You are not the target audience; therefore, the message fails to communicate.

-.- -. --- .--

-.-- --- ..- .-.

.- ..- -.. .. . -. -.-. .

A Navy radio operator during World War I would have understood this code. The operator's audience shared a common mission: to transmit classified military messages over long distances. In short, the Navy radio operator communicated in Morse code to another military operator whose job it was to decode the message. The military operator is the **target audience,** the audience for which the message is written.

To communicate successfully, you must speak the "language" of your audience. Failure to speak in terms your reader understands creates a barrier that prevents communication, much the same way the Morse code keeps you from understanding its message. To know how best to communicate with your reader, you must know who your audience is. Your audience may be a **specific audience** (a single person or a group whose point of view is the same), or your audience may be a **multiple audience** (readers whose points of view differ). Once you know your audience, you can plan ways to appeal to your reader(s).

© Digital Vision/Getty Images

To help you target the needs of a specific group, gather information about the **demographics** of the group—information such as the age, sex, income, and educational level of your group. If you are planning to advertise a new day care center, for example, your target audience would be working parents with young children. You might look at census data to find out where to advertise your new center. If you are designing a website for amateur astronomers, for instance, explore topics astronomers are interested in—for example, star charts, planetary events, observatory information, and recommendations for telescopes.

As a writer, the relationship with your readers is also important. Are they customers, managers, peers, or subordinates? Your relationship will determine how you write your document—the tone you use, the formality of your document, and its medium.

The reader's needs determine what kind of information the writer supplies. When your manager needs to know the cost of hiring an administrative assistant, you provide cost. When the maintenance crew wants to know which mosquito repellent to use, you research repellents and send the crew members an e-mail with your recommendation. When the audience is unsure of its needs, the writer helps the audience think through the communication situation.

In technical writing, one rule dominates: *The needs and wants of your audience dictate every decision you make as a writer.* To make effective decisions, writers exercise **rhetorical sensitivity,** adapting a message to the audience's needs and wants and framing it within a relevant context. Sometimes the writer's position is a precarious one: A writer must balance the needs of her audience without sacrificing the integrity and intent of her message. Lionel may want a higher line of credit, but if the customer representative researching his request determines his income does not warrant a higher line, she must refuse his request.

Analyze Your Target Audience

Sometimes your audience is a specific person or a group with a common interest. After you identify the readers in your target audience, consider how their knowledge level, roles, interests, cultural background, and personalities may influence what you write and how you write it. Age, experience, attitude, organizational distance, income, and politics may affect the language you choose to communicate successfully. Targeting the special needs of a specific audience requires a writer to consider several factors at once. Understanding your audience's knowledge level, role, interests, cultural background, and personality is the first step to successful communication.

Attending to the needs and wants of your audience is much like attending to a special guest in your home. You are aware of this person's presence, and you make every effort to make this person feel welcomed. For example, a Spanish-speaking exchange student from Chile spoke English moderately well and enjoyed playing the guitar. His American host family attended to his needs and wants by defining unfamiliar words and borrowing a guitar for him to play. Just as the host family gave special consideration to the Chilean student, you should consider your audience by making every effort to **accommodate** (adjust to, make concessions for) your audience's needs and wants.

Knowledge Level

What people know and how well they know it varies widely from one person to the next. As such, knowledge level can be high, low, or moderate. It can be technical or nontechnical. Ask yourself what your readers know or do not know about your subject. If you tell them what they already know, you risk wasting their time (not to mention yours). Yet if you omit something they need to know, you have not done your job.

For example, the knowledge level of Josh's parents prevented them from understanding a medical report. After two-year-old Josh fell down a flight of stairs at home, his distraught parents took him to the emergency room. Josh's emergency room report read: "The child suffered from contusions and lacerations." *Contusions* and *lacerations* are familiar terms to doctors and nurses. For Josh's parents, however, the medical **jargon** (the highly specialized language of a discipline or technical field) did not communicate as effectively as these everyday terms familiar to most parents: *The child suffered from cuts and bruises*. The medical jargon was confusing, making Josh's injury seem worse than it was.

Experience, age, and expertise can affect how much someone knows. Josh's parents lacked the experience and background of a doctor or nurse. And because of his age, Josh did not understand medical terms. Likewise, the technician who X-rayed Josh's finger knew how to position it to get the best picture but lacked the expert knowledge of the engineer who designed the machine.

Role

Consider your reader's **role** or area of responsibility before you begin writing. What is your reader's job or position in the workplace? Role or job title affects not only knowledge level but also the information your reader thinks is important.

Understand your reader's role and accommodate it. Accountants are concerned about their company's finances. If you write a recommendation to the accounting office about a planned purchase, you should accommodate the accountant's role by including information about cost. The technician who reads the same report may be more interested in how to operate equipment being purchased, having little concern about the cost. For the technician, you should include sufficient information about the technical specifications of the equipment.

© Yuri Arcurs, 2009/Shutterstock

Interest

When your readers are interested in your subject, they read with greater motivation and enthusiasm. Where you find common interest, your writing task is easier, for your reader becomes your automatic ally. Where there is no apparent interest, look for ways to identify with readers and offer an objective yet focused message.

Interest can be affected by age, experience, cultural background, and role. Your interests now are different from what they were ten years ago because you have a wider range of experiences. The camping and fishing trips you enjoyed as a child may have been replaced by long motor trips and concerts as a young adult. If everyone in your family enjoys eating black beans and rice, you may have a taste for those foods because of your background. Now your role is to be a student. When you join the workforce, your interests will be determined in part by your professional role.

Cultural Background

Culture—the special beliefs, customs, and values specific to a particular group of people or to a particular region—affects what an audience considers to be proper behavior. Many beliefs regarding human relations are affected by an individual's cultural background. By failing to consider someone's cultural background, you risk offending your reader and erecting barriers to communication. Your goal is to open the lines of communication and reach out to all of your readers.

In the United States, regional cultural differences affect communication. In the South, many parents insist that their children say, "Yes, ma'am" and "No, sir" to their elders as a sign of respect and proper etiquette. Other regions of the country do not rely as heavily on these endearments. While "Yes, ma'am" and "Yes, sir" are expected as polite gestures in one region of the country, the expressions may sound out of place—even offensive—in another region. Some people begin a telephone conversation with small talk, asking a person about his family as a prelude to conducting business. Yet other people consider such small talk too personal or an inefficient use of time.

U.S. businesses are becoming increasingly global. U.S-based businesses have interests abroad in countries such as Mexico, Argentina, Turkey, and India. Many documents are read by audiences outside the United States whose cultural differences affect communication. Where U.S business personnel perceive directness as a sign of open and honest business dealings, other cultures consider this approach brash and insensitive. Where U.S business relies heavily on written agreements ("put it in writing" and "read the fine print"), other cultures trust oral communication. Understanding these differences is imperative to accommodating your audience's cultural background.

Personality

Personality can be affected by culture, heredity, age, experience, and role. Also, someone's personality can shape his or her work habits. A legal researcher who prefers to work alone may appreciate receiving instructions via e-mail. Someone who prefers working in a group may want to receive oral instructions in a meeting so he can share his reaction with others. For him, e-mail may be a nuisance. When communicating, you may not know your readers well enough to make judgments about their personalities. But if you do, you can tailor your communication style appropriately.

Mayur is a successful manager. Part of his success comes from analyzing the personalities of his subordinates and supervisors. He knows his supervisor likes to make decisions based on credible research. When Mayur talks to her, he is direct and presents only the facts. When Mayur writes to her, his tone is objective, and he includes ample statistical data. In fact, the company's new medical plan is the result of Mayur's detailed proposal. Mayur's line manager, on the other hand, is easygoing and wants to know the bottom line. E-mails to him are short, infrequent, and friendly. The line manager is not interested in details, prefers a visit to an e-mail, and is hurt if the tone is too formal. Mayur has a good relationship with this line manager, who might otherwise be suspicious of a supervisor.

Before you begin to write a technical document, analyze your audience to determine their special needs. Use the questions in Table 2.1 to help you decide what to remember about your reader(s). When you have answered the questions, summarize what is most important to your audience. Then follow the suggestions in the second column for adjusting to your audience's needs.

Table 2.1

ASK THESE QUESTIONS	MAKE THESE ACCOMMODATIONS
Knowledge Level	
What does my reader already know about the topic? Is my reader an expert, a technician, or a lay reader? What does my reader need to know? What does my reader want to know?	Add particular knowledge that your audience does not have. Leave out or quickly summarize knowledge your audience already has. Decide how much technical language to include. Use informal definitions or a glossary if necessary. Present complex information visually.
Interests	
How strong is my reader's interest in my topic? Are my reader's priorities different from mine or the same as mine? Is my reader likely to agree with my point of view?	Appeal to known interests or try to create interest. Express agreement with and understanding of a point of view when possible. Provide evidence to help sway others to your point of view.
Role	
Is my reader's role • to make decisions or implement a plan? • to operate equipment, encode data, train others? • to create or design or invent? Is my communication going to management, to a peer, or to a supervisee?	Include knowledge the role requires—planning parameters for managers, technical details for technicians. Write different sections for different roles. Be diplomatic with management, courteous yet straightforward with a peer, and respectful and direct with someone you supervise.
Cultural Background	
What is my reader's cultural background? What are my reader's beliefs? Are my reader's beliefs different from mine or the same as mine?	Understand how culture affects someone's beliefs and decisions. Learn about the cultural background of your audience and adhere to the cultural norms of that audience as much as possible.
Personality	
What kind of personality does my reader have? Is my reader analytical, quiet, or outgoing? Does my reader prefer having details or seeing the big picture?	Adjust tone and medium to personality. Provide facts, order, and evidence for the analytically minded; a personal touch for facilitators; and ideas and the overall picture for creative thinkers.

Meeting the Needs of a Multiple Audience

Shakespeare was arguably the greatest writer who ever lived. His success depended on his wit, knowledge of theater, and understanding of his audience. As a businessperson, Shakespeare knew he had to please England's royal family as well as the peasants who came to see his plays. He had to appeal to young and old, to men and women, to the educated and the uneducated. In the sixteenth century, Shakespeare wrote successfully to a multiple audience, an audience made up of multiple interests, with members whose needs and wants sometimes conflicted with one another.

Typical Reader

A person or group of people who want or need specific information.

Writer's Focus

Analyzing the rhetorical situation and the audience's needs and providing information in the best possible way for the audience to understand.

Today technical writers face a similar challenge writing to an audience that can include executives, managers, and administrative assistants. In his day, Shakespeare was clever—he wrote different parts of the same play for different people. Today his "different parts for different folks" strategy is used by technical writers too. But technical writers go one step further. They "label" the parts with headings, short titles preceding sections of the document to alert readers to the information written for them.

Another strategy for meeting the diverse needs of a multiple audience is to determine who comes first—whose needs are most important. To decide what data to focus on as you write, divide your audience into two groups: **primary audience** and **secondary audience**. Think of the primary audience as readers or listeners to whom you are responsible first and the secondary audience as readers or listeners to whom you are responsible after having met the needs of the primary audience. Both audiences are important, but as a writer, you must organize your tasks according to some kind of priority.

PRIMARY AUDIENCE	SECONDARY AUDIENCE
• Asked for or authorized the writing of the document	• Will be affected by the document in some way
• Will make decisions based on the information in the document	• Is interested in the decisions made or the information in the document
• Will request or take action based on information in the document	• May use some information for a purpose different from the document's purpose
• Will likely read the entire document	• May read selected portions

Walsh Plastics is considering building a plant in Thailand. Suppose you are the writer of the feasibility report analyzing the move for the company. Walsh's executives and the company lawyer who must decide whether to open a factory in a foreign country constitute the primary audience. The architect who will design the new plant, the sales representatives who will move, and the managers who will train new workers make up the secondary audience. How will you address each audience's needs and wants?

The following criteria may help identify the primary and secondary audiences for your writing projects.

Magdalena, a software engineer, faced the challenging task of writing a proposal and developing the software for the inventory management system of a local school system. The primary audience, the director, contracted services with Magdalena, specified what the software needed to do, and decided who would be trained to use it. The secondary audience included assistants who would key data, the programmer who would modify the software as needed, and the superintendent who would confirm that Magdalena had fulfilled her contract terms. How would Magdalena write a document for readers with such diverse backgrounds, professional roles, and technical expertise? To accommodate all of their needs, she wrote different parts of the report for different people. Table 2.2 reveals the adjustments Magdalena made to accommodate the needs of the multiple audience. Chapters 12 and 13 will cover long reports with different headings written to accommodate a multiple audience.

Table 2.2

READER'S ROLES AND NEEDS	MAGDALENA'S ADJUSTMENT TO READER
As the *approver,* the **superintendent** needs to know whether the money spent on the programmer's services was responsibly invested and whether the terms of the contract have been completed.	Magdalena writes a *cover memo* briefly summarizing the report, describing the program, and outlining advantages to the school system. She uses little or no technical language, carefully defining any technical terms.
As the *decision maker* and *manager,* the **director** needs an overview of the program to see whether the specifications agreed upon have been met and to receive a demonstration of the product.	Magdalena writes the **Executive Summary**, which presents the most important information in the report. She includes some technical language and gives a formal demonstration of the program.
Despite *varied roles,* **all of the readers** need to understand the purpose of the manual and those parts that will help each of them.	In the **Introduction**, Magdalena explains the purpose of the proposal and its organization. She uses little or no technical language.
As the *technician,* the **programmer** needs to understand the program structure, to know how best to extend the functionality of the program, and to know how users interface with the program.	Magdalena documents her programming with UML diagrams and places this information in the **Appendix**. She invites the programmer to the training session for assistants.
As *end users,* the **administrative assistants** need to understand how to key, manipulate, and find data as quickly as possible.	Magdalena writes **procedures** that explain how to use the program. She uses short commands, occasional explanations, and screen shots. She then follows up with a training session on how to use the program.
Magdalena's audience is **diverse,** including a range of ages and technological experience.	Magdalena stores the report, the documentation, and presentation on Google Docs, giving everyone access so her readers have options for reviewing the material.

Sometimes, though, when a document is short, you can simply revise it for each audience and send it separately. For example, an e-mail from the director of information systems to the network administrators telling them to bring down the network Friday afternoon for routine maintenance specified in detail what the staff should do. At the end of the email, the director reminded her staff that users would be notified to log off by noon.

Before the director sent the e-mail to users, however, she shortened the message. Instead of specifying the work to be done, she asked users to log off by noon, announced that the maintenance was routine, and thanked them for their cooperation and patience. The reminder of the network outage in the bimonthly newsletter was even briefer. By the time she finished, she had revised her message for three different audiences.

Writing to a multiple audience, then, requires careful analysis of each possible audience member followed by a workable plan. Writing "different parts for different folks," focusing on the needs of the primary audience, and rewriting short documents are all strategies available to the technical writer. Remember, too, that an audience that you did not consider could read your document. Therefore, you must anticipate every possible audience member and adjust accordingly.

Focus on Ethics

As a writer, to avoid biased language, you must be aware of stereotypes in your writing. Sometimes the stereotype is so engrained in the culture that you do not realize you are using biased language. You probably know you should avoid sexist language in your writing (referring to men and women differently), but stereotypes include more than gender. People also can be stereotyped because of race, sexual orientation, age, physical or mental abilities, religion, ethnicity, and weight.

In your writing, strive to present everyone as being equal. First, avoid sexist language by referring to men and women the same way. For example, do not assume that all doctors are men and that all nurses are women. Avoid using examples that reinforce stereotypes.

Second, do not mention a person's physical characteristics if they are not relevant. If you would not say, "Our new software developer is Max, a smart white man without disabilities," then do not say, "Our new software developer is Sandra, a smart white woman with physical disabilities."

Sometimes you are not aware of the biased language. If you are not sure whether you have used stereotypes in your writing, ask another person to look over the document.

Think Critically

What are the possible consequences of stereotyping people?

⬡ STOP AND THINK 2.1

Think of an issue about which you feel passionate—your candidate for Student Government Association president, pet adoptions, a political issue, or something else that is important to you. Suppose you had to convince the entire student body to agree with you. What kinds of adjustments would you make to appeal to your multiple audiences?

2.2 PLANNING YOUR DOCUMENT'S PURPOSE, SCOPE, AND MEDIUM

Understanding who your audience is and what they need and want is an important part of your job as a writer. However, you have other decisions to make before you are ready to write. Early in the writing process, determine the purpose of your document, its scope, and the medium you will use.

Purpose

Purpose is defined as a specific end or outcome. It is what a writer wants a reader to do after reading a document. In technical writing, the purpose is to inform and/or persuade. Because much technical writing is intended to persuade, you need to consider your topic from the readers' points of view. How will your readers react to the information you provide? For them, is the information good or bad news? With whom or what are you competing for your readers' attention? Is there a time limit for responding? Are your readers required to read your document? In other words, how hard must you work to get and keep your readers' attention? You should address these and other concerns as you think about the purpose of your document.

To determine the specific purpose of your writing assignment, ask yourself some basic questions:

- What do I want to inform my readers about?

- What do I want to persuade or convince them of?

- What do I want to happen as a result of this message?

To determine the purpose of your writing, ask additional questions to figure out what you want to happen when someone reads your document. What do you want your readers to do? What do you want them to know, to buy, to believe, to give? What would you like them to learn to do or change their minds about? Would you like them to stop doing something or start doing something? When you answer those questions, you will know the purpose of your document.

A statement of purpose may be to inform citizens of the latest employment trends or to convince the public to purchase smoke alarms. The persuasive purpose also implies providing information. Thus, a purpose to persuade becomes a purpose to inform, too. To convince bank customers to invest their money in money market accounts, you also must inform them about the advantages of such accounts. To convince the public to purchase smoke alarms requires evidence that smoke alarms save lives.

A statement of purpose on the same topic can vary for each audience. Consider the new employee evaluation system at Fabre Perfume Industries. Every employee is evaluated. Therefore, the purpose of the new *Employee Evaluation Manual* is to describe the procedure so that all employees understand how they will be evaluated.

However, because supervisors must conduct the evaluations, they receive the new *Employee Evaluation Manual* <u>and</u> the *Evaluation Procedures Manual*. The purpose of the *Procedures Manual* is to inform supervisors

Suppose a local newspaper reporter had interviewed you about the incident you wrote about in the Write to Learn activity. How does knowing the story will appear in print for a wider audience affect what you say and do not say? Suppose you were being interviewed before a live television audience. What adjustments would you make for a live broadcast?

about the new process for conducting evaluations—how to locate the online forms, where to send them, and what the deadlines are. The topic—new evaluations—is the same, but supervisors need additional information to implement the new guidelines.

Scope

© Vuk Vukmirovic, 2009/Shutterstock

Once you have a clear, stated purpose, you must decide the following: How thorough will my coverage be? What information do I include and omit? Here you use your audience analysis and statement of purpose to make decisions about the **scope** of your writing—the extent of treatment, activity, or influence—that is, what is and is not included.

Suppose you are writing instructions telling car owners how to change a tire. You have settled on this statement of purpose: The user should be able to change a tire after reading my instructions. If you wonder whether to include information about how to select a dependable tire or how often to rotate tires, you could review your statement of purpose and say to yourself: No, my purpose is to explain how to change a tire, not to sell tires or inform users about proper tire maintenance. If you are wondering whether to mention that changing a tire is not difficult and is an important survival skill, you can ask yourself this question: Will this information help me achieve my purpose with this audience? In other words, will it help my drivers change a tire? The answer is yes. Motivating your reader to follow instructions does support your purpose.

Medium

Finally, you need to choose a medium for delivering your message. The **medium** is the means by which information is conveyed (for example, a television commercial). What kind of document will you produce? Will it be printed? What medium will accomplish your purpose and appeal to your audience?

Today's choices for media range from traditional media—such as print, television, and radio—to online media, including websites, social media, and e-mail. While technology offers us more channels through which to communicate, traditional channels continue to play a role. Consumers of traditional media are largely passive, but consumers of online media are more engaged, seeking out information using smartphones, tablets, and laptops. As a result, writers can choose the best medium for their message from a variety of options—as long as they understand the advantages and disadvantages of each.

Landin Technical Institute promoted its Graphic Arts program 25 years ago using what was available—traditional media. A simple trifold brochure was displayed in a rack and mailed to potential students, black-and-white memos circulated through campus mail, and announcements pinned to bulletin boards kept everyone informed. Occasionally news of the program was aired on television or radio.

Today news about the Graphic Arts program, such as degree requirements and student activities, still uses these traditional media.

However, as Figure 2.2 illustrates, the message is now expanded upon, separated into parts, and repurposed into digital media for different audiences needing different information.

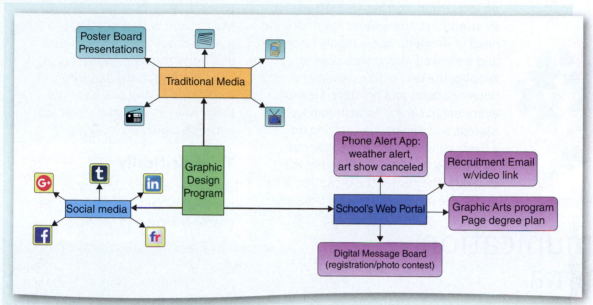

Figure 2.2 Traditional and Online Media

Everyone, including Americans with disabilities, has access to program requirements on the college's website. Abbreviated announcements for the fall fundraiser and the spring portfolio show slide across digital message boards throughout campus and emerge on the department's Facebook page. Award-winning art photos are housed on Flicker. Users rely on phone apps for reminders; advisory committees use Google+ polls for assessments and Meet for meetings. On her blog, one instructor highlights student achievements, which are truncated for recruitment e-mails accompanied by a short video. Potential employment opportunities appear on the department chair's LinkedIn profile.

Each time the basic message is repurposed, part of it remains the same, but other parts shift to adapt to another medium. The ease with which a message can be reworked and redistributed connects readers to information they want quickly. Central to this communication flow are the writers who select appropriate media and produce the text.

As a writer, you have decisions to make: Do you need detailed instructions or a quick reference sheet? PowerPoint® slides or a webinar? Do you need to post your document on the Web or send it as an e-mail attachment? Is there any benefit to mailing a long printed proposal?

As you are making your decision, ask yourself these questions:

1. What media are available to me?

2. What media does my audience typically use?

3. Is the medium appropriate for my audience, message, and purpose?

4. Is the time and money required to produce the medium worth the possible outcome?

Communication
Dilemma

Marcus and Sophia are chemists conducting experiments for Wuxi Pharmaceuticals on how bacteria ward off viral invaders. They just left the lab to attend a retirement reception for the head of maintenance, a highly respected and well-liked man responsible for keeping the lab facilities running during power outages and holidays. Nearly everyone has come to wish him well. Marcus and Sophia are carrying on a lively conversation, excited about something that happened in the lab that day. They enter the reception area and settle into a corner with Uma, the public relations officer, and Drew, the new webmaster, who is looking uncomfortable in such a large group. During the presentation, Marcus and Sophia continue to talk quietly about the CRISPR-based immunity and RNA interference in higher organisms, ignoring everything taking place around them. Marcus sees Uma looking at him with a puzzled look.

Think Critically

Why do you think Uma looks puzzled? What advice would you give to Marcus and Sophia?

To help you decide what medium is appropriate, find out what kind of media are typically used in your organization. Your local department of social services may use e-mail for routine communication and interoffice mail for intake reports. The state agency, however, may expect e-mail attachments for monthly participation reports. Work at the national level may best be presented on a website from which slide presentations and flyers can be downloaded and printed.

While many businesses have state-of-the-art computer equipment and fast Internet connections, some small businesses, such as Air Care's home heating and air-conditioning business, may have only a computer, a printer, and a minimum amount of accounting and word processing software. You, like Ramon, the owner of Air Care, may find yourself in a field for which you are well prepared professionally but not as adept with desktop publishing. Perhaps well-designed templates for sales proposals, invoices, and interoffice memos meet the needs of this environment.

© kemie/iStockphoto.com

The **format** of your medium deals with the details of the document's arrangement: the type of document, its length, the preferred style manual, and its organization. Just as your English instructor may prefer that your essays be written a particular way, your employer also may prefer that your document be written a certain way. Your English instructor may require papers to be keyed and double-spaced using the guidelines from the *MLA Handbook for Writers of Research Papers*. Your business or psychology instructor may require another style guide, such as *the*

Chicago Manual of Style or the *Publication Manual of the American Psychological Association.*

An employer may expect you to follow a company style sheet (with suggested headings and a specified way to present data) and include the company letterhead (with the logo, address, and slogan). Forms and procedures can be posted on a company's intranet web server where templates set up for page layouts ensure design consistency. Furthermore, the level of formality may depend on the subject matter, the audience, and company standards. Some formal and legal correspondence outside and inside an organization still uses a business letter requiring a signature, while most routine correspondence depends on e-mail, texting, and phone calls.

© Andrey Arkusha, 2009/Shutterstock

Technical writers have many avenues with which to convey information. Writers' many choices provide them with creative and innovative solutions to any communication challenge. Table 2.3 shows some of the choices for a medium once the purpose and scope have been determined.

Table 2.3

PURPOSE	SCOPE		MEDIUM
To Convince Reader(s) to . . .	**Includes . . .**	**Does *Not* Include . . .**	**Possible Choices**
Prepare for hurricane (residents of North Carolina)	Emergency supplies, hurricane routes, shelters, procedures	Routes/shelters for states other than North Carolina	Brochure, newspaper insert, television, local news/weather app
Operate Brand X scanner (new non-tech-savvy owner)	Information for scanning photos and texts	Information for any brand other than X; instructions for how to repair	Short user's manual, online help, downloadable pdf documents
Stop smoking with nicotine patch (smoker of ten years)	Information about the nicotine patch	Information about other methods such as gum, willpower, and hypnosis	Pharmaceutical insert for nicotine patch, website with motivational video
Eat nutritious meals (teens)	Simple, quick recipes to meet basic nutrition needs; foods teens typically like	Recipes for heart patients, diabetics, or aging population	Spiral-bound cookbook with CD, Recipe App pin, YouTube recipes
Book a vacation (middle-class families)	Vacation spots with group activities and fun parks; reduced rates	Vacation spots with long flights or honeymoon plans	Magazine article, brochure, Buzzfeed, Expedia website and app

(continues)

Table 2.3 *(Continued)*

PURPOSE	SCOPE		MEDIUM
To Convince Reader(s) to . . .	**Includes . . .**	**Does *Not* Include . . .**	**Possible Choices**
Seek information about financial aid (high school seniors)	Information about parental income and college plans	Opinions about fairness of financial aid	Studentaid.gov, phone call, banking websites
Sell stained-glass window ornaments (home decorators)	Photos, description, ordering information, and pricing	Complete details on how each is made and cost of materials	Etsy, Pinterest, eBay, online chatroom
Complain about a credit card company fraud (victim)	Details and documentation of the fraudulent practice	High interest rates on a store credit card	Letter, phone call, online form

STOP AND THINK 2.2

Analyze an assignment that one of your instructors has given you. What are the purpose, scope, and medium of the assignment?

CHAPTER REVIEW

Summary

1. The audience's needs and wants should dictate every decision a writer makes. Writers think through the rhetorical situation which prompts a response, or rhetorical act. Logos, ethos, pathos, and kairos are strategies employed to appeal to an audience.

2. A specific audience is a single reader or a group of readers with a common purpose. Knowledge level, roles, interests, cultural background, personality, and format affect communication with a specific audience.

3. A multiple audience is made up of readers with different points of view. Analyzing knowledge level, roles, interests, cultural background, personality, and format are still important when communicating with a multiple audience.

4. A writer must analyze his or her audience and then decide how to accommodate the readers' needs and wants.

5. Early in the writing process, a writer must determine the purpose, scope, and medium.

Checklist

- Is my audience a specific audience or a multiple audience?
- Have I identified the rhetorical situation and possible appeals?
- Have I analyzed the knowledge level, roles, interests, cultural background, and personality of my audience?
- If I am dealing with a multiple audience, have I selected a strategy for accommodating their needs and wants?
- Have I put into words the purpose of my writing assignment?
- Have I determined the scope of my writing assignment by deciding what it should and should not include?
- Have I found an appropriate medium for the writing assignment?
- Have I selected an appropriate format for the audience and purpose of the writing assignment?
- Have I checked for stereotypes in my writing?

Build Your Foundation

1. To make you more aware of audience, answer the following questions: Who might be the target audience for these TV shows, networks, or stations? To what groups of people might they appeal? Why?

Grey's Anatomy	*Monday Night Football*	*Country Music Television*
60 Minutes	*Jeopardy*	*Nick at Nite*
American Idol	*Survivor*	*The History Channel*

2. Consider the following terms. If any are unfamiliar to you, look them up in a dictionary or ask your family or friends what they mean. Which audience(s) would understand these terms?

blitz	QWERTY	curl	sauté
goalie	billabong	dunk	arabesque
a cappella	compost	angioplasty	starboard

3. Look through the comic section of a newspaper. Which comic strips appeal to which audiences? How do you know? For each comic strip, list the target audience and features that help you identify the audience.

4. Bring several issues of your favorite magazine to class, or access a magazine online. Spend 15–20 minutes looking at the table of contents and browsing through the articles and advertisements. After considering the following questions, write a few paragraphs analyzing one magazine for audience and purpose.

   a. What is the purpose of the magazine? Who is the intended audience?
   b. What are four things the editors of the magazine have done to accommodate their readers' needs and wants? In other words, how have the editors appealed to their readers?
   c. Do you like the way the magazine has tried to appeal to its readers? Why do you believe the appeal is or is not successful? Locate appeals to logos, ethos, and pathos.
   d. What suggestions do you have for improving the appeal of the magazine?
   e. Do you notice stereotypes in the magazine, particularly in the advertisements? If so, what are they?

5. Suggest an appropriate audience and medium for the following situations:

   a. Nadia wants members of her scuba diving club to know the latest diving news.
   b. Thaddeus is responsible for selling manufactured homes in his territory.
   c. The County Health Department wants to tell the public how to prevent the flu.

6. Who are the primary and secondary audiences in the following situations?

   a. Aruna Amin, an advertising consultant, has been hired to write a series of ads to educate young people about the danger of using cell phones while driving.
   b. Lu-yin Chang, a professional technical writer, is working on a catalog for Pickernel Camping, a national outfitter of camping supplies.

Your Turn

1. Divide into teams of three or four students. Use the following scenario to answer items a and b.

   Sam, Kaito, and Meg have just started publishing *TV Highlights,* a weekly magazine. Sam sells the advertising. Kaito, a graphic designer, is responsible for the artwork. Kaito's uncle is the owner. He makes most of the decisions but often defers to Kaito's opinions. Meg is the accountant.

   Think about the role each person performs in this small company. How do each person's responsibilities affect decisions? How does each person's role affect how he or she communicates with the other people in the company? Also, who is the target audience for *TV Highlights?*

   a. Kaito wants a four-color cover on glossy paper for the first issue because he thinks the first issue should look impressive. Meg, on the other hand, believes a four-color glossy cover is too expensive. Sam says the advertisers do not care how many colors are on the cover. They want only the local high school's blue and red colors to be represented. Meg decides to write a report to Kaito's uncle recommending a two-color cover for the first few issues. Who is Meg's audience for the report? What should she remember about her audience? What kind of information might she include to convince Kaito's uncle (and Kaito)? Should she include information about Sam's concerns? Why or why not?

b. Franz Bohm, a freelance writer, has written to Kaito, asking what topics interest the magazine's readers. The magazine is written for a rural audience in New England. The average reader is a teen-aged girl. In what types of articles do you think the readers of *TV Highlights* are interested?

2. Write an e-mail to your employer requesting time off for a special event, such as homecoming or a family vacation. Then switch roles. Write an e-mail from the employer to you denying the time off. How do your messages differ?

3. Write a letter to the president of the United States about a particular policy you like (or do not like). Tell a friend what you like (or do not like) about the same policy. How does your language change?

Community Connection

1. Interview the editor or a news reporter for a local news agency—newspaper, radio, or television. What are the demographics—the specific breakdown of the members of the audience—by such identifiers as age, sex, income, and race? How do the demographics affect the news reported? How does the writer appeal to this multiple audience? How does the medium affect the message? Ask about one broadcast or column in particular. Who is the specific audience? What is the purpose, scope, or medium? Write a one-page question-and-answer (Q&A) of the interview.

2. Interview someone from another country or another part of the United States. Ask about differences in the culture, such as food, celebrations, customs, and manners. Research the person's culture. Write a list of suggestions that would help an area business communicate more effectively with this person. For example, what would a real estate broker need to know to work well with this person?

EXPLORE THE NET

Visit Cyborlink, a website offering advice on international business etiquette, to learn tips on how to conduct business in over 100 countries. Choose one country unfamiliar to you. Report on cultural norms such as what to wear, how to greet people, when and how to present gifts, and how to behave when conducting business in another country. Take a look at Hofstede's Dimension of Culture Scales on the website. How does the United States rank on the scale? Compare the United States' ranking to two other countries.

3 TECHNICAL RESEARCH

Goals

- Distinguish the difference between researching at school and at work
- Identify and locate secondary sources
- Document secondary sources
- Evaluate sources
- Take notes from sources
- Collect primary data

Terms

Write to Learn

Think about a time when you wanted or needed to know more about a topic. What was the reason for your research? What did researching the topic involve? In other words, how did you conduct the research? Did you begin with an online search? Did your research include a survey, an experiment, or an interview? What did you learn from your research activities? Were you intimidated by the research process?

 FOCUS on Technical Research

Read Figure 3.1 on the next page and answer these questions:

- In what order are the entries placed? Why?
- Why do some entries include a date of access?
- Of the sources listed, which ones did the researchers find online? in print?
- Which source is most recent?

What If?

How would the model change if . . .

- The researchers were planning to publish their work in a newspaper or publication without a focus on science?
- The audience were interested only in the most recent findings on the topic?

WORKING BIBLIOGRAPHY

Ben-Barak, I. Radiation-Proof Microbe Uses Its Powers for Good. *Sydney Morning Herald* Nov. 6, 2008, first ed.: p. A24. Newspaper Source Plus. https://www.ebscohost.com/public /newspaper-source-plus (accessed Mar 13, 2017).

Dong, X.; Tian, B.; Dai, S.; Li, T.; Guo, L.; Tan, Z.; Jiao, Z.; Jin, Q.; Wang, Y.; Hua, Y. Expression of PprI from *Deinococcus Radiodurans* Improves Lactic Acid Production and *Stress Tolerance in Lactococcus Lactis*. *PLoS One* Nov 2015, pp. 1–16. ProQuest. www.proquest.com (accessed Mar 20, 2017).

Galhardo, R.S.; Rosenberg, S.M. Extreme Genome Repair. *Cell* 2009, 136, pp. 998–1000.

GuanJun, G.; Lu, F.; YueJin, H. Engineering *Deinococcus Radiodurans* into Biosensor to Monitor Radioactivity and Genotoxicity in Environment. *Chinese Science Bulletin* 2008, pp. 1675–81. Academic Search Premier. https://www.ebscohost.com/academic/academic-search-premier (accessed April 23, 2017).

Fialka, John J. Position Available: Indestructible Bugs to Eat Nuclear Waste: Scientists Envision New Role for Sturdy Bacteria Breed: Creating "Super Conan." *Wall Street Journal* 16 Nov. 2004, eastern ed.: A1.

Impey, C. *The Living Cosmos: Our Search for Life in the Universe.* Random House: New York, 2007.

Leonetti, J.; Matic, I. Use of Bacteria for the Production of Bioenergy. US 9181564, US 20110104766, May 22, 2009.

Rodrigues, V.D.; Torres, T.; Ottoboni, L.M. Bacterial Diversity Assessment in Soil of an Active Brazilian Copper Mine Using High-Throughput Sequencing of 16S rDNA Amplicons. *Antonie van Leeuwenhoek* Nov. 2014, pp 879–90. ProQuest. www.proquest.com (accessed April 1, 2017).

Shrivastav, Snehlata. BARC Scientists Utilizing N-Science for Benefit of Masses [Nagpur]. *The Times of India [Online]* Feb 25, 2014, p 8. ProQuest. www.proquest.com (accessed May 3, 2017).

Tough Bug Reveals Key to Radiation Resistance. *New Scientist* [Online] March 24, 2007, p. 21. MasterFILE Premier. https://www.ebscohost.com/academic/masterfile-premier (accessed May 8, 2017).

Figure 3.1 Sample Working Bibliography using American Chemical Society (ACS) Style Guide

Writing @Work

Courtesy of Mark Sonya Parrish

CareerClusters
PATHWAYS TO COLLEGE & CAREER READINESS
Education & Training

Source: The Center to Advance CTE

Sonya Parrish is a teaching associate and doctoral student in literature at Miami University in Oxford, Ohio. She has taught first-year college composition courses for three years. She researches primary and secondary sources regularly for her roles as graduate student and English teacher and incorporates technical writing in the syllabus for her composition courses.

Sonya's scholarly research includes hunting through digital archives, essays, and books by other scholars and through the literature in her field. "I rely heavily on using print sources in which I can write notes, underline important points or quotes, and make comments in the margins. I also compile notes from texts into Word documents that present the information in a more unified and organized manner."

Sonya teaches her students to evaluate sources using five criteria: authorship, objectivity, knowledge, accuracy, and relevance. When evaluating websites, Sonya helps her students see the way in which information on the Web is authored and constructed.

Different kinds of sites—such as .org and .edu sites—deliver different kinds of information to different audiences in different ways.

When scholarly research responds thoughtfully to other scholars' work, it creates a dialogue that requires proper documentation. "Writers should acknowledge others who have provided them with information on a given topic," according to Sonya. "They should also think about their audience's expectations of accuracy and honesty in writing." She uses GPS navigation instructions as a metaphor for what proper citations should do: show the reader what "path" the author took in constructing his or her argument and prove that the path is credible. Another scholar or teacher, like Sonya, can then pick up the hunt for information using the bibliographical trail left by other authors.

Think Critically

1. If Sonya were getting an advanced degree in biology or architecture, would she rely as heavily on printed source material? Why or why not?

2. Suppose Sonya is teaching a section about Maya Angelou's poetry. Give an example of a primary source and a secondary source that Sonya might use.

Printed with permission of Sonya Parrish

Writing in Education and Training

People who work in education and training usually need strong communication skills. One of their roles is to share their skills with learners, whether those learners are young people in primary or secondary schools, adults in colleges and universities, or adults in the workplace or in other areas of society. Whether a student in second grade or an engineer who requires training on a new computer-assisted drafting (CAD) program, every student should receive clear, accurate, detailed, and complete instruction in a form which he or she can easily understand. In addition, educators and trainers must engage their audiences, so they need the ability to use technology effectively to convey a clear message. Another role of education and training professionals is to advance the body of knowledge in their fields. Thus, these professionals write reports and journal articles as well as books using the style manual accepted by professionals in the given field to disseminate research findings and new ideas and interpretations. For instance, a biology professor who wants to publish an article on her most recent research results could use CBE (Council of Biology Editors) style, the manual issued by the Council of Science Editors. An art or history professor wanting to submit a manuscript for publication might use the University of Chicago's *Chicago Manual of Style,* while a Spanish or American literature researcher would likely use the Modern Language Association's *MLA Handbook for Writers of Research Papers.*

3.1 CONDUCTING TECHNICAL RESEARCH

Information is everywhere: on the Web, on the television, on the radio, in your textbook, on CDs and DVDs, in magazines and newsletters, and on the lips of doctors, professors, parents, and friends. You sit in front of an electronic device, such as a computer, tablet, or smartphone, where you may access a world full of information. If you want to know something, you only have to look in the right place.

The problem that technical researchers face is not a scarcity of information; it is more likely to be an overwhelming amount of information. The problem is in understanding what information they need, where it is, how it is stored, how to retrieve it, and what to do with it after they find it. The process of conducting research can be delineated as a series of steps, but like other parts of the writing process, in practice, the process is fluid, unfolding as you go.

Typical Reader

A person looking for honest, accurate answers to questions about a topic.

Writer's Focus

Locating information from appropriate sources; evaluating its credibility; synthesizing that research into a coherent document, presentation, or discussion; and using proper documentation.

3.2 RESEARCHING AT WORK

 WARM UP

Employees rely on the information they collect to solve problems, to make decisions, to answer questions, and to perform many other functions at work. On the job, research is usually involved in all of the following situations (and more):

- Developing a new product
- Handling a production problem
- Purchasing equipment or services
- Establishing safety procedures
- Securing corporate data
- Planning an advertising campaign

Writing on the job provides information to help the business operate effectively. Unlike academic writing, its purpose is not to show the writer's knowledge of the topic.

For example, if a nurse writes a fact sheet explaining how patients should manage their diabetes, the nurse is not writing to show how much he knows about the subject but to teach patients how to stay healthy. If a chef creates standard operating procedures, she does not write the document to impress readers with how much she learned in school but rather to ensure food safety. All of the information that writers and researchers gather and present is used for effective job performance. Useful information presented effectively can determine whether an enterprise is successful or unsuccessful.

Before you can write at work, you may need to conduct research. In fact, many decisions and actions at work require more information than you have at hand. You probably begin by determining what you already know. Then considering

Recall research tasks you may have done in a work or school setting. For each task, what was the purpose of the research? How was the workplace research different from research you have done for pleasure or at school? For example, how is researching the best ways to remove a virus from a client's laptop different from finding more information about your favorite singer or sports star?

© Stephen Coburn/Shutterstock

your audience, purpose, and scope, you gather and evaluate new information and likely form conclusions about the material you read. Before you conduct the research, you must make sure you know who, what, where, when, why, and how. For example, who is involved, and who will use your research? What do these people need to know? Where will you search for information—within or outside your organization or both? Why are you researching this topic? How will you collect information, and how will it be used? You also need a strategy for

- Finding and evaluating the right material and the best sources.

- Conducting the research and reading efficiently.

- Carefully and accurately recording the information you find so that you do not accidentally plagiarize or violate the owner's copyright.

- Documenting where you found the information so that you or someone else can find it again.

Researchers may find some data easily, such as production figures that are readily available on the corporate network. Sometimes, though, researchers must search extensively for information.

Employees have two basic sources of information: secondary sources and primary sources.

Secondary sources are indirect or secondhand reports of information, such as the description of an event the writer or speaker did not witness. When a newspaper reporter describes what executives of a closing textile plant said, that description is a secondary source. **Primary sources,** on the other hand, are direct or firsthand reports of facts or observations, such as an eyewitness account or a diary. The writer or speaker is the one who witnessed the event or developed the idea.

For example, hearing a company president, rather than a reporter, give reasons for a plant's closing is primary information. Likewise, a journal is a firsthand account of the writer's experiences and is, therefore, a primary source. However, if you use ideas from another person's journal in a report on healthy lifestyles, the borrowed ideas become secondary data in your report because you did not experience or observe them yourself.

Researchers generally start with secondary sources because they often give general overviews and offer useful background information. Secondary sources are usually easier and less expensive to consult than primary sources. The overviews these sources can give help researchers understand what is already known about the topic. A problem-solver may even learn that someone has already discovered a solution.

STOP AND THINK 3.2

How is researching at work different from researching at school? Why do professionals conduct research? What kinds of research might you do in your intended career?

3.3 FINDING SECONDARY DATA

To solve most problems, your first step is to explore the available secondary data. After all, you do not want to reinvent the wheel. If the answer already exists, you do not need to spend time, effort, and money to rediscover it.

While using our smartphones for simple online research is so commonplace that "to google" has become an acceptable verb, researchers should be aware of a variety of ways to access secondary information.

For work-related research, you will probably use one or more of the following sources of secondary data: your organization's correspondence and report **archives** (collections or repositories of documents), a library catalog, periodicals, and general reference materials. While these secondary data sources may be available in print (sometimes called *hard copy*), most will be available in print and electronic files.

Correspondence and Report Archives

A logical place to begin looking for an answer to a problem is in the organization where the problem exists. Most organizations keep archives of correspondence and reports. Especially in large organizations, archives are generally maintained locally or remotely in an electronic format on the organization's intranet so that people who need the information have access but the files are not available to the public. On the other hand, some highly regulated organizations, such as pharmaceutical companies, may be required to keep print as well as electronic copies of essential information.

Employees may use archived documents to learn about the history of the problem or topic. They may find letters, memos, or reports explaining when problems were first noted, what kinds of investigation were conducted, and whether a solution was successful.

When the research topic does not have a history, relevant facts and statistics may be found in a variety of sources within the organization's records.

Library Catalog

The researcher's next stop is the company's library or a public or academic library. Some large businesses have an in-house or corporate library that contains specialized materials relating to the business it serves. In addition to company-produced reports such as production figures, accident reports, and personnel information, these internal libraries typically hold materials that employees need in order to stay current in the field in which they work. A software company's library may contain books and journals specializing in software development and marketing. Because these company libraries focus specifically on the needs of employees, they do not compete with public or other libraries by carrying all types of reading and research materials. They often contain more electronic than paper resources. If no in-house library is available to the company's problem solvers, they must go to an academic, online, research, municipal, or regional library.

As a new sales representative, you are going to Japan to meet your first prospective customer. If you know little about Japanese people and customs, where can you find what you need to know? Where would you find whether you should take the customer a gift and what kind of gift you should present? List several things you need to know and where you can find the information.

Whether in a corporate, public, or research library, employees looking for secondary data may start locating materials through the library catalog. The library catalog helps researchers find books, pamphlets, periodicals, audiovisual materials, and other holdings. In fact, it is now common practice for libraries also to catalog certain websites and other electronic sources such as e-books. Most libraries have computerized catalogs that are searchable by subject, title, and author and sometimes by other categories such as date or keyword. Most catalog systems also send requested entries to a printer for printing the records. Generally, libraries have integrated systems so that the online catalog can tell where a book is located and whether it has been checked out.

After the user keys the author's name, a title, or a subject, the online catalog displays a list of sources and their locations. Because materials are often cataloged using authorized subject headings from the Library of Congress Subject Headings, using keywords found in this reference can make a search more effective. If a search yields one book with useful information, a new search using the keywords found in that book's entry will likely produce other helpful sources.

If a researcher finds that a particular book is not in the library, the researcher may request that the book be ordered from another library through an interlibrary loan. The book also may be found online through a subscription database that offers online access to full-text books.

Most online library catalogs are user-friendly, but you should not hesitate to ask a librarian for help. Librarians can explain how to use the equipment, what the standard subject headings are, and how to search so you find what you need quickly and efficiently. Remember that the catalog will lead you to sources for background and in-depth information. For more recent data, use periodicals or Internet sources.

Communication
Technologies

When you visit a library, besides the physical library, you also have access to thousands of other libraries throughout the world. WorldCat, an Online Computer Library Center, Inc. (OCLC) product, links you to the collections of more than 71,000 (and growing) member libraries of OCLC, giving you access to more than 2 billion records for books, manuscript collections, audiovisual materials, and computer files in a variety of languages. It is the world's largest network of library content and services. Through WorldCat, you can search many libraries at once and find an item available at a library near you; download and use research articles and digital files, such as audiobooks; and even link to "Ask a Librarian" for help with your research.

Think Critically

Does access to so much information in many different media present problems for researchers? Explain.

Periodicals

Magazines, journals, newsletters, and newspapers are called **periodicals** because they are published at specified intervals of time. (Journals are magazines that are published for a scholarly or academic audience.) When you need current information, periodicals—whether online or in print—are one type of source you should seek. Periodicals are more current than books, but newspapers, especially daily papers, generally provide even more current information than periodicals. In addition, many periodicals, such as *Newsweek* and *The New York Times,* are published on the Internet and in print.

The next question is how to find the articles you need in the periodicals. Library catalogs tell you what print periodicals the library holds in different subject areas, but to find specific articles, you need to search an index or a database.

In the past, indexes, printed on paper and bound as books or magazines, were time-consuming to use. Today most periodical searches are conducted electronically. Many web-based databases, available to libraries by subscription, index periodical content. Gale, EBSCOhost, ProQuest, and Elsevier are some of the best-known database providers. In addition, many of these databases are no longer just indexes; they now provide a large amount of full-text content from periodical articles, books, encyclopedias, and more. Some of the databases, such as LexisNexis and Academic Search Premier, are general; others are subject-specific, such as SIRS, which includes publications dealing with the social sciences, and ICE Video Library, produced by International Clinical Educators, Inc., a product which supports physical and occupational therapy training. In addition, some databases, such as America's Newspapers and Newspaper Source Plus, specialize in newspapers, and these two databases index and include actual articles.

You can access other indexes through a service provider such as OCLC (Online Computer Library Center, Inc.). For example, WorldCat, mentioned earlier, is an OCLC index of physical holdings (recordings, tapes, books, papers, and dissertations). WorldCat users may locate materials at other libraries and place an interlibrary loan request.

General Reference Materials

General reference materials such as encyclopedias, dictionaries, handbooks, almanacs, and fact books are quick ways to get information. Many users rely on easy access to general reference sources for background information. They may first check those that are available online, such as *Grolier Online Encyclopedia* or *Merriam-Webster Online.* However, a library usually offers more comprehensive resources either in the print reference collection or online in subscription databases.

Some websites even offer access to reference tools. For example, the *Encyclopedia Britannica* website provides an encyclopedia, a dictionary, and an atlas. Also, Bartleby.com gives users access to several reference tools, including dictionaries, thesauruses, fact books, and books of quotations. Some materials continue to be available on DVD, such as *World Book Multimedia Encyclopedia*®, but the easy access to Internet materials is lessening the need for CD and DVD materials.

Reference materials come in general interest versions. Some examples include *World Book Encyclopedia, Encyclopedia Britannica,* and *Webster's Dictionary.* Others are special interest versions, such as *Ethnic Dress in the United States: A Cultural Encyclopedia* (2015) and *The Lupus Encyclopedia: A Comprehensive Guide for Patients and Families* (2014). In addition, *The Encyclopedia of Educational Technology,* a website created and maintained by San Diego State University, covers performance, training, and instructional design and technology.

Electronic Resources

In addition to periodical databases, indexes, and online general reference materials such as encyclopedias and dictionaries, computers connected to the Internet provide a wealth of information on countless topics. Because the Internet is a worldwide collection of computer networks, it is an information highway connecting government, military, educational, and commercial organizations and private citizens to a range of services and resources. Therefore, you can get information from a huge variety of sources over the Internet. The World Wide Web (WWW or the Web) is one system for accessing information via the Internet. The Web uses HTTP, a protocol for transmitting data, and browsers such as Internet Explorer® and Firefox® to locate web documents called web pages that may be linked to each other with hyperlinks. Web documents often contain graphics, sounds, text, and video. Many programs work optimally in Chrome because it is Google-based.

Users with access to the Internet may participate in bulletin boards, e-mail, LISTSERVs, social networking, blogs, wikis (a collection of web pages to which any user may add or delete content), social media, and other means of exchanging information. If, for example, someone had problems with his or her car and was not able to resolve the issue with the car dealer, the car owner could retrieve consumer information from the manufacturer, advocacy groups, legal professionals, and other consumers online.

tacojim/iStockphoto.com

Finding Electronic Information

As a researcher, how do you get to the tremendous amount of information on the Internet? You can search the Web using a search engine such as Yahoo, Google, or Mozilla Firefox in much the same way you search a database using keywords and topics.

However, search engines do not look through all information on the World Wide Web. Each engine searches only a portion of all of the sites. Even metasearch engines such as Ixquick Metasearch, Dogpile, Mamma, and Yippy do not cover the entire Web.

While search engines cover only a portion of the Web, a researcher's concern often is how to filter through so much information to find what is useful. Search engines use "spiders" to go out periodically and view web pages and links on sites; an "index" that catalogs words, Internet addresses, and other information about the pages the spider finds; and software to filter through all of the pages in the index to find matches when a search is requested. Because the "spider" goes out every few days or weeks, it detects changes made to web pages. However, until the information has been indexed, it is not available for researchers.

Because each search engine visits and indexes different sites and is updated at different times, you should routinely use at least three search engines. Then you can compare the results of your searches to determine which search engines are most effective.

Even after you have used three search engines, some Web information may evade your search. For example, *invisible Web* or *deep Web* refers to sites that are not registered or typically searched by search engines. USA.gov is an example of a deep web search engine that focuses on government documents. The wealth of information to be found in government documents also may require special search strategies. Other helpful tools include the Catalog of U.S. Government Publications (http://catalog.gpo.gov) and FedStats (www.fedstats.gov), or you may consult a government documents librarian.

Searching with Keywords

Choose specific, precise keywords; then consider using the advanced or custom (terms may vary with search engines) search procedures to refine your search. The guidelines in the custom search or the Help section of the search engine should explain how to use logic or keyword connectors to limit or expand your search. While the following connectors are typical, check the guidelines for each search engine you use.

Use these strategies TO LIMIT A SEARCH:

When you connect keywords with **AND,** the search yields both keywords.

Using **+ (the plus sign)** gets the same results.

Ex: juvenile AND diabetes   Yields: Sites that deal with juvenile
Ex: juvenile **1** diabetes   diabetes only

When you connect keywords with **NOT**, the search yields the first keyword, not the second. Using **– (the minus sign)** gets the same results.

Ex: diabetes NOT juvenile
Ex: diabetes – juvenile

Yields: Sites that deal with any type of diabetes except juvenile

When you surround keywords with quotation marks ("keyword keyword"), the search yields the same keywords in the same order beside each other.

Ex: "capital punishment"

Yields: Sites that include the same term, *capital punishment*, but not *capital* alone or *punishment* alone

Use these strategies TO EXPAND A SEARCH:

When you connect keywords with **OR**, the search yields either keyword.

Ex: diabetes OR juvenile

Yields: Sites that contain diabetes and/or juvenile as the topic

When you place an asterisk (*) after the word, the search yields words that contain the base or root word.

Ex: biblio*

Yields: Sites that include *bibliography, bibliographer, bibliophile, bibliotheca,* and so on

Remember that you can get the same data in many different ways. One researcher may find an article by skimming a journal from the library shelf. Another researcher may do an online search in the library or on his or her home or office computer. Still another researcher may find a link to an online journal in a discussion group. Explore the many tools available to you for research.

STOP AND THINK 3.3

Using the list you drafted in the Warm Up on page 53, underline the information that would come from secondary sources. For those underlined items, add any other sources or methods you can think of for accessing information.

 WARM UP

3.4 DOCUMENTING SECONDARY SOURCES

Has someone else, intentionally or accidentally, received credit for your ideas or work? If so, how did you feel? If not, describe how you might feel.

Documentation is a system of giving credit to another person (writer or speaker) for his or her work. It is using a citation system to note whose ideas or words the writer is using and where he or she found them. Responsible writers document ideas and materials they borrow or use.

Plagiarism is the act of using another person's words and/or ideas without properly documenting or giving credit. While plagiarism is a serious academic offense, sometimes causing students to fail a course or to be expelled from school, it is even more serious in the workplace. Theft of another person's work often results in lost jobs, lawsuits, and ruined reputations.

For instance, Doris Kearns Goodwin, a respected historian who won the Pulitzer Prize for History in 1995, taught and served on the Board of Overseers at Harvard, assisted President Lyndon Johnson with his memoirs, and won many awards, admitted to plagiarism in a book she wrote in 1987.

Despite a long career with many achievements and honors, this admission caused Goodwin to be ridiculed in public, scorned by her peers, and subjected to significant financial loss. The University of Delaware withdrew its invitation for her to speak at graduation; PBS placed her on indefinite leave from the Jim Lehrer news show; she had to defend the credibility of her other books; and her publisher had to pay Lynne McTaggart, the author of the book from which Goodwin had extensively plagiarized. More recently, Melania Trump's 2016 speech for the Republican National Convention was found to plagiarize portions of Michelle Obama's 2008 Democratic National Convention speech. Copying parts of Obama's speech caused embarrassment for Melania Trump and her husband's campaign as well as triggered the resignation of Meredith McIver, the writer who assisted Trump with the speech. As you can see, plagiarism, intentional or accidental, can be damaging.

You may ask, "What exactly do I document?" You document anything you use from another person's work, including art work. Remember, if you do not document, you are no longer borrowing; you are stealing and will be treated as a thief of intellectual property. Therefore, to keep your credibility, reputation, and job, document borrowed phrases, sentences, or ideas in the form of summaries, paraphrases, and direct quotations. For instance, if you reported on the environmental impact of a new soy ink for your company's publications division, you would document researched facts, contradictory statements, and others' unique ideas.

On the other hand, you do not need to document common knowledge or information that your audience typically knows. Common knowledge,

You and your friend Armando began a desktop publishing company to create marketing materials for local entrepreneurs and small businesses. Your company's work involves contacting the businesses, designing the posters and web marketing materials, and publishing and distributing the materials. Armando worked on creating the marketing materials for a Fine Arts major at his college who creates and sells silver jewelry to help pay for educational expenses. The client requested publicity for a show and sale he has planned for the end of the academic year. When you look over the finished promotional products, you notice Armando included drawings of the jewelry and its creator produced by another student. You feel uneasy about publishing these materials without the permission of the drawings' artist, but you know that you cannot reach the student artist in time to ask permission before the copy must be delivered to the printer and the website updated; otherwise, a delay will cause the promotion to be too late to draw customers to the show and sale.

Think Critically

How can you find out whether you and Armando are breaking copyright laws if you decide to publish the drawings?

Communication
Dilemma

however, may differ for each audience, particularly expert audiences. For instance, the fact that Bill Gates is chief executive officer of Microsoft Corporation is certainly common knowledge for an audience of computer engineers. However, Gates's management philosophy might not be common knowledge for the engineers, but it could be for business school graduates. If information is common knowledge for your target audience, you do not need to document it. The same information directed to a different audience may not be common knowledge and, therefore, would need to be documented.

The writer's field determines the documentation format. For example, Modern Language Association (MLA) format, which is most likely taught in your English class, is the documentation system used in the humanities. Among the many other documentation systems are the American Psychological Association (APA) system for social sciences, the American Medical Association (AMA) system for medicine, and the Council of Science Editors (CSE) system for the physical sciences. Most fields have a style manual. A style manual is a book of rules for developing a document, including formatting and documentation. *The Chicago Manual of Style,* the stylebook of the University of Chicago Press, is the preferred style manual for many technical fields, including anthropology.

Because each documentation system has a particular format, consult your instructor (or employer) for the appropriate style manual. For example, if as a human resources officer you investigate the effectiveness of a test used to screen job applicants (a psychology-related topic), you probably will use American Psychological Association (APA) style. However, a report outlining the water quality of a prospective site for a trout farm (a biology-related topic) may require that you use Council of Science Editors (CSE) style guidelines.

All documentation systems explain how to identify each source. However, the emphasis, order, and punctuation may be different. For example, the APA and CSE styles emphasize publication dates in citations because dates are critical in the sciences. MLA style emphasizes the author and location (page numbers) in the text.

Documentation comes in two parts: (1) the Works Cited or References (or bibliography), a list of sources at the end of the document, and (2) the internal citations. The documentation process begins with a working bibliography. The opening model for this chapter, Figure 3.1 on page 49, is a working bibliography. In addition, some writers choose to add notes or descriptions following each source in a bibliography to develop an annotated bibliography. Figure 3.2 is an excerpt of a student's annotated bibliography.

Not only are annotated bibliographies a useful tool for the researcher, they also may be used for sharing information with students, colleagues, and others. For instance, an expert on the use of silk in clothing design might share an annotated bibliography with someone newly interested in the subject, providing a "jump start" for that person's learning. Moreover, professionals also may use annotated bibliographies, adding and deleting sources as needed, on relevant subjects to help themselves stay abreast of developments in the field.

Renita Sears

Professor Benjamin Frye

ENG 231.01IN

30 December 20_ _

Annotated Bibliography: Using Insects in Organic Gardening

Brown, John. Personal interview. 31 Jan. 2018.

In a two–hour discussion, Mr. Brown, a master gardener trained by the North Carolina Extension Service, answered questions about his experiences using insects in gardening. He expressed his enthusiasm for employing insects in fighting bugs that eat vegetation as well as fruit in the garden. His experience with ladybugs was especially helpful.

"Earthworms for Profit." *Journal of Horticultural Sciences* 32 (2017): 232–238.
      Academic Search Elite. Web. 21 Oct. 2015.

This article, developed to encourage people to consider earthworm farming, is written for an expert audience. It provides facts, investments costs, and other considerations that experts might use in presentations to potential investors and farmers.

Green, Al, and Harvey Wall. *Aphids: Little Critters with a Big Bite*. Los Angeles:
      Caltech UP, 2017. Print.

Authors Green and Wall present 210 pages explaining how insects may be used to control aphids in vegetable and flower gardens. The book, written with experienced gardeners in mind, argues that the audience should use insects rather than chemicals to combat infestations of aphids. Doing so, they explain, saves the environment for everyone and preserves the health of those working and eating in the garden.

Figure 3.2 Annotated Bibliography Excerpt in MLA Style

Bibliography and Works Cited

A bibliography (also called Works Cited in MLA and References in APA) is a list of sources used in researching a topic. While collecting data, researchers develop a working bibliography. They continue to locate and add new sources to the list during the research process. Sometimes they delete a source from the list when they find one that is more recent, more authoritative, or more reliable.

When the research is finished, writers use the list's final form to prepare a bibliography. A bibliography has three purposes: (1) It establishes credibility by showing readers what sources you consulted; (2) it allows others to find your information path so they can continue or evaluate the study; and (3) it gives credit to other people's thoughts, words, and sentences that you used.

As you look at secondary sources, you develop a paper or an electronic working bibliography. Most writers prefer to maintain bibliographic data electronically. Computer software allows you to add, delete, or move sources

sdominick/iStockphoto.com

easily. In addition, software is available that automatically puts source information into the appropriate form according to the style manual you are using. Users, however, should always check citations for accuracy as the software may not be accurate every time. Hypertext programs can show images of cards where users key bibliographic information. If you find a source when you don't have a laptop or tablet, you can enter publication information for each source on a 3" × 5" index card. Cards allow you to arrange entries easily to be keyed into the final source list.

As you develop bibliographic entries, follow the style manual's model that most nearly matches the type of source you are using. For example, if you have used a book with three authors, find a model that matches a book with three authors. Then follow the model carefully. Avoid relying on memory to guide bibliographic entry creation; with so many source types and models, it is safer to trust the style manual than memory. Also, after a bit of time has passed, review your bibliographic entry with the style manual's model and the information from your source. If you find any discrepancies or errors, correct them.

After you complete the research and draft the document, you remove from the bibliography the sources you did not use. You place sources you did use in appropriate order. For MLA, use alphabetical order by the first author's last name or by the word that appears at the beginning of the entry (often a title) if the author is not given. Other systems arrange sources differently. This ordered list of sources is placed at the end of the document, presentation, or report.

Internal Citations

People will assume that ideas are yours unless they see a citation in the text. **Citations** are written indications of the source of borrowed ideas or materials. Enter internal documentation immediately after each summary, paraphrase, and direct quotation to tell your reader where you found the information. Internal citations in APA consist of the author's last name (or a shortened form of the title if no author is named), year of publication, and page number. When the author's name is mentioned in the sentence, only the date and page numbers are included in the parenthetical citation. As in APA, internal citations in MLA consist of the author's last name (or a shortened form of the title if no author is named) and the page number. When the author's name is mentioned in the introductory sentence, only the page numbers are included in the citation. Likewise, in ACS, internal citations include the author's name and the year of publication; the date is a part of the citation because science readers care about how recent information is. Readers then use the author's name or the title to find the full bibliographic entry in the alphabetical listing of references or works cited. Place the citation at the end of the sentence (or group of sentences) containing the source material in your document. Enclose the citation in parentheses and place the period after the ending parenthesis, as shown in Figure 3.3.

Scientists who first found Deinococcus radiodurans in an irradiated can of meat in 1956 were surprised. Irradiating food, they thought, would preserve it, yet this pink bacteria was creating a nasty bulge in the can. Then in 1996, scientists working around a nuclear waste tank in Savannah River, South Carolina, found the same tough bacteria (which came to be known as Conan the Bacterium) growing on a rod in the tank. Because this bacterium can not only survive but thrive in "some of Earth's most inhospitable environments," the United States Department of Energy believes it may be used as a solution to the potential $260 billion cleanup of nuclear waste sites across the country (Fialka 2004).

Researchers are just beginning to understand how Deinococcus radiodurans survives radiation and what other uses it may have. According to Chris Impey's The Living Cosmos, this bacterium can repair damage to its DNA quickly, typically in 24 hours, by storing five or more copies of its genome ready to be replicated (2007). One scientist for the Uniformed Services University suggests that, if people and animals can develop repair systems similar to Deinococcus radiodurans, they too can withstand higher doses of radiation. Avoiding radiation sickness would be helpful, for example, in cancer treatment and space travel (Tough Bug 2009). Another use was found by a group of researchers in China who have genetically modified Deinococcus radiodurans with a green florescence protein to create a biosensor that glows when "biological hazards of radioactive and toxic pollutants" are present (GuanJun et al. 2009).

Several exciting new uses have been proposed recently. Several French researchers were granted a patent in 2015 for modifying Deinococcus radiodurans so that it could be used to create bioenergy from biomass waste on a large scale and in a reliable and affordable manner (Leonetti and Matic, 2009). Scientists are even using Deinococcus radiodurans to improve food supply. Lactic acid, produced by lactic acid bacteria, provides a sour flavoring element in sour cream, buttermilk, various fruits, molasses, and wine. It is commercially produced and is frequently used as a flavoring agent and preservative in foods and beverages as well as a raw material in some pharmaceuticals. By using Deinococcus radiodurans, the researchers were able to enhance production of lactic acid and increase the acid's tolerance to environmental stressors (Dong et al., 2015). Another use of Deinococcus radiodurans is to determine the various bacterial populations in and around an active copper mine in Brazil (Rodrigues et al., 2014). As the scientific community discovers all that it can do, Conan the Bacterium may be a superhero after all!

Excerpt from Research Document— Internal Citations in ACS Style

References

Dong, X.; Tian, B.; Dai, S.; Li, T.; Guo, L.; Tan, Z.; Jiao, Z.; Jin, Q.; Wang, Y.; Hua, Y. Expression of PprI from *Deinococcus Radiodurans* Improves Lactic Acid Production and Stress Tolerance in *Lactococcus Lactis*. *PLoS One* Nov 2015, pp. 1–16. ProQuest. www.proquest.com (accessed Mar 20, 2017).

Fialka, John J. "Position Available: Indestructible Bugs to Eat Nuclear Waste: Scientists Envision New Role for Sturdy Bacteria Breed: Creating 'Super Conan.'" *Wall Street Journal* 16 Nov. 2004, eastern ed.: A1.

GuanJun, G.; Lu, F.; YueJin, H. Engineering *Deinococcus Radiodurans* into Biosensor to Monitor Radioactivity and Genotoxicity in Environment. *Chinese Science Bulletin* 2008, pp. 1675–81. Academic Search Premier. https://www.ebscohost.com /academic/academic-search-premier (accessed April 23, 2017).

Impey, C. *The Living Cosmos: Our Search for Life in the Universe*. Random House: New York, 2007.

Leonetti, J.; Matic, I. Use of bacteria for the production of bioenergy. US 9181564, US 20110104766, May 22, 2009.

Rodrigues, V.D.; Torres, T.; Ottoboni, L.M. Bacterial Diversity Assessment in Soil of an Active Brazilian Copper Mine Using High-Throughput Sequencing of 16S rDNA Amplicons. *Antonie van Leeuwenhoek* Nov. 2014, pp. 879–90. ProQuest. www.proquest.com (accessed April 1, 2017).

Tough Bug Reveals Key to Radiation Resistance. *New Scientist* [Online] March 24, 2007, p. 21. MasterFILE Premier. https://www .ebscohost.com/academic/masterfile-premier (accessed May 8, 2017).

Excerpt from References List

Figure 3.3 Internal Citations and References in ACS Style

STOP AND THINK 3.4

What happens when writers incorrectly or incompletely cite sources? What are the costs to businesses? to professionals?

Have you ever made a decision based on information someone else provided you, only to have a poor outcome because the information was not accurate or true? If so, how did you feel about the person who gave you the information initially? Did you continue to use or share information that he or she told you? How do you decide whose information to use and whose to disregard?

As you have discovered, not everything that appears in print (or on your digital devices or TV) is true. In fact, many mistakes, untruths, and half-truths are published. For instance, a financial planner who uses information from an unreliable source to make faulty investments for her clients will not stay in business very long. So when you conduct research, choose your data sources critically and carefully.

These guidelines for evaluating sources will help you get started.

Publication Date

When you want to know the most recent discoveries and happenings in a particular area, you need up-to-date information. Therefore, you must check publication dates. The data in a book may be even older than the copyright date indicates because some books take two or more years to be published. Likewise, websites without dates may not have been checked or revised in several years.

Author's Credentials

Lending ethos or ethical appeal, an author's reputation is an important element in determining the value of a potential source. An author or authors with a strong and positive reputation can add credibility to your writing. Furthermore, the methods and resources used by an author or editor have the ability to help or harm your writing.

Reputation

Often the preface or introduction of a book outlines the education and experience of the writers or editors. Likewise, magazine and journal articles sometimes include brief biographies. Check websites, particularly the beginning and ending pages, for an author's biography and credentials. If the publication gives no information about the author or editor, consider factors such as the reputation of the journal, publisher, or associated business or organization. Online information needs to include a credible publisher or sponsor. This information is generally located at the bottom of the page. Ask if the topic at hand is an area of expertise for the author or source.

A brief online search will likely offer insight into an author's credentials, accomplishments, associations, flaws, and more. You also can check an author's reputation in reference sources such as *Who's Who in America*, *Contemporary Authors*, *Who's Who in Science*, and *Who's Who in Small Business and Entrepreneurship Worldwide*. Some of these references, such as *Contemporary Authors*, are found online.

Based on what you learn about the author's credentials, determine whether he or she qualifies as an expert in the field. If you have two sources on the same topic, you might find one author to be more credible than the other.

Methods and Resources

Usually, in the introduction of a book or in the opening paragraphs of an article, the author or editor will explain the methods used to reach the

acte
cor...
rming to
conduct —eth'
eth·ics (eth'iks) *n.* 1
rds of conduct
ith *sing.* or *pl.*
morals a partic...
group,
E·thi·o...

Focus on
Ethics

Another aspect of borrowing or using others' words and ideas involves copyright. Copyright legally protects the rights of writers or creators and gives them a way to control how their work is used. Copyright applies only to tangible and original expression, not to oral presentations.

Using copyrighted work requires special considerations. If the way you plan to use someone's words or ideas fits the definition of fair use, you may use the work without paying for it or getting permission. Yet you still must give credit to the creator. Fair use guidelines are special exceptions that allow others to use a portion of a writer's work in a limited way. Fair use evaluates the purpose and nature of the new use, the character of the copyrighted work, the percentage of the work being used, and the effect of the use on the original's marketability. Ultimately, fair use requires that the new user not damage the original or profit from its use.

When you are uncertain about whether to request copyright permission or to document a source, consult other writers, your supervisor or mentor at work, or others with experience in the field. If you are still in doubt, it is better to request permission and to document. No writer or professional has ruined his or her reputation or career by overdocumenting, but many have by not documenting.

Think Critically

If you find a cartoon in the Sunday newspaper, should you document or request permission before using it to introduce a concept or highlight a point in a report you are writing?

conclusions. If you believe those methods are sound, the book or article gains credibility as a potential source. If you believe those methods are flawed, the book or article loses credibility. Likewise, you may evaluate a potential source by the resources its author uses. Resources may be mentioned in the text and listed in the works cited or bibliography.

Depth and Coverage

Determine whether the source covers the topic in a way that is appropriate for your audience's and your needs. Does the text explore the topic deeply enough and in enough detail to be useful? Is it too technical, or does it provide only a surface treatment? Is the source a popular or commercial publication or a scholarly publication? Scholarly sources, such as peer-reviewed journals and university press or academic publications, generally offer more thorough and reliable information.

In addition, you should look critically at the tone and presentation of source material. Favor those sources that present all sides (opposing views) of an issue in an objective tone. Obvious biases, lack of logical reasoning, little or weak evidence, or unbalanced treatment are all reasons to look for other sources.

Special Considerations for Electronic Sources

These guidelines pertain to many sources, but the ever-increasing availability of electronic materials means that researchers are spending more time and effort searching online. Therefore, you should give special consideration to evaluating electronic sources. Because its materials are not screened in any way, the Internet contains more trash than treasure. Remember that anyone, from the bored 10-year-old next door to the busy physics professor, can post a website.

You will find the following guidelines to be useful in evaluating electronic information:

- **Is an author or sponsoring group listed?** Are credentials or experiences noted to show that the author is an expert on the subject covered? Is the author or sponsor mentioned in other sources? If no author or sponsor is given, a critical reader might wonder why. For instance, an animal rights supporter could post an anonymous site exaggerating abusive aspects of corporate farming methods. Without knowing the author and his or her agenda, readers might not recognize the bias of the site.

- **What is the electronic address?** The abbreviation in the web address should show where the source originates. Several examples follow.

Educational institution	.edu
Nonprofit organization	.org
Government organization	.gov
Military	.mil
For-profit or commercial organization	.com

Sites sponsored by schools are usually scholarly and objective, providing reliable information. Government-sponsored sites—whether local, state,

twohumans/iStockphoto.com

national, or international—typically present reliable information, such as U.S. census data. However, these sites may be biased. For example, the president controls the press secretary's message and the focus of a given story.

Likewise, many nonprofit organizations such as the American Lung Association maintain trustworthy sites, but some may be biased by the organization's agenda. For example, the website of the National Rifle Association is unlikely to provide statistics on the number of children killed by guns in their homes but is more likely to show how many burglaries are stopped by homeowners with guns. However, commercial sites are almost always biased. After all, readers cannot expect a web page sponsored by Gerber® to explain to parents why they should not feed Gerber® baby food to their children.

- **What are the references and/or links?** Does the website include a list of sources used in preparing the page that readers can check? Are links to other reputable, reliable sites included? Are the links to scholarly sites or to commercial or obviously biased sites?

- **Is there balance and a clear purpose?** Does the site present the subject fairly? Does it include opposing viewpoints? Is the design clear and careful to aid the reader's understanding, or does the design encourage strong reactions or confusion? Offensive images and cluttered, irrelevant information may be intended to create a particular response from users. For instance, viewers are more likely to have an emotional reaction than a logical response to an image of caged animals in a medical research facility. Understanding a site's purpose—to sell ideas, products, or services; to share knowledge; or to incite strong reactions—can help determine how reliable the information is.

- **What do design and presentation suggest?** If the site is well-designed and effective, the data it contains is more likely to have been treated with the same care and effort. Similarly, a site that demonstrates effective communication skills—free of grammar and spelling errors—is more likely to gain a reader's trust.

- **When was the site last updated?** Researchers should note the date of the last update, if one is provided, or the copyright date. If no date is provided, then viewers should be aware that the information contained on the site could be inaccurate by current standards and outdated. Sometimes sites are orphaned or abandoned.

 STOP AND THINK 3.5

Read this case and consider possible outcomes: Colleen received time and money to study the effects of genetically modified grain, used for livestock food in commercial farming, on the wild animals in the areas surrounding the farms. Her report requesting permission for this project was based primarily on one study published in an animal science journal. Over the last year, this study was largely discredited in scholarly journals.

WARM UP 3.6 TAKING NOTES FROM SOURCES

Examine the notes you take during class. About what percentage of the notes are written in the instructor's or the speaker's exact words? About what percentage is written in your own words—your interpretation of the instructor's or speaker's comments? Are any of the notes your ideas or perhaps conclusions you came to as a result of something someone else said? What percentage would you estimate?

Employees doing research note information they collect, just as you do when writing a paper in school. When you discover data you believe will be helpful, write complete, careful notes. Generally, researchers take notes electronically using a tablet or laptop. The computer user can transfer notes to the first draft of the report without having to rekey them. Also, researchers working with online notes can copy and paste material they want to quote directly into the draft research document. Many versions of note-taking software, some free to users and some for purchase, are available. OneNote by Microsoft, for instance, allows users to insert typed text, pictures, and e-mails, as well as audio and video notes. These notes are saved as individual pages, which are organized with sections that are placed within notebooks. Its search features can pull from text, images, and audio files. In addition, its ability to be used offline with synchronization and merging allows groups to collaborate efficiently. Evernote is another program that one can use to take notes. The user can share data between devices even if he or she does not have Microsoft Office on his or her device. On the other hand, some researchers still prefer to use 4" × 6" note cards for notetaking because they say the process of writing longhand on paper helps them with the critical thinking process and because note cards are easy to arrange and carry. However, researchers who choose this method must be especially careful when keying in the information from the cards to the research document.

You should read your source material carefully before making any notes. Understanding your sources thoroughly is an important part of being a successful researcher.

Read the excerpt in Figure 3.4 from an article describing a genetically engineered bacterium developed from *Deinococcus radiodurans*. John J. Fialka wrote the article "Position Available: Indestructible Bugs to Eat Nuclear Waste" for *The Wall Street Journal*. You will find the complete

The original Conan proved to be a wimp among extremophiles. It could handle radiation but not the solvent toluene and other chemicals normally found in bomb makers' wastes. So in 1997, the Energy Department started work on a genetically manipulated bug that researchers called Super Conan.

Super Conan now lives in a petri dish at the Uniformed Services University of the Health Sciences, a U.S. military research facility in Bethesda, MD. It can handle nasty chemicals as well as radiation, but the researcher who developed it, Michael J. Daly, says that the government is afraid to let it out.

"We're at a point where we could do some field trials," he says, adding that his sponsors at the Energy Department doubt that the public is ready for the release of the laboratory-engineered bug into the environment. It might eat nuclear wastes, but they worry about what else it might do, he says.

Figure 3.4 Excerpt from a Published Article

bibliographic entry on page 49 in the sample working bibliography. This passage will be used to discuss note taking.

For each note, using software or index cards, include (1) the information you want to use—only one idea per note or card, (2) the topic, and (3) the source and page number(s) from which you took the data. Figures 3.5, 3.6, and 3.7 illustrate the way some researchers develop notes.

You can use borrowed information in your notes three ways:

1. Summary

2. Paraphrase

3. Direct quotation

Summary

To **summarize** is to condense longer material, keeping essential or main ideas and omitting unnecessary parts such as examples and illustrations. Be consistent with the source's idea, but use your words. When conducting job-related research, you might summarize a journal article or a chapter of a book that is helpful at supporting evidence in a report. The original material might be an entire book, but your summary could be a few paragraphs or one sentence. The note in Figure 3.5 summarizes the original material you read in the article about a bacterium.

Fear of environmental damage from Super Conan   Fialka A1

To be able to deal with some of the defense industry's wastes, the Energy Department used the radiation-resistant Conan and genetically engineered the bacterium to handle hazardous chemicals left from bomb making. But now the government is unwilling to release this Super Conan for field testing for fear of unknown environmental effects.

Figure 3.5 Summary Note

Paraphrase

To **paraphrase** is to present someone else's idea in one's own words, phrases, and sentence structure. While a summary should be shorter than the original material, a paraphrase generally is about the same length or even a bit longer than the original. A writer paraphrases when the material supports a point but is not unique or dramatic enough to be quoted. Most of the materials writers use from other sources are paraphrased. Paraphrasing allows writers to include other people's thinking while putting the borrowed ideas into their own words and sentences. As you practice paraphrasing, you may find the following process helpful:

1. Read the original carefully.

2. Put it aside.

3. Write the idea in your own way.

4. Compare your version with the original.

5. Make certain you have used your own words and sentence structure and have accurately conveyed the author's idea. (Borrowing three or more words in a row is quoting and requires quotation marks.)

Figure 3.6 contains a paraphrase of the last two sentences from the excerpt on bacterium. Notice that the wording and sentence structure are significantly different. Changing or moving a word or two is not effective paraphrasing. Avoid plagiarism by stating the borrowed idea in your own way, choosing words and sentence structure you would normally use, and properly crediting the author of the source.

No field trials for Super Conan   Fialka A1

According to Michael J. Daly, the developer of Super Conan, the Energy Department refuses to field-test the bacterium for fear that it might eat not only the nuclear waste it was designed to eat, but also some things it was not intended to destroy.

Figure 3.6 Paraphrase Note

Direct Quotation

Direct quotation, the third way writers incorporate material into their documents, is the use of borrowed ideas, words, phrases, and sentences exactly as they appear in the original document. However, you do not want to overuse quotations. Avoid a cut-and-paste patchwork style by making less than 10–15 percent of your document direct quotations. Copy phrases and sentences directly only when you cannot present the idea as well in your own words. For instance, if the original writer or speaker chose unusual words or composed unique or dramatic sentences, you may want your reader to get the flavor of the original by quoting directly. Another reason for using direct quotation is to enhance your credibility by using the words of a well-known authority. Figure 3.7 is a model of a note using direct quotation.

Description of *D. radiodurans*   Fialka A1
One reporter describes *Deinococcus radiodurans* as "a wimp among extremophiles."

Figure 3.7 Direct Quotation Note

Introduce Quotations

Writers introduce quotations to make the writing smooth. Do not let quoted sentences stand alone. You can integrate quotations into your text with words such as "according to one expert" and "Greg Markham claims" or with complete sentences such as the following: During the 2015–2016 campaign, Donald Trump rebuffed his critics: "Anyone who thinks my story is anywhere near over is sadly mistaken."

Indicate Added or Omitted Material

When you need to add to or edit a direct quotation for clarity or conciseness, use brackets to set your changes apart from the quoted words, as in the sentences below.

> **Original:** "After the board meeting in which a 2 percent fine was approved, she signed her resignation letter."

> **Addition for clarity:** "After the board meeting in which a 2 percent fine was approved, [Maureen O'Keefe] signed her resignation letter," explained Mayor Pro-tem Harold Epps.

You may need to quote only part of a sentence. In that case, use an ellipsis—three spaced dots—to show where you omitted words from the original. However, if you include a paraphrase of the idea (rather than omit it), you do not need an ellipsis. If the reason for O'Keefe's resignation is not important to your work, you might quote the source this way:

> **Omission:** "After the board meeting . . . , [Maureen O'Keefe] signed her resignation letter."

The ellipsis shows that something—in this case, the clause "in which a 2 percent fine was approved"—was left out of the quotation.

STOP AND THINK 3.6

When should research writers use direct quotation? Would you use an ellipsis or brackets to indicate that you left out part of a quoted sentence?

3.7 COLLECTING PRIMARY DATA

 WARM UP

Many job-related problems or questions are too unique or too current for secondary sources to answer. A commercial fisher may learn more about a new net's effectiveness by talking to other users and experimenting than by reading the literature on nets. To solve some work-related concerns, primary data may be more help. Primary data is gathered through field research: surveys, interviews, observation, and experimentation. Some field research is conducted in person, some by telephone, and some online.

Surveys

Surveys gather facts, beliefs, attitudes, and opinions from people. Many businesses rely on surveys to collect information for decision making. One example is a questionnaire accompanying a product registration form for small appliances such as hair dryers or coffee makers. The manufacturer uses the data to determine who is buying the product, how the buyer learned of the product (what advertising method worked), and how satisfied the buyer is.

A survey works only when you know what you want to learn before you begin. For example, if your goal is to learn students' preferences for cafeteria snack bar food, you may not want to ask for their favorite food. If you do, their responses may not be appropriate for a cafeteria or snack bar, such as flaming kabobs and baked Alaska. Once you decide what you want to learn, you should compile your survey by (1) carefully selecting your audience or **respondents** (people chosen to answer questions), (2) deciding how you will administer your survey, and (3) carefully planning your questions. Finally, you will report the results of your survey.

Compile Your Survey

When you choose an audience, you must select a sample broad enough to represent that audience. A **population** is the target group from which a researcher wants to gather data. The owner of a garden center who wants to know whether customers will use a repotting service would have a population of all of the business's customers. If the owner cannot question all customers due to expense, time, or distance, she may choose a sample to provide representative answers. A **sample** is a subgroup with the same characteristics as the entire population. Keep in mind that the sample must be small enough for you to tabulate and analyze the results but large enough to provide meaningful results. In some situations, companies hire specially trained people or companies to design and conduct surveys.

Once you know your audience, the next step is to decide how to administer the survey. You can administer questionnaires in person, by mail, by telephone, online, or by e-mail. Today many businesses survey online or by e-mail. While sites such as SurveyMonkey and SurveyGizmo can make developing and administering surveys faster and easier than other methods, remember that you still need to make the critical decisions about how your audience perceives the company you represent and the questions being asked of them. Zoho.com is another tool used for surveys. (Realize that these sites normally have free polling results, but you may have to pay for charts and analyses.)

© Georgejmclittle/Shutterstock

Your decision about delivery method is based on the kind of data you seek, how much time you have, and what your budget is. If you are asking personal or controversial questions, you should use a confidential mailed survey to ensure a higher return rate. Also, although many people believe their e-mail and online responses are private, electronic communication is far from secure. In fact, in the workplace, employers have the right to access information on company computers, which means that your e-mail and online work is subject to scrutiny. If time is a concern, telephone, online, e-mail, and in-person surveys provide faster responses than mail surveys. Also remember that all survey methods can be costly.

Carefully planned, effective survey instruments increase the rate of responses received. Thus, it is important to consider the following suggestions as you prepare surveys:

- **Explain why you need the information and how it will be used.** Because you are asking respondents to share data, they have the right to know what you plan to do with the information. In a cover letter or an opening paragraph, explain what prompted the survey. Then describe the benefits. Estimate the time required to complete the survey. Many surveys also offer to send results of the study to respondents or tell respondents where they can find the published results.

- **Convince your audience to participate.** After all, you are requesting their time and thoughts. They may wonder what you are giving them in return. You might offer an incentive such as coupons, free merchandise or services, improved or additional services, or discounts.

- **Logically order questions beginning with easy-to-answer items.** If respondents have difficulty with the first questions, they are not likely to continue. The initial questions should ask for information that is easy to recall and not too personal. Also arrange questions in logical groupings to aid respondents' memory, as in the following questions:

  - In what county do you live?

  - How long have you lived there?

- **Ask only necessary questions.** If you do not need the answer, do not ask the question. For example, do not ask about income if income is not relevant to the data you seek. People will not respond if they believe you are wasting their time.

- **Write clear and nonleading questions.** For responses to be useful, questions must be clear and precise. Compare the following two questions:

  - Do you shop by mail often?

  - How often do you shop by mail each month?

With the first question, the respondent will answer based on his or her definition of "often." That answer may not be useful. Likewise, questions should not lead respondents to particular answers. Consider the following questions as an illustration:

  - Don't you believe that the cost of class rings is outrageous?

  - Why don't you buy your lunch in the school cafeteria?

The wording suggests a particular answer. Consider changing it as follows:

- Do you believe the cost of class rings is reasonable or unreasonable?
- Is cost a factor in your decision not to purchase lunch in the school cafeteria? Or
- Which of the following are factors in your decision not to purchase lunch in the school cafeteria?

Cost   Food choice

Time   Other _____

- **Make the purpose of the question clear.** If the survey is to learn about consumers' reactions to your newspaper's new type style, do not ask general questions such as "Why did you purchase this newspaper?" Answers to that general question may vary tremendously from "It was the cheapest one on the newsstand" to "It is the one my father reads." Such responses will not help you find what you want to know—whether people like the new type style.

- **Prefer facts to opinions.** When designing questions, seek facts whenever possible. Facts provide stronger, more credible evidence. For example, ask "Do you purchase from a mail-order catalog at least once a month?" rather than "Do you like mail-order shopping?" However, sometimes opinions provide useful information, as in a satisfaction survey.

- **Stick to one topic per question.** While you might be tempted to include several issues in one question, the answers will be useless if you do not know to which topic the person is responding. Suppose respondents say yes to the question, "Are you ever concerned for your safety as you walk through the parking deck and up the stairs into the Sollenberger Building at night?" You do not know what concerns the respondents—the deck, the stairs, the building, or the darkness.

- **Plan for tabulation.** Remember that once responses come in, you need to evaluate and interpret them. Your job will be easier if you design questions whose answers are stated as numbers. When you already know the range of possible answers, **close-ended questions** (questions that restrict the number of possible answers) such as those in Figure 3.8 allow for a limited number of responses and are easy to tabulate.

1. Do you live within five miles of one of our stores?
   Yes_____   No_____
2. Please indicate your level of satisfaction with your purchase.
   a. Extremely Satisfied < >
   b. Satisfied < >
   c. Somewhat Satisfied < >
   d. Somewhat Dissatisfied < >
   e. Dissatisfied < >
   f. Extremely Dissatisfied < >

Figure 3.8 Close-Ended Questions

Although more difficult to tabulate, **open-ended questions** encourage the respondent to provide any answer he or she likes; the question gives no suggested answers. These questions are sometimes necessary to discover respondents' thoughts and feelings. Unexpected attitudes or information may be uncovered this way as well.

Open-ended questions ask respondents to supply words, sentences, or short essays, as in the following examples:

- How do you think RFG's board should respond to the new regulations?
- What could Apgard do to improve service to you and your organization?

Leave adequate space for answers when asking open-ended questions.

Figure 3.9 gives examples of different types of questions.

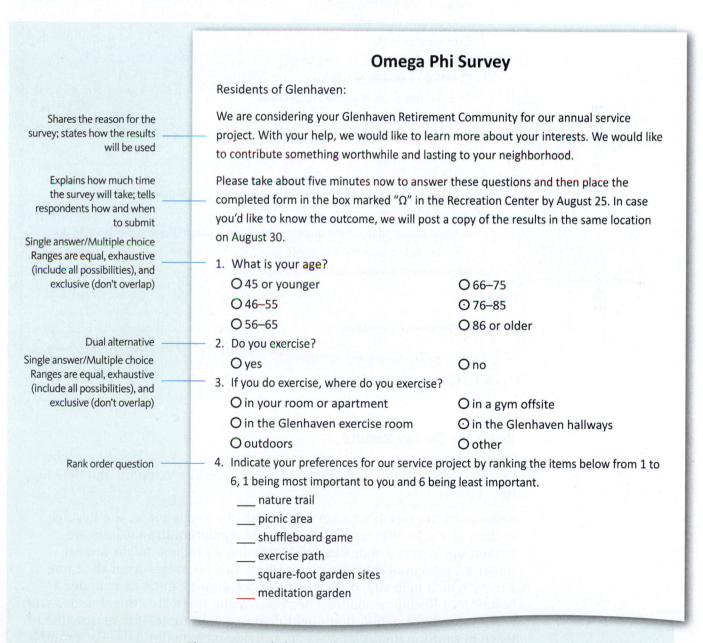

Omega Phi Survey

Residents of Glenhaven:

We are considering your Glenhaven Retirement Community for our annual service project. With your help, we would like to learn more about your interests. We would like to contribute something worthwhile and lasting to your neighborhood.

Please take about five minutes now to answer these questions and then place the completed form in the box marked "Ω" in the Recreation Center by August 25. In case you'd like to know the outcome, we will post a copy of the results in the same location on August 30.

1. What is your age?
   - ○ 45 or younger
   - ○ 46–55
   - ○ 56–65
   - ○ 66–75
   - ⊙ 76–85
   - ○ 86 or older

2. Do you exercise?
   - ○ yes
   - ○ no

3. If you do exercise, where do you exercise?
   - ○ in your room or apartment
   - ○ in the Glenhaven exercise room
   - ○ outdoors
   - ○ in a gym offsite
   - ⊙ in the Glenhaven hallways
   - ○ other

4. Indicate your preferences for our service project by ranking the items below from 1 to 6, 1 being most important to you and 6 being least important.
   - ___ nature trail
   - ___ picnic area
   - ___ shuffleboard game
   - ___ exercise path
   - ___ square-foot garden sites
   - ___ meditation garden

Labels at left:

Shares the reason for the survey; states how the results will be used

Explains how much time the survey will take; tells respondents how and when to submit

Single answer/Multiple choice Ranges are equal, exhaustive (include all possibilities), and exclusive (don't overlap)

Dual alternative

Single answer/Multiple choice Ranges are equal, exhaustive (include all possibilities), and exclusive (don't overlap)

Rank order question

Figure 3.9 Mailed Survey *(continues)*

Single answer/multiple choice

Single answer/multiple choice. Notice the middle ground or neutral choice, "No opinion"

Multiple answer. Notice the option for adding a choice not provided

Close-ended question

Open-ended question

Open-ended question

5. Check the item that best reflects the way you would complete this sentence: If a new outdoor area is installed in the community, I am...
    ○ willing to spend two hours or more per month to maintain it
    ○ willing to pay $35 (or less) per year to hire maintenance
    ○ not willing to maintain the area

6. Spending time outdoors is important to my health and well-being.
    ○ strongly Agree   ○ disagree
    ⊙ agree   ○ strongly disagree
    ○ no opinion

7. What goal or goals do you hope to achieve if your preferred outdoor area is installed? Mark all that apply.
    ☐ to become more active
    ☐ to socialize more
    ☐ to spend time outside of my home
    ☐ to learn new skills or activities
    ☐ to become more reflective and peaceful
    ☐ other _____

8. Are you satisfied with the outdoor facilities now available at Glenhaven?
    ○ Yes
    ○ No

9. a. If you answered YES to the question above, what part of the outdoor facilities do you enjoy?
    b. If you answered NO to the question above, what part of the outdoor facilities do you want to see added or improved?

10. What outdoor activities do you enjoy most?

Thank you for your participation!

Figure 3.9 (continued) Mailed Survey

Write the Survey Results

When you report the results of a survey, you make several decisions: where in your document to report the results, which results to report, and how to report the results.

Sometimes the results of a survey appear in a single place, the Results section of a scientific report, for example. Sometimes the results are broken up: Responses dealing with defining a problem might appear under a Problem or Background heading. But responses from the same survey which help support a particular solution might appear under a Solution or Recommendations heading. While there are ethical issues with leaving out information that might disprove your topic, it is reasonable to leave out information that does not provide meaningful data. For example, data in your marketing survey showing customers are not interested in your new line of shoes should be included. But the confusing data about shoe sizes can be deleted when the respondents did not know their European shoe sizes.

For example, data from the Omega Phi survey could be reported in these ways:

Graph: Data from question 3 might be presented in a bar graph. Such information would be introduced with a sentence like "Figure 2.1 shows how important spending time outdoors is to the residents."

Percentages: Data from question 5 could be reported as written percentages with commentary to draw the reader's attention. While residents responded with equal emphasis to most of the goals for an outdoor project (16–19 percent each)—desire to become more active, to socialize more, to spend time outside my home, and to learn new skills or activities—surprisingly 29 percent expressed the desire to meditate.

Summaries: Data from the open question could be summarized without quoting everyone. When asked which outdoor activities residents enjoyed most, the majority of residents included short walks and sitting in the garden as favorites.

Quotations: One memorable quotation is reproduced here. One resident says, "Sitting in the sun brightens my day more than any other activity at Glenhaven."

Interviews

Interviews, like surveys, are an excellent source of primary data. Interviews give you access to experts' facts, opinions, and attitudes that you might not find any other way. However, interviewing can be time-consuming and costly.

Compile Your Interview

To make the process as successful as possible, use the following guidelines:

- **Define your purpose.** Know what information you want from each interviewee. Write down the purpose and review it before talking to the interviewee.

- **Make an appointment.** Telephone, write, or e-mail the respondent to describe the topic and to request an interview. Whether you will be interviewing someone by telephone, by mail, by e-mail, or in person, ask the respondent in advance for a convenient time to conduct the interview. If the interview will be in person, offer to visit the respondent or to arrange a suitable place to conduct the interview. If the interview will be via mail or e-mail, agree on a time frame for sending questions and receiving answers. For interviews by instant messaging, set an appointed time. Make certain that the respondent understands the topic and that you have allowed reasonable preparation time. Moreover, be professional in your appearance, writing, and speaking.

© Alissa Kumarova/Shutterstock

- **Do your homework.** Do not expect the respondent to make all of the effort. Learn as much as possible about the topic before you conduct the interview.

- **Plan and write your questions.** Prepare questions to draw out specific detailed information. Avoid vague questions such as "How do you feel about responding to emergency calls involving hazardous materials?" Instead, ask clear, specific questions, such as "What training has prepared you for emergencies involving toxic gases?" In addition, avoid questions that require a yes or no response because they do not encourage the speaker to elaborate. Also avoid questions that reflect an opinion or bias, such as "Isn't it true that management overemphasizes shop safety?" Instead, ask for the respondent's views: "In regard to shop safety, does management underemphasize, overemphasize, or adequately emphasize?" Further, avoid using "feel" in a question, as in the previous sample item, unless truly seeking information related to an emotion.

  Be prepared to include follow-up or clarification questions when they are needed. Especially consider follow-up questions following a "yes/ no" item. Use your list of questions, but don't be bound to them. If the interviewee introduces a new topic or direction of interest to you, pursue it. Likewise, if the interviewee rambles or strays from your topic, be ready to politely and gently redirect. For instance, you could move the interviewee back to the topic by saying, "Considering the highway construction project, when do you expect the board to approve the land acquisition?" or "We've talked about the strike; now let's move to discussing the allegations of mismanagement." Also, follow-up questions can ask for examples or best, worst, or most memorable experiences.

  Many interviewers develop questions on a tablet or laptop. This method lets them read the questions from the machine and record answers on it as the interview takes place. Some interviewers write questions on one sheet of paper and record answers on another. Other interviewers prefer to write each question and its answer on a note card. An audio recorder often is helpful, but ask permission to record the interview before you begin. There are several ways to record using a phone or a tablet. Most devices have built-in recording apps. In addition, OneNote is an app that allows you to take notes, draw, and record. Choose the system that works best for you.

- **Conduct the interview in a competent and courteous manner.** Remember, you are in control, and the success of the session depends on you, not the respondent. Make sure you do the following:

  - Arrive on time.
  - Introduce yourself.
  - Dress appropriately.
  - Speak in a clear, distinct voice.

- Explain the purpose of the interview

- Begin with questions that ask for facts rather than feelings or personal matters.

- Ask about the present; then ease into questions requiring memory of the past.

- Stay on track; stick to the topic.

- If interviewee speaks off topic, be prepared to pursue unexpected and interesting topics by asking follow-up questions.

- Take notes, but not excessively.

- Listen attentively.

- Ask for clarification or more complete details if needed.

- Be assertive but not arrogant.

- If using a recorder, check to be certain it is working properly.

- Ask one question at a time.

- Avoid showing reactions (shock, agreement) to the interviewee's responses.

- Encourage responses with forward posture, head nods, and "uh huhs."

- Avoid small talk.

- Thank the respondent for his or her time.

- Offer a handshake as you leave.

- Add a more complete summary to your notes as soon as you leave.

Write the Interview Results

Similar to reporting survey data, you have to make decisions about where, what, and how to report interview results.

As with the survey, you don't necessarily have to place all the survey data in the same place in your document. Sometimes it might fit under a results or data collection heading. Other times, it's best to separate what you've learned into different sections of your paper, a good story in the introduction and discussion of a problem under a problem section. And while you're obligated to report the interview honestly, if one response did not provide meaningful data, you may omit that response.

People report interview data in a number of ways. When you write about your interview, you

1. Can use a question-and-answer (Q and A) format. For some purposes, a Q and A format is sufficient for recording the results of an interview. You see this format frequently in magazines and hear it on television. However, even if you leave out questions that did not reveal much data and edit answers to avoid repetition, this format is lengthy. If you're asked just to report on an interview that is not a part of a longer report, then the Q and A might be a good idea. If you are reporting orally on what you learned from an interview, then a Q and A format might not be good.

EX: An interview with Morgan O'Shannon on December 29, 2017, gives us some insight into how an individual uses eBay for buying and selling personal items.

Q What prompted you to use eBay the first time?
A I was searching for good deals on automotive parts and accessories.

Q What was the first item you bought?
A A high pressure, steel braided hose for my car.

Q What kinds of things have you bought on eBay?
A Automotive parts and accessories, electronics . . . computer parts, audio-video equipment. Also collectibles, novelties and figurines—as presents mostly.

Q What kind of collectibles did you buy?
A Presents like the penguin candle holders for my Mom. I'm a Dale Earnhardt fan, so I've bought racing memorabilia.

2. Can integrate responses into your report. This format is perhaps the best for your reader. Here you use the information from the interview *when you need it* in the report. You don't have to write the answers in the same order you asked them, and you don't have to include every question and answer in your report. A proposal regarding the shipping and receiving operations might use information from the same interview in different sections:

   • in the Problem section of the proposal to report on problems created by slow service

   • in the Solutions section of the proposal to report on ways to improving the efficiency

   • in the Background section of the proposal to report on the history of this problem

Information from the interview on how another company handles ordering might be left out entirely.

Example: Morgan O'Shannon, a 28-year-old eBay user, describes some of the items he has purchased on eBay. He has bought automotive parts, electronics, computer parts, audio-video equipment, and collectibles. When pressed about the kind of collectibles a young man might purchase, Morgan said he found gifts on eBay, one gift, in particular for his mom, a pair of penguin candleholders—since she collects penguins. A fan of Dale Earnhardt Senior and Junior, he has also bought racing memorabilia.

In writing the results of an interview, the writer will likely use a lot of "he/ she (or Mr./Ms. X) says" introductions with quotations and paraphrases:

   • The director of shipping, Mr. Amean, says, "Our processes for inventorying goods received has improved since the purchase of a bar code reader."

   • He went on to express concern over the security of the warehouse.

Observation

In addition to surveying and interviewing, observing is another method of collecting primary data. Professionals frequently rely on observation to solve problems in their jobs. Medical professionals observe patients to diagnose illnesses. Crop scientists observe the numbers and types of weeds and insects in a field to decide whether the crop should be sprayed. Highway departments count vehicles to decide where to place traffic signals. However, you need to be careful when gathering data by observation. Observers may be biased, or subjects may act differently if they know they are being studied. Further, you should strive to interpret data objectively. Do not begin with preconceived ideas.

Plan Your Observation

To collect credible data by observation, use the following guidelines:

- **Train observers in what to look for, what to record, and how to record.** If you wanted to know about traffic at a certain intersection, you would train people to count vehicles; in addition, you would need to tell the observers the rules. For example, how would they count enclosed-bed trucks such as moving vans? If one observer counted these trucks with passenger vehicles, another counted the trucks with commercial vehicles, and the third did not count the trucks at all, the data would be flawed. Also make sure that all observers are using terms the same way. For example, what is "peak period"? If you tell observers that the peak period is from 11 A.M. until 2:30 P.M., their counts for peak period will be useful data because each observer counted during the same time frame.

- **Make systematic observations.** For instance, if the observers counting vehicles work only from 7 A.M. to 9 A.M. and from 4 P.M. to 6 P.M., will you get an accurate picture? Because many people are commuting to work and school during these times, you are likely to get inflated numbers.

- **Observe only external actions.** You cannot project internal actions or reasoning. For example, you may observe that 24 percent more people displayed flags this Independence Day than last, but you cannot say that more people are flying flags because they feel more patriotic. Report only actions or events you can see.

- **Quantify findings whenever possible.** Being able to assign statistics adds credibility, showing that an action or event was consistent.

- **Support your observations.** If you cannot quantify, support generalizations with details, examples, and illustrations. You might even make drawings or take photographs. A note-taking and recording app, such as OneNote or Evernote, would allow you to access information across devices as well as to search for specific information.

While observation can be a valuable source of primary data, consider the time, equipment, and cost. For instance, hiring and training people to count vehicles can be time-consuming and expensive. Even if you decide to place a mechanical device across the highway to count vehicles, it must be paid for, and it will not describe the vehicles.

Write the Observation Results

Sometimes observation results are reported simply and directly, perhaps with statistics, such as in traffic counts. In other circumstances, observation results may be reported in a full formal document. In this document, the introduction provides the date and purpose of the observation. Under the heading "Procedure," the writer describes the procedure used for the observation. Under "Results," the writer explains what was observed, or what happened. Under "Conclusions," the writer discusses in present tense the conclusions drawn based on the observations.

Experimentation

Experimentation is the act of causing an event so that an observer can test an assumption or a hypothesis (a statement of what the tester believes will happen). Experiments test whether a change in one factor causes another factor to change. For example, if the owner of a car-cleaning business wants to know whether his current car wax or a new product gives the longest-lasting shine, he might polish half a car with the current wax and the other half with the new wax. He then would check the car periodically for shine.

Employees frequently use experiments in the workplace. Manufacturers often test new products in limited markets to see whether the products will be successful. Managers may compare a current operating plan in one plant with a new plan in another plant. Researchers may gather samples of air, water, soil, food, medicines, body tissues, or even construction materials for testing.

Planning Your Experiment

As with observation, experimenters must be careful to avoid elements that will make the experiment and its results invalid. Sometimes other factors or variables can affect the results of an experiment. For instance, using different cleaners on the two halves of the car would affect the results of the wax study. Using adults for conducting clinical trials of a drug meant for children would not provide meaningful information about how the drug will work on pediatric patients. Therefore, when you design an experiment, try to eliminate as many outside factors as you can.

Objectivity is very important in experimentation as well. Interpret data collected objectively. Do not start with preconceived ideas of the experiment's outcome. And remember to use passive voice when writing about experiments; passive voice keeps the focus on the experiment rather than the person conducting the experiment.

Surveys, interviews, observation, and experimentation all serve as useful tools for acquiring information, and many researchers use a combination of those methods. Remember the stain on the wool sweater in the Warm Up at the beginning of this section? Even an everyday problem such as how best to clean a favorite garment, may require you to interview, observe, and experiment to find a solution.

Validity and Reliability

To maintain credibility, primary researchers look for valid and reliable data. **Valid data** are data that provide an accurate measurement of what an individual intends to measure.

For example, a clothing store owner wanted to know whether her business would attract as many customers as it did on weekdays if it were open on Sunday. She devised a test to collect data. The Sunday she chose was during a weekend when two big football games were being played in town and visitors filled area hotels. Comparing the number of customers on that

Sunday with the number of weekday customers would not generate valid data. The large number of visitors in town on that particular Sunday would influence the results.

Reliable data are data that provide results that can be duplicated under similar circumstances. If you explain that mixing two liquid chemicals will create a solid, then other people can try the same test. If they follow your procedures, the mixed liquids should solidify. Being able to repeat the test with the same results represents reliable data.

Write the Experiment Results

Experiment results may be reported simply, as in this sentence: When the Altima is driven with the ADW gas additive, the engine chokes and shuts off approximately once every 20 minutes. However, the writer also may have a need to report results more formally, as seen in science lab reports. For more information and a model, see "Science Lab Reports" in Chapter 9, pages 249–252.

STOP AND THINK 3.7

What are three methods of collecting primary data? Why should you plan observations?

3 CHAPTER REVIEW

Summary

1. Researching at work involves finding information to help people solve problems, make informed decisions, answer questions, and perform many other functions.

2. Secondary data, or reports of information from someone other than the witness or the person directly involved, are usually found in a business, school, or public library through print or electronic means.

3. Writers must give credit for borrowed material by documenting the source. Failure to credit others for their words and ideas means risking reputation, employment, legal action, and financial reward.

4. Writers should evaluate sources by checking publication dates, the author's credentials, and the author's methods and resources.

5. As researchers find useful material, they take notes using one method or a combination of three methods—summary, paraphrase, and direct quotation—on note cards or a computer.

6. Primary data, or information direct from the person involved, may be collected by surveys, interviews, observation, and experimentation.

Checklist

- Have I defined the problem or need for information?
- Have I considered what information I already have?
- Have I reviewed information available in my organization's archives relating to my problem or need?
- Have I viewed the library catalog, online when accessible or in the library when not accessible online?
- Have I searched periodical indexes and databases for more recent secondary sources?
- Have I relied on general reference materials, electronic or in print, for quick background information and for references to other sources?
- Have I searched the Web using strategies to filter for useful information? Have I found the most current information?
- Have I given credit, using an appropriate style system, for borrowed words and ideas unless the information is considered common knowledge or is material in the public domain?
- Have I evaluated all sources of information before using the data?
- Have I taken notes using summary, paraphrase, and direct quotation?
- Have I considered collecting primary data using surveys, interviews, observations, and/or experimentation to find information not available through other sources? Have I planned for validity and reliability?

Build Your Foundation

1. Using the style appropriate for your field or the one your instructor suggests, compose a note card for each item.

   a. On page 14 of the magazine *Farm Review*, Edward F. Rademacher's and Janet Schwartz's article "Hog Farmers and Homeowners: Zoning Solutions" notes that municipal and regional governments are "legislating distance" between the farms' waste lagoons and residential areas. The article appears in the November 2015 issue of the magazine.

   b. In her 2016 book *Commercial Flower Production*, Dr. Iyana P. Nuez writes, "Careful record keeping and close observation are the key to disease management." The book is 283 pages long, and this statement appears on page 259. The book was published by Delmar, a publisher located in New York.

2. Using the style appropriate for your field or the one your instructor suggests, paraphrase items a and b. Write a direct quotation using item c. Remember to include documentation and an introduction or integration so that readers will know the context from which the information came.

   a. "The Center for Marine Conservation reported that volunteers scouring ocean beaches and inland shorelines cleaned up more than 7 million pieces of trash, including cigarette butts, bottles, cans, lightbulbs, syringes, and plastic bags." Found in a magazine article by Cindianne Jernigan, "Cleaning Up," *Natural State*, Volume 8, Issue 43, page 105.

   b. "Yesterday the Highway Department reported approval of a plan to open an 8.5-mile corridor between Henderson and Mount Clemmons. However, the new road may be a little bumpy because two sections of experimental asphalt, one designed to combat hydroplaning and the other made of crumbled tire rubber, are being used." Found in a newspaper article by Bill Rogers, *The Hartford Daily Trumpet* (Hartford, Illinois), August 29, 2015, page B2.

   c. "Storage is so cheap now that photographers have no excuse for not backing up their images. Arrange backup to be redundant and automatic. Store photos in at least three ways, with one of those being off premises." Found in a magazine article by Dee Kay, "Preserving Your Best Photos," *Photography Solutions*, Volume 10, Issue 12, June 2016, page 209.

3. Choose a technical or scientific topic (for example, taxation of Internet sales, irradiation or genetic engineering of food supply, or cosmetic use of Botox®). Find five sources, print and electronic, on the topic. Develop a working bibliography with each source listed in correct MLA or APA bibliographic form or the style your instructor wants you to use.

4. You are calling Ash Staton to set up an interview about a new type of home security system he invented. What arrangements should you discuss with him? List three things you should cover when you contact him to set up the interview.

5. Revise these questions to make them effective for an interview.

   a. Do you run for exercise?
   b. Isn't selling tissue removed during surgery illegal and immoral?
   c. What would your response be if the market declines more than 10 percent and if employees are threatening a strike?
      a. Revise these questions to make them effective for a survey. Do you enjoy winter sports?
      b. Do employees at Sera Corporation earn a reasonable salary?
      c. Do students like the new recreation center?

6. Identify a company where you might like to work and gather information that would help you apply for a job there. For instance, learn about products, services, and activities. Research the way the company is organized, its business philosophy, and its niche in the marketplace. Write a report that would be helpful to other students who might be interested in seeking employment there.

Your Turn

1. Think of a subject or hobby about which you know a great deal. In a brief essay, describe how you acquired your knowledge.

2. Find three specialized reference sources (for example, a medical dictionary or an aerospace encyclopedia) relating to your future career field or a topic of interest. (At least one of these reference sources should be online.) List the reference sources and a description of what each one offers.

3. Collect questionnaires for class analysis. Determine effective techniques as well as weaknesses in the surveys' strategies.

4. Watch a televised or video-recorded interview. Note the strategies the interviewer uses to make the interview effective.

5. Using the same keyword, use three Internet search engines. Bring to class the first ten listings that each search showed and compare the results.

6. Go to the Help section of any Internet search engine. Learn how this particular system works. Share what you learn with your classmates.

7. Using a full-text database available in your college or community library, find and print an article relating to your career field or to a term project. Write a summary of the article and bring the summary and the article to class. Explain to your peers how the information in the article impacts your professional or academic plans.

8. Choose a topic relating to your career field. Search for secondary information to provide basic background information. Write an essay summarizing your findings and prepare a bibliography.

9. Prepare questions and interview someone in your field of interest. From that person, collect information about a particular research project he or she undertook. Ask about methods, difficulties, and the outcome of the research. Record your findings on your sheet of prepared questions.

10. Although the University of Chicago Press online edition does not replace the book edition of *The Chicago Manual of Style,* you can still get information on how to cite books, electronic resources, journals, and newspapers. Visit the The Chicago Manual of Style Online site for the 15th and 16th editions. Go to "Chicago-Style Citation Quick Guide," and then click on the "Author-Date" button at mid-page. Using material in your possession, such as a book or magazine you are reading, create a reference list entry and parenthetical citation using the appropriate model.

11. A number of websites offer help with using the Modern Language Association's style, such as Cornell University's Library (https://www.library.cornell.edu/research/citation/mla) and Purdue's Online Writing Lab (https://owl.english.purdue.edu/owl/resource/747/01/). Also visit the website of the Modern Language Association (MLA). Go to "FAQ About MLA Style" in the Modern Language Association site to find answers to the following questions related to using MLA style:

    - How does a researcher cite a tweet?

    - How many spaces should follow a period or other ending mark of punctuation?

    - Does the current MLA style guide use underlining or italics, for example, to indicate a book title or website?

12. In a small group, identify an issue at your school.

    a. Using an online survey tool such as SurveyMonkey or SuveyGizmo, develop a survey to collect facts and opinions about the issue.
    b. Establish your audience and administer the survey electronically or in person.
    c. Tabulate the survey results.
    d. Present the survey results in a report or in graphic form.

Community Connection

1. Choose a product that your school or a community organization uses and compare it to a similar product. Keeping that product in mind, design an experiment to test a question. Write a report on the experiment design, the findings of the experiment, or both. Make sure you collect valid and reliable data.

2. Identify a problem at school, in your community, or at work.

   Examples:
   Does our campus have adequate parking (or on-campus transportation) for the student population?

   How can a person use leftovers to lower his or her food costs?

   Are students safe on campus? Or do they feel security measures on campus are adequate?

   a. Decide what information you need to solve the problem.

   b. Determine how and where to find the information.
   c. Conduct the necessary research.
   d. Report orally or in writing on your findings.

EXPLORE THE NET

Many colleges and universities offer help to researchers through their libraries and online writing centers. Visit "Research Help" at Cornell University Library and read about citation management. What citation management programs are used at Cornell? Also view the Annotated Bibliography Tutorial. What distinguished an annotation from an abstract? Next visit UCLA Library or Purdue Online Writing Lab. Name two or three services or aids these sites offer a researcher.

4 WRITING PROCESS

Goals

- Identify a writing process that suits your writing style
- Plan your document
- Draft and revise your document
- Edit and publish your document
- Collaborate constructively with others

Terms

Write to Learn

Think of a process with which you are familiar that involves several steps and some time to complete. The process could be anything from making a craft or troubleshooting a computer to painting a room or learning a football play. In one page, answer these questions about your process: What steps do you follow? Must you retrace your steps? Are some steps more important or enjoyable than others? How did you learn this process? Does the process get easier the more you do it? Explain.

FOCUS on Writing Process

Read Figure 4.1 on the next page and answer these questions:

- Can you identify this document as an early draft? Explain.
- For whom are the editing notes and questions?
- What kinds of problems do the editing notes address?
- Do you see any problems that the editing notes do not cover? Explain.
- Do your early drafts resemble this draft? If so, in what way?

What If?

How would the model change if

- The model represented an earlier or later draft?
- The draft were handwritten?
- The draft included comments from several readers?
- The model were missing a relevant piece of research?

need a title

Our brains begin as a single cell shortly after conception, and then begin dividing in a process we call meiosis. From this process *what process? Elaborate.* comes a brain that has much in common with other human brains, but is also different. Some brains are able to think visually. Others' have musical or linguistic talent. And others' have athletic ability. *Develop first paragraph. Use examples. Show that brain is remarkabale! Tone—sense of wonder?*

Their is still much we do not know about the brian, but scientists are learning more about it all the time. The brain has over trillion nerve cells of two types: glial and nerve cells. The adult human brain is a wet, fragile, pink mass—feels like play dough. It can seem to stop time by recapturing a memory. It has enough energy to power a lightbulb. *good info here* It weigh a little over three pounds, is shaped like a walnut, and fits into the palm of your hand. It works constantly. Represents 2% of body weight and consumes 20% of our calories and 25 % of our oxygen. It works unceasingly. When it "thinks" harder, it uses more fuel. It physically changes as it adapts to its enviroment. *sent are choppy—fix later* It has moreconnections, between cells. It forms more dendrites, between the neurons. It needs oxygen, glucose, and water to operate. ~~The basic structure of the brain is pretty common knowledge. Its is divided into 3 parts, the forebrain, the midbrain, and hindbrain.~~ *Do I need this?*

Purpose of paper missing—no thesis

Find photo or diagram of brain?

Some spell/punc/sent errors. Fix later

 Figure 4.1 Sample First Draft of an Introduction in a Report

Writing @Work

Manufacturing

Source: The Center to Advance CTE

Andrew Yoder has been a book production editor for Rowman & Littlefield Publishers in Lanham, Maryland, for nine years. He shepherds books through copyediting, proofreading, indexing, cover production, and finally manufacturing. Most of his technical communication involves e-mailing authors, freelancers, and in-house colleagues. He also is a book author and freelance writer and editor.

To begin a writing project, Andrew first gathers all of the resources he needs into one electronic file, organizes the contents of the file into smaller themed sections, and then finds the best section with which to start. "I'll occasionally read the quotes [in the file] and try to think about different angles and sections while doing mind-numbing tasks like mowing my yard."

Recently, Andrew talked with his fellow Rowman & Littlefield editors about how they approach writing. Each editor takes a different approach: "One colleague said she writes out a very detailed outline that serves as a draft replacement. Another coworker said that she

doesn't draft; she just writes. That's me. Any revising that I do is more like copyediting than working from a draft."

Authors should not be afraid of the copy editor's red pen. After Andrew sends one of his own completed manuscripts to his copy editor, he hopes to receive a great many questions and corrections that will improve the book. "Some authors are offended when someone edits their work or asks questions, but I'd rather have a copy editor find mistakes in my work than have a reader find them." Furthermore, says Andrew, "The biggest enemy of revising or editing material is a large ego."

Think Critically

1. How would your instructors react if you had outside copy editors correct your work before you turned it in? Why is writing at school different from writing on the job?

2. Look at the section in this chapter "Writing Is Different for Everyone" on page 92. Why do different people use different approaches to writing assignments?

Printed with permission of Andrew Yoder

Writing in Manufacturing

Manufacturers use machines and robots to automate products, such as pharmaceuticals, furniture, hardware, or household appliances, on a massive scale. Industrial production managers, also called quality control systems managers, oversee the daily operations of a manufacturing facility. They collect and summarize information, documenting evidence of successful and failed processes along with corrective actions. To see if an intervention, such as a robotic arm, assists productivity or slows down the process, the manager records observations and analyzes results much as a scientist records the results of an experiment.

Production managers set up and enforce efficient processes. "Process is everything,"

says Bill Hofler, a manager with over 15 years of manufacturing experience. "The process must be standardized so that it produces a quality product every time. We improve the process bit by bit by reducing or adding a step, upgrading the machinery, or eliminating waste." Consistent quality depends on repeating the same process by following an SOP, or standard operating procedure to include a detailed set of instructions complete with any necessary diagrams or flow charts.

Managers also assist with production reports and troubleshooting. Production reports analyze all costs associated with a product, including labor, materials, and overhead, to ensure financial feasibility and a suitable profit margin. When quality is compromised as in a defective garment or a cracked tile, the manager determines why, offers solutions, and reports findings to senior management.

4.1 A PROCESS FOR TECHNICAL WRITING

So far, you've learned why people write at work; how to plan for audience, purpose, scope, and medium; and how to conduct research. Now that you are ready to write, how do you begin? Where will the words come from to fill the pages of your document? They will come from completing the stages of writing your document—the **writing process.** This process includes planning, drafting and revising, and copyediting.

The writing process used by technical writers has much in common with the writing process used by any writer—an essayist, a novelist, a journalist, or a songwriter. However, each genre brings its own challenges. Along with considering audience, purpose, and medium, technical writers must spend the early stages carefully planning their writing. Working with technical data requires thinking not only about words but also about graphics and page design. Furthermore, technical writers often work collaboratively. Sophisticated software becomes an integral part of the process too. In practice, the technical writing process builds on the writing process with which you are already familiar.

To learn about the technical writing process, you will follow the decisions Jenna makes as she participates in a research project for educators in her state. Jenna begins the project by herself, but others soon join her effort. A middle school science teacher, Jenna is the team leader for a group of instructors given the task of researching new teaching methods for science teachers. The team will publish its findings in a journal, present them at a statewide conference, and house student activities on the state's public education web portal. To complete the project, the team will engage in **collaborative writing,** or writing with others as a group.

This chapter follows Jenna through each stage of the process, from coming up with her idea in the planning stage to polishing the final paper in the publishing stage. The sample document on page 89 shows an early draft of the introduction to the paper. Other models in the chapter illustrate changes Jenna made to this draft as she worked through the writing process.

To manage the stages of the technical writing process effectively, you should understand three characteristics of the process: It moves back and forth between predictable stages, it requires sufficient time to complete, and it varies from one person to the next. If you understand how the process works, you can customize each stage to fit your personality and thinking style.

© Monkey Business Images/Shutterstock

Writing Is Recursive

Writing is an act of creativity. Although the overall process does advance from planning to the publication of a final document, in practice writing does not usually move forward smoothly from one step to the next. It's an untidy process, as the writer moves back and forth between predictable stages. In other words, writing is not linear; it is **recursive,** or circular, in nature.

For example, you plan an article about new city bus routes and begin to write. Then you discover you overlooked the route in your own neighborhood. You go back to the research stage and gather more information. Next, you hear about some citizens who are not happy with the proposed routes. You circle back and change your purpose to reflect their discontent. After interviewing a few concerned citizens, you revise the article again.

Texts change, sometimes dramatically, as the writer moves through the different stages of the writing process. In some stages, writers expand documents, generating ideas and words without judging their usefulness. During other stages, writers make judgments, cutting some words and keeping others. Sometimes, as writers gather information, new ideas may even cause them to change their strategy, perhaps moving from an inductive to a deductive organizational plan.

Writing Takes Time

Writing takes time. Most writers need a certain amount of time to let ideas "cook" in their heads. The process can be compared to baking bread. You gather ingredients, mix them, knead the dough, and place the dough in a warm place to rise. However, you cannot make the dough rise; it rises in its own time because you set the process in motion. Like the bread, your ideas need time to incubate. The other stages take time too. It may take you two weeks to conduct research and only one day to write a rough draft, but the revising may take another week. When you write, you must allow time to cycle through this process.

Writing Is Different for Everyone

While the writing process does have stages, what people do in each stage differs from one person to the next. How people feel about the stages differs too. Some enjoy the prewriting and planning and dislike the revising. Others enjoy the revising but are frustrated by the planning. Some writers contemplate ideas mentally before committing words to paper and then write slowly with little revision. Others write words quickly, composing many drafts.

Writing Is a Conversation

When you speak to people face to face, it's clear you are holding a conversation, with ideas bouncing from one person to the next: the more people, the more talking, the more varied the responses. Even the person who says nothing is part of the conversation, for he is engaged, thinking, and even responding with facial expressions. Before you know it, views shift or become more deeply entrenched. It's easy to see the give and take of a conversation you can hear and see. But what about the seemingly isolated act of writing? Isn't the outcome the same—this give and take of ideas? However, instead of only two or three people, now the conversation broadens to include all the readers.

The discussion among homeowner Semenya and contractors Ronisha and Arthur about installing radiant floor heat in the bathroom takes several turns. Semenya asks questions about costs. Ronisha and Arthur explain how the floor is installed. The three are talking when the designer joins them and points out the appeal of quiet heat and the resale value. The ideas flow, one person's response piggy-backing on another's input. The conversation helps Semenya make decisions. The electrician who arrived late is largely silent, yet she is still engaged in the conversation, taking mental notes.

A similar but more expansive process is taking place elsewhere as potential customers first read about Radiant Heat's heating mats online and either decide against the product or question representatives via chat rooms or phone calls. It would be difficult to determine the number of people engaged in this rather simple conversation, for even the potential customers who decided against the heating system were part of it.

As a writer, you do not simply convey information to unresponsive readers. You join a much larger conversation which adds your bit of expertise, your questions, and your insights to an ever growing and changing registry of knowledge. Writing, then, contributes to and constructs knowledge.

Writing Is an Act of Discovery

Anyone who has written an angry e-mail and then chosen (wisely) not to send it when he discovered he overreacted has experienced writing as discovery. Anyone who has brainstormed a written list of possible names for a website until she stumbled upon the perfect one has experienced writing as discovery. Through writing we search: We seek the hidden agenda, the kernel of truth, the sterling idea. Somehow, writing allows us to dive deep into our brains and pull out a gem. Or maybe writing simply allows the gem to quietly surface. Either way, writing is a treasure hunt helping us unearth something of value.

Writing Is an Adventure

Writing—like many journeys—is an adventure. Any task, from rebuilding a car engine to taking a math course, is fraught with the ups and downs of reward and frustration. Our effort is broken down into steps: problems to be solved, compromises to be negotiated. We apply the knowledge we have and seek out what we do not know. Sometimes we don't know what to do next, so we ask questions, wrestle with uncertainty, and ponder our circumstances. Then we try something and it doesn't work, so we try something else. The auto parts store does not have the right spark plugs in stock, so we go to other stores and look online. There's not enough time to master all the formulas before the math test, so we master the most important ones and take practice tests.

So it is with writing. It's work. We persevere, building confidence in our ability, making decisions, developing a style, putting something of ourselves into our words. Sooner or later we come to a stopping point: We've done our best. We have something of which to be proud. When we embark on our next writing project, we apply what we've learned about our writing process—and things go a little more smoothly.

Writing Is Influenced by the Writer's Background

We say technical writing is objective. We say technical writing deals largely with facts. Certainly, while objectivity and factual reporting are the intent, all writing starts with the self, the writer—what the writer knows, what the writer thinks is important. We learn to consider our reader's cultural background, age, role, knowledge level, and interests; yet we must also consider how our cultural background, our upbringing, our age, our interests, our roles influence what we say—and then we strive to keep those influences from interfering with the message.

For instance, Ophelia is asked to research energy sources for Mowhawk's newest manufacturing plant. A supporter of sustainable energy sources, Ophelia is tempted to provide more data for solar panels and must consciously balance her report to include traditional energy sources as well.

 STOP AND THINK 4.1

Explain the recursive nature of the writing process. What is meant referring to writing as a conversation? Why is the process different for everyone?

 WARM UP   ## 4.2 PLANNING

Everybody makes plans. People plan how to spend an afternoon or what to wear. They plan major events—weddings, graduations, parties. What are the benefits of having a plan? Are there drawbacks to having a plan? If so, what are they?

Like other tasks, writing is easier when you have a plan. **Planning** is the first stage of the writing process, when a writer thinks of an idea and prepares to develop and research it.

Choosing a Topic

Your first task is to choose a topic. Sometimes your employer or instructor will give you a topic with some guidelines. For example, a trainer in the home office of Pajoli's Pizza franchise is asked to write an operating manual for the entire chain. The manual includes the home office specifications (for example, how to open and close the restaurant, how to prepare each dish, and how to calculate food costs). Therefore, the research plan is straightforward: Interview managers, observe them in action, and write the procedures step by step.

When the topic is given to you, learn as much as possible about the assignment. Ask about audience, purpose, scope, and medium. Note any gaps in the analysis, ask questions, and make changes based on new information. For example, based on the observation that some restaurant owners are Hispanic, the writer for Pajoli's manual plans for a Spanish translation. Also, if the pizza franchise decides to use touch-screen kiosks in the dining area, instructions for maintaining the kiosks will be added to the manual.

Working with someone else's idea can simplify the planning stage. Sometimes, though, your writing task is not prescribed. Your employer or instructor may give you general guidelines and expect you to come up with ideas and a plan.

Freewriting, mapping, and journaling are strategies that can help you choose a topic. For example, your assignment could be like Jenna's. When Jenna was given her task, she was not given a specific topic. To help her select a topic, Jenna used freewriting and journaling.

Freewriting

Freewriting is writing freely to discover an idea. You write what comes to mind without judging what you have written or worrying about grammar or sentence structure. Three variations of freewriting are open freewriting, focused freewriting, and looping.

With open freewriting, you write about anything and see where your writing takes you. Jenna's open freewriting finally brings her to a possible topic in the last few sentences shown in Figure 4.2.

> What am I interested in? Today, not much today. Let's see. Okay, let's find a topic for the research. Could write about problem solving. Hmmm. Also saw on Discovery Channel a segment about the brain and learning disabilities. Hmmm. I have a learning disability. Maybe I could research that. Yeah—why do I have a learning disability, and what instruction works best for me? That would help instructors in the classroom.

Figure 4.2 Jenna's Open Freewriting

With focused freewriting, you choose a topic and freely associate ideas with that topic. This exercise, too, helps Jenna discover an idea. An example of Jenna's focused freewriting is shown in Figure 4.3.

> TOPIC: Learning: How do students learn best—with good instructors when the students are motivated? What makes a good instructor? One who has enthusiasm, one who knows the subject, one who knows how students learn, knows students' learning styles. Who was my best instructor? Mr. Kohl. But what made him good? Why do students not learn? What happens in the brain when someone learns? Do we know the answer to that question? Maybe if we knew how the brain learns, instructors could do something to improve that process.

Figure 4.3 Jenna's Focused Freewriting

With the looping technique, you write for five minutes, stop, and summarize in a sentence what you have written. Staying focused on the summary sentence, you write again for five minutes, stop, and summarize. Then you repeat the process until ideas appear, as they do in Figure 4.4.

> First Loop (write for 5 minutes): Tired, sleepy, head hurts, had a hard time paying attention to the stock market seminar—too much math. I wish I had gone to the counseling workshop—more my style. My sister would like this though; she is good with math—a math whiz. Why is that? Why do some people learn some things more easily than others? (Stop and wait a few minutes.)

Figure 4.4 Jenna's Looping Technique *(continues)*

Typical Reader

A person or people needing specific information presented in a well-organized, coherent document.

Writer's Focus

Working toward a well-organized, coherent document beginning with the idea and planning stages through the drafting, revising, and publishing stages.

> Second Loop (write for 5 minutes): Why *do some people learn some things more easily than others?* Who else? Renee is good at karate; Jon is good with cars but dislikes English. Why? Was Einstein's brain different from everybody else's? If I knew, would it help me and others learn math? What would help me with my learning problems in math? (Stop and wait a few minutes.)
>
> Third Loop: Jenna could summarize the last idea and begin freewriting again to start another loop.

Figure 4.4 (continued) Jenna's Looping Technique

Journaling

Another way to find an idea is to write in a journal regularly. Figure 4.5 shows a journal entry Jenna writes one morning.

> I had this strange dream last night that I was late to class. Everyone was taking the exam, and I had only 10 minutes to finish it. I panicked, but then I saw three students get up and act out one of the problems. I saw more students writing on the board. In the back, I saw students talking in a group. Suddenly, the class became three classes—you know how weird dreams can be. Somehow I knew these students were learning. What does that mean? Maybe that people learn in different ways. There must be some kind of brain research on it.

Figure 4.5 Jenna's Writing Journal

Jenna notes in several of her entries, she has come back to the question of what happens in the brain when people learn. Because she does not know much about brain research, she decides she would like to know more about it. At this point, she selects brain-based teaching as a possible topic.

Shaping an Idea

After you choose a topic, you can begin **shaping** the topic by giving it some direction. When you are shaping an idea, answer several questions: Is the idea narrowed or focused enough? How can I develop this idea? What are the subtopics or parts of the idea? How can I organize these subtopics?

Questioning, reading, mapping, and outlining will help you focus your idea and figure out subtopics.

Questioning

Jenna uses questioning to shape her idea. Who will benefit from learning about this topic? Clearly, instructors can benefit, but what do they need to know? When and where can they use this information? Why does learning take place? How can instructors improve classroom learning? After asking these questions, Jenna decides that the "why" and "how" answers are important for shaping her idea. She also approaches her colleagues to get their points of view.

To proceed with a clear understanding of what is most important, a writer should review the rhetorical situation. Midway through the project, when the process takes an unexpected turn because of new information or a difficult circumstance, the writer can use these questions to make decisions about how to proceed. Figure 4.6 lists rhetorical questions and how they apply to Jenna's project.

JENNA'S RHETORICAL SITUATION	
Purpose	What do I want to accomplish with this document? How significant is this communication task?
Jenna's Purpose	*To improve teaching and learning of science in the middle grades*
Context	What is the background, the larger framework or situation into which this communication fits?
Jenna's Context	*The need to prepare students for careers in science, technology, engineering, and math (STEM)*
Audience	Who is this document created for? Who is the intended audience?
Jenna's Audience	*Busy teachers with middle-grade science students*
Persona	What best describes the role of the author? How does the author establish credibility?
Jenna's Persona	*A mentor who will strive to present the best research available in accessible, easy-to-follow text*
Evidence	What kind of research is needed to produce this piece?
Jenna's Evidence	*Research from neural medical journals and teaching methodology, classroom observations, and interviews*
Media	Through which channel or channels will the communication be delivered?
Jenna's Media	*The white paper required by the grant and teaching activities housed on a web portal*
Structure	What is the best way to organize this information and keep the reader's attention?
Jenna's Structure	*Representing only research and activities which prove to be the most practical and the most appealing to teachers and their students*

Figure 4.6 Jenna's Rhetorical Situation

Reading

Jenna finds some direction from the reading journal she's been keeping as she reads about her topic. She tags some pages with sticky notes when she finds information that might help her shape her topic. When she feels stuck, she uses a search engine or online database to plug in a topic to see what might come up. An example is shown in Figure 4.7 on the following page.

Mapping

Jenna also uses cluster mapping to shape her ideas. She begins with her topic in the middle and allows ideas to radiate from the center, drawing lines to connect related topics. As she lists topics, her list grows into other clusters and generates more ideas for topics. Jenna can then see at a glance the major ideas, their subtopics, and the relationship of the subtopics to the major

"Improving Our Classrooms" (Fall 2015) article: Talks about how windows of opportunity for learning open and close in the growing brain. Example: The neurons for learning language are active until about age 10. After that, neurons not used die out.

Brains Help4Teachers newsletter (July 2015): Virtual lectures during class may aid retention.

How the Brain Learns (2011) by Sousa: Sousa stresses how the brain constantly adjusts to its environment. Gives many teaching suggestions for the classroom.

Figure 4.7 Additional Research Notes from Jenna's Reading Journal

ideas. For example, she notices the amount of sleep students get and the instructor's method of delivery both affect retention. She also sees the need to clarify the differences between retention and learning. Figure 4.8 shows Jenna's concept map.

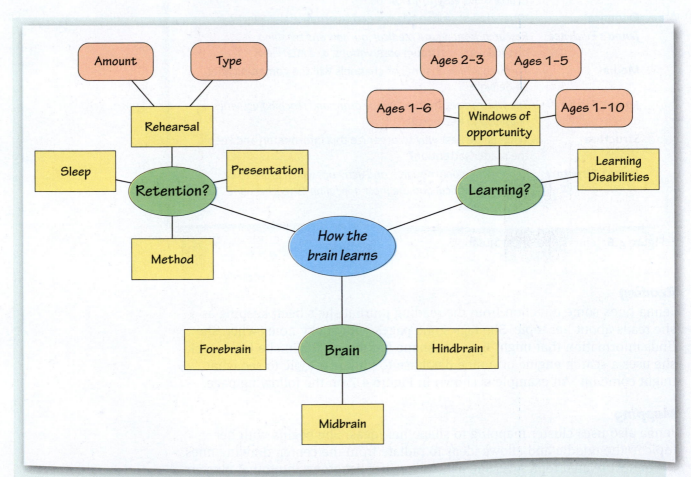

Figure 4.8 Jenna's Concept Map

After looking closely at the cluster, Jenna must narrow her choices and decide which subtopics to include and which to omit. Not all the ideas are relevant to her purpose, that is, to facilitate learning in a middle school classroom. She decides not to include learning disabilities because most schools have disability support programs with their own resources. She also decides to leave out early brain development since her students are older.

Outlining

From the cluster map, Jenna develops a **tentative outline**. This outline is an informal, changeable plan for organizing topics and subtopics. Notice the outline in Figure 4.9 is not a formal one (although it could be), yet it gives Jenna a focus for her paper's topics and subtopics.

Introduction—some interesting facts about the brain—to get students'
attention

   – Basic Brain Anatomy—explain basic parts of the brain and
      what each part does

   – How neurons work—how a neuron fires and passes information
      from one to another

   – Relate basic brain anatomy and neurons' firing to how the brain
      learns (Show the actual changes in brain anatomy)

   – Retention—what factors affect retention?

     + Amount of sleep

     + Timing of information presented

     + Rehearsal

       - Type of rehearsal

       - Length of rehearsal

   – Student Activities

Figure 4.9 Jenna's Tentative Outline

As you outline topics, consider how to organize them. The document type and purpose may dictate the organizational pattern. Typical organizing principles include the following:

- **Chronological order** for presenting topics or events in the order in which they occur (or occurred), as in the development of a product or the history of an event

- **Spatial order** for arranging items in space, as in a description of an office, a factory, a landscape design, or a home

- **Causal order** for presenting causes and effects, as in a presentation of reasons for an event or the consequences of an action

- **Comparing and contrasting for examining similarities and/or differences,** as in the recommendation of one product or action over another

- **Classifying** or breaking something down into parts, as in an analysis of venture feasibility or product usefulness

- **Problem and solution for proposing a course of action to resolve an issue,** as in a definition or an analysis of a problem followed by a workable solution

Other ways to organize data include strategies that meet your readers' needs as well as your purpose for writing. These strategies include the following:

- **General to specific** (or specific to general). Does your audience need the big picture or the details first?

- **Background before new information.** Do the members of your audience need to know a little history or be given a context to prepare them for something new or different?

- **Familiar to less familiar.** Will your readers be more receptive to new data or different processes if you present the familiar, more easily understood information first?

- **Simplest to most complex** (or most complex to simplest). Do your readers already understand the complex ideas, or do they need to be led to them logically?

- **Most important to least important** (or least important to most important). Will your audience benefit from reading the most important idea first or last?

Often using one organizational strategy is not enough. Longer, more complex documents may require one section to be organized differently from another section. In such cases, a combination of methods works best. Jenna considers using a combination of methods for her document, as follows:

- **Problem and solution:** Jenna presents the problem of lower science achievement and offers brain-based teaching as a solution.

- **Cause-to-effect order:** Jenna plans to develop her argument with the reasons instructors should change lesson plans and the effects those changes may have on student learning.

- **Background before new information:** Jenna believes instructors need to understand the newest research about the brain before she presents the teaching strategies based on that research.

© Antonio Guillem/Shutterstock

- **Simplest to most complex:** Because instructors are busy, Jenna plans to introduce simpler ideas first, which can be incorporated quickly into lesson plans, before moving on to strategies that require more time to implement.

Consider which headings (short titles in a manuscript that identify a topic) you will use and what the final document will look like. A heading is appropriate when you have one or more paragraphs on a single topic that likely corresponds to the outline you wrote. The document type—a report, a resume, a brochure, a web page—also will dictate your headings. After reviewing her tentative outline, Jenna converts her topics to a parallel structure and plans to use the headings shown in Figure 4.10. Using these headings as guides, Jenna spends the next few weeks researching, taking notes, and organizing those notes. (See Chapter 3 for guides to research and note taking.)

How the Brain Is Structured (first-level heading)

How Neurons Create Memories (first-level heading)

How Brain Structure and Activity Affect Learning (first-level heading)

How to Aid Retention (first-level heading)

    Amount of Sleep (second-level heading)

    Timing of Information Presented (second-level heading)

    Amount and Type of Rehearsal (second-level heading)

Classroom Activities

Figure 4.10 Jenna's Tentative List of Headings

 STOP AND THINK 4.2

What strategies for freewriting and shaping have you used in the past? Which ones work best for you? Does this chapter present some methods you have not tried? If so, which ones?

4.3 DRAFTING AND REVISING

 WARM UP

Now that you have a plan and research about your topic, you are ready to write. This part of the writing process is called the drafting and revising stage. Review your audience analysis and purpose for writing. Keep your audience and purpose in the back of your mind as you draft and revise.

Drafting

Drafting is the second stage of the writing process. When drafting, you write the first, second, and third (or more) versions of your document. As soon as you begin to write, you are writing a first **draft**—an early version of a document that is subject to change. Do not put off writing because you are waiting for the perfect first sentence to come to mind. Just start writing. The order in which you write does not matter. What does matter is the order in which the reader reads, so you can start anywhere and fill in gaps later for your reader. Force a few words until they start to flow. Drafting is like trying new paint: You do not know whether you like the color until you see it on the wall.

The Introduction

While the introduction might not be the first part you write, it is the first part your readers will see. It sets the tone and determines how receptive your readers are to the information you present. Use the introduction to

Do you have difficulty writing the first words in a draft, or do the words come fairly quickly? How long does it take you to write a two-page first draft on a familiar topic?

- **Relate to your readers** by discussing a situation you and your readers have in common.

- **Hold your readers' attention** with startling statistics or an eye-opening quotation.

- **Forecast** the topics and information you will cover.

- **Identify questions** that are answered in the document.

- **Define the problem to be solved** by explaining what the problem is and why it exists

- **Provide the background of the situation** with a brief description of events leading up to the need for this document.

- **Offer a research overview** by introducing the major headings and telling where and how the research was conducted.

The Body

As you write, you decide how to support your subtopics in the body of your paper. When thinking about ways to elaborate, explain, or prove your points, ask yourself what your readers need. Do they need

- **Long or short examples**—specific occurrences that happened or could happen?

- **Testimonials**—real-life stories from people who can attest to or support a view?

- **Quotations**—statements from people who are often authorities on a topic?

- **Statistics**—numerical data, percentages, and/or test results to support a view?

- **Historical facts**—verifiable information researched by credible scholars?

- **Financial facts or estimates**—financial reports, trends, and/or economic news?

The Conclusion

Use your conclusion to do what the document type requires. Proposals may need a reminder of the solution; sales letters may need a call to action; a recommendation may need a summary of key points and a possible decision; a research paper may answer questions posed earlier in the document.

Revising

When you finish drafting, it's time to revise your document. When **revising**, read your document and make changes to content, organization, and word choice. Use your audience analysis and purpose statement to guide you. Because the content affects the other revision strategies, start by revising content and then move to organization and sentence structure.

After you print a first draft, put it aside for a while. Come back to the draft at a later time and read it again to decide what does and does not work. Make notes on the draft. Draw arrows when you see, for example, that the third paragraph should be next to the sixth paragraph and the example in the second paragraph should be in the fifth paragraph. Cross out phrases, sentences, and paragraphs which distract from your message and can be deleted.

Consider improving page design and adding graphics. Perhaps a list can be bulleted and set apart from the margin to draw attention and make information more accessible. Can numerical data be clarified in a pie or bar graph? Can a carefully placed photo create human interest and support your message? Should a flow chart be placed closer to your description of a process? Attractive page design and meaningful visuals enhance the readability of your document.

Writing can be an untidy process, as Figure 4.11 illustrates. This document is the second draft of Jenna's introduction.

How the Brain Processes Information *good title*

Three to four weeks after the sperm and egg unite, one of the cell layers of the embryo thickens and develops into a flat neural plate. From this place comes a thinking mechanism that has much in common with other human brains, but that also differs in remarkable ways. Some brains are wired to envision and build bridges, skyscrapers, and superhighways. Others' create the songs of our youth, the art we hang on our walls, and the motion pictures that define our age. Still others' manage the linguistic marvels of a best-selling novel or the complex motor skills of an ice skater. *Much better! ¶ has good examples. Tone shows sense of wonder.*

Add transition Their is still much we do not know about the brian. *topic sent weak*

The adult human brain is a wet, fragile, pink mass. It can seem to stop time by recapturing a memory. It has enough energy to power a lightbulb. It weigh a little over three pounds, is shaped like a walnut, and fits into the palm of your hand. It works constantly. Represents 2% of body weight and consumes 20% of our calories and 25 % of our oxygen. It works unceasingly. *choppy sent. Need variety. Use sent comb* When it "thinks" harder, it uses more fuel. It physically changes as it adapts to its enviroment. It has more connections, between cells. It forms more dendrites, between neurons. It needs oxygen, glucose, and water to operate. *This ¶ lacks unity—has 2 ideas: physical description and how brain works.*

Need to lead up to thesis If we understand how the brain learns, we can improve our methods of teaching.

Several errors, typos—fix later. Revise one step at a time.

Figure 4.11 Jenna's Second Draft of the Introduction

Figure 4.12 provides a hierarchy of questions to ask while you revise. The questions begin with the general content before moving to sentence structure, mechanics, and grammar.

CONTENT QUESTIONS FOR REVISION

Do I have enough or too much information for my reader? Do I need to conduct more research or delete something?

Is my information clear? Do I need to revise for clarity?

Is my introduction effective? Do I need to revise to attract my readers' attention?

Is my purpose clear? Do I need to add a sentence that explains the purpose?

Do my details logically support my purpose?

ORGANIZATIONAL QUESTIONS FOR REVISION

Is the information in the best logical order for my reader? Do I need to move paragraphs or sections? Are my paragraphs and sections unified?

Do I need to remove sentences that do not fit the purpose?

Do sections and paragraphs have topic sentences? Do I need to add topic sentences?

Are transitions clear between sections and paragraphs? Do I need to add transition sentences or phrases?

Does my conclusion logically end the document?

READABILITY QUESTIONS FOR ANALYSIS

Does my writing flow from one sentence and paragraph to the next?

Are sentences varied by length and type? Would my sentences be more interesting if I combined them?

Have I selected the best words? Do I need to replace overused words? Do I need to define terms?

Figure 4.12 Hierarchy of Questions for Revision

STOP AND THINK 4.3

What are the three most helpful pieces of advice in this section? Why do you find them helpful?

WARM UP

4.4 COPYEDITING AND PUBLISHING

What is your impression when you find errors in a newspaper or textbook?

How important is an error-free document? In business, a professional image indicates a professional, responsible institution behind the image. In the absence of a person, the document represents a company, in effect becoming the face of that company. If the face has smudges and errors, the impression is negative. If the face is clean and attractive, the impression is positive. Therefore, after you have planned, drafted, and revised your document, you must take care of the finishing touches by copyediting and publishing your writing. **Copyediting** involves proofreading a document for correctness in word choice, spelling, grammar, and mechanics. **Publishing** is the last step, when you send your document to the person or people who need or requested it.

Copyediting

After you have revised for content, organization, and word choice, it is time for copyediting, one of the final stages of the writing process. In this stage, you carefully proofread your document and polish it. Figure 4.13 lists copyediting questions to ask yourself as you correct a document.

Do I have any sentence problems—fragments, run-ons, or comma splices?

Is the punctuation correct?

Have I used words correctly? Have I double-checked frequently misused words?

Have I spelled the words correctly?

Is the documentation of sources accurate?

Does the document look professional?

Is the page design balanced and attractive?

Is the formatting consistent?

Figure 4.13 Copyediting Questions for Analysis

Use several methods when proofreading for errors. To catch those errors you may not notice as you read silently, read your draft aloud to find fragments, grammatical errors, and awkward sentences. You also can read the draft backward, starting with the last sentence of the paper and moving toward the beginning. In addition, if you know a good grammarian and speller, ask that person to help you copyedit. Today you can use a number of electronic aids for copyediting. Most word processing programs underline misspelled words and possible grammatical issues as you enter text, alerting you to errors. You can correct errors as you go, or you can wait until you finish the document to run spelling and grammar checks. Not only do these programs locate misspelled words, but they provide a list of possible corrections as well.

However, the spell-checker does not select the best word for you. For example, it does not flag an improper use of *their* or *there* if the word is spelled correctly but used incorrectly. Also, technology creates new uses for existing words which spell-checkers cannot verify. For instance, we can no longer assume "feed?" has something to do with food because today it often refers to a collection of news stories. "Viral" is not necessarily a description of a nasty cold but is thumbs up for a story or photo posted and reposted online in rapid-fire succession.

The grammar checker operates the same way. It flags sentences that may have problems, but you must understand grammar to know whether to change the wording. For example, grammar programs point out the use of passive voice. Deciding whether to rework the sentence requires an understanding of passive and active voice. If you are unsure about proper usage, consult a current English handbook or a reputable online source.

Other electronic aids include a dictionary (for parts of speech or meanings of words) and a thesaurus. A thesaurus is handy when you know that a better word exists for the one you have used or when you have overused a word and need a synonym. However, words have subtle differences in meaning. *Roget's Thesaurus* lists *steal* as a synonym for *borrow*, but you cannot use the two words interchangeably. Always use a dictionary to double-check definitions. Otherwise, your use may be awkward or inaccurate.

Publishing

When you have finished copyediting your document, you are ready to publish. In this final stage, make sure the document looks professional, is ready on time, is presented in the form your reader needs, and uses sources correctly.

If your reader expects a printed product, print the document on good paper, using a high-quality printer and print cartridge or toner. To meet your deadline, have the document ready several days ahead of time to allow for mishaps—the printer not working, the cartridge running out of ink, or the power going out. If you are sending a document to a print shop, know how much time the printer needs. For documents that require signatures of others in your organization, as many proposals do, allow adequate time for meeting with and requesting signatures of these busy people.

If the medium is electronic, you may be able to upload, send, or post in less time than it takes to publish a printed document; however, be prepared to contend with technology mishaps—from the ice storm compromising a remote server to the forgotten password needing to be reset. Protect your files: Save in multiple places, maintain virus software, and keep passwords up to date. Publish the file using valid file formats, such as PDF, doc/docx, JPEG, or RTF. Follow established protocol (accepted behavior) and netiquette (online manners) for your electronic submission, whether it's uploading through an application, posting to a website, inserting links to sources or tables, or using e-mail to supply a link to the document or to send as an attachment. Create polite and professional e-mail text and copy appropriate people.

Document your sources using the proper style manual for the discipline. Separate style guides have been developed for fields such as the humanities, the social sciences, law, medicine, and engineering. Electronic publications, webpages, and government publications have their own publishing preferences. Style guides also vary by country, with different publication guidelines for Australian English and Canadian English, for example. Do not risk plagiarizing your document. Sometimes acknowledging a source requires receiving written or verbal permission. When in doubt, seek permission to use someone else's work and document your source.

Figure 4.14 shows the final draft of Jenna's introduction. Compare this version with the sample document on page 89 to see the changes Jenna made throughout the writing process.

How the Brain Processes Information

Three to five weeks after the sperm and egg unite, one of the cell layers of the embryo thickens and develops into a flat neural place. From this place comes a thinking mechanism that has much in common with other human brains but that also differs in remarkable ways. Some brains are wired to envision and build bridges, skyscrapers, and superhighways. Others create the songs of our youth, the art on our walls, and the motion pictures in our theaters. Still others manage the linguistic marvels of a best-selling novel or the complex motors skills of an ice skater.

Despite its obvious importance to our lives, there is still much we do not know about the brain. What we do know, however, is fascinating. We know it can reverse time by reliving a memory. We know it has enough energy to power a light bulb. A wet, fragile, pink mass, the brain is shaped like a walnut (Figure 1) and can fit into the palm of your hand. Weighing a little over 3 pounds, it comprises only 2 percent of your body weight but consumes 20 percent of your calories and oxygen. When it "thinks" harder, it actually uses more fuel.

Figure 1 Human Brain

© hidesy/Shutterstock

Working around the clock, the brain constantly reshapes itself as a result of experience. It physically changes as it adapts to its environment—most noticeably in the number of connections, called dendrites, which it forms between its cells, called neurons. So when learning takes place, the brain is physically altered forever. Because the brain is where learning begins and ends, an understanding of this process can help us become better instructors and learners.

Figure 4.14 Final Draft of the Introduction

 STOP AND THINK 4.4

What kinds of mistakes do you tend to miss when you copyedit your writing? Make a list of those mistakes and practice looking for them in a draft.

4.5 WRITING COLLABORATIVELY

 WARM UP

Many writing projects—newsletters, proposals, research projects, brochures, and webpages—are produced collaboratively. The more complex and longer your project, the more likely you will work with others. Often writing produced collaboratively is better than anything anyone could have written individually. Interdependence is necessary in today's work environment. You are stronger when you use others' strengths along with your own.

The topic of your writing project may require the input of people from several disciplines. Each person brings a special area of expertise to the

Describe an experience when you worked as part of a group or team. What role did you and the others play? What was the final outcome? Could you have accomplished the final outcome by yourself? Explain.

project—whether it is medical, technical, political, or socioeconomic or the ability to write and design graphics. Applying for a grant to aid a hospital in a rural community might involve the following people:

Chief Surgeon Dr. Emily Coltrain	to address medical needs and equipment
Hospital administrator Ray Guevara	to address hospital and equipment costs
Two members of the hospital's board of trustees (an educator and a prominent business leader)	to represent community concerns
City council member Julia McNeil	to represent city and local business concerns
Senator Colin Elkins	to foster political support
Architect Holden Wacamau	to design the hospital trauma center requested in the grant
Communication Liaison Kermit Angelo	to solicit support using social media
Professional grant writer Paula Solinski	to gather data from different areas to write, revise, edit, and publish the grant

A collaborative effort may be required not only for a long document but also for a short piece of writing. A monthly departmental newsletter, for example, may include short articles from different employees with one editor putting the newsletter together—much the same way a newspaper editor collects articles from reporters.

Advantages of Collaboration

Employees pool their resources because they produce their best work in conjunction with others. In short, collaboration works and works well because a team

- **Brings together different kinds of knowledge.** In this age of specialization, no one person has all of the answers. The more knowledge you can tap, the more credible your final project will be.

- **Brings together different talents.** Some people can depict information graphically; others are better at interviewing to get information; others write well. Members can offer the team what they do best.

- **Allows different perspectives and viewpoints.** Different perspectives can offer wisdom and balance.

- **Improves work relationships.** During a work project, people form friendships, empathize with each other's work problems, and may be able to help with solutions.

- **Is enjoyable.** People who get along in a group and successfully produce results have fun working with each other.

- **Keeps one person from being responsible for the entire project.** Often the work seems less stressful because the responsibility is shared.

Disadvantages of Collaboration

The rewards of collaboration are well-documented, but group work can have its pitfalls. For instance, working with others

- **Can be a dreaded event.** While most people enjoy working in a group, someone who does not get along with a group member may feel anxious about the experience. Some people prefer to work by themselves, and group interaction is frustrating for them.

- **Can include conflict.** However, some disagreements over content or procedure can be productive because they encourage more talking and thinking to reach the best outcome. Groups that learn to manage conflicts can work through them without creating ill will.

- **Can take longer than people working alone.** Group communication often requires more time to talk over solutions, collect data from different people, read drafts, and work through conflict. On the other hand, a well-organized group may complete a project more quickly.

- **Can take away personal motivation.** Someone who has only a small interest in the group project may not care about the outcome and thus will not be productive.

- **Can encourage groupthink.** Groupthink is the tendency of group members to conform to the group's preferences without thinking through an issue individually. The danger of groupthink is members may be lulled into believing they are producing a superior product when, in reality, their unwillingness to confront tough issues yields a mediocre product. Groupthink results when people do not care enough about the project to risk confrontation or when people do not know how to manage conflict and therefore avoid it.

- **Can lead to unequal workloads.** Some task-oriented personalities will jump in to get the job done. Illness may keep someone else from working on the project. Sometimes members who know more about certain areas of the project assume more responsibility because of their specialized knowledge. In some instances, members do not pull their weight. Inequity in workloads may lead to resentment.

- **Can produce fragmented writing.** If different parts of a document are written by different people with little agreement on how the writing should be organized or without a designated editor, coherence and readability may suffer.

Despite the pitfalls, collaboration is necessary in the workplace. Employees who learn to work together show their managers and teammates they know how to accomplish a task with others. Many job descriptions ask for individuals with people skills, and job interviews include questions about the applicant's ability to work with others. Being a team player is one of the most important skills for today's job market.

Organizing Collaborative Projects

How do five or six people write one document? A collaborative writing project can be organized in one or more of the following ways.

- **Different people write different parts and use one editor.** Jenna's team eventually selected topics for the white paper required by the grant funding the project. Most members wrote between 10 and 20 pages with accompanying graphics on their topics, as listed here:

Brian	Methodology and evaluation
Jenna	Brain research
Ray	Multiple intelligences
Mercedes	Teaching and learning styles
Sudomo	Technology in the classroom
Everyone	Classroom activities
C. J.	Webmaster for project

Because Jenna agreed to be the final editor, team members uploaded their sections to the Google Docs pages Jenna set up for the project and commented on each other's drafts, color coding their comments by team member. Jenna kept a watchful eye over this phase, asking questions and encouraging members to rewrite portions or clarify their data. Once the collaboration ended, Jenna downloaded the project into a Microsoft® Word document and revised it to promote consistency in tone, documentation, and formatting. Then she uploaded the document once more to Google Docs so so the team could make last-minute changes. Once the changes were complete, Jenna converted the files to Word and sent an e-mail with the paper attached as a zipped file to the agency funding the research.

The system Jenna and her team used works well when topics can be distributed and when people agree ahead of time on matters of style, length, purpose, scope, and medium.

Communication
Technologies

Online mind mapping software such as Mindmeister and Bubbl.us can help individuals brainstorm and shape ideas visually. A cloud-based technology, Mindmeisiter offers mobile apps for both iOS and Android devices and allows real-time collaboration from all members of your team. Mindmeister can carry a project from ideas to writing to presentation. Focusing primarily on mind mapping, the web-based and iOS Bubble.us app is an easy-to-use tool enabling a new user to generate a map within minutes. Both Mindmeister and Bubbl.us offer free and paid subscriptions. By using mapping software in the early stages of your writing process, you can see your ideas emerge, organize, and evolve.

Think Critically

What advantages might mind mapping have over other ways to generate and shape ideas, such as freewriting or journaling?

Focus on Ethics

Trust within a group is one of the most important factors in its success. Work to create trust by following these ethical guidelines:

Be responsible. Keep your word; do what you say you are going to do.

Be loyal. Avoid talking about others in the group to other group members or to people outside the group.

Be honest. Make sure any research you bring to the group is properly documented. If you do not provide a source, your entire group could get into trouble for plagiarism.

Be respectful. Keep an open mind when individuals express opinions different from your own. Practice common courtesy. Show concern for others, say please and thank you, and apologize when necessary.

Be fair. Complete a reasonable share of work. Do not expect someone else to do more than a fair and reasonable share, and do not take credit for another group member's work.

Think Critically

Is it possible for these guidelines to conflict with one another? For example, is it possible for loyalty to conflict with honesty? How does the use of collaborative software such as Google Docs affect the team's ability to trust each other? Explain your answer.

■ **Different people submit data to a central person who compiles the information.** For example, the grant writer for the rural hospital could collect information from others' notes, charts, spreadsheets, interview results, and rough drafts. Paula might need a letter written by the grant committee chair, but she would write most of the draft herself. After writing the final draft, she would send it to committee members for their feedback.

This system works well when the writing is specialized. As a specialist in the grant-writing field, Paula is a paid consultant who knows the parameters of her grants, has experience pulling usable data from different sources, and understands how politics affect the awarding of grants.

■ **Different people write different stages.** The first writer brainstorms ideas, organizes subtopics, determines research questions, and then passes the information to the second writer, who gathers the research. The second writer conducts more research and passes all the research to the third writer. The third writer writes the first draft and passes the draft to the fourth writer, who revises it. The fifth and last writer edits the final draft and publishes it.

A textbook chapter could be written this way, with the editor suggesting topics, a research assistant collecting data, the author writing the chapter, and the editor copyediting and publishing. Professional Adobe Acrobat would allow team members to comment on other writers' submissions as they received them. This system works well with a team whose members are in the same field, who get along well, and who understand the writing process.

■ **Groups divide research tasks and come together to write.** A committee of four team members divided research investigating an institution's compliance with financial regulations. The first meeting in the department chair's office took two hours as the team generated an outline for the project on a white board. By the time the meeting was over, the white board was cluttered and smudged—with three different handwritings, strikeovers, partial erasures, and lines connecting ideas. The group met the next week. One team member wrote a sentence, and another changed a word in that sentence, while yet another team member keyed the sentence. Everyone gave suggestions, including the person keying the information. In two hours, their draft was written and e-mailed to the company's communication director for copy editing. This system works well for projects with a predetermined format and for people with outgoing personalities who do not waste time haggling over word choice.

When writing a longer document, a group may need to meet regularly—either in face-to-face or virtual meetings. To organize tasks for a longer document, use the first meeting (or the first several meetings) to do the following:

- Create a vision
- Clarify the group's purpose
- Analyze the audience
- Determine the scope
- Select the medium and style guide
- Set meeting times and places
- Decide on the research plan
- Set goals and assigned tasks
- Share contact information
- Set the timeline for work

A leader or chairperson can set the meeting agendas, write minutes, keep the group on task, and act as a spokesperson. A good leader will make sure everyone has a voice in determining the goals of the project and the format for the meetings. When people help make decisions, they are more likely to support those decisions.

Using Collaboration Tools

Writers use collaboration tools such as wikis, co-authoring software, and online meeting spaces.

- **Wikis** such as Wikispaces, Media Wiki, and Google Sites assist groups in storing and sharing information from files, links, sources, video, and photos. From any location, all members of the team can upload data to a single location where it can be retrieved and revised from a computer or mobile device.

- **Co-authoring software** such Google Docs allow several writers to author and edit a text **synchronously** (at the same time) or **asynchronously** (at different times in different locations). Google Docs also works well with Microsoft Office files. Word documents can be uploaded to Google Docs and then downloaded back into Office for final publication for readers requiring a Word document. Word 2016 includes a real-time co-authoring version to more easily manage collaboration.

- **Online meeting** spaces such as Webex, GoToMeeting, and Google Hangouts enable people in different locations with varying schedules the flexibility of virtual meetings. Phone conferencing using Skype, FaceTime, and GoogleTalk facilitates long-distance discussions. Instant messaging, texting, and e-mail, while not venues for long conversations, can help a group plan the next meeting time and place or adjust when a meeting must be rescheduled.

Using Positive Work Habits

Once meetings get under way, your leader and teammates will count on your participation. To be a productive group member, you need sound work habits and effective communication skills. The following practices will show team members they can count on you:

- **Complete your share of the work.** Do whatever tasks are necessary to help the group, whether it is making phone calls, taking notes, looking up information, or creating graphics.

- **Come prepared to each meeting.** Review the agenda and come with suggestions, a notebook, or a laptop to show you have done your homework and know what will happen at the meeting.

- **Be interested in the project.** Give positive feedback. Show you care about the final outcome.

- **Be on time to meetings.** If you cannot be on time, let your leader or a group member know beforehand. If you are habitually late to meetings, your group members might think you do not care about the project.

- **Do not take criticism personally.** Remember, your goal is to produce a quality product. When someone questions your suggestions, see the questions as a way to improve the final outcome, not as a criticism of you. If you demonstrate the ability to handle constructive criticism, you will have an easier time offering it.

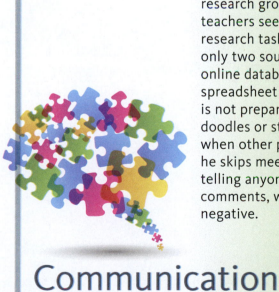

Brian is a new teacher in Jenna's research group. While the other teachers seem engaged in their research tasks, Brian has posted only two sources from the school's online databases to the Google Docs spreadsheet Jenna established. He is not prepared for meetings and doodles or stares out the window when other people talk. Sometimes he skips meetings altogether without telling anyone beforehand. His comments, when he gives them, are negative.

Jenna thinks Brian's behavior is getting in the way of the group's progress. She also believes he is frustrating the other team members, who are working hard to make the project a success. She has overheard some of the members talking about what a poor team player Brian is.

Jenna is worried. She does not want Brian's work habits to affect the final outcome of the team.

Think Critically

What should Jenna do?

Communication
Dilemma

Healthy work habits are important to building group relationships, but communication skills are important too. Your teammates cannot read your mind, but they can hear words and read body language. To contribute to the success of your team, be honest and respectful in your communication.

The number one requirement for group cohesion is trust. The second requirement is a shared group vision with enthusiasm for the outcome. As a reliable team member and a responsive communicator, you will build trust and thus create the positive synergy which leads to success.

Now that you understand the writing process, options for organizing collaborative projects, and strategies for effective collaboration, you are ready to work on any writing project by yourself or with others. The more you practice the writing process, the more adept you will become at using it to accomplish your objectives. You also will experience the camaraderie that comes from working with others to achieve a common goal.

STOP AND THINK 4.5

Using the suggestions for good work habits, take a personal inventory of your own work habits. Which ones produce positive results? Which ones need improvement?

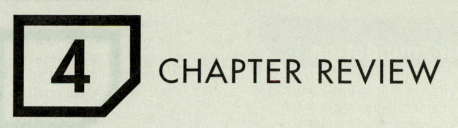

4 CHAPTER REVIEW

Summary

1. The writing process is a creative act that moves back and forth between predictable stages, requires sufficient time to complete, and varies from one person to the next.

2. The first stage of the writing process, planning, begins with freewriting to generate ideas and moves to shaping to narrow a topic and organize the ideas.

3. Shaping strategies include questioning, reading, mapping, outlining, and reviewing the rhetorical situation.

4. The second stage of the writing process is drafting and revising. The process involves writing a draft, analyzing its strengths and weaknesses, and revising the draft. The drafting and revising stage may be repeated two, three, four, or more times.

5. Writers revise drafts in a hierarchy from big to little to make changes that affect the content and organization first before they make changes that affect sentences, words, spelling, and grammar.

6. Copyediting includes reading carefully for errors and correcting them. Publishing presents the reader with the final version, a professional-looking document complete with sources in the form the reader has specified.

7. In today's workplace, collaborative writing projects take advantage of each team member's strengths and varying view points. Effective teams avoid common pitfalls of collaboration, organize their writing tasks, and maintain positive work habits.

Checklist

- Do I understand the writing process?
- Have I considered how to adjust the writing process to meet my personality and thinking style?
- Have I identified the planning strategies that work for me?
- Have I used shaping strategies to narrow my topic, generate subtopics, and organize them?
- Have I read and analyzed the first draft according to "big to little"—from content, organization, and sentences to words and mechanics?
- Have I revised my first draft?
- Have I written as many drafts as I need to create a well-written document that meets the needs and wants of my audience?
- Have I copyedited my document to find all errors?
- Have I published my document so that it is error-free and professional?

Build Your Foundation

1. How is writing like one of these processes: climbing a mountain, growing a plant, training a dog, or learning a song?

2. Listed below are the steps of the writing process. Rank them from easiest to most difficult for you, with 1 being easiest and 8 being most difficult. Rank them again for the time each one takes, with 1 taking the least time and 8 taking the most time. Which stage is most important? Why?

   Prewriting   Researching   Revising 1   Copyediting
   Shaping   Drafting   Revising 2   Publishing

3. Keep a writing journal each day for five days. Write in it for 15 minutes at a time. At the end of five days, underline topics about which you might consider writing. Choose one topic and practice mapping to come up with subtopics.

4. Use open freewriting, focused freewriting, or looping to come up with a topic for research. Then practice focused freewriting on your topic to help shape the idea. Another option is to practice focused freewriting on one of these topics: the environment, sports, music, or health.

5. Read an article or blog, listen to a podcast, or view a video. Using the rhetorical questions posed in the chapter, analyze the communication situation.

6. Map your own writing process. Compare your process to a neighbor's, an instructor's, or a family member's.

7. Answer these questions about your writing process.

   a. Where and when do you prefer to write? Do you prefer silence?
   b. Does the computer help or hinder your writing process? Explain.
   c. How do you prepare to write? Consider such tasks as playing music, gathering materials, making a sandwich, getting a beverage, or organizing your desk.
   d. What is the best piece of writing you ever wrote? Describe your process. How did you know the writing was good?
   e. How do you know you have finished revising and are ready to publish?

8. Think of as many synonyms as you can for the following words. When you are finished coming up with synonyms on your own, consult a thesaurus for additional synonyms.

circumstance	run	shirt	end
excellence	communicate	document	building
describe	pleasant	fuel	employment

9. Use a variety of ways to combine the following short sentences into longer ones to add variety to the sentence structure. Then add a suitable topic sentence, a concluding sentence, and an appropriate transition to create a smoother flow of ideas.

   Luis has been offered two jobs. One job is at the movie theater. The other job is at the golf course. He might take the job at the movie theater. He would work at the concession stand. He would sell popcorn, beverages, and candy. He could take the job at the golf course. He would work at the golf pro shop. He would sell golf balls, tees, and other golfing supplies. One job pays more per hour. The golf course pays more per hour. The golf course is ten miles from Luis's home. The job at the movie theater pays $0.50 less per hour. It is a block from Luis's house.

Your Turn

1. Write two paragraphs, one discussing what you like about writing and the other discussing what you do not like about writing. Write one paragraph by hand on notebook paper and the other using a word processor. How does your writing process change?

2. Write a paragraph describing your favorite place by dictating your words to someone else. How does speaking aloud affect your writing process?

3. Write an essay or a paragraph on a topic of your choice. After you complete one draft, exchange papers with at least two of your classmates. Ask them to make comments using the list of questions for copyediting in this chapter.

4. Select one of the following topics and write a one-page essay: Why people should exercise regularly, why people should stay informed about news events, or why people should recycle. Then practice writing collaboratively by dividing the topic into stages. Writer 1 will prewrite and organize three subtopics and pass the prewriting to Writer 2. Writer 2 will write the first draft and pass the draft to Writer 3. Writer 3 will revise and pass the revision to Writer 4, who will edit the revision, make changes, and submit the final draft.

5. In small groups, write a letter to the editor of your local newspaper, expressing your views on a current event (for example, a choice of a political candidate, the way your tax dollars are spent, or a community concern). Individually, brainstorm ideas, organize your ideas, and take notes. In one session, write the letter as a group. Ask one person to copyedit the final version, bringing it back to class for the group to see.

6. Think of the last time you worked on a group project. What kind of experience did you have? What were the benefits of working with this group? What were the drawbacks? What could you do differently the next time you are part of a group to make sure you have a positive experience? Write a one- to two-page analysis.

Community Connection

1. Interview a writer in your area (a reporter, technical writer, local novelist, or public relations expert) about his or her writing process. Does the writer come up with topics, or does someone else provide them? What advice, if any, does the writer have for your classmates? What technology does the writer find most helpful? Summarize the writer's process and share your findings with the class. If possible, bring to class something the writer has written. Better yet, invite the writer to class to talk about the writing process.

2. Help another person with all or part of the writing process for a writing project. You might help a family member or a member of Big Brothers Big Sisters or AmeriCorp. Coach the person through the stages of the writing process. Write a description of your experience.

3. Interview employees in your area, asking how often they work collaboratively, what kinds of projects they complete collaboratively, which technology aids they use, and how they organize tasks.

EXPLORE THE  **NET**

Choose five boldfaced terms from the chapter. Then visit the Merriam-Webster online dictionary and use the thesaurus to find one or two synonyms for each term you chose. Do the synonyms help you remember the definitions of the terms? Explain.

5 CORRESPONDENCE

Goals

- Identify correspondence
- Analyze and target the audience for correspondence
- Prewrite for correspondence
- Prepare for and determine how to format text messages, e-mails, memorandums (memos), and letters
- Understand and use strategies for composing good news, bad news, and persuasive messages

Terms

Write to Learn

Consider information you share with others in any work situation, whether a collaborative paper or class project, a task you manage at home, or paid employment. For example, do you need to schedule a meeting or set a deadline? Is time a factor in the communication method? Is a record of your communication important? Is your communication usually face to face, over the phone, in notes or letters, by e-mail, over social media, or through other means? With one task in mind, write a few paragraphs about what and how you communicate.

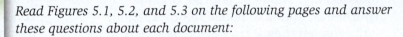

FOCUS on Brief Correspondence

Read Figures 5.1, 5.2, and 5.3 on the following pages and answer these questions about each document:

- Where is the main idea in the e-mail? in the memo? in the letter?
- How is the message organized in the memo? in the letter?

What If?

How would the model change if . . .

- The recipients of the e-mail were less familiar with the project?
- The memo writer needed a more immediate response from the reader?
- The letter writer were declining the student's scholarship application?

E-mail

From:	Johnson Edwards	C:	Robert Bruley
To:	Alignment Team	BC:	
Subject:	Beginning alignment work		
Attachment:	Common critical processes.docx		

Good morning!

Please add a list of your area's critical processes to the attached Google document. The first step in our project is to identify common areas among our work units.

 Figure 5.1 Sample E-mail

Kendall Developers, LLC
Suite 1543, Norwalk Towers
442 Martin Luther King Boulevard
Johnson City, Texas 074431

To: Billy Franklin

From: Ellen Anderson   *ESA*

Date: 7 May 20--

Subject: Changes in Deverville site plans required by new city regulations

Billy, after a conversation with Arden Sorbak, Deverville Planning Director, today, I think we should review our site plans for the new discount mall.

1. We had planned for 238 parking spaces with 24 handicapped spaces. The new city guidelines will require 5% more overall parking.
2. The set back lines on the north side of the site allow 80 feet from the property line to the building; however, according to Sorbak, we need to allow 105 feet because of the drainage embankment.
3. The city planning and zoning committee also has some questions about the landscaping plans. In particular, they want to be certain the trees on the street side of the building do not create debris or hazards for drivers and that they are esthetically consistent with the city plantings along the streets in that area.

Please review the newly adopted city guidelines, make the necessary adjustments in our plans, and deliver copies to me and Sorbak. We'll need those new plans in three weeks, no later than Friday, 29 May 20--, in order for them to be presented for approval at the next Planning and Zoning Committee meeting. That time frame will allow us to be on the agenda for this next meeting.

We'll all be happy to see these plans recorded with a stamp of approval and this project under construction!

ESA /cah

Figure 5.2 Sample Memo

Landover Community College

Office of the Dean of Students
Telephone (919) 555-0443
Fax Number (919) 555-0140

October 26, 20—

Ms. Regina Williams
P.O. Box 2453
Taylor, NC 28590

Dear Ms. Williams:

I am pleased to award you an $1800 Student Government Association Scholarship to attend Landover Community College for the 2018–2019 academic year. The selection committee recognizes your achievements and your need for assistance in reaching your academic goals.

The funds will be disbursed during the upcoming academic year. These monies will be available for you to use during preregistration and registration for tuition and fees, as designated in the scholarship. Any remaining funds may be used to purchase books, supplies, or other school-related items in the Landover bookstore. Remaining funds will be given to you approximately four to eight weeks after registration.

I warmly congratulate you and wish you every possible success. We look forward to having you as a student at Landover. If you have any questions, feel free to contact Mr. Rudy Conway, Financial Aid Director, in Room 345 of the Thomas Hannam Building or call (295) 555-0164.

Sincerely,

Simone Sanchez

Dr. Simone Sanchez

Dean of Students

SMS/trp

P.O. Drawer 2877 • Farmville • North Carolina • 27555-2877

An Equal Opportunity/Affirmative Action Institution

Figure 5.3 Sample Letter: Positive Message

Writing @Work

CareerClusters®
PATHWAYS TO COLLEGE & CAREER READINESS
Finance

Source: The Center to Advance CTE

Saren Erdmann is an information technology project manager for US Bank. Saren's primary responsibilities include managing software installations and enhancements for US Bank's branch locations. She identifies project stakeholders, coordinates and runs all project-related meetings and communications, documents each project, and assesses risks and solutions that keep initiatives running as smoothly as possible.

Because most of Saren's stakeholders are located in remote offices, she must coordinate with them via phone calls, e-mails, or instant messaging. Saren is quick to note the dangers of miscommunication when exchanging notes with colleagues in short digital texts. "Since the written word can be interpreted in so many ways, it is very important to be clear," she advises.

To write with clarity, Saren recommends keeping messages short and to the point and using a professional tone. Her rule of thumb is that "no matter how well you know someone, you must always maintain a level of professionalism when sending written communication at work."

However, a little humor carefully delivered to a friendly audience won't hurt: "If I have been working with someone for a long time and we have a personal relationship, my work-related communications to them are slightly more relaxed, but still business-appropriate."

Project managers like Saren are agile at juggling correspondence. They multitask, prioritize which items need an immediate response, and have a strategy for managing items on the back burner. "I am bombarded with so much correspondence on a daily basis that it is difficult to absorb everything I receive right away. I am careful to archive all project documentation and correspondence in a central location. If I need to refresh my memory or read an original communication I missed, I can find the information in my files."

Think Critically

1. Research the word *stakeholder*. What is the original meaning? How is it used in this profile?

2. Why is clear writing so important to Saren? How does she keep her writing clear?

Printed with permission of Saren Erdmann.

Writing in Finance

Communicating in the financial services industry offers a number of challenges and opportunities unique to this time. Some of the challenges include the loss of trust in institutions following the 2007–2009 financial crisis and the demand from consumers for immediate, tailored, and transparent communication, much like what they receive on personal and social media sites. In addition, this industry has historically been quite conservative and continues to experience greater regulation and oversight. However, according to Julia Sahin, an account executive with Edelman New York, these challenges present opportunities. Sahin describes several trends that will influence communication in banking and financial services: (1) While financial services is a highly regulated industry, social media may be used in engaging and compliant ways. (2) As new communication methods are developed, financial institutions must be open to new ways

of reaching and maintaining their customers. (3) Financial institutions must find ways to provide consumers with the "transparent communication, responsiveness, and genuine conviction" customers say they want. (4) Financial institutions can use social media to learn the reasoning behind consumers' decisions and where they look for information when making financial decisions. Technological advances are likely to improve the access to this type of data. (5) A new generation of customers is bringing new expectations of the industry, such as real-time communication and access to transactions on mobile platforms. Sahin believes the innovations to meet the new demands will be developed from outside the industry, and she advises financial institutions to build on these external partnerships and be open-minded in order to stay relevant with customers.

Adapted from Sahin, Julia. "Five Communication Trends in the Financial Services Industry." Posted 12 Feb. 2015. Edelman. Web. 1 Jan. 2016. http://www.edelman.com/post/five-communications-trends-financial-services-industry/

5.1 INTRODUCTION TO ELECTRONIC CORRESPONDENCE, MEMOS, AND LETTERS

 WARM UP

Communication is essential for being able to act and make decisions in the business world. People must be able to share information. Although some communication can take place face to face, a great deal of communication is conducted through instant and text messages, e-mails, blogs, memos, and letters. All of these may be used for brief correspondence. However, each one has its own distinguishing characteristics. For instance, instant and text messaging, blogs, and e-mail are the fastest and most efficient means of written communication. A writer can compose a message, send it electronically anywhere in the world that has Internet access, and receive an answer almost immediately.

Unlike electronic correspondence, memos and letters take more time. Of the two, memos are more efficient than letters, primarily because memos have fewer formal parts and because they are usually directed to an audience in the same organization as the sender. Memos also invite a speedy response. In some situations, receivers write a response on the memo they have received and send it back to the writers. In contrast, letters may have many parts and may be sent by postal service or a commercial carrier to readers outside the organization.

All correspondence seeks the **goodwill** of readers. Goodwill is the value of doing things that create mutual admiration and respect. It is the feeling of friendship. In addition, writers of brief correspondence practice the principles of effective communication.

Goodwill

Goodwill is the act of making and keeping a friend. Goodwill is a feeling of good intentions. Effective business correspondence fosters goodwill through its word choice and message. You can create goodwill in writing the same way you create the bonds of a friendship.

Goodwill, like friendship, is created by being honest and polite. It is fostered by doing what you say you will do when you say you will do it. Business friendships grow in an atmosphere of mutual respect and trust. You also foster goodwill by attending to correspondence as quickly as you can. In short, you generate goodwill by treating your reader the same way you would like to be treated.

Principles of Effective Communication

In addition to generating goodwill, brief correspondence should be helpful to readers. Table 5.1 on the folllowing page suggests some of the characteristics of effective correspondence as well as traits to avoid in instant and text messages, e-mails, blogs, memos, and letters.

Following conventional format and using standard English help make a positive impression on your reader. To ensure that the information in your

Imagine what the world would be like if people could not retain information or share ideas. For example, what would scientific knowledge be today if people had not been able to build on the discoveries of previous generations?

Typical Reader

A busy employee needing accurate, complete information delivered quickly in an easy-to-read document so that he or she can perform a job and contribute to the organization.

Writer's Focus

Responding quickly to convey pertinent and accurate information that adds to the work flow and builds goodwill.

Table 5.1

Communicate Effectively and Develop Goodwill With . . .	Communicate Ineffectively and Hinder Goodwill With . . .
Concise language	Fuzzy, unnecessary words that take up readers' time with details they do not need
Accuracy and completeness	Inaccurate, incomplete information, creating misunderstandings and problems to be solved later
Professional appearance	Sloppy appearance, making you and your organization appear incompetent and careless
Conventional format	Unfamiliar format that confuses the reader and makes your intent unclear
Logical organization	Illogical organization, frustrating readers' efforts to follow your thinking
Positive, polite tone and "you" attitude	Accusing, sarcastic, or flippant tone; concerned only with the writer's point of view
Standard English usage	Grammatical and punctuation errors and misspelled words, causing you and your organization to appear uneducated and/or careless

correspondence is well organized, complete, and free of errors, reread the document before you send it. If you are unsure whether your message is clear and easy to understand, ask a colleague to read your correspondence and to provide feedback.

Electronic correspondence, memos, and letters not only help get the job done but also serve as a way to evaluate the writer's performance. Managers and administrators can tell from an employee's messages whether that employee is solving or creating problems, communicating with or confusing readers, building or ruining relationships, and getting the job done or making no progress.

Suitable Tone and Humor

Brief correspondence usually has a conversational, informal tone. In fact, in this type of correspondence, it is appropriate to use *I*, the first-person pronoun. "You're busy, so I'll be brief" is the opening sentence of an effective sales letter for a magazine. Note the focus on the reader, the use of first person, and the casual tone. Readers are more likely to cooperate when the message sounds as if a person, rather than a machine, wrote it. This informal writing style is similar to a conversation you might have with a friend if that conversation were polished slightly.

Use humor to create goodwill in difficult situations or with uncooperative audiences. For example, a club leader at school might use humor to convince students to volunteer to donate blood even if they have not donated before or are afraid to do so.

However, writers should be cautious about using humor. As useful as it can be, humor used carelessly may be harmful. For example, a manager whose daughter died in a work-related accident is not likely to laugh when her quality assurance officer writes that the government safety inspectors "are going to kill us." Writers of electronic communication must be especially careful with regards to humor. What seems funny to a sender may be flat or even rude to a receiver who does not understand the cultural or historical nuances of the message. Consider audience, situation, the character of the relationship, and the method of delivery before deciding whether to use humor.

STOP AND THINK 5.1

Reflect on these questions: What is goodwill? Why is it important? Is a formal tone ever appropriate for brief correspondence?

5.2 WHO READS CORRESPONDENCE?

 WARM UP

Almost everyone in the workplace (and almost everyone outside the work world as well) reads correspondence. The readers of electronic messages, memos, and letters have similar characteristics. All of them expect the communication to be brief, to target a specific reader or readers, to have a specific purpose, and to follow standard format.

Some correspondence is sent to a multiple audience, and some is written with a specific audience in mind. If the reader is only one person, meet the needs of that person. Use language and information that he will understand and answer questions that this reader would ask if she were present. If an audience is made up of a group of readers, consider the needs of all of them.

Regardless of how well you know your readers, use the table on page 36 in Chapter 2 to help you focus on your audience. If you know little about your audience, learn as much as you can. Ask others what they know about your audience or read correspondence your audience has written. If you cannot learn much about your audience, assume a serious or neutral tone.

Keep your language moderately simple and natural. Work especially hard to build goodwill.

Messaging

Instant and text messages are becoming more acceptable as a form of business communication, primarily because of the speed with which senders and receivers can deal with information. Because readers may be internal or external to the writer's organization, the writer may know a great deal, a little bit, or almost nothing about the reader. Therefore, senders must anticipate expectations of the audience, particularly the readers' expectations as to how formal the message should be. An employee may send an instant message or a text message with incomplete sentences and extensive abbreviations (for example, B4 for "before" or NRN for "No reply necessary") to a supervisor. If that supervisor does not approve of such informality and does not understand the message, the communication is

Imagine writing an e-mail or a note filled with private jokes, insider stories, or juicy gossip to your closest friend. Now imagine that message being misdirected to your parent, guardian, supervisor, or instructor. Consider the consequences.

likely to be strained and create a poor impression. Even though instant or text messages may be very brief and informal, they need to be clear and to provide the readers with the information they need. They should not create barriers to future effective communication.

Instant and text messages are becoming an important avenue for business communication. For example, the U.S. government uses SnapFresh, a text message and mobile web app, to help recipients of the Supplemental Nutrition Assistance Program (SNAP) find stores and markets that accept food stamps. Also, many political campaigns use messaging to "get out the vote" and to mobilize volunteers. Many advertisers use text messages to send coupon codes, flash sale announcements, and discount notices to consumers. Used carefully, with perhaps one to three contacts per month, rather than daily, this type of marketing campaign can be effective and inexpensive.

Many employees use instant messaging with colleagues, particularly when collaborating on a task. With instant messaging, the employee uses his or her contact list, called a buddy or friend list, to see who is online and ready to communicate. Instant messaging participants can see messages immediately, so they don't have to wait to check e-mail. On the other hand, your audience for a text message may not be available when you send your text. Wait a reasonable time for a response before sending another message. In addition, keep messages brief. If you have a long, complex message, send it as an attachment via e-mail or through some other medium.

E-mails

For personal as well as professional correspondence, e-mail has become a common way to communicate. Readers may be inside or outside the writer's organization. Thus, writers know some readers well and others not at all. Because readers often receive a great deal of e-mail in a day, they expect writers to focus on a point and to keep the message brief without omitting essential information. Readers expect messages to be relevant and clear. They will not waste their time with messages that are incomplete, confusing, or unclear.

Blogs

Readers of blogs might be anyone who is interested in the topic presented by the blog. In effect, the blog is correspondence because the sponsor or writer presents information, the reader may respond to the information, and the writer then answers the question, clarifies the discussion, or adds more information. Thus, the blog includes the give and take of correspondence, as Figure 5.4 shows.

Some readers may find the blog as a result of searching for information on its topic; others may find the blog through links in social media sites, such as Facebook and Twitter.

Readers expect blogs to be current (updated regularly), sensitive to the culture of the online community, and accurate. Audiences expect bloggers who are wrong to apologize. Blogs that sell, rather than inform, often turn off the audience. In addition, readers expect blogs to contain concise, clear information with links to other information, which they may choose to

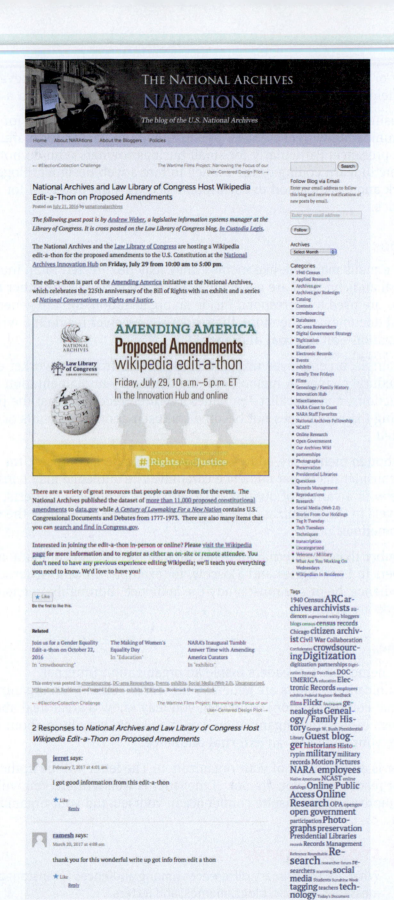

Figure 5.4 Model of Correspondence between Blog Writer and Audience Source: https://narations.blogs.archives.gov/2016/07/21/national-archives-and-law-library-of-congress-host-wikipedia-edit-a-thon-on-proposed-amendments/

follow or not. Readers also expect bloggers to use keywords relevant to their field so that the blog's information may be easily found in a search.

For business owners, blogging is an easy and low-cost solution for communicating with customers, vendors, and others and for maintaining a web presence. Particularly for small business owners who do not have the time to learn coding or the money to hire a web designer, blogging is a quick and easy method of correspondence with the potential for a large audience.

Memos

While e-mails may look like memos, they may be directed to an internal or external audience and are generally read on a screen. On the other hand, memos are used to correspond inside an organization and are generally printed documents. Therefore, the reader is a receiver inside the writer's organization—an **internal audience**.

For example, an employee might receive a memo from a coworker explaining a procedural change. A memo outlining the facts—implementation time, date, actions, and checklist—provides a written record so that the person receiving the notice does not become confused about the details of what is expected.

Even though memos are addressed to people inside a company, the writer must consider his or her audience carefully. The audience may consist of people with a variety of outlooks, backgrounds, opinions, interests, roles, and levels in the organization. Sometimes the writer will know the readers and sometimes not.

Remember that the internal audience of an international company may have members in Los Angeles and Moscow, for example. Once a writer identifies the audience, he or she must study the audience thoroughly to ensure that its needs are met.

Letters

While memos are for readers inside an organization (internal communication), letters are generally for readers outside an organization (external communication). Although you may know a great deal about members inside your organization, you may know very little about readers outside your company, an **external audience**.

A letter is an extension of your organization. The letter will be in the presence of your reader when you are not. If the letter is well written, you will make a good impression and inspire confidence in yourself and your organization.

STOP AND THINK 5.2

What are the primary differences among audiences for instant and text messages, e-mails, blogs, memos, and letters?

5.3 PLANNING CORRESPONDENCE

 **WARM UP**

Prewriting for any correspondence involves planning to communicate with readers who have diverse needs and expectations. Some situations call for quick, spontaneous, informal communication as seen in texts and tweets. Others call for thoughtful, deliberate, formal communication as seen in some memos and letters. The following considerations will help you plan effective correspondence.

Author's Purpose

After analyzing your audience, ask yourself these questions before you write:

- What do I want the receiver to do or think after she reads this correspondence?

- What do I want to accomplish with this message?

- What is the main point and context for this message?

- Does my reader need background information? If so, how much?

- Do I need to make the message simpler for this audience? What definitions or explanations will the audience need?

- Is this reader familiar with the subject matter? Does the reader have previous experience with this idea?

- What questions should my correspondence answer?

In addition to answering these questions, you should take notes on the details you need for your correspondence. Gather the facts, such as situation background, events that occurred, problems created, order/part numbers, accurate descriptions, or questions to ask. Find out the name, title, and correct spelling and address of the person to whom you are writing. Double-check to make sure the information you have gathered is accurate and complete.

Using the answers to these questions, put your ideas on paper. Some writers prefer a list, such as the kind a person makes for grocery shopping. Other writers like to use freewriting. Remember that freewriting is writing everything that comes to mind. Because this is the creative part of writing, you should not be critical of your ideas. Get all of the ideas, brilliant or otherwise, on paper.

Whichever technique you use will generate a collection of ideas you want to cover in the message or body. With all of the ideas before you, you can start to be critical. Cut the ones that are unnecessary and change those that do not communicate exactly what you want to say. Prewriting is also the time to rank ideas. Consider your purpose and the organization that will best help you achieve it. Decide what you will place first, second, third, and so on.

Furthermore, writers sometimes need documentation (proof) of discussions, decisions, or actions. Perhaps you or your company would like something

Think about the planning involved in hosting a party or preparing a meal. What kind of party or meal might result if you do not plan? Likewise, how effective can your correspondence be if you do not plan?

more substantial or concrete than e-mails to back up an offer that was made during a meeting with a vendor or an action that was taken following a safety review. Memos or letters would serve that purpose. Your document should include all of the specific details—for example, names, product numbers, shipping information, dates, times, and locations—that your audience may need now or in the future.

Reader's Schedule

Remember that busy professionals may receive a great volume of correspondence. Thus, you should make your writing work for you if you want it to be read. Subject lines, such as those in e-mails and memos, must be specific and descriptive. They should clearly show the readers how the topic relates to them. If your subject line is poorly written, the reader may choose to delete your message without reading it.

Formality

In your planning, also consider the reader's expectations for formality. If you are sending a message to people in your organization, you are likely to know the formality they expect by referring to other correspondence. For instance, the corporate climate may be formal, in which case readers might expect complete sentences, correct punctuation, and few or no abbreviations.

However, others with whom you communicate may be more comfortable with informal messages—incomplete sentences, little punctuation, and the many abbreviations writers have developed to make online exchanges fast, such as BTW for "by the way" and HAND for "Have a nice day." Be careful to learn what readers expect before sending informal messages; it is usually better to be too formal than too informal.

As internal correspondence, memos may, in some circumstances, be informal. In other circumstances, memos may be formal. Letters, on the other hand, are usually formal.

Because letters typically address external audiences, letter writers should inform the reader of all relevant information. For instance, the reader may not be as aware of history and background as other readers inside the organization are. The reader is not likely to know insider language, or jargon. The reader may not be aware of corporate policies, organizational culture, chain of command, or other elements that are important in understanding the issues being discussed. In addition, when a writer is communicating with an unfamiliar audience, the writer should "put his or her best foot forward" by carefully choosing words, gauging tone, and focusing on the purpose of the correspondence.

When letters are used internally for special circumstances such as promotions, dismissals, recommendations, or disciplinary matters, writers should plan for an even higher level of formality because of the importance of the subject and the legal implications.

In general, formal documents do not use the following:

- Contractions
- Clichés
- Personal or emotional commentary
- Conversational speech
- Abbreviations
- Short, simple sentences

Length

In addition to level of formality, plan the length of your messages to meet readers' needs and expectations. Most cellular carriers such as AT&T and Verizon no longer limit the number of characters that may be used in a text message. However, depending on the device receiving the message, your text may be divided into two message boxes. When planning, keep limitations in mind as well as the frustration your receiver would experience in trying to read a long message on a phone. Likewise, because people generally read e-mail from a computer screen rather than printing hard copies, keep your messages as brief as possible so that people can read the text without scrolling through several pages. Short messages also allow for easier response. If you have a long, involved message, consider sending it as multiple text messages or e-mails. Another option is to create a document with a word processor and send the document as an attachment.

As with planning electronic messages, prewriting memos requires writers to consider the audience's expectations. Readers usually expect memos to be brief and to cover one topic. However, the need to be brief should not override substance. Make sure the memo explains the topic fully—whether it offers a solution to a problem, outlines a change in procedures or policies, or deals with other business concerns.

Privacy and Security

Also consider privacy and security, especially when planning electronic correspondence. Little electronic communication is truly private. Employees using company equipment—computers, tablets, and phones—to send messages or e-mail and to post blogs should keep in mind that the message or post belongs to (and represents) the company. Even people e-mailing from their personal electronic devices may not have the privacy they expect because of hackers, worms, and viruses. In addition, people who use Forward, Reply All, and Blind Copy with e-mail should be particularly sensitive to the privacy of others with whom they correspond. For example, Dale sends a message that he thought was private to Jin-ho, but Jin-ho forwards the message to Neva. As a result, Dale's privacy was compromised because Neva now knows something Dale might not have wanted her to know.

© Ldprod/Shutterstock

Emotions

Moreover, plan for handling emotions effectively. Do not flame. (When writers are harshly criticizing each other, they are flaming.) Avoid messaging, e-mailing, or posting when you are angry. Wait until you can handle the issue logically rather than emotionally. Using all capital letters generally equates to shouting, so use this style only when you intend to shout. For emphasis, you can surround a word or phrase with asterisks or white space.

Another way to convey feelings is through the use of emoticons, symbols created on the keyboard to convey emotions, such as :-), the smiley face. Yet writers must carefully consider how readers will react to the feelings expressed in a communication because feelings can be misinterpreted or misunderstood.

Manners

Finally, learn about good manners and etiquette in cyberspace, also known as *netiquette.* Keep in mind, though, that rules of etiquette may vary from one medium to another. For example, abbreviations may be approved for some business uses of instant messaging but discouraged for use in other media. Table 5.2 lists some of the rules of netiquette.

Table 5.2

Do	Don't
Read and respond promptly. If you need time to reply, respond to say that you received the message and note when you will reply.	Write long, complex messages; readers expect text messages and e-mail to be brief.
Represent yourself and others well and fairly.	Write anything that you would not say in front of any person, including those people discussed in the message, e-mail, or blog.
Communicate as clearly and rationally as possible. Remember that readers will not have your tone of voice or body language to help them interpret your meaning.	Include offensive, obscene, or illegal content.
Keep the correspondence thread when replying so that readers will be able to follow the line of discussion.	Quote large blocks of irrelevant text.
Develop a descriptive, precise subject line so that readers can predict the message, file the correspondence, and find it later.	Key in all capital letters (seen as shouting) or in all lowercase letters (perceived as lazy).
Keep your virus protection current so you do not to forward problems to others.	Believe or forward every urban legend and cyber myth that comes your way.
Respect others' bandwidth and download times.	Forward jokes and chain messages without being certain that the recipient wants them.

STOP AND THINK 5.3

Why are electronic correspondence privacy and security issues important to consider when prewriting?

5.4 FORMATTING

In much the same way fancy type identifies a formal invitation, the formatting features of instant and text messages, e-mails, blogs, memos, and letters help readers recognize the type of correspondence they are viewing. Specific elements are unique to each type. For example, instant and text messages, because they typically are viewed on a phone screen, are usually brief and simple blocks of text. E-mails may look like memos, but they typically include e-mail addresses for the sender and receiver. Memos are recognizable by their headings (To, From, Date, and Subject). Likewise, the mark of a letter is the inside and return addresses, salutation, and complimentary close—features that are familiar to audiences.

Think about the information readers want to know when they receive messages. What are their questions? Compare that answer to the elements of formatting for instant and text messages, e-mails, blogs, memos, and letters. For example, the first thought of audiences receiving a message is often, "Who is sending me this communication?"

Messaging and E-mail

Writers usually do not need to be concerned about formatting decisions when they create electronic correspondence because the application or cellular and e-mail software providers have already made most of the decisions. Most programs, such as Microsoft® Outlook Express®, simply ask the writer to click a light-colored line or a blank box and key the intended receiver or subject line. Most programs automatically insert the sender's name or address and date. However, writers should plan for differences between sender and receiver in e-mail software. Avoid complex formatting such as bulleted lists, tables, italics, or underlining unless you know that the recipient's software can read them.

While software does take care of most formatting decisions for e-correspondence, memos and letters require more formatting decisions.

Memos

A draft of a memo begins with a standard format of headings followed by the body, or message. Like the addresses and salutation in a letter (Dear Mr. Najafi), headings make a document recognizable as a memo. Four elements appear at the top of a memo, as shown in Figure 5.5.

TO:

FROM:

DATE:

SUBJECT:

Figure 5.5 Memo Headings

However, in some cases, headings may not appear in that order. When you begin work, your new employer may give you a style manual that shows you a different format the company prefers.

Memo templates are included in most word processing software. Microsoft Word 2016, for instance, provides online access to memo templates and a wizard to help writers create memos. The advantages of working with memo templates are that they are simple to use (even for writers with no experience), are easily modified, and provide attractive document design.

At the same time, these familiar templates have a number of shortcomings, such as overused design (readers will likely recognize the template) and decisions made without the writer's input or consideration. Because writers do not need to think about design or headings, sometimes these "plug-and-play" templates encourage writers not to think about other decisions related to their message. Ineffective communication may be the result.

TO Line

In the TO section, you name your audience. You may name one person, such as Joanna Tschiegg, or you may name a group, such as the Employee Benefits Committee or the Sterile Manufacturing Division. On occasion, you may need to name several readers who are not connected by a unit or committee. In this case, you may simply list their names.

The list of receivers' names may be presented a couple of ways. When you are sending a memo to more than one person, key all names on one line, connecting them with commas, or key the names in a list, as shown in Figure 5.6.

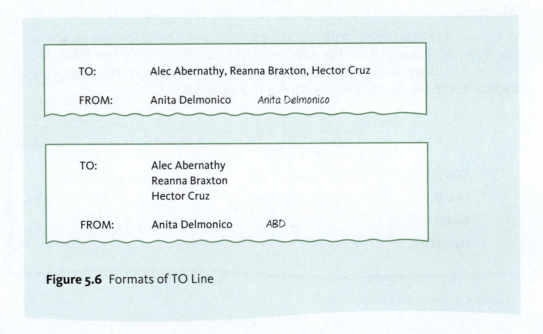

Figure 5.6 Formats of TO Line

When you are sending a memo to a large number of people, use a distribution list. This format is shown in Figure 5.7.

TO: IT Supervisors

FROM: Porter Harrington   *Porter Harrington*

              Distribution List
                  Delonte Alston
                  Daniel Baron
                  Toyomi Narita
                  Omar Moya

Figure 5.7 Format of TO Line with Distribution List

When you list several people's names, enter them in alphabetical order or **hierarchical order**, from the top to the bottom of the organizational chart. In hierarchical order, the people of greatest recognition and responsibility in the organization, such as the president and vice president, are listed first. Other employees are listed in decreasing order of rank within the organization. Remember, however, if the hierarchal list contains two employees of the same rank, such as two directors, you should place their names in alphabetical order so as not to offend either person.

FROM Line

After the FROM heading, you list the name or names of the sender of the message. If you are the only person responsible for the message, your name appears. If the memo comes from a group, the group or unit name is listed, such as FROM: Wooster Jazz Band.

You are sitting at your desk at Phoenix Fabrication when you receive a text from a person you met at the last Chamber of Commerce after-hours meet-and-greet on your work cell phone. He wants to know if you are interested in joining an investment club. You had been thinking of learning more about the stock market and investing, so this offer grabs your attention.

Just when you are about to reply, you remember that your boss cautioned you about using company time to conduct personal business. You think that perhaps this one quick personal text will not be a problem, and you do not want to miss the opportunity to join the investment club. You think to yourself that the acquaintance did contact you at work first; you did not ask him to contact you there. After all, how will anyone know you sent the text?

Think Critically

Should you reply to your acquaintance? How? Explain.

Communication
Dilemma

Some memos are from several people who are not part of a group. In this case, list the names of each sender in a line joined by commas or in columns, again in alphabetical or hierarchical order. Remember to write your initials or sign your full name after the keyed name in the FROM section, as shown in Figure 5.6 and 5.7.

Initialing or signing memos is especially important when they deal with important legal or organizational matters. Memos become legal documents that can be used in a court of law when they are signed and dated. Your initials or signature also tells the reader that you have reviewed the memo and accept responsibility for the message, particularly if someone else keyed it.

Dateline

The dateline usually appears after TO and FROM and before the subject line. You can choose between two styles for writing the date: international (also called military in the United States) or traditional.

International date style is becoming increasingly popular in technical documents because of economy. International style requires no commas. In this style, the writer gives the day first, the month next, and the year last, as in 12 May 2017. Another reason for its increasing popularity is that it is more clearly understood by readers outside the United States, most of whom use this style.

The traditional month–day–year style used in the United States, as in June 4, 1955, and April 1, 2011, gives the month, the date, a comma, and the year.

Subject Line

In most memos, the subject line logically appears as the last of the headings. It announces the point of the memo immediately before you develop that point. You may see terms such as *Reference*, *Regarding*, or *Re* (which comes from the Latin *res*, meaning "thing" or "matter"), used the same way as the word *subject*. However, some readers consider those terms archaic. In addition to helping the reader predict the topic, the subject line distinguishes one message from another and focuses the writer on one main idea.

Predict   The subject line should allow readers to predict what the memo will say. In other words, it reflects the main idea discussed in the body. Be as specific as you can when composing the subject line. A subject line that reads "Insurance" does little to help the reader predict what the memo will cover. That subject line is too general to provide insight. "Dental Insurance Open Enrollment Period Set for 18–29 June 2018" is precise enough to tell readers what to expect and to encourage them to read the message. Make the wording as specific as possible, as in the following examples:

Use *Minutes of Strategic Planning Meeting*	instead of	*Minutes* or *Meeting*
Use *Questions about Requisitions*	instead of	*Questions* or *Requisitions*
Use *Incident in the Carpentry Shop on May 4*	instead of	*Incident in Carpentry Shop*

The subject line should not be a complete sentence, but a phrase or a clause—more like a newspaper headline.

Distinguish   In addition to helping the reader predict the subject of the memo, the subject line should clarify the difference between one memo and many others. For instance, servers at a restaurant may read many memos during the year that deal with menu items. Therefore, if the subject line says only "Menu Changes," the server reading it will not immediately know that this message is different from last week's memo. Instead, specific subject lines such as "Italian Items Added to Menu for June" or "Lobster Price Increase" or "Salmon Unavailable Until April 20" tell the server exactly what to expect the message to cover.

Focus   The subject line also aids the writer. Writing a subject line forces the writer to focus on the most important idea. Furthermore, it allows the writer to check the message of the memo against the subject line. The message should cover the same idea the subject line announces. Effective subject lines (with important words first) are critical for the message to get the attention you want it to receive. Moreover, this advice for writing effective subject lines is important not only for memos but also for e-mails.

A memo should cover only one main point. Writers who have two messages for the same audience should write two memos for the following reasons. First, if a memo has more than one message, the reader cannot determine what is truly important. Second, the busy reader may find the first idea, assume that it is the only important information, and stop reading. Third, the memo might be so long that it intimidates readers. Readers generally expect memos to be one to four paragraphs long. Finally, some messages are inappropriate to combine, as Figure 5.8 illustrates.

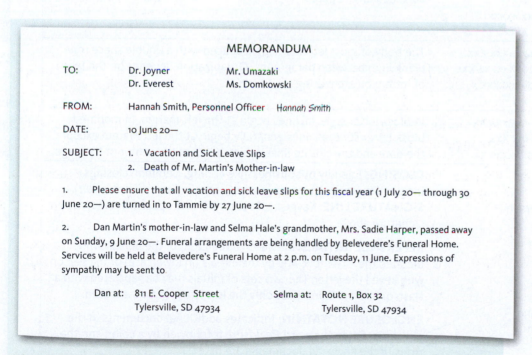

Figure 5.8 *Ineffective* Memo with Two Main Ideas

Letters

All letters share a similar format. They are constructed using basic parts and may be written in one of several styles.

Letter Parts

Figure 5.9 illustrates and describes the basic parts of a letter: heading, dateline, inside address, salutation, body, complimentary closing, signature, and reference initials.

Jefferson Gas and Appliance HWY 17 South P.O. Box 11 Washington, NC 27889-1107 13 July 20—	**INSIDE ADDRESS:** Complete address of the sender as a return address (personal business letter). A letterhead (company/organization letter) includes the company name, logo, address, and other optional information such and telephone and fax numbers.
	DATELINE: Date the letter was written.
Ms. Rhea Tankard Manager Malloy's Manufacturing 1023 West Main Street Washington, NC 27889-5043	**LETTER ADDRESS:** Professional (for example, Dr., Rev., Capt.) or courtesy title (Mr., Miss, Ms., or Mrs.), correct name (first name/first initial and last name), title, and address of the person to whom you are writing (no abbreviations). Name here should match the name used in the salutation.
Dear Ms. Tankard Subject: Contract for . . .	**SALUTATION:** Name of the person you want to read your letter. Typically uses professional (for example, Rev., Capt., Chief) or courtesy title (Mr., Miss, Ms., or Mrs.) and last name.
	SUBJECT LINE (optional): Focuses on the topic of the letter.
Xx xxxxx xxxxxxxxx xxx Xxxxxxx xxxxxxx xxxx Xxxxxxxxxxx xx xxxxxx x xxxxxx xxx Xx xxx xxxxx xxxxxxxx xx xxx xxxx	**BODY:** Usually two to five paragraphs long but can be several pages and may use headings similar to reports. The letter should look balanced on the page.
X xxxx xxxxxxxx xxxxxx Xxx xxxx xxxxxxx xxxx Xxxxxx xxx xxxxxxxxxx Xxxxx xxxxxx x xxxxxx x	The body of most letters is single-spaced with a double space (one blank line) between paragraphs. Organization depends on the type of letter you are writing.
Xxxxx xxxxxxxx xxx xxx Xx xxxxx xxxxxxx xxxx Xxx xxxxxx x xxxxxx Xxxxx xx	In block letter style, all lines begin at the left margin. In modified block letter style, all lines generally begin at the left margin except the date and the closing lines, which begin at the center of the page.
Sincerely yours W. B. (Jeff) Jefferson President WBJ/pjm Enclosures (3) c: Sofia Arellano Jay Reardon	**CLOSING:** Friendly but businesslike ending. Common closings include *Sincerely, Yours truly,* and *Cordially* (never *Thank you*). **SIGNATURE LINE:** Keyed name and title with space for handwritten signature above. **REFERENCE INITIALS:** Initials (in uppercase) of the person who dictated the letter followed by the initials (in lowercase) of the person who keyed the letter. The two sets of initials may be separated with a slash or a colon. Sometimes only the lowercase initials are used. **ENCLOSURE NOTATION:** Indicates additional documents in the envelope. Often the word *Enclosure* is followed by a colon and the titles of the enclosed documents are listed. **COPY NOTATION:** Indicates that a copy has been sent to another person or to other people.

Figure 5.9 Letter Parts

For letters longer than one page, subsequent pages generally include headers to keep readers oriented, as those shown in Figure 5.10.

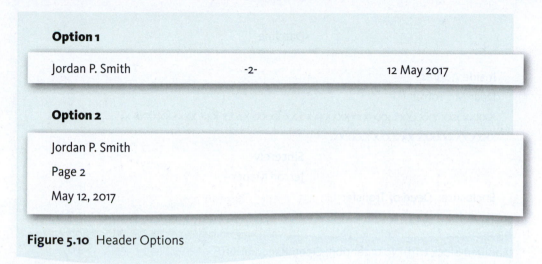

Option 1

Jordan P. Smith	-2-	12 May 2017

Option 2

Jordan P. Smith

Page 2

May 12, 2017

Figure 5.10 Header Options

Letter Styles

Letter styles vary. Business letters are usually written on letterhead stationery in block or modified block letter style. Personal letters include return addresses instead of letterheads and may be written in block or modified block letter style.

Block letter style aligns the return address, dateline, and closing at the left margin. Paragraphs are not indented. It is easy to key but may look off-balance. In **modified block letter style**, the dateline and closing begin at the horizontal center of the page. Paragraphs begin at the left margin. This style may be more difficult to key, but it looks more symmetrical on the page. Figure 5.11 illustrates basic differences in block and modified block letter style.

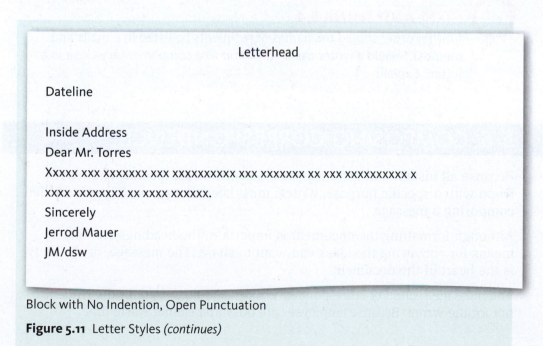

Letterhead

Dateline

Inside Address
Dear Mr. Torres
Xxxxx xxx xxxxxxx xxx xxxxxxxxxx xxx xxxxxxx xx xxx xxxxxxxxxx x xxxx xxxxxxxx xx xxxx xxxxx.
Sincerely
Jerrod Mauer
JM/dsw

Block with No Indention, Open Punctuation

Figure 5.11 Letter Styles *(continues)*

Letterhead

Dateline

Inside Address
Dear Mr. Torres
Xxxxx xxx xxxxxxx xxx xxxxxxxxx xxx xxxxxx xx xxx xxxxxxxxx x
xxxx xxxxxxxx xx xxxx xxxxxx.

Sincerely
Jerrod Mauer

Enclosure: Deed of Transfer

Modified block with No Indention, Open Punctuation

Figure 5.11 (continued) Letter Styles

Two punctuation styles are used in business letters: open and mixed. Open punctuation means that no punctuation marks are used after the salutation and the complimentary close. Open punctuation is considered a time-saving style and is used with block letter style. Mixed punctuation may be used with modified block letter style, in which case the salutation and complimentary close are followed by punctuation marks. The proper punctuation with this style is a comma after the complimentary close and a colon (for business letters) or a comma (for personal letters) after the salutation.

 STOP AND THINK 5.4

In what order should the names of recipients be listed in e-mails and memos? Should a writer use *Thank you* as a complimentary close in a letter? Explain.

 WARM UP   **5.5 COMPOSING CORRESPONDENCE**

Because all instant and text messages, e-mails, blogs, memos, and letters begin with a specific purpose, writers must keep that purpose in mind when composing a message.

Although formatting the document is important, the headings are only a means for conveying the ideas you want to share. The message, or the body, is the heart of the document.

The message section of correspondence should be organized for the reader, not for the writer. Because employees are busy and cannot waste time,

Sending a personal e-mail that reveals proprietary information (ideas the company owns) might cost you your good standing with your colleagues or even your job. It might subject you to legal action as well. Do not say anything in an e-mail that you would not say directly to a person, and do not write anything that might embarrass you or your organization, regardless of who reads it. E-mail can be deleted, but it never really disappears and may be forwarded anywhere to anyone. Most networks (the sender's and the receiver's) archive and back up all e-mail.

In addition, some people might think that a simple e-mail reply to a friend outside the company is not so bad. If so, then you might ask, "Where do we draw the line?" and "Who draws the line?" If using the office computer to answer personal messages is fine, then is it all right to use the company car to pick up your dry cleaning or to use the corporate credit card to pay for that dry cleaning? Can you use the office copy machine to photocopy brochures for your weekend real estate business? Can you use time you have at work to go online to order a gift for your brother's birthday or to pay your personal water bill? What about using the company phone to make a couple of calls to your grandparents who live in South Africa?

Using company time and equipment to conduct personal business is unwise. You could be fired, and it could ruin your reputation, making it difficult for you to find future employment. It also could get your company in trouble legally.

Focus on Ethics

eth·ics (eth′iks) *n.* 1 ...rds of conduct ...ith *sing.* or *pl.* morals ... a partic... group,

Think Critically

What is the harm in telling a friend about a new project at work that your supervisor has assigned to you?

---

correspondence should be organized accordingly. Imagine a busy decision-maker opening an e-mail that she expects to be one page, only to discover that the message is more than four pages long. The receiver may decide not to spend time scrolling through and reading the four pages, especially when she expects an e-mail to be brief. Writers who frustrate their readers or who fail to meet their readers' expectations are not likely to be successful in achieving goals.

Organize ideas to suit the message. Some messages are best presented in a straightforward manner. Others, when presented bluntly and directly, are likely to offend readers. And still others, such as persuasive messages, require more motivation than a direct approach provides. The strategies for informative and good news messages, negative or bad news messages, and persuasive messages are useful in writing instant and text messages, e-mails, blogs, memos, and letters.

Informative and Good News Messages

Brief correspondence usually gives the audience information that is pleasant—or at least acceptable. Pronouncements of good news, routine letters of inquiry, responses to letters of inquiry, and letters of appreciation all use a similar positive organizational structure.

You can expect the readers of a good news message to be in a receptive mood as they read your correspondence. Because your news is responsible for their pleasant mood, these readers are easy to approach. Therefore, the strategy is direct: Present the main idea first. Explanations, background information, and supplementary ideas follow the main idea.

Figure 5.2 on page 120 and the e-mail from the production manager at Gene-tech Laboratories in Figure 5.12 are examples of the direct approach to organizing informative and good news messages. The model letter in Figure 5.2 conveys good news to Regina Williams, the recipient of an $1800 scholarship to a local community college. In that letter, the tone is enthusiastic, while the tone of the following memo is more neutral or matter-of-fact.

MEMO

TO:	All Gene-tech Lab Employees
FROM:	Jamir Cayton, Production Manager Jamir Cayton *Jamir Cayton*
DATE:	November 15, 20 —
SUBJECT:	Deadline to Turn In Leased Chemical Lab Garments

Main idea—what the writer wants the reader to do

Please turn in by 5pm on December 7, 20—, all leased chemical lab garments checked out to you. The garments should be delivered to Room AC2407.

We signed a contract and will receive service from a new cleaning company, D & W Garment Care Center, effective December 8, 20—. Benefits of the change you should notice are

Explanation and supplementary ideas—why the writer is requesting this action and what effect it will have on the reader

- Perfume- and starch-free garments.
- An additional coat each week.
- Immediate replacement of worn or damaged garments.

Inform your department head if you need to report lost or damaged garments.

Figure 5.12 Memo Using the Good News Strategy (Direct Approach)

Figure 5.13 shows the body of an e-mail of inquiry. Correspondence of inquiry, while employing a more neutral tone, still represents a positive message because it shows an interest in a concept, product, or service.

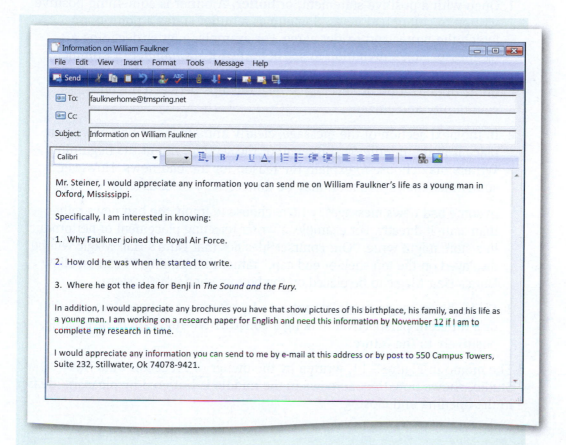

Information on William Faulkner

File Edit View Insert Format Tools Message Help

Send

To: faulknerhome@trnspring.net

Cc:

Subject: Information on William Faulkner

Calibri

Mr. Steiner, I would appreciate any information you can send me on William Faulkner's life as a young man in Oxford, Mississippi.

Specifically, I am interested in knowing:

1. Why Faulkner joined the Royal Air Force.

2. How old he was when he started to write.

3. Where he got the idea for Benji in *The Sound and the Fury.*

In addition, I would appreciate any brochures you have that show pictures of his birthplace, his family, and his life as a young man. I am working on a research paper for English and need this information by November 12 if I am to complete my research in time.

I would appreciate any information you can send to me by e-mail at this address or by post to 550 Campus Towers, Suite 232, Stillwater, Ok 74078-9421.

Figure 5.13 Positive Message: E-mail of Inquiry

Bad News Messages

Occasionally, the purpose of an instant or text message, an e-mail, a blog, a memo, or a letter is to share negative news—information readers will not be pleased to get, such as employee layoffs or unpopular policy changes. Negative messages can range from serious to mildly disappointing. A letter with a negative message may refuse a request, delay an order, or register a complaint.

Readers usually are not expecting bad news, and in this case, the direct approach is not the best choice. If readers see the bad news immediately, the disappointment may be so great that they miss or ignore the explanation entirely. A bad news message must relay the bad news and still try to maintain the reader's goodwill.

Therefore, the strategy of bad news messages is indirect. You can soften bad news by surrounding it with pleasant ideas in the following ways:

1. Open with a positive statement, or **buffer**. A buffer is something positive written to soften bad news. Sometimes a buffer states a point upon which the writer and reader agree. For example, a letter declining a businessperson's invitation to speak to the local Chamber of Commerce might mention the excellent work the Chamber does or the importance of the organization in developing relationships between the business community and citizens.

2. In the next section of the message, clearly announce the bad news, but place it in the middle or at the end of the section, not at the beginning. Writers may choose to explain the reason for the bad news. However, sometimes the explanation may be unnecessary or counterproductive.

   In some bad news messages, writers choose to imply the bad news rather than state it directly. For example, a writer rejecting placement of her product in a store might write, "Our contract specifies that Dura's Hair Magic will be displayed on the top shelf or end cap," rather than stating, "I cannot allow Dura's Hair Magic to be placed on the bottom shelf in your store."

3. Close the message on a pleasant note by offering an alternative solution or a different perspective, making a constructive suggestion, or looking positively to the future.

The memo in Figure 5.14, written by the owner of Precision Cuts Hair Studio, shows how the bad news in the middle is buffered by pleasant ideas in the opening and closing.

Precision Cuts Hair Studio

Memo

TO: All Stylists

FROM: Monza Hairston   MCH
            Owner and Manager

DATE: 6 June 20—

SUBJECT: Fashioning a Positive and Professional Image

Buffer—positive statement about creativity, something about which reader and writer agree

Being creative folks, we enjoy expressing our individuality in the way we dress. It is stylish and fun to dress flamboyantly.

Bad news statement—new policy that is likely to be unpopular

Some of us, using those creative energies, have been talking about ways to improve our professional image. Toward this end, the shop will adopt a uniform dress policy beginning on the first working day of next month, Monday, 2 July 20–. You may choose from solid navy and solid white outfits or outfits combining the two colors.

Positive close—benefits employees may enjoy

Besides enhancing the shop's professional image, the new policy will save you money because your personal clothes will not be subjected to the chemicals you use every day. Since you will not be using as much creative energy on clothing selection, you can lavish it on clients to make our shop the most popular one in town!

Figure 5.14 Bad News Memo

The opening buffer protects the reader from the bad news; a positive closing ends on a friendly note; and the bad news is strategically sandwiched between the two, where it is least likely to become the reader's focus.

Figure 5.15 shows a negative news e-mail. Abraham Bizmark of Bizmark Gold Studio writes to La'Neice Jackson, president of D'Oro Jewelry Stores.

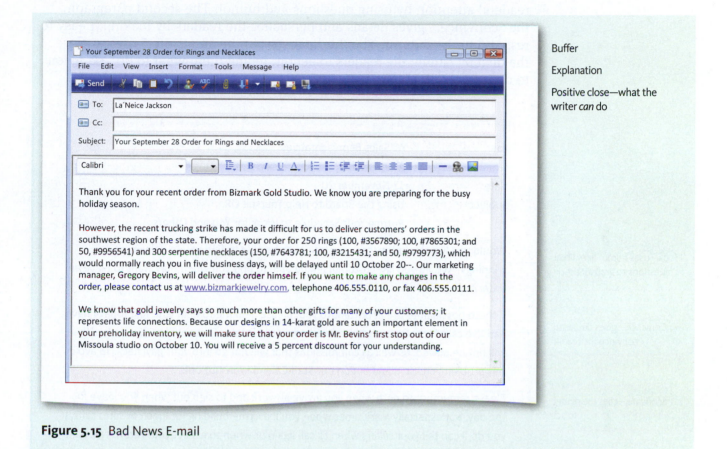

Buffer

Explanation

Positive close—what the writer *can* do

Figure 5.15 Bad News E-mail

Letters of complaint also are examples of correspondence containing negative news. When an individual has a legitimate complaint, the challenge is to present the complaint without alienating the reader. Most complaint letters also include a request to make things right, sometimes a refund, an exchange, extra service, or at least an assurance that the problem will not recur.

Persuasive Messages

A persuasive message is any correspondence in which the sender attempts to convince the receiver to agree with the writer. Persuasive messages are often used to sell products or services. Persuasive messages also include requests for assistance, support, or participation, such as a request for an employment recommendation or an invitation to participate in a charity's telethon.

Sometimes readers are receptive to the message—for example, the homeowner who wants to replace her leaky, rattling windows will eagerly listen to the salesperson who is telling her about the advantages of replacement windows. However, some audiences are not at all receptive to the persuasive message. Perhaps a previous experience or a lack of interest causes the audience to be hostile. In either case, the strategy of the persuasive message must not only gain the audience's attention but also convince the audience to agree with the message.

The memo in Figure 5.16, written by a sales director, shows a persuasive strategy at work. Notice how the opening paragraph, the "hook," grabs the readers' attention by using questions and humor. The second paragraph, the "convince," gives details and persuades the readers by making it easy to respond to the request. The third paragraph, the "motivate," tries to close the deal by calling the readers to action, telling them what to do and when to do it.

to:	All Sales Representatives
from:	Anson Archer *AA*
date:	12 November 20—
subject:	Using the Board to Help Yourself OR
	Putting Your Schedule to Work for You and Others

Hook—uses humor and direct questions to grab attention

Would you like the lottery representatives to be able to find you to deliver your winnings? Would you like customers to be able to find you when they want to place an order?

Convince—gives details to convince the reader

If these possibilities are important to you, please help me to <u>help you</u>. Just today I have had five calls for sales representatives I could not locate. That could be five orders that will not be placed, as well as commissions that will not go into your paycheck. To avoid this problem, check in and out on our Staff Calendar on Outlook.

Motivate—calls the reader to act

Please remember to note when you arrive at work and to sign out when you leave for the day, but especially mark times when you leave the building for lunch or sales calls. If you do, I can tell your callers when to call again or when to expect your return call. And I'll even hold your lottery winnings until you return!

Figure 5.16 Persuasive Message in E-mail

Persuasion means that you make your idea, plan, product, or service look appealing. Presenting false information is unethical, but it is considered good business sense to present the strengths of an idea or a product in a persuasive letter or a sales letter. To make your idea, plan, product, or service seem appealing, write sales messages according to the following organizational plan:

- **Hook** your reader's attention.
- **Convince** your audience of the advantages or benefits.
- **Motivate** your reader to action!

HOOK Your Reader's Attention   **Hooks** are attention-getters. That is, they are words designed to engage the reader. Hooks are designed to make the reader open the message and begin to read. Hooks may even start on the envelope of a sales letter (for example, an envelope that reads "Pay to the order of" in front of the recipient's name or "Free Gift Inside"). The hook may continue after the reader opens the letter.

Sometimes an announcement written in boldface precedes the message. The first line of the body sounds exciting. Throughout the letter, the writer "pulls out all the stops." Some information is boldfaced, underlined, bulleted, shadowed with color, or set apart from the text. Some persuasive messages use headings and different fonts. Some have borders, pictures, or graphics—anything to capture the readers' attention. Figure 5.17 illustrates some familiar attention-getters.

Figure 5.17 Hooks in Sales Message

The appeals of the attention-getters vary. Some appeal to the desire to get something for nothing. Some appeal to the reader's sense of compassion, need for security, or desire for prestige. Some appeal to the reader's curiosity.

CONVINCE Your Reader   This section, generally the longest part of the correspondence, usually begins with facts because decisions are most often based on facts—solid evidence. But the persuading does not end with the facts.

Advertisers describe their product (sometimes including visuals) to help readers understand but also to provide a favorable impression of the product. It is unethical (and illegal) for an advertiser to lie, but the words are usually written to sell—to create a favorable impression and a desire for the product or service. Likewise, persuasive writers who want to sell an idea or a concept must explain the idea clearly so that readers will see its worthiness.

A persuasive message should offer convincing evidence of the merits of the idea, product, or service. Facts, figures, and statistics can provide objective proof. **Testimonials** are personal stories or people's statements (often famous people) that a concept, product, or service worked for them. Sometimes advertisers try to compel readers to try their product free for a limited time. The advertisers hope the product will convince readers to keep the product and pay for it. Often enclosures such as brochures with pictures, order forms, or more testimonials are included. Sometimes a sales message is not just an e-mail, letter, or memo; it is an entire collection of materials.

MOTIVATE Your Reader to Act Finally, the writer must try to motivate the reader to do something—go to the phone and dial a number, say yes to a requisition, get in his or her car and drive to the store, send an e-mail of approval, write a check, or fill in a credit card number. To move the reader to action, persuasive message writers make this part as convenient as they can. You have probably heard motivators similar to these:

- An operator is waiting to take your call.

- Buy now and save 15% off the cover price.

- Send your tax-deductible contribution and help a homeless person find shelter from the cold.

Figure 5.18 is a persuasive letter from *Easy Home Cooking* magazine trying to convince Phoebe Nelson to subscribe. Using testimonials, a

---

EASY HOME COOKING Magazine
224 North Leming Road • Richmond, Virginia 26310
Phone 202-555-0171 • FAX 202-555-0190

April 17, 20–

Phoebe L. Nelson
764 Lord Fulford Drive
Boling, NH 57878-7873

Dear Phoebe:

As a preferred customer in the Culinary Arts Association family, we know that you like to prepare healthy, economical meals for your family and that you are busy and don't have time to waste. Also realizing that you're creative and enjoy fine food, we thought you would be interested in EASY HOME COOKING Magazine, one of America's most progressive magazines for the young home chef.

Here is what others are saying about us:
"EASY HOME COOKING Magazine is creating a buzz among the young professional set. They have high expectations, and this publication delivers."
        -GOURMET

"EASY HOME COOKING's design is impressive ... Its 'culinary school' features rank number one."
        -Shireen Braddock, American Culinary Institute

"This is the kind of magazine I wish I had started!"
        - Emerille

EASY HOME COOKING offers 433 recipes; 52 weekly meal planners; 50 culinary school workshop features, each of which explains and teaches a basic skill; and 70 tips. Pages are laminated to handle spills and splatters and come in an attractive 81/2 x 11-inch binder. All of the materials are printed in easy-to-read large type and come with color photographs showing garnishing and serving ideas.

With our easy payment plans, you don't want to miss this special opportunity to spice up your time in the kitchen. EASY HOME COOKING can be delivered to you each month for less than you spend on a sincle cappuccino at your favorite coffee emporium!

Want to learn more? Send us the enclosed card, and we will tell you more. Find out why EASY HOME COOKING is the right decision for you
.
Sincerely,

Marilyn L Zavala

Marilyn L. Zavala
Editor-in-Chief, EASY HOME COOKING

Figure 5.18 Sales Letter

strong focus on Phoebe's needs and interests, and facts, the letter is persuasive. In addition, the use of an enclosed reply card makes it easy for Phoebe to say yes.

STOP AND THINK 5.5

The Warm Up contained the following statement: "Dear Arnie: You're fired." Why is the direct approach not effective for bad news messages? What is a call to action in persuasive messages?

Communication
Technologies

You are in the midst of a worldwide intelligent network. Communication tools are wireless and increasingly smaller, including more features and functionality. Smartphones and handheld computers allow you to fax, call, e-mail, and surf the Internet as well as send graphics, videos, and messages anywhere in the world. The use of such devices allows you to conduct business and communicate with people anywhere at any time.

Think Critically

Describe some benefits and challenges of being constantly connected to people and your job.

5 CHAPTER REVIEW

Summary

1. Forms of brief correspondence—instant and text messages, e-mails, blogs, memos, and letters—are essential tools in the business world.

2. Writers must analyze and appropriately address the audience in all brief correspondence by maintaining goodwill, following principles of effective communication, using a suitable tone, and using humor effectively.

3. Considering audience needs and expectations, determining goals, thinking about technology and the situation, and freewriting are prewriting steps that ensure successful writing of brief correspondence.

4. Each type of brief correspondence uses specific formatting that distinguishes it from other correspondence.

5. To organize the body, writers must consider the type of message and the reader's needs. Writers use a direct approach in good news messages, an indirect approach to buffer unpleasant news in bad news messages, and a "hook, convince, motivate" strategy for persuasive messages.

Checklist

- Have I identified and analyzed my audience? If I am addressing a multilevel audience, have I planned to meet the needs of each group or type of reader?

- Did I establish my purpose or goal in this correspondence?

- Did I use freewriting to generate the information I want to share with the audience?

- Did I develop an organizational plan? Does it take into account good news, bad news, or a persuasive message?

- Does my correspondence follow the correct format and use consistent style? Does it contain the correct parts?

- Is the tone and level of formality appropriate to the audience?

- Have I asked a respected peer to read my correspondence and give specific feedback on the impact and effectiveness of my message?

- Did I proofread the headings for completeness and accuracy?

- Did I proofread the message for errors in spelling, keying, grammar, and punctuation?

- When the correspondence was acceptable, did I sign my name or, if appropriate, write my initials to the right of my keyed name?

Build Your Foundation

1. Here are eight parts to a good news letter announcing that Tessa Heilig has won a cruise to the Caribbean. However, the parts are mixed up. Rewrite the letter, putting the sentences in proper order. Several combinations may be possible.

   a. To claim your prize, you must call 1-800-CRUISES before April 18 and provide the operators with proof of identity.
   b. You have just won an all-expenses-paid cruise to the Caribbean!
   c. Congratulations, Tessa. We look forward to helping you arrange the vacation of your life!
   d. Enjoy a variety of on-board recreational activities, delectable meals, and superb entertainment at our expense.
   e. Your name, Tessa Heilig, was drawn out of 456,897 entries to be our top-prize winner in the Colombo Publishers Sweepstakes.
   f. Colombo has reserved four nights and five days for you and a guest.
   g. You must schedule your trip between June 1 and September 21, 20—.
   h. Pack your bags, Tessa, and don't forget the sunscreen!

2. Read the following writing situations. Select the details you need; then write the headings for each memo.

   a. You are the manager for your school's soccer team. Normally, you coordinate the packing of equipment and supplies for traveling to away games. However, for the next conference game to be played at Midland on May 9, you will be out of state attending your cousin's wedding. So you are writing a memo to Coach Robin Lytle and your two assistant managers, Diego Alvarez and Carey Johansen, to remind them of what needs to be done in your absence.
   b. You are Connie Famosa, manager of A Helping Hand, a residential cleaning service in San Alto, New Mexico. Six full-time and fifteen part-time employees are under your supervision. To thank the entire staff for their service, you plan to hold a picnic in your backyard. The event will take place on October 1, 20—, from 5 P.M. to 8 P.M. You are writing a memo today to invite all employees and their families to the picnic.

3. Marcus Robiskie of the ABC Detective Agency has just located Akilah Massaquoi's car, stolen three months ago from a shopping mall. List information you would include in a letter to Akilah from Marcus announcing the good news. Make up the addresses. Before making your list, use your imagination to answer these questions: How can Akilah get her car back? When can she get her car back? How did the detective find the car? How does Akilah feel?

4. Compose and send an e-mail or a letter of inquiry to request some information. Consider a research project for another class, a question about a product you own, or a question about a place you want to visit. Share the correspondence and response with the class.

Your Turn

1. Write a memo from Christa Brinkdopke, chief of installation services for Fox Cablevision, to Eric Monroe, an employee under her supervision. Eric has just completed 25 years of service with Fox Cablevision, and Christa wants to show her support for his work. Eric has had perfect attendance for the last three years, and his customer evaluations are consistently positive.

2. As assistant to your Quality Assurance Team at World Wide Insurance, you are in charge of scheduling meetings. The chair, Ruben Flores, has asked you to call a meeting for Monday afternoon, April 24, 20—. He wants the group to discuss a recent employee concern regarding unsafe exercise equipment in the Employee Wellness Center. Ruben would like the Quality Assurance Team to gather in Room 124-C at 4:15 P.M. He expects the meeting to end at 5 P.M. Write a memo announcing the meeting.

3. You are chief food scientist for Lehigh Bakery in Anderson, Wisconsin. Duane Carlson, president of the Logan Dairy Cooperative, a farmer-owned and farmer-operated sales organization under contract to sell its entire production to your company, has invited you to speak to his members regarding the effect of certain veterinary medicines on the taste of dairy products. On the date the Cooperative requested, Thursday, January 18, 20—, you are already scheduled to attend a meeting of the American Association of Bakers. Write a memo declining the invitation to speak to the Cooperative.

4. Plan and draft two e-mails that announce a new flextime program at Bauman Industries. The program will allow workers to share the responsibilities of one position among two or three people. Print the e-mails to give to your instructor or to share with your classmates or team.

   a. One e-mail should target and address the managerial staff of the company. Before composing the e-mail, consider the needs, concerns, questions, and biases of this audience.
   b. The second e-mail should target and address all employees of the company. Remember that you will need to meet the needs and answer the questions of all readers without offending anyone.

5. Go to the L-Soft website at http://www.lsoft.com/resources/ stellaremailtips.asp for twelve tips on developing effective e-mail list communication. Also view the history of listserv at http://www.lsoft .com/corporate/history-listserv.asp on the same website. Then address these two questions: (1)How might these twelve tips be useful in your career? (2) Knowing the history of L-Soft and listserv, what would be different in your experience if Eric Thomas had not created his software?

Community Connection

1. Ask an administrator or organization in your school if you can help edit and revise one piece of brief correspondence.

   a. After receiving the document, interview the writer or writers. Make sure you ask about the target audience and the purpose of the correspondence.

   b. Edit and revise the document. Then share it with a group of classmates or your entire class. Collect feedback from your peers.

   c. Edit and revise using the comments from your peers. Then submit the revised draft to the administrator or organization.

   d. Again collect feedback regarding the changes you made.

2. Contact a nonprofit organization or local government agency.

   a. Using a form letter or an e-mail from the agency, such as requests for contributions or welcome messages to new members or volunteers, analyze the target audience and the strategy used in the message.

   b. Offer to write a letter, a memo, or an e-mail, such as a message encouraging people to volunteer or to donate yard sale items.

3. Review a blog or Twitter account of a local business or nonprofit organization.

   a. What is its audience and purpose?

   b. Do you think it is an effective correspondence with the audience?

   c. What, if anything, would you suggest to improve the postings?

EXPLORE THE **NET**

To learn about writing processes for many types of correspondence, including business letters, e-mails, and memos, check out Writing Guides at Colorado State University's online writing center, Writing@CSU. Writing in Business provides guides for your e-mails, letters, memos, and more. Review the instruction and examples for types of letters. Given the types discussed in this chapter—good news, bad news, and persuasive—into what category do these letters covered by Writing@CSU fall?

Adjustment letter

Application letter

Inquiry letter

6 DOCUMENT DESIGN AND GRAPHICS

Goals

- Design an effective document for the audience and purpose
- Determine the audience and purpose of graphics
- Format graphics to make them easy to understand
- Construct graphics for the audience and purpose

Terms

Write to Learn

Using words only, write directions from your school to your home. Then draw a map with arrows to show the same route. Which is easier to understand—the written directions or the map? In a short journal entry, explain why.

FOCUS on Document Design and Graphics

Read Figure 6.1 on the next page and answer these questions.

- Describe what you see on the page. What percentage of information is devoted to words? to graphics?
- Has anything special been done with the words to make them stand out? If so, which words, and why do they stand out?
- Do the graphics help present the message? Explain.
- Where do the words explain or introduce the graphics?

What If?

How would the model change if . . .

- The medium were a 24" × 36" poster or trifold brochure?
- A PowerPoint® presentation provided this information?
- The insert were designed for second-graders?

Tornado Safety Plan

Tornadoes can strike with little warning. To keep you and your students safe, review the Mecklenburg County Tornado Safety Plan and share it with your students.

Alert System
Designated school personnel will receive phone, e-mail, and radio alerts to indicate a tornado watch or warning.

Tornado Watch
Conditions are favorable for a tornado.
Tornado Warning
A tornado has been spotted or indicated on radar.

If a tornado warning is issued, the alarm will sound—**three long blasts**.

Designated Personnel
Table 1 lists contact information for the designated safety personnel.

Personnel	Phone Numbers
Dr. C. Webber, Superintendent	704-555-0114
Dr. R. Gaskins, Principal ELS	704-555-0115
V. Romerez, Safety Officer ELS	704-555-0116
Dr. T. Mazurka, Principal EHS	704-555-0117
K. Isenhour, Safety Officer EHS	704-555-0118
Dr. C. Shaut, Principal EMS	704-555-0119
S. Cho, Safety Officer EMS	704-555-0120

Table 1. Emergency Contacts

Once a tornado warning has been issued, designated personnel will tune in to one of the local stations below and stay tuned until the danger has passed.

WKIX FM Radio 91.5
WNRT TV Channel 8

Safety Procedure
If a warning is issued, the designated safety personnel will sound the alert. When you hear the alert—**three long blasts**—move to safety immediately.

1. Instruct students to walk calmly in single file to the nearest designated Safety Zone in your building.
2. As you leave the classroom, turn off the lights and close the door. DO NOT stop to open the windows. Spend your time getting to safety.

Safety Zones
Each school has posted signs in hallways showing the location of the Safety Zones. The orange signs, like the one in Figure 1, have the words *SAFETY ZONE* and an arrow directing students to the appropriate area in their school. Become familiar with the signs and the location of designated Safety Zones.

Figure 1 Safety Zone Sign

"Duck and Cover" Position
When students arrive at the Safety Zone, instruct them to get on their knees facing the interior walls. Students should assume the "duck and cover" position (duck and cover the head) illustrated in Figure 2.

Figure 2. "Duck and Cover" Position

 Figure 6.1 Sample Document with Graphics

Writing @Work

Courtesy of Aidan Grey

CareerClusters
PATHWAYS TO COLLEGE & CAREER READINESS
Arts, A/V Technology & Communications
Source: The Center to Advance CTE

Aidan Grey is a freelance graphic designer in Denver, Colorado, and former director of photography for Home&Abroad (H&A), a travel planning website. He has 13 years of graphics expertise, including contracting with photographers, publishing images in print and on the Web, and designing logos.

Aidan believes that a picture is worth a thousand words, but not necessarily in English. "There's a different kind of eloquence in graphics because we get to use many additional 'languages' simultaneously— color, texture, composition, line, light. Red is one 'word' and says one kind of thing, while blue is another and says other things." In other words, it's important to be sensitive to the "linguistics" and semiology (signs and symbols) of images.

The various constraints that Aidan considers when working with graphics include content, color, licensing and copyright, cost, lighting, size, and composition. He judges which constraints to prioritize on a project-by-project basis but always gives credit when using others'

work: "You're never going to get in trouble for crediting someone properly."

Knowing when images hurt your content is as important as knowing when they enhance it. "Images are not helpful when they are too busy and when they contradict the desired message," cautions Aidan. For example, "If your report is about why the company is not meeting goals, images of smiling, happy people can send a decidedly wrong message." Images should enhance and complement the message of the text they accompany.

Aidan's graphic design work requires him to use communication skills along with his graphics virtuosity. At H&A, for example, he wrote contracts, form letters, manuals, and e-mail messages and even translated documents into other languages for investors.

Think Critically

1. With a partner, select a photograph in this book to analyze. Individually, jot down some notes about the "languages" the photo uses.

2. Compare notes with your partner. Does the photograph "say" more than you thought at first? Explain.

Printed with permission of Aidan Grey.

Writing in the Arts, A/V Technology, & Communications

Did you ever stop to think who comes up with slogans like these?

- When there is no tomorrow. FedEx

- Just do it. Nike

- It's finger lickin' good! Kentucky Fried Chicken

The product or service represented by each is immediately recognizable, its brand successfully established with the help of a copywriter. Copywriters do more than come up with catchy phrases, though. They compose ad copy, the text for traditional, print, and online marketing campaigns. They write jingles and scripts for radio and TV ads, create direct mail correspondence, and write text for websites and social media.

Writers strategize a campaign using AIDA (qtd. in Strong 85), text that gets the readers' *attention,* keeps their *interest,* taps into their *desire,* and propels them into *action.* To compose persuasive copy, writers must understand what motivates people to act and also be able to whittle a twenty-five-word description down to the most essential ten words. For a successful promotion, writers familiarize themselves with a client's USP (unique selling proposition)—what's different about a product or service and how it benefits a customer (Reeves). Good copy may come to a writer in a flash, but more often it comes after research, brainstorming ideas, and composing multiple drafts.

6.1 DESIGNING THE DOCUMENT

A cluttered room with poorly designed lighting can make it difficult for people to find what they are looking for. A cluttered document with poorly designed elements can put readers in the same predicament. Readers may be discouraged if they cannot find the information they need quickly and easily.

When you write, you make many decisions—what to write, how to organize, which words to use, and so on. Indeed, words are important to any writer, but in technical writing, *how the words look on the page is just as important as what the words say.* If they want readers to stay focused, good technical writers learn to design pages that are visually friendly.

For example, the 1" × 3" plastic tab inserted into Lorenzo's potted rosebush included six steps for planting and 57 tiny words squeezed onto the tab. Lorenzo could not read the tiny words, so he threw away the tab and dug a hole deep enough to plant the root-ball of the bush several inches below the ground. Stephanie, Lorenzo's next-door neighbor, showed him the 2" × 3" set of instructions that came tied around a branch of her new rosebush. With a couple of illustrations and print big enough for Lorenzo to see, he read the caution against burying the root-ball too deeply and adjusted the hole he had dug. In a few months, both neighbors had beautiful roses, thanks to Stephanie's better-designed and thus more effective instructions.

Figure 6.2 shows the two sets of instructions—one poorly designed and the other designed with the reader's needs in mind. The writer of instructions for commercial potting plants must consider the eyesight of home gardeners who find themselves squinting when trying to read small print.

Compare the appearance of different search engines. How is Google's home page different from Bing's? How is Ask's home page different from Yahoo's? Look at the color scheme, layout, and number of graphics on the page. Which site is most appealing to you? Why?

Tea Rose

Find an area that receives full sun. Use rich, well-drained soil that contains organic matter. Dig a hole slightly wider than the root-ball. Plant the bush so that the top of the root-ball is exposed. Do not cover the root-ball. Water the area thoroughly and fertilize twice a year: in spring and in late summer.

Tea Rose

1. Find an area that receives full sun.
2. Use rich, well-drained soil that contains organic matter.
3. Dig a hole slightly wider than the root-ball.
4. Plant the bush so that the top of the root-ball is exposed. *Do not* cover the root-ball.
5. Water the area thoroughly
6. Fertilize twice a year: in spring and in late summer.

Figure 6.2 Examples of Poorly Designed and Well-Designed Instructions

Design Elements

In addition to words, writers use **design elements** to aid comprehension and keep the reader's interest. Design elements affect page layout, the decisions writers make about arranging white space, text, headings, and graphics on their chosen medium to create a visually appealing reading experience.

White Space

White space is blank space with no text or graphics. It rests the eyes, separates chunks of information, and makes a document look inviting. Writers can create white space in margins, between paragraphs, before and after itemized lists, between columns, and around graphics.

Text

Text refers to the words printed on the page. Readers read text more quickly if it is left-justified with ragged-right edges, meaning that the text is flush with the left margin of the page and uneven along the right margin. This page is set up with left justification and ragged-right edges. Figure 6.3 shows differences in page justification.

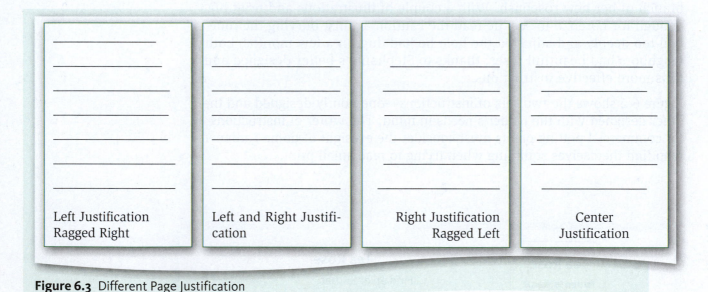

Left Justification Ragged Right   Left and Right Justification   Right Justification Ragged Left   Center Justification

Figure 6.3 Different Page Justification

Type fonts, the design and shape of letters, are divided into serif and sans serif. (Sans is French for "without.") *Serif* refers to letters with distinguishing lines or "tails" (like the text in this sentence), making it easy to see the differences between one letter and another. Sans *serif* refers to letters with few distinguishing lines and no "tails" (like the text in this sentence). Sans serif fonts are appropriate for something short, such as a title or heading. The major headings in this book use a sans serif font.

Size is measured in points, with a large point number (14 or 16) used for a larger letter. Text in 10 or 12 points is a comfortable reading size for most people. So for print body text, such as the paragraphs in this textbook, choose a 10- to 12-point serif font that mixes capital and lowercase letters. Documents in all caps are difficult to read. Hence, all caps should be used only for emphasis or for a title or major heading, such as the headings in this textbook. For online material, use a serif font in 16 points or higher.

Figure 6.4 shows a variety of popular serif and sans serif fonts.

SANS SERIF FONTS	POINT SIZE	SERIF FONTS	POINT SIZE
Arial	16 point	Garamond	16 point
Calibri	14 point	Times New Roman	14 point
Verdana	12 point	Georgia	12 point
Century Gothic	10 point	Courier	10 point

Figure 6.4 Sans Serif and Serif Fonts in Different Sizes

Highlighting features are print styles, such as **boldface,** <u>underline</u>, *italics,* and CAPITAL LETTERS, which draw attention to words and phrases. Use these highlighting features sparingly. Overuse clutters the page and distracts the reader, drawing attention away from your message.

Another tool for focusing the reader's attention is an itemized list. To itemize a list, set up a list separate from the text. The list may be indented from the left margin. Bullets (● □ √) or numbers often precede each item in the list. Use a numbered list when the sequence of items is important. Otherwise, use a bulleted list.

For example, in Figure 6.5, Mr. Gorham sends his students an e-mail, giving them last-minute instructions for their trip to France. He boldfaces the word *double-check* and sets up a bulleted list to draw attention to the five items the students must pack.

The following items are essential for a smooth, trouble-free trip. Check and **double-check** to make sure you have packed these items:

- Your passport—you will not be allowed on the plane without it
- Your money—credit card, traveler's checks, and some currency
- Your medical insurance card
- Any medication you routinely take
- Emergency telephone numbers, such as for canceling a lost or stolen credit card

Figure 6.5 Use of Boldface and Bullets in a Letter

Headings

Headings are short titles that introduce the main idea of a selected portion of text. Like a formal outline, headings help your reader see the organization of a document in one glance. Instead of Roman numerals, capital letters, and Arabic numerals to show divisions and subdivisions, the size and placement of headings show the organization. Most reports use a system of two headings (first-degree headings and second-degree headings), but they can use more. For example, this textbook uses a system of four headings for chapters.

Graphics

Graphics are visual representations of information. They include many familiar visual aids such as tables, line graphs, pie graphs, and diagrams. But they also include more sophisticated and less familiar aids such as schematics, pictographs, decision charts, and Internet graphics.

Graphics are used in technical writing whenever information can be expressed better in a visual form than in words alone. Sometimes a graphic is used by itself, as in the traffic signs you see on your way to work or school. For technical writers, a graphic is often combined with text to convey meaning.

Whether you use graphics alone or with text, considerations of purpose and audience guide your decision and influence which graphic is appropriate for your document. The last section of this chapter introduces you to some of the more familiar and easy-to-design graphics.

Medium

In addition to considering white space, headings, and graphics, writers choose the best medium for their documents. Possible choices include paper media (for example, heavy stock, 8 1/2" × 11", or an insert) or electronic media (for example, e-mail, social media, or web app). Again, purpose and audience determine which medium you choose. In turn, the medium also influences the design.

For example, the city mayor mailed a one-page survey to her constituents to find out voter opinions on key issues. On one side was the survey; on the other was the return address with prepaid postage. After completing the survey, readers could refold and reseal the document and drop it in the mail. For constituents using social media, the survey link was posted on Facebook—and reposted once a week to stay in the public's eye until enough responses were collected and shared. The purpose (receiving information quickly from as many citizens as possible) influenced the choice of media (the envelope design and Facebook's electronic submission). The envelope design also determined placement of the survey, address, and prepaid postage. Similarly, Facebook allowed repeated posting of the survey link and easy tabulation.

© c., 2009/Shutterstock

STOP AND THINK 6.1

Why do white space, ragged-right edges, serif font, and headings make text easy to read? What is the purpose of highlighting features?

6.2 WHO READS GRAPHICS?

A picture is indeed worth a thousand words. Graphics can clarify information quickly. At one glance, your readers can perceive more information than they would with words alone. Most complex technical material can be simplified with a graphic: a table, a drawing, a diagram, or a graph. Where academic readers rely heavily on words to understand meaning, technical readers often rely on words *and* graphics.

Audience

Technical subjects such as engineering, marketing, and medicine rely heavily on data presented visually. Some concepts cannot be relayed without a graphic. Therefore, readers of technical documents expect to see graphic aids in their reading. However, readers vary in their ability to understand graphics. While international readers may have difficulty with some vocabulary, they can often comprehend a graphic quickly. As with decisions about text, decisions about graphics depend on what your readers can understand and what they already know.

Generally, the more data in a graphic, the more difficult it is to read. When choosing which graphic your audience will best understand, ask these questions:

- How much does my reader know about the subject?

- How interested is my reader in the subject?

- Do my readers need or expect technical information expressed visually as graphics? Or will my audience be confused by graphics?

- Does my audience's reading level tend to be higher (tenth grade or higher) or lower (ninth grade or lower)?

- How will my reader access the graphic, through traditional or online media?

Purpose and Objectives

Audience is only one consideration when selecting a graphic. You also must consider your rhetorical situation, especially the purpose of your graphic as well as how much and what kind of information you want to convey.

To determine which graphics best complement your message, ask yourself these two questions:

- What is the purpose of the writing?

- How can graphics help achieve that purpose?

Then choose the graphic that best meets your needs.

Typical Reader

A person requiring visual representations of technical data to aid comprehension.

Writer's Focus

Presenting complex information visually, using page design to enhance readability, and matching graphics to audience and purpose.

To help you select an appropriate graphic, look at the Purpose column in Table 6.1 and decide what you want to accomplish. Maybe you want your reader to operate a digital camera. To achieve that purpose, you want your reader to see what the camera looks like and where each button is. Drawing the mechanism of the camera with clearly labeled parts would help achieve that purpose. Do you need to show numbers to your readers in an easy-to-read format? If so, a formal table would serve your purpose.

Table 6.1

Purpose	Graphic
Present a small amount of numerical data	informal table
Present numbers in easy-to-read rows and columns	formal table
Explain an idea using words set up in rows and columns	verbal table
Contrast data to highlight differences	bar graph or pictograph
Contrast two or more sets of data to highlight differences	multiple bar graph
Follow a trend over time	line graph
Compare two or more trends and show how data is related	multiple line graph
Illustrate how the whole is divided into parts or how the parts relate to the whole	pie graph or divided column graph
Educate quickly with an attractive combination of texts and visuals	information graphic
Explain a process	flowchart
Demonstrate a decision-making process	decision flowchart
Present the structure of an organization	organizational flowchart
Confirm a schedule of tasks	Gantt chart
Demonstrate an idea using a symbol	icon
Illustrate representative details of an object or a mechanism	diagram or line drawing
Show how something actually looks	photo

STOP AND THINK 6.2

What are some questions to ask about your audience to help you select an appropriate graphic? Using Table 6.1, identify three graphics you frequently see in textbooks. What is the purpose of each graphic?

6.3 DESIGNING GRAPHICS

WARM UP

Graphics add critical information to your text and become part of the overall appearance of a document. Good writers create a flow between words and graphics that unifies a document, allowing readers to move along without interruption. To help your reader interpret graphics quickly and easily, you should keep graphics simple and neat, integrate graphics with text, give credit for borrowed graphics, and use color effectively.

Keep Graphics Neat and Simple

The quality of a graphic is a factor in how carefully it is read. A neat, clean graphic is easy to read and interpret. Leave enough white space around the graphic so the page looks organized, and make the graphic large enough so the reader can see all parts clearly. Align decimals when they are presented in columns, as shown in the numbers below.

Look closely at the graphics in the following sections of this chapter. What do you notice about each one? What do the graphics have in common? Notice some of the differences. In which graphics do the differences occur?

8.3

0.525

98.6

27.0

In general, a graphic should have one main point. Including two simple graphics to illustrate two concepts is better than using one cluttered graphic to illustrate too many concepts. Figure 6.6 is an example of a cluttered

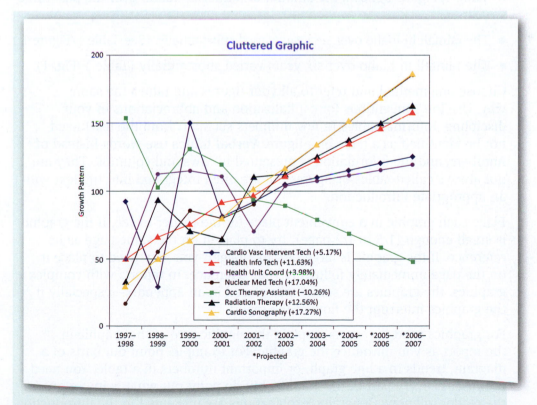

Figure 6.6 Example of Cluttered Graphic

graphic that is nearly unreadable. With too many colored lines, it looks more like a robotic weapon from a science fiction movie than a line graph predicting trends in community college majors.

Provide Keys to Measurements

Explain how your data is measured and offer clues about what the data means. Depending on the purpose and the tradition, distance can be measured in light years (NASA), kilometers (China), miles (USA), or nautical miles (sailors). Your pictograph may have five icons of bears for one region, but if your reader does not know that one icon represents 100 bears, she may underestimate the population. Your line graph has four lines, all different colors. What does each color represent? To help your reader understand your graphic, tell how your data is measured and offer short definitions, explanatory footnotes, or legends (quick guides to symbols or colors used).

Integrate Graphics with Text

Clearly refer to each graphic by figure or table number in the text *before* you place it on the page and *as soon as* your reader needs to look at it. Use the word *figure* to refer to any graphic that is not a formal table. Use the word *table* to refer to a formal table (a table with rules and titles). Number figures consecutively throughout. Number tables consecutively—but separately from figures—throughout. Call your reader's attention to figures or tables by incorporating references into your text, using parentheses, or creating stand-alone sentences as follows:

- Table 1/Figure 1 shows the amount of rainfall in Idaho over the past three years.

- The rainfall in Idaho over six years varied substantially. (See Table 1/Figure 1.)

- The rainfall in Idaho over six years varied substantially (Table 1/Fig. 1).

Choose one method and refer to all your figures and tables the same way. Use the conventions for capitalization and abbreviations of your discipline. Informal tables (a few numbers set apart from the text) need not be identified as a table or a figure. **Verbal tables** use words instead of numbers, and the information is presented in rows and columns. They are not always called tables or figures but are often integrated into the text with an appropriate introduction.

Place each graphic in a convenient place for the reader to see. If the graphic is small enough (1/5 to 1/2 page), try to place it on the same page as its reference. If the graphic is large (3/4 to 1 page), you may need to place it on the page immediately following your reference. In reports with complex graphics, the graphics are sometimes placed in an appendix—especially if the graphics interrupt the flow of the report.

For graphics used in reports, explain the significance of the graphic in the report as you introduce the graphic. For example, point out parts of a diagram, trends in a line graph, or important numbers in a table. You need not discuss every part of the graphic, but do point out what is important for the reader to know. Generally, explanations are presented in the introduction preceding the graphic. More complex graphics may require discussion before and after placement of the graphic.

Communication
Technologies

Websites such as Gratisography, New Old Stock, Jay Mantri, and Superfamous offer free images, graphics, and photographs without copyright restrictions. Artists here give up their rights to their creations under Creative Common Public Domain Dedication (CC0 1.0 Universal). Some images do require attribution (giving credit to the artist), but others do not. Most of these sites are searchable, making it easy to find the perfect image for anyone wanting to build a website or create a design.

Think Critically

Why is it important to make sure you do not need permission before you use an image? Why might you want to attribute a photo to the photographer responsible for the image, even if attribution is not requested?

Provide a title for every graphic, except for informal tables that are simply indented from the margin. Table titles and figure titles are often centered below the figure. However, placement may vary. Choose a placement and be consistent throughout the document. Use specific names for titles so readers understand what they are to learn from the graphic. For example, use

Salary Distribution for 2015–2017– *not just* Salaries

Regal Powerboat Model OTY-453–*not just* Powerboat

© Krivosheev Vitaly/Shutterstock

Give credit for a graphic if you do not compile it yourself or if you compile it using borrowed data. Place the word *Source* below your figure. Include the bibliographical reference for the source as you would a footnote or an endnote and specify if you have permission to reprint the graphic (e.g., "Reprinted with permission") or if you have changed the graphic in some way (e.g., "adapted from Williams, 2016, p. 64").

Use Color Effectively

Color often attracts a reader's attention before the words attract his attention. Color is a powerful design tool that can be used to:

- **Indicate a document's organization.** By using the same color for major headings, you give your readers visual cues to the overall organization of a document and help them scan quickly for information.

- **Emphasize or clarify an important point.** When using a color for a key word, a phrase, an idea, or part of a graphic, you draw your reader's attention to important information. You also can use color to signify a change or to guide readers through a process.

- **Support your text's meaning.** By using certain colors consistently to convey specific information, your reader begins to associate the color with the meaning (red with danger, for example) and therefore understands the text more quickly.

- **Make your document attractive.** By using colors to break up black-and-white text, your page will look more appealing.

- **Improve visibility for visually impaired readers.** Use contrasting colors to enable visually impaired readers to see your color scheme. Comply with ADA regulations by avoiding reds and greens together for readers who are red/green colorblind.

With a click of the mouse, you can change color from blue to green or green to red, for example. But be careful. Like any technical writing tool, color can be misused. To use color effectively:

- **Avoid overusing color.** More than three or four colors (including black and white as two colors) can overwhelm a reader, and using one color (other than black) too often can be distracting.

- **Apply color consistently to elements throughout a document.** For example, if you set major headings in red and set key words in black boldface, do not suddenly switch a major heading to blue or a key word to red boldface.

- **Remain sensitive to cultural identifications with colors.** International audiences associate colors differently from American audiences. For instance, Americans associate green with go (traffic lights) and red with danger (fire trucks and stop signs). However, green is a holy color to a Muslim and red is a sign of mourning to a South African.

- **Avoid unusual combinations of colors.** Some colors, such as purple on a blue background and orange on red, are difficult to read.

 STOP AND THINK 6.3
Why should graphics be neat and simple? Identify three ways to refer to graphics in your text. How can colors be misused in a document?

 WARM UP

When you look at a page with text and a graphic, which do you read first—the text or the graphic? Do you ever read the text without looking at the graphic? Do you ever look at the graphic without reading the text? Explain your preference.

6.4 CONSTRUCTING GRAPHICS

As a technical writer selecting graphics for a document, you have many options from which to choose. You make those choices by considering which graphics are most appropriate for different audiences and purposes. This section shows you how one writer selected graphics for different audiences in a series of articles promoting good health practices.

Theresa, a nutritionist and freelance writer, is working on several different writing and promotional assignments. One article is for *Mind and Body,* an online magazine for fitness trainers and instructors. These readers have a solid background in physical education, a keen interest in the subject, a college reading level, and experience interpreting graphics. The second article will appear in *Fitness*, a newspaper delivered monthly to junior high classrooms. These readers have less knowledge about good health practices and may not be as motivated to make healthy lifestyle choices. As younger readers, their reading level is lower than that of the fitness trainers and instructors, and their experience reading graphics is limited.

Theresa's other assignments include writing a monthly newsletter for her clients, giving a speech at a middle school, creating a website, and organizing a health fair event. Theresa sometimes uses her clients' stories in her publications—with their permission, of course.

This section will take you step by step through Theresa's decision-making process as she decides how to disseminate information to her different audiences.

Constructing Tables

Tables are used to present words or numbers organized into categories of columns and rows. Tables, one of the most popular graphic aids, can be informal or formal. A verbal table, often called a chart, is a variation of the formal table, categorizing words instead of numbers into columns and rows.

Informal Table

An **informal table** is a graphic that uses rows and columns drawn without rules (lines) or stubs (column headings). In an informal table, the information flows with the text. The explanation of the graphic is a brief summary of the information presented in the graphic.

Theresa's latest article to the young readers of *Fitness* gives examples of healthy food choices and calorie estimates. To present average calorie needs quickly, Theresa uses an informal table. The informal table is a good choice because the information is simple (only two items to consider) and is appropriate for her younger audience. Figure 6.7 shows the informal table and its written introduction.

The Dietary Guidelines for Americans recommends the following calorie needs for moderately active boys and girls aged 13:

Daily Calories for Boys	2200
Daily Calories for Girls	2000

Figure 6.7 Model of Informal Table

Formal Table

A **formal table** is an arrangement of information in rows and columns with rules (lines drawn). It is typically used to organize numbers, words, or other data in a consistent format. Numerical information, in particular, can be difficult to follow without the structure of a table.

Theresa uses part of a table from a book, *Exercise and You,* to inform the readers of *Mind and Body* about recommended training rates for aerobic exercise. The older and more knowledgeable audience will likely understand the detailed numerical data and be motivated to use the information. Figure 6.8 is the table Theresa adapted from the data in the publication, along with her brief introduction. The introduction describes what kind of information is included in the table but does not explain every item. The table, with a short introduction, is self-explanatory.

Tips for Constructing Tables

- Use only as many rules as necessary to read the graphic. Use short titles, called stubs, to name each column. For tables with lots of rows and columns, consider shading at regular intervals to aid comprehension.

- Make the table symmetrical, balancing words, white space, and numbers.

- Add footnotes with clarifying notes to help a reader interpret the data.

- If an outside source was used, write the word *source* underneath table followed by a footnoted bibliographic entry.

Table 1 shows the recommended heart rates by age during exercise. The athlete's training rate is for only the fittest athletes. The average training rate is recommended for a healthy person beginning a fitness program.

Table 1. Recommended Heart Rates during Aerobic Exercise

| | TRAINING RATES[a] | | |
AGE	MAXIMUM HEART RATE	ATHLETE, 85%[b]	ATHLETE, 85%
20	200	170	160
22	198	168	158
24	196	167	157
26	194	165	155
28	192	163	154

Source: Adapted from Alan Grayson and Suzanne Brazinski, *Exercise and You,* Clearview, ND: Mountain Press, 2017, 72.

[a]Based on average heart rates of 72 beats per minute for males and 80 beats per minute for females
[b]Percentages represent percents of maximum heart rates in Column 2

Figure 6.8 Model of Formal Table and Introduction

Verbal Table

As already stated, a verbal table, also known as a chart, is similar to a formal table with its rows and columns. Like a formal table, it uses stubs and may include footnotes and bibliographic information if taken from another source. It is different, though, in the kinds of data included. Formal tables use numerals; verbal tables use words. Some writers refer to a verbal table as simply a table and number it. Other writers are less formal, referring to a chart, for example, without numbering it.

Theresa wants to emphasize to her younger audience the dangers of poor eating habits. She could write this information in a paragraph, but she decides that a chart presents the information more efficiently. So Theresa constructs the chart in Figure 6.9 and writes a one-sentence introduction. For her middle-school readers, she stays away from longer medical terms such *as hypertension, atherosclerosis,* and *gastroenterological disease.*

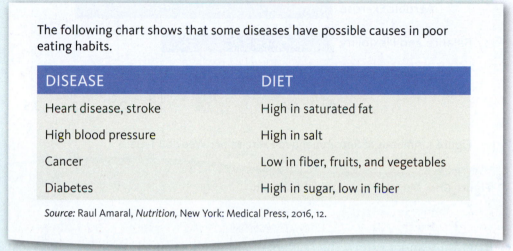

The following chart shows that some diseases have possible causes in poor eating habits.

DISEASE	DIET
Heart disease, stroke	High in saturated fat
High blood pressure	High in salt
Cancer	Low in fiber, fruits, and vegetables
Diabetes	High in sugar, low in fiber

Source: Raul Amaral, *Nutrition,* New York: Medical Press, 2016, 12.

Figure 6.9 Model of a Verbal Table with Introduction

Constructing Graphs

A graph is a visual aid that shows the relationships among numerical data. Five types of graphs are bar graphs, pictographs, Gantt charts, line graphs, pie graphs, and information graphics.

Bar Graph

The **bar graph** is a graph that uses a horizontal axis and a vertical axis to compare numerical data presented in rectangular columns or bars. The bars can run vertically or horizontally. While both vertical and horizontal graphs can depict the same data, horizontal columns allow more room to accommodate longer labels. Sometimes the decision to use a horizontal graph may depend on where the graph fits best, the need to break up text, or the graph's proximity to other visual aids.

Theresa receives some good advice about how to vary her exercise routine from a gym teacher and posts the advice on her blog as a horizontal bar graph. She has more space on the vertical axis to write the name of each category.

Figure 6.10 shows Theresa's horizontal graph along with her introduction.

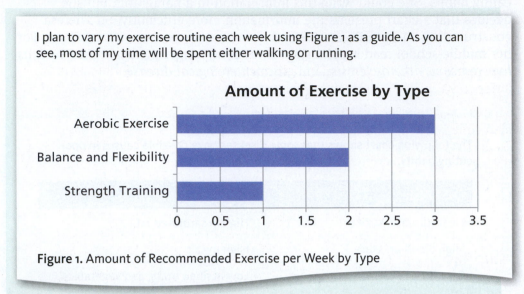

I plan to vary my exercise routine each week using Figure 1 as a guide. As you can see, most of my time will be spent either walking or running.

Amount of Exercise by Type

Figure 1. Amount of Recommended Exercise per Week by Type

Figure 6.10 Model of Horizontal Bar Graph

Theresa wants to show the readers of *Fitness* how much weight a client lost each week for the first three months. Because the bar graph is relatively easy to read, it is appropriate for the *Fitness* readers. Figure 6.11 shows the bar graph Theresa designed, along with the introduction advising her readers which numbers to pay attention to.

Figure 2 shows the progression of pounds lost for 12 weeks. Notice the greatest amount of weight loss occurred during the first four weeks (11.9 total). After six weeks, weight loss was negligible (only .3 pounds).After eight weeks, weight loss resumed at a slower but steady pace (4.6 total).

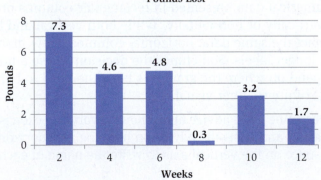

Figure 2. Pounds Lost per Week (12 weeks)

Typically, the body will lose more weight at first because of sustained metabolism and significant water loss. Several weeks into the weight-loss program, a person's metabolism slows down the amount of loss to protect the body from harm. Weight loss will stabilize if a person continues to manage diet and exercise.

Figure 6.11 Model of Bar Graph with Introduction

In her bar graph, Theresa uses the vertical axis for the dependent variable (the number of pounds lost) and the horizontal axis for the independent variable (the number of weeks). The dependent variable changes depending on, or relative to, the independent variable. Here the pounds lost depend on the number of weeks the client stays with her routine. Typically, a vertical axis represents the dependent variable and a horizontal axis represents the independent variable. Often the horizontal axis depicts time or distance.

Theresa is careful to label both axes ("Pounds," "Weeks") for the reader. She also added the specific number of pounds atop each bar for easy reference. To do so is not necessary, but Theresa thought her readers would appreciate seeing the numbers. The decision to add specific numbers depends on who your readers are and how much detail they need. Additional tick marks between pounds to mark individual ounces or half pounds were not added because the graph was understandable without them. The bars are the same width with the space between the bars approximately one-half the bar width.

Notice how Theresa introduces the graphic before she places it in her article and continues her explanation after the graphic. Dividing the discussion this way breaks up her lengthy explanation.

Multiple Bar Graph

To compare fat loss to lean body mass (LBM), Theresa uses the **multiple bar graph** in Figure 6.12, a bar graph with more than one bar (called a **bar cluster**) for each measurement. With three bars, this graph is relatively easy to read for the older readers, but Theresa wants to challenge her younger readers to see the difference in the more dramatic fat loss and slower gains in LBM.

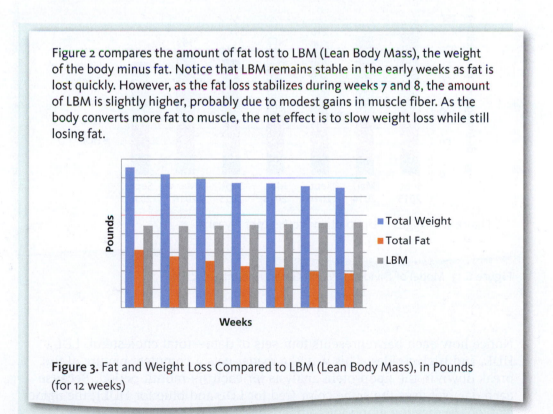

Figure 2 compares the amount of fat lost to LBM (Lean Body Mass), the weight of the body minus fat. Notice that LBM remains stable in the early weeks as fat is lost quickly. However, as the fat loss stabilizes during weeks 7 and 8, the amount of LBM is slightly higher, probably due to modest gains in muscle fiber. As the body converts more fat to muscle, the net effect is to slow weight loss while still losing fat.

Figure 3. Fat and Weight Loss Compared to LBM (Lean Body Mass), in Pounds (for 12 weeks)

Figure 6.12 Model of a Multiple Bar Graph with Introduction

The multiple bar graph uses two sets of bars on a horizontal and vertical axis to compare several sets of numerical data. With some bars taller than others, the bar graph depicts differences dramatically. Again, the introduction points out what is most important to the reader.

Each bar is a different color. A key is provided to explain what each color represents. Also, Theresa decides not to add the specific pounds atop each bar as she did in the single bar graph because the numbers make the graph difficult to read.

Divided Column Graph

The **divided column graph** is a type of bar graph that shows how all the parts in each column relate to a total quantity.

Mind and Body wants to publish a success story of someone who lowered cholesterol levels. For this article Theresa provides a divided column graph illustrating how diet and exercise contributed to her client's improved cholesterol numbers. This audience is studying factors affecting HDL (good cholesterol) and LDL (bad cholesterol) and will understand the medical jargon. Figure 6.13 shows the divided column graph along with the introduction.

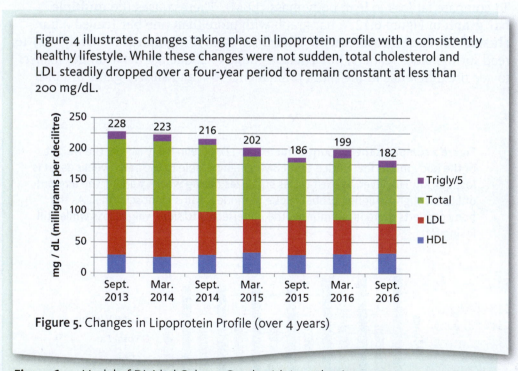

Figure 4 illustrates changes taking place in lipoprotein profile with a consistently healthy lifestyle. While these changes were not sudden, total cholesterol and LDL steadily dropped over a four-year period to remain constant at less than 200 mg/dL.

Figure 5. Changes in Lipoprotein Profile (over 4 years)

Figure 6.13 Model of Divided Column Graph with Introduction

Notice how each bar represents four sets of data—total cholesterol, LDL, HDL, and triglycerides. This way the reader gets a complete picture of the break down in the lipoprotein analysis for each six-month period. Because each data set uses the same color (red for LDL and blue for HDL), the reader can look across the graph for comparisons.

Histogram

The **histogram** is a type of bar graph. Instead of specific numbers, however, this graph uses ranges of numbers derived from the data collected rather than separate categories. A histogram is appropriate for depicting the frequency of an occurrence.

Theresa has been hired as a consultant by the local gym to research equipment needs and programs for the new wing. To begin her research, she wants to know who uses the current facility—which age groups frequent the gym now. So she includes the histogram in Figure 6.14 in her report.

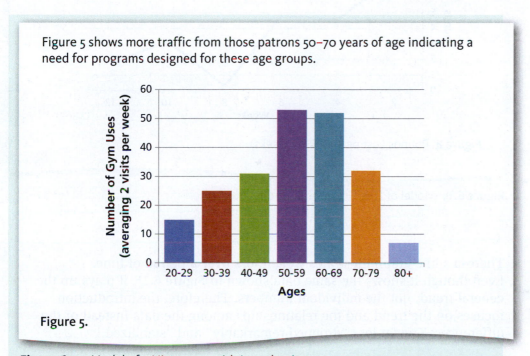

Figure 5 shows more traffic from those patrons 50–70 years of age indicating a need for programs designed for these age groups.

Figure 5.

Figure 6.14 Model of a Histogram with Introduction

Line Graph

The line graph is similar to a bar graph in that it uses a horizontal axis and a vertical axis to compare numerical data. Instead of bars, however, this graph uses a line that depicts a trend.

Theresa can use a **line graph** to show the same data she used in the bar graph. A line graph uses a horizontal axis and a vertical axis to show a trend or relationship among numbers. Theresa must decide which graph is more appropriate for her readers. To experiment with a different graph, she plotted the same eight-week fat-loss data on a line graph.

Figure 6.15 shows the same data in a line graph that Figure 6.11 shows in a bar graph.

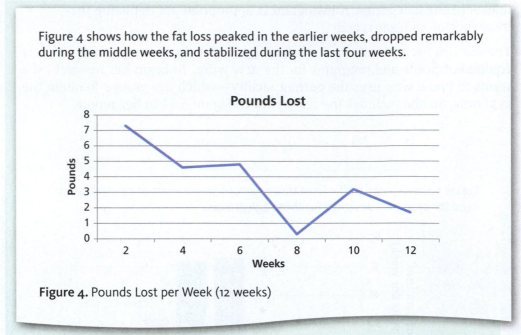

Figure 4 shows how the fat loss peaked in the earlier weeks, dropped remarkably during the middle weeks, and stabilized during the last four weeks.

Pounds Lost

Figure 4. Pounds Lost per Week (12 weeks)

Figure 6.15 Model of Line Graph with Introduction

Theresa's line graph illustrates weight loss over a period of time. Even though it shows the same data shown in Figure 6.11, it plays up the general trend, not the individual numbers. Therefore, the introduction focuses on the trend and the relationships among the data instead of the differences: The fat loss "dropped remarkably" and "stabilized."

Communication
Dilemma

You work as a wedding planner for I Do Wedding Consulting. Your manager, Rachel, is proud of the way you communicate with clients to find out and provide exactly what they want for their wedding day. The company has recently expanded to include international clients, and Rachel has put you in charge of marketing the company's services to Chinese couples who want a westernized wedding.

You decide to create an international section on I Do's website showcasing weddings you have planned. Because you believe the most beautiful weddings are all white, you have included photos with arrangements of white roses and other white flowers. Several months later, Rachel is puzzled. Not a single Chinese couple has made an appointment.

Think Critically

Why was the photo gallery not effective for the target audience? You may need to research color associations in other countries to learn why the gallery was not an effective marketing tool.

This graph would be appropriate for either audience because the trend is easily interpreted, but Theresa decides not to use this line graph for either article. She believes that the bar graph is more appropriate for the inexperienced readers of Fitness because she wants to highlight differences in weight lost. Instead, for her Fitness audience, Theresa considers using the multiple line graph shown in Figure 6.16.

Multiple Line Graph

Theresa's Figure 6.16 puts the same information from the multiple bar graph in Figure 6.12 into a **multiple line graph**. A multiple line graph uses more than one line to compare data. Be careful not to clutter the graph with too many lines, or it may be difficult to read. Multiple lines are usually presented in different colors or line schemes—dotted, hyphenated, or straight. Theresa's multiple line graph compares three sets of data.

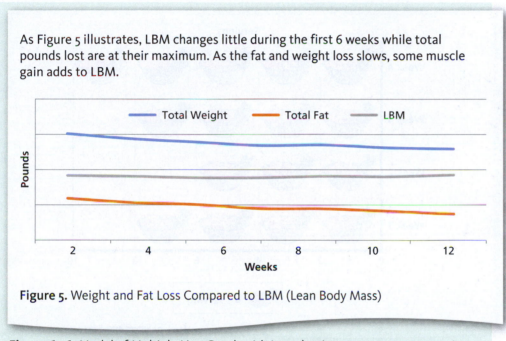

As Figure 5 illustrates, LBM changes little during the first 6 weeks while total pounds lost are at their maximum. As the fat and weight loss slows, some muscle gain adds to LBM.

Figure 5. Weight and Fat Loss Compared to LBM (Lean Body Mass)

Figure 6.16 Model of Multiple Line Graph with Introduction

Theresa thinks the physical education majors would be interested in seeing how the three sets of data interact with each other and would have the educational background to understand the relationship among weight loss, fat loss, and LBM. While she will provide her *Fitness* readers with the same information in two bar graphs, she will provide the information to her *Mind and Body* readers in one multiple line graph. Theresa always chooses her graphics by considering the needs of her audience as well as her own purpose for writing.

Notice how the multiple line graph illustrates the **relationships** among weight loss, fat loss, and LBM rather than the **differences**. Again, the introduction emphasizes how each variable affects the other and provides Theresa the opportunity to make these connections visually clear to her readers. Remember, writers use introductions to direct their readers' attention to pertinent data points.

Pictograph

A **pictograph** is a special kind of bar graph that uses pictures instead of bars to represent data. Like bar graphs, pictographs show differences in related data. In addition, pictographs add color and interest, are easy to read, and are especially appropriate for nonnative speakers of English. To be clear, the pictures or icons must be easily recognized and distinguishable from one another.

Employees of Grow Organic Consortium competed with other area businesses to see which company's employees could come closest to eating eight servings of fruits and vegetables every day for a month. Several weeks into the competition, Theresa presents the results on her blog using the pictograph shown in Figure 6.17. She decides to use the pictograph in her monthly newsletter to spur other companies to step up the pace.

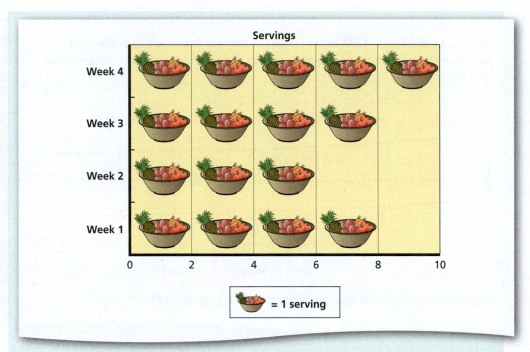

Figure 6.17 Average Consumption of Fruits and Vegetables for Four Weeks at Grow Organic Consortium—Model of Pictograph with Introduction

Like the bar and line graphs, the pictograph uses horizontal and vertical axes to present data. The colorful fruits and vegetables will appeal to Theresa's general audience. The approximate numbers are rounded to the nearest quarter serving. However, if precision is important, a pictograph would not be the best choice. In Figure 6.17, Theresa turns the graph to present the data horizontally so that her audience can read the data like a calendar.

Information Graphic

To combine text and graphics to present factual information quickly, Theresa finds this **information graphic** (also infographic) from the CDC, shown in Figure 6.18. When she talks to her middle-school audience, she hopes students will pay attention to the colorful and interesting information contained in the poster.

Figure 6.18 Example of Information Graphic Source: http://makinghealtheasier.org/burntolearn

During her talk, Theresa points to relevant sections, being careful to attribute the graphic to the CDC. The slogan, 60-minute clock, and report card reinforce the message: Physical activity improves grades. The design and colors direct the flow of the message from the graphics to the text.

Some appropriate infographics can be found online; others may have to be created using design software such as Easel.ly or Piktochart. A more sophisticated infographic is the poster presentation, used in academic circles to display the major findings of a research project.

Tips for Constructing Graphs

- Avoid data overload. In general, limit pie wedges to seven and bar clusters and divisions to five. Use your judgment: If your graph looks busy to you, it's probably too busy for your reader.

- In general, begin vertical and horizontal axes at 0 to avoid distorting data. Exceptions include larger graphs with gaps in relevant data that would create extra white space. For these, visually split a line to discontinue the axis and pick up with a different number.

- Design infographics to include the most important information with relevant graphs in an attractive, balanced layout. Size varies. Most print versions are larger: 11" × 14", 48" × 96" (poster), or three- or four-panel display.

- Provide bibliographic information if an outside source was used.

Pie Graph

To represent what percentages of total daily food intake should consist of fat, protein, and carbohydrates, Theresa draws a pie graph, shown in Figure 6.19 on the following page. A **pie graph** is a circular graphic that shows how parts relate to the whole.

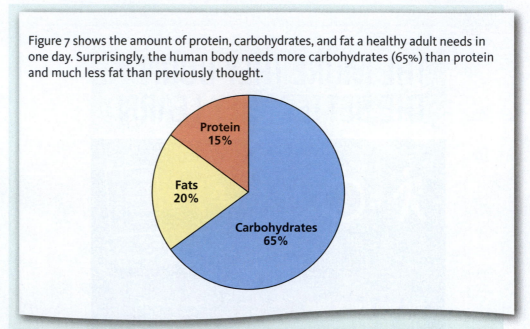

Figure 7 shows the amount of protein, carbohydrates, and fat a healthy adult needs in one day. Surprisingly, the human body needs more carbohydrates (65%) than protein and much less fat than previously thought.

Figure 6.19 Model of Pie Graph with Introduction

The whole totals 100 percent, with each piece of the pie representing a percentage of the whole. A pie graph should contain no more than seven sections. Notice the pieces of the pie move clockwise from the twelve o'clock position from largest to smallest, visually the most satisfying order for the wedges. Sometimes wedges are presented in a different order with a smaller one appearing before a larger one—but only if the logic in your text warrants. For example, the age ranges of a retirement neighborhood were presented in order of ages: < 15, 16–30, 31–45, 46–60, 61–75, 76 + . Even though the wedges representing ages 61–75 and 76 + were larger, they appeared last on the pie to sequence the age ranges.

The introduction repeats the actual percentages in the pie and points out the significance of those numbers. The readers of *Mind and Body* already know these percentages and do not need to be reminded of them. So Theresa decides not to use the pie graph for this more knowledgeable audience but does include it for her *Fitness* readers.

Theresa creates an **exploding pie graph** in Figure 6.20 for the readers of *Fitness* and *Mind and Body*. An exploding pie graph separates, or "explodes," one wedge from the circle, thus drawing attention to this piece of the pie. Theresa thinks that the younger readers need a reality check about consumption of soft drinks and that the *Mind and Body* readers should be alert to consumers' growing dependency on soft drinks.

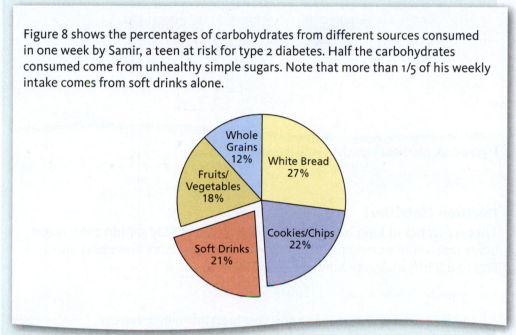

Figure 8 shows the percentages of carbohydrates from different sources consumed in one week by Samir, a teen at risk for type 2 diabetes. Half the carbohydrates consumed come from unhealthy simple sugars. Note that more than 1/5 of his weekly intake comes from soft drinks alone.

Whole Grains 12%

White Bread 27%

Fruits/ Vegetables 18%

Cookies/Chips 22%

Soft Drinks 21%

Figure 6.20 Model of Exploding Pie Graph with Introduction

Theresa explodes the soft drinks wedge by separating it from the rest of the pie and shading it orange to signal a dangerous overconsumption. Even with a few extra pieces and a separated part, any audience will be able to understand the pie easily.

Constructing Charts

A **chart** is a drawing with boxes, words, and lines to show a process or an organizational structure. Three popular charts include the flowchart, decision flowchart, and organizational chart.

Flowchart

Theresa wants a quick way to show the complex process of converting glucose to fat. She knows that the readers of *Mind and Body* already understand what happens to food the body does not use, but the readers of Fitness are unaware of this process. She chooses a **flowchart,** shown in

Figure 6.21, to illustrate this process to her less knowledgeable readers. In a flowchart, the lines and arrows show a process or series of steps. Theresa's introduction summarizes the process.

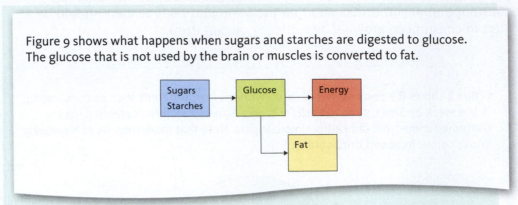

Figure 9 shows what happens when sugars and starches are digested to glucose. The glucose that is not used by the brain or muscles is converted to fat.

Figure 6.21 Model of Flowchart with Introduction

Decision Flowchart

Theresa wants to help her *Mind and Body* readers stay within their target heart rate while exercising. So she creates the **decision flowchart** shown in Figure 6.22 to illustrate how to adjust heart rates.

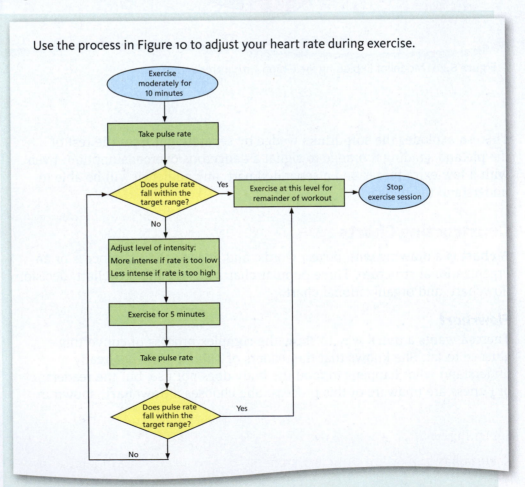

Use the process in Figure 10 to adjust your heart rate during exercise.

Figure 6.22 Model of Decision Flowchart with Introduction

A decision flowchart is a special flowchart that uses symbols to indicate critical parts of making a decision. Flowcharts should cover only the major steps involved in decision making, not the details. Include any important details in the discussion about the flowchart. Also, don't confuse your reader with too many symbols and provide a key for the symbols, if necessary.

Theresa uses standard symbols to indicate parts of the decision-making process: Ovals designate where the process starts and ends, rectangles or squares designate activities, diamonds designate places to make decisions, and arrows direct the flow of the process. Colors applied consistently signal critical parts of the process, but readers could understand the chart without color. The flow of information moves up and down and from left to right.

Organizational Chart

Theresa was asked to speak to a student body during an assembly. To make students aware of the school's Wellness Center, she creates an **organizational chart**. An organizational chart is a drawing with boxes, words, and lines to show how an organization is structured. Theresa's chart, in Figure 6.23, shows the hierarchy of the Wellness Center's employees.

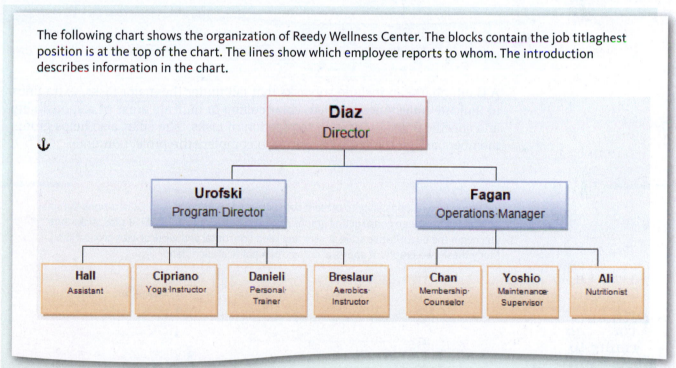

Figure 6.23 Model of Organizational Chart with Introduction

Gantt Chart

A **Gantt chart** is a bar graph used to schedule the major tasks of a complex project. Named for Henry Gantt, who developed it, the chart uses bars to depict the length of time needed to complete each task.

Theresa has been asked to chair a committee to organize a health fair for the retirees of her community. The team will meet in July to plan the fair, which will take place on September 23 and 24. At the second meeting, Theresa passes out the Gantt chart shown in Figure 6.24. Theresa's chart provides the schedule for completing the tasks. To make sure the committee will have everything accomplished by September 23, Theresa completed the schedule by working backwards—from the date of the fair back through time to the July planning meetings. Her chronological list shows that some later tasks are dependent on the completion of earlier tasks.

Planning Schedule for Health Fair September 23 and 24

Task	July	August	September
Plan Events	■		
Arrange Venue		■	
Contact Vendors	■		
Arrange Security		■	
Sign Vendor Agreements		■	
Advertise Event			■
Set Up Booths/Tents			■
Hold Health Fair			■

Figure 6.24 Health Fair Planning Schedule—Model of Gantt Chart

A Gantt chart can include subtasks that fall under the major tasks, extra lines to indicate milestones reached, color coding to indicate areas of responsibility, and specific dates to indicate completion of tasks. The chart also helps group members assign the tasks necessary to complete the project on time.

Writers have a responsibility to present data accurately without creating distortions that may be misleading. When constructing graphs drawn on horizontal and vertical axes, make sure you begin the quantitative scale at zero and keep horizontal and vertical axes proportional. Study these two graphs of approval ratings for a political candidate.

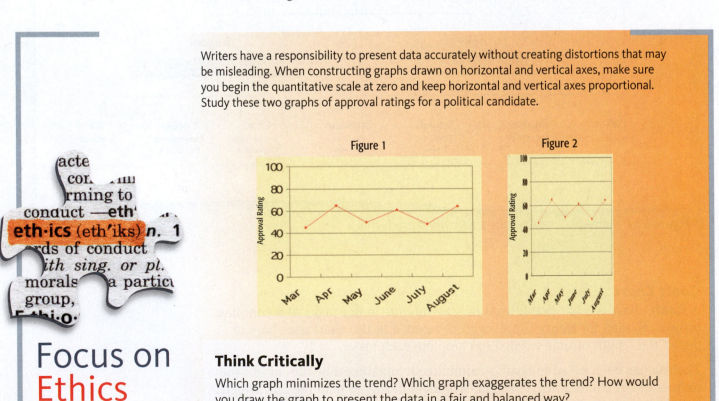

acte **con**... **rming to** **conduct** —**eth'**... **eth·ics** (eth'iks) *n.* 1 ...**rds of conduct** ...ith *sing.* or *pl.* **morals** a partic... **group,**

Focus on Ethics

Think Critically

Which graph minimizes the trend? Which graph exaggerates the trend? How would you draw the graph to present the data in a fair and balanced way?

Theresa keeps her chart simple. She presents it as a tentative schedule, realizing that the timeline may change. Also, because the schedule is not part of a written report but is simply distributed to the committee members for consideration, it has no figure title or number.

Constructing Diagrams and Pictures

Other choices for visual aids include diagrams, drawings, and pictures. A diagram, drawing, or photo shows how something looks or how it operates. Icons are used to give information quickly or direct a reader's attention.

Diagram

For her *Mind and Body* article, Theresa uses a **diagram**—a line drawing—shown in Figure 6.25 to show how triglycerides (fat) look in the bloodstream. She believes that her *Mind and Body* readers have the background for this information and hopes the diagram will reinforce the dangers of a diet that is high in fat.

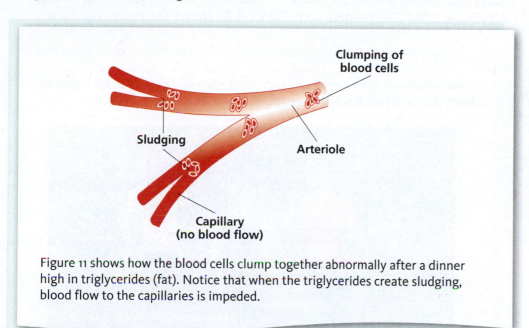

Figure 11 shows how the blood cells clump together abnormally after a dinner high in triglycerides (fat). Notice that when the triglycerides create sludging, blood flow to the capillaries is impeded.

Figure 6.25 Model of a Diagram with Introduction

Notice the use of **callouts,** names of specific parts of a diagram that are connected to the diagram or drawing with lines. The drawing represents a simplified version of the blood arteriole and capillaries. Adding other particles in the bloodstream would complicate the graphic. Here Theresa drew only what was needed to make her point.

Icon

An **icon** is a simple picture or drawing that represents an idea or a concept. Often the rendering uses clip art, drawings available for free or at a nominal cost. Some symbols such as the "no smoking" or "wheelchair accessible" signs are recognized worldwide. The symbols also can signal a recurring idea in a newsletter, brochure, or web app.

In her weekly blog, Theresa uses the icons shown in the margin. These icons will alert readers to the exercise tips and recipes. Using the icons, readers can turn to them immediately without reading the text to find the tips and recipes. Because the icons are simple symbols used to direct readers to text, they do not require figure numbers, captions, or titles. As symbols directing readers to certain types of information, they are not substitutes for research.

Photograph

A photograph can be inserted into a document when it is important to show in detail what something looks like. Photographs can also reveal emotion. To be effective, the photo should be clear and focus on a particular idea or message.

Theresa uses social media to promote a healthy lifestyle. Because she believes exercising with others encourages people to continue their exercise plan, she decides to post a photograph of coworkers taking a walk after work. Her photo also helps create the mood she is after, that is, depicting *Fitness* in a fun and positive way. Figure 6.26 shows the photo she chose.

Tips for Constructing Diagrams and Pictures

- Keep diagrams as simple as possible.

- Use simple, clear callouts for diagrams.

- Reproduce photos with sufficient pixels (at least 300 pixels per inch) to create crisp, clear images.

- Ask permission before publishing photos. Permission may not be necessary, but you will not know unless you ask.

Some workers at Sampsun Marine Industries, shown in Figure 6.2, get together every day for a walk through the park.

Figure 6.26 Photograph of Employee Walk with Introduction

STOP AND THINK 6.4

Which chart shows a process? an organizational hierarchy? the way something looks? What are the advantages and disadvantages of using a photograph?

CHAPTER REVIEW

Summary

1. To create effective document design, (a) use adequate white space, (b) use left justification with ragged-right edges, (c) use a 10- to 12-point serif font that mixes capital and lowercase letters, (d) determine a workable system of headings, (e) use highlighting techniques to draw attention to important information, and (f) consider appropriate media.

2. Graphics should be neat and placed in a convenient location for the reader (usually after they are first mentioned in the text). Graphics require an introduction, appropriate figure and table captions and numbers, a citation for the source when necessary, aligned decimals, and effective use of color. Graphics presented by themselves (as in a poster or a sign) do not require labels and numbers.

3. Each type of graphic has a purpose that can be matched to writing objectives and audience needs.

4. Effective graphics include informal, formal, and verbal tables; bar graphs, line graphs, pictographs, pie graphs, and infographics; flowcharts, organizational charts, Gantt charts; diagrams; icons; and photographs.

Checklist

- Have I determined my writing objectives and found a graphic to match?
- Have I designed my page with adequate white space, left justification and ragged-right edges, a 10- to 12-point serif font, capital and lowercase letters, a workable system of headings, and appropriate highlighting features?
- Have I selected appropriate graphics?
- Have I selected an appropriate medium for my writing objectives?
- Have I constructed the graphic neatly?
- Have I referred to the graphic properly as a table or figure?
- Have I placed the graphic in a convenient place for the reader?
- Have I provided a specific title for each graph, chart, and formal table?
- Have I numbered the graphics consecutively?
- Have I given credit for a graphic found in an outside source?
- Have I explained the significance of the graphic?
- Have I kept the graphic as simple as possible?
- Have I used color effectively?
- Have I constructed each graphic according to the required criteria for each?

Build Your Foundation

1. Examine several of your textbooks for design features. Describe each design. Which book has the best design? Why?

2. Create a slide presentation or scrapbook of graphics from newspapers, magazines, or websites. Using your checklist, decide whether the graphics present the data effectively. Note different types of graphics that may not be specifically covered in this chapter. Into which category of graphics does each fall?

3. Create a slide presentation with five infographics found online to share with your classmates. Rank them from most effective to least. Consider design elements such as color, type, and placement of graphics and how well they blend with or support the message. How useful is the information to your readers or to the general public? Include the source information in each slide.

4. Suggest the best graphic to use for presenting the following situations. In addition, try to construct the graphic.

   a. Lamar emailed his father and listed his latest test scores in calculus: Chapter 1, 83; Chapter 2, 79; Chapter 3, 92.
   b. Using a pedometer, Thanh compared the miles she walked during a school week to the miles she walked during her vacation. School: May 25, 1.3; May 26, 1.9; May 27, 2.7; May 28, 1.6; May 29, 2.5. Vacation: June 1, 0.6; June 2, 1.2; June 3, 0.9; June 4, 1.4; June 5, 2.0.
   c. Gahiji wrote his parents to tell them how he spent the $1,250 they gave him for his first month of college: $850, books and educational supplies; $65, snacks and pizza; $210, dorm accessories (rug, poster, bedding); $46, entertainment; $40, parking fine; $39, unspent funds.
   d. Crystal, head cashier for a grocery store, must show her coworkers the procedure for gaining approval for a customer check over $300: Inform the customer about store policy, verify the identity of the customer with a photo ID, ensure that the information on the check is correct, get two phone numbers from the customer, write your initials on the check, and call the manager to approve the check.
   e. Alessandra must show her physics instructor the structure of a hydrogen atom and the location of protons, neutrons, and electrons.
   f. Patrick is designing a travel brochure for future Peace Corps volunteers. He wants to show how eager students were to learn English in a Philippine village last summer.
   g. Sasha is giving a Prezi® presentation on the growth of fish farms in her state. Five years ago there were 120 farms; four years ago, 200 farms; three years ago, 250 farms; two years ago, 350 farms; and now, 560 farms. She needs an attractive opening slide.
   h. In July, Zach is collaborating with three other researchers to write an article for an academic journal. To be published in the December issue, the article must be accepted by October 10. To meet this deadline, Zach plans these tasks: review of literature conducted, draft written, draft sent to editor, draft sent to reviewers, draft revised, article resubmitted, and article published.

Your Turn

1. Write a brief article explaining the significance of a special photo. Incorporate the photo correctly into your article.

2. Convert the following survey information from 450 employees at GM Bio Tech into a pie graph. Top concerns include the following: 175 want a flex schedule, 50 want onsite child care services, 75 would like an exercise room, 50 want a lunch counter, and 100 want a merit-based salary system.

3. Use the information from Table 1 (following) to generate graphics. For each graph, write a brief introduction. Title and number each graphic properly.

   • A pie graph of the bottled water, diet soft drinks, and regular soft drinks consumed in 2005. Total the gallons of water and soft drinks and compute the percentages.

- A table citing the use of caffeinated beverages—including tea, coffee, diet carbonated, and regular carbonated—since 1980
- An informal table with the whole milk, other milk, and total milk consumed in 1975
- A bar graph showing the total number of carbonated beverages consumed from 1985 to 2010
- A double bar graph showing the consumption of tea and coffee since 1975
- A pictograph showing water consumption from 1990 to 2010
- A line graph showing the amount of bottled water consumed since 1980
- A double line graph showing the consumption for whole milk and other milk since 1975. Do you notice a trend? Explain.
- A multiple line graph showing the consumption of bottled water, diet carbonated drinks, and regular carbonated drinks consumed from 1985 to 2010. Do you see a relationship among this data? Explain.

2. Create a flyer or brochure to advertise an area event, to educate people on a topic, or to alert them to some danger in your area. Suggestions include an upcoming rabies clinic, evacuation routes, boating safety, a musical or charity event. Follow principles of document design and use graphics to convey meaning and support your message. Ask permission to post your document in appropriate places.

EXPLORE THE NET

The American Institute of Graphic Arts (AIGA) is a professional organization for design artists. Visit AIGA.com. What kinds of information does the site offer? Find one article about diversity in design, and tell three things you learned. Then fill in this blank with at least five verbs from the AIGA site: AIGA is celebrating 100 year of design that _____ .

Community Connection

1. Create an information graphic on a topic of interest for an organization in your community—such as medical center, school, or club. Use graphics software or attach your information and photos to a poster. Ask if you can display your information graphic.

Works Cited

Reeves, Rosser. *Reality in Advertising*. New York: Knopf, 1961.

Strong, Edward K. *The Psychology of Selling and Advertising*. New York: McGraw Hill, 1925.

Table 1 Beverage Consumption, 1975–2010

Beverage	1975	1980	1985	1990	1995	2000	2005	2010
Whole Milk	21	17	14	11	9	8	7	6
Other Milk	8	11	12	15	15	14	14	15
Tea	8	7	7	7	8	8	8	20
Coffee	31	26	27	27	20	26	24	23
Bottled Water	NA	3	5	9	12	17	26	29
Diet Soft Drinks	NA	NA	10	14	14	14	15	NA
Regular Soft Drinks	NA	NA	31	33	37	39	36	NA

All numbers rounded to the nearest gallon per capita.
Source: Adapted from USDA/Economics Research Service. "Food Availability Data System: Beverages." February 1, 2015.

7 WRITING FOR THE WEB

Goals

- Plan web pages
- Organize and design web pages
- Write text for web pages
- Write specialized web content

Terms

animation, p. 197
blog, p. 208
demographics, p. 192
discussion forum, p. 209
FAQ, p. 205
home page, p. 192
hyperlink, p. 194
interactive, p. 191
Internet, p. 191
keywords, p. 202
RSS, p. 208
satisficing, p. 192
scannable, p. 201
social media, p. 207
usability, p. 196
Web Accessibility Initiative (WAI), p. 198
wiki, p. 208
World Wide Web, p. 191

FOCUS

Focus on Writing for the Web

Read Figure 7.1 on the next page and answer these questions:

- What is the reason for the site?
- Describe the color scheme. How do the colors make you feel?
- Does the page look balanced? Why or why not?
- What information is on the page? Is it easy to find? Explain.
- If you were a newcomer to the site, which part would you visit? If you had visited the site before, which part might you revisit?
- What combination of text and graphics do you see?

What If?

How would the model change if. . . .

- The site provided FAFSA forms for different majors or different schools?
- An upcoming deadline was given for submission of FAFSA forms?
- The site highlighted college graduates who had used financial aid?
- The site hosted its own discussion forum?

Get help paying for college

Submit a Free Application for Federal Student Aid (FAFSA)

New to the FAFSA?

Start A New FAFSA

Returning User?

- Make a correction
- Add a school
- View your Student Aid Report (SAR), and more...

Login

College Scorecard
Information on college costs, graduation, and post-college earnings.

Deadlines
Information about your deadlines.

School Code Search
Find your college's school code. Also find detailed information about your college.

FAFSA Filing Options
Learn about the other options for filing your FAFSA.

Site Last Updated: Sunday, February 5, 2017

Announcements

- The IRS Data Retrieval Tool is unavailable at this time. We regret any inconvenience.

To fill out a FAFSA, you can manually input your tax

Thinking About College?

 Use *FAFSA4caster* to see how federal student aid can help you pay for college!

 Check out how Federal Student Aid can put you on a path to success. View Videos on *YouTube* or Download the Accessible Videos

Due to scheduled site maintenance, FAFSA on the Web will be unavailable every Sunday from 3 a.m. to 11 a.m. (Eastern Time). We apologize for any inconvenience this may cause.

FOIA | Privacy | Security | Notices

WhiteHouse.gov | USA.gov | ED.gov

 Figure 7.1 Sample Web page Source: https://fafsa.ed.gov/

Writing @Work

© Ingrid Breyer

CareerClusters®
PATHWAYS TO COLLEGE & CAREER READINESS
Hospitality & Tourism

Source: The Center to Advance CTE

Michael Luongo is an experienced and prolific freelance travel writer based in New York City. For ten years, he has been publishing his work in magazines, in newspapers, in books, and on the Web. He works with all kinds of publishers, from prestigious ones such as *The New York Times* to specialized and small ethnic publishers.

A versatile writer like Michael knows how important it is to adjust one's writing style and format for publication on the Web. His rule of thumb is that if you have to print something out to read it, it's too long to be readable on a screen. In addition, paragraphs in web articles must be shorter than they usually are in print.

"Think of ways to divide your work into pithy bits that are full of information and catchy," suggests Michael, "such as top tens and other 'listy' ways of writing." Michael also believes that avoiding the wordiness and punctuation of complete sentences increases readability and highlights the important content.

Web copy must also be interactive and clickable—full of words and images that contain links to other related material. According to Michael, "You want to make your work so clickable that a reader will lose all sense of time with it."

Michael's advice to those who want to publish on the Web is to start publishing on the Web. "Create your own website or blog first—since you can control it—and use your name or your specialty as a part of the website or blog name. You should always reserve your name. com as soon as you can." For example, Michael's website is www.michaelluongo.com. "It's your calling card; your portfolio; and, in my case, part of my dream work as a travel writer."

Think Critically

1. Do you agree with Michael about the length of writing on web pages? Explain.

2. Starting with Michael's advice in this feature, create a "top ten" list of rules and tips for writing on the Web.

Printed with permission of Michael Luongo.

Writing in Hospitality & Tourism

Event planners plan gatherings for a variety of occasions, such as week-long conventions and trade shows or evening celebrations and fundraisers. The job outlook is promising, with employment expected to increase 10 percent from 2014 to 2024 (Bureau).

Event planners market their services with both print and online media. Ads in the yellow pages, attractive brochures, business cards, and direct mail reach out to local customers. Other customers look for assistance online. Therefore, an inviting website and social media, particularly Pinterest and Facebook, describing services and posting photos are essential.

Successful promotion demands a concise style, persuasive writing skills, and a professional image to appeal to the logos and ethos of the audience.

To execute an event, entrepreneurs combine expertise in document design with thorough research. Designing theme sites, décor, and invitations calls for visual creativity. Knowledge of the audience—what's needed and wanted—is critical, for organizing a wedding entails different expectations from planning a Relay for Life fundraiser. Assessing customers' needs and evaluating the success of an event call for analytical skills. Staying organized and on top of all the details—the caterer, the entertainment, RSVP responses—can be aided with project management apps such as Planning Pod or Bizzabo.

7.1 GETTING STARTED ON WEB PAGES

How do you read a novel? How do you read a website? Do you read both in the same way, or do you read them differently? Explain.

Over 3.4 billion people worldwide, close to half the world's population, use the Internet (Miniwatts). Knowing how to write for these users will give you a critical advantage in the workplace. As a reader of Internet lore, you have first-hand experience of what works and what an online audience looks for; thus, your familiarity with web writing conventions will help you get started on your own web pages.

Although the terms *the Web* (for **World Wide Web,** a collection of online resources) and **Internet** are often used interchangeably, they are not synonymous. The Internet, a global system of networks, is the infrastructure on which the World Wide Web as well as other protocols, including e-mail and instant messaging, travel. Think of the Internet as the train track and the Web as one of the trains running on the track.

Reading Web Pages

Because of the **interactive** nature of the Internet, with pages that respond to user input, users read online material differently from the way they read printed text. People read books and magazines in a linear fashion from one page to the next. However, web readers scan pages across the top center, then down from left to right in the shape of an F, looking for keywords. Instead of turning pages, readers follow links, jumping from one page to another and one site to another, wherever their interests take them. In this way, readers control the flow of information, and no two readers read a website the same way.

On the FAFSA home page illustrated in Figure 7.1, the short, direct headline catches the reader's attention: "Get help paying for college." Two questions above the fold line (upper half of the page) start the discussion: "New to the FAFSA?" or "Returning User?" One student answers yes by clicking "Start a New FAFSA," and another answers no by clicking "Login for a Returning User." The interaction is more like a conversation as the web page communicates with different users in different ways. A viewer opens the conversation by accessing the site. The site, or its behind-the-scenes sponsor, poses topics for discussion by writing text and creating links.

Brand X Pictures/Getty Images

Online readers want speed and convenience. Most find ten seconds too long to wait for a page to load. If the site glitters with animation but does not give viewers the information they seek, they are not likely to return. Furthermore, readers prefer not to scroll horizontally (to the right) or too far vertically (down) to find information.

Web readers can be fickle but determined. They move ahead and then backtrack if they discover they were better off on the page before; therefore, the option to go back a page or back home means wrong turns can be corrected easily. Furthermore, memories are short; thus, links on each page and web browsing history remind readers where they've been. Surprisingly, they often overlook larger boxes and banners in favor of smaller textual links. Finally, their impatience leads to decisions by **satisficing,** a term coined by Herbert Simon to describe the tendency of a consumer to choose a quick solution that is good enough rather than invest time in figuring out the best solution.

To navigate quickly, readers pick up clues from one page to help them understand the next page. As a web writer, you must be familiar with these clues and adjust your writing to this different way of reading and accessing data. Indeed, the savvy web writer understands this reader, for he, too, has been in the reader's shoes.

Planning Web Pages

To write text for the Web, you need to think through the basics of planning a document: What is your purpose? Who is your audience? Your challenge is to achieve your purpose and meet the needs of your audience.

What Is Your Purpose?

In Chapter 2, you learned to determine the purpose of your writing early in the process and to use your purpose to guide you as you make decisions about your document. Here, too, determining your purpose is important. What do you want to happen as a result of this document? In other words, why does your website or web page exist? What is the reason for your post or discussion?

The purpose of most technical writing is to inform or persuade. In web writing, the purpose might expand to include other goals, such as offering a service, defining an image, soliciting opinions, creating a community, or entertaining people. One commercial site informs customers about cell phone plans, provides a service by recording minutes used, and persuades customers to purchase a smartphone. Your bank's website projects an image of a responsible, conservative institution. Facebook brings people together, and YouTube entertains as well as informs.

Effective sites establish their purpose on the **home page** (the first page of a website)—often as a slogan and photo. Overton's logo (a swirling blue O reminiscent of a wave) and slogan ("Launching Life on the River Since 1976") in Figure 7.2 clearly identify this company with boating and water sports. Blue reminds viewers of water, and the splashes of red along with the laughing faces support the company's image of a fun, outdoor lifestyle. With sales promotions, live chat, 1-800 number, tabs, and shopping cart conveniently located, Overton's is ready to take your order.

Who Are Your Readers?

Online readers come from all over the world, with English, Chinese, Spanish, and Japanese as the four most popular languages. The audience may include many readers looking for news headlines on CNN or a single stock broker looking for Exxon Mobil's performance in the S&P 500.

Defining the audience for your web-based project will help you get started on your writing. Who is your target audience? Describe this audience as specifically as you can. What are the **demographics**, or defining characteristics, of your audience? In other words, where do they live; how old are they; what is their income; are they male, female, married, or single?

Figure 7.2 Website with a Clear Purpose Source: http://www.overtons.com/

After you have defined your target audience, consider how you can best appeal to your audience. Ask yourself these questions:

- What information does my audience need, expect, and want?
- What will my audience do with this information?
- What appeals will convince my audience that my goods and services have value?

Some members of your audience will have the latest technology; others will not. When planning your site, consider monitor settings, Internet connection speeds, special requirements of tablets and smartphones, and browsers used by your target audience. Plan for a variety of technology setups—including PCs and Macs—and test your page in different browsers (for example, Internet Explorer®, Safari®, and Mozilla Firefox®). Recent development of responsive web design makes this task easier by adjusting scripts, resolution, and image size automatically to different devices.

Keep in mind anyone anywhere in the world can read whatever you put on a web page. You may think you are selling hand tools to the residents of southern Oklahoma, but do not be surprised to receive orders from China or Northern Ireland; thus, text and graphics should be designed with the international visitor in mind. The Internet is always open to anyone with a computer and an Internet connection.

STOP AND THINK 7.1

How do visitors read a page on the Web? What issues should a web designer be concerned about when planning a web page?

7.2 ORGANIZING AND DESIGNING WEB PAGES

Now that you have a clear purpose and a good understanding of your target audience, it is time to organize your material and design your page.

Organizing Web Pages

To begin organizing your website, use sticky notes or index cards to list everything you want to include—no more than one item or image per note or card. Group your items into similar categories, considering the importance of each idea to your users. Place your notes on a white board or bulletin board so you can move them around until you have an outline that works—with topics and subtopics. Your sticky notes become a story board, a visual organizer to help settle on a logical order for your topics. Common ways to organize information on a website are by category, task, product, date/time, or department.

Once you have an outline, you can figure out how to structure your website. A simple site may move forward in a linear fashion from one page to the next, similar to a flowchart. Other sites organize pages in a hierarchy, similar to an organizational chart or a hub-and-spokes configuration. In the hierarchy, information flows progressively from top to bottom from the home page to a second or third tier in increasing levels of detail. With the hub, information flows outward from a central point.

However you organize your pages, you will need a system of navigation. **Hyperlinks**, also called links, are a word, phrase, or graphic used to link,

Focus on Ethics

Claudia is setting up a website for her floral business, Claudia's Creations. She is in a hurry to get the site up and running. She wants to show some of the sprays, wedding bouquets, and dish gardens she has created, but she cannot find the pictures she took of them. So she searches the Web and finds designs that she likes on two websites: Floral Fantasia and Flowers by Chenda. Claudia decides to use some of the designs from those sites on her own website until she finds her misplaced pictures or takes new ones.

Think Critically

What might happen if Claudia's customers discover that she used flower designs from other sites?

or join, pages within a site or to an external site, allowing viewers to move easily from page to page. Depending on the browser settings, hyperlinks can be a different color, underlined, or graphical. The goal is to make information accessible in three or four mouse clicks.

External links can enrich a subject with information from another site and reduce content on a page. However, if you plan to use external links, inform your readers they are leaving your site and moving to another one. If you use an external link, make certain the link works. It is frustrating for viewers to click on a dead link that does not take them to the page you intended. There is no copyright infringement for providing links to other sites. However, it is illegal to provide a link to a site representing any form of illicit activity.

Not every site uses external links, but every site should include a clear system of internal links to take viewers to pages within the site. Without clear navigation, readers can get lost, wondering how to get back to a page they found interesting. Table 7.1 explains some common ways to provide internal links.

Table 7.1

Home Page Link	Takes user to the opening page of a site. A home page link should be on every page of a site.
Top/Previous or Next Page/Arrow	Helps readers go to the top of the page, back one screen, or forward to the next screen. Links may appear as text or as navigational arrows or pointers.
Jump Links	Enables readers to move immediately to desired information further up or down the page without scrolling. Such links allow users to "jump" to the top or bottom of the page or to various headings.
Breadcrumb Trails	Tracks pages the viewer has accessed—in order near the top of the page. The viewer can click any link in the trail to return quickly to a previous page.
Site Map or Index	Shows a hierarchal list (in words or phrases) of information on the site—similar to a table of contents. Users click a link to view a specific page quickly without having to sift through multiple levels of pages.
Navigation Bar	A list of links—words, tabs, or pictures—that span the top, sides, or bottom of a page and direct users to other pages.
Drop-Down Menu	A word or phrase that opens, or pulls down, a list of options when a user clicks the word or the arrow. Drop-down menus use space efficiently because the list of options is hidden and does not clutter the page.
Search	Allows the user to enter keywords and search for pages in the site. Search features save the user time.
Footer (Meets WAI Guidelines, Defined Later in the Chapter)	Links presented as small text at the bottom of the page—along with other pertinent data (phone numbers, copyright information, and mailing address).

Figure 7.3 illustrates links—including navigation bars, drop-down menus, various articles, and search features—on the home page of the National Endowment for the Arts website. A site map (not shown) appears in the footer of this page.

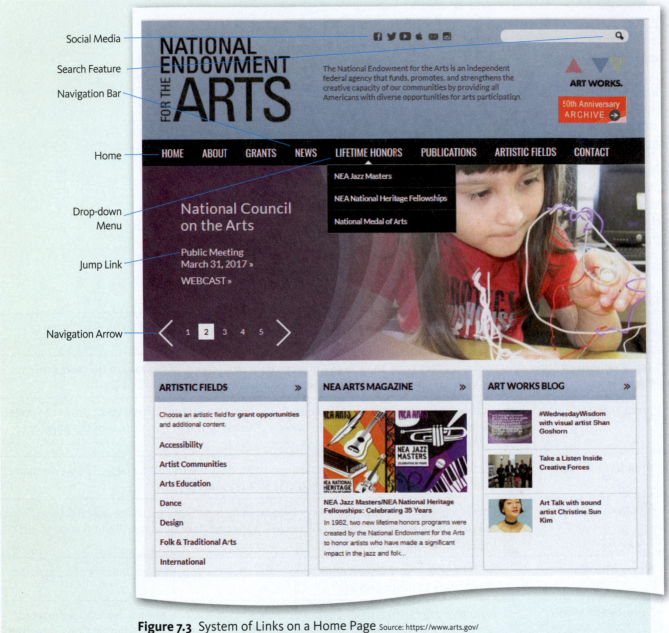

Figure 7.3 System of Links on a Home Page Source: https://www.arts.gov/

Designing Web Pages

If users do not have a good experience the first time they access a site, they may not return. Establish **usability**—the ease with which an audience can access and use a site—as your top design principle. In addition to ease of use, web pages should look attractive—uncluttered, symmetric, and inviting. Use the following principles when designing your website.

Header

Create a header, the banner spanning the top of a web page, to set the appropriate image and tone for your site. A site advertising scented candles may use a photo of lit candles, pastel colors, and a simple script font to create a relaxing scene. A site advertising sports cars, on the other hand, might use bright colors, a photo of a red Corvette, and a bold font to evoke excitement.

Page Layout

To help readers scan for information, organize information under relevant headings. If your page is long—more than a couple of scrolls–consider one of these options:

- Divide information into multiple shorter pages with corresponding links to those pages. This strategy works well when your content is different and potentially long enough to justify sending your viewer to another page, such as a vintage comic book site, which classifies comics by publishers (Marvel, DC, and others).

- Divide information by headings, and insert page jumps to those headings further down the page. Place a table of contents or list of topics in a single area of the page. This strategy works well if the information is so complex that breaking it up would distract the reader from the message. Wikipedia articles employ this system with a table of contents on the left side.

In either case, place the most important information for any page—the title, purpose, key navigational elements, and search features—near the top so readers see it before scrolling vertically. Do not set up pages so visitors have to scroll horizontally.

Line Length

A shorter line length reduces eye movement needed to scan the text. The ideal line length is approximately half the width of the screen, or between 50 and 70 characters (or 10 to 12 words) per line.

Graphics

Graphics break up the text, attract the reader's attention, and offer instant identification with the purpose of the website. Use graphics to provide visual relief, to support your content and image, and to create an attractive site. A site focusing on the fun and challenge of a rock-climbing club would not use a photo of a beginner halfway up a wall panicked at the prospect of rappelling back down.

Graphics take time to load, and too many graphics may discourage people from investigating a site. To speed up the download time of graphics, use one of the following formats for compressing files: GIF (Graphics Interchange Format) and JPEG (Joint Photographic Experts Group). Use smaller logos as opposed to larger background logos. If more detail is necessary, enable users to click the picture to see the full size.

Multimedia

Pages can use **animation** (text or graphics that move), audio, and video to direct the reader's attention. Although the movement and audio create interest, too much movement can distract your reader, so use multimedia sparingly. Furthermore, if the extra graphics result in the page taking a long time to load, you may lose visitors.

Tables and Grids

Use tables or grids to organize text and graphics. Rows and columns give the page a uniform, clean, professional appearance. Data can go inside cells, and one table can be nested inside another. Invisible tables form the skeleton that holds the site together. Use borders around the page or around the grids to draw boundaries between sections or omit borders for a more seamless look.

Fonts

Font sizes and styles affect screen legibility. Sans serif fonts are usually recommended for online text because they look more distinct on a screen. Avoid all capital letters and boldfaced blocks of text because these styles slow down the reader and are the equivalent of YELLING.

As with printed text, you can emphasize important words or phrases with boldface or italics as long as you do not overuse such tactics. Overuse will diminish the relative importance of each term you've selected for emphasis. Be wary of using underlining. Most viewers associate it with links and expect to be able to click to access another page.

Colors

Colors evoke a variety of emotional responses. When building a website, select color to create an inviting look to reflect the site's purpose. The color scheme should also take into account the target audience's cultural associations with color. For example, red, often associated with the devil in the United States, is the color of wealth and good luck in China.

Review, too, the color wheel and opt for colors that complement one another—for example, yellow and purple or blue and orange. Avoid too many colors and pick a neutral, white, or very dark background color with contrasting colors for the text. Accent colors can direct visitors to important content.

Consistency

You teach the user how to read your site by repeating certain patterns. Repetition allows readers to anticipate the site's structure. To achieve consistency, make sure your pages look similar and employ the same design features positioned in the same place on every page. A company name and logo that appears in the top left corner of one page, for example, should appear in the top left corner of every page. If the text is dark blue on a light blue background, do not experiment by changing the scheme on another page to dark blue text on a white background.

Accessibility

Plan a site that follows the Web Content Accessibility Guidelines (WCAG) 2.0. These guidelines are part of the **Web Accessibility Initiative (WAI).** Its goal is to make web content available to users with a wide range of disabilities, including visual and hearing impairments, learning disabilities, cognitive and movement limitations, speech disabilities, and combinations of disabilities. For example, alternative text descriptions for graphics and video captions enable visually impaired learners to read a web page.

The Vermont state page shown in Figure 7.4 illustrates the principles of good website design. It is organized with vertical and horizontal grids or panels with the largest panel slightly to the left of center. The panels are

Figure 7.4 Example of a Well-Designed Page Source: http://www.vermont.gov/

symmetric and consistent to give structure yet varied enough to generate interest. The name of the state is prominently displayed in large brown letters in the upper left corner under an outline of green hills. The banner across the top featuring orange, red, and gold autumn trees against gray-blue mountains sets the color scheme for the other borders, photos, and backgrounds on the site. Sans serif text using few words per line comprises informational links. Larger headings appear in dark serif font on a white background or white serif font on a dark background. To encourage efficient reader interaction, the site is packed with easy-to-identify links, including a small Home link, Help & FAQs, and opportunities to share the page. Accessibility links, a site map, and other information line the bottom of the web page (not shown here).

STOP AND THINK 7.2

List at least five design principles for the Web. How should color be used? What are some technology considerations?

How do you read a book? How do you read a web page? Do you read them the same way? Explain.

In many ways, writing for the Web is similar to writing text for any other technical document, except that a web page is viewed on a screen, not on an 8½" × 11" sheet of paper. The screen influences the appearance of pages in important ways. Writing scannable text will help your readers find what they need.

Strategies for Pages

Use the following strategies to keep your pages organized and focused on your audience.

Page Title

Come up with a short, descriptive title for your website—something visitors can read quickly in a browser title bar. Make every word count to identify your purpose in 80 characters or less. Give each page within the site its own short, descriptive title. On the Vermont website in Figure 7.4, for example, each page has a unique title, such as "Agriculture & Environment" and "Travel & Recreation." If you visit these pages, they will be listed in the order in which they were viewed under "History" in the browser window. If readers bookmark a page (or save to Favorites), the website and page titles are stored. Content-rich titles that identify what's on the site can optimize search engine results for your enterprise.

Audience

Know your target audience and write directly to that audience. Compare these two sentences from a job-hunting website for displaced workers:

Original: The JDW site has been set up to help displaced workers find jobs in their immediate geographical areas whether their expertise is in construction, sales, or engineering.

Revision: If you have lost your job, we can help—no matter what your area of expertise or where you live.

The original example talks about the website. The revised example talks to the reader, offering sympathy and help. It's your job to start the dialogue by reaching out to your reader and making her feel connected.

Inverted Pyramid

State important points before you provide detailed supporting information. An article appearing on the *Scientific American* site is written in an inverted pyramid organizational pattern. The title ("Strong Future Forecast for Renewable Energy") announcing the main idea is followed by the subtitle, which narrows the article down to the growth of certain types of energy, specifically wind and solar. From here, author Benjamin Hulac moves from most important to least, citing rising investments before he moves to specific initiatives from particular companies, interviews from key people, and obstacles to be overcome. The inverted pyramid allows viewers to see the most important content before they scroll down the page. This way, if viewers jump ahead without scrolling, they have been exposed to the most important information.

Typical Reader

A person anywhere in the world with a computer and an Internet connection who is scanning pages, clicking links, and expecting to find specific information quickly and easily.

Writer's Focus

Organizing information, writing scannable text, designing attractive pages, and providing users several ways to access the information.

Facts, Not Hype

To keep your web page as informative as possible, report facts and avoid the hype of an overdone sales appeal. People want information they can use.

> **Original:** Are you sitting at home wondering when you'll meet that special person? Skin Rejuvenation promises to restore skin scarred from acne or sun damage. Order your jar today and get ready for an adventure!

> **Revision:** Skin Rejuvenation moisturizer is easily absorbed, thereby reducing winter chafing by 15%.

Original Phrases

Avoid web clichés such as "Click here" or "Check out this site." A link can be easily made a seamless part of a sentence, as the following examples show:

> **Original:** Click <u>here</u> to learn how variations in temperature affect the success of gel coat application.

> **Revision:** Variations in <u>temperature</u> affect the success of gel coat application.

Standard English

Use standard English and follow rules of correct punctuation and usage. Nothing ruins the credibility of a web page—and its writer—more than errors.

Scannable Text

Except when the site posts an article or a resume, say as much as you can in as few words as possible. Your goal is to create **scannable** text to enable readers to locate important words and phrases—or keywords—quickly and effortlessly. To reduce words and make your text scannable, follow these suggestions.

Short Paragraphs

Write short paragraphs that stand out and can be quickly skimmed and absorbed, usually six to eight lines. A single, well-worded sentence can stand alone as a paragraph. See the visual relief in the thumbnail sketch in Figure 7.5 where one longer paragraph is separated into three.

Figure 7.5 Long versus Short Paragraphs

Short Sentences

While sentences can vary in length, aim for an average of 20 to 25 words per sentence. The revised sentence below is much clearer and easier to read when it is written as two shorter sentences.

> **Original:** Set in the rustic Craghill Mountains near the small town of Wilcox, Tennessee, Spring Village, conveniently located close to a transportation center, medical center, and cultural alcove, is a caring community for seniors.

> **Revision:** Set in the rustic Craghill Mountains near the small town of Wilcox, Tennessee, Spring Village is a caring community for seniors. It is conveniently located close to a transportation center, medical center, and cultural alcove.

Headings

Create short but informative headings to help readers identify topics and decide at a glance what they want to read. Headings also provide transitions to the next topic, alerting the reader to shift from one idea to another. For example, to help readers locate information in its web page, the Community Orchestra provides three headings: Upcoming Performances, How to Join, and Director's Notes.

Paragraphs to Lists

Use bulleted lists to break up paragraphs, reduce the amount of text, and emphasize important content. The following list of e-mail "don'ts" is easier to scan than the paragraph with the same information.

> **Original:** Respect your e-mail recipient's privacy and time by not sending chain e-mails. They are hoaxes and waste your reader's time. It is presumptuous to send attachments or other people's e-mail addresses unless you have permission to do so. Sending multiple postings to people who are not interested wastes time and takes up storage space. Finally, do not "Reply to All" unless it is necessary.

> **Revision:** To respect proper e-mail netiquette, don't

> - send chain e-mails.
> - send attachments or other people's e-mail addresses unless you have permission to do so.
> - send multiple postings to people who are not interested.
> - "Reply to All" unless it is necessary.

Keywords

To help search engines and your audience find your website, embed **keywords** in the first 50 words of your text. Keywords are important words, which describe particular content and subject areas. To quickly locate information, readers scan text looking for keywords and phrases. Keywords for a mythology website include *Joseph Campbell, The Hero*

Communication Technologies

Google Analytics is a free service from Google to track activity on your website to help you get to know your visitors. With Google Analytics, you can see who is visiting, where they come from, how they found your site, which pages they read, how long they stayed, what device they used to access your site, and how many bounced off after viewing only one page. After evaluating traffic patterns on your site, you can adjust content to increase activity. To help you learn how to use this tool, the Analytics Academy on Google's website offers training.

Thinking Critically

What are the implications of a high bounce rate for your site? What steps might you take to lower the bounce rate?

with a Thousand Faces, myths, hero, Departure, Initiation, Return, Call to Adventure, and Healing and Reconciliation. Which of the following versions does a better job of including more of these keywords in the first 50 words?

Original: Joseph Campbell compared myths of the hero from all over the world. He found similarities in the myths and identified twelve stages of the hero's journey. Below are Campbell's stages with short explanations. The explanations and stages are typical of the journey but may not be found in all [50 words] myths. The stories and their plots are similar, but the characters and circumstances differ. Campbell's work is compelling. For more information, see his landmark book *The Hero with a Thousand Faces* [75 words].

Revision: In his book *The Hero with a Thousand Faces*, Joseph Campbell identifies twelve stages in myths of the hero's journey. The journey takes place in three parts: hero's Departure, Initiation into the journey, and Return to improve society. From the Call to Adventure through Healing and Reconciliation, the hero receives Supernatural Aid [50 words], passes into the Darkness of the Realm of Night. . . .

In the original version, Campbell's book is not even mentioned until after 75 words into the passage. The second passage is more concise, relaying significant information and key phrases in every sentence.

All of these suggestions have one goal—to make relevant information easily available.

 STOP AND THINK 7.3
Explain three overall writing strategies for web pages. Explain five ways to write scannable text.

Describe your experiences with two of these situations: (1) choosing a theme for a prom, a dance, a reunion, or a holiday event; (2) keeping a journal; (3) answering the same questions over and over; (4) collaborating on a project; or (5) writing posts on Facebook.

The Web offers a new medium for established ways of communicating. The type of writing is not altogether new, but when the audience and medium change, good writers adapt. The result? New avenues of writing for existing genres. Six of these adaptations are outlined next: home page, blog, FAQ, wiki, social media, and video sharing.

Home Page

Think of your website as a theme park. Your park may have many areas—rides, a petting zoo, edutainment, restaurants, and more, or only a single nature trail. The home page of your website is like the entrance to the park. Because you want many visitors, you design an inviting entrance, one that reflects the theme and offers basic information to help people navigate the site. Like a home page, there may be several ways to get from one area to the next inside the park. The following tips can help you develop text for a home page:

- **Create a headline and slogan or subheading.** Get the reader's attention and announce your purpose. How can a visitor benefit from your product or service? A meaningful title and catchy slogan can brand the site, establishing product and company recognition at a glance. For example, a website devoted to video production replaced its title and slogan with something more appealing, as follows:

    Original: Title "Videographer" with slogan "We offer expert video productions."

    Revision: Title "Keepsake Video" with slogan "Keeping your memories alive."

- **Write a short introduction and conclusion.** The introduction explains the purpose of your website and, most importantly, how your audience can benefit from your merchandise. The conclusion brings the page to a close. Consider the introduction and conclusion on the Keepsake Videos site.

    Introduction: "Need your event captured for posterity? We offer professional video production services for your special event."

    Conclusion: "Allow us to help you preserve your special moments."

- **Consider adding short articles.** You may want to include Frequently Asked Questions (FAQs), tips, or a blog on your website. On the Keepsake Video site, a FAQ answers questions about the video process, tips suggest ways to stage a production, and a weekly blog describes the latest trends.

- **Consider adding links suited to your business.** Add items typically used to market your enterprise, such as a gallery, testimonials, games, special sales, or social media. Keepsake Video included a gallery of short films and testimonials from satisfied customers and added a link to Facebook and Instagram.

■ **Include essential information.** A home page should incorporate the following information:

- Contact information telling readers how to communicate with the owner of the site—e-mail, phone number, and/or street address.

- A logo or graphic that helps "brand" the site, creating product and company recognition at a glance.

- An About section describing the organization and providing some of its history.

- A system of navigation to help readers find their way around the site.

- A date (usually at the bottom) showing the last time the site was updated.

- Any disclaimers or privacy/security statements—what kind of information may be collected by the site and what monitoring systems may be in use to track information.

Figure 7.6 shows the home page of Hold Fast Custom Builders, a small construction business. Its design is simple, yet it has all the characteristics of an effective home page: a logo slogan, appropriate photos, and essential information.

Figure 7.6 Example of a Home Page Source: Hold Fast Custom Builders

FAQ

FAQ, pronounced *fak* or *f-a-q*, is an acronym for *Frequently Asked Questions* (and *Frequently Answered Questions*). A FAQ is what its name implies— questions asked often enough to warrant publishing so other people can benefit from the answers. For an archive of FAQs, visit the Internet FAQ Archives online.

You may want to use a FAQ for a website. If you routinely respond to customer service calls, written FAQs can help you answer questions about your product.

To compile a FAQ,

- Determine the most frequently asked questions. What do your readers ask? What do your customers ask? What do they want to know?

- Ask the question the way your readers will ask the question. Use the readers' terms—the readers' vocabulary.

- Set up a consistent format to set questions apart from the answers—perhaps boldfacing questions and providing adequate white space between questions and answers.

- Keep the answers relatively short. One or two sentences is preferable, but no more than a couple of paragraphs. Embed links to other pages on your site or to external sites for more detailed information. Organize questions in order of importance or in chronological order for your reader.

- Proofread for clarity and correctness to keep your FAQ professional.

- On a website, place the FAQ where your readers can easily find it—in links on the side, at the bottom, near Help items, or close to information about which readers may be curious.

- Update your FAQ periodically to keep the information current.

Communication
Dilemma

Julian Mills, a local politician and long-standing member of the Sandhills community, is on the Board of Trustees for Hope Center Hospital. He maintains a blog on his political initiatives, including the construction of the hospital's new cardiac wing. So far, he has expressed concern over the cost of the wing, delays, and decisions about equipment. Overall, though, he supports the construction and is proud to have played a role in such a state-of-the art facility. A local reporter, Sabrina Klein, also keeps a blog about area events. Her husband happens to be an architect for the company contracted to build the cardiac wing. In her blog, Sabrina criticizes Julian, saying, "Mr. Mills . . . nitpicks about decisions and micromanages the day-to-day operations of the board. He knows nothing about construction and is clearly pushing a political agenda. He should step down from the board." Julian, understandably angered by the remarks, wonders what, if anything, he should do about the remarks.

Think Critically

What factors should Mills consider before he decides whether to respond?

7.5 SOCIAL MEDIA CONTENT

Social media is web-based software that allows users to share content with others in an online community. These sites include popular ones such as Facebook and Pinterest as well as blogs, wikis, discussion forums, and even video sharing.

Popular Social Media

The popularity of Facebook, Pinterest, and Twitter offers opportunities for marketing and networking. While advice for writing in all social media is similar, you should investigate the site's particular advantages and adjust content accordingly. For example, Twitter's posts are limited to 140 words or less, Pinterest depends heavily on photos, and Facebook adds new features, such a professional connections and groups, frequently. All offer ways for viewers to interact with each other via the web.

Consider the following suggestions to market your product or service using social media:

- Craft a compelling headline to stimulate curiosity.
- Upload an attractive and interesting photo(s) to create a desire or need.
- Write directly to your reader in a conversational style. For example, contractions and second person "you" contribute to a friendly and natural tone. Target your audience by setting up groups with common interests.
- Avoid inflammatory or inaccurate posts that would harm your credibility.
- Share links to articles or other sites to educate followers.
- Interact with others to connect with potential clients and professional partners. Build goodwill by complimenting other posts and adding thoughtful, authentic comments.

Notice how the Small Cakes Facebook page in Figure 7.7 creates desire for baked goods with photos of cupcakes, iced and decorated.

Figure 7.7 Appealing Facebook Photo for Small Cakes Source: https://www.facebook.com/smallcakesgreenvillenc/

Blogs

Similar to a journal or diary, a **blog** (short for *weblog*) is a website with periodic commentary or news posted in reverse chronological order. A blogger is usually an individual with special knowledge or passion about a topic. Because viewers can respond, a blog is not only a source of information but also an online community. In addition, a blog may include links and graphics.

There are as many blogs as there are content areas. A doctor posts her administrative struggles, a news reporter posts commentaries about the day's events, and a businessperson posts progress on the development of a new product. The writing style used on a blog is informal. As with any web material, blogs should be read with a critical eye. Some blog conversations provide current, credible, and insightful news. Others merely vent and ramble.

Many platforms house blogs for the average person, including LiveJournal, Blogger, Wordpress, and Tumblr. To post an informative and reputable blog,

- Write blogs on topics you know about or about which you are passionate. Compose meaningful, accurate articles focused on satisfying a desire or need for information.

- Lend credibility to your posts by including your credentials—your experience, expertise, degrees, awards, or special expertise.

- Contribute regularly to build a following, but do not overwhelm readers with too many posts.

- Create an easy-to-remember short name that represents you and/or your subject.

- Communicate with people on other blogs to generate interest.

- Make your blog site attractive and interesting with appropriate color and photos.

- Let your personality come through in your photos and natural writing style.

- Use **RSS** (Really Simple Syndication), a standardized web feed format to send the content of your blog directly to your followers so they will not have to visit your website to get updates.

Wikis

A **wiki** uses special software that allows a number of users to collaboratively author web pages, usually according to a set of guidelines. Some wikis, such as Wikipedia and Familypedia, provide open access to anyone. Other wikis are closed, and only people granted access can contribute. AskDrWiki, for example, is a medical wiki which allows only professionals to edit content. A wiki can foster creative collaboration for a process, such as programming code. Writers use wikis, too, to post articles and allow other writers to edit them.

If you are interested in participating in a wiki,

- Read several articles so you know how the text is written and edited.

- Become familiar with the process for editing articles in the wiki.

- Keep your tone neutral, polite, and civil—even when you disagree.

- Work toward consensus as you edit.

- Include references for information from other sources.

Discussion Forums

Operating like an electronic bulletin board, a **discussion forum** is a place where users can discuss items of interest or get specific questions answered. On the Apple website, for example, a discussion forum attempts to answer questions about Apple products and applications. A person who is having difficulty downloading iTunes might post a question and receive responses through this forum. Online discussion forums exist for nearly every topic imaginable—the stock market, art, architecture, business, family, science, and more. The major news networks house online discussion forums. In addition, forums can be found on Google Groups and are an integral part of online classes.

To interact with a discussion forum on a topic of interest,

- Read other posts to see how people generally respond.

- Supply as much information as possible when posting a concern or opinion.

- Provide accurate information when responding to a concern or opinion.

- Think critically about others' responses. Not every response is credible.

- Practice good technical writing style with succinct, correct, and respectful prose.

Whatever kind of text you write for the Web, keep in mind two guiding principles—the needs of your readers and the limited space on the screen. To keep readers engaged, design attractive sites that support your message and deliver concise, valuable information.

Video Sharing

The option to create and share video has turned many into amateur production artists. Two sites in particular, YouTube and Vimeo, host short videos for entertainment and education. A technical writer might be asked to write a script for a video presentation. Suitable subjects for filming include testimonials, how-to guides, and virtual tours. Follow these suggestions to write text for a short, five- to six-minute video:

- Choose a clever, short title for your video.

- Create a storyboard, a list of video segments you'll need for the video. You might try sticky notes with one shot per note or notes pinned to a bulletin board. Move them around until you have found the best order. Number or label each shot.

- Write the script for each shot. Be sure the correct script goes with the corresponding visual.

  - Use the language your audience is mostly likely to understand. Most people viewing a video for instructional purposes lack prior knowledge of the topic.

- Use an informal style. The speaker(s) are talking to the viewer, not lecturing. Write directly to your audience, using the pronoun *you* and keeping sentences relatively short.

- Motivate your reader with positive comments about her ability to complete the video task. Interject humor when appropriate.

- Let the video do the "talking" when possible. Sometimes too many spoken words can detract from the action in the film.

■ Consider adding closed captioning to address WAI guidelines.

■ Add production information, such as who produced the video, what sources were used, who is in the video, how long it lasts, and the date of production.

 STOP AND THINK 7.4

Name five types of writing assignments adapted especially for the Web. Choose two and describe them in detail.

7 CHAPTER REVIEW

Summary

1. When creating a web page, know how users read and interact with material, determine your purpose, define your audience, and find out the technology limitations of your audience.

2. When organizing and designing a web page, choose a system of navigation, assign headings, create attractive web pages that are easy to use, and maintain a consistent and accessible design.

3. When writing web pages, create unique page titles, write to your audience, organize using an inverted pyramid, compile factual content, use original language, write standard English, and construct scannable text. Write short paragraphs and sentences, organize information under headings, and use lists and keywords.

4. When writing home pages, blogs, wikis, FAQs, or social media posts, follow established protocols.

Checklist

- Have I defined my audience?

- Have I written web pages that adjust to the unusual way readers read them?

- Have I considered the technology limitations of my audience?

- Have I determined my purpose and included it in a slogan on the website?

- Do my text and graphics support my purpose?

- Have I organized my website using a workable system of internal links?

- Have I designed attractive web pages with easy-to-locate information for visitors to my site?

- Do my pages load quickly?

- Have I written text that uses unique page titles, is written directly to my audience, organizes material in an inverted pyramid, is factual, avoids clichés, and uses standard English?

- Have I written scannable text with short paragraphs, informative headings, lists, and keywords in the first 50 words?

- Have I followed standard protocol for my home page, blog, FAQ, wiki, and discussion forum?

Build Your Foundation

1. Rewrite these sentences, breaking them into shorter sentences and deleting extra words.

   a. We offer Spanish tutorials and practice for the beginner as well as the intermediate Spanish learner on a variety of topics so a traveler can feel comfortable traveling in a Spanish-speaking country.

   b. Take time to visit our website at www.homedezigns.com to see the latest collection of living room, bedroom, and kitchen furniture along with accessories such as lamps, vases, and art—from contemporary to traditional.

   c. Because water conservation is important, there are many ways people can help conserve water, including taking showers instead of taking baths and running the washer and running the dishwasher only when they are full.

   d. Spruce up your resume, network with the right people, and organize your job search to increase your chances of finding a job so it does not take you the normal four to six months to find one.

2. Brainstorm possible slogans, color schemes, graphics, and links for one of these sites. Conduct research if you need to familiarize yourself with the type of business. Share your written plan with the class.

   a. Nehu's Chiropractic Care, new to the area, wants a site that describes services and teaches the public about the value of chiropractic care.

   b. Krischler's Insurance Services offers personal and commercial policies, including car, home, long-term care, life, and commercial, for a small community.

   c. Beach Getaway is a real estate agency specializing in ocean view rentals for family vacations.

   d. Eastern Music Company sells musical instruments to school bands.

   e. Helping Handz is a charity organization in North Dakota that collects winter coats for children in grades K–12.

3. Improve the following block of text by breaking it up into three paragraphs and shortening some of the sentences.

   Global warming—the explanation goes something like this: Energy from the sun heats the earth, and then some of that energy is sent back into space in the form of infrared radiation. A portion of that outgoing radiation, though, is blocked from escaping into space by the earth's relatively thin atmosphere—a good thing because the infrared radiation that remains stabilizes the earth's temperature. A problem occurs when the atmosphere, subjected to increasing amounts of carbon dioxide and other greenhouse gases, thickens to trap more of the sun's infrared energy, preventing its escape from Earth. More trapped energy raises global temperatures—thus the term *global warming*. Global warming can drastically alter the climate. The predictions are frightening: melting polar ice caps, rising ocean levels, category 5 hurricanes. Are these dire predictions true? Are we really in a period of global warming? The body of scientific evidence does suggest that global warming is a reality.

4. Go to "About Wikipedia" to learn more about this open source wiki. Make a list of what you learn.

5. On the FAFSA home page are links to how-to videos assisting students with the financial aid process. View and evaluate how well one of these videos achieves its purpose. Rate the video with one to five stars (with five stars representing the best) and explain your verdict.

Your Turn

1. Create a sketch of a home page on a topic of interest. Draw your page, cut pictures out of magazines, download art, include names or graphics for relevant links, and come up with the slogan. If you are familiar with HTML code or a web authoring system such as WordPress, Weebly, or Wix, design the page yourself.

2. Find two websites—one that follows most of the guidelines presented in the chapter and

one that does not. Write a one-page analysis explaining why one website is more effective than the other. Use bulleted lists to set up your comparison and introduce each list with a couple of sentences.

3. Write a FAQ on a topic of your choice. Choose from your school, your major, your job, or any topic with which you are familiar.

4. Use the following topic to practice the collaboration required by a wiki. Working with four of your classmates, enter the passage in a word processor. Send the file to each member of your group—perhaps over several days. Each person should find one or two errors and add one or two pieces of information to make the passage more interesting. Remember to provide references if you quote or introduce new information.

Henry David Thoreau was born July 17, 1812, and died May 6, 1862. He was an American poet, essayist, naturalist, and song writer. He was a strict abolitionist. His transcentral views can be seen in his lectures and most notably in his book *Weldene*. Perhaps his most influential work is "Civil Disobedience," which was inspired by his time spent in Portugal. "Civil Disobedience" influenced such political leaders as George Washington, Martin Luther King, and Mahatma Gradson.

5. For this mock wiki, work in groups of five. In your group, pass around the terms one at a time—perhaps over several days. Each person defines two terms and adds one or two pieces of information or deletes information deemed inaccurate, vague, poorly worded, or unnecessary.

| blog | wiki | breadcrumb trails | Wikipedia |
| RSS | hyperlink | discussion forum | keywords |

6. Write a discussion response to these questions: How has the Internet helped you in your education? What have you learned from this chapter?

7. Write a FAQ about a topic related to your school or community—such as how to establish residency, how to join a community group, or how to select an area restaurant. Ask if your FAQ can be placed on the organization's website or place your FAQ in a central location such as a bulletin board.

Community Connection

1. Help your neighbors lower their monthly bills—maybe energy, food or transportation costs. Use a government- or university-sponsored website to research your topic. Write a list of "Top 10 (or choose another number) Ways to Lower _____" or "10 Ways to Improve _____." Use e-mail or social media to get the word out.

2. Create a Facebook page for a charity or a community event. Choose an appropriate banner and photo. Insert links to other site or articles about the charity.

EXPLORE THE NET

Join a discussion group on Google Groups you find interesting. Respond using the strategies presented in the chapter. Print your responses and submit them to your instructor.

Works Cited

Bureau of Labor Statistics. "Meeting, Convention, and Event Planners." *Occupational Outlook Handbook*, 15 Dec. 2015, https://www.bls.gov/ooh/business-and-financial/meeting-convention-and-event-planners.htm. Accessed 12 Mar. 2016.

Hulac, Benjamin. "Strong Future Forecast for Renewable Energy." *Scientific American.* Rpt. from Climatewire with permission from Environment & Energy Publishing. 27 Apr. 2015, https://www.scientificamerican.com/article/strong-future-forecast-for-renewable-energy/. Accessed 12 Jan. 2016.

Miniwatts Marketing Group. *Internet World Stats.* 28 Feb. 2017, http://www.internetworldstats.com/surfing.htm. Accessed 3 Mar. 2017.

8

INFORMATIVE REPORTS

Goals

- Write two types of summaries and an abstract
- Create a mechanism description with a visual and a process description
- Write a periodic report, a progress report, and a news release

Terms

Write to Learn

Think about where you are on the path of your educational goals. Perhaps your career will require a two-year associate or a four-year bachelor's degree—or a master's or doctorate degree. Write several paragraphs answering these questions: What have you achieved toward reaching your educational goals? What do you still need to do to reach those goals? When will you reach your goals? What problems are you experiencing? Your audience can be your parents or guardians, a scholarship committee, or other people who have supported your educational career.

FOCUS on Informative Reports

Read Figures 8.1 and 8.2 on the following pages and answer these questions:

- What is the purpose? Does the writer ask the reader to do anything?
- Can you determine the audience for whom each of these reports was intended?
- What would make the reports more useful and easier to read?
- In what fields might reports of this nature be needed?

What If?

How would the model change if . . .

- The readers were lacking in background knowledge?
- The subject of the technical description were an object, not a process?
- The process description were more complex and longer?

Technical Process Description: How a Surge Protector Works

Nominal voltage for most common electrical devices is 120 volts. A surge protector is used to protect electrical equipment from transient surges and spikes which exceed the nominal voltage limits of connected equipment (i.e., a TV) and can cause catastrophic failure of sensitive internal components.

Normal Flow

When supplied voltage is within "normal" ranges, electricity flows through the ungrounded "hot" wire in the surge protector, through the appliance, and back through the neutral wire in the surge protector, thus completing the circuit. A component called a metal oxide varistor, or MOV, diverts the extra voltage to the grounding wire during a surge or spike; during normal flow, the MOV in the surge protector does nothing.

Surge of Duration

When a surge occurs, the voltage significantly exceeds our required level (120 volts, in this example). Surges can be caused by inconsistency or failure of power company equipment, a vehicle accident which takes out a nearby transformer, or a lightning strike. The MOV in the surge protector will redirect the excess voltage to ground, thereby preventing it from reaching and damaging the connected equipment. In the event a sustained spike occurs, a fuse or circuit breaker in the surge protector will become overloaded (by design) and blow or trip, completely severing the power circuit and preventing the excess current from reaching the connected device(s).

Figure 8.1 Technical Process Description: How a Surge Protector Works

Process Description: Clinical Development of Noroviruses

Noroviruses cause acute gastroenteritis in persons of all ages. The illness typically begins after an incubation period of 12–48 hours and is characterized by acute onset, nonbloody diarrhea, vomiting, nausea, and abdominal cramps. Some persons might experience only vomiting or diarrhea. Low-grade fever and body aches also might be associated with infection, and thus the term "stomach flu" often is used to describe the illness, although there is no biologic association with influenza. Although symptoms might be severe, they typically resolve without treatment after 1–3 days in otherwise healthy persons.

However, more prolonged courses of illness lasting 4–6 days can occur, particularly among young children, elderly persons, and hospitalized patients. Approximately 10% of persons with norovirus gastroenteritis seek medical attention, which might include hospitalization and treatment for dehydration with oral or intravenous fluid therapy. Norovirus-associated deaths have been reported among elderly persons and in the context of outbreaks in long-term–care facilities. Necrotizing enterocolitis in neonates, chronic diarrhea in immunosuppressed patients, and postinfectious irritable bowel syndrome also have been reported in association with norovirus infection; however, more data from analytic studies are needed to confirm a causal link with these conditions.

Norovirus is shed primarily in the stool but also can be found in the vomitus of infected persons, although it is unclear if detection of virus alone indicates a risk for transmission. The virus can be detected in stool for an average of 4 weeks following infection, although peak viral shedding occurs 2–5 days after infection, with a viral load of approximately 100 billion viral copies per gram of feces. However, given the lack of a cell culture system or small animal model for human norovirus, whether these viruses represent infectious virus is unknown, and therefore the time after illness at which an infected person is no longer contagious also is unknown. Furthermore, up to 30% of norovirus infections are asymptomatic, and asymptomatic persons can shed virus, albeit at lower titers than symptomatic persons. The role of asymptomatic infection in transmission and outbreaks of norovirus remains unclear.

Excerpt from United States. Dept. of Health and Human Services. Centers for Disease Control and Prevention. *Morbidity and Mortality Report Weekly:* Recommendations and Reports. "Updated Norovirus Outbreak Management and Disease Prevention Guidelines." 60.3, 4 Mar. 2011: 1–11. Web. 27 Feb. 2016.

Figure 8.2 Technical Process Description: Clinical Development of Noroviruses
Source: United States. Dept. of Health and Human Services. Centers for Disease Control and Prevention. Morbidity and Mortality Report Weekly: Recommendations and Reports. "Updated Norovirus Outbreak Management and Disease Prevention Guidelines." 60.3 4 Mar. 2011. 1–11. Web. 27 Feb. 2016.

Paige Heller is a physical therapist at an outpatient orthopedic clinic in Sedona, Arizona. She treats patients daily and provides written documentation for each visit, including daily evaluation notes, periodic progress reports, and discharge summaries.

Paige's writing must be clear and concise, yet thorough and rich in detail. "A good physical therapy document needs to be readable by a varied audience that includes the patient, other physicians, and employers. These reports may also be used for legal purposes, so they must include large amounts of information in a small amount of writing."

To write a report that is brief and that contains all necessary information, Paige follows the "SOAP" formula for writing bulleted clinical notes. Each letter stands for its own bulleted item in the note:

- S stands for subjective—the first bullet states what the patient reports.
- O stands for objective—the second bullet states what the therapist observes and tests.
- A stands for assessment—the third bullet is an analysis of the S and O points.
- P stands for plan—the last bullet is a future/intended course of treatment.

Just as Paige writes her reports so they are useful for other practicing therapists and physicians, she must read others' reports in order to provide the most advanced and tested treatment possible. "Physical therapy is an evidence-based practice, which means we dictate our treatments according to the results of research and studies in the field. I frequently access online medical journals to review such reports. I also read physician reports of surgeries or diagnostics to better understand a patient's condition or injury." In other words, Paige's technical writing proficiency depends in part on her technical reading skills. In turn, other physical therapy professionals rely on Paige's technical writing ability, which is why accurate documentation is so important.

Writing @Work

Courtesy of Paige Heller

Health Science
CareerClusters
PATHWAYS TO COLLEGE & CAREER READINESS

Source: The Center to Advance CTE

Think Critically

1. Why are the S and O bullets critical in Paige's physical therapy reports?

2. Why is the A bullet needed? Why is it important to assess the first two bullets?

Printed with permission of Paige Heller

Professionals who work and write in the fields of health sciences must be measured, precise, and careful in what they write. While the professional may seem to have one primary audience, such as a physician writing a medical note on an injured patient for her physical therapist, the professional must bear in mind that many other readers may use the medical notes. For instance, other members of the patient's healthcare team may read the note for implications related to their areas of treatment, the health insurance staff may read it for use in determining eligibility for benefits, and lawyers advocating for and against the patient's receiving disability benefits may use the notes. The writer would not want to create problems or unjust perceptions. In addition, most writers in healthcare professions need to write concisely; many forms, which often do not allow a great deal of space, are used, and readers in the fields expect essential information to be given clearly and directly. Further, a professional lexicon is imperative. Professionals in healthcare will use a specialized vocabulary and will expect others in the field to understand and use the same kind of professional language.

Writing in Health Science

8.1 GETTING STARTED ON INFORMATIVE REPORTS

Recall the last movie or play you watched. How would you respond if a friend asked, "What was the show about?" Using what you remember about the show, write the answer you would give to your friend.

Professionals in business and industry use specialized reports to convey information about their work. This chapter presents the most frequently used informative reports: summaries and abstracts, mechanism and process descriptions, progress and periodic reports, and news releases. These specialized reports use standard forms. Once you learn how to use them, you can develop reports using information from jobs or personal experience.

8.2 SUMMARY AND ABSTRACT

Typical Reader

Any person, whether manager, technician, or client/customer, who wants access to an overview of more detailed information, whether a company report, a journal article, a book, or another document.

Writer's Focus

Clearly presenting major ideas and, when needed, essential supporting information in a readable manner to enable users to understand the central points of a longer document.

A **summary** is a condensed version of a document. When writing an essay, you generate details to develop or support a thesis and topic sentences. Summaries require writers to do the opposite: Keep only general information and the most important details.

Abstracts are more condensed than summaries, often reducing documents to a thesis. The length depends on the audience's needs and expectations.

Some summaries and abstracts stand alone; others begin a longer technical document. By condensing the report's highlights before the audience reads the details, summaries save the audience time. People at upper levels of an organization may choose to read only the summary sections of longer reports. They do so because their interest is in the big picture or health of the organization rather than the details or technical aspects of day-to-day operations.

Some employees use summaries to stay on top of the latest research and developments in their fields. These employees summarize publications in the career field as they emerge and file them for future reference.

To write a summary or an abstract:

a. When an oral presentation is given, take notes during the presentation or soon afterward. Thus, you are less likely to forget what the speaker said.

b. With a written document, read the document twice—or as many times as necessary to fully understand the content. As you read the second time, highlight the main ideas or cross out everything (all details) except the main ideas. Paraphrase (put the author's ideas in your words) main ideas. For longer summaries, choose a few important details to include. For abstracts, condense the paraphrased material.

c. In the summary's first sentence, include the thesis or main point of the document using your own words and sentence structure.

d. Make clear what you are summarizing. With an article, introduce the source in the first sentence by including the title and author's name. For a speech or meeting, credit the speaker, sponsoring organization, facilitator, or moderator in the opening sentence.

Figure 8.3 is an article that an employee reads so the employee can summarize it for his supervisor and/or for his files for future reference. Figure 8.4 contains two summaries and an abstract of the article in Figure 8.3.

A Faster Way to Clean Roots

Agronomists, plant pathologists, and botanists—to name a few—are interested in the effects of soil and crop management practices on crop root systems. But before they can begin their studies, scientists usually have to spend time and energy cleaning soil off the roots. A new invention by the Agricultural Research Service (ARS) may help.

Soil scientist Joseph G. Benjamin, of ARS's Central Great Plains Research Station in Akron, Colorado, has created a root washer with a rotary design to automate and speed up the process. Other devices require more attention from the operator. The new device can clean up to 24 samples at a time, more than previous washers.

The washing cycle starts when a technician places a sample of soil and roots in the machine's chambers. As the sample rotates within the machine, it is dipped into and sprayed with water to remove the soil. Mud exits from the back of the machine. The cycle takes about 90 minutes, and the roots, which are not damaged by the machine, are then ready for study. "The root washer works well to easily and quickly separate plant roots and other organic materials from the soil," Benjamin says. He also points out that compared to other washers, his device can wash larger samples.

Once the roots are clean, a flatbed scanner is used to digitize their images for scientists to analyze with computer software. Through mathematical equations, Benjamin is able to determine the surface area of the roots contained in the sample. As Benjamin points out, "The human eye is still the best discriminator at determining what materials are roots and what are not." Benjamin's root washer is an enlarged version of a weed-seed washer invented by weed scientist Lori J. Wiles and others in ARS's Water Management Unit at Fort Collins, Colorado. Before her invention, nothing was available commercially to quickly wash soil from seeds.

FIGURE 8.3 Article to Be Summarized Source: Elstein, David. United States. Dept. of Agriculture. "A Faster Way to Clean Roots." *Agricultural Research:* 2004 (52.1). Web. 10 Dec. 2009.

LONG SUMMARY OF "A FASTER WAY TO CLEAN ROOTS"

In "A Faster Way to Clean Roots," David Elstein announces a technological breakthrough for people who study plants and crop management. While scientists normally use considerable time cleaning dirt from plant roots by hand before the plants can be studied, a machine created by soil scientist Joseph G. Benjamin offers help.

Benjamin developed a device to rotate and clean 24 plants at once, decreasing the need for scientists to handle the plants and speeding the process. During washing, the machine dunks and shoots water at the roots but does not harm or change the root system. The water takes the mud with it when it drains from the machine.

When the clean roots are removed from the new machine, Benjamin's device uses a flatbed scanner, computer software, and mathematical equations to calculate the surface area of the roots. However, the inventor notes that the machine is not as effective as the human eye at distinguishing roots from other materials.

Benjamin based the design of his invention on a weed-seed washer invented by scientist Lori J. Wiles and colleagues at the ARS Water Management Research Unit in Fort Collins, Colorado.

Figure 8.4 Examples of Summaries and Abstract *(continues)*

SHORT SUMMARY OF "A FASTER WAY TO CLEAN ROOTS"

In "A Faster Way to Clean Roots," David Elstein announces a technological breakthrough for people who study plants and crop management. Before soil scientist Joseph G. Benjamin's creation of a machine to clean soil and organic matter from plant roots, scientists had to painstakingly remove the dirt from the root system of plants they wanted to study. Benjamin's invention does not damage the roots, and it mechanizes and speeds the preparation. Compared to other machines, Benjamin's rotary-design wash cycle prepares 24 samples for study faster and with less handling. When the plants are clean, Benjamin's device uses a flatbed scanner, computer software, and mathematical equations to calculate the roots' surface area.

ABSTRACT OF "A FASTER WAY TO CLEAN ROOTS"

In "A Faster Way to Clean Roots," David Elstein announces a technological breakthrough for people who study plants and crop management: soil scientist Joseph G. Benjamin's creation of a machine to clean soil and organic matter from plant roots without damaging the roots.

Figure 8.4 (continued) Examples of Summaries and Abstract

e. Decide whether your audience needs a few details or only main ideas. For long summaries, include only details that are especially important. For short summaries, leave out details. For abstracts, include only the most important general ideas. Be concise. Reduce the original document to the main idea in a few sentences.

f. Keep your summary information proportional to the original. If the author spent four paragraphs on one topic and two paragraphs on another, your summary should give proportional time and emphasis. For example, in your summary or abstract, do not include more information from the two-paragraph topic than from the four-paragraph topic.

g. Write in present tense.

h. Paraphrase; do not copy word for word.

i. Quote sparingly, if at all, and use quotation marks correctly.

j. Provide transitions to keep the summary from sounding choppy.

Do not give your opinion. A summary or an abstract should be objective.

STOP AND THINK 8.2

If a summary includes three of an article's five main points, is it effective? Why or why not?

8.3 MECHANISM DESCRIPTION

 WARM UP

Examine the pen or pencil you are using to take notes. Briefly describe its parts and their functions.

A **mechanism description** describes the main parts of a device or machine. It explains what the purpose of the mechanism and overall design is, what the parts are, what they look like, and what their function is. It does not tell users how to operate the machine as instructions would.

Mechanism descriptions are used in catalogs, instruction manuals, product packaging, and employee training. Examples of mechanisms in the workplace include car parts, furniture, kitchen tools, doorstops, pencil sharpeners, and more sophisticated machines such as an engine or a DVD player. Mechanism descriptions are often included with instructions in product packaging.

Consumers can find a mechanism description in a manual that comes with new equipment, such as a computer or can opener. This description tells what the parts are, how they fit together, and what their functions are. Technicians and operators use the description to become familiar with the characteristics of the machine and to troubleshoot problems. New employees use a mechanism description to learn job responsibilities and safety procedures. Decision makers use mechanism descriptions to reach informed decisions, perhaps comparing current equipment with equipment proposed for purchase.

Figure 8.5 is a mechanism description that a community college electronics student produced to demonstrate his understanding of an everyday object that people use. The audience for the report was the instructor, other electronics students, and anyone curious about how things work.

Typical Reader

Either a technician or a professional needing technical specifications for a mechanism; any person who needs to understand how a mechanism works.

Writer's Focus

Writing thorough and clear descriptions and explanations in a readable format with accurate, precise details, including measurements, materials, and appropriate graphics.

Surge Protector: A Mechanism Description

People who set up computers and printers, sound equipment, or almost any type of electronics often include a surge protector in the purchase. Most surge protectors, also known as surge suppressors, are a small box with several utility outlets, a power switch, and a three-wire cord for plugging into a wall outlet, allowing users to plug multiple electronic devices into one power outlet. More importantly, they protect the electronics (and the users) from surges in power. A power surge is an increase in the flow of current caused by an increase in voltage above the 120 standard volts used in the United States. An increase in voltage lasting three nanoseconds (billionths of a second) is a surge. An increase lasting only one or two nanoseconds is a spike. A surge or spike that is high enough can destroy an electronic device by overloading sensitive internal components. Surge protectors keep this destruction from occurring.

Figure 8.5 Mechanism Description: A Surge Protector *(continues)*

Figure 1 shows a basic surge protector consisting of six main internal parts: hot wire, neutral wire, grounding wire, metal oxide varistor, fuse, and toroidal choke coil.

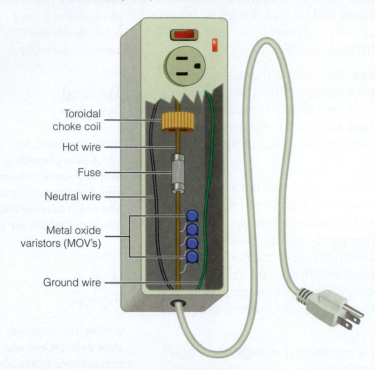

Figure 1 Internal View of a Basic Surge Protector

Hot Wire

In a surge protector—as well as in an electrical circuit, a hot wire is one-half of the circuit conductor (ungrounded circuit conductor). It supplies a road for the electricity to reach its destination.

Neutral Wire

While the hot wire supplies the path to the destination, the neutral wire provides a path back "home." Electricity is always seeking the shortest path back to the earth and has to run in a "circle" to be a complete circuit.

Grounding Wire

Ground wires and fuses are standard safety features in electrical circuits and appliances. They protect the electrical system from damage as well as the users from electrical shock. A ground wire in an electrical device such as a surge protector provides an electrical pathway to the earth that is separate from the normal current-carrying wires—the hot and neutral. In the event the neutral wire is damaged or broken, the grounding wire provides a secondary path back to earth, preventing the user from becoming that path.

Metal Oxide Varistor

In the most common type of surge protector, a component called a metal oxide varistor, or MOV, diverts the extra voltage during a surge or spike to the grounding wire. As you can see in Figure 1, an MOV forms a connection between the hot wire and the grounding wire. An MOV is an inductive device with three parts: a piece of metal oxide material in the middle joined to the power and grounding line by two semiconductors. The purpose of MOVs is to resist or limit the change in current.

Fuse

Fuses limit the current which can flow in a circuit. The metal filament in the fuse melts, thus breaking the circuit. Ideally, that connection will be broken before the extra power "fries" anything plugged into the surge protector.

Toroidal Choke Coil

Toroidal choke coils are passive electronic components, typically consisting of a ring-shaped magnetic core of highly magnetically permeable material, such as iron powder or ferrite, around which wire is coiled to make an inductor. The purpose of the toroidal choke coil in a surge protector is to limit or resist a change in current. Along with the fuse, it is a safety component.

Adapted from http://electronics.howstuffworks.com/gadgets/home/surge-protector.htm/printable

Figure 8.5 (continued) Mechanism Description: A Surge Protector

To write a mechanism description,

1. Take notes, describing every part in detail. Assume that you are on the telephone. You must describe a mechanism that the listener has not seen.

2. Use **spatial order**. That is, explain the parts from left to right, right to left, top to bottom, bottom to top, or whatever pattern is logical.

3. Open with an overall physical description of the mechanism, a statement that identifies its general purpose (what it is designed to do), and a preview of its parts.

© Blend Images/JupiterImages

4. Divide the mechanism into its parts and discuss each part under a separate heading. Use proper names of the parts. Place headings in the same order you used in the preview list.

5. Provide a precise physical description of the parts. Include size, color, location, and material (what the mechanism is made of).

6. Include the purpose or function of each part.

7. Provide a graphic of the mechanism. Include exploded (enlarged) views of parts that are too small to be easily seen. Add callouts to label each part.

8. Use active voice whenever possible.

Do not explain how to operate the mechanism. Instead, describe what it does, what it looks like, what its parts are, and what they look like and do.

 STOP AND THINK 8.3

In a mechanism description, should a writer describe a metal disk as (a) about the size of a penny or (2) 1/2″ in diameter? What organizational pattern is used in mechanism descriptions?

James Berry, a pediatric occupational therapist, is tempted to give a parent a glowing report even though the three-year-old patient is not making significant improvement in therapy sessions. Mr. Berry likes the parent and does not want to add to the parent's stress.

Think Critically

What are possible effects of misinformation in Mr. Berry's reports?

Communication
Dilemma

Consider what happens during registration at your school. What are the steps?

Typical Reader

Either a technician or a professional needing to understand specific steps in a process; any person who needs to understand what happens and the order in which it happens in a process.

Writer's Focus

Writing clear, complete, and well-organized descriptions of what happens in a process in a readable format and including graphics, when appropriate.

Process descriptions usually explain events that happen through time without the reader's taking action, such as photosynthesis, yeast growth in bread production, or the election of a U.S. president. Unlike instructions that tell the reader how to do something, a process description explains what happens in an activity over time, how a machine or an event works. Two examples of process descriptions appear at the beginning of this chapter on pages 215–216.

Employees often find process descriptions in manuals, reports, and policy documents. For instance, an employee manual might describe the process by which an employee is hired, fired, promoted, placed on probation, and retired. In a manufacturing facility, reports may describe the process used to create the manufactured product or the flow of materials through the plant. Users may have a great deal of background knowledge or almost none. These readers could use the process description to make a decision, such as a change in the movement of materials in a manufacturing process to improve efficiency or reduce labor costs, or to improve understanding of what happens, as in a greater understanding of what happens to select a new pope.

Generally, the process description begins with a brief introduction defining the process, sometimes in only one sentence, and outlining the scope and purpose of the document. It also usually previews the major pieces or steps in the process. If you think an image, such as a flowchart, might help the reader comprehend the process, place it with the introduction.

Following the introduction, the body answers, "How does it happen?" It begins with a purpose or function of that step or part followed by details, step-by-step or part-by-part detailed descriptions of the activity.

Conclude the process description by summarizing principal steps or parts. If appropriate, discuss the value of the process or its effect on things.

To write your process description,

- Organize steps or parts chronologically. If the process is a continuous cycle, such as rain and condensation, then you may begin with any major step and continue through.

- Use present tense.

- Explain any cause-and-effect relationships in the process. For example, if reaching a temperature of –10 degrees F triggers a shut-down on the conveyor belt, then explain the cause(s) and the effect(s).

- Divide any step or part into substeps or subparts as needed to include detailed descriptions.

- Avoid requests or commands.

- Avoid the pronoun *you*.

- Use graphics within steps when they will aid the reader and clarify the description.

STOP AND THINK 8.4

How does a process description differ from instructions?

8.5 PERIODIC REPORTS

Periodic reports explain accomplishments for all projects of a work group or of an entire organization over a specified time period. For instance, when you listened to your governor make a State of the State address or the president make a State of the Union address, you heard a periodic report. These speeches explore the many ongoing projects of the state or nation for the year. Periodic reports may cover different periods: a week (weekly), a month (monthly), three months (quarterly), six months (semiannually), or more.

Businesses and nonprofit organizations use periodic reports to inform shareholders, clients, vendors, donors, and employees of the organization's accomplishments and challenges. Figure 8.6 is an example of a periodic report prepared by a student intern.

Consider the organizations you belong to, participate in, or are concerned about. How do you learn about the status, or "health," of the organization?

Memorandum

March 5, 20—

To: Miss Helen Wooten, Adviser
From: Ove Jensen, Student Intern
Subject: Job Shadowing a Radiologic Technologist at Grove Park Hospital

February has been a productive period in my second month of job-shadowing Ms. Antoinette Clavelle, radiologic technologist at Grove Park Hospital. The month was filled with action and variety. I observed work in the Neonatal Intensive Care Unit, the MRI (Magnetic Resonance Imaging) section, and the Radiology Lab. In addition, I completed one of the three research papers required for earning academic credit.

Gives highlights of entire report.

Neonatal Intensive Care Unit

During my first session with Ms. Clavelle last month, which took place in the Neonatal Intensive Care Unit, I watched radiologists work with medically fragile premature and newborn babies. Ms. Clavelle used an ultrasound machine to obtain images of the brains of two patients.

I further observed Ms. Clavelle use a portable X-ray device to take film of the chest and abdomen of another young patient. Some of the infants in this unit weigh as little as 1 pound and are connected to many pieces of support equipment, such as respirators and heart monitors. These patients present unique challenges to radiologic technologies.

Provides as many specifics as possible, is organized from most important information to least important information.

MRI Section

Since Ms. Clavelle is a rotation supervisor, I was able to observe the operation of the MRI machine while she worked in that area. This room-sized piece of imaging equipment serves a variety of purposes in diagnosing patients' problems. During the four hours I shadowed Ms. Clavelle in the MRI section, she worked with the following patients:

1. An 82-year-old stroke patient,
2. A 14-year-old auto crash victim with head trauma,
3. A quarterback for the university football team with a knee injury, and
4. A 36-year-old woman suffering back pain.

Everything about this machine is computer-driven, so I became a little restless in the control room while the patients were undergoing treatment. The problem was that I did

Notes and explains problem area.

Figure 8.6 Periodic Report *(continues)*

Miss Helen Wooten   Page 2   March 5, 20—

not understand the computer jargon used by the technologists, nor did I understand what I was seeing when I looked at the images on the computer screen. Many of the technologists were in a hurry and did not have time to explain the images to me.

Radiology Lab

Observing Ms. Clavelle in the Radiology Lab gave me an opportunity to witness a wide range of uses of radiologic technology as well as to see the necessity for accurate reporting. A patient's well-being may depend on the technologist's communication skills.

Researched Reports

As my goal is to earn academic credit toward graduation, I am submitting one researched report, "Using Ultrasound in Diagnosing Brain Hemorrhage," along with this monthly report. I am researching now for the second report and plan to finish it by the end of March. I should have the final paper completed by the end of April or the first week in May.

Conclusion

My experiences with Ms. Clavelle in February were worthwhile and exciting. In fact, after observing technologists use several types of equipment, I have found that my interest is greatest in ultrasound, and I am considering work in that area as a career goal. When we meet next, I would like to discuss the educational requirements for such a career and the possibility of shadowing someone during the spring semester who works only with ultrasound.

Looks forward to the next report and meeting.

Figure 8.6 (continued) Periodic Report

Typical Reader

Any person involved with or interested in the organization, such as employees or shareholders, who would like to know about the activities and accomplishments of the organization.

Writer's Focus

Presenting a logically organized, detailed description of the activities of the organization during the reporting period.

To write periodic reports,

1. Consider all activities and accomplishments of the organization for the specified time period. Begin by noting the time period. Are you sharing information about the last two weeks, the past month, or the fiscal year? (A **fiscal year** is the operating year, such as the academic year, which often runs from July 1 through June 30.)

2. Meet your audience's needs. What are the audience's concerns, history with the writer and the project or organization, and roles?

3. Organize tasks so you can report them logically. Once lists are complete, categories of tasks become subheadings under a major heading. Organize so the reader can find important information easily.

4. Format for the audience. Many longer periodic reports are manuscript-formatted, appearing like an essay or a book with a title. These reports offer the formality and distance appropriate for a diverse audience. When written for an internal reader, a short periodic report may be formatted as a memo. For an external reader, the report may be formatted as a letter.

5. For the introduction, develop an overview that briefly presents the highlights of the report. Mention each idea included in a major heading. Also state the reporting period, the time for which the document describes activities or progress.

6. For the body, compose a section for each activity category or type of work undertaken during the reporting period, with section headings and sometimes subheadings organized from most important to least important. For instance, the monthly activity report of a U.S. Navy recruiter might include the following work areas (and headings): Job Fairs, School-Based Meetings, Office Conferences, and Public Speaking Events. Under each heading, the recruiter describes, from most to least important, accomplishments during the reporting period. In the rest of the report, the recruiter may note problems encountered.

7. In the conclusion, highlight any key ideas and refer to the next report.

8. Check for accuracy, particularly in statistics and names.

9. Use lists, numbered or set in columns, whenever possible to ensure easier reading.

10. Divide long discussions into paragraphs to reflect groups of ideas.

STOP AND THINK 8.5

What three types of information are usually included in the introduction of a periodic report?

8.6 PROGRESS REPORTS

 WARM UP

Periodic report writers should *not* include their opinions, instead providing facts and allowing readers to draw their own conclusions.

Like periodic reports, **progress reports** are documents that report progress for a period of time. Unlike periodic reports, which cover all of an organization's work, a progress report describes what has been done during a specified time on only one project, such as work on the construction of a building. A progress report covers in detail all achievements as well as plans for the upcoming reporting period toward completing one project.

Anyone in an organization may need to report progress made on a project. Readers may use information in a progress report to make decisions, to take actions, or to file for future reference.

Think about the grade reports you receive from school. What is the writer's purpose in presenting this report? Determine the relationship between the writer and the audience. Now think about how grade reports changed as you progressed through your academic career from elementary to middle school to your current level of schooling. What do the changes indicate?

Figure 8.7 shows a progress report.

Memorandum

To:	Yearbook Staff Members
From:	Yearbook Staff Trip Committee
Date:	February 1, 20—
Subject:	Progress Report 3: Planning for Trip to Disney World

Since our yearbook staff trip to Disney World is less than two months away, we are working hard to make an enjoyable adventure possible. This report outlines the accomplishments, the work remaining, and one problem encountered during January.

WORK COMPLETED   (January 1–February 1, 20—)

We are marking a few things off the to-do list. If we can maintain the current level of enthusiasm, we will get there.

Finances

The staff sponsored two doughnut sales to add $350 to the travel fund.

Reservations

Three buses from the White Goose Line have been reserved at a cost of $800 each. In addition, reservations have been made for three nights at the Disney Dunes Hotel and a deposit of $500 has been paid to the hotel.

Chaperones

University policy requires 11 instructors or parents to accompany groups the size of our staff on overnight trips. To satisfy that requirement, four instructors, their spouses, and three parents have agreed to serve as chaperones.

WORK SCHEDULED

The primary responsibilities remaining are earning the rest of the money required for the trip and making additional reservations.

Finances

The fund balance now contains $9,675 of the $11,000 we need to earn for the trip. Five other fund-raising projects have been scheduled before the trip. However, if the future projects are as successful as the last two, we may raise the remaining $1,325 after only three projects have been completed.

Reservations

We will order two-day passes for Disney World and one-day tickets for Sea World next week. Also, Ms. Zhao will make reservations for the Yearbook Banquet at Seaside Restaurant. The Banquet Committee will request a buffet for Saturday evening.

Indicates that this is the third progress report on this project; notes the report topic.

The Introduction describes the project being reported on, gives the reporting period, and states the purpose of the report.

Covers what has been done on the project.

Covers work yet to be done.

Provides as many specifics as possible, is organized from most important information to least important information.

The Work Completed may include subheads if the work accomplished falls under two or more categories. Omits the subhead Chaperones under Work Scheduled because nothing else concerning chaperones needs to be done.

Figure 8.7 Model of an Internal Progress Report *(continues)*

Yearbook Staff Members   Page 2   February 1, 20—

PROBLEMS/PROJECTIONS

The University Board has agreed to consider our request to be excused from classes early on the day we leave. Otherwise, we cannot reach Orlando before three o'clock in the morning. If we arrive in the middle of the night, we will probably waste the day planned for Disney World catching up on sleep. We might think of changing the schedule if the Board denies our request. Other plans are proceeding as expected, and we should have all work for the trip completed by March 16, two weeks before departure.

Explains any difficulties that may affect the project; gives a revised completion date if problems have caused delay.

Figure 8.7 (continued) Model of an Internal Progress Report

To write a progress report:

1. Organize a progress report to answer the readers' most important questions first. Use the following outline to plan for progress reports. Under each heading, the writer may add subheadings if several ideas will be covered in that section.

HEADING IN REPORT	WHAT THAT SECTION COVERS
Introduction	Report topic, purpose, and reporting period
Work Completed	What has been done
Work Scheduled	What needs to be done
Problems/Projections	What has gone wrong and when the work will be finished

2. In the opening or introductory section of the progress report,

   - Name the project.

   - Indicate the **reporting period**, which is the time the report covers.

   - State the purpose of the report (to tell readers the status of the project).

3. Use *I* or *we*—first person—where appropriate. You take responsibility for your actions and opinions by using *I*. Using *I* or *we* is not only acceptable but also encouraged.

In the Work Completed section,

   - Note again the time period you cover. (This is optional; if it is included, it usually appears beside the heading or in the opening sentence of the section.)

   - Use past tense verbs.

   - Use subheadings (to separate tasks) or bulleted lists. When three or more tasks or topics are included in this section, subheadings are necessary. When only one or two tasks are included, subheadings are optional.

   Provide sufficient details and explanations about each job completed. Because your reader is probably most concerned about what you have done on the project, ensure that this section is clear and accurate.

Typical Reader

Anyone inside or outside the writer's organization needing information on progress toward completion of a task.

Writer's Focus

Clearly describing achievements and plans toward completing a task in a standard organizational plan.

Place your most important ideas first. After all, this is your opportunity to tell what you have achieved.

4. In the Work Scheduled section,

- Tell your audience what work needs to be done in the next reporting period.

- Use future tense verbs.

- Separate and emphasize each major task or job with subheadings, as you did in the Work Completed section. Remember to use subheadings when you have three or more tasks. Otherwise, subheadings are optional.

5. In the Problems section,

- Describe any obstacles to completing the job. Inform the reader of anything that has affected the quality or quantity of work.

- Describe these problems in a bulleted or numbered list or present them in paragraphs.

- Be honest and direct.

- Report just the facts unless you need to assign responsibility for problems. Remember that finger-pointing can be counterproductive.

In the Projections section, give readers a new completion date if problems have stalled the project so that the original date cannot be met.

STOP AND THINK 8.6
While both periodic and progress reports are issued periodically or in set increments of time, how are the two reports different?

WARM UP

8.7 NEWS RELEASES

Recall news relating to business or industry you have seen, heard, or read in the last week from television, radio, print, or online media. With that news in mind, answer the following questions: What parts of the story do you remember? What made the story memorable? What elements of the story do you think business or industry provided? What elements were probably the result of a reporter's investigation?

News releases, also called press releases, are reports of events or facts prepared for the **media**, which are systems or means of mass communication. The goal of the release is to inform the public of, for example, an employee promotion or a company expansion.

One type of press release is the public service announcement (PSA). **PSAs** differ from other news releases in that they present facts beneficial to the public. PSAs, for example, announce Red Cross blood drives, city council meetings, fundraisers, and other public events. People and organizations send news releases to the media to share information with the public.

In many large organizations, **public relations**, the communication between a company and the outside world, is handled by departments that write news releases to help the company maintain a positive image. For instance, if a company executive is involved in a scandal, the public relations staff may prepare a news release to present the company's view and restore public confidence.

In smaller organizations without public relations departments, any employee may write a news release. The maintenance director might write a release describing the company's recycling efforts, a retail manager might cover the store's planned expansion, and a volunteer group's administrative assistant might outline the organization's upcoming fundraising project.

Because the writer sends the release to select news agencies, the first readers are editors and news directors. They decide whether the news release will run. If the information is newsworthy and the release is well written so that little editing is required, the chance that it will be published increases. Other influential factors include space and time constraints.

If the release is published, the second audience is the public. The public is anyone who reads a newspaper or magazine, watches television, uses the Internet, or listens to the radio. Specialized media agencies receive news releases targeting a particular audience, so the second audience might also be a select group.

For instance, you are probably familiar with television stations that target specific people: MTV targets music lovers; TNN attracts country music fans; CNN focuses on people interested in world, economic, and political news; and the Disney Channel targets children. Audiences are looking for the same thing—timely and interesting information.

Figure 8.8 shows a news release with a triangle indicating the part of the release an editor chose to publish. The last two paragraphs, which contained the least important information, were cut.

Typical Reader

Any person who appreciates news.

Writer's Focus

Planning and writing a news release that is effective enough in content, style, organization, and format to win the news editor's approval for publication and that is interesting enough to gain the attention of the ultimate audience; organizing so that essential information comes first and is not lost if the editor must cut the story because of space or time constraints.

STERLING
Public Information Office

City of Sterling
Office of the Mayor
1156 West McGill Street
Sterling, IL 61081-1908
Phone: 815-555-0197
Fax: 815-555-0177

NEWS RELEASE   Contact: Adam Riggs, Mayor's Office
                                               815.555.0197
                                               ariggs@city_of_sterling_il.gov

August 23, 20—

For Immediate Release

ROLLER ART DONATES SKATE PARK TO CITY

STERLING, IL — Roller Art has donated $100,000 to Sterling for the development of a park especially designed for in-line and roller-skating enthusiasts. The park will feature two oval tracks for straightforward skating and another area with five ramps for trick skating.

The 2.45-acre park site is located three blocks west of the city office quad. Roller Art deeded this undeveloped land to the city two years ago.

Construction on the property is expected to begin within the month, and Mayor Manuella Huerta says that the park, to be named Roller Royale, will be open by early summer.

Robert Nowicki, spokesperson for Roller Art, said that his company is happy to be able to give back to the community that has helped Roller Art become successful. Roller Art employs 48 people who design and manufacture roller skates.

Roller Art has a history of giving to Sterling. In its nine years of doing business in the community, the company has donated a total of $425,000 to the city and an equal amount to local nonprofit groups.

The local company has the top-selling in-line skates on the market, Rold World. Rold World, developed after years of research, combines speed with the maximum in directional control.

-30-

Figure 8.8 Model News Release Cut by Editor

To write a news release,

1. Begin by analyzing the audience. Consider the editor or news director as well as the target audience.

2. Answer the classic reporter's questions: Who? What? When? Where? Why? and How? With answers to those questions, you have the most important information to include in the news release.

Figure 8.9 shows an illustration of this idea-packed opening for a news release. Notice where the reporter's questions are addressed.

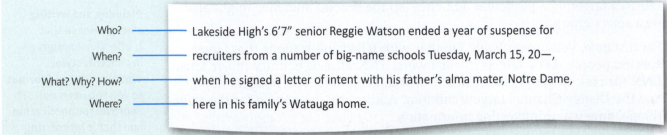

Who?	Lakeside High's 6'7" senior Reggie Watson ended a year of suspense for
When?	recruiters from a number of big-name schools Tuesday, March 15, 20—,
What? Why? How?	when he signed a letter of intent with his father's alma mater, Notre Dame,
Where?	here in his family's Watauga home.

Figure 8.9 Reporter's Questions in News Release Opening

3. Beyond the reporter's questions, ask yourself these questions: (1) What will interest my audience? (2) What will grab their attention? (3) What would they ask if they could?

4. Plan for accuracy. Check your prewriting notes for accuracy in the following:

- Facts
- Numbers and statistics
- Names
- Locations

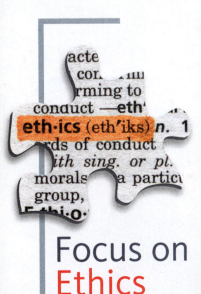

Focus on Ethics

Isaac Nonn is a volunteer campaign worker for a candidate running for the state legislature. Isaac's candidate is slipping in the polls, and the opposition is gaining in popularity. Isaac recently received a packet in the mail from an anonymous sender, indicating that the opposition candidate was expelled from college for cheating before she transferred to the university from which she ultimately graduated. Isaac is thinking about forwarding the materials to local media outlets—perhaps anonymously.

Think Critically

How should Isaac handle the situation?

- Quotations
- Completeness ("the whole truth")

With correct text, releases will have a greater chance of being published.

5. Plan for credibility. Exaggerations are overstatements or additions beyond the truth that can ruin a person's credibility. Instead, use information that can be verified. Avoid superlatives such as *the best, the fastest*, and *the worst* unless you can document or prove the statement. If your release opens with "R. J. Birch, the fastest 10K runner in the state," make sure you have her race times or other proof of your statement.

6. Compose the headline carefully because it will be read first. Include an active verb. Use present tense for current events, past tense for events already concluded, and future tense for scheduled activities. For example, the headline HALIFAX ACADEMY TO HOST STAR TREK CONVENTION uses an active verb that indicates future time (to host) because the event has not yet occurred. Be aware that your news release will compete with others for space or airtime (time to deliver a news story). Thus, the headline is your chance to make a positive first impression on the reader.

7. Open the body of the release with a **hook**—catchy wording or an idea that attracts attention. Dynamic wording or an intriguing idea seizes the audience's attention. Below are hooks used to open news releases.

- The nets are still hanging in Memorial Coliseum after last night's City League upset, but only because the Knights expect to return for them during the playoffs.
- When 600 first-year students show up for orientation at Schantz College on Saturday, they will receive something besides their dorm assignments.
- The Easter Bunny Brought What?

Those opening sentences attract attention so readers or listeners will want to know more.

8. Order ideas from most important to least important and begin with the important answers to the reporter's questions. Organizing from most to least important achieves several purposes:

- You make editors' work easier and the story's publication more likely.

- You help readers find the most important information quickly and easily—even if they do not read the entire article.

- Making cuts is easier, and you have more control of how they are made.

    If a news director has 20 seconds of airtime and your news release is 30 seconds, the news director must cut 10 seconds or choose not to use it. Likewise, print editors sometimes must cut inches to fit releases into the space available.

© Zoriah/The Image Works

9. Format news releases so information the reader needs stands out, editors can make changes easily, and news anchors (who might read the text on the air) can easily follow the document. For illustrative purposes, the release is divided into three units: the top of the page or introductory information, the body or story, and pagination cues. Refer to Figure 8.10.

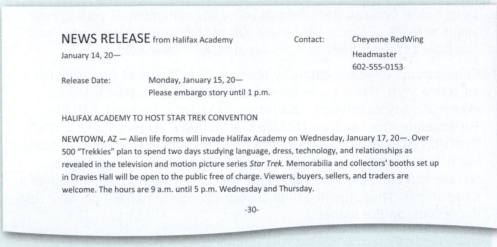

NEWS RELEASE from Halifax Academy   Contact: Cheyenne RedWing

January 14, 20—   Headmaster
602-555-0153

Release Date: Monday, January 15, 20—
Please embargo story until 1 p.m.

HALIFAX ACADEMY TO HOST STAR TREK CONVENTION

NEWTOWN, AZ — Alien life forms will invade Halifax Academy on Wednesday, January 17, 20—. Over 500 "Trekkies" plan to spend two days studying language, dress, technology, and relationships as revealed in the television and motion picture series *Star Trek*. Memorabilia and collectors' booths set up in Dravies Hall will be open to the public free of charge. Viewers, buyers, sellers, and traders are welcome. The hours are 9 a.m. until 5 p.m. Wednesday and Thursday.

-30-

Figure 8.10 News Release Format

10. **Properly format introductory information.** Many large companies create letterhead for news releases. It is printed with the company name, postal and web addresses, telephone number, logo, and the words NEWS RELEASE. If your organization does not have special letterhead, use plain 8 1/2" × 11" paper. Use the following guidelines for introductory format:

   - Begin with the words NEWS RELEASE in all capital letters. Key the source of the document in initial caps if letterhead is not used.

   - Key *Contact* and a colon flush right across from NEWS RELEASE. After the colon, enter the name of the person responsible for the release as well as the person's job title and phone number.

   - Record the date the document was written beneath NEWS RELEASE.

   - Use *For Immediate Release* or place *Release Date* and a colon at the left margin under the date. After the colon, key the date and the specific time the information should be made public.

   - Writers occasionally request a release to be held for a period of time before publication. If you want a story to be held, beneath or beside the release date, key *Please hold until* [desired release time] or *Please embargo story until* [desired release time]. **Embargo** means "to withhold or delay publication."

   - Give the news agency a suggested headline in all capital letters.

11. To format the body of a release, preface it with a **dateline**, which identifies the location of the story. Key the dateline in all capital letters. In Figure 8.10, NEWTOWN, AZ is where the story takes place. After the location, (1) leave a space, (2) key a dash, and (3) leave another space.

12. Use pagination cues, a special code to help readers follow the text and read from one page to another. To use these cues,

- Key the word *-more-* centered at the bottom of the page when the release will be continued on the next page.

- End news releases with *-30-* or ### centered after the last line.

Do not promote a product or a service in your release. If you are tempted to do so, remind yourself that news is who did what, where, when, why, and how, while advertisements are how new, improved, or cost-effective something might be. Editors rarely publish releases that read like sales literature.

STOP AND THINK 8.7

Before a news release is published, what reader or readers must approve it?

8 CHAPTER REVIEW

Summary

1. Summaries and abstracts are condensed versions of longer documents. In a summary, the writer clearly and logically presents only main ideas. The length of the original and the writer's purpose determine the length. Abstracts are shorter than summaries and cover the main idea of the original.

2. A mechanism description describes the main parts of a device or mechanism and explains the purpose of the mechanism and overall design, the various parts, the way they look, and their functions.

3. Process descriptions explain events that happen through time without the reader taking action or what happens in an activity over time or how a machine or an event works.

4. Periodic reports describe the progress of all ongoing projects in an organization or organization division during a specified time period.

5. Progress reports describe the status of one project for a specified period. Progress and periodic reports require writers to consider the interests of the audience and the schedule of the project or the organization.

6. News or press releases are reports of events or facts prepared by employees to send to the media. The goal of the release is to have the media outlets publish the story and inform the public.

Checklist

- Have I designed, organized, and written the document with the audience in mind?
- Have I analyzed my audience(s) and determined what readers need?
- Is my format appropriate for the audience and the situation?
- Have I included relevant background information?
- Have I used a logical and appropriate organizational plan?
- Are the ideas under each heading organized appropriately?
- Is the information complete and accurate?
- Have I used lists where appropriate for ease of reading?
- Have I made my document easy to read by using descriptive headings? Do the headings follow parallel structure?
- Do I present accurate, specific details?
- Have I remained objective throughout the document?
- Have I presented problems as facts, not accusations?

Build Your Foundation

1. Write a one-sentence summary of one of the following well-known fairy tales: "Little Red Riding Hood," "Cinderella," "Sleeping Beauty," "Goldilocks and the Three Bears," or "The Three Little Pigs." Compare your summary with those of your classmates. If you read the story rather than working from memory, remember to use your own words.

2. The statements listed in items *a–j* will go into a progress report. Identify each statement as *Work Completed, Work Scheduled,* or *Problems/ Projections.*

   a. We have purchased a site license from NetBright for our network.
   b. The DVD, which was delivered last Friday, was damaged in shipping so that it is inoperable.
   c. The technicians installed antivirus protection on all computers.
   d. If all work scheduled is completed as we expect, the network will be ready for the team orientation on September 23.
   e. This week the system director will order the serial cable we need.
   f. The hardware security system we requested was $300 over budget.
   g. Each computer will be named so that users can easily identify it.
   h. A system administrator must be trained before we can operate fully.
   i. We connected the shared printer to the network and tested it.
   j. We forgot to order a surge protector for the smart board, so we cannot use this equipment until the order arrives next week.

3. Some of the following sentences are vague, and some include the writer's opinions. Revise each sentence to make it specific and factual. Invent details as needed.

   a. The calibrator is several minutes off schedule.
   b. The phenomenal response to our new online safety education program shows that this new program will benefit employees.
   c. To get to the Human Resources office, go down the hall a bit and turn left.
   d. The line was down for a while last Friday because of an issue with water.
   e. We can assemble the original air purifier in 45 minutes, but the stylized case of the new model results in a much longer assembly time than we planned.

4. Evaluate your progress on a hobby or collection. For instance, if you build sound systems, explain the pieces of equipment (e.g., speakers and receivers) you have acquired and describe the equipment you will add. If you collect baseball cards or comic books, note the cards or books you own now and the items you want to trade or buy. Make notes about your progress. Then share those notes with your classmates.

Your Turn

1. Write a long summary, a short summary, and an abstract on one of the following: a magazine or journal article, a textbook chapter, a sporting event, a meeting, a TV show, a movie, a classroom lecture, or a speech. The material you use for the summaries and abstract might relate to your chosen career field, a recent news event, or a topic suggested by your instructor.

2. List five mechanisms you know well. These may be mechanisms you use at work, at home, or at school. Consider using simple devices or a single mechanism within a larger, more complex machine. Write a mechanism description for one of the items. In your report, include a diagram of the mechanism. Remember that a borrowed image must include a citation to give credit for the source of the image.

3. Write a periodic report using the following information.

   As the Drafting Club chair, you receive organization funds from the Student Government Association (SGA). You report to the SGA twice a semester to tell them what the club is doing. Your next report is due January 6, 20—. In this report, you will discuss Professional Pursuits, Service, and Membership. The club is more active than ever. Over the holidays, five members attended the American Institute of Building Design meeting in Pensacola, Florida, and brought back information to share with other members. The club began the school year with 21 members, and two students joined during the second semester. This year's service project is to plan the city's first Habitat for Humanity house. Club members have completed the exterior drawings and submitted them for approval. They will finish the interior drawings before the school year ends. All 23 members of the club have participated in this service project.

4. Think of groups to which you belong: a family, a club, a neighborhood, a school. With one group and a particular time period in mind, plan and write a periodic report for a specific audience. Describe the ongoing activities for your group or for your unit of the larger organization.

5. Consider any project you are working on at home, school, or work as a topic for a progress report. Your audience will be a person or group of people who have an interest in or make decisions about the project. Use the appropriate format and organization for the topic and audience.

6. If you are seeking a summer or part-time job, applying for admission to a school, or working on a project, write a progress report to the appropriate person about how you are accomplishing your goals.

7. Contact several businesses or governmental agencies to request a copy of the organization's annual report, a periodic report outlining the status of the organization that is presented annually to shareholders, employees, vendors, and others. Analyze these reports to determine whether they fit the guidelines for periodic reports in this chapter.

Community Connection

1. Visit a nonprofit organization in your area. Learn about the mission and needs of the organization. Then locate a journal or newspaper article that is relevant to the nonprofit—an article you think might help with the organization's mission or goals. Write a one- to three-paragraph summary of the article. After submitting the article and your summary to your instructor for review, present the article and your revised and edited summary to the nonprofit's personnel.

2. Write a news release for your school or another organization with which you are affiliated to announce an upcoming event, an accomplishment, or other newsworthy information. Submit the release to your instructor and class. If appropriate after careful revision and editing, submit it to a local news agency for publication.

EXPLORE THE NET

The U.S. Food and Drug Administration (FDA) publishes a website containing links to FDA press releases from 2004 to the present. If you search for "US FDA press release archive," you will find topics ranging from food and drug research to biologics and radiation protection. Find a news release that interests you; print and read it. Write several paragraphs in which you explain if and how it uses the guidelines for effective news releases.

9 INVESTIGATIVE REPORTS

Goals

- Develop a trip report that meets the needs of the audience
- Compose an effective incident report
- Compose science reports
- Compose forensic reports

Terms

conclusion, p. 251
deductive reasoning, p. 249
forensic reports, p. 253
incident reports, p. 243
inductive reasoning, p. 249
objectivity, p. 251
passive voice, p. 250
result, p. 251
scientific method, p. 249
trip reports, p. 245

Write to Learn

Consider an investigation you made recently. Perhaps you had a problem with a piece of equipment and had to investigate what caused the problem. Or maybe you attended a workshop, a seminar, or an off-campus lecture or looked for a new apartment and needed to tell others what you learned. Or perhaps you tried a new recipe for your family or took part in a clinical trial. Think about your impressions of what is required to effectively report on an investigation. Write a paragraph describing the audience that needs to learn about this situation. List three to five pieces or types of information your audience may need. Write your impression of how your audience will use the information.

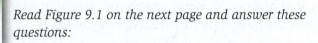

FOCUS on Investigative Reports

Read Figure 9.1 on the next page and answer these questions:

- When did the incident occur?
- What is the date of the incident mentioned?
- What is the main idea? In other words, what was the incident?
- What kind of information is contained in the Outcomes section?

What If?

How would the model change if . . .

- The information was intended for only one reader—an administrator at the hospital?
- The person who improperly installed the probe was not known?

HOPE
Hospital
www.hopehospital.org

4200 Hillcrest Road • Bath, ME 04530-5990
Phone: 207.555.0169 • Fax: 207.555.0170

Report on Incident in Clinical Laboratory

Summary

On Wednesday, July 7, 20—, a technician improperly installed the sampling probe on the Olympus Chemistry Analyzer, causing the probe to bend and rendering the machine inoperable. After the vice president granted approval for the $1,206 replacement probe, it was purchased and installed on Friday, July 9, 20—. The technician has been cleared through drug testing, and the incident was declared Operator Error Without Prejudice (according to the Hope Hospital Employee Policy Manual). Clinical Laboratory managers designed in-service training and proper installation posters to prevent this incident from recurring.

Description

On Wednesday, July 7, 20—, during the regular daily maintenance on all instrumentation, Todd Ely, Laboratory Technician II, improperly installed the Olympus Chemistry Analyzer's sampling probe. Because it was improperly placed, the probe hit the side of the specimen sampling cup, causing the probe to bend. As a result, the bent probe could not aspirate samples.

Outcomes

Without the Olympus Chemistry Analyzer, one of three machines in the lab used for testing blood, urine, and other bodily fluids, the hospital experienced delayed turnaround times for critical patient test results. Some tests were delayed as much as four hours.

Approval to purchase a new probe was requested through the executive level because the cost of $1,206 placed the purchase in the Nonbudgeted Capital Equipment category. Approval was granted on Thursday, July 8, 20—, and the probe was ordered and shipped overnight. It arrived at 10:30 a.m. on Friday, July 9, 20—, and was installed immediately. The machine then worked properly.

Todd Ely was drug-tested as standard operating procedure dictates. Because his test was negative, he is continuing with his duties. The vice president declared the incident Operator Error Without Prejudice.

Conclusion

As a result of this incident, all technicians participated in an in-service on proper installation of sampling probes on the Olympus and the other two machines. In addition, a visual showing proper placement is now posted beside all three machines to remind technicians how to install sampling probes correctly.

Figure 9.1 Sample Incident Report

Writing @Work

Courtesy of Anna Linnenberger

CareerClusters®
PATHWAYS TO COLLEGE & CAREER READINESS
Science, Technology, Engineering & Mathematics
Source: The Center to Advance CTE

Anna Linnenberger works for a small Colorado-based optics research company called Boulder Nonlinear Systems (BNS). BNS builds spatial light modulators, which are essentially programmable lenses that can be used, for example, for satellite laser communications, data encryption, and optical tweezers for biological research.

At BNS, Anna is responsible for developing software, overseeing customer support, testing new products, writing proposals and reports, and running funded projects that are under way. According to Anna, "Writing skills are surprisingly underemphasized in engineering classes. Although I have a BS in computer engineering and am working toward a doctorate in electrical engineering, I learned most of my writing skills on the job from senior engineers."

Even with expert help, Anna finds proposals difficult to write well: "Not only are you often writing about a subtopic that you are not an expert on, but your audience is a proposal reviewer who probably isn't an expert either. So it can be challenging to propose an idea persuasively and clearly to your target audience."

For Anna, reporting on research projects that are under way is much easier than writing proposals. "Each research project requires progress reports and final reports that are written according to a predefined formula or outline. You are writing to the funding agency's technical point person for your project. They basically want to know that their money is being spent to develop the technology you proposed and that things are moving forward at a reasonable pace."

The writing style for Anna's engineering reports is minimalist: "Write clearly and get to the point quickly. You don't want to be wordy, and you never use first-person point of view such as 'I did this' or 'we did that.' All technical terms need to be defined the first time you use them." Anna hopes that her reports and proposals are used to "further optics research in new directions."

Think Critically

1. Go to BNS's website. Has the company explained its mission so that a nontechnical person can understand it? Does BNS need to explain its mission? Why or why not?

2. Why do you think writing skills are underemphasized in engineering classes? Do you think most engineers write as much as Anna does? Explain.

Printed with permission of Anna Linnenberger

Writing in Science, Technology, Engineering, and Mathematics

Writers in the fields of science, technology, engineering, and mathematics (STEM) often are communicating very complex and technical information, sometimes to an expert audience and sometimes to a general or lay audience unfamiliar with terms and concepts. They need to be able to effectively communicate with both audiences. When these STEM professionals, through research or practice, discover information that needs to be shared with other experts in their field, they must meet their audience's expectations—clear, concise, well and logically organized writing that uses the jargon and the concepts understood by STEM experts. Readers do not appreciate feeling as if they are being "talked down to." Likewise, STEM writers must be able to express complex technical and scientific ideas in ways that the general reader who does not possess technical knowledge can understand. For example, scientists may need to write proposals seeking funding for research from an audience

unfamiliar with the science, technologists might need to explain equipment and how to operate it to an audience who lacks a technology background, engineers may need to sell a design to clients who do not know engineering concepts or terms, and mathematicians may need to use a complex mathematical analysis to solve a problem for people who do not understand how or why the formula can help them. Consider the television series *NUMB3RS*, which aired from 2005 to 2010. This American crime drama involves a young genius college professor, Charlie Eppes, who helps his brother, Don, an FBI agent, solve crimes using math. Although Don and the other FBI agents are intelligent and expert at their jobs, they do not easily understand Charlie's suggestions for ways math can help with a particular crime. However, Charlie is quite good at finding analogies or simple ways to interpret complex mathematics. In one episode, Charlie explains affinity analysis and association rule data mining by describing how one supermarket increased diaper sales by placing them in the aisle beside beer coolers after the store had discovered that most diapers are purchased along with beer—by men on or near the weekends.

9.1 INCIDENT REPORT

Incident reports, also called accident reports, describe an unusual incident or occurrence. The incident could be an accident, a surprise inspection, the outburst of an angry employee or customer, or a near-accident. When police write the details of a fender bender, they are writing an incident report. When an instructor "writes up" a student for missing class, he or she is writing an incident report.

The report must be carefully written to reflect what really happened, for it can become legal evidence used in court. It also must be written to accommodate the needs of a variety of readers. These readers may be heads of companies, managers, oversight organizations such as the U.S. Food and Drug Administration, insurance companies, and criminal justice personnel. Incident reports are used by many professionals. Anyone who is responsible for overseeing the safety of personnel, the public, operations, and equipment; for preventing accidents; or for dealing with the aftermath of accidents might read an incident report.

Incident reports communicate a precise description of what happened and provide a record for later reference. They also are written to help employees and organizations see what is occurring so they can formulate plans to prevent the incident from occurring again.

Figure 9.2 on the following page recounts an incident at a food production plant. The most likely readers are supervisors, managers, company heads, and food safety inspectors. Other possible readers are consumer groups, news agencies, representatives of insurance companies, criminal proceedings personnel, and union representatives. Because of the potential for many different readers, some distant from the writer, the report is formal, using an appropriate manuscript format.

To write an incident report:

1. Begin with a brief summary of what happened.

2. Add *Background* as a heading if information about events leading up to the incident would be helpful to your readers. Some incident reports combine the summary and background and do not use a separate heading for this part if it is short.

3. Under *Description,* tell exactly what happened in chronological order. Make sure you cover the reporter's questions: Who? What? When? Where? Why? and How?

4. Be honest and objective.

5. Use the Outcome section to provide the observable incident results.

6. Use the Conclusion section to tell what was learned from the incident and how to prevent it from happening again.

To get started, carefully note any evidence. Interview people separately who witnessed or who know about the incident. Do *not* include information you cannot verify.

Imagine a familiar scene: Children are playing together when something is broken. When an adult arrives, he or she asks, "What happened?" What responses do the children provide? Will all of the children give the same account? Will some responses be more useful to the questioner than others? If so, how and why? Describe similar situations from your work or academic life.

Typical Reader

Anyone who is responsible for safety or who must handle a situation after an accident or incident.

Writer's Focus

Writing precise, detailed, and objective information that answers the audience's questions and is organized to be easily read and used.

Summarizes what happened

Provides a more detailed narrative of the incident; covers the incident from beginning to end; answers the major questions Who? What? When? Where? Why? and How?

Tells what happened as a result of the incident; may repeat some information stated in the Description

Explains what has been learned as a result of this experience and what will help prevent a similar incident

GRANDMA'S GOODIES
www.grandgoodies.com

1146 Stanton Road
Copley, OH 44312-0148

Phone: 330-555-0122
Fax: 330-555-0133

INCIDENT OF CONTAMINATION, MIXING OPERATIONS

Summary
On January 31, 20—, between 8:00 a.m. and 10:15 a.m., Number 4 flour bin was contaminated by water leaking through a small hole in an overhead steam exhaust pipe, but no permanent damage was done to the facility or equipment. The contamination was isolated to the one bin, and the contents were discarded. After thorough testing, production resumed after ten hours. The report of contamination and all test results were filed in the plant office for regulatory review.

Description
On January 31, 20—, Alexine Blanc and Julio de Mola were preparing a batch of Double Devilish Chocolate Brownie mix. At 10:15 a.m., Blanc noticed clumps in the Number 4 flour bin. Because all dry ingredients supplied to Grandma's have anti-caking additives, Blanc and de Mola knew something was wrong.

As procedure dictates, Blanc informed Val Witt, Director of Mixing Operations. Witt stopped mixing operations and requested an emergency shut-off in Packaging. Nonessential personnel were dismissed. Witt directed a complete investigation. Ten 4-ounce samples from clumps in Bin 4 were sent to the laboratory for testing. Witt also tested five 4-ounce samples from each of the remaining bins.

After Witt talked with Jason Jarvis, Manager of Packaging, Jarvis ordered samples from 5 percent of the products packaged that day.

At 11:30 a.m., the lab tests indicated that the substance causing clumping in the flour contained water and metal rust particles. No foreign substances were found in the samples from the other six bins, nor did the tests show any problems with the samples from packaged goods.

The information about the foreign materials in Bin 4 led investigators to look for leaks over the bin. A piping company, Adair Contractors, located and repaired a 1/16-inch diameter hole in the juncture where two exhaust pipes meet.

Outcome
All materials in Number 4 flour bin were discarded. The empty bin was thoroughly sanitized before use. Once cleared by the laboratory, other bins were placed back in operation. Production was off-line for ten hours on January 31, 20—. None of the contaminated materials were packaged or shipped to consumers. No one was injured or sickened because of the incident.

Conclusion
In the future, bin covers will be closed tightly until batch mixing begins. Because the piping contractor has guaranteed the repair work for one year, I do not anticipate more leaking from this area. However, I do recommend a thorough inspection of the entire exhaust pipe system. In addition, I believe systematic testing of all ingredients would further ensure our promise of quality products.

Figure 9.2 Example of Incident Report

STOP AND THINK 9.1
The reporter's questions should be answered in the Description section of an incident report. What are the questions?

9.2 TRIP REPORT

Trip reports tell supervisors and coworkers what was gained from a business trip. Trip reports are a condensed narrative. Often the report does not include everything about the trip, only those parts that are most useful to the organization. In this way, the trip report is similar to a summary because the writer includes only the essential details about the trip.

Businesses often send workers to conferences to learn the latest developments in their field. Sometimes associates visit other businesses to negotiate deals or to learn about operations. A trip is an investigation, a research mission from which the findings must be shared with others. Typically, trip reports provide managers with critical information resulting from a trip. In addition, coworkers may use information from trip reports to do their jobs.

Figure 9.3 is a trip report from Lily Lang detailing her findings from a business trip to China. While in China, she met with current and potential vendors for her company—a manufacturer and a wholesaler of hammocks, rugs, and other household and outdoor furnishings.

Suppose you are planning a vacation to a place from which someone you know just returned. What questions would you ask that person? Do you think that person's experience might enhance your trip in some way? If so, how?

Typical Reader

Managers and administrators (and sometimes coworkers and clients/customers) who need information acquired during a trip to make decisions and plans.

Writer's Focus

Creating clear, well-organized, and focused information and constantly considering the audience's needs and roles.

MEMO TO: Cristina Santana, Vice President, Operations

FROM: Lily Lang, Pan Asian Liaison   LL

DATE: 6 November 20—

SUBJECT: Vendor Investigation Trip to China, 1–12 October 2017

My mission in China was to visit potential and existing suppliers. I visited potential fabric suppliers to determine their capability to provide fabrics for our company's hammocks and outdoor furniture. I also visited our rug vendor to inspect finished products before they were shipped and to gain knowledge about hand-hooked rugs for educating customers so they can better appreciate our product. I also planned to develop relationships to improve our business.

Potential Vendors

Lixin Textile Enterprises, Fabric Supplier in Beijing   3 October 2017

After meeting with Mr. Guo, the business owner, and Mr. Guo's sales manager, Sally, and touring the facilities, I realized that Lifestyle Fabulous should not pursue a relationship with this organization. Although this supplier had an impressive office building and display room as well as an impressive website, I soon discovered that the company is a trading company that owns no factories. The owner said that he owned three fabric factories in China, but later I discovered through conversations and observations that Mr. Guo's relationship with the factories was that of vendor and customer. I had my suspicion validated by Mr Guo's assistant.

Hongyue Textile Co., Ltd., Fabric Supplier in Beijing   4 October 2017

Hongyue Textiles should be considered as a supplier. This company was not a scheduled visit. I visited this fabric factory with Mr. Guo and Sally; I discovered during the visit that the factory owner, Mr. Wang, is willing to do business with me directly or through Mr. Guo's company. Mr. Wang owns a weaving factory and a printing factory with a total of 300 employees. Mr. Wang seems to be an honest person. His price is better than that

Figure 9.3 Example of Trip Report *(continues)*

of the Taiwanese fabric supplier with whom we currently contract, and his minimal order quantity also is more desirable. (See details in Attachment A.) For paper-printing polyester fabrics, solid olefin fabrics, and jacquard olefin fabrics, Hongyue Textiles has potential as a supplier to us for the following reasons:

- UV stability rate for both solid olefin and jacquard olefin fabrics satisfies our requirements for outdoor furniture. (See Attachment B for colorfastness testing report.)
- Production lead time is 35 days after receiving purchase order.
- Sample lead time is five to seven days after receiving artwork.
- Minimal order quantity is 10,000 meters with up to eight colors per design.
- Payment requires no deposit and 100 percent invoice value at the sight of bill of lading and other shipping documents. (See Attachment C for details.)

However, I would not trust Hongyue with pigment-printed fabric because its R&D department had only three to five people and the company does not have a workshop for pigment printing. That work is outsourced.

Existing Vendors
Jinfeng Rugs Co., Ltd., Our Hand-Hooked Rug Vendor in Tinjin
6 October 2017

I met with Dan (the broker) and Lu (the owner). We discussed the following issues:
- The supplier lacks creativity and has no ideas for new products.
  - So that we will be inspired by seeing others' rug designs, Dan will e-mail me pictures of rugs he sells to European customers and rugs he sees in market.

- The yarn usage does not match well with the rug weight.
  - We weighed the backing and calculated the glue consumption and yarn waste to come up with a new figure. In the future, Dan will use this figure of 0.2645 lb per square yard.

- The finished rugs looked great, but I did some simple burning and tearing tests to the polyester yarns because the rug testing report was not yet available.
  - The flame from the yarn burning looked different from that of the test sample I ran in the United States.
  - I called the yarn vendor immediately to request a testing report on colorfastness and content. The report must be presented to me when I visit the yarn supplier.
  - I e-mailed our accounting department to hold the yarn payment.

- Dan and Lu asked me to solve their problem with yarn inventory as soon as possible.
  - We need to use 70,000 pounds of yarns in two months because Jinfeng's import registration will expire in June and renewal will require a large sum for deposit.
  - One way to use the yarn is to come up with more rug designs so our salespeople can strive for some big orders. I will ask Beth to look into this. Another option is to send the yarns to the United States.

Anji Xiaofeng Bamboo Products, the Haining Bamboo Vendor With Whom We Contracted in March 2016
9 October 2017

I had a productive meeting with Zhang Liang, the owner, and Ye Qin, the CFO. We discussed the following issues:

- Moldy boxes
  - The vendor will reimburse us 100 percent.
  - Liang and Qin presented the weather report to prove that it was a sunny day when they delivered the container to Shanghai Port. The suddenly changing temperature from inside the Shanghai warehouse

Figure 9.3 (continued) Example of Trip Report *(continues)*

to outdoors on the water in January may have had something to do with the mold, especially when the wooden boxes had been neither fumigated nor heat treated.

o   I will ask Mr. Branch whether we should share the loss since this company has been a reliable and honest vendor.

- Single bamboo rocker
    o   The sample looked beautiful, but did not display enough bamboo patterns because it was made with heavy bamboo.
    o   The labor cost for weaving the rope seat and back was too high. Zhang Liang believed that the weavers would become more efficient after they got used to the weaving patterns and the labor cost would decrease by 30 percent after the first shipment.
    o   I asked Zhang to ship the finished sample to us immediately and make another sample with regular bamboo instead of heavy bamboo.

Jiahua Bamboo and Wooden Furniture, Ltd., a Second Bamboo Vendor in Anji (With Whom We Have Contracted for One Year)

10 October 2017

Mr. Gu, his assistant, and I met; our discussion helped answer my questions relating to our bamboo products. We discussed the following subjects:

- Why is bamboo furniture more expensive than wooden when bamboo is easier to grow than trees?
    o   Bamboo is an eco-friendly product, and its demand far exceeds its supply.

- What type of bamboo is the best choice for outdoor furniture?
    o   Heavy bamboo is the best choice, but heavy bamboo does not show the natural beauty of regular bamboo.
    o   Regular bamboo is not a good choice for outdoor furniture because its color fades and it does not withstand all types of weather—the strips held together with glue come unglued. Also, if the starch-soluble carbohydrate sugars and extractives were not completely removed from bamboo, the furniture would attract bristletails. Although heavy bamboo may be durable for outdoor furniture, it would not be worth the high price.
    o   Mr. Gu considers me a good friend and wanted to continue the friendship, which is why he suggested that we not buy outdoor furniture made with bamboo even though he is the bamboo vendor.

- Follow-up: Should we conduct more research and reconsider importing outdoor bamboo furniture? I will share information with our sales and marketing department.

Conclusion

The trip was successful. After meeting with potential rug vendors, I recommend Hongyue Textiles to Lifestyle Fabulous. In addition, I identified a serious concern relating to our hand-hooked rug vendor and acquired valuable new information about bamboo products.

Recommendation

I recommend that we negotiate a contract with Hongyue Textiles, follow up on the polyester rug test results from the Shanghai testing center, develop more rug designs so that Jinfeng Rugs can use the yarn inventory before its import registration expires in June, and conduct market research to determine desirable characteristics and marketability of bamboo products.

Figure 9.3 (continued) Example of Trip Report

To write a trip report:

1. Report information your audience will find most useful. You do not need to include all of the details of the trip, only what your audience requires.

2. Preview the report in your introduction.

3. Cover the reporter's questions as you write the report: Who? What? When? Where? Why? and How? Write a section for each major concept or activity to be reported.

4. Include a heading for each section (major concept or activity) in the report body.

5. Use bulleted lists for important events or knowledge gained.

6. Decide whether your report needs Conclusions and/or Recommendations sections. Some trip reports require both, others neither, and some only one.

   - Use Conclusions to summarize the trip benefits or findings.
   - Use Recommendations to suggest further action(s).

7. Choose chronological order or order of importance.

8. Use active voice and first person—*I* or *we*—to make the report sound natural.

Do *not* try to retell every element of a trip. In addition, do *not* include information that has no relevance to your audience, such as the chance meeting of a childhood friend or the fabulous Indian restaurant you discovered.

Prepare for writing a trip report before you leave. Find out what the purpose of the trip is and what your organization expects you to learn. Investigate these concerns during your trip and address them in the report.

STOP AND THINK 9.2

How do writers decide what to cover in a trip report?

Communication
Technologies

New technologies have made modern scientific research possible. The developments of advanced instrumentation and experimental techniques have provided researchers the means to collect many forms of qualitative and quantitative data. Computer programs such as molecular modeling programs, Ab Initio quantum chemistry software, Mathcad, and Maple help process and analyze huge amounts of data. Other software programs for data analysis include R, Python, RapidMiner, and Google Fusion Tables.

Think Critically

Research one of these programs and explain how this program helps researchers make new discoveries in science, technology, engineering, or mathematics.

9.3 SCIENCE LAB REPORTS

The best science is born of a curiosity about the world along with the creative thinking to figure things out. Scientific findings, however, add little to people's collective knowledge unless someone records what was done and what happened in a science report. In the classroom, lab reports become the vehicles for testing knowledge of concepts and procedures. In professional disciplines, lab reports become the basis of science articles submitted to major journals such as *Analytical Chemistry* and *Journal of Forensic Sciences*.

The steps of the **scientific method** dictate the structure of science reports. The scientific method uses both inductive and deductive reasoning. Reasoning from a particular observation (I sneeze every time I am around a rose) to a general conclusion (Therefore, I think roses make me sneeze) is called **inductive reasoning**. Reasoning from a general conclusion (I think roses make me sneeze) to a particular situation (I probably won't sneeze if I give my mother candy instead of roses) is called **deductive reasoning**. Using inductive reasoning, scientists arrive at a tentative hypothesis, then use deductive reasoning to test that hypothesis for validity. The science report is the written record of this process.

While some differences exist in the structure of a science report among various disciplines—names for a heading or the addition of a section—a science report always answers these questions: What was the purpose of the lab? What materials were used? What procedure was followed? What were the results? What were the conclusions?

Organize

As you review the notes taken during your experiment or procedure, organize your information into these sections:

- **Introduction:** Tells the purpose or the objective of the lab (what the lab is expected to prove) and can provide background of the situation under investigation, tells under whose authority the lab was conducted, and provides relevant dates. The introduction does not always have a separate heading in shorter reports.

- **Materials and Method** (also called *Experimental Section, Methodology,* or *Procedures*): Lists materials, items, evidence, and/or instruments used. This section describes the procedure and includes relevant calculations. Materials can be presented in a separate heading from *Methodology* if the report is long.

- **Results and Discussion** (or just *Results*): Presents test results with relevant calculations, including any accompanying graphics such as tables or graphs. This section presents the results and explains why things happened. Results can be presented in a separate heading from *Discussion* if the report is long.

How do your science classes differ from your other classes (such as English, history, business, or physical education)? Explain why you think these differences exist.

Typical Reader

- **A scientist or professional interested in learning and critiquing the latest research in the field.**
- **An educator testing students' knowledge of a concept or process.**
Both readers respect, understand, and follow the scientific method.

Writer's Focus

Setting up sound research design, recording results methodically, analyzing data, and drawing logical conclusions. Presenting research objectively, following the principles of the scientific method.

Focus on Ethics

Clinical trials are research studies that test the effectiveness of new drugs, equipment, vaccines, and medical procedures. Many of these trials are funded by private companies. Usually, these companies want to sell the medicines or equipment related to the study.

Changing or "fudging" data can be tempting for funding organizations when results of a lab experiment are unexpected or difficult to understand. Ideally, clinical trials and tests from several sources would show similar results. If that is the case, the results are considered to be true, or valid. Sometimes, though, studies show conflicting results.

Jacob Krishner is the president of AM Pharmaceuticals. His company sponsored a clinical trial for a vaccine to protect against the zika virus. Three other trials had already indicated the effectiveness of the vaccine. The most recent study, done on a relatively small sample and conducted by a group of recently hired research scientists, shows that the drug might have a serious side effect. The company has invested a great deal of money in this project.

Think Critically

What should Krishner do? Does he accept the latest test results? Does he manufacture the vaccine based on the other three studies? What should he consider as he makes his decision?

■ **Conclusion(s)**: Includes a brief summary that tells how the test results, findings, and analyses meet the objectives of the lab. This section tells what was learned or gained from the experiment.

Write

After organizing your data, you are ready to write. In most cases, you will be writing to an expert in the field. (An exception is forensics, which may require explanations for the lay reader too.) So you will most likely use the scientific jargon of the field. When writing, remember to:

1. Use precision when describing procedures or offering numerical calculations.

✓ **Precise**
The tadpole measured 3.15 cm long.

✗ **Approximate**
The tadpole measured about 3 cm long.

2. Use **passive voice** (the verb *to be* + the past participle of the verb) when describing the methodology or procedures. Passive voice focuses on the process and keeps the report objective.

✓ **Passive Voice**
Tiny shifts in blood flow to parts of the brain were detected with functional MRI.

✗ **Active Voice**
Using functional MRI, we detected tiny shifts in blood flow to parts of the brain.

3. Maintain **objectivity** by describing observable results without letting personal bias or emotions influence your observations.

✓ **Objectivity**	✗ **Personal Bias or Emotions**
The client fidgeted, her eyes darted around the room, and she pursed her lips tightly.	The client was clearly angry.

4. Separate observable results (the facts) in the Results section from conclusions drawn (what the facts mean) in the Conclusions section. A result is not the same as a conclusion. A **result** is simply what happened. A **conclusion** goes beyond what happened and requires the researcher to draw an inference and interpret the data.

✓ **Results**	✗ **Conclusion**
The patient's temperature remained stable, ranging from 97.5° to 98.1° over the last 48 hours.	The patient is no longer contagious.

5. Document any sources that were used and provide a list of references.

6. When required by the discipline and length of the lab, consider adding:

- A Theory section if the lab relies on extensive theory.

- An Instrumentation section if the lab tests equipment.

- A Calculations section if the lab uses lengthy mathematical computations.

- A Recommendation section if future research is warranted.

- An Appendix (a separate section at the end of the report) if complex data such as tables and graphs would otherwise disrupt the flow of the report.

7. Use the straightforward language of the science report.

- ***To*** Verb + ***What*** **Phrases:** *To determine the differences* between several aquatic ecosystems, samples were taken in November from three sites in Georgia.

- **Lists:** A survey was sent to 150 students, 25 instructors, and 50 parents.

- **Description of Processes:** The *blood was drawn* from the patient's finger and placed on the slide. The *sample was examined* under a microscope.

- **Cause-to-Effect Reasoning:** The *data* from the table *suggests that* the resolution is highest with the pH 7/45% meOH buffer solution (alpha = 3.35).

Do not include results in the Conclusions section or conclusions in the Results section. Do not allow your personal bias to influence the conclusions you draw. Finally, do not leave out any relevant data. Record results exactly as they happen. Figure 9.4 shows a science lab report.

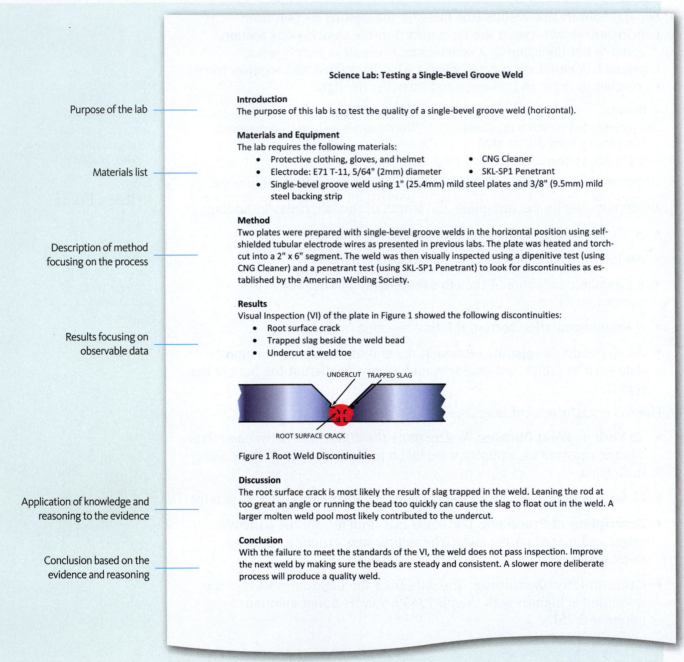

Purpose of the lab

Materials list

Description of method focusing on the process

Results focusing on observable data

Application of knowledge and reasoning to the evidence

Conclusion based on the evidence and reasoning

Science Lab: Testing a Single-Bevel Groove Weld

Introduction
The purpose of this lab is to test the quality of a single-bevel groove weld (horizontal).

Materials and Equipment
The lab requires the following materials:

- Protective clothing, gloves, and helmet
- Electrode: E71 T-11, 5/64" (2mm) diameter
- Single-bevel groove weld using 1" (25.4mm) mild steel plates and 3/8" (9.5mm) mild steel backing strip
- CNG Cleaner
- SKL-SP1 Penetrant

Method
Two plates were prepared with single-bevel groove welds in the horizontal position using self-shielded tubular electrode wires as presented in previous labs. The plate was heated and torch-cut into a 2" x 6" segment. The weld was then visually inspected using a dipenitive test (using CNG Cleaner) and a penetrant test (using SKL-SP1 Penetrant) to look for discontinuities as established by the American Welding Society.

Results
Visual Inspection (VI) of the plate in Figure 1 showed the following discontinuities:

- Root surface crack
- Trapped slag beside the weld bead
- Undercut at weld toe

UNDERCUT   TRAPPED SLAG

ROOT SURFACE CRACK

Figure 1 Root Weld Discontinuities

Discussion
The root surface crack is most likely the result of slag trapped in the weld. Leaning the rod at too great an angle or running the bead too quickly can cause the slag to float out in the weld. A larger molten weld pool most likely contributed to the undercut.

Conclusion
With the failure to meet the standards of the VI, the weld does not pass inspection. Improve the next weld by making sure the beads are steady and consistent. A slower more deliberate process will produce a quality weld.

Figure 9.4 Science Lab Report

STOP AND THINK 9.3
What is the difference between results and conclusions? Why do writers of science lab reports use passive voice?

9.4 FORENSIC REPORTS

Forensic reports are investigative reports that analyze evidence for legal purposes. From the Latin *forensic* ("of the forum," or "public"), forensics is the branch of science that uses scientific principles and methodology to evaluate various kinds of evidence. Forensic science includes a variety of specialties, including the study of handwriting, fingerprinting, blood, ballistics, tire treads, and computer hard drives. While television shows such as *NCIS, CSI,* and *Bones* have made forensic work in a crime lab popular, noncriminal investigations use forensic science as well. Highly trained in their respective fields, forensic experts write reports and often testify in legal proceedings.

As a specialized type of science lab, forensic reports strictly adhere to the scientific method—similar to the science lab reports discussed in the preceding section. Attention to detail, reliance on test procedures, objective analysis, documented research, careful reporting, and observations based on evidence are all important. Ethical considerations are vital as the forensic specialist strives to present evidence without making unnecessary assumptions or unproven interpretations. The facts must speak for themselves.

How do you make judgments about people and events? Do you base your opinions on evidence, intuition, or a combination of both? Explain.

Typical Reader

A member of a legal proceeding who must make a decision, decide the fate of a defendant, discover the truth, or make critical decisions based on the best evidence available.

Writer's Focus

Investigating objectively and thoroughly, presenting expert opinion clearly, and explaining complex processes to people not familiar with the field.

Communication
Dilemma

Akira Mehrs, the director of Experience Science, must write an incident report about an altercation that occurred between an employee whom she respects a great deal and a customer. Darrell French, a science guide, was accepting payment from Dawn Morton for entrance fees for her daughter and five friends. When Ms. Morton followed the girls into the aquarium area, she became excited, first asking and then demanding that Mr. French allow her daughter to pet one of the otters. She kept saying that it was the only request her daughter had for her birthday. Mr. French explained that the otters are wild animals and should not be touched. Ms. Morton's continuing demands were bothering other visitors, and other children, hearing her comments, began asking to hold and pet the animals. Mr. French told Ms. Morton that she would be asked to leave if she did not remove her hand from the otter tank. When the woman began to shout at him, Mr. French walked away, leaving Ms. Mehrs to handle the situation. When Ms. Mehrs sits down to write the incident report, she considers omitting the fact that Mr. French walked away from his station because she realizes that that fact will detract from his service record.

Think Critically

Should Ms. Mehrs omit details from the report to protect her employee? Why or why not?

Figure 9.5 shows a forensic report.

Numbers used to identify evidence; purpose of the report

Objective, precise description of the evidence

Parenthetical documentation used throughout to cite sources

Table used to compile results for easy reference

Evidence-based conclusions

Credentials of forensic anthropologist

APA style used to cite references in forensic science

Forensic Anthropology Report
14 December 20—

RHUML 2009-135-I-00 Red Haven University Medical Laboratory
The basis of this report is to clarify the sex of skeletal remains #2008-114-I-05.

Description of Remains
The remains exhibit variations in erosion and completeness. Remains #2008-114-I-05 are relatively complete. There is noticeable macro-porosity (large pores) on the auricular surface where the two hips connect to the tail bone (Buikstra and Ubelaker 1994), and stage 2 (Behrensmeyer 1978) fracturing is visible on the left radial pubis outside the pubic bone. The right ischium (lower hip) is fractured on the distal portion (bottom edge); roughly 70% of it is missing.

Sex Determination
Individual 2008-114-I-05 has a low and flat iliac crest, the main reason females have wider hips. The subpubic angle is U-shaped, and the sciatic notch is wide open. Both are characteristic traits associated with females (Buikstra and Ubelaker 1994). See Table 1 for attributes for sex determination.

Table 1 Attributes for Sex Determination

Os Coxa Attributes	2008-114-I-05	Result
Ilium	Low, flat	Female-like
Subpubic angle	U-shaped	Female-like
Sciatic notch	Wide	Female-like

(Adapted from Krogman 1962)

Observations
After examining the individual, it is clear that a female is represented. Based on the evidence, individual 2008-114-I-05 exhibits traits that are common with females.

Compiled by
Ian Peters, PhD, Anthropologist
Red Haven University Medical Laboratories

References Cited
Behrensmeyer, A. K. (1978). Taphonomic and Ecologic Information from Bone Weathering. *Paleobiology* 4:150–162.
Buikstra, J. E., Ubelaker, D. H. (1994). *Standards for Data Collection from Human Skeletal Remains*. Fayetteville. AR: Arkansas Archeological Survey Research Series 44.
Krogman, W. M. (1962). The Human Skeleton in Forensic Medicine. Springfield, IL: Charles C. Thomas.

Figure 9.5 Forensic Report

To write a forensic report:

1. Identify the credentials of the expert (name, title, education, and sometimes years of experience). This information can be included at the beginning or end of a report. As part of court testimony, the credentials are subject to careful scrutiny by the prosecuting and defense attorneys.

2. Identify the specimens under investigation, usually by number. These specimens may become exhibits in a case.

3. Organize the report according to the principles of the basic forensic report, as follows:

   - **Evidence:** A description of the evidence collected.

   - **Method:** A description of the method or procedure used to test the evidence, using charts, graphs, photos, and/or diagrams as necessary.

   - **Observation** (sometimes called *Interpretation, Results,* or *Conclusion*): The conclusions that can be reasonably drawn from the evidence. The report also notes if the evidence is not conclusive or if evidence is missing.

4. Write descriptions, discussion, and observations using the basic principles of scientific and technical communication: Use specific and precise measurements and vocabulary. Remain objective and focus on the process and the data.

5. Use strategies for communicating unfamiliar information to a lay audience. Explain terms as you write, provide quick definitions (in parentheses or in the next sentence), explain scientific concepts using common analogies, and break down complex processes step-by-step.

6. Provide headings and subheadings as necessary. For example, if you are asked to determine the number, sex, age, and condition of a set of bones, the report might include these headings: *Number, Sex, Age,* and *Condition of Remains.*

7. Provide references as they are used. You can cite references with parenthetical citations and a list of references at the end.

Do not allow prejudice or bias to influence your findings. Rely on evidence, not conjecture. Do not draw inferences if the evidence is incomplete. Simply point out that the evidence is insufficient.

 STOP AND THINK 9.4

Why is it important for forensic specialists to include their credentials in a forensic report?

9 CHAPTER REVIEW

Summary

1. Trip reports tell supervisors and coworkers what was gained from a business trip. The report includes only those details of the trip that are most helpful for the audience.

2. Incident reports, also called accident reports, describe an accident or an unusual incident or occurrence.

3. Lab reports answer these questions: What was the purpose of the lab? What materials were used? What was the procedure? What were the results? What are the conclusions?

4. Forensic reports give the credentials of the examiner, describe evidence, describe the method used to examine the evidence, and make observations.

Checklist

- Have I analyzed my audience(s) and determined what readers need to know?

- Have I designed, organized, and written the document with the audience in mind?

- Is my format appropriate for the audience and the situation?

- Have I included relevant background information?

- Are the data under each heading organized appropriately?

- Is the information complete and accurate?

- Have I presented problems as facts, not accusations?

Build Your Foundation

1. Are these statements subjective or objective? Explain.

   a. This is the best English class I have ever taken.
   b. This class covers the basic style and formatting of technical writing.
   c. The patient seemed angry, probably because of something that happened on the way to the office.
   d. The temperature is in the mid-80s with 20 mile per hour winds from the southwest.

2. Some of the sentences below are vague, and some include the writer's opinions. Revise each sentence to make it specific and factual. Invent details as needed.

   a. The calibrator is several minutes off schedule.
   b. The phenomenal response to our new automated response system shows that this program will benefit employees.
   c. To get to Human Resources, go down the hall a bit and turn left.
   d. The line was down for a while on Friday because of some lecture on safety.

3. Are the statements listed below observable results? Respond *yes* or *no*.

   a. The manager plans to review quality standards with all employees.
   b. The olive trees have lost 80 percent of their leaves.
   c. Mr. Domingues regrets his decision to close the recapping unit.
   d. After the robbery, the Gallery Movie Theater closed.
   e. The front line operator failed to read the Caution statement.

4. What type of graphics do these statements call for? Consider calculations, figures, and tables.

   a. The experiments were designed to demonstrate the properties of inverse functions. We experimented with several types of functions, including transcendental functions and polynomial expressions.
   b. The area of the platinum disk was found using simple algebra.
   c. An energy flow diagram (see Figure 2) was developed illustrating the energy flow and the student's position on the food web.
   d. The circuit in Figure 3 uses an op-amp as a multiplier.

5. Which part of the following statements could be more precise?

   a. The bear drank from the water hole several times in the afternoon.
   b. The decibels were tested at levels too low for human ears.
   c. The robin sat on a few eggs in its nest for a couple of weeks.
   d. The CPU costs around $374, the monitor costs about $89, and the printer costs $68.99 plus shipping and handling.

6. Where do these sentences belong in a lab report—under *Introduction, Materials and Method, Results, Discussion,* or *Conclusions?*

    a. For this activity, four potatoes, four pieces of wood, four cans, and a flame were used to determine evidence of carbon.
    b. The larger the food supply, the larger the individual guppies in the population.
    c. The data for absorbencies in Table 1 show excellent correlation and a strong linear relationship (R = 1.00) for Plot 1.

7. To practice explaining complex information to a lay audience, find a way to explain these laws of physics to a 6-year-old.

    a. Conservation of Matter: Matter is neither created nor destroyed.
    b. Third Law of Motion: For every action, there is an equal and opposite reaction.
    c. First Law of Motion: A body persists in its state of rest or of uniform motion unless acted upon by an external unbalanced force.

8. Think of ways to explain these complex processes so that a lay reader can easily understand the process. (You may need to do research first to understand the concept.) Look for a common occurrence or description to use as an analogy:

    a. How the subconscious affects a person's behavior
    b. How the human eye sees
    c. How lightning is formed
    d. How sleet develops

Your Turn

1. Think of a time when something went wrong—perhaps a problem at school or work. After identifying and analyzing your audience, write an incident report describing the incident and what you learned.

2. Visit a place of interest—perhaps a college, a business, a museum, or a sporting event. Think of questions to ask during your trip. Write a trip report to a real or fictional supervisor, answering the questions.

3. Conduct a science experiment at home. Get ideas from books, a science instructor, or online sources (Steve Spangler Science, ScienceBob, 40 Cool Science Experiments, or others). Take notes and write a lab report for English class.

4. Think of something about which you would like to know more—when your car gets better gas mileage or whether one brand or type of sunscreen works better than another. Ask a science instructor to help you design an experiment. Perform the experiment and write a lab report.

Community Connection

1. Volunteer at a day care center, for a reading program, or for another activity. Write an incident report based on an event you witnessed or learned of. Address the report to the leader of the organization.

2. If you have a chance to travel to a conference, a seminar, a workshop, or another event, provide a trip report to the sponsors of the trip. Ask your classmates and/or instructor to help edit and revise the report.

3. Interview someone who performs experiments, conducts labs or medical tests, or examines evidence (a police officer or a medical examiner, for example). Ask how reports are written, how evidence is handled, and how the scientific method is used. Discuss the difficulty of remaining objective. Share a short written or oral report of your findings with your class.

4. Attend a court proceeding for a criminal case and take notes. How do forensic specialists provide expert testimony? Interview a lawyer and ask about the importance of forensic testimony and the procedure for admitting it into evidence. Tell your classmates how your findings compare with the chapter's information about forensic reports.

EXPLORE THE NET

WorldWideScience.org has a mission to accelerate scientific discovery and progress by providing a global gateway for one-stop searching of scientific databases and portals from around the world. A user is able to search many data sources around the world with a single query and then translate the resulting materials into a language the user understands. *WorldWideScience.org* offers real-time searching of over 100 databases and portals of scientific literature published in many languages from more than 70 countries. In addition, translation of multilingual scientific literature is available through the site. The Office of Scientific and Technical Information (OSTI), a unit of the Office of Science within the U.S. Department of Energy, created and maintains the site for the WorldWideScience Alliance.

How many languages are currently supported on the site?

After selecting a topic you are interested in from the basic sciences, energy, medicine, agriculture, or environment, conduct a search. Results will be delivered in order of relevance to your query. What article or material appears as your first (or most relevant) result? Now try to translate one of the articles in your response list.

10 INSTRUCTIONS

Write to Learn

Think of the last time you followed instructions. Maybe the instructions were from an instructor, your parent or guardian, your employer, a textbook, or an online manual. In a brief journal entry, answer these questions: Under what circumstances did you read the instructions? Were the instructions easy or difficult to follow? Explain. How did you resolve any problems that resulted from poorly written instructions? If graphics were included, what kind were they? Were they helpful? Why or why not?

 FOCUS on Instructions

Read Figure 10.1 on the following pages and answer these questions:

- How does the writer make it clear what to do first, second, and so on?
- How many actions does each step represent?
- How does each step begin?
- What is the purpose in Section 5 of the boxed warning in red at the top of the page when other specific warnings appear beneath it?

What If?

How would the model change if . . .

- The user were a beginner in the field?
- The user was not a strong native speaker of English?
- The instructions were spoken rather than written?

4 MOUNTING TIRE ON RIM/WHEEL ASSEMBLY

TUBELESS; SINGLE-PIECE

4A. Before mounting, be sure that the tire is properly matched to the rim. These photo examples show the rim/wheel size stamp.

⚠️ **WARNING** NEVER assemble a tire and rim unless you have positively identified and correctly matched the tire and rim diameter. If an attempt is made to seat the tire bead by inflating on a mismatched rim/wheel, the tire bead will break with explosive force and may result in serious injury or death.

4B. Identify the short side of the drop center well. Single-piece tubeless rims and wheels must be mounted from the short side of the drop center well. On steel disc wheels, the short side is typically located opposite the disc. Aluminum wheels typically have symmetrical drop centers so tires can be mounted from either side. However, on certain 19.5-inch

aluminum wheels, the short side of the drop center well is located on the disc side.

4C. Place the wheel on the floor with the short side of the drop center well facing up. **Lubricate** the tire beads and rim surfaces.

4D. Push the tire on the rim opposite the valve stem and use the curved end of the tire iron to pry the bottom bead over the rim flange.

4E. Apply pressure to the bead opposite the valve stem making sure the bead is completely in the drop center well.

4F. Taking small bites, use the curved end of the tire iron to pry the top bead over the rim flange. Keep the bead in the drop center well with your foot or a bead-locking device. Continue until the top bead is fully mounted over the rim flange.

BEFORE INFLATING TIRE RIM/WHEEL ASSEMBLY, THE TIRE MUST BE PROPERLY MOUNTED.

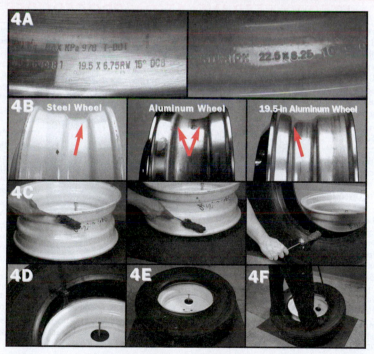

DEMOUNTING AND MOUNTING PROCEDURES
FOR TUBELESS TRUCK AND BUS TIRES
PAGE 5

Figure 10.1 OSHA Tire Changing Instructions *(continues)* Source: Excerpted from OSHA 3421-10R 2014: Servicing Multi-Piece and Single-Piece Rim Wheels: 29 CFR 1910.177. Demounting and Mounting Procedures for Tubeless Truck and Bus Tires; Demounting and Mounting Procedures for Tube-Type Truck and Bus Tires; Multi-Piece Rim Matching Chart. Source: Occupational Safety and Health Administration, U.S. Department of Labor.

5 INFLATING TIRE RIM/WHEEL ASSEMBLY

> ⚠️ **WARNING** TIRE AND RIM SERVICING CAN BE DANGEROUS AND MUST ONLY BE PERFORMED BY TRAINED PERSONNEL USING PROPER PROCEDURES AND TOOLS. FAILURE TO READ AND COMPLY WITH ALL OF THESE PROCEDURES MAY RESULT IN SERIOUS INJURY OR DEATH TO YOU AND OTHERS.

⚠️**WARNING** **NEVER** use starter fluid, ether, gasoline, or other flammable materials and/or accelerants to lubricate or to seat the beads of a tire. This practice can cause the explosive separation of the tire/wheel during servicing or during highway use, which may result in serious injury or death.

⚠️**WARNING** **ALWAYS** inflate the tire rim/wheel assembly in a restraining device with the valve core removed. The air line assembly must consist of the following components: a clip-on air chuck, an in-line valve with a pressure gauge or presettable regulator, and sufficient hose length to keep the technician outside the trajectory during inflation. (See "Trajectory" WARNING below.) **DO NOT** rest or lean any part of your body against the restraining device during inflation. Failure to use a restraining device when inflating a tire rim/wheel assembly is not only a violation of OSHA regulation 1910.177, but also a DANGEROUS PRACTICE that may result in serious injury or death.

⚠️**WARNING** During inflation, if ANY sidewall undulations or bulges appear or if ANY snapping, cracking or popping noises occur — **STOP! DO NOT** approach tire. Before removing from restraining device, completely deflate tire remotely. Remove clip-on air chuck. Mark tire as damaged for potential "zipper rupture". Render tire unservicable, non-repairable and scrap.

⚠️**WARNING** **NEVER** inflate beyond 40 psi to seat any tire beads. **NEVER** stand, lean, or reach over the tire rim/wheel assembly in the restraining device during inflation. Even if a tire is in a restraining device, inflating beyond 40 psi when trying to seat the beads is a DANGEROUS PRACTICE that may break a tire bead or the rim/wheel with explosive force and possibly result in serious injury or death.

STEP-BY-STEP INFLATION PROCEDURES

1. Before inflating any tire rim/wheel assembly, be sure to read, understand and comply with ALL WARNINGS.

2. After mounting the tire on the rim, use a compressed air tank with quick release valve to seal the beads. **Do not exceed 5 psi before placing the assembly in a restraining device.**

3. Place the assembly in an OSHA-compliant restraining device, such as a tire safety cage. Photo 5A is an example of one type of a restraining device. Manufacturers recommend that restrain- ing devices be freestanding and located at least one foot away from any flat or solid surface.

4. Inflate the tire, with the valve core removed, using a clip-on air chuck with an in-line valve or pressure regulator and a sufficent length of hose. **Inflate to 20 psi** in restraining device. **IMPORTANT!** Look for distortions, undulations, or other irregularities in the tire sidewall, such as in Photo 5C. Listen for any popping or snapping sounds. If ANY of these conditions are present — **STOP! DO NOT** approach tire. Before removing from restraining device, completely deflate tire remotely. Remove clip-on air chuck. Mark tire as damaged for potential "zipper rupture". Render tire unservicable, non-repairable and scrap.

5. Visually inspect tire rim/wheel assemblies throughout the inflation process for improper seating. When inflating a tire, stay out of the trajectory. See "Trajectory" WARNING below. **DO NOT** stand or lean any part of your body against, or reach over, the restraining device during inflation.

6. Continue to inflate until the beads are seated on the rim/wheel. Inspect both sides of the tire to be sure that the beads are evenly seated. **NEVER** inflate beyond 40 psi to seat any tire beads. If the beads are not seated at 40 psi — **STOP!** Completely deflate, remove from the restraining device, and determine the problem. Reposition the tire on the rim, relubricate, and reinflate.

7. After the tire beads are seated, continue to inflate the tire to its recommended inflation pressure. **IMPORTANT!** Look for distortions, undulations, or other irregularities in the tire sidewall, such as in Photo 5D. Listen for any popping or snapping sounds. If ANY of these conditions are present — **STOP! DO NOT** approach tire. Before removing from restraining device, completely deflate tire remotely. Remove clip-on air chuck. Mark tire as damaged for potential "zipper rupture". Render tire unservicable, non-repairable and scrap.

8. If none of these "zipper" conditions are present, **remove clip-on air chuck, install the valve core, and adjust the inflation pressure** to the recommended operating inflation pressure.

9. Before removing the tire rim/wheel assembly from the restraining device, always visually inspect for proper seating of the beads and all parts.

10. Conduct a final inspection. Check for air leaks. Install a suitable valve cap.

DEMOUNTING AND MOUNTING PROCEDURES
FOR TUBELESS TRUCK AND BUS TIRES
PAGE 6

Figure 10.1 (continued) OSHA Tire Changing Instructions Souce: Excerpted from OSHA 3421-10R 2014: Servicing Multi-Piece and Single-Piece Rim Wheels: 29 CFR 1910.177. Demounting and Mounting Procedures for Tubeless Truck and Bus Tires; Demounting and Mounting Procedures for Tube-Type Truck and Bus Tires; Multi-Piece Rim Matching Chart. Source: Occupational Safety and Health Administration, U.S. Department of Labor.

Writing @Work

Courtesy of Stephen Freas

CareerClusters®
PATHWAYS TO COLLEGE & CAREER READINESS
Information Technology

Source: The Center to Advance CTE

Aaron Wartner is an application and database administrator for Accenture, an IT consulting firm in Cincinnati, Ohio. In his role, he is responsible for maintaining a digital planning system used by Accenture's customers.

Aaron's job creates a link between customers who use Accenture's technology and the technology itself. He has the tricky task of communicating both with his "techy" colleagues and with clients. "Much of my time is spent e-mailing information to or requesting action from my coworkers. I also write instructions for customers' scheduled maintenance activities that describe how to perform the work, how to coordinate with other teams, and the timing for each action."

Writing technical instructions that are easy to follow is not an easy task. "Instructions must be interpreted the same way by every reader to be successful," says Aaron. "So they must be understandable, and the intent must be clear. Consistency in describing objects and activities and careful use of technical jargon are a few ways I try to meet these goals."

Aaron begins writing a set of instructions for a certain task by doing that task himself.

"I start by walking through the process to understand the flow of steps and to make sure that what I am doing will work. I identify and record each basic step as I go, preserving the order of steps. Once I have all of the steps, I create an outline of the process. Finally, I word the instructions for each step based on who the intended audience is."

After Aaron finishes a set of instructions, he follows them in his company's test system to make sure they work. "Having a test system allows us to fix errors in our instructions before they reach customers."

Think Critically

1. Do you think Aaron expected to do so much writing in his job? Explain.

2. Convert Aaron's description of the process he follows (paragraphs 4 and 5) into a simple set of instructions.

Printed with permission of Aaron Wartner

Writing in Information Technology

With the invention of the World Wide Web and the introduction of the Internet in the 1990s, society entered the Information or Digital Revolution. Just as the Industrial Revolution gave rise to traditional industry, the Digital Revolution brought a society based on the development and use of information. Thus, one's ability to find, analyze, interpret, and use data greatly impacts one's ability to be successful. Because communication across the world is simple, inexpensive, and available, the world has become a smaller place, which makes workers who can effectively use and communicate about data valuable. Therefore, workers in the United States compete with workers in China, India, Japan, and all other parts of the world in the Information Age. Students dreaming of a bright and successful future will focus on building research skills, communicating technical information clearly and concisely, and utilizing data to achieve goals.

WARM UP

10.1 GETTING STARTED ON INSTRUCTIONS

Do you usually read instructions before you attempt a procedure? Why or why not?

Typical Reader

Any person, whether technician, professional, or client/customer, who needs to follow guidelines, procedures, or directions to complete a task.

Writer's Focus

Analyzing a process to present clear, detailed, and precise instructions with appropriate explanations, cautions, warnings, and graphic elements to enable users to follow steps successfully to complete a task.

Imagine you just purchased a new cabinet for your home theater system. You want to assemble the cabinet before your friends arrive to watch a movie. You have two hours to put the cabinet together. Because you are on a tight schedule, you begin to assemble the furniture without looking at the instructions. "It can't be that hard," you mumble under your breath. You are certain that reading the instructions will slow you down. An hour and a half later, you are still trying to connect the pieces. You are frantic because your guests will be knocking on your door in 30 minutes—and the cabinet is still in pieces on the floor. Finally, you look at the **instructions**, the sequence of steps explaining how to complete a task.

Who Reads Instructions?

People who read instructions need to perform a task or understand how someone else performs that task. The server being asked to close a restaurant needs to know the procedure for doing so. The surveyor measuring a road for underground pipes needs to know how to determine traffic patterns. You, assembling your newly purchased home theater cabinet, need to know how to set it up as quickly as possible.

You can empathize with a reader trying to follow a set of instructions. Instructions, with their graphics and technical language, can be intimidating. Consequently, some readers read instructions carefully, paying close attention to every word.

On the other hand, many readers, similar to you in the previous situation, are impatient, trying to go through the steps without reading them first. Some readers, thinking they are familiar with the procedure, read only a few steps and think they know what to do. Other readers rely more on the graphics than the words for information.

Whatever their approach, readers trust the writer to give them accurate, precise information in the proper sequence. Some instructions—electrical installation and medical procedures, for example—can be matters of life or death. For example, the instructions for installing a new light fixture can put a do-it-yourself installer in danger of electric shock if the instructions fail to say, "Before installing the fixture, turn off all electrical power running to the fixture." In those cases, readers trust writers with their lives and with the lives and safety of others.

Because your reader trusts you, you must make sure that your instructions are accurate and thorough. The amount of detail depends on how much knowledge your audience has about the process. A beginner, for example, needs more detail than someone with experience. Effective instructions keep readers motivated to read carefully.

Planning Instructions

Before writing your own instructions, you must understand the procedure about which you are writing. If you understand the procedure, you will be better able to explain it to someone else. If you do not understand the procedure, your readers probably will not understand it either. When possible, work through the process yourself to see where your readers may get tripped up.

Use the following suggestions to analyze the process and to better understand the steps, the series of actions required to complete the process:

- Create a flowchart with steps to the process. Write what someone should do first, second, third, and so on. Do not to skip any steps. Add and remove steps as needed.

- In your mind, work the process backward. What is the purpose of the procedure? What is done last, next to last, third to last, and so on?

- Watch a member of your target audience performing the task for the first time. Take notes. What is the first step? What is the most difficult step? Which step or steps does the person misunderstand? Would additional information make things clearer? Interview this person after he or she has completed the procedure. Ask for suggestions to help you write a clear set of instructions.

- In your planning, you also should consider the situation or circumstances under which users will be reading and following your instructions. For instance, a student undergoing fire and rescue training in a safe learning environment under the supervision of an instructor is likely to feel less stress and pressure in following the instructions for using a fire extinguisher than a homeowner working alone to put out a kitchen fire. Effective instructions will meet the needs of users in both circumstances.

STOP AND THINK 10.1

If a friend wanted to borrow your vehicle, would your operating instructions differ if the friend were 20 years older than you are? If the friend had just received his or her first driver's license? If the friend were from a country where vehicles operate on the left side of the road?

10.2 ORGANIZING AND FORMATTING INSTRUCTIONS

WARM UP

How do you prefer to receive a set of instructions? Do you want to read written steps or to be told how to do something? Do you prefer watching someone perform a procedure or looking at pictures or a drawing of what to do?

Now that you have analyzed the steps for your instructions, organize your information into sections for your reader. Then place that information into a sequence of chronological steps and an easy-to-read format.

Organizing Instructions

All instructions include steps of procedures and appropriate explanations along with additional details to clarify the procedure. However, instructions often contain other parts as well. Whether to include these parts depends on the audience and the purpose of the instructions.

Different writing situations require different organizational strategies. Although most instructions begin with an introduction, some do not. For example, the manual for a new car may contain an introduction at the beginning, but not for each major section. Furthermore, not all instructions require a list of materials. For example, telling someone how to use a blender would require only familiarity with the appliance, not a list of materials. But telling someone how to make pancakes would require a list of materials and ingredients.

Some instructions might require **cautions**, statements to indicate which actions might harm the mechanism. Others might require stronger **warnings**, statements to indicate which actions might injure or harm someone trying to follow the instructions. When you delete a file from your computer, a caution appears to ask whether you really want to send the file to the trash bin. The instructions telling you how to administer flea and tick protection to your cat warn about the danger of the product coming in contact with your skin. Even your bag of microwave popcorn has a warning: "HANDLE CAREFULLY—CONTAINS HOT AIR AND STEAM." You, too, are responsible for including proper cautions and warnings with any instructions you write.

Use Table 10.1 to determine what elements to add to instructions.

Table 10.1

Include	If
Cautions	Your reader could damage equipment by doing a step incorrectly. Insert cautions in your text before readers are likely to do anything harmful. Often a symbol or graphic accompanies the caution.
Definitions	Your reader must learn new terms to perform the procedure. Define six or more terms in a separate list or glossary. Define fewer than six terms when you first use the term.
Less Explanation	Your reader has performed the process before or the process is an emergency procedure in which reading explanations would prevent the reader from acting quickly.
More Explanation	Your reader is performing the process for the first time, the procedure is complicated, or the reader needs to know more to perform the procedure correctly.
Graphics	A picture, diagram, or flowchart would make the instructions easier to follow. Place a graphic as close as possible to the step it illustrates—above, below, or beside. Avoid placing the graphic on another page or at the end of the instructions.
Introduction	Your reader would benefit from any or all of the following information: background, purpose (what readers will be able to do when they finish), intended audience, scope (what the instructions do and do not cover), organization, best way to read the instructions, assumptions about readers' knowledge or abilities, and/or motivation to read the instructions carefully. An introduction, when included, appears at the beginning of the document.
Materials/Tools	Your reader should gather materials, tools, or ingredients before following your instructions. Place this list before the steps.
Notes/Tips	Additional but not essential information would aid your reader's understanding. Include a note immediately after the step to which it pertains.
Warnings	Your reader could get hurt by overlooking a step or not doing a step correctly. Place warnings before the reader is likely to do anything dangerous, often at the top of the instructions and again before any step which might be dangerous. Often a symbol or graphic that represents danger accompanies the warning.

Formatting Instructions

Because readers are likely to be varied and are often impatient, the format of your instructions should be easy to read. Use plenty of white space to make instructions look accessible. Number your steps using Arabic numerals (1, 2, 3, and so on) and align the steps in a list.

Another effective way to make instructions easy to use is to incorporate graphics such as flowcharts and diagrams. Graphics simplify a process and are useful for an intermediate reader who has performed the process before and needs only a quick refresher. Graphics aid the beginner as well, who will rely on both graphics and text to follow the procedure correctly. Sometimes different parts of a mechanism are shown at different times in the steps. Refer to your graphics with an explanatory statement, such as "Refer to Figure 1 to see the location of buttons on the DVD player." You may add callouts that point to specific parts of your diagram to help readers find the parts you are discussing. Instructions that include referral statements cue the reader to look at the graphic at the appropriate time.

Formats may vary. For example, simple instructions may include only a one-sentence introduction and a list of numbered steps. Some instructions may contain only pictures. More complex instructions require several sections and graphics. A numbered list is preferred to define steps that must be completed in a certain order, although some instructions use letters or bullets to indicate steps.

Online instructions often use a layered approach to formatting. For instance, the basic steps in a procedure are shown in a list on a page. That list then includes links to other pages where more information or more detailed instructions appear. Figure 10.2 shows a page from the U.S. Department of

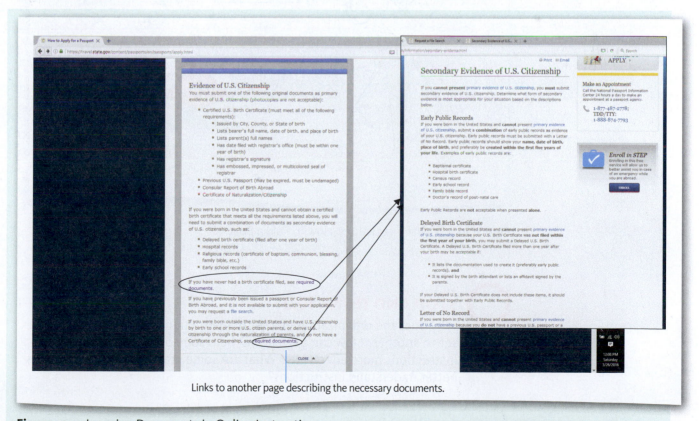

Links to another page describing the necessary documents.

Figure 10.2 Layering Documents in Online Instructions Source: travel.state.gov, U.S Department of State, Bureau of Consular Affairs.

State's Consular Affairs website, which provides instructions for applying for a passport. Note the terms in blue, such as "required documents," are links to other pages providing more specific information related to each term. In this case, "required documents" links to a page titled "Secondary Evidence of US Citizenship" that describes the types of documents that might be used for passport application if primary evidence of citizenship is not available.

Figure 10.3 below illustrates a simple format for instructions a simple format for instructions an elementary school teacher or a recreation therapist might use.

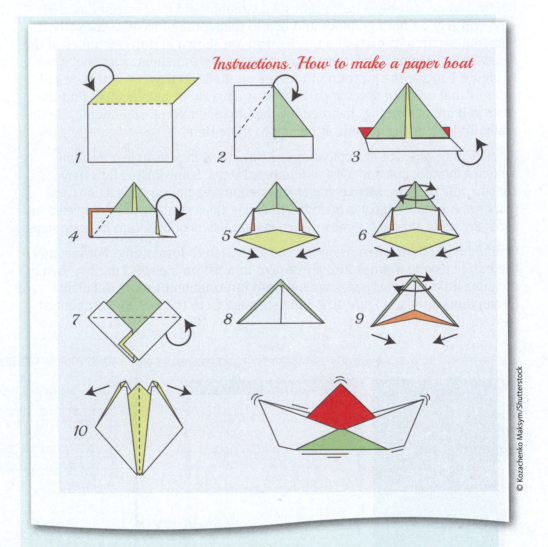

Figure 10.3 Visual Instructions: How to Fold a Boat

 STOP AND THINK 10.2

Why does the organization of a set of instructions change from one set to another? How can page layout help someone read and follow instructions more effectively? What are some graphics that help readers better understand instructions?

10.3 COMPOSING INSTRUCTIONS

Organization, format, and graphics may vary, but all instructions require chronological steps. Except for instructions written for experienced readers, most instructions require explanations to accompany the steps.

Steps

A **step** is the action that a reader performs—what the reader actually does. Steps have a consistent and unique structure. Use the following guidelines for writing steps:

1. Make sure steps proceed *forward in time*—numbered, or in some cases lettered—with no backtracking to pick up a step that was forgotten.

✓ Forward in Time	✗ Backtracking
a. Buckle your seat belt.	a. Insert the key into the ignition switch.
b. Insert the key into the ignition switch.	b. Turn the key forward until the engine starts.
c. Turn the key forward until the engine starts.	c. Buckle your seat belt before you turn the key forward.

2. Begin each step with an active-voice verb in the **imperative mood** (a command: verb + object) and use second person (stated or understood "you" as the subject).

✓ Action Verb to Start	✗ No Verb to Start
Trim the tip of the dog's nail.*	The tip of the dog's nails should be trimmed.

* You can begin with a modifying word or phrase, as in "Carefully trim the tip of the dog's nail" or "To ensure a pain-free procedure, trim the tip of the dog's nail."

Communication Technologies

Many companies use interactive video to train employees. This choice saves companies money by avoiding costly travel expenses when employees must go to another location for specialized training. Interactive video places instructional material online or on DVD. Employees view the instruction, study it at their own pace, and interact by keying answers or comments. Training is available on a host of topics, including sales techniques, museum operations, and information technologies.

Think Critically

List the pros and cons of face-to-face training sessions in a classroom setting and of distance-learning training with interactive video.

3. Use short sentences, which keep your reader focused on one step at a time. An overly complex or compound-complex sentence can create confusion.

✓ **Short Sentences**	✗ **Long Sentence**
Install a smoke detector inside each bedroom in which an occupant sleeps with the door closed. Smoke blocked by the door might not sound an alarm in the hallway. Also, the sleeper might not hear an alarm coming from another area of the house.	Install a smoke detector inside each bedroom in which an occupant sleeps with the door closed because smoke blocked by the door might not sound the alarm in the hallway and the sleeper might not hear an alarm coming from another area of the house.

4. Write only one instruction (one action) for each step.

Exception: If two steps are closely tied to each other in time, reading them in the same step might be easier for the reader: "Release the clutch. At the same time, press the accelerator."

✓ **One Instruction per Step**	✗ **More Than One Instruction per Step**
a. Place your chin on the chin rest. b. Look at the light.	Place your chin on the chin rest and look at the light.

5. Make sure each step is truly a step—an action, something to do. A description implies action, but it does not direct the reader to actually do something.

✓ **An Action**	✗ **A Description**
Grasp the rope when it comes back to you.	The rope will come back to you.

6. Keep the natural articles *a*, *an*, and *the*.

✓ **With Articles**	✗ **Without Articles**
Send the electrician a notice to connect power to the house.	Send electrician notice to connect power to house.

7. Include precise, specific details (measurements, sizes, locations, time, parts, and restatement in more familiar language) to show your reader exactly what to do.

✓ **Sufficient Details**	✗ **Not Sufficient Details**
Loosen the chain to provide 3/8" of movement, or "give," between the front and rear sprockets.	Loosen the chain to provide some movement, or "give," in the chain.

8. Place any necessary explanations after the step. Placing the step first keeps the reader on task.

✓ **Explanation after Step**	✗ **Explanation before Step**
Touch the number pad to enter the weight of the food to be defrosted. Make sure you enter the weight in pounds and tenths of pounds.	Make* sure you enter the weight in pounds and tenths of pounds. Touch the number pad to enter the weight of the food to be defrosted.

*Although *Make* is a verb, it does not indicate a step but explains how to enter the weight.

9. Use substeps when a major step is too broad to be clearly understood by your reader.

✓ **Use of Substeps**	✗ **Overgeneralized Step***
Play a G major chord.	Play a G major chord.

a. Place your third finger on the third fret of the bottom string.

b. Place your second finger on the second fret of the fifth string.

c. Place your third finger on the third fret of the first string.

* Whether to use substeps depends on your audience's knowledge and experience with the procedure.

Explanations

An **explanation** is an extension of the step it explains. An explanation uses the same number as the step it follows and is written immediately after the step.

1. Write the step. Then write the explanation if it is needed.

2. Write another step. Then write the explanation if it is needed.

3. Write another step. Then write the explanation if it is needed.

The number and type of explanations depend on your reader's previous experience. Not every step requires an explanation, but well-placed explanations guide and motivate your reader. Often explanations are written as a note following the step. Typical explanations include the following:

- What not to do and why

  Darken the appropriate oval with a No. 2 pencil. Do not place stray pencil marks on the answer sheet. The computerized scanner may read the stray mark as an error.

  Note: Warnings and cautions are important enough to include before the step that may cause a problem if it is not completed correctly.

- Why a step is important

  Rinse the boiled egg with cold water as soon as you remove it from boiling water. The cold water will cause the egg to contract from the shell, making the egg easier to peel.

- What happens when the reader does something

  (1) Press PROGRAM on the remote control. The MENU will appear on the TV screen. (2) To autoscan for a channel, press CHANNEL SCAN once on the remote control. The tuner scans the channels stored in the tuner's memory, stopping on each channel for about two seconds.

- How to perform the action—more detail

  Tighten the axle nuts. Make sure they are tight. No space should be visible between the inner nut, the wheel slip, and the axle nuts. If there is space, tighten the axle nuts more securely.

- What terms to define

  Beat the eggs until frothy, or until they look like sea foam. *or* A digital signal transmits electrical data using binary code, or "off" and "on" pulses.

Note: If you have a number of definitions (approximately six or more), consider adding a separate section labeled "Definitions" or "Glossary." If you have fewer than six, define them as you write or place them in the introduction.

- How to make a decision

Wrap a small section of hair around the curling iron. If you want curls to flip up, wrap the hair backward (away from the shoulders). If you want curls to curve under, wrap the hair down (toward the shoulders).

Note: Branching the two methods into substeps is another possibility:

1. Wrap a small section of hair around the curling iron.

    a. If you want curls to flip up, wrap the hair backward.

    b. If you want curls to curve under, wrap the hair face forward.

Because some readers need more details, you must think carefully about how much explanation to add. Consider answers to the questions that follow.

- What should readers not do? Why?

- Would readers be more likely to perform the steps correctly if they knew the significance of the action, the reason for performing the step, or more about the process?

- Would pointing out what should happen when readers execute a step help them? (The first time you performed the process, how did you know you had performed a step correctly?)

- Does the reader need help making a decision? Should some steps be subdivided into if/then scenarios? Refer to the curling iron example in the previous list.

- Would the reader benefit from a brief definition?

- What questions will readers have?

- What are the most crucial steps—those steps that *must* be done correctly?

Finally, think back to the first time you performed the procedure and how awkward it felt to be a beginner.

- What did you do wrong the first time you performed the process?

- What questions did you have the first time you performed the process?

Field Tests

Always **field-test** your instructions by asking several people to try them before you send your final copy. Your field testers can provide you with valuable feedback by noting wording that is not clear, steps that are out of sequence, or steps that have been left out altogether. To administer a field test, also called a usability test, you must select a test method, design the test, select test subjects, and make revisions based on the data.

Concurrent testing and retrospective testing, discussed next, are two field tests that evaluate how effectively users can perform your instructions.

Concurrent Testing

Concurrent testing evaluates a product while it is being used or an activity while it is being performed. In a concurrent test, you observe your subjects reading and performing your instructions. You measure such things as their accuracy, speed, recall, and attitude.

Rhonda adapted an informal method of concurrent testing to evaluate instructions she wrote. Her instructions told AmeriCorps volunteers how to find the campsite for their training retreat. To make sure all 50 volunteers would find the site, she asked three classmates to follow her directions using a map she had drawn. Two classmates did not arrive at the campsite because they turned onto Riverside Road instead of Riverview Road. As a result, Rhonda knew that she needed to revise her instructions to emphasize the name of the correct road and to caution drivers against making the wrong turn. Because of the information Rhonda learned, all AmeriCorps volunteers found their way.

Concurrent testing for longer instructions involves a more formal procedure. For example, Arturo, the service manager for Satellite Dish Subsidiaries, wants to make sure that his instructions for installing a satellite dish for TV and Internet service are clear. He selects five test subjects in a rural community who range in age from 20 to 45 because these are the types of people who will likely be installing the dish. He then watches each person install the dish, taking notes about errors, comments, questions, and frustrations. After watching the five subjects perform the installation, Arturo knows that two of them had difficulty mounting the dish in the correct location at the proper angle. He realizes that his steps about placement are confusing because each step contains too much information. So he makes the steps shorter and adds a roof diagram to show suggested areas for placement.

To design a useful concurrent study, decide whether your subjects should complete the whole procedure or just selected tasks. Rhonda and Arturo asked their subjects to perform the entire task. On the other hand, a usability study focuses only on selected tasks. One usability study of a website advertising cars asked users to find the "sale of the day," descriptions of used models, and information about warranties.

As you observe your test subjects, ask yourself these questions:

- Were the subjects able to do what the instructions told them to do?

- How long did the subjects take to complete the task?

- How many mistakes did the subjects make?

- What steps were most difficult? least difficult?

- Were the subjects frustrated at any time? If so, explain.

- What did the subjects remember about the task 15 minutes after completing it?

- What did the subjects remember about the task 24 hours after completing it?

You also can ask subjects to verbalize their thoughts, reading the instructions aloud and saying whatever comes to mind. Through this window to subjects' thoughts, you see how they are reacting to each step. You may want to record their performance so you can review it more closely later.

Retrospective Testing

A second way to test instructions is through the use of **retrospective testing**— asking subjects to complete a questionnaire or to answer questions about a task *after* they have performed it. Many field tests use a concurrent test along with a retrospective test. This way testers gain additional insights into the behavior of test subjects.

Surveys often are used for retrospective testing. Remember that a survey can include different types of questions. Figure 10.4 shows questions that Kelsey plans to ask his loan officers after they have field-tested his procedures for completing a car loan application.

Retrospective Test Questions

Question Types	Questions
Multiple Choice	Was the introduction informative? Yes____ No____
	After filling in the applicant's name, address, Social Security number, and telephone number (steps 1–4), the next step was to
	a. Enter the amount of money requested.
	b. Include the value of the car.
	c. Enter the current interest rate.
Likert Scale	Rank on a scale of 1–10 (with 10 being most satisfied and 1 being least satisfied) your satisfaction with the completeness* of this document.
	1 2 3 4 5 6 7 8 9 10
Short Answer	Describe the first step you performed.
	After reading step 6 (*perhaps a critical step such as entering gross income*), what did you think you were supposed to do?
Open	What suggestions do you have for improvement?
	What was the most difficult section? Why?

*Kelsey could ask about clarity of the wording or usefulness of the graphics.

Figure 10.4 Survey Questions for a Retrospective Field Test

Regardless of the test method you use, select a reasonable sample of subjects. To ask senior accountants to test instructions for using a machine lathe is not practical because they would not use the instructions. You would ask senior accountants to test instructions for new accounting software. Some experts recommend using at least five testers, but others do not believe that five testers is enough—especially for a longer document such as a manual or for interactive media on a website. After completing your field test, you should compile your data, list problems from most frequent to least frequent, and devise solutions.

Online Instructions

No doubt you have used **online instructions**, or computer-based instructions, to order concert tickets, to track a UPS delivery, to set up e-mail and social media accounts, or to complete a job application. Online instructions allow users to find out something, to get something, or to learn something quickly.

Online instructions include help menus and web-based instructions. Help menus are one of the most popular types of online instructions. Most computer programs feature a help menu, typically in the upper right corner of the screen, or balloon help, the explanation that appears when you scroll over a menu item. Think about your educational career. You may recall using tutorials on a website to teach yourself grammar, keyboarding, or a foreign language.

To write online instructions, keep in mind the strategies presented in this chapter for writing and explaining steps, using white space and graphics, and providing cautions and warnings. In addition to the guidelines for writing paper-based instructions, online instructions should:

- Limit each unit of instruction to one screen size so it is not necessary for the user to scroll down the page.

- Use consistent design—font, font sizes, colors, graphics, and headers— so the reader learns to anticipate the organization and feels comfortable navigating.

- Provide a tree or map of the site and topics so readers can see the site at a glance and link to areas of interest.

- Insert navigational aids such as links to the home page and to other pages listed in the site map.

- Use keyword searches with several synonyms for the same action.

- Evaluate the usefulness of the instructions with a field test, revising the instructions if necessary.

Communication
Dilemma

You have just landed a job as a trainer for an international company that makes engines for jet airplanes. Your job is to train new engineers, line managers, and other employees to assemble specific engine parts. This coming Monday you will conduct your first training session online. You review the training materials developed before you joined the company to prepare for the session. Then, on Friday afternoon before the scheduled training, your manager tells you that many employees taking the training are not from the United States. Participants live in Taiwan, Germany, and Japan. Your boss explains that translators will work to help the trainees who do not speak English. But you wonder if these participants will benefit from the training at the level or rate they need to.

Think Critically

How might you revise your training materials so that international employees will better understand? Are the answers to online questions at the session's end enough evidence to certify participants in the processes for which they were trained?

Also, if you are teaching users to perform tasks on a screen, configure instructions so they do not take up the entire screen. By configuring your instructions this way, you allow users to work on the screen while they read the instructions.

STOP AND THINK 10.3

How are steps written? What kind of information do explanations contain? What kind of information makes instructions precise? Why is field testing important? How can a writer field-test instructions? What strategies should you keep in mind when writing online instructions?

Focus on Ethics

When you pick up a prescription from the pharmacy, you receive an insert that gives you information about the drug—instructions for use, proper doses, side effects, and risks. By giving patients and doctors more information on which to base judgments about good health, drug companies accept an ethical responsibility to protect their consumers. Warnings appear on the inserts in order of risk severity:

- Contraindications

- Warnings

- Precautions

- Adverse reactions

In addition to these four risk categories, the FDA requires another category for selected drugs to indicate special problems that may lead to serious injury or death. These problems are displayed prominently in a box as a warning to consumers and physicians. Based on clinical data, the black box warning alerts physicians to carefully monitor the health of patients taking these drugs.

Think Critically

Why are the warnings given to both consumers and physicians?

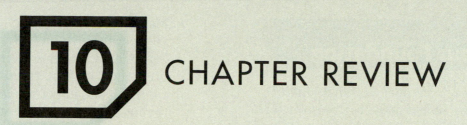

CHAPTER REVIEW

Summary

1. Readers of instructions can be in a hurry, so writers must learn to compensate with carefully planned writing. Readers trust writers to be accurate and safety-conscious and to provide adequate explanation in their instructions.

2. All instructions contain itemized steps. Most instructions contain an introduction and graphics. The process and the audience determine whether a list of materials, warnings, cautions, notes, or definitions should be included.

3. Instructions are written in short chronological sentences using active voice and imperative mood. Each step must show an action. Explanations follow steps and tell what not to do, why a step is performed, what the results of a step are, and how to complete a step. Explanations should provide enough detail to enable the reader to perform the step correctly and safely. When creating online instructions, the writer should limit each unit of instruction to one screen, use a consistent design (font, colors, and graphics), provide a tree or map of the site and topics, insert navigational aids on the home page, and configure instructions so that users performing tasks on the screen can see them while working.

Checklist

- Do I thoroughly understand the procedure about which I am writing?

- Did I consider using graphics?

- Did I consider using an introduction, a list of materials, cautions, warnings, and notes?

- Have I written steps that move forward in time? Do my steps begin with a verb that commands? Have I used short sentences that include only one action per step? Are my steps truly steps, or things to do? Have I kept the articles *a*, *an*, and *the*?

- Have I considered including explanations that tell what not to do and why? that include significant details to help the reader understand why a step is important? that tell the reader how to make a decision? that include descriptions of what will happen when the reader does something? that give enough details on how something should be done?

- Have I included enough precise details (for example, distances, sizes, places, or time)?

- Have I considered whether online instructions would be appropriate for my audience? Have I followed the additional guidelines for online instructions?

- Did I field-test my instructions with my target audience?

Build Your Foundation

1. Examine each step below. What kind of information would make each instruction more specific?

   a. Rotate the tool several times around the wire, leaving the spring closed.
   b. Draw part of an oval for the head.
   c. If the fitting has a tub spout, make a hole in the wall.
   d. Clean the vehicle before you return it to the lot.
   e. Beat the meringue until stiff peaks form.
   f. Place the selvages of the material together.

2. Break up each sentence into shorter sentences that reflect one step per sentence.

   a. Remove the cover from the mic; press the transmit button on the mic; and by using a small screwdriver with a plastic or wooden handle, adjust the transmitting frequency.
   b. Take the two upper sections of the handle and using the shortest bolt with the nut provided, fasten them together as shown in the illustration in Figure 1.
   c. Read the passage and locate all nouns, underlining them with a single line.

3. Rewrite these steps so that each one begins with a verb in active voice and imperative mood. (The "you" can be understood.)

   a. The cook should touch the AUTO DEFROST pad to begin the defrosting process.
   b. When you want to play, you should press the START button.
   c. The aquarium floor requires a layer of gravel that, sloping from back to front, is about 6 to 8 centimeters deep at the front wall.
   d. We want you to come to the front of the room and use the available podium.

4. Label each of the following as steps, explanations, cautions, or warnings.

   a. When paddling, keep the canoe in line with the current.
   b. Make sure the supply voltage matches the voltage specified on the rating plate.
   c. Separate dark clothes from light clothes to prevent colors from running.
   d. Do not overload your dryer. For efficient drying, clothes need to tumble freely.
   e. When you have recorded your message, press the pound key.
   f. When the virus protection window appears, click OK immediately to decontaminate your drive. Failure to heed the virus warnings may cause you to lose data and contaminate other devices.
   g. To determine how tight the fasteners need to be, see the Torque Range chart in the back of this book.

5. Which of these guidelines for writing instructions apply to all instructions (print and online)? Which apply only to online instructions?

   a. Make sure each step represents only one action unless the actions are so closely related that they need to be in the same step.
   b. Limit each unit of instruction to one screen size.
   c. Evaluate the usefulness of your instructions with a field test.
   d. Use a consistent design for each screen.
   e. Provide a tree or map of your site and topics.
   f. Do not omit *a*, *an*, and *the*.
   g. Eliminate your reader's need to scroll down the page.
   h. Insert navigational aids such as links to important pages.
   i. Include appropriate cautions, warnings, and notes.
   j. Use active-voice verbs in imperative mood for steps.

6. For a beginner using a word processing program such as Microsoft® Word, list help topics that a beginner might need to use. *Hint:* Find the Question Mark icon, often on the tool bar across the top of the page, to see a list of help topics.

7. Visit WebMD.com to see online instructions for preventing the common cold. Are the instructions clear? Explain.

Your Turn

1. In small groups, write instructions for any of the following processes (or another process with which you are familiar). Analyze your audience, follow the guidelines for composing instructions, and provide ample explanations.

making a bed	cleaning a room	changing the oil/tires
setting up a tent	using a calculator	playing a video game
setting up an aquarium	lifting weight	constructing a craft
brushing your teeth	mowing the lawn	changing a diaper
administering first aid	creating artwork	doing a yoga move

2. You have been asked to write online help instructions for a word processing program you know well. Write your instructions for one of these processes:

   a. Setting a password to open or modify a document
   b. Inserting footnotes
   c. Changing the margins
   d. Adding a header with automatic pagination
   e. Viewing two pages side by side
   f. Wrapping text around a photograph

Community Connection

1. Based on your experience and interviews with other students, write instructions for new students that explain how to register for classes or for a particular program.

Although your school probably has registration instructions, the document you develop should be an "insider's guide" of insights that you and other students have gained about more direct methods, pitfalls, situations to avoid, and classes to take together and classes to avoid taking in the same term. For the new students, define unfamiliar terms and give precise locations and descriptions.

2. Visit a nonprofit organization in your community and learn about the procedures and processes used there. Ask if you can help by developing written instructions for a task or procedure, such as steps for closing the facility at the end of the day, making an enlargement on the copier, orienting a volunteer, or answering an office telephone.

EXPLORE THE NET

The Plain Language Action and Information Network (PLAIN) is a government initiative mandating the use of plain, clear language in government documents. The plainlanguage.gov site offers writing tips for making procedures easy to follow.

Do a search for the No Gobbledygook Awards or the Clearmark Awards and read about them. Read a document written by a winner of one of these awards. In a journal entry or method of your instructor's choosing, describe how the document exemplifies the use of plain language.

11 EMPLOYMENT COMMUNICATION

Goals

- Plan employment communication
- Format and organize a resume
- Choose a type of resume
- Compose a resume
- Compose employment letters
- Create a web presence

Terms

Write to Learn

Place yourself in the future, ten years from now. Write a one-page description of your life. Where do you live? What talents and interests have you pursued? What kind of job do you have? Are you happy with your job? How much money do you make? How did you create this life? In other words, how did you get here?

FOCUS on Employment Communication

Read Figure 11.1 on the next page and answer these questions:

- Glance at the resume for ten seconds and then look away. What do you remember? In other words, what stands out?
- Does the resume look balanced and attractive? Explain.
- What information is included in each major section?
- How does Matt's work experience relate to his job objective?
- Matt paid for some of his college expenses and worked as a volunteer. What does this information say about Matt as a person?

What If?

How would the model change if . . .

- Matt had 15 years experience in the computer industry? 10 years in the restaurant business? 5 years of military experience?
- Matt had won an academic scholarship or an award for web design?
- Matt were applying for a faculty position or a graphic arts position?

Matthew R. Abboud
mabboud@email.mcc.edu
mattabboud.com

Temporary
67B Lakeside Apartments
San Soma, New Mexico 87103
(505) 555-0173

Permanent
803 Princeton Road
Little Rock, Arkansas 87103
(505) 555-6729

OBJECTIVE   Computer programmer in an industrial environment

QUALIFICATIONS
- 3 years' experience in networking and computer support
- AAS degree in Computer Programming
- Experience with HTML5, Javascript, Angular JS, and CSS
- Proficient in ASP.NET, C#, and C++

EDUCATION   Maddox Community College, San Soma, New Mexico
AAS, anticipated graduation May 2017
Major: Computer Programming, GPA 3.9/4.0

Major Courses

Advanced Tech Support	Hardware/Software	Systems Analysis/Design
Windows Admin I	Support	Database Management
LINUX.UNIX	Advanced C++	Intro to Programming/Logic
Technical Writing	Web Development Tools	Interpersonal Communication

CO-OP EXPERIENCE   **Wadell Computing Solutions**   **January 2016–Present**
Columbia, New Mexico
- Design and develop test specifications for mobile applications
- Evaluate existing computerized systems to improve efficiency
- Serve on Quality Assurance Team within IT department

Landcaster Microsystems   **July 2015–December 2015**
San Soma, New Mexico
- Installed and configured Windows operating systems and server
- Used JQuery to select and manipulate HTML elements
- Maintained PL/SQL database
- Answered Help Desk calls

OTHER EXPERIENCE   **Earned half of college expenses**   **2014–2017**
Auto Express, San Soma, New Mexico, Sales Clerk
AG Shirt Factory, Gabriel, New Mexico, Production Line Worker

VOLUNTEER   Special Olympics—Gabriel, New Mexico   **2014**
WORK   Big Brother—San Soma, New Mexico   **2011–2013**

Figure 11.1   Matthew Abboud Resume

Writing @Work

Courtesy of Kate Houck

CareerClusters®
PATHWAYS TO COLLEGE & CAREER READINESS

Business Management & Administration
Source: The Center to Advance CTE

Kate Houck manages the Implementation Team for Employment Law Training, a San Francisco–based company that provides employers with online compliance training. In addition to a BA in political science, she has extensive experience evaluating job applicants, interviewing, and hiring employees for companies ranging from Internet startups to Fortune 500s.

"The biggest challenge in reviewing a stack of resumes is culling the wheat from the chaff," explains Kate. "I look for a resume that has a good layout and concise, engaging statements about relevant experience and accomplishments. It should also demonstrate passion for or expertise in something. You can usually teach someone to do a job, but it is harder to teach someone to be an employee who cares."

The most glaring mistakes to avoid in a resume or cover letter are the easiest ones to prevent. Kate emphasizes that these documents "should have no typos or spelling errors. If you mess this up, you are just being careless." She also recommends that job candidates google themselves to eliminate undesirable public listings: "It may not be fair, but your online presence serves as a sort of reference in today's electronic age. So if there is anything posted that you don't want an employer to see, make sure it is under a pseudonym or restricted access; otherwise, it's fair game."

Having seen so many resumes has taught Kate precisely what makes a great resume and how to make her own resume float to the top of the pile: "The top two things I try to convey in my resume are competence and excellence. I not only highlight what I have done at each job, but also provide evidence that shows how I surpassed the objectives for that position. I don't want to be just a performer on my resume or at work; I want to be a star."

Think Critically

1. Does your resume meet Kate's standards for "good layout and concise, engaging statements about relevant experience and accomplishments"? Why or why not?

2. Would Kate see that you have "passion for or expertise in something?" How can you change your resume so that someone like Kate puts it at the top of the stack?

Printed with permission of Kate Houck

Writing in Business Management and Administration

A college administrator must balance sound educational practices with the bottom line. Local, state, and national government agencies control funding; thus, all communication requires an understanding of political processes. Persuasive tactics are tailored to the audience and, hence, to the party in power. Collaborating with others to set up bond referendums, campaigns, and fundraisers can bring in money for new programs, updated equipment, or library resources.

A college administrator may write letters, performance appraisals, recommendations, strategic plans, and grant proposals. Regular newspaper columns or newsletters, TV and radio interviews, commencement and impromptu speeches inform constituents of current events and present a professional image for the college. A flexible communication style enables an administrator to officiate at a building dedication and later address a school-wide emergency, such as a gas leak. Facilitating relationships with messages of appreciation, congratulatory notes, and condolences helps maintain strong networks.

Jim Garland, former physics professor and university president, says his thinking and thus his writing shifted once he left the classroom. As a physics professor he wrote about "narrow topics and explor[ed] them in excruciating depth." As a college administrator he had to also grasp the big picture and "bring diverse points of view together in service to multifaceted goals." He encourages administrators to give their full attention to issues with "real substance," the crises, layoffs, and inevitable social issues (qtd. in Toor).

11.1 GETTING STARTED ON EMPLOYMENT COMMUNICATION

 WARM UP

The job you seek may be a long-awaited dream job or a part-time job to help pay expenses while you attend school. Whatever the job, you will need attractive and well-crafted employment communication to highlight your strengths for the job market. You will use your technical writing skills to analyze your audience's needs and then persuade your audience that you can fulfill those needs.

Employment communication includes a **resume** (a one- or two-page summary of your qualifications), a **cover letter** (to accompany the resume), a **follow-up letter** (to thank the employer for the interview and to summarize your qualifications), and possibly a **resignation letter** (to announce your intention to resign). You can improve your chances of getting hired by creating an **employment ePortfolio** and registering with select social media and job posting sites. Employment documents are important because they:

- Create a professional, favorable impression.

- Allow you to control the presentation of your skills on paper and online.

- Encourage an employer to call you to arrange an interview.

To get started on employment communication, assess your strengths, learn what you can about a prospective employer, and choose your references. Then consider the employer's perspective and expectations.

Assess Your Strengths

Good employment communication begins with self-assessment. Consider your skills, aptitudes, education, interests, and experience. Use the following questions to help you determine your strengths as an employee:

- **Education:** What is your grade point average (GPA)? Which classes have prepared you for a particular job? What degrees do you hold? Where did you go to school, and when did you graduate?

- **Employment:** What jobs have you held? Write the job title, city and state, and dates for each job you now have or have previously held. Describe your duties and any job-related projects. Be specific.

- **Accomplishments:** List your accomplishments (scholastic, job-related, extracurricular, or community) over the last several years. Include any honors or awards you received. What skills do these accomplishments and honors illustrate? Would these skills be useful in the workplace?

- **Skills:** What are your talents? What can you do well? Are you a good problem solver, an innovative thinker, or an effective communicator? Do you have specialized skill sets—with computers, machinery, sales? Make a list, even if it overlaps with something you have already written.

If you were the chief executive officer of a successful corporation, what kinds of employees would you hire? What would you want to see on a resume?

Typical Reader

A busy manager scanning employment communication for key information.

Writer's Focus

Capturing the manager's attention by placing the most important qualifications in carefully designed and error-free employment documents.

- **Character or personality traits:** Are you dependable, honest, and flexible? Are you outgoing, calm, and optimistic? Do you have a sense of humor?

When you finish your assessment, consider which responses would impress a prospective employer. Now you have a better idea of what makes you valuable as an employee.

Research Your Prospective Employer

Learn all you can about your prospective employer, the company, and the job. Look for the company's website and browse. Call the human resources office if you have questions about the company's hiring practices. Do you know anyone who works for or used to work for this organization? You also can find information about major American companies in *Hoover's 500: Profiles of America's Largest Business Enterprises.*

As you research, look for answers to the following questions:

- Who will be responsible for making the decision to hire you—an individual or a committee? If it is an individual, what position does that person hold? What skills is this person looking for in an employee?

- What can you find out about the company—its mission statement, current projects, or past accomplishments? How is it organized? What other jobs are open?

- What can you learn about the position for which you are applying? What would you be expected to do, and with whom would you work?

Ideally, you will be applying for a specific job with a particular company—a Social Worker II position at the Richmond Department of Social Services, for example. In reality, though, you also may send out a number of resumes to different organizations for a certain kind of job. In these cases, you may not have time to research the jobs and organizations in depth.

Choose Your References

A reference is a person who knows you well enough to vouch for your skills and your character. This person should feel comfortable making positive statements about your work performance, giving examples of your accomplishments, and answering specific questions from a prospective employer.

Choose three to five people to include as references. Work references—people for whom you have actually worked—make the best references. After all, your employer is interested in knowing how well you perform on the job. Furthermore, educational references such as instructors, advisers, and guidance counselors also can attest to your abilities. Including one personal reference, someone (not a relative) who

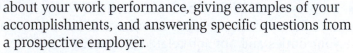
© technotr/iStockphoto.com

knows you well outside the workplace, is acceptable as long as you also include strong work references.

Before you list someone as a reference, ask the person to agree to serve as a reference for you. If this person hesitates or says no, ask someone else.

The trend today is not to include references on the resume but, instead, to have a list prepared in case you are asked to provide names. Then if you are granted an interview, you can offer your list at that time.

Who Reads Employment Communication?

To write the best employment communication possible, you must understand your audience by considering the employer's perspective and expectations.

Employer's Perspective

Generally, employers seek someone whose credentials qualify him for the position, whose personality fits with the current staff, and whose career plan complements the company's goals. Employers are interested in an applicant's education, experience, skills, and work habits. Employers also want employees who have personal and professional integrity.

Your employment materials show employers you have the skills they need. At this stage, the resume, letter, application, and web presence are the only means employers have of knowing who you are and what you can do for them. Therefore, you want to make a positive first impression with your communication.

© stray_cat/iStockphoto.com

If you have done a good job of showcasing your professional strengths, you may be contacted for an interview. During the interview, you have an opportunity to convince an employer you are the best candidate for the job. An employer will screen applicants carefully, selecting only a few to interview. Thus, the goal of resumes and e-materials is to establish credibility and create enough interest to be granted an interview. The goal of the interview is to persuade an employer to hire you.

Audience awareness is especially important when you are writing employment materials. Focusing on the needs of your reader may be difficult because the resume is primarily about you, the writer. Nonetheless, because the reader is the decision maker, her needs are most important. Place yourself in the shoes of this person, the one responsible for hiring you. Keywords in the vacancy announcement will influence your choices about what to include in your initial employment package.

Employer's Expectations

Your prospective employer expects your communication to conform to standard employment protocol. Employment communication must

- Contain no errors. Resumes with misspellings, typos, and punctuation errors are routinely cast aside during initial screenings.

- Look neat and professional. For example, a resume whose print is too light makes the writer look careless, as does an e-mail using two different fonts. All print resumes should use

  quality printers and paper. All online communication should be organized using consistent formatting.

- Follow accepted conventions. A resume that is too long or too short, for example, or an ePortfolio lacking appropriate sections, creates a negative impression. A writer who does not take the time to research the proper way to send professional materials for a particular career path casts doubt on his value as an employee.

- Emphasize your best qualities (even if you think you may be bragging).

STOP AND THINK 11.1

Choose three people who might agree to be references for you. What do you think these people would say about you? Are they familiar with your career goals? Why do employers discard some resumes initially? Why do employers read selected employment communication carefully?

WARM UP

11.2 FORMATTING AND ORGANIZING RESUMES

Congratulations! You have been voted Most Likely to Succeed from your graduating class. A short article appears about you in your yearbook. What does the article say? Why are you most likely to succeed?

Because employers may spend no more than 15 to 45 seconds looking at your resume during the initial screening, you must make the resume memorable. Here you have the chance to demonstrate your skills with page design using special features, appropriate headings, and organizational schemes.

Making Your Resume Stand Out

Have you ever noticed how some words in a newspaper or magazine ad jump out at you—those words in large bold type surrounded by white space? The ad is designed to create an immediate impression in a small amount of space.

Like any advertisement, the resume must impress a reader in limited space. Ultimately, you are designing an ad and selling yourself, your skills, and your expertise to a prospective employer. You want your most impressive qualifications to jump out at the reader during the first glance at your resume. For a high school student or a recent college graduate, the resume should be only one page long. For people with several years of impressive work experience, a two-page resume is acceptable. Some careers, such as university professorships, require a longer curriculum vitae. Electronic resumes, too, may be longer because they are generally scanned by software for initial screening and not by human eyes.

Part of the design strategy, then, is to consider how the resume looks. White space allowing ample margins results in a resume that is uncluttered and easy to read. Special features such as **boldfacing**, underlining, *italicizing*, CAPITALIZING, bullets (•), or asterisks (*) make important information stand out. But too many special features can make your resume appear cluttered and busy. The resume should look symmetric and balanced with easy-to-find headings. The most important part of your resume, your name, should be prominently positioned using larger boldfaced type.

Choose an easy-to-read font—something in a 10- to 12-point font for print and 14-point for online. Times New Roman serif font is still the standby for print media, but sans serif fonts such as Arial, Helvetica, or Calibri are easier to read online.

Consider setting up your resume as a table (hide the grid lines) with information in columns and rows. You can place side headings in the first column and different sections in rows. Because side headings take up more space, if you have additional information, you may want to center or left-justify your headings. Templates can give your resume a professional look, but they may not distinguish your resume from others who use the same template.

Look at versions of resumes in this chapter as well as resumes on the Web and in career books. Choose a layout that works for the amount of information and the headings you decide to use. Your goal is to make your resume stand out.

Deciding Which Headings to Include

Making decisions about which headings to include is like making decisions about your daily wardrobe. You must put on certain clothes—jeans, shirts, shoes, socks—whatever your basic wardrobe consists of. However, you can choose accessories—jewelry, caps, scarves, belts—to express your individuality, those things that set you apart from others. Similarly, a resume must include basic information. However, optional headings, like accessories, highlight your strengths, minimize your weaknesses, and set your resume apart from others.

Basic Information

Basic information consists of your identification, education, and work experience.

- **Identification:** Include your name, complete address (permanent and temporary, if applicable), telephone number(s), and e-mail address. If you have constructed a career ePortfolio website, include that address here.

- **Education:** Include the name, city, and state of the school from which you graduated; dates of attendance and graduation or expected date of graduation; and your major or course of study. Sometimes it is helpful to list specific courses you took, as well as academic honors, your overall GPA or the GPA in your major classes (particularly if the GPA is good), and any extracurricular activities. If you already have a postsecondary degree, it is not necessary to list your high school degree.

- **Work Experience:** Include the name, city, and state of the organization and the position or title and description of duties if they are related to the job for which you are applying. You also may add promotions and skill sets. Above all, emphasize your accomplishments.

Optional Headings

Many different names for headings can appear on resumes. All of them give your prospective employer a better idea of what you can do. Table 11.1 suggests some optional headings and offers a rationale for using each one.

Table 11.1

Possible Headings	Purpose	Rationale for Use
Job Objective Objective Career Objective Professional Objective	To identify the job or position for which you are applying	Use if the employer must determine what job or category of jobs you are qualified for and if you can compose an interesting and specific statement
Skills/Abilities Professional Skills Leadership Skills Technical Skills Computer Skills	To highlight skills in a chronological presentation or in place of a chronological presentation	Use if you desire to showcase special skill sets, especially those skills not reflected in other sections. Here is an opportunity to highlight those skills listed in the vacancy announcement.
Military Experience Military Service ROTC	To summarize military experience	Definitely use if you have military experience. Military personnel are reputed to be dependable and hard-working. Some companies give preference to veterans.
Work Experience Other Work Experience Related Experience Computer Experience Volunteer Work	To include experience not directly related to the job or to differentiate between different kinds of applicable work experience	Use if the experience shows a consistent work history or if the experience is remarkable in some way. Experience not directly related to the job listing shows your dependability and ability to learn and work with others.
Accomplishments Honors Awards Achievements	To enhance your resume with your unique accomplishments	Definitely use if you have awards, recognitions, and honors that complement educational and work-related descriptions but do not seem to fit under either.
Summary Major Qualifications Summary of Skills	To summarize your qualifications in three to five bullets or in a short description	Use if you decide to specifically relate your qualifications to the qualifications in the job listing.

Organizational Strategies

Two organizational strategies govern the writing of all resumes: reverse chronological order and priority order.

Reverse Chronological Order

Some parts of the resume are presented in **reverse chronological order** (backward through time). The priority here is time; that is, what is most recent is considered to be most important. In particular, past jobs and schools attended should be listed in reverse chronological order. For example, when presenting your work experience, list your most recent job first, your second most recent job second, and continue back through time until you have listed all jobs, the most relevant jobs (if you have a long work history), or jobs spanning the last 10 years.

Priority Order

Major sections are presented in **priority order**—from most important to least important. Whatever you present as most important should be the credentials you consider to be most important *to the prospective employer*. In some cases, it's reasonable to prioritize impressive work experience over education by positioning work experience before education.

If you are a recent graduate without much work experience, you may position education first as the most important qualification. If you use a skills summary, place it early in the resume. That way, employers who quickly skim your resume can focus on your major qualifications even if they do not read further.

Within each section, lists of skills, duties, awards, and accomplishments also are organized from most important to least important.

STOP AND THINK 11.2

Which optional headings can be included in a resume, and why would someone use them?

11.3 TYPES OF RESUMES

WARM UP

There are two fundamental ways to arrange information on: through time or by skill. The **chronological resume** organizes information in reverse chronological order—or backward in time through a person's education and employment record—with the most recent information presented first. Instead of organizing information around time, the **functional resume** organizes information around a person's unique skills, giving an applicant the opportunity to highlight special abilities or experience. This resume may have a section devoted to technical skills, sales abilities, or leadership skills. Some resumes are a combination of chronological and functional resumes, highlighting special skills in one area and using a chronological presentation for the work history. Resumes can be printed and mailed to an employer. More often, they are sent or posted electronically.

Consider the different ways information can be organized. For example, when you study history, how is the information organized? When you study math, how is the information organized?

Chronological Resume

A chronological resume offers an approach that most employers recognize and accept. This resume

- Provides a history of employment (regardless of the job) and education in reverse chronological order.

- Accounts for every year the applicant is out of school, with no gaps in time.

- Tends to emphasize dates in the resume's design.

- Uses predictable headings.

- Places education and work experience early in the resume.

The chronological resume offers several advantages. First, it is familiar and readily accepted by employers. Second, it can be read quickly. Third, it draws attention to a steady and impressive work history.

Although the chronological resume is widely used, it is not ideal for everyone. First, a lengthy work history may produce a lengthy resume. Second, the structured format could limit someone whose qualifications do not fit into its framework. For example, it may not be flexible enough for someone with little or no work experience. Third, it may be so similar to other resumes that nothing distinguishes it from them.

Matt's resume in the opening model is an example of a chronological resume. Matt is applying for his first full-time job after graduation. With less than two years of related programming experience, he believes his degree is his strongest asset and his co-op experience is his next strongest asset. The dates, separated from the main text of the resume, stand out. He lists other work experience last because it is not as impressive as his co-op experience. Notice he does not describe his other work experience because it does not relate directly to his job objective. Most employers would understand what these part-time jobs entail and would note them only because they show Matt's work ethic.

Functional Resume

Resumes organized according to function or purpose are more flexible than chronological resumes. Tailored to suit the requirements of a particular job, a functional resume

- Summarizes the most important qualifications for the job.

- May not account for every year out of school.

- Emphasizes skills, accomplishments, and job titles regardless of time frame.

- Uses less predictable headings designed for the job.

- May present education and work experience later in the resume.

The functional resume offers several advantages. First, it helps the employer judge what skills and accomplishments are useful for the job. Second, the functional resume can be used in a variety of circumstances. For example, functional resumes are useful when you have plenty of work experience and skills that would take up too much space on a chronological resume. Finally, functional resumes offer a flexible structure when applying for a job for which you have no formal education but for which you have marketable skills. For example, you may have learned carpentry skills from your father but do not have a degree.

The flexibility of a functional resume can minimize time lapses in education or job experience, time you may have to account during an interview. Be prepared to explain any lapses quickly and discuss the constructive things you did while out of work, such as taking classes or volunteering. Do not complain about being laid off, and don't talk about problems you may have had with your former supervisor.

Juanita's resume in Figure 11.2 is a functional resume. Juanita's circumstances are different from Matt's. Juanita is not applying for her first full-time job upon graduating from college; she is applying for her first part-time job while she is in high school. Because she does not have a degree yet, her job skills are more important than her education. She has little

---

Juanita Manuel
Route 5, Box 332   Charles, Ohio 44637
(414) 555-0195   (414) 555-7268
jmanuel@email.net

Job Objective

Part-time position as an administrative assistant

Office Skills

- Office procedures
- Interpersonal skills
- Customer service
- Business correspondence
- Records management

Computer Skills

- Microsoft Office Professional 2016
- QuickBooks Pro 2016
- Microsoft Publisher 2016
- FileMaker Pro14

Office Experience

MANUEL'S FLOWERS, July 2012-Present
Part-Time Assistant in family-owned business: Answer phone, process orders, assist customers, order supplies, encode data using QuickBooks

BETA CLUB, October 2014-2016
Treasurer: Maintained account ledger, created annual budget, balanced budget, wrote checks

JUNIOR MAGAZINE SALES, January 2014-March 2015
Co-chair: Directed sales staff, planned advertising campaign, sold magazines

Education

Wanoca High School, Charles, Ohio. Anticipated date of graduation, June 2017
Office Technology Curriculum
Courses in Accounting, Office Management, Computer Technologies, Microsoft Office Professional 2016, and Business Writing

Activities

Future Business Leaders of America, Vice-President, August 2015—June 2016
Soccer, Track, Softball, August 2014—2017
Volunteer Reader for the Blind, August 2006—2010

Honors and Achievements

Winner Advertising Competition, FBLA, 2015
Runner Up Wanoca Spelling Bee, 2013

Figure 11.2 Functional Resume

work experience, so she capitalizes on her club and volunteer work to show she can handle office responsibilities. A skills approach works best for her circumstances.

Electronic Resume

Technology has changed and continues to change the way people look for and apply for jobs. An **electronic resume** is a chronological or functional resume that has been reformatted to be sent electronically. Since employers are on different trajectories with technology, adapt by producing several versions of the same resume (for people *and* machines) and by researching current resume practices when you begin your job search.

An electronic resume may take one of the following forms:

- **E-mail resume:** Sent as a formatted attachment to an e-mail or as part of an e-mail message

- **ASCII text resume:** Sent with special text formatting as an attachment to or part of an e-mail

- **Scannable resume:** Sent as an attachment to an e-mail, part of an e-mail message, or mailed (but eventually scanned by an optical reader or a keyword search)

- **Online resume:** Posted on a company's website or career hub or posted on an applicant's website

- **Video resume:** Sent or posted electronically and useful especially for the performing arts or careers relying on presentation skills such as teaching or sales

E-mail Resume

Sending a resume as an e-mail attachment is a popular and efficient way to contact an employer who controls the hiring process. A department chair and small business owner who screen resumes *themselves* might respond, but it's less likely a large company with an HR department or a job listing service would. It pays to know your employer's process for reviewing applications.

A resume can be sent as an e-mail attachment that saves your formatting. However, unless you know your employer uses Word, for example, it's safer to send a resume as a PDF (Portable Document Format, .pdf) document. Use Word or another program to create the document, and then resave as a PDF. This way, anyone without the latest Word upgrade can read the file. It may also be smart to save your resume with an RTF (Rich Text Format, .rtf) extension. This way, anyone without a PDF reader can open your RTF file. Using this process, there is little difference in the actual appearance of the electronic resume and the print resume. The only difference is the file format.

It's not likely you'll need to embed the resume inside an email message; but just in case, you can save a resume as a TXT (text, .txt) file, and copy and paste it into the e-mail message. You'll lose some formatting; however, your resume will be on its way.

ASCII Text Resume

If your company does not use a job listing service or a government posting agency, you need other strategies for sending your resume electronically.

A **text file** is versatile. It can be sent a variety of ways and can be read by people *and* machines. While the text file is not as pretty as a formatted Word document, you can show off your resourcefulness by making the most of the options available to you. This way, if the printed text file makes its way to your employer, the document will be more attractive. You can format to a limited degree by using the following suggestions:

- Use plain fonts (for example, large, open, "no tails" fonts such as Arial or Calibri) or consider Courier, a fixed font with each character taking up the same amount of space.

- Use 10- to 14-point font size.

- Use one column, flush with the left margin; do not use side headings or tables.

- Consider using a series of +++ or *** or === or ^^^ to divide the major sections of your resume (between Education and Experience, for example).

- Use capital letters for heading titles and other important information.

- Avoid boldface, italics, underlining, and other characters not on the keyboard.

- Use the space bar instead of tab keys.

- Use asterisks, dashes, or hyphens instead of regular bullets.

- Use wide margins set for 60 characters (1" left, 2.5" right).

- Use commas to indicate small breaks, semicolons to indicate breaks in a longer list, colons to set up a list, and periods to end sections.

Communication
Technologies

Want to shore up your interview skills while you walk the dog? Help is available for both Android and Apple devices with Job Interview Questions and Answers from Career Confidential. It's an interactive video app to give you practice with "tough interview questions in an easy-to-use mock interview format." You can practice and compare your answers to suggestions supplied by a professional coach. Play Store also offers 101 HR Interview Questions from Programmerworld with 16 categories of questions.

With The SimuGator, an iTunes app with over 50 questions, users can experience various interviewing styles from different interviewers.

Think Critically

What is the benefit to using an app to help you practice your interview skills? Is there some way the app could hurt your performance during an interview?

Figure 11.3 shows Barbara's chronological resume formatted as an ASCII text file.

```
BARBARA NIEVES
607 Windy Road, Apt. 307
Cypress Bay, FL 32761
(501) 555-9780
bnieves@email.net
bnieves.com

SUMMARY
Versatile background in retail, banking, and travel industries. Strong people skills. Team player. Work well
under pressure. Ability to organize tasks and people. Ability to learn new skills.


=================================================================================================

EXPERIENCE
K.W. Flooring and Windows, Cypress Bay, FL, 8/08 to Present.
Retail Manager: Sell carpet, flooring, storm windows; manage sales staff, order supplies and inventory;
screen resumes; key in documents; operate office machines; coordinate appointments; answer, screen,
and route telephone calls.

Northeast American Bank, Central Islip, NY, 6/04 to 6/08
District Specialist: Acted as a liaison between regional and branch offices, worked on special projects,
solved customer problems, gathered data, prepared reports, handled 10-line telephone with heavy traffic,
keyed in notes and correspondence, entered information into data base, and scheduled appointments.
Customer Service Representative: Opened new accounts; issued travelers checks, US Savings bonds,
certificates of deposit, foreign drafts and currency; maintained vault supplies, processed collections,
screened mail.
Teller: Balanced transactions, handled large sums of money, assisted in routine customer transactions,
resolved customer access issues.

Rothgar Travel Agency, Patchogue, NY, 1/02 to 5/08.
Travel Agent: Handled in person and by telephone all travel arrangements for individuals and tour groups.
Supervised bus tours and traveled.


=================================================================================================

EDUCATION
Fifer County Community College, Lincoln, NY, 1997, AAS Accounting
Baskin County Junior College, Cypress Bay, FL, 2006, 42 credits toward AAS Business Administration


=================================================================================================

VOLUNTEER WORK
Beaufort City Schools, Classroom volunteer 2012-2016
Relay for Life, Organized fund raiser and teams 2010-2015
Options for Domestic Violence, Organized fund raiser 2009
Angel Tree Ministry, Organized gift-giving for 150 children 2007-2012
```

Figure 11.3 Electronic Resume as ACCII Text File

Scannable Resume

Scannable resumes are mailed as a print document, sent as an e-mail, or posted online to be scanned electronically for **keywords**, significant words included in the vacancy announcement. A keyword search compares qualifications on the resume to qualifications the employer needs and determines whether the resume has enough matches to warrant a closer reading.

It's best to insert keywords throughout your resume, but a separate section of keywords can be added either to the top or the bottom of the resume if you are not able to include all the relevant words in your job descriptions.

Use the suggestions for formatting an ASCII text resume with these differences:

- If you print the resume, use dark black ink on white paper.
- If you mail the resume, do not staple or fold pages and use a large envelope so the resume lies flat.

Online Resume

An **online resume** is posted on a website. Typically, the website is one you build, one your company or school hosts, or one sponsored by a web-based job-hunting service such as Monster Worldwide, Indeed, or CareerBuilder. Online job-hunting services provide instructions for posting web-based resumes. Those instructions may include uploading a scannable resume.

With an ePortfolio, you can post your resume and set up links to projects, references, or professional affiliations. Send your resume—print, e-mail, or scannable—and note that you have a website in your cover letter or e-mail. Include your website address at the top of your resume along with your address and telephone number.

Video Resume

A **video resume** is a short film during which you talk about your credentials and accomplishments. Video resumes are especially appropriate for the performing arts or careers relying on presentation skills, such as teaching, or careers in which interpersonal skills are vital, such as sales.

Videos take time to load and view, so brevity and careful selection of scenes and script are important. A video for the position of tour guide, for example, should not include the 20-minute talk on the Lincoln Memorial. However, a 45-second clip of the introduction to the Lincoln Memorial and another 30-second clip of the glass-making shop at Williamsburg would be a better choice. The script should be well rehearsed. Speech should be clear, correct, relaxed, and natural.

Ask a professional to produce your video. A poorly produced video will not create a favorable impression.

 STOP AND THINK 11.3

Describe the different ways to send an electronic resume. Under what circumstances would you convert a resume to a text file? Who might consider producing a video resume?

11.4 COMPOSING RESUMES

 WARM UP

After you have analyzed your audience and assessed your strengths as an employee, you are ready to compose the parts of your resume. Writing a resume means working through drafts until you have written a professional document with *no errors*.

Have you ever written a perfect paper—an essay, a letter, a short report? Is it possible to write something with no errors? Explain.

Word Choice

When writing a resume, present information in as few words as possible. The word choice in a resume may be unlike anything you have written before. A resume has its own grammar rules: Sentences and paragraphs are not used because they take too long to read. Instead, resumes are written in fragments, lists, descriptive phrases, and verbs. Resume language is both general and specific, with carefully chosen details.

Nouns or Nouns + Descriptive Phrases

For naming *Activities, Honors, Achievements*, and *Awards*, use a list of nouns or nouns + descriptive phrases.

ACTIVITIES: Key Club treasurer, Girl Scout leader, member Lions Club

AFFILIATIONS: Key Club, Girl Scouts, Lions Club

SKILLS:

- Knowledge of both Windows and Mac OS environments
- Ability to program using jQuery and Javascript frameworks
- Experience with mobile Web development

Verb + What

Verb + what is a quick, effective phrase to describe skills, qualifications, and work experience. Use action verbs to stress what you can do for an employer. Performance is more impressive than qualifications. The greater the variety of verbs, the more dynamic and effective the resume. Add details to the phrase to show more specific information.

Make sure the lists use consistent tenses: present tense for jobs you currently hold and past tense for jobs you no longer hold. If you have (or had) a title, include the title before your list of duties followed by a colon. Also organize your list of duties in order of importance.

Present Tense Verbs Describes Jobs You Currently Hold

train personnel	install software	perform audit
provide child care	service equipment	manage office staff

Past Tense Verbs Describes Jobs You No Longer Hold

designed ad copy	analyzed sales	assisted customers
planned events	maintained data base	evaluated procedures

Job Titles before Duties

Cashier: Operated register, greeted customers, and took orders

Shift Manager: Supervised 15 workers, enforced safety measures, and calculated payroll

Table 11.2 shows other action verbs you may want to consider.

Table 11.2

accomplished	coordinated	generated	reduced
achieved	counseled	identified	revised
administered	designed	increased	saved
attained	developed	investigated	solved
budgeted	devised	maintained	streamlined
built	established	mentored	strengthened
calculated	evaluated	organized	taught
completed	formulated	planned	trained
contributed	fulfilled	promoted	wrote

Specific Language

Think of your resume as the first piece of evidence a potential employer sees regarding your unique skills. As evidence, it should come with sufficient proof of your credentials and accomplishments. The proof comes in those specific, quantifiable bits of information you incorporate into your resume.

What you choose to include in these roughly 160 to 350 words (for a one-page resume) proves your qualifications and tailors your resume to the skills an employer needs. A job or career objective should be customized for the job you seek and could express a passion, an area of interest, or a line of advancement. If you are responding to a vacancy announcement, indicate the position for which you are applying in your statement. Likewise, duties should be specific and focus on accomplishments, not just a list of your responsibilities. Avoid over generalized statements.

✓ Specific Language	✗ Vague Language
To secure a position as a loan officer in a local credit union (names the position and the particular kind of institution)	To work as a professional in a modern banking environment
To work part-time as a tour guide for a seventeenth-century governor's palace (responds specifically to the job announcement)	To obtain a summer part-time position
A seasonal wildland firefighter in an engine crew (specific job title and position)	A firefighter
Ensured compliance with EPA and OSHA regulations (responds to query for experience with EPA and OSHA)	Enforced safety regulations
Met all 10 performance standards from 2001 to 2010 (specifies how many and when)	Consistently met performance standards

Parallel Structure

When setting up headings, providing information, or creating lists for resumes, use **parallel structure** (repetition of the same grammatical structure already in use). Parallel structure provides consistency, enabling your reader to anticipate your structure.

This means if you begin your employment history with a job title, list the job title first with every job. If you begin your employment history with the name of the company and the job title second, list the company name first and the job title second for each job.

Descriptions also should be written in parallel structure.

✓ **Parallel**	✗ **Nonparallel**
Answered calls from field technicians, created service bulletins, analyzed warranty claims, authorized warranty repairs and modifications, communicated with design engineers.	I answered calls from field technicians. Was responsible for service bulletins. Duties included warranty claims analysis and warranty authorization numbers for specific repairs and modifications. Close communication with design engineers was ongoing.

Keywords for Scannable Resumes

When selecting keywords for a scannable resume, the rules of resume writing change. A print resume relies on verbs to demonstrate skills performed. The scannable resume, on the other hand, relies on nouns to list skills, qualifications, and job titles in your descriptions of qualifications and experience. Following are some examples of keywords.

Skills: C++ programming, graphic design, marketing, statistical analysis, training, database management, communication, problem solving, management, organization, attention to detail

Job titles: Computer specialist, manager, supervisor, director, administrative assistant, chair, facilitator, nurse's aide, machinist, research assistant

Qualifications: Membership in professional organizations, licenses, certifications, degrees, awards

Using several synonyms for one word increases the chances that your keywords will match those of your employer. For example, because the words *hair stylist* and *cosmetologist* are synonyms, you should include both terms for a resume that will be scanned. Scanning programs are very literal, though. For example, if the company asks for experience with Microsoft Office Suite, do not write "proficient in Word, Excel, and PowerPoint." Those terms may not match without the words "Microsoft Office Suite."

A machine can scan a three-page resume as quickly as a one-page resume. Thus, when in doubt, include more rather than less information in a scannable resume. Print resumes save time for the reader by restricting length and using concise wording, whereas scannable resumes are thorough.

Punctuation

Because resumes do not contain complete sentences, applying traditional punctuation rules can be tricky. If one piece of information ends naturally on a single line, end marks are usually omitted. For other marks of punctuation,

- Use periods to break up large blocks of text or to indicate a change in information.

- Use colons to introduce lists.

- Use commas to separate simple lists of three or more items.

- Use semicolons to separate complex lists (lists that already contain commas) of three or more items.

Refer to the models in this chapter to see how the resumes are punctuated. Whatever system you adopt, use consistent punctuation throughout your resume.

STOP AND THINK 11.4

What is the hardest part of writing a resume? Why? How does the wording of an essay differ from that of a resume? How does a traditional print resume differ from a scannable resume? What are the advantages of an electronic resume?

11.5 COMPOSING EMPLOYMENT LETTERS

 WARM UP

Employment letters—or corresponding e-mail messages—give you another opportunity to present your skills. Unlike the resume, these letters are written in traditional paragraphs and complete sentences, also showing the employer how well you write. Three types of employment letters are (1) cover letters to accompany the resume and to highlight the applicant's strengths, (2) follow-up letters to thank the employer for the interview, (3) and in some cases, resignation letters to announce a person's intention to leave a company.

Look closely at the cover letter in Figure 11.4 (page 302) that Matt wrote to accompany his resume. How is this cover letter like a sales letter?

Cover Letter

A cover letter is a sales letter, a persuasive message that sells *you* as the product or service. As stated in Chapter 5, sales letters are composed of a hook, a sell, and a motivation to action. Likewise, a cover letter is composed of an opening (an attention-getter or a hook), a summary of qualifications (the proof or sell), and a request for an interview (motivation to action).

A cover letter may be mailed with other employment materials, but more often the information is included as an e-mail message with the resume attached. Or it could be a section of your ePortfolio. Regardless of how you send the letter, the organization of the message is the same. Remember, a professional e-mail starts and ends with a proper greeting (Dear __) and closing (Best regards).

Opening

The first paragraph should grab the reader's attention by

1. Stating your interest in the job.

2. Describing your qualifications in a way that sets you apart from other applicants.

3. Explaining how you found out about the job.

4. Quickly summarizing your major qualifications for the job.

Most cover letters are **solicited**; that is, they are requested or advertised. With solicited positions, refer to the advertised vacancy announcement in the opening sentence.

Sometimes, however, you may submit an **unsolicited letter**. In this case, you are looking for employment with an organization that has not solicited or advertised a vacancy. Not all companies advertise their jobs, and you will not know whether there is an opening unless you ask. You never know what might happen: Your skills may be in such demand that a company creates a position for you. Writing an opening to an unsolicited letter is more of a challenge; you must generate interest immediately. Name-dropping may stimulate interest, or a dynamic opening can emphasize your advantages.

Solicited Letter Opening (refers to advertisement in the opening sentence)	**Unsolicited Letter Opening (generates interest with name dropping and a unique background)**
A radiography degree and three years' experience at Unity Systems Health Care qualify me for the radiography position you advertised recently on Tri-Point Hospital's online vacancy announcements.	Dr. Yu Zeng suggested I contact you about an opening in your radiology department. With degrees and certifications in medical sonography, radiography, echocardiography, and computed tomography/magnetic resonance imaging, think how valuable my services would be to a small rural hospital with a limited staff. My bedside manner is impressive, and I am available for employment.

Summary of Qualifications

The second and third paragraphs justify your claim to be a first-rate candidate by proving your credentials. The letter is not meant to be a copy of your resume. The letter should emphasize qualifications but not repeat the resume word for word. To offer proof that you can perform the job, include the following in these paragraphs:

1. Description of your education.

2. Selected highlights of appropriate work experience.

3. Brief list of job-related skills including technical, professional, and/or people skills.

4. Explanation of some ability, skill set, or goal not mentioned in your resume.

If you are a recent graduate, your education paragraph will come immediately after your opening paragraph. It will specify your degree and major course of study and may include relevant courses, accomplishments, and areas of expertise. If you have been in the work force for several years, your work experience will come immediately after the opening paragraph and describe relevant jobs and major work-related accomplishments. In the letter, you also have the opportunity to add information about your character, work habits, and people skills, along with any other information you believe is relevant to the job.

© sjlocke/iStockphoto.com

Request for Interview

The last paragraph in the cover letter motivates the reader to action by asking for an interview and making it convenient to contact you. To conclude,

1. Refer to your attached or enclosed resume.

2. Ask for an interview.

3. Tell how and when you can be reached by including your phone number(s), e-mail address, and, if applicable, ePortolio address.

When composing your cover letter or introductory e-mail, vary your sentence structure. Although it is easy to begin every sentence with *I* when writing about yourself, try to begin some sentences with other words. For variety, consider beginning sentences with prepositional phrases, introductory clauses, and transitional words.

Communication
Dilemma

Grant, age 28, spent two years in the state penitentiary for shoplifting when he was 19 years old. Since that time, he attended classes, obtaining an associate degree in accounting, and spent three years in the U.S. Army. He now has a family and is an involved and respected member of his community.

Grant is applying for a job with D & J Accounting. The application asks if he has ever been convicted of a crime. Since his shoplifting offense, Grant has been a law-abiding citizen.

Think Critically

What are the possible consequences if Grant does not reveal the shoplifting incident? What are the possible consequences if he does? What do you think Grant should do?

Figure 11.4 shows a cover letter Matt wrote to Hailey O'Dell, personnel director at Monarch Electronic Industries. Matt's letter gets his reader's attention with a confident opening. He offers an understanding of the work environment and tells where he found the job announcement. Then Matt uses two paragraphs to explain how his education and work experience make him a good match for Monarch. In the last two paragraphs, Matt includes his desire to relocate, reveals knowledge of and interest in the company, includes contact information, and requests an interview. Note the variety in sentence structure in Matt's letter.

> 67B Lakeside Apartments
> San Soma, NM 87103
> 15 June 20–
>
> Ms. Hailey O'Dell, Personnel Director
> Monarch Electronic Industries
> 3902 West Broad Street
> Charleston, AK 72203
>
> Dear Ms. O'Dell:
>
> My skills and qualifications are a good match for the System Programmer/Analyst position posted 6 October on LinkedIN for your company. With co-op experience at a company similar to Monarch's, I have first-hand knowledge of the challenges of working in an industrial setting.
>
> I earned an AAS degree in Computer Programming from Maddox Community College. At Madddox's virtual computing lab, I learned to program using C++, C#, Java, and Angular JS. In addition, I gained experience with Microsoft Office 2016 as many of our class assignments were completed using an application in the Office suite. Before I graduated, I served on a quality assurance team to set up help desk protocols.
>
> In addition to my education, I have experience meeting the computing needs of business and industry. At Wadell Computing Solutions, I used C# and C++ to design and develop test specifications for mobile applications. At Landcaster Microsystems, I installed and configured operating systems using Windows 8/Professional and Windows Server 2012. After several rotations at the help desk, my supervisor praised my problem-solving and customer service skills.
>
> Last year, I attended a conference sponsored by Web Accessibility Initiative to familiarize myself with Web Content Accessibility Guidelines. Monarch's track record as a leader in making the Web accessible is well documented. I would welcome an opportunity to help in this initiative.
>
> My resume is attached for your consideration. I would be happy to schedule an interview to discuss my qualifications. Having grown up in Little Rock, I would welcome an opportunity to relocate to my home state. You may reach me at (501) 555-0172 after 3:00 p.m., e-mail me at mabboud@email.mcc.edu, or visit my ePortfolio at mattabboud.com.
>
> Sincerely,
>
> *Matthew Abboud*
>
> Matthew Abboud

Figure 11.4 Cover Letter

Follow-Up Letter

It's customary to send a follow-up letter or e-mail, sometimes known as a thank-you letter, immediately after a job interview. The follow-up should

1. Thank the employer for the interview.

2. Remind the employer of something positive that took place during the interview.

3. Explain why you are the best candidate for the job.

4. Express continuing interest in the job.

Follow-up correspondence tells prospective employers you are still interested and reminds them of your qualifications. With e-mail, make sure you use an appropriate, specific subject line (for example, *Follow-up to Interview*). Figure 11.5 shows a follow-up letter Matt wrote to Ms. O'Dell after his interview.

67B Lakeside Apartments
San Soma, NM 87103
29 August 20—

Ms. Hailey O'Dell, Personnel Director
Monarch Electronic Industries
3902 West Broad Street
Charleston, AK 72203

Dear Ms. O'Dell

Thank you for considering me for the position of computer programmer with your company. I enjoyed touring your facility and discussing ways to improve the SQL server database. As you may remember, I have had two years' experience with installing and configuring operating systems, in particular with Windows 2012 and would have no trouble assisting you with the upgrade to Windows 2016. I would welcome the opportunity to put my knowledge to work for your company.

My desire is to return to my home in Arkansas, and I am willing to relocate to any of your subsidiaries in the state. I look forward to hearing from you soon. If you have additional questions about my qualifications, please call me at (505) 555-0173, or e-mail me at mabboud@email.mcc.edu.

Sincerely,

Matthew Abboud

Matthew Abboud

Figure 11.5 Follow-up Message

Resignation Letter

Whatever your reason for leaving a job, writing a letter of resignation to inform your current employer of your plans is a professional courtesy.

Focus on Ethics

Recently, the city manager of a small town was fired because he listed a degree in city planning on his resume he did not actually have. Being two classes short of a college degree, he decided close enough was as good as the degree—except that it was not. It was a lie.

Many people have skeletons in their closets: a court conviction, a substance abuse problem, or an unfinished degree. It is true that on paper, someone with a conviction does not look as credible as the person with a sterling record. Someone without the proper degree does not look as qualified as the person with the degree. However, the truth is better than any lie fabricated to cover up a misdeed.

If a person cannot be trusted to complete employment data honestly, then this candidate is not a good risk for a company.

Falsifying employment data carries serious consequences, such as immediate termination or prosecution. Some events in the distant past may have little bearing on the current circumstances (like a DWI ten years ago or a family member's prison sentence) and need not be disclosed. However, if you are asked about something, do not lie.

Think Critically

What are the consequences for the city manager and the citizens of the town?

A well-written letter of resignation that gives reasonable notice helps ensure goodwill between you and your current employer. Later, when asked for a reference, your employer will be more inclined to supply a positive one. To write a letter of resignation, follow these guidelines:

- Announce your intention to leave the company. Be clear you are writing a letter of resignation.

- State the last day you will work. Make sure that date provides enough notice according to company policy and your knowledge of company operations.

- Use courteous and professional language.

- Compliment your employer and the company. Thank your supervisor for any opportunities or special help provided. If you are leaving because you are dissatisfied with the work environment, find something positive to say about the organization, even if it is brief.

- Offer to help the company prepare for your absence. You could train your replacement or complete work projects in advance.

- Volunteer a reason for leaving only if you feel comfortable doing so.

- Close with something positive. Thank your employer once more or say something positive about your upcoming plans.

Montel wrote the letter in Figure 11.6 to Donald Shappel, the director of Charter Disability Services, resigning the position he has held for nine years. Montel has enjoyed a close working relationship with his supervisor.

1080 Oak Trace Road
Atlanta, GA 30317-6690
November 30, 20—

Donald Shappel, Director
Charter Disability Services
503 North Chester Street
Atlanta, GA 30322-1005

Dear Donald

Please accept this letter of resignation, effective two months from now. January 30, 20—, will officially be my last day as interpreter for the hearing impaired for Charter Disability Services. My wife has accepted an administrative position at Dare Regional Hospital in Hopewell, Virginia. After much discussion, we believe it is in our best interest to move to her job location.

I have enjoyed the nine years working as lead interpreter. Your guidance, in particular, has enabled me to learn new skills and grow professionally. I am proud to have been a part of the Charter team and to have contributed to its fine work as an advocate for disability services.

Before I leave, I will complete the annual evaluations of my clients. Furthermore, I will be happy to spend my last week training my replacement. After I leave, I will be available by phone to answer any questions.

Again, thank you for the opportunity to work for Charter Disability Services. My wife and I will miss you and the staff, but we look forward to new opportunities in Virginia.

Sincerely

Montel Newsome

Montel Newsome

Figure 11.6 Letter of Resignation

STOP AND THINK 11.5

What is the purpose of a cover letter and a follow-up letter? Why should you give as much notice as possible in a letter of resignation?

11.6 CREATING A WEB PRESENCE

Establishing a web presence for your employment credentials may be essential to your job search. Job seekers can set up a web presence in two ways: (1) An ePortfolio is a convenient vehicle for displaying the full range of your qualifications. (2) Social media, such as LinkedIn, Facebook, and Twitter, expand your network, making it more likely an employer will contact you.

ePortfolio

Many job hunters post their resumes on websites that contain not only their resume, but also links to work samples and other career-related artifacts. These websites are sometimes known as electronic portfolios, or ePortfolios. Employers can view your resume and work samples quickly and need not wait for you to send them.

Creating a career ePortfolio has a number of advantages, giving you the opportunity to market yourself in greater detail by

- Showing off a more complete picture of your qualifications with nontraditional employment artifacts, such as work samples, academic papers, and photos.

- Revealing your personality and thus a sense of the person behind the resume

- Granting you a possible competitive edge as a person who can organize information and leverage technology

- Exposing your credentials to multiple search engines

Constructing an ePortfolio furnishes another outlet for promoting your credentials. You might get started by adapting a print portfolio to web media. Once you have an ePortfolio, update it regularly—even after you've landed a job—so it's ready to view for a promotion or for your next job search.

Content

An ePortfolio should contain traditional career-related artifacts as well as appropriate nontraditional materials. Traditional artifacts include the items already discussed, a resume, letter of application, letters of reference, transcripts and certifications, and contact information. Some credentials are career-specific. For example, a network engineer may want to add scanned copies of certifications. A journalist may want to include links to articles.

In addition to traditional documentation, an ePortfolio gives you an opportunity to include a wider range of artifacts, including less traditional items to prove your value as an employee.

- **About Me:** Tell your story—enough to distinguish you from others and encourage someone to read further. Include a flattering but professional head shot. Mention education, experience, and accomplishments briefly but in the *context* of explaining how you got here, what your goals are, and where your interests lie. Figure 11.7 shows excerpts from Sophia Cuomo's About Me section for her ePortfolio.

To write an About Me section, relate life events to the larger context of your career path. Sophia, a bio tech student, personalizes her story by responding to these prompts:

What led to your career choice? I remember my grandparents' struggle to produce soybeans on the family farm in east Texas during the drought of 2000. Growing up on that farm, I decided I wanted to work to reduce the effects of drought on crops.

What are your career passions? My research interests lie in the development of new soybean cultivars. As an intern at Smyethon Farms, I assisted in a study manipulating soybean genes to genetically engineer a drought-resistant variety. Up early to take soil samples and measure soybean growth, I was thrilled to observe the data evolve.

What are your hobbies? I've always enjoyed watching a plant grow from a seedling to maturity. Check out my blog, *Garden Varieties*, with tips for the gardeners in east Texas.

Can you inject your personality? Last summer, I successfully cross-bred two tomato varieties, named Merry and Pippin after two of my favorite characters in the *Lord of the Rings*.

Is there a quote that inspires you? Abraham Lincoln once said, "The best way to predict your future is to create it." I envision a future in which everyone has enough to eat and drink. My AA degree in Bio Technology is a step toward that future.

Figure 11.7 About Me

- **Writing samples:** Include your best academic and professional papers, ones related to your career. Revise them, if necessary, to present the best impression. Employers want to know you have writing skills, so here is your chance to demonstrate how well you write. Convert all files to PDF.

- **Skills:** If you have a particular skill set—such as leadership, teaching, or technical expertise—you may want to devote a separate page this skill. Uploading a video is a possibility if you have good public speaking skills.

- **Work Samples:** Include descriptions of projects and research you've completed, such as a website you designed or satisfaction survey you conducted, along with relevant examples of your work. Employers want to see what you've accomplished.

- **Photos:** Add photos of a finished project—like a robot, a set of house plans, or a refinished car. Photos of you volunteering, working on a team, or receiving an award can be an asset—as long they show your accomplishments and skills.

While these pages are typical, there are many ways to make the portfolio uniquely your own. Rename a section, add a section, and combine others to fit your experience. For example, writing samples might be placed under work samples. Photos can appear anywhere. You might organize your portfolio by different types of skills, such as leadership or teaching. If you have written a personal philosophy, include it.

Appearance and Organization

Your ePortfolio is a website and should use design principles for documents and web pages outlined in Chapters 6 and 7. Selecting a theme appropriate for your career, choosing consistent colors and formatting, and using readable fonts will make your ePortfolio attractive and organized. To assist your reader in locating and understanding content easily,

- Add a table of contents—either as a side bar or easy-to-find links on your page

- Explain the context for each artifact—a quick description of the assignment in your architectural design class or the background for your proposal to introduce confidential shredding at your workplace.

Figure 11.8 shows how Sophie Cuomo organized her ePortfolio by designing a home page to reflect her interests and offer relevant links.

Figure 11.8 ePortfolio Home Page

Ethical and Legal Cautions

Finally, to decide whether an ePortfolio is right for you, consider these ethical and legal cautions:

- Uploading photos has its downside: Employers can now see you; and while you are legally protected from discrimination (age, race, gender), you will not know if a photo of you is the reason an unscrupulous employer refuses to interview you. On the other hand, your photo may make you more competitive.

- It's never a good idea to post personal information, like your address, your age, or phone number, on a website. Create a form that allows a potential employer to contact you. The contact will come to your e-mail address.

- While you are granted certain educational license when presenting images from the Web for a class project, you are not granted educational license when hosting your own website. If you use photos of others or artifacts related to a group project, get permission to use the items. If you want to use an image, research the creator of that image and ask permission.

Social Media

With nearly two-thirds of Americans using it (Perrin), social media is a powerful tool for your job search and career development. Parker, reporting for Jobcast, notes 94 percent of their clients use media to recruit.

To use social media effectively for job hunting, examine your rhetorical situation. What is the purpose of the site, and how can you use this medium help you reach your target audience? What persona or image do you want to project? What are the conventions you can use? Which appeals work best?

Leveraging LinkedIn, Facebook, and Twitter can increase your chances of success by exposing your credentials to a larger but more targeted audience. The more connections (friends, coworkers, family, other professionals) you have, the larger your network, and the better your chances of finding a potential employer. Present yourself as a person of integrity. Use documents and work history as evidence of your competence.

LinkedIn is the premier site for your job search as it is widely used by both recruiters and job hunters. Its many services include housing your profile, hosting a job board, distributing helpful articles and advice, and extending your network. You can research companies, contribute to a blog, and upload slides. Become familiar with the site and what it can do for you.

Facebook and Twitter can complement your LinkedIn profile. Facebook is not designed expressly for job hunting, but its many followers widen your network. Interestingly, employers often resort to Facebook as part of their screening process for applicants, so delete any posts or photos that might make you look irresponsible, and keep new status updates respectable. Choose "Friends" under Facebook's privacy settings.

Twitter can help you follow occupational trends, network with others of like-minded interests, as well as give you another place to house your profile. You can also search for a job using hashtags.

Plan your activity on all social media sites carefully.

- **Create a credible, authentic, marketable profile**. When you get ready to join a site or update a profile on social media,
  - Personalize your profile, if possible, by entering a headline or handle that best names your area of expertise.
  - Upload a professional picture of yourself, a headshot, with a nice smile.

- Include a complete but concisely worded profile—all your work experience with details about what you did. Add any awards, promotions, and degrees. Focus on accomplishments.

- Use your best writing skills: Make sure there are *no* errors in your writing. Keep your tone professional but positive and engaging. Include keywords in your descriptions.

- Update your information regularly so it stays current.

- Include relevant links to (1) your ePortfolio, (2) other social media sites you use, and/or (3) web-based projects or ventures.

■ **Connect with others.** Ask others to join your network, be your friend, or follow you:

- Choose professionals in your field, alumni, friends, and coworkers. Even though more people mean more connections, it's best to choose reputable people who can help you achieve your goals.

- When someone asks you to join the network or group, respond promptly.

- Compliment others using the site's protocols: Offer and request recommendations, "like" posts, or re-tweet.

■ **Get involved.** It's not enough to craft a winning portfolio. You must participate in the site's activities:

- Join groups that interest you.

- Post job-related articles, updates, or accomplishments.

- Respond to others' posts with short, meaningful, personalized messages.

- If you are a good writer with credible expertise, use LinkedIn's Pulse blog or share your own blog on Facebook and Twitter.

Remember, everything you post should be correct, professional, and accurate. Your online activity helps establish your ethos, your reputation as a responsible, knowledgeable person someone would like to hire.

 STOP AND THINK 11.6

Name several ways to create a web presence for your employment materials. What kinds of information might be included in an ePortfolio? an About Me section? a social media profile?

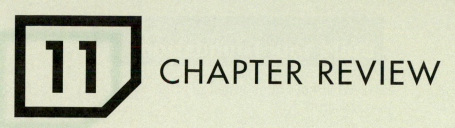

CHAPTER REVIEW

Summary

1. You get started on employment communication by assessing your strengths, researching the prospective employer, choosing your references, and understanding your audience.

2. For a resume to stand out, it should look symmetric, include ample white space, and use an easy-to-read font. Basic headings include Identification, Education, and Work Experience. Optional headings enhance the resume and tailor it to the job description. Information is organized in reverse chronological order and priority order.

3. Resumes are arranged as chronological resumes or functional resumes and may be formatted as electronic resumes.

4. Resumes are written using parallel phrases and lists as opposed to sentences and paragraphs.

5. Three types of letters and employment-related e-mail are cover letters/messages, follow-up letters/messages, and resignation letters.

6. Creating a web presence for your employment materials with an ePortfolio and social media can improve your job prospects.

Checklist

- Are all documents (resume, cover letter, follow-up letter, and e-mail) free from grammar, spelling, and punctuation errors?

- Are all documents reader-centered rather than writer-centered?

- Have I addressed the job qualifications (either the qualifications listed in an employment ad or the qualifications I think the job requires)?

- Have I chosen the most effective resume for my situation: chronological, functional, or electronic?

- Is my writing organized to reflect my strengths?

- Does the first sentence in my cover letter or message grab the reader's attention?

- Does my cover letter or message explain how I possess the necessary skills for the job and refer to any skills mentioned in the ad or job description?

- Did I give enough information so that I could be reached easily?

- Is the tone in my cover letter or message and follow-up letter or message positive and polite?

- Have I addressed my communication to the proper person?

- Have I complimented the supervisor and the company in my letter of resignation?

- Is my ePortfolio attractive, professional, and engaging with an appropriate, work-related photo?

- Do my social media sites include all relevant employment materials? Are my posts credible, professional, and well-written?

Build Your Foundation

1. What kind of information is left out of each of the following resume excerpts?

   a. Identification

   Maria Valencia
   589 Mohican Avenue
   Providence, RI

   b. Experience

   Denton's Sport Shop,
   York, NE
   Ordered inventory
   Kept business ledger
   Calculated payroll

   c. Education

   Danville Technical College
   Associate in Applied
   Science GPA: 3.5/4.0

   d. Major Resume Headings

   Work Experience
   Skills
   Volunteer Work
   Professional Affiliations

2. For each situation, decide whether a chronological or functional resume is appropriate. Suggest possible sections or headings for each situation.

   a. Boota worked for eight years as a dental hygienist. She stopped work for ten years while her children were small. She worked part-time in a day care center for three of those years and volunteered at her children's schools. She also kept the accounting ledger for her husband's restaurant. Now at 38, she has just completed an associate degree in accounting with a GPA of 3.9.

   b. Marcine just graduated with a degree in occupational therapy. Before she went to school, she worked as a carpenter's helper.

   c. Lyle retired from the Air Force two years ago and has taken a few marketing courses. As a teenager and young adult, he worked in his father's printing company. He is applying to be a sales representative for a publishing company.

3. For Francisco's resume, write the Work Experience section for the following three jobs. They span approximately five years. Make up any information that is missing.

   a. Francisco worked at Oleander Juice Bar. He took orders for and prepared juice drinks. He also operated the cash register and balanced the register each night. He became the crew manager after six months.

   b. Francisco worked for Complete Lawn Care. He mowed lawns for several businesses and residences. Part of his job included trimming bushes and raking leaves. He learned how to plant flowers and bushes and to apply insecticides and fertilizer.

   c. Working for Lucky Horse Stables, he groomed horses; cleaned out the stalls; fed, walked, and trained horses; and provided them with basic medical care.

4. Help the following individuals word their job objective statements.

   a. Lara wants to work as a nurse practitioner. She likes children and has experience working in a children's hospital.

  b. Henri has credentials in electronics and theater and is currently enrolled in an audio engineer program. He wants to work the sound system for musical groups.

  c. Molly's goal is to work with children with autism. She is applying to a highly renowned educational center.

5. Revise the following descriptions of work history to reduce the number of words. Make sure you use parallel structure.

  a. HVAC Technician: I installed air conditioning systems, including running the duct work and running and connecting electrical and gas supply lines. Assisted in construction of company storage facility. We were offered contracts to replace insulation on hurricane-damaged homes.

  b. Recording Engineer: To edit and master recordings in CD-R media. Work to design package and labeling CDs. Produce and sell CDs at public concerts. Operated PA and computerized lighting systems for Little Theater Productions.

  c. Music Director: I directed choir during rehearsals and performances and selected music for weekly performances for the choir. Also, I ordered music from companies. When there was a special occasion, I put together a cantata of musical selections. The organ and piano—I played them, too, and sometimes handbells. Oh, and I sang for weddings.

6. Select a partner in your class with whom to share your strengths as an employee. How do your strengths differ? Give each other suggestions for which strengths to highlight in a resume or cover letter.

7. In groups of four, write a Work Experience section for the entire group using the strategies in the chapter. Include at least one job each member has held—whether full- or part-time.

8. Following is an ad for an administrative assistant. Following the ad is a draft of a cover letter for the position. Decide whether the excerpt addresses every qualification in the advertisement. What, if anything, is left out?

> ADMINISTRATIVE ASSISTANT High-energy, detail-oriented team player for our Greenville office to learn many office responsibilities. Prefer knowledge of Microsoft Office. Send resume to . . .

As a graduate of Taggart Technical Institute, I have gained skills in word processing. In particular, I have worked extensively with all aspects of Microsoft® Office.

I also am familiar with the most up-to-date office management systems. A part-time job with Apex Industries gave me the opportunity to work in an office with an efficient office manager. From the office manager, I learned important tips about filing, turning out timely correspondence, and scheduling appointments.

9. The following sentences from cover letters do not provide the details that prove the skill or qualification listed. What information should be added?

    a. I have educational experience with personal computers and basic programming.

    b. I have worked in my family's construction business for the past seven years, so I have extensive knowledge of how a building should be put together. I have worked on every phase of a job.

    c. I am a 2017 graduate of Vancouver Community College with an associate degree in medical office technology. Throughout my college career, I gained many skills.

10. Zeno is preparing to apply for a construction job. On his worksheet, he has listed the following seven people as possible references. Read the descriptions and help him decide which references to use.

- Jack Garriet: Zeno's high school drafting teacher
- Rosie Montero: Zeno's neighbor and an administrative assistant at the high school
- Dr. Gretchen Walker: head of local Habitat for Humanity, for which Zeno has volunteered (Habitat for Humanity helps build and finance houses for people who could not otherwise afford them.)
- Rochelle Currier: Zeno's neighbor and an architect; she supervised a high school construction project on which Zeno worked
- Roy Janak: manager of Kemp Building Supplies; sold supplies to Zeno
- Meredith McDougan: Zeno's 12th-grade English teacher
- Chevron Tucker: Zeno's uncle and a member of the clergy

11. Interview a parent or friend who is successfully employed. Find out what kind of resume this person wrote, what process was used by the hiring company, and what the interview was like. Has resume writing changed since this person was hired? Share your findings with the class.

Your Turn

1. Pretend you have just completed the degree (with a high GPA) you have always wanted. Create a resume and cover letter to apply for your dream job.

2. Write a functional resume highlighting your skills for a job in your field. Use Juanita's resume as a model. Write a cover letter to accompany it.

3. Rewrite the resume you wrote for item 12 or 13 as an electronic resume. Choose between a text file resume or a scannable resume.

4. Write a letter of resignation for a job you have had for five years.

5. Write a resume and cover letter for someone who has been in the work force at least five years. Take notes to assess this person's strengths using the questions at the beginning of the chapter. Ask the employee to give you a description of a job he or she would like to have along with a job objective. Does this person need a chronological or a functional resume?

6. As a first step toward setting up your own ePortfolio, write an About Me section. Start by introducing yourself and your field of study. What drew

you to your career path? What are you passionate about? What makes you unique? Why should someone want to know more about you?

7. What sections would you include in an ePortfolio? Share an appropriate photograph with your class.

Community Connection

1. Visit your local Employment Security Commission to learn about the local job market and how applicants find and apply for jobs. What jobs are available? How does an applicant apply for a job? What is the unemployment rate? What suggestions do case workers have for applicants? Prepare a short report for the class about what you learn.

2. Become familiar with your college's placement center or a head-hunting agency. Find out what services are offered and how to register for them. Is there a fee? Do services come with a guarantee? Is there an online job site? Share what you learn with the class in a short oral report.

EXPLORE THE NET

The *Occupational Outlook Handbook*, published annually by the U.S. Department of Labor, gives information about the job outlook, median salaries, and job conditions. Locate this source online and research two occupations that interest you. After looking at the educational requirements and job outlook, list the pros and cons of pursuing one of these careers.

Works Cited

Parker, Samara. "26 Social Recruiting Stats and Facts." *Jobcast*, 28 July 2014, www.jobcast.net/26-social-recruiting-stats-and-facts/. Accessed 03 Jan. 2016.

Perrin, Andrew. "Social Media Usage: 2005–2015." *Pew Research Center*, 8 Oct. 2015, www.pewinternet.org/2015/10/08/social-networking-usage-2005-2015/. Accessed 02 Jan. 2016.

Toor, Rachel. "Bad Writing by Administrators." *The Chronicle of Higher Education*, 4 Jan. 2016, www.chronicle.com/article/Bad-Writing-by-Administrators/234791. Accessed 3 Mar. 2016.

12 PRESENTATIONS

Goals

- Understand audience and formality
- Plan for audience, topic, graphic aids, location, time, and stage fright
- Determine how to organize and compose presentations
- Prepare outline, notes, and appearance
- Rehearse for a presentation
- Present with confidence
- Organize a group presentation

Terms

adrenaline, p. 325
anecdote, p. 327
auditory, p. 332
direct approach, p. 326
external audiences, p. 319
feedback, p. 333
formal presentations, p. 319
indirect approach, p. 326
informal presentations, p. 319
internal audiences, p. 319
rhetorical question, p. 327

Write to Learn

Recall speakers whose performances you have enjoyed. For instance, you may have had an instructor who held your attention from the moment you entered the classroom. Perhaps you appreciated a speaker at a club meeting or special event. What made these speakers effective communicators? List the qualities and actions that helped these speakers to be effective. For instance, consider these questions: What did the speaker do to get your attention at the beginning? What did the speaker provide as visual support so you could better understand the message?

 FOCUS on Presentations

Read Figure 12.1 on the next page and answer these questions:

- Who is the intended audience?
- What does the title contribute to the slide?
- Why did the authors put the information in the notes section?
- Would the presentation be improved if each graphic on the top slide were on a separate slide?
- Do any elements of this presentation suggest it was developed for face-to-face delivery or for a webinar?

What If?

How would the model change if . . .

- The writers had intended to deliver the presentation only face to face?
- Readers were unfamiliar with the Americans with Disabilities Act or the needs of a diverse community?
- All audience members were experts in disability services?

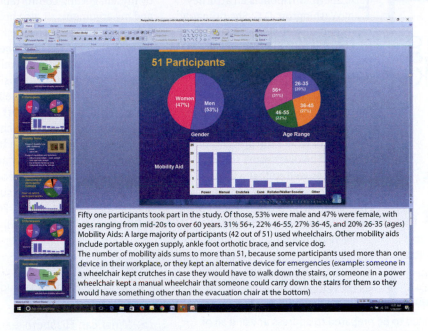

Fifty one participants took part in the study. Of those, 53% were male and 47% were female, with ages ranging from mid-20s to over 60 years. 31% 56+, 22% 46-55, 27% 36-45, and 20% 26-35 (ages) Mobility Aids: A large majority of participants (42 out of 51) used wheelchairs. Other mobility aids include portable oxygen supply, ankle foot orthotic brace, and service dog.
The number of mobility aids sums to more than 51, because some participants used more than one device in their workplace, or they kept an alternative device for emergencies (example: someone in a wheelchair kept crutches in case they would have to walk down the stairs, or someone in a power wheelchair kept a manual wheelchair that someone could carry down the stairs for them so they would have something other than the evacuation chair at the bottom)

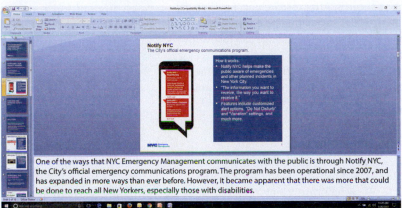

One of the ways that NYC Emergency Management communicates with the public is through Notify NYC, the City's official emergency communications program. The program has been operational since 2007, and has expanded in more ways than ever before. However, it became apparent that there was more that could be done to reach all New Yorkers, especially those with disabilities.

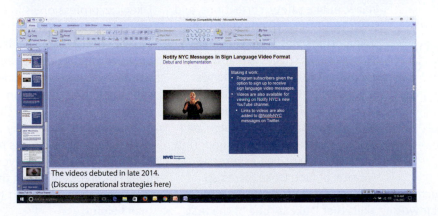

The videos debuted in late 2014.
(Discuss operational strategies here)

Figure 12.1 Sample Presentation (PowerPoint) Graphics Source: *Perspective of Occupants with Mobility Impairments on Fire Evacuation and Elevators*. United States. Dept. of Commerce. National Institute of Standards and Technology. ADA National Network/FEMA Webinar Series. 8 Dec. 2016. Web. 29 Jan. 2017.

Writing @Work

Courtesy of Elizabeth K. Tripodi

CareerClusters®
PATHWAYS TO COLLEGE & CAREER READINESS
Law, Public Safety, Corrections & Security
Source: The Center to Advance CTE

Elizabeth K. Tripodi is an attorney in Washington, D.C. She primarily represents shareholders of publicly traded companies in lawsuits against the company when there has been fraud.

For Elizabeth, a successful presentation is multifaceted: "A good presentation immediately provides an overview of where the presentation is going. It involves some sort of visual aid as well so that a listener is engaged both aurally and visually. Finally, I think anecdotes always make a presentation more interesting."

When preparing a presentation, Elizabeth meticulously researches and outlines her material. "Research is such a key element, especially when preparing for a hearing before a judge. You need to be prepared to address any and all of the judge's concerns. After researching, I outline my presentation. Following an outline ensures that I'm clear, concise, and that my audience can follow my reasoning."

"After outlining, it's practice, practice, practice," says Elizabeth. "I like to start rehearsing in a room by myself, getting comfortable with the material and my arguments. It also helps me to hear my own voice," she notes. "I often ask other attorneys to pretend they are the judge hearing my case so that I can practice performing well under pressure and reacting to various scenarios."

Elizabeth knows that delivering a great presentation depends in part on connecting with your audience. "If I know what the audience expects, I will tailor my presentation to them. In addition, I think eye contact with your audience is essential. Be comfortable with your material and try not to read from a script. Finally, make sure your presentation style suits your personality. For me, it's about seeming professional, friendly, and intelligent."

Think Critically

1. Who are Elizabeth's audiences in the courtroom?

2. What can Elizabeth learn by practicing in front of someone who role-plays the judge? What does she risk if she does not practice this way?

Printed with permission of Elizabeth Tripodi

Writing in Law, Public Safety, Corrections, & Security

Accurate, clear, relevant, specific, and concise information is crucial in law, public safety, corrections, and security. In fact, effective writing is so important that Duke University's School of Law suggests that it might be "the greatest challenge of legal education." The School of Law provides first-year students with a Legal Analysis, Research, and Writing Program, which is supported by the Legal Writing Resources website. In fact, Duke places so much emphasis on helping students develop their writing skills that Duke is "one of the first top-tier law schools to employ writing faculty (with substantial degrees, skills, and experience in the practice of law) whose first professional commitment is teaching; at a number of other top-tier schools, these courses are still taught by upper-class law students, recent law graduates, or practitioners who serve as adjunct professors." Likewise, professionals in corrections and public safety have a need for refined communication skills. Because many incidents now are recorded on video and sometimes audio as well, report writers who ramble; include jargon, text language, subjective thoughts, or unclear abbreviations; write too much and bury the essential facts; or copy reports written by others are likely to have their shoddy reports revealed by district attorneys or defense lawyers. If the information does not precisely match the video and/or audio recording, then the report becomes more harmful than helpful.

Source: From "Legal Writing at Duke Law School." *Duke Law*. Web. 9 Feb. 2017. https://law.duke.edu/curriculum/legalwriting/ ToersBijns, Carl. "Report Writing for Correctional Officers." *Corrections.com: Where Criminal Justice Never Sleeps*. Web. 9 Feb. 2017. http://www.corrections.com/news/article/30175-report-writing-for-correctional-officers

12.1 GETTING STARTED ON PRESENTATIONS

WARM UP

What presentations or public speaking do you expect to do in your career?

The success with which you handle oral reporting may determine whether you are successful in your profession. You may have the best new product idea for your company. However, for your idea to become a reality, you must communicate it to the management team and convince the team members to try the product. This chapter explains how to plan, organize, compose, prepare, rehearse, and present oral reports effectively.

The higher up the corporate ladder you move, the more likely you are to give presentations, either face-to-face or electronically. The audience, formality, and purpose may vary. For instance, you may give presentations to **internal audiences** (listeners within the presenter's organization). Your audience may be colleagues above or below you in the organizational hierarchy—or both. You also may give presentations to **external audiences** (listeners outside the speaker's organization), such as suppliers, vendors, collaborators, partners, and customers.

Some oral presentations will be as informal as an impromptu gathering where you answer questions. These spontaneous **informal presentations** occur without preparation or rehearsal. Instead, you use your experience and knowledge to provide insight. Listeners will expect thought and clarity, but they will not expect you to recall precise details. Other presentations will be elaborate and carefully prepared sessions. These **formal presentations**, planned in advance and rehearsed, are usually scheduled for an online event, an office, an auditorium, or a conference room. These locations may include tools for the presenter's use—ranging from a podium and microphone, to more high-tech aids such as SMART Board™ interactive whiteboards and LCD projectors. Formal presentations often include material for distribution, posters, product samples or models, and multimedia slides.

During your career, you may be asked to present solutions to problems; results of investigations; policies or procedures; progress on projects; benefits of ideas, products, or services; or training seminars.

Typical Reader

Any person or employee needing information delivered verbally, often with graphic aids to enhance the message.

Writer's Focus

Providing clear information in an accessible format targeted to the audience's needs and delivered appropriately for the situation.

STOP AND THINK 12.1

What are some of the differences between informal and formal presentations?

Communication Dilemma

Shelton Corbett and Jody Kolema were assigned to make a presentation before their company's board of directors on new licensing guidelines. Because of other projects taking longer than expected, Shelton and Jody are behind schedule in planning their presentation. As they begin rehearsing with slides, Jody realizes that Shelton has used examples of employees doing questionable or illegal actions related to licensing in which the employees' identities are barely disguised. In other words, Shelton is almost accusing certain employees.

Think Critically

What action, if any, should Jody take?

WARM UP | 12.2 PLANNING

The planning stage is essential in the creation of presentations. This is the stage in which you analyze your audience, develop a topic, create effective graphic aids, assess the location, plan your time, and anticipate stage fright.

Audience

Analyzing your audience is as important in oral presentations as it is in written reports. You need to know your listeners in order to connect with them.

Begin your audience analysis by asking why you are making the presentation and what you want to achieve. You must understand the goal if you want to reach it. For instance, Will's manager asked him to comment on a new pillow display. Will explained at length how he thought the pillows were too soft when, in fact, all the manager wanted to know was whether the display was sturdy and safe. If Will had understood that his manager was asking about the staging of the display, Will could have answered appropriately.

Once your purpose is clear, try answering the following questions:

- Who is the audience—customers? clients? technical experts? managers? sales staff? product developers?

- What is the audience's role? How will the audience use the information?

- Will the audience be a single person, a small group, or a large group?

- If the audience is a group, is that group made up of the same types or roles (all engineers or all sales staff), or is it diverse?

- Is the audience more comfortable with words or with numbers and statistics?

- What impresses the audience?

- What are the audience's expectations?

- Will the audience use the information themselves or pass it along to others?

- How much, if anything, does the audience already know about the topic?

- Is the audience familiar with the jargon related to this topic? Or will you need to define and explain technical aspects of the presentation?

- How comfortable is the audience with technology? Does the audience expect multimedia in the presentation?

- What history does the audience have with this topic? Is the audience likely to begin with an approving, neutral, or hostile attitude?

The better you know your audience, the more effective you can be in meeting the audience's needs and achieving your purpose.

Topic

Sometimes speakers choose their own topics. However, when asked to speak at work (and in school), you often are assigned a topic. In business, managers often ask employees to prepare a written document such as a progress report, a solution to a problem, or an incident report. After submitting the written report, the employee may be asked to make an oral presentation.

For example, Edith Frost, a machinist at Tarboro Machine Corporation, wrote a report that suggested three new safety measures for all machine operators. She submitted the report to the plant safety officer and the vice president. Edith's supervisor then asked her to present her plan at the next managers' meeting.

© NejroN/iStockphoto.com

Graphic Aids

Research suggests that an audience takes in less than 25 percent of what a speaker says. One way to increase your audience's comprehension is by using graphic aids. Graphic aids clarify ideas and highlight important information, allowing audiences to both see and hear the message.

While presentation software, such as PowerPoint, Prezi, PowToon, and others, is frequently used in presentations, slideshows or electronic media are not required. Some speakers prefer to take the stage without slides, perhaps using objects, posters, and even people to demonstrate their points.

Guidelines for Choosing What to Illustrate

When you think of adding graphic aids, you must decide what to illustrate. Use these questions to help you:

- What information is most important? What needs to be emphasized?

- What data is most complex or most difficult to understand?

- What concepts, statistics, or figures are particularly important?

Once you answer those questions, you will have selected the ideas your audience needs to understand and, as a result, determined what ideas to illustrate. The next question is how best to illustrate a particular idea.

Types of Graphic Aids

Graphic aids can include photographs, line drawings, charts, tables, objects, multimedia, and more. For instance, a presenter discussing environmental hazards might use a flip chart to diagram the amount of chemicals found in groundwater. A student speaking to her classmates about erroneous ideas associated with cerebral palsy brought her brother, a police detective with cerebral palsy, to class as a graphic aid.

The various types of graphic aids—flip charts, transparencies, slides, multimedia, dry erase boards, handouts, physical objects, and more—ra`nge from simple and inexpensive to complex and costly.

The time and cost of development must be considered along with effectiveness when choosing graphic aids. You do not want to spend a great deal of time or money to create a working prototype of a new product when no action or decision is expected. The time and expense could not be justified for a simple informational presentation. However, the investment might be reasonable if production or funding decisions were to be made.

© Photodisc/Getty Images

In addition to time and cost, the location (room or space) and audience size are factors in determining the types of graphics to use. For example, flip charts and posters are appropriate for small audiences in close spaces. Objects, demonstrations, marker boards, and transparencies may work well with a medium-sized group as long as everyone can see the graphic easily. In large meeting facilities, multimedia presentations and films provide images that are large enough for everyone to see.

Other factors to consider are artistic talent (yours or your company's) and equipment. If your organization has a graphic arts department that can produce quality graphs, charts, photographs, films, or electronic aids, your only challenge may be selecting the ideas you want illustrated and choosing from your options. On the other hand, you may have to rely on your own skills and talent. When professionals are not available, you may need to choose a simple graphic aid because you can prepare it easily and well. That is, you might create a simple slide presentation instead of planning, developing, and editing a film that includes sound and captions.

Guidelines for Creating Graphic Aids

When you develop graphics, keep your audience's needs in mind. The following guidelines will help you:

- Make the graphic large enough for everyone to see easily—even people sitting in the back or the corners of the room.

- Do not crowd numbers or images on a graphic aid.

- Remember that although attractive design counts, the message is more important.

- Consider handouts to which the audience can refer later.

The following tips are specifically for use with presentation software such as PowerPoint®:

- Select landscape layout for your slides. It gives you longer lines for your text.

- Give each slide a title or heading.

- Select a font that the audience can easily read from a distance, such as **Times New Roman Bold** or **Arial Black.**

- Use serif fonts to improve readability. Because sans serif fonts present a cleaner, crisper image, use these fonts for titles of slides.

  - Serif Font (with feet or bars)

    - Times

    - Bookman

  - Sans Serif (without feet, bars)

    - Arial, **Arial Black**

    - Calibri

- Choose a font size that is readable and that suggests the importance of elements on the slide. Generally, these sizes are appropriate:

  - Titles: 24–36 points

  - Other text: 18–24 points

  - Source notes: 14–16 points

- Capitalize the first letter of important words in titles of slides. Words that are in all uppercase letters are difficult to read.

- Keep slides simple and uncluttered. Use phrases and keywords, and limit the number of lines on a slide to six or fewer. In slide creation, less is best! Remember that the speaker is the show; the slide is only meant to support the speaker. In fact, effective slides often do not tell enough of the story to be meaningful without the speaker's narrative. See the sample slide on the left in Figure 12.2. The few words on the screen add to the impact of the message. Now compare the slide on the right, cluttered with words and bullets, to the slide on the left. Which one do you think would have the greatest impact on the audience?

Few Words slide   Cluttered slide

Figure 12.2 An Effective Slide Using Few Words Compared to an Ineffective Cluttered Slide

- In bulleted lists, capitalize only the initial letter of the first word (and, of course, proper nouns and proper adjectives).

- Use the Notes section as a reminder of your next point; specific facts, figures, or quotations; cues when someone else will be advancing the slide; or reminders such as "Make eye contact."

- If you have clip art or an image that supports the text on a slide, place it in the lower right corner. But never add images that do not carry meaning for your message; otherwise, they only clutter and confuse meaning.

- If you use transition effects between slides, make the effect meaningful. Always limit use of transitions and animations.

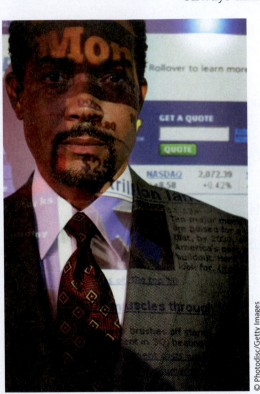

© Photodisc/Getty Images

- On your speaker's notes pages, number the slides so you can quickly move to a particular slide when someone asks a question.

- Do not preset timings in your slides. If you advance the slides manually, you can pace yourself rather than force your speech to fit the predetermined increment of time for each slide.

Location

Presenters also should plan for the presentation's location, which can be very important. For example, if you will be making a union presentation to a construction crew at an outdoor job site, using a projector and screen probably is not an option. If you are using a small conference room to make a presentation about new soccer league rules, demonstrating an illegal shot block could be difficult.

In addition to their own needs regarding location, presenters should plan for the audience's needs as well. Answer the following questions about the location to prepare for your presentation.

Speaker's Considerations

- Is a speaker's podium available? Is a table or space available for handouts and demonstration tools?

- Will you be standing directly in front of the audience, or will you be sitting in front of or with the audience?

- Is the stage elevated, or are you on the same level as the audience?

- How much space does the room encompass? How well does sound carry? How loudly will you need to speak in order to be heard?

- If a microphone is needed, is it a wireless, podium, or handheld mic?

- Is audiovisual equipment installed, or must you bring your own?

- Is available equipment compatible with your software and hardware?

- Will you need passwords, keys, or codes to access the equipment, software, or Internet?

- How much space do you have for moving around during your presentation?

- Are people available to help you with equipment or to distribute handouts?

- Will someone introduce you, or will you introduce yourself?

Audience's Considerations

- Is the location difficult to find or reach? Are directions available?

- Is the location accessible for people with disabilities?

- If needed, are restrooms and refreshments available? Where? Will you need to make those announcements as you begin, or will someone else do so?

- Will all members of the audience be able to see and hear?

- Is the location appropriate and comfortable (design, lighting, temperature) for the type of presentation?

- Will the audience be seated or standing?

- Are the seats arranged appropriately for the group in attendance?

Time

Presenters should plan to meet the time expectations of the audience. If you are invited to present, the person who invites you should let you know how much time you have to speak. If the host does not give you a time, ask. Speakers who ignore audience expectations often lose the audience's attention. For example, when you go to class, you expect the class to be conducted within the typical time period. How would students respond if their instructor kept the class 30 minutes beyond the usual time? Listeners often respond by fidgeting, focusing on distractions, and sometimes even walking out. Keep listeners' attention by complying with the time frame you are given.

Also plan for the proper rate of speaking. Speak slowly when you share difficult or complex ideas and pause after each major section or idea. Nervous speakers tend to talk too fast and may frustrate the audience. To avoid this problem, be aware of your pacing.

Stage Fright

You may think it odd that a textbook tells you to plan for stage fright when most people want to avoid it. Yet stage fright is not something to eliminate; it is energy you should use. Many professional speakers will tell you that you cannot eliminate nervous reactions when speaking. Those reactions, they say, are natural responses to stress. Instead of trying to suppress stage fright, let it work for you. To harness this energy, you should:

- Recognize and plan for how your body responds to anxiety.

- Anticipate excess **adrenaline** (a stimulant that excites and creates extra energy) to give your introduction and important points extra emphasis.

 STOP AND THINK 12.2

Would an audience of your classmates be more interested in how school policy affects taxpayers or how school policy affects students? Explain.

WARM UP | 12.3 ORGANIZING AND COMPOSING

Think of messages you have prepared to give orally, such as planning to ask someone for a date or a favor. Under what circumstances would it be better to communicate an important message in writing? Under what circumstances would it be better to communicate an important message in a formal oral presentation? In a brief journal entry, explain the differences and similarities between oral and written composition.

When you are making a presentation, listeners cannot refer to a previous page if they find your ideas unclear or confusing. Therefore, you should organize and compose your oral presentations for the listeners' situation and needs.

Selecting an Organizational Plan

For most presentations, you will probably use the **direct approach**. With the direct approach, you state the main idea first and then explain and support that idea with details. Stating the main idea first lets your listeners know what your subject is, what points you will make, and how you will proceed.

On the other hand, if you know that your audience opposes the point that you support or if you want to be especially persuasive, consider using the **indirect approach**. With an indirect approach, you gradually build your evidence, convincing the audience of your point, which you state at the end of your presentation.

Previewing Organization

Regardless of organizational strategy, give the audience a preview so they know what plan you are following. The preview is like a map showing a driver where to turn and how far to go. Your preview explains the order of your ideas. Here are two examples of typical preview statements:

- This recommendation contains four major parts: review, staffing, operational policy, and production.

- The SOP for student interns involves completing treatment plans, writing care instructions, and recording patient progress.

Speakers may use a slide, such as the one in Figure 12.3 below, to introduce the topics that will be covered:

Figure 12.3 Preview Slide

Composing the Introduction

Listeners typically recall the first and last points they hear. Therefore, plan for a strong introduction and conclusion. If you are uncertain how to introduce your presentation, think as your audience might. What would get your attention? You would want to know the topic; the points the speaker will support; and how this issue affects you, the listener. Your introduction should announce the topic and points you will make. In addition, you want to give the listeners something to which they can relate—some connection. For example, an address by a woman to her town's commissioners began this way: "My friend Marquita died last month. She should not have been in the path of a car going 45 miles per hour, nor should any of your children, grandchildren, or neighbors. Our town must protect its citizens by providing bicycle paths and enforcing helmet laws."

Depending on your audience and purpose, try one of several introductions, but remember that the strategy works only if the idea is clearly relevant to your presentation's topic:

- A direct quotation, usually from a well-known source

- A **rhetorical question**—a question designed to provoke thought; a question for which the speaker expects no answer

- A startling fact or statistic to grab a listener's attention

- A statement you then disprove

- An **anecdote,** a humorous story

For example, if you were making a class presentation on the advantages of modern medicine, you might begin this way:

> If you were born in the United States in 1990, you had a life expectancy of 75.4 years. On the other hand, people born in 1970 were expected to live only 70.8 years. According to these statistics, you will outlive your mother and father by 4.6 years. (United States: National Center for Health Statistics)

The startling fact that the audience's generation is expected to live 4.6 years longer than their parents' should grab the listeners' attention, particularly because these statistics relate to the audience's mortality.

Composing the Body

These guidelines will help you compose the body of an oral presentation:

- Address people. Include the words *you* and *your* early and often.

- Use words your audience will know. Define unfamiliar terms.

- Use simpler sentences than you use when writing.

- Give listeners information they want or need and fully explain its relevance.

- Emphasize main points. Because listeners take in only a small percentage of what they hear, repeat or restate essential ideas.

- Announce transitions so the audience will not miss the connection from one point to the next.

- Answer questions you think your audience is likely to ask.
- Stay within your time limit, meeting the audience's expectations.

Composing the Conclusion

Conclusions are important because they are the last point the audience will hear. Therefore, they require as much planning as introductions do. An effective conclusion should hold the audience's attention, summarize key points, and call for action, if any is requested.

STOP AND THINK 12.3

John wants to persuade his parents, who do not allow him to drive long distances alone, to let him drive 55 miles to a basketball tournament. The ideas that John plans to share with his parents are that (1) driving is the least expensive and safest way to get to the tournament, (2) he has behaved responsibly when given other opportunities, and (3) the bus does not travel to the location. Place these ideas in the most effective order for John to present to his parents.

 WARM UP

Think about your experiences speaking both with and without notes. If possible, discuss these experiences in small groups. Review the benefits of using notes and problems you have had with them.

12.4 PREPARING

After you complete the planning process, you need to prepare notes and your image. Doing so will help ensure that you deliver an effective presentation. Risks are huge if you neglect your preparation. Without notes, you are left with only your memory, which sometimes fails under stress. Without personal preparation, you may become preoccupied with your clothing or hair, feeling greater frustration and losing ground with the audience.

Outlines and Notes

A practiced performance with an outline or notes yields an informal, conversational style. Speakers may generate an outline using presentation software such as Microsoft® PowerPoint® or develop an outline using a word processor or a pen. With an outline or notes on index cards or paper, you will be able to talk to your audience, not read to them.

To reach this point, you must organize your ideas effectively. If you were writing a report, your next step would be to compose sentences, build paragraphs, and create a document. For an oral presentation, however, you should avoid extended writing. A complete paper with sentences and dense paragraphs might encourage you to read the text rather than interact with your audience. Or fearing that you might lose your place in all of that text, you might avoid the text entirely and try to speak from memory.

An outline or notes should show each main point in your presentation. Under each main point, list facts, figures, or quotations that support the point. For precision and accuracy, do not trust your memory for such specific information in front of an audience.

For example, the outline in Figure 12.4 shows one section of a report on progress for upgrading warehouse computers.

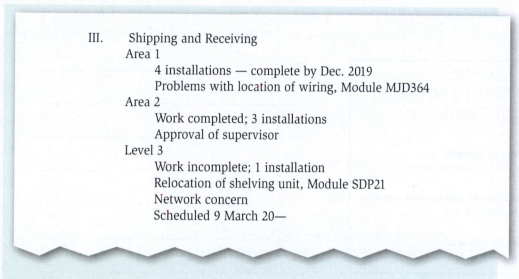

III.   Shipping and Receiving
         Area 1
                 4 installations — complete by Dec. 2019
                 Problems with location of wiring, Module MJD364
         Area 2
                 Work completed; 3 installations
                 Approval of supervisor
         Level 3
                 Work incomplete; 1 installation
                 Relocation of shelving unit, Module SDP21
                 Network concern
                 Scheduled 9 March 20—

Figure 12.4 Excerpt from a Presentation Outline

For the first point of an outline or a note card, write a word or phrase that will trigger your memory. Then go on to the next point of your speech. These talking points will help you to have a conversation with your audience and keep you from straying from your message or omitting crucial ideas.

For each idea, prepare a point in an outline or on a note card similar to the one in Figure 12.5. This card reminds the speaker that this section of the talk is about contributions employees of the school make to the institution's foundation. The card is particularly helpful because the speaker would want to report the statistics accurately.

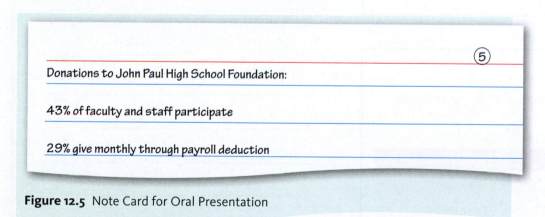

⑤

Donations to John Paul High School Foundation:

43% of faculty and staff participate

29% give monthly through payroll deduction

Figure 12.5 Note Card for Oral Presentation

If you are developing computer slides for a presentation, most software allows you to add notes. These notes reinforce the logical flow of the discussion and highlight details such as statistics, quotations, and important facts. For instance, PowerPoint® allows you to print handouts with two, three, four, six, or nine slides per page, including space for notes.

Figure 12.6 shows a PowerPoint® handout. You can use it to add notes for yourself, or you can give it to the audience so they can write notes as you talk.

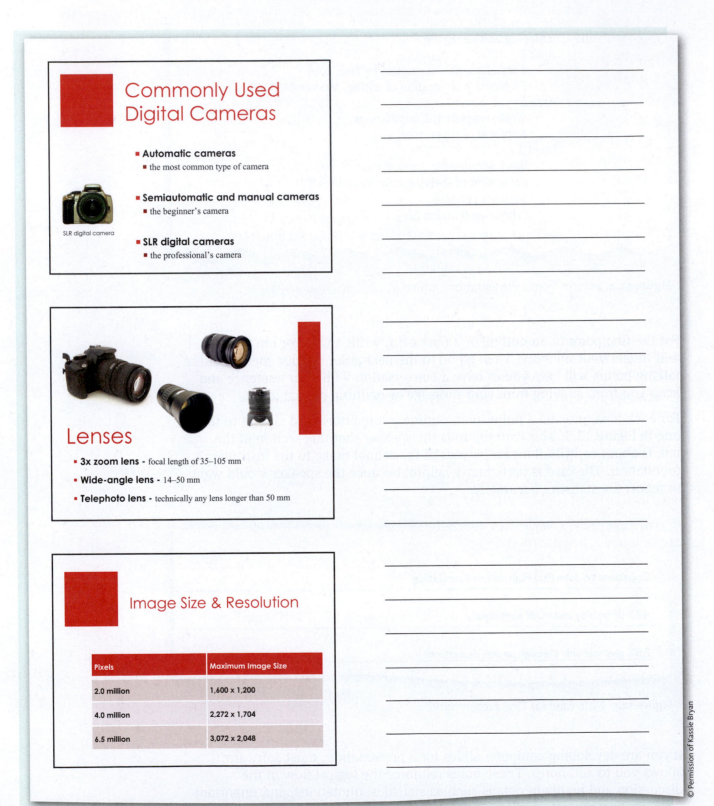

Figure 12.6 PowerPoint® Handout with Space for Notes

When preparing outlines or notes, remember these important points:

- Do not write notes as complete sentences or long phrases. Even experienced speakers would be tempted to read these.

- Prepare neat notes that are surrounded by adequate white space. Use large print so you can read the notes easily.

- Structure notes uniformly: Use numbered lists, bulleted lists, or outline form.

- If you are using cards, write only one idea on each card. If you are using printed notes or outlines, use a large, easy-to-read serif font.

- Number notes or cards from beginning to end. On note cards, place the card number in the upper right corner, as shown in Figure 12.5 on page 329. Should the cards become disorganized, you can sort them quickly.

- Use outlines and notes to spark your memory. By glancing at the words, you will be able to look at your audience and deliver a portion of your speech. Thus, you can converse with the audience using a polished approach.

Personal Appearance

In addition to note cards and graphic aids, image has a big impact on the way listeners receive a speaker's message. You probably know how appearance can affect communication in everyday situations. For example, think about the way a salesperson might treat you if you are wearing dirty jeans and a ragged hoodie. If you have not experienced this treatment yourself, you likely have seen other people treated differently because of their clothing or grooming.

When you select clothing for a presentation, consider the audience's expectations and the situation in which you will be speaking. For instance, someone addressing city council would probably dress as formally as its members do (in business attire). On the other hand, a speaker addressing children at a youth center would dress more casually. Whatever you wear, make sure you are comfortable in the outfit. If you feel good about the way you look, you will speak with confidence.

If you have done everything you can to prepare for success, you are ready to move to the rehearsal phase.

STOP AND THINK 12.4
Would running shorts ever be appropriate dress for a presentation? Explain.

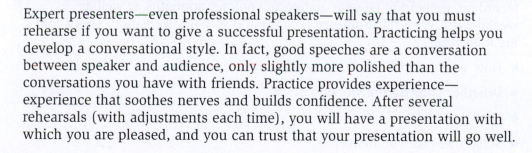

12.5 REHEARSING

WARM UP

Expert presenters—even professional speakers—will say that you must rehearse if you want to give a successful presentation. Practicing helps you develop a conversational style. In fact, good speeches are a conversation between speaker and audience, only slightly more polished than the conversations you have with friends. Practice provides experience— experience that soothes nerves and builds confidence. After several rehearsals (with adjustments each time), you will have a presentation with which you are pleased, and you can trust that your presentation will go well.

Think about other skills you have developed—sports, music, or art. How much practice is enough? What does this tell you about oral presentations? Respond to these questions in a brief journal entry.

Using your note cards and graphic aids, you should practice your speech. When you first deliver the talk, you can identify parts you like and dislike. Delivering the speech a second time, you can change what you do not like. When you are comfortable with your delivery, you have rehearsed enough. You have reached a conversational style.

Speakers practice their speeches in different ways, including using an audio recorder, a mirror, a video camera, or a live audience. With experience, you will decide which methods work best for you.

Using an Audio Recorder

After recording your presentation, take a break. Later, with the benefit of time and a fresh perspective, listen to your recording for the following:

- Rate (how fast you talked)
- Volume (how loudly or softly you talked)
- Pronunciation (how distinct your words were)
- Inflections (what your changes in pitch and tone were)
- Time (how much time you took to present your ideas)

If you find that you are talking too rapidly, something that often occurs when people are nervous, adjust your pacing. Change your volume so everyone can hear you but will not think you are yelling. Listen and correct pronunciation, particularly of unfamiliar or challenging words. Avoid speaking in monotone by varying your pitch and tone appropriately for the message. Finally, check the length of your rehearsed presentation to ensure that you are within your time limit.

Using a Mirror

Watch yourself in a mirror as you practice your presentation. Put yourself in the role of the audience. What do you see that will enhance or detract from the message? Check for the following:

- Appropriate facial expressions. For example, do not grin when delivering sad news such as suicide rates. Likewise, do not finish your presentation without having changed expressions.
- Effective use of your body and hands. (Do your hand movements emphasize major points, or do they tend to distract your listener from the topic?)

Using a Video Recording

Do not review the presentation immediately. Wait until you have more perspective—perhaps in an hour or the next day. When you do view the recording, pretend to be your audience. Look for strengths as well as weaknesses. With this **auditory** (sound) and visual information, check for the following:

- How you sound
- Whether your pacing works
- How you look
- What message you deliver

Using a Live Audience

Ask a friend or family member to listen to you practice your presentation. After delivering the speech, invite **feedback**—comments and suggestions to help you improve. Asking specific questions often will help you get more useful feedback. Try some of these questions:

- What was my speech topic?
- What point did I try to prove?
- Did I make eye contact?
- Did I speak loudly enough?
- Did I tend to use verbal tics such as *and, uh, um,* or *like*?
- Was my conclusion effective?
- Did I pronounce words correctly?

STOP AND THINK 12.5

While an audio recorder provides useful feedback when you are rehearsing a speech, what does it not tell you? In small groups, discuss your answers.

12.6 PRESENTING

 WARM UP

Discuss these questions with your classmates: Can oral presentations be fun? How can you make presenting fun?

Once you have thoroughly prepared, check the environment to ensure the best situation and present with confidence.

Checking the Room

Arrive early for your presentation. During that time, make sure listeners will be comfortable and can see clearly and hear well. Consider seating, lighting, temperature, equipment, and graphic aids.

Seating

Check the arrangement of chairs. Are they arranged so that you can communicate effectively? For example, if you want group discussion, the chairs should be placed so that people can see each other. Also, everyone in the room should be able to see you (and any other presenters) easily.

Lighting

Make sure your audience will have enough light to see and take notes. Correct any glaring and overly bright spots. In a room that is lighted properly, your audience can concentrate on your message.

Temperature

Check the temperature controls. People who are uncomfortably hot or cold will not be good listeners.

Equipment and Graphic Aids

Check all equipment to make sure it is working properly and prepare for problems. Remember Murphy's Law: If something can go wrong, it will!

Focus on Ethics

You live in an age in which most business is global. That means that at some point in your career, you may have an opportunity to attend a meeting in Japan, give a presentation in Australia, or create and present a training course via videoconference for an audience in Brazil.

Because more business is being conducted globally, knowing methods for effective presentations across cultures is extremely important. Beginning with the presentation planning stage, you must be aware of how cultural practices and expectations of the audience are different from your own. Research the audience's culture and plan for differences to ensure that your presentation is well received.

For example, while presenting to an international audience, you should be aware of gestures that are not universal. In Greece, nodding your head up and down means "no," not "yes." In Australia, a "thumbs-up" gesture is considered inappropriate.

You also should research the formality of the culture. Jokes are not appropriate for some audiences. Dressing formally makes other audiences uncomfortable.

No matter what cultural differences you face, the most important rule to remember is to respect those differences.

Think Critically

What are some cultural differences evident in your community? How does being aware of them give you the opportunity to be a more effective communicator?

Make sure you have an extra bulb for the projector, markers, and anything else you might need.

Before the event, determine how you will post or display your materials. Consider visibility and access when arranging your graphic aids. Graphics need to be located so that

- Everyone in the room can easily see them.
- You can point to the graphics as you talk.
- You can reach equipment to make adjustments, such as turning up the volume.
- The equipment has a power supply.

Also, if you intend to post slides or graphics online for your audience to access after the presentation, post them and ensure that they are accessible before the presentation.

Delivering the Message

Having prepared for the presentation, you are ready to enjoy talking with your audience. Use the following pointers to help you deliver an effective message:

- Use appropriate facial expressions.

- Maintain eye contact, which shows your interest and concern.

- Explain every graphic. Tell people exactly what you want them to understand.

- Post or distribute handouts only when you want the audience to use or read them. You may ask someone to distribute them for you.

- Consult your notes, but do not read from them.

- Continue to talk even when something goes wrong. Recover as best you can, but go on. Do not call attention to a mistake by apologizing.

- Remember that your audience wants you to succeed. Your audience's desire for an effective presentation, along with the self-confidence you gained from being fully prepared, will ensure a positive experience.

- Give your audience an opportunity to ask questions if the program and time allow. If you cannot answer a question, respond in a positive way: "I'm sorry that I don't have the answer to your question, but I'll be happy to check my sources and answer you later this week."

STOP AND THINK 12.6

Should you display your poster before you begin to speak? Is eye contact with your audience desirable? Explain.

Communication Technologies

In today's age of global communications, many presentation teams are made up of members from across the globe. Therefore, presenters must have a way to keep track of presentation documents and ideas. They also must have a quick way to distribute the most current documents and keep team members up to date. That is where virtual office space comes into play. This space can be on the Web or on the company's intranet. It allows the storage of shared files as well as space for discussion groups. Members also can use virtual bulletin boards to post the latest updates.

Think Critically

What are advantages and disadvantages of having office space on the Web? on an organization's intranet?

Imagine that three employees walk into a meeting, each expecting to make a sales presentation. Each expects to make his or her own presentation, but when they arrive at the meeting, the three are asked to speak jointly. How do you think the presentation will go?

Presenting with others requires special consideration. Collaboration provides many opportunities to share diverse perspectives and expertise. However, group presentations require careful planning if they are to be effective. Collaborators must act as a team and plan for developing a topic, setting time limits, moving between speakers, providing graphic aids and handouts, answering questions, and managing the presentation.

Dividing the Topic

When collaborating on a presentation, speakers must plan roles and responsibilities. One important issue to discuss is who will be responsible for presenting what information. For example, three employees making a planning proposal might divide the discussion this way: Speaker 1—introduction of speakers, their qualifications, and the problem prompting the proposal; Speaker 2—the proposed solution and the budget; Speaker 3—the conclusion and the requested action. Therefore, the division of topics may dictate the order of presenters.

In addition, sometimes a speaker's expertise will require that he or she deal with a particular aspect, such as an accountant explaining a budget. If speakers are equally qualified to present the material, the group must define other reasons for assigning roles.

Setting Time Limits

The same way individual speakers must stay within a time limit when making a presentation, group presenters also have an obligation to stay within a time frame. After the group determines the length of the entire presentation, the members should decide the time allotted each member, keeping in mind the material each member will cover and its relative significance. Given a 30-minute slot in the agenda, the team members presenting the planning proposal might divide their time this way:

Speaker 1	Introduction of speakers and their qualifications; problem prompting the proposal	10 minutes
Speaker 2	Proposed solution and budget	15 minutes
Speaker 3	Conclusion and requested action	5 minutes

Speaker 2 is allotted the most time because explaining the proposed plan and justifying its budget are critical. If the audience does not understand this information, the proposal may not be approved. In addition, Speaker 2 must prove that a significant problem exists. Speaker 3 needs less time, not because concluding is unimportant, but because conclusions should be direct and brief, giving the audience time to ask questions.

Members of groups should be even more careful than individual speakers to stay within their time limit. If one speaker exceeds his or her time limit, another presenter is left with less time.

Transitioning Between Speakers

Audiences expect to be introduced to speakers. In a group presentation, the speakers may choose to have another person introduce them or to introduce themselves at the beginning of the session. Another option is for each presenter to be introduced as he or she begins to speak.

When various speakers are answering questions, listeners prefer to be reminded of the responding speaker's name. Often a moderator will name the presenter as the moderator asks him or her to address a question, such as "Dr. Quan, would you like to answer the question on profiling?"

Providing Graphic Aids and Handouts

Group presenters should discuss the use of graphic aids and handouts when planning their presentation. Coordinating the appearance of slides, transparencies, and handouts adds to the professionalism of a group presentation. For example, members could agree to use one slide template; a certain color, scheme, or typeface; or the same headers and footers. Members should decide when to distribute handouts. Will all handouts be provided to listeners at one time, or will each presenter be responsible for distributing his or her own handouts? Because some speakers do not want the audience reading handouts while they speak, they may prefer to distribute all handouts at the end of the presentation. Other speakers may want the audience to have copies of materials so they can take notes during the discussion. Speakers should discuss and agree on a plan before the presentation.

Speakers also must decide what equipment they will need. For instance, when two speakers plan to use overhead transparencies and the third speaker wants an LCD projector, they should agree on where to place the equipment and whether any equipment must be moved between presentations. Presenters using the same multimedia equipment should know their software needs and make sure the equipment is compatible.

Answering Questions

Group presenters should anticipate questions and plan how to answer them. In some presentations, the group may allow each speaker to take questions when the speaker ends his or her portion. Other groups will answer questions only after all presenters have completed their speeches. Presenters also should know whether a moderator will assign each question to a particular presenter or whether the presenters will select questions. Speakers are wise to plan answers for questions they expect to be asked. Therefore, collaborators might divide the topic areas so that each presenter can prepare for questions in a certain area.

Groups may perform more effectively with leadership. Thus, many groups have a lead presenter, a chairperson, or someone who manages the process. The lead presenter often represents the group in discussions with meeting planners and acts as liaison, then corresponds with group members to keep them informed. The lead presenter sometimes speaks first, previewing the presentation or stating objectives, or last, summarizing key points and moderating questions. The lead presenter may have other responsibilities, including the following:

- Keeping speakers on schedule; calling time for those who talk too long.

- Keeping questions moving; preventing arguments and the monopolization of discussions.

- Responding to requests for more information; mailing materials.

An effective leader will ensure that all group members' talents are used and that all opinions are heard.

STOP AND THINK 12.7

In a collaborative presentation, how do speakers determine who will speak when? Do groups need a lead presenter or chairperson? Why or why not?

12 CHAPTER REVIEW

Summary

1. Your ability to effectively present your ideas orally to others will affect your success in the workplace.

2. Plan for your audience, topic, graphic aids, location, and stage fright.

3. Use audience analysis to organize as well as to compose the presentation's introduction, body, and conclusion.

4. Preparing involves creating an outline or notes and making adjustments to your image.

5. After planning, organizing, composing, and preparing, rehearse using a variety of methods to polish your presentation.

6. Check the seating, lighting, temperature, equipment, and graphic aids to create the best possible listening environment.

7. When presenting as part of a team, think about how the team will divide the topic among presenters; what amount of time to allot each speaker; how to move between speakers; how to handle graphics, handouts, and questions; and who will manage the presentation process.

Checklist

- Have I carefully analyzed my audience and clearly defined and focused the topic?

- Have I planned how I can effectively use my response to stage fright?

- Have I composed a strong and effective introduction? body? conclusion?

- Will my outline or notes allow me to deliver a conversational performance instead of reading a speech or speaking without aid?

- What type of graphic will be most effective for enhancing critical or complex ideas and for speaking to a group?

- Have I prepared for an appropriate and professional appearance?

- Have I rehearsed and gathered feedback for improvement?

- Have I checked the room for seating, lighting, temperature, equipment, and graphics?

- Have I effectively delivered the message using facial expressions, eye contact, graphics and handouts, notes, confidence, and questions?

- For a collaborative presentation, have my team and I divided the topic among speakers, established time limits, planned transitions, coordinated graphics and handouts, planned for questions, and considered the selection of a team leader or chairperson?

Build Your Foundation

1. Your supervisor has asked you to speak to her church's women's circle about Mexico and your work there as a Habitat for Humanity volunteer. The meetings usually last one hour. If your supervisor tells you to talk as long as you like, what factors might you consider when deciding on length?

2. Mrs. Nicoletti, a counselor, has asked you to explain to a group of 35 first-year students how to complete their registration cards. The entire process involves using decisions the students have made previously and entering data on a preprinted form. Choose a room in your school with which you are familiar and imagine this location. What would be the most effective way to arrange chairs for this presentation? Consider graphics you might use. Consider how much, if at all, you want the students consulting with each other. Other factors could be the room's size and the location of permanent features such as built-in cabinets. Write a description of how you would arrange the room or draw the layout you think would be best.

3. Using one of the topics below or a topic your instructor supplies, develop an idea for an effective attention-getting introduction for your peers, other students in your school. Remember to state your topic and to preview the points you will make in order to connect with your audience.

cost of prescription drugs	the Internet and entertainment	mass transit in rural or urban United States
globalization	employment in fast food	local pollution concerns

4. Fast-forward your life several years and imagine a time when your supervisor first says to you, "Great job on this report! Now you can present the report at the _____ meeting." (Fill in the blank with managers', stockholders', team, committee, or some other group.) Suppose you have six weeks before the date of the presentation. Develop a timeline with the tasks you will undertake to prepare for an effective oral presentation. The plan should identify what you will do and when you will do it during the six weeks. Remember that you already have a written report, but you need to develop an oral presentation appropriate for a different audience. Also remember that this is your first professional presentation, so you want adequate rehearsal time to build your confidence level.

5. Select or create a graphic aid that you can use in a two-minute presentation to clarify or emphasize an idea. For example, you might bring a tool to class and demonstrate how to use it. Or you could draw a graph or chart and explain the process or statistics it illustrates. You also could show a photograph, poster, or painting and explain the idea or concept it supports.

Your Turn

1. Review an oral report you presented recently—in school or elsewhere, formal or informal. List some changes you would make to improve your effectiveness if you were to present it again.

2. Attend a presentation at school, in the community, or at work. If a live presentation is not possible, watch a video of a speaker, perhaps a politician, an editorial commentator, or an infomercial promoter. As you view the presentation, make two lists: (1) positive elements that make the speech work and (2) negative elements, things that detract from the presentation's effectiveness.

3. Choose a written report you completed recently or find a model in a textbook. Write an essay about decisions and changes you would make to present the written information in an oral report.

4. Research a career you are considering. Look for information on employers, salaries, working conditions, educational requirements, and hiring rates. You could

go to the library, talk with a counselor, visit someone working in the field, or talk with an instructor in the curriculum area. When you have as much data as you need, think about making an oral presentation to classmates who might be interested in the same career.

a. Write a brief analysis of your audience.

b. Decide on the main idea for your presentation. Write it in one complete sentence.

c. List at least two ideas for information that could be enhanced with a graphic aid.

d. Create at least one of the graphic aids listed in item c.

e. Prepare the outline or notes you would use for this presentation.

5. Plan a speech that you could deliver to your graduating class. Consider audience and purpose when planning the speech. Will you need graphic aids? If so, what kind of graphic aids would be appropriate? Share your topic and notes with other students to gain feedback. Finally, deliver the speech to your peers and ask for additional feedback.

2. Choose a cause for which you are concerned or passionate, such as recycling, a soup kitchen, or proper hand washing. Develop and deliver a presentation. The audience might be your class, a club, or another group.

3. As a representative of your school, offer to make a presentation at a local library or community center on a topic of interest to the public. You might choose a topic related to your school and its activities, such as academic or athletic programs, clubs and other activities, the arts (a planned theater production), diversity among students, or contributing factors for your school's excellence. Or you could suggest a topic that interests you and that you think would interest others. Plan and prepare for the presentation, rehearsing in front of your classmates. Using their feedback, adjust your graphic aids and delivery. If you can get permission from a person in authority, deliver the presentation at the library or community center. Otherwise, deliver the presentation to your classmates.

Community Connection

1. Visit a senior center or a child care center in your area. Interview people to determine topics of interest for the seniors or children. After doing research (if needed) and collecting information, develop and deliver a presentation at the center. Remember that you will probably need the staff's permission and help to arrange a time and setting. Also consider the attention span of your audience.

EXPLORE THE NET

In an article published in 2003 in the magazine *Wired*, Edward Tufte makes some pointed comments about the use of presentation software and PowerPoint® in particular. Search for "Edward Tufte and PowerPoint Is Evil and Wired" to find the article online. After reading Tufte's article, write a brief paper discussing whether you agree or disagree with his commentary.

13 RECOMMENDATION REPORTS

Write to Learn

Think of the last time you had to choose between two things. Maybe you had to decide between two classes or two restaurants. In a one-page journal entry, describe the process you used to make your decision, including your comparisons and evaluations.

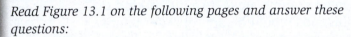

FOCUS **On Recommendation Reports**

Read Figure 13.1 on the following pages and answer these questions:

- What two items are being compared?
- On what factors (also known as criteria) is the recommendation based?
- Why is this report presented in memo format?

What If?

How would the model change if . . .

- The writers were not concerned about the environment?
- The audience (decision-maker) was opposed to the idea of purchasing a car for courier service?

Interstate Development

MEMO TO:	Roberta Boyles
FROM:	Lorraine Nevelle and Rodrigo Reyes *LBN RAR*
DATE:	July 15, 20--
SUBJECT:	Purchase Recommendation for Courier Service Vehicle

INTRODUCTION

The purpose of this report is to recommend which new vehicle the Courier Service for Interstate Development (doing business as Urban Girl Clothing) should purchase. The vehicle currently used to circulate documents and product among the six downtown retail stores, a 2009 Ford Fiesta, poses a safety hazard to the drivers and pedestrians because of brake and transmission problems. It also does not present a positive image for the company because four wrecks have left it dented and rusty. We have narrowed our choices to two hybrid cars: 2017 Ford Fusion Hybrid SE and 2017 Chevy Volt Hybrid. To determine which vehicle to recommend, we developed the following criteria:

1. Safety
2. Function
3. Cost
4. Efficiency and Environmental Impact

RECOMMENDATION

We recommend that the Courier Service purchase the 2017 Ford Fusion Hybrid SE. First, both vehicles have been proven safe, but the Fusion Hybrid SE is likely to earn the same safety awards as its 2016 model. Second, this car offers a great deal of interior and trunk space for transporting goods, considerably more than the competition. Third, the cost of the Fusion Hybrid is within the allocated budget and is likely to be less (including rebates and discounts) than that of the Chevy Volt. Fourth, the Ford Fusion Hybrid, with an electric motor that can reach speeds up to 47 miles per hour, seldom engages the gas engine in city driving, achieving 44 miles per gallon. Yet, its 188 horsepower engine (electric and gas) provides all the power drivers need.

SCOPE

Interstate Development's directors have suggested that we rank safety as the first criterion. The wellbeing of our employees and the public is our first priority.

 Figure 13.1 Sample Recommendation Report *(continues)*

Roberta Boyles
Page 2
July 15, 20—

Function is our second criterion. The car we purchase must be able to transport bulky and heavy loads of product and display items as well as personnel the 11 miles or less between each of our six stores.

To make sure we stay within budget, we have ranked our third criterion as cost. The directors have allocated $29,500 for a new Courier Service vehicle.

Efficiency and environmental impact are our fourth criterion. The directors have set the goal of reducing our carbon footprint by 20 percent over the next five years. We would like the new vehicle to contribute to that effort.

The remainder of this report will compare both cars to the three criteria.

DISCUSSION

Safety

A new vehicle must include:

a.   Driver, front side, and passenger side airbags and knee bags for driver and front passenger.

b.   Antilock brake system.

c.   Vehicle stability control system.

2017 Ford Fusion Hybrid SE. According to the Ford web site and sales brochures from a local dealership, the Fusion Hybrid has front seat side and curtain airbags as well as driver and front passenger knee airbags as standard equipment. The Fusion also includes 4-wheel antilock brakes and Advance Trac electronic stability control as well as a rearview camera and SYNC with Voice-Activated Communication and Entertainment System to allow hands-free operation of phones and music systems.

The Fusion has earned a 5-star (where 5 is the best) overall rating from the National Highway Traffic Safety Administration.

2017 Chevy Volt Hybrid. The Volt's standard equipment includes all the airbags Fusion has along with thorax side-impact seat-mounted bags, antilock brakes, and stability control.

Conclusion. While both vehicles meet the subcriteria for safety, the Fusion Hybrid SE has a higher safety rating from the National Highway Traffic Safety Administration because of the 2017 design features, some of which are carried over from 2016, when the car also earned safety awards.

 Figure 13.1 (continued) Sample Recommendation Report *(continues)*

Roberta Boyles
Page 3
July 15, 20—

Function

The new vehicle will be driven almost entirely inside the city to deliver documents, boxes or single items of clothing, display materials, and occasionally personnel. Thus, the car needs to be large enough to accommodate packages as well as people comfortably and safely.

2017 Ford Fusion Hybrid SE. The Fusion Hybrid seats five and has front legroom of 44.3 inches and rear legroom of 38.3 inches. It has a trunk volume of 12 cubic feet.

2017 Chevy Volt Hybrid. The Volt Hybrid seats five and has front legroom of 42.7 inches and rear legroom of 34.3 inches. It has a trunk volume of 10.6 cubic feet.

Conclusion. Both vehicles are designed to seat five people, yet the Ford Fusion Hybrid has greater space for occupants and small items. In addition, the Fusion has a larger trunk volume for transporting larger boxes and display elements, such as mannequins.

Cost

Since the directors allocated $29,500 in the budget for this purchase, the cost of the vehicle must not exceed that amount.

2017 Ford Fusion Hybrid SE. The Manufacturer Suggested Retail Price (MSRP) for the Fusion Hybrid is $25,299. The two local Ford dealers have a $725 destination fee.

2017 Chevy Volt Hybrid. The MSRP for the Chevy Volt is $32,683. The local Chevrolet dealer has a $750 destination fee.

Conclusion. The Ford Fusion Hybrid SE meets the third criterion; the Chevy Volt exceeds the budget by $3,183. The prices listed are MSRP and do not include rebates or tax incentives for purchasing hybrid/fuel efficient cars.

Efficiency and Environmental Impact

The new vehicle must be efficient and environmentally friendly. Interstate Development's directors suggest the following features:

- Hybrid or all electric engine
- Fuel economy
- Low environmental impact

Figure 13.1 (continued) Sample Recommendation Report *(continues)*

Roberta Boyles
Page 4
July 15, 20—

Table 1 depicts a comparison of subcriteria for both vehicles.

FEATURES	Ford Fusion Hybrid SE	Chevy Volt Hybrid
Engine	2.0L Atkinson-4 cylinder 188 horsepower Multi-point fuel injection	1.5L CVT-Inline-4 149 horsepower Direct fuel injection
MPG	44city/41 highway	43 city/42 highway
Transition, electric to gas	electric up to 47mph	electric up to 45 mph

Table 1. Comparison of Efficiency Features

2017 Ford Fusion Hybrid SE. The Fusion Hybrid boasts 44 miles per gallon in the city where its electric motor can be used up to speeds of 47 miles per hour. Since the car can reach speeds of up to 47 miles per hour on the electric motor, it rarely needs to use the gas engine in city driving. A bonus is that its "eco-friendly" cloth seats are recycled fabric.

2017 Chevy Volt Hybrid. Although the Volt Hybrid meets the subcriteria, its statistics are similar, but do not match those of the Fusion Hybrid SE.

Conclusion. The Ford Fusion Hybrid SE meets and exceeds our subcriteria for efficiency and low environmental impact.

 Figure 13.1 (continued) Sample Recommendation Report

Anne Nickel is a brand engagement consultant in London, England, for a global brand-building company called The Brand Union. Her job requires a combination of marketing and management skills. She advises clients about what they need to change inside their organization to fit and promote their brand.

In her role, Anne writes recommendation reports to help clients learn how to strategically adjust their marketing campaigns, business practices, communication methods, and reward policies. According to Anne, these reports combine information gathered through other kinds of writing. "In order to write a recommendation report, one also has to write interview questions, interview notes, an implementation plan, and briefs for the design team that tell them what to produce for the client. So it requires a diverse writing skill set."

She believes that persuasive documents like these need to do many things at once to have the desired effect on their audience. "Recommendation reports require both rational and emotional persuasion. Case studies and statistics can be used as evidence for rational persuasion. Visuals, like graphics and video, help emotional persuasion by bringing life to ideas beyond the words used to enunciate them."

Anne emphasizes that brilliant evidence and graphics will not do anything for your report if you fail to address the correct audience. "It is important to direct your recommendation to a person who will be open to your ideas and support them. Sometimes this person is the top decision maker and in control of the budget, but other times it is someone who has the connections or authority to be a cheerleader for your ideas and pitch them to the powers that be."

Courtesy of Anne Nickel

CareerClusters®
PATHWAYS TO COLLEGE & CAREER READINESS
Marketing

Source: The Center to Advance CTE

Think Critically

1. Think of a brand that you use regularly. Why do you continue to choose it over other brands? Is it style, prestige, price, value, habit, loyalty, convenience, or something else? How much of your choice is rational (that is, based on the actual qualities of the product)?

2. What recommendations do you have for the brand? Think about ways the manufacturer could sell more of the product, add features that consumers like you would pay more for, reduce its environmental impact, and so on.

Printed with permission of Anne Nickel

Professionals in marketing must be constantly aware of audience. First, they must identify the audience and get to know them as well as possible so they can try to establish a connection. Good marketers listen to their audience. They learn the language (the terms) the audience uses to more effectively move readers or viewers to action. In addition, marketers must focus; they must be able to convey a clear and engaging idea quickly. Finally, marketers must understand the purpose of their communication and tell the audience exactly what to do: call the toll-free number, submit a Facebook like, register online, or submit a review.

Writing in Marketing

13.1 WHAT IS A RECOMMENDATION REPORT?

Look at the sample recommendation report that introduces this chapter. Where is the actual recommendation made? Is this a logical place for the recommendation? Why or why not?

Typical Reader

Someone who must make a choice between several options; a decision maker who is seeking accurate, specific information focused on prioritized factors for each option.

Writer's Focus

Meeting the reader's needs by addressing the reader's prioritized factors for each option in a clear, detailed, accurate manner and by organizing the information logically and presenting it in the standard organizational plan for recommendation reports.

The **recommendation report** is a problem-and-solution report, a written answer to a need that arises in the workplace. Most problems, however, have more than one solution. The recommendation report suggests the best solution to a problem or need. It helps readers make a choice. Employees write recommendation reports to help decision makers choose the best solution. Recommendation reports help people solve large and small problems, from constructing a building to selecting a new computer.

Sometimes the recommendation is the purchase of equipment. In the sample at the beginning of the chapter, Lorraine Nevelle and Rodrigo Reyes examine two vehicles and recommend the 2017 Ford Fusion Hybrid SE for Interstate Development's courier service. Throughout this chapter, you will look more closely at some of the decisions Lorraine and Rodrigo made while writing their report.

Sometimes a recommendation report proposes a course of action. For example, Hennepin Logging has decided to expand and has narrowed the location of its new plant to three towns in Virginia. The report compares and contrasts the three sites against the **criteria**—factors on which a decision is based—the company thinks are important and recommends a location. You will see how the writer gathers data and plans the report.

The last time you bought school supplies, you chose from among several alternatives. Knowing that you needed a three-ring binder, you probably examined several different three-ring notebooks. The choice you made depended on factors you considered important and may have included cost, special features such as clipboards or zippered pencil pouches, durability, and color. Companies go through the same thinking process when they make choices.

Decision makers who have the power to implement your recommendations read recommendation reports. Sometimes one person reads the report, and a committee or board often votes on recommendations. The report is usually written to a supervisor, but sometimes recommendations are made to coworkers.

The report can be **solicited** (asked for) or **unsolicited** (not asked for). In solicited reports, your reader asks you to analyze several alternatives. This reader understands the need and will be more receptive to your suggestions.

In an unsolicited report, your audience is not expecting your recommendations. You may have difficulty gauging this reader's reaction. Your reader may be receptive and appreciate your initiative in helping to make decisions. On the other hand, your audience may be unwilling to accept your recommendations for a variety of reasons. For example, Kamelia, a production supervisor at a large wholesale nursery, was asked by her manager to help select the walkie-talkies to be issued to all employees. Because Kamelia's supervisor was already committed to purchasing the walkie-talkies, he was receptive to her recommendation.

However, Troy received a different reaction from his supervisor. Troy, a landscape maintenance technician, took the initiative to develop a recommendation report in which he suggested buying an all-terrain vehicle (ATV). Troy believed the ATV would be helpful in carrying chemicals for spraying, moving new plants, and getting around the grounds to inspect for pests. However, his employer, who had not requested the recommendation report, did not agree that an ATV was necessary or would improve the quality of work. Troy's audience was not receptive to his recommendation.

An analysis of your audience's attitude may affect how you organize your report. A **receptive audience**, readers who are open to ideas or suggestions, will be ready to read the recommendation early in the report (as is presented in the sample at the beginning of this chapter). An **unreceptive audience**, readers who are not open to ideas or suggestions, will require more careful research and supporting information up front, with the recommendation coming last. You need to lead this reader carefully to your recommendation. Table 13.1 shows the strategies for accommodating receptive and unreceptive audiences.

Table 13.1

Receptive Audience	Unreceptive Audience
Introduction	Introduction
Recommendation	Scope
Scope	Discussion with more details
Discussion with limited details	Recommendation

Recommendation reports are persuasive. **Persuasive writing**, writing to convince others, requires that you analyze audiences carefully, for your job is to convince your reader to act on your recommendation. Researched facts, opinions of authorities, and logical thinking are the tools you need to be convincing. Learn what information your reader expects in the final report and how detailed the research should be. For example, in the earlier situation, Kamelia knew that her audience approved of purchasing the new equipment but had not chosen the brand or model. As a result, she could focus her report on comparing the types of walkie-talkies.

Troy, on the other hand, did not have his audience's support from the beginning. He was concerned not only with comparing the different ATVs but also with convincing the decision maker that ATVs were needed. Further, if Troy had analyzed the audience, he would have learned that three years earlier employees inside the planting sheds had ordered two golf carts to move flats of seedlings from area to area. But the carts were removed when employees were found to be playing with and abusing them. If Troy had been aware of the previous incident, he could have prepared his report to account for this history and explain how it would not be repeated.

 STOP AND THINK 13.1

If the reader of the vehicle recommendation had been unreceptive, where would you have placed the recommendation section? Why must writers of persuasive reports analyze audiences carefully?

Blaine Schroeder is an accountant for Gildstein's Business Managers. He has the difficult job of recommending to his supervisor which construction company should construct a small office building: Wilmore Construction Company Inc. or Galloway Builders. Wilmore is a larger company and has a better reputation for finishing tasks on schedule.

Bids from both companies fall within Gildstein's budget, but the office building must be completed in time for holiday sales. Galloway Builders is owned by Schroeder's brother-in-law,

Ethan Galloway. The Galloways have a child with a serious medical condition and really need the money they would earn from this contract. Schroeder's wife wants him to recommend her brother's company for the job. She claims that families should take care of one another.

Think Critically

What should Blaine Schroeder do?

Communication
Dilemma

 WARM UP ## 13.2 STARTING A RECOMMENDATION REPORT

Some television commercials help viewers define a problem. Some commercials demonstrate problems about which people already know. Other commercials show problems that listeners may not have considered before. List some problems that commercials define. For example, an ad selling mouthwash may make people wonder whether they have bad breath.

After you have analyzed your audience, you must define your problem, brainstorm solutions, and devise criteria.

Define Your Problem

In a solicited report, the person or group who requested the recommendation report has identified the problem. The problem is usually evident, but put it into words anyway. In the opening sample report, Lorraine and Rodrigo stated the problem: "The vehicle currently used to circulate documents and product among the six downtown retail stores, a 2009 Ford Fiesta, poses a safety hazard to the drivers and pedestrians because of brake and transmission problems. It also does not present a positive image for the company because four accidents have left it dented and rusty."

In an unsolicited report, the problem may need more explanation. Unlike the solicited report, the unsolicited report is not requested. No one except the report writer has noticed the problem or considered solutions. Therefore, you must make certain that readers see the problem and its importance clearly. If the problem needs more explanation than one or two sentences, consider placing the explanation in a separate paragraph or paragraphs in the introduction.

State the problem as specifically and precisely as possible. For example, "The roof of Roosevelt Farms Bed and Breakfast leaked during the October 2, 2013, hurricane and stained the dining room ceiling" is a better problem statement than "Roosevelt Farms Bed and Breakfast had a leak."

Brainstorm Solutions

Now brainstorm solutions to the problem, including other stakeholders as appropriate. You may need others to help you generate possible solutions. Explain the problem to your colleagues and tell them you would like their ideas. Tell them that the focus is creative problem solving and that the time for criticism will come later.

Take notes as ideas emerge. You could act as moderator to keep the group on track and stop any criticism that creeps in. Narrow the choices to two or three. You may use others' advice to help narrow the choices.

When Lorraine and Rodrigo brainstormed solutions to the vehicle problem, they discussed repairing and repainting the 2009 Fiesta and generated a list of six potential vehicles. They eliminated the old vehicle as not being worth the investment and narrowed the list to two when they decided that an all-electric vehicle would cost too much.

The search for solutions also may require research. Professional journals and newsletters, LISTSERVs, government documents, interviews, and company reports may reveal findings that influence your recommendations. Seek as much information as you need to brainstorm solutions.

Devise Criteria

As you narrow your solution choices, decide what criteria to use. Interview people about what is important to consider when making your choice. Ask all concerned—administration or management, workers, and people who have used one of the solutions. Getting opinions is important so that the solution you recommend works for everyone.

Roneika West was asked to write a report for Hennepin Hard Wood to recommend a town in Virginia for the construction of a new plant. After several meetings, three sites were selected as possible locations. Roneika consulted with others to help her devise criteria. Table 13.2 shows some of the preliminary information she gathered by consulting Hennepin's management, the workers who will relocate, and a furniture manufacturer who buys wood from the company.

Table 13.2

From	Town Should Have
Administration	10-acre plot of land Available workforce Adequate power supply
Workers who will relocate	Effective, successful schools Affordable housing
Local furniture manufacturer	Safe roads Consistent, adequate water supply

From this preliminary list, Roneika was able to classify like items under larger categories. The categories—resources, utilities, and living conditions—became the criteria for her first draft. The smaller units under each category that help to define each criterion (singular of *criteria*) became the **subcriteria**, or more specific categories of criteria, as follows:

Resources	Utilities	Living Conditions
land	power	schools
workforce	water	housing
roads		

Next, Roneika worked to further define each of the subcriteria. Again, she went back to her colleagues and asked these questions: What is a fair price for the land? How many people are needed in the workforce? What kind of labor is needed, skilled or unskilled?

If your list of criteria is longer than four or five items, reevaluate their importance to limit your list to no more than five. Working with more than five criteria might overwhelm your readers.

STOP AND THINK 13.2

Should writers of solicited recommendation reports define the problem? Is brainstorming for solutions best done alone or in collaboration? Think about an explanation.

WARM UP

13.3 FORMATTING AND ORGANIZING RECOMMENDATION REPORTS

Look closely at the headings in the sample recommendation report beginning on page 343. What kind of information goes under each heading?

The recommendation report is a highly structured report that uses a consistent outline and a comparison/contrast discussion. You may have seen such reports written as multipage paper documents. However, the best format for a recommendation report may not be a multipage paper document. In fact, you have many formatting choices for these types of reports.

If you are submitting a report to a prospective client, you might send it as an e-mail attachment, post it to a website, or provide hyperlinks in a Microsoft® Word document. As with other decisions, you should base your choice of format on the audience's needs.

For instance, an audience that frequently uses the Internet would appreciate the ease and speed of having access to an online report. In contrast, some readers are more comfortable with a traditional print document; thus, the writer could submit a paper copy or send the document as an e-mail attachment that could be easily printed. Whatever the format, recommendation reports follow the same basic outline.

Outline

The recommendation report consists of introductory material, a recommendation (summary of discussion), scope (what the report covers and why), and discussion (analysis of criteria—the factors used in making the decision).

Introduction

The introductory section:

- States the purpose of the report.

- Briefly explains the problem.

- Narrows the choice to two or three items.

- Gives a criteria list.

- Previews the rest of the report.

- May include the investigation method.

The model introduction in Figure 13.2 orients the readers to the information in the body of the report—the site recommendation for a real estate license review course. This model introduction explains the history and the problem, the recommended solution, the criteria, and the investigation method.

MEMO

TO: Marcia Yates, President, Realtors Association

FROM: Reggie Thaxton, Site Coordinator *RST*

DATE: November 22, 20—

SUBJECT: Site Recommendation for March 20— License Review Course

At the June 20— Realtors Association meeting, the board agreed to sponsor a review course to be held in March before the spring licensing exam. Board members believed that a six-hour review course held before the state licensing exam would increase the pass rate, helping members to move from salesperson to broker. You asked that I send you my site recommendation by the end of November so that you could include the announcement, prices, and registration information in the December newsletter.

This recommendation report suggests the site that I believe will meet our needs. After consulting with the Visitors Bureau and other meeting planners as well as examining sales brochures from meeting facilities, I narrowed the options to two locations: the Paradise Hilton and the Narona Garden Club. Each meeting space has been evaluated using the criteria listed below, from most important to least important element, suggested by board members:

1. Location

2. Cost of meeting rooms

3. Equipment

4. Food service

Figure 13.2 Sample Introduction

Recommendation

The recommendation section of the report:

- Makes the recommendation.

- Uses criteria to summarize reasons for the recommendation.

Because readers want the important information first, the recommendation section appears early in the report unless the report is unsolicited.

As Figure 13.3 shows, this section may be brief. In longer reports describing more complex situations, the section could be several paragraphs. If you offer multiple recommendations, number and list them.

Recommendation

I recommend that the March 20— review course be held in the meeting room of the Paradise Hilton. This venue offers a central location, a reasonable cost for use of the facilities (when the hotel caters the luncheon), access to requested electronics with on-site technicians for service, and hot and cold menus.

Figure 13.3 Sample Recommendation

Scope

The scope section:

- Lists criteria, in descending order from most important to least important, that were given in the introduction.

- Explains why the criteria were chosen and why they are ranked as they are.

This discussion assures writers and readers that they agree on important factors in the decision. This section also explains how information is analyzed, as shown in Figure 13.4 in the description of criteria and explanation of why each criterion was chosen.

SCOPE

Board members noted that location is critical because most of our members who are registered to take the exam are already employed in the business and will not want to be away from work any longer than necessary. Therefore, the driving time to this review session should be as short as possible. Location is the first criterion.

Since the cost of meeting rooms for the course must be passed on to participants through registration fees, the price for use of the facility must be reasonable. Thus, charges for the use of rooms are the second criterion. Presenters who will teach the review courses have requested an overhead projector with a screen and a computer with a projection system. To be certain the electronics work in the meeting rooms, I prefer that the facility provide them so that we do not need to rent them or ask presenters to bring their own equipment. Availability of equipment, therefore, is the third criterion.

To fit six hours of training into a one-day drive-in format, board members suggested that the program and its pricing include a meal and refreshments for two breaks. For that reason, in-house food service is the fourth criterion. The recommendation report will compare the Paradise Hilton and the Narona Garden Club to these criteria:

1. Location

2. Charges for the use of rooms

3. Availability of equipment

4. In-house food service

Figure 13.4 Sample Scope Section

Discussion

The discussion section:

■ Analyzes each of the criteria thoroughly.

■ Draws conclusions about which item is better for each criterion.

Organize the discussion section of the report by criteria, starting with the most important and moving to the least important. Give each criterion a major heading. Each criterion is introduced with an explanation of essential elements or features. Then each item being considered is compared to the ideal set in the introduction. Finally, a conclusion shows the results of the comparison for the criterion. Figure 13.5 presents one part of a discussion section.

DISCUSSION

Location

The site for the review course should be within a one-hour drive for all members in our region. The location should be easily accessible from a major highway and well marked on the city bypass.

Paradise Hilton. The Paradise Hilton, in the historic district in the city center, is five minutes from Interstate A1 and within 45–50 minutes of all members. The hotel has many billboards advertising its location on major highways outside and within the city. In addition, the state highway signs direct travelers from the bypasses to this hotel and two other hotels in the historic area. Visitors say that the Paradise Hilton is easy to find.

Narona Garden Club. The Narona Garden Club is located in a residential neighborhood just south of the capitol and southwest of the historic area. It is within an hour's drive for our members. While many signs in the city point to its location, no signs on the highway and only one on each bypass make this location difficult for out-of-town visitors to find.

Conclusion. While both locations meet the criteria, the Paradise Hilton is most central and is easier to find because of better signage.

Figure 13.5 Discussion Section

Remember, receptive readers are interested primarily in the recommendation, which is why it appears early in the report. Unreceptive readers, however, are more likely to be persuaded if the recommendation is placed last, after the supporting evidence in the discussion.

Comparison/Contrast Discussion

Most recommendation reports follow an organizational plan called *point by point,* as in the sample report at the beginning of the chapter.

Point-by-point organization zigzags from one item to the next, comparing or contrasting some aspect of one item to the same aspect of another item. Under the safety heading in the opening sample report, the writers compare the safety features of the two cars. Both vehicles are collected under one point, or criterion—in this case, safety. Figure 13.6 shows the zigzag from one item to another.

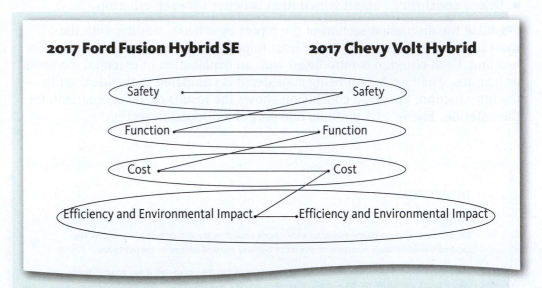

Figure 13.6 Point-by-Point Organization

Table 13.3 links a general outline for this section (left column) to the headings in the discussion section (right column) in the model report.

Table 13.3

Criterion 1	Safety
Item 1: Explain everything about item 1.	2017 Ford Fusion Hybrid SE
Item 2: Explain everything about item 2.	2017 Chevy Volt Hybrid
Conclusion: Which item is better and why?	Conclusion
Criterion 2	**Function**
Item 1: Explain everything about item 1.	2017 Ford Fusion Hybrid SE
Item 2: Explain everything about item 2.	2017 Chevy Volt Hybrid
Conclusion: Which item is better and why?	Conclusion
Criterion 3	**Cost**
Item 1: Explain everything about item 1.	2017 Ford Fusion Hybrid SE
Item 2: Explain everything about item 2.	2017 Chevy Volt Hybrid
Conclusion: Which item is better and why?	Conclusion
Criterion 4	**Efficiency and Environmental Impact**
Item 1: Explain everything about item 1.	2017 Ford Fusion Hybrid SE
Item 2: Explain everything about item 2.	2017 Chevy Volt Hybrid
Conclusion: Which item is better and why?	Conclusion

Appendixes

Appendixes are another component of some recommendation reports. **Appendixes**, the plural of *appendix*, are supplementary materials that appear at the end of a document. Report writers may decide to attach information, documents, or supporting materials they believe will aid the audience in understanding the report.

Each document or supplementary item is entered and labeled as a separate appendix. Usually, elements that become appendixes are not directly involved in the report but are closely aligned to information presented.

For instance, a recommendation report suggesting the hiring of four part-time salesclerks rather than one full-time employee could include a company salary scale as Appendix A and a chart of employee shifts and positions as Appendix B. Some information drawn from these documents would probably be used in the report, but the entire documents might be too distracting to include. So they would appear at the end of the document as appendixes, where readers may refer to them.

References

Recommendation reports that include statistics, expert opinions, and other information from outside sources often include a Works Cited or list of sources.

STOP AND THINK 13.3

What heading of a recommendation report contains the most diverse information? What does it mean to "provide a preview of the rest of the report"? Which part of the report will be most difficult for you to write? Why?

Focus on Ethics

Writers, especially writers of recommendation reports, should consider the interests of all stakeholders, or all parties and people involved in an issue. Because the decisions made based on the information and analysis in the recommendation report could affect the stakeholders, a report that represents the views of only one person or a few people is unfair. A report that does not represent all stakeholders could even be detrimental to the health of an organization or a company.

Highway construction is an example in which many opinions and perspectives result in the best recommendation. Building a new road affects many people. The highway can improve or destroy businesses, increase or decrease property values, bypass or relocate homes, and change the character of communities.

Public hearings, city council meetings, and other gatherings are usually held for people to review the choice of plans and to hear other people's ideas. The process takes a great deal of time, possibly five or ten years or more. However, the process is vital to the fairness of all stakeholders.

Imagine a system in which roads and highways or schools are built with no opportunity for citizens to provide input. If only one person or group is represented in the decision making, many unanticipated problems could result.

Think Critically

Think of some decisions that excluded certain stakeholders. How might these situations have affected excluded stakeholders?

Imagine that your school is looking for a new mascot. In small groups, design an ideal mascot. How did you select the mascot? How did you decide which mascot would best represent your school?

While decisions about formatting and organizing a recommendation report are likely to have an impact on readers' perceptions, those elements are secondary to decisions made in composing: setting criteria, evaluating criteria, and researching criteria.

Setting Criteria

Criteria, the factors on which you base a decision, play an important role in the recommendation report. Table 13.4 shows where and how criteria are used.

Table 13.4

Criteria Are . . .		
Introduced	in the	Introduction
Summarized	in the	Recommendation
Explained and ranked (Why chosen and ranked?)	in the	Scope
Evaluated (one by one)	in the	Discussion

The criteria you choose depend on what you, your audience, and your colleagues think is important. Safety, function, cost, and efficiency and environmental impact are important factors in the choice of a new car for Interstate Development, as noted in the introduction of the report at the

Communication
Technologies

Some recommendation reports are long, formal, and directed to a large and diverse audience. In such cases, these reports are often published online instead of, or in addition to, being published in print. View online one such recommendation by the New Jersey Teen Driver Study Commission at http://www.nj.gov/oag/hts/downloads/TDSC_Report_web.pdf. Since this recommendation report presented these 47 recommendations to the New Jersey governor and legislature in 2008, many actions and programs have been developed to improve safety for teen drivers.

If you are interested in seeing the effects of this recommendation report, go to http://www.nj.gov/oag/hts/teen-driver-report-updates.html.

Think Critically

After reviewing the report, make a list of similarities and differences between the New Jersey report and the sample recommendation report beginning on page 343.

beginning of this chapter. After you select criteria, you must present them in a logical, consistent way.

All criteria must be presented with a name, a **rank** (the relative importance of one criterion to another), and a **standard** (a means of defining and limiting a criterion). Choose a simple name, usually a noun that is parallel to the other criteria. Some reports use questions such as *What is the cost?* and *How safe is this option?*

Give each criterion a rank to show its relative importance to the other criteria. Which is the most important criterion? the second most important? the third most important? List them in descending order, from most to least important. The rank of criteria may change depending on the circumstances.

For example, younger workers with families moving with the Hennepin Logging operations to Virginia might rank the criteria for an acceptable town as schools (first), family entertainment (second), and medical facilities (third). Older workers might rank the criteria as medical facilities (first), family entertainment (second), and schools (third).

Finally, determine the standards of (or limits to) the criteria. For example, if Interstate Development will not pay more than $29,500 for a vehicle, then that amount, $29,500, sets the standard for cost. If families moving with Hennepin Logging to Virginia expect a class A trauma center to be within a half hour's drive of the town, an accredited trauma center with a class A certification within a 25-mile radius could be the standard for medical facilities.

You may need help refining your criteria. In the opening sample report, Figure 13.1, beginning on page 343, the vehicle had to meet several subcriteria under safety. Seek ideas and opinions from as many stakeholders as possible. In your report, list subcriteria when you get to the appropriate criterion section. Like criteria, subcriteria should be listed in descending order of importance.

In the opening recommendation report, the vehicle had to meet several subcriteria under safety. Because the decision makers consider safety to be of primary concern, it is ranked as the first criterion. The standard is security for passengers and cargo. Subcriteria include driver, front side, and passenger airbags as well as knee airbags, an antilock braking system, and a stability control system. The recommendation is based on findings related to the criteria and subcriteria. Table 13.5 summarizes how to develop the criteria in your report.

Table 13.5

Name	A noun, noun phrase, or question
Rank	Criteria listed from most important to least important
Standard	A limit that clarifies each criterion (cost, size, quantity, and so on)
Subcriteria	A list of more detailed criteria that fall under one criterion heading

Evaluating Criteria

Evaluating criteria is a step-by-step process. Jacob is comparing the safety features of two swing sets for his daycare center: Play Time Gym Set and Kiddie Swing Set. Consider the three subheadings—Play Time Gym Set, Kiddie Swing Set, and Conclusion—under the criterion *Safety* in a recommendation report comparing playground equipment for a day-care center. Under *Play Time Gym Set,* the writers discuss the safety subcriteria for one set of swings. Under *Kiddie Swing Set,* the writers discuss the same safety subcriteria for another set of swings. Table 13.6 shows how, through discussion, the writers check off the subcriteria one by one.

Table 13.6

The Play Time Gym Set Meets the Subcriteria Easily.		
Smooth edges	✔	It has plastic seats with rounded edges.
Secure cap covers	✔	Fewer caps are needed because of the round edges.
Slide under 10 feet	✔	Slide is 6 feet long.
Inability to absorb heat	✔	Slide is plastic and will not absorb heat.
The Kiddie Swing Set Does Not Meet All of the Subcriteria		
Smooth edges	✘	It has galvanized frames with few rounded edges.
Secure cap covers	✘	More cap covers are needed.
Slide under 10 feet	✔	Slide is 6 feet long.
Inability to absorb heat	✘	Slide is metal and will absorb heat from the sun.

The checklist shows at a glance that the Play Time Gym Set more completely meets the preschool's needs for safety. The Play Time Gym Set meets four out of four needs; the Kiddie Swing Set meets one out of four needs. A simple count shows that the Play Time Gym Set wins in the safety category. After the comparison is made, the results are easy to summarize in the conclusion, which follows the discussion of each item.

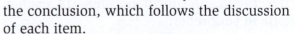
© niddai/iStockphoto.com

Suppose the Kiddie Swing Set had met only the special features and cost criteria and the Play Time Gym Set had met only the safety criteria. Then you would make a judgment call. Safety is ranked as the first concern, more important than special features and cost. Therefore, you would likely recommend the Play Time Gym Set.

Suppose, however, that both items meet the criteria. Then you should look for some deciding factor. Maybe the cost of one item is lower. Maybe the delivery is quicker or the guarantee is better. In those rare cases where there is no real difference between the two items, you are free to recommend either one—or you may want to set other criteria.

Researching Criteria

Research data for a recommendation report can come from a variety of places. Much of the research you conduct for a recommendation report will be field research in which you use surveys, interviews, observations, and visits. Websites, manuals, and catalogs can provide product information. Print media in the library can be useful too. *Consumer Reports,* government publications, business indexes, professional journals, and the many ways to research electronically also can provide data you need.

Roneika West, in her recommendation report to Hennepin Logging, used several sources. She interviewed coworkers and workers at another logging operation. She surveyed the employees who would move to the new site. Roneika visited the three towns in Virginia and interviewed town officials. She reviewed government tax base documents on the Internet. Sometimes personnel, sales brochures, a visit to a store, or sales representatives provide all of the information the writers need.

Be alert to opportunities to present research data in graphics. The opening sample report uses tables of features. Other possibilities for graphics are pictures or diagrams of equipment, pie graphs of survey results, and bar graphs to compare items.

STOP AND THINK 13.4

Consider the sources you might use to research the following recommendation report topics: bass fishing boats, navigation software, and uniforms for nurses.

13 CHAPTER REVIEW

Summary

1. Decision makers read recommendation reports. Reports can be solicited (asked for) or unsolicited (not asked for). For receptive audiences, place the recommendation section early in the report. For unreceptive audiences, place the recommendation section later in the report.

2. Writers get started on a recommendation report by defining the problem, generating possible solutions, and devising criteria. They interview colleagues and others to help with the prewriting process.

3. The recommendation report follows a tight structure using a consistent outline and a comparison/contrast discussion. The major sections include an introduction, the recommendation, the scope, a thorough discussion, and appendixes. The comparison/contrast organization follows a point-by-point pattern that discusses all solutions under one heading or criterion. The recommendation report may be presented in one of many different formats based on the audience's needs.

4. Criteria are presented in the introduction, summarized in the recommendation, explained in the scope, and thoroughly analyzed in the discussion.

Checklist

- Have I devised a reasonable set of criteria by which to judge the items under analysis?

- Have I further defined the criteria by setting standards and including appropriate subcriteria?

- Does my introduction give the purpose of the report, define the problem, narrow choices, and introduce criteria in order of importance?

- Have I considered whether my audience is receptive or unreceptive? If the audience is unreceptive, did I make the necessary adjustments to accommodate an unreceptive audience?

- Does the scope explain why the criteria were chosen and why they were ranked as they were?

- Is the organization of the discussion clear? Does it follow a point-by-point organizational pattern?

- Have I used graphics appropriately? Is the document attractive?

- Have I considered the appropriate format for my audience and the appendixes that would help the audience make an informed decision?

- Have I included a Works Cited or reference list, if one is needed?

Build Your Foundation

1. Using the Internet, research one of the products listed below. Then determine an audience, a person or group that might use the product. Using the information you gather on different types or models and different manufacturers' products, devise a reasonable set of criteria by which to judge the items under analysis. Name and describe the audience and list the criteria in order of importance. Also explain each criterion and why it was selected.

   a. Golf clubs or tennis racket
   b. Smartphone
   c. Slow cooker (crock pot)
   d. Digital camera
   e. A cosmetic product (for men or women)
   f. Backpack

2. Suppose you work for a real estate management company. In one of the office buildings your company manages, the heating and air conditioning unit stopped working today. The technician assigned to repair the equipment says that the unit cannot be fixed and should be replaced. The tenant cannot run her business without adequate heating, so she expects immediate action. The technician suggests TempPro heating units as well as Environease machines. He says that both are good products, each with a five-year warranty.

   a. Other than warranty, what criteria might the real estate management company establish?
   b. Suggest a standard for one of the criteria.
   c. Write a problem statement for a recommendation report using this situation. Add specific information as needed.
   d. What graphics might be useful in the recommendation report developed in this case?

3. Sunee's doctor has told her to eat a nutritious diet low in fat, cholesterol, and salt and high in complex carbohydrates. Help her evaluate the butter substitutes listed below in the two columns on the right based on the criteria on the left. What conclusion can you draw from your evaluation?

Substitute	Margarine (1 tbsp)	Table spread (1 tbsp)
#1 Low in fat	17% fat	11% fat
#2 Low in cholesterol	0% cholesterol	0% cholesterol
#3 Low in salt	4% salt	5% salt
#4 High in complex carbohydrates	0% complex carbohydrates	0% complex carbohydrates

4. Revise the following recommendations section:

   After thoroughly studying the options, I recommend the following actions: closing the drive-through payment window, reducing the day-shift staff by one employee, encouraging more use of the computerized self-serve stations in the office, and using student interns to teach patrons how convenient and easy the online options are to use. Otherwise, I suggest we do nothing at this time and study our operations for other possible solutions.

Your Turn

In small groups, use one of the following scenarios to answer items 1–5. You do not need to use the same scenario for all five questions.

a. You are on the Entertainment Committee to decide which band to hire for the annual Holiday Ball. According to the survey you sent, employees are evenly divided on which of three groups to choose: Newton Jazz Ensemble, Midnight City Rock Band, or Down and Dusty Country Band.

b. You are on the Hampton Scholarship Committee. Hampton Company gives a $1,000 scholarship to a deserving student every year. The guidance counselor has chosen Dario Mesa and Allison Jurevicius as the top two contenders for the scholarship. You and the committee must select one of these students.

c. As a member of Ammsco Chemical's Quality Circle, you must decide what microwave to buy for the new employee lounge. You have narrowed your choice to two: the Trimstyle Model 1400 and the Even Cook Model 1550. You, along with the members of your Quality Circle team, must choose the new microwave.

1. Write an introduction to a recommendation report for item a, b, or c. Add details as needed. Look at the model and at the outline under "Formatting and Organizing Recommendation Reports" in this chapter. You may begin your introduction with "The purpose of this report is to. . . ."

2. For any two of the preceding scenarios, brainstorm a list of criteria. Narrow your list to the top three or four. Rank them in order from most important to least important.

3. Choose one of the lists of criteria from item 2. Apply a standard, or limit, to each of the criteria. Devise subcriteria for one of the criteria.

4. In an oral or written scope section, tell your classmates why you chose your criteria and why you ranked them the way you did.

5. Generate an outline for two of the scenarios. Follow the format shown below. For now, make your best guess for the conclusion under each criterion.

Criterion 1	Criterion 2	Criterion 3
Item 1	Item 1	Item 1
Item 2	Item 2	Item 2
Conclusion	Conclusion	Conclusion

6. Request from your school or district administration a copy of a recommendation report that was denied. Review the report using the guidelines in this chapter. Write an explanation of why you believe the report is ineffective and what you would do to improve it.

Community Connection

1. List some problems or opportunities in your community. Focus for a moment on the one you care about most. Could two or three courses of action solve this problem? Write a report to your city official recommending a course of action. Research your courses of action using the library or other resources.

2. Ask several local businesses for examples of recommendation reports they have used. Review the reports and compare them to the guidelines covered in this chapter. Choose one report to critique. Discuss its strengths and weaknesses, and share your findings with the class.

3. Identify a faculty or staff member at your school who is preparing to make a decision, perhaps what to purchase (such as a new microscope for the science lab) or which selection to make (such as the speaker for graduation or a band for Homecoming). Ask the decision maker for the opportunity to prepare a recommendation report based on the situation. With permission to proceed, complete the following tasks:

   a. Interview the stakeholders. Using your interview notes, create a document that defines what each stakeholder seeks in a solution.
   b. Use the information gathered from stakeholders to devise criteria.
   c. Brainstorm potential solutions and research the two that look to be most promising.
   d. Develop your recommendation report comparing the two solutions to the criteria.
   e. Seek constructive criticism from your classmates and instructor.
   f. Revise the report.
   g. Submit the revised recommendation report to the decision maker and to your instructor.

4. Check with your schools' clubs and organizations to learn about any products or services they are considering. For example, if one of the clubs or organizations is planning a dance or performance, perhaps the group will be searching for a band, a DJ, a karaoke machine, or stage sets. Ask if you can do the research and write a recommendation report. Remember that you will need to interview some of the organization's leaders to establish criteria. After developing the report, submit it to your instructor and/or classmates for their review. Revise, edit, and then submit it to the organization. Ask for the group's feedback and final decision.

5. Local governments are likely to use recommendation reports to make decisions about many things, from purchasing vans and buses to contracting with paint companies. For that reason, arrange an appointment to interview someone in city government who writes recommendation reports. During the interview, ask about the research, the writing process, and the final document. If possible, get a copy of a report and have the interviewee explain its development. Focus on skills that will help you become a better report writer. Write a summary of the important information you gained during the interview.

6. With a partner, write a recommendation report to a local agency in which you suggest an action or a decision that will improve circumstances for a group of people or all citizens of the community.

EXPLORE THE NET

Review one or more of the sites listed below. Each of them involves computerized decision aids, a digital analysis, and recommendations for the user. The first describes a digital aid for women deciding on a birth process, the second describes a patent application for a computerized system that would provide purchase recommendations and connect the consumer directly to the manufacturer, and the third discusses implications of computer recommendations for the treatment of concussions. After reviewing the sites, write an essay or journal entry, as your instructor directs, in which you discuss the merits or the potential problems with computerized decision aids.

"Clinical Research Reports Outline Clinical Trials and Studies Findings from Mashhad University of Medical Sciences (the Impact of a Computerized Decision Aid on Empowering Pregnant Women for Choosing Vaginal Versus Cesarean Section Delivery: Study Protocol for a . . .)." *Computer Weekly News* (2015): 370. ProQuest. Web. 27 Dec. 2015.

"Patents; 'E-Commerce System and Method' in Patent Application Approval Process (USPTO 20150356588)." *Computer Weekly News* (2015): 626. ProQuest. Web. 27 Dec. 2015.

Usha, Lee M. "The Big Business of Treating Brain Injuries." *Boston Globe* (Online): 1. 17 Dec. 2015. ProQuest. Web. 27 Dec. 2015.

14 PROPOSALS

Goals

- Define proposals and determine their purpose
- Plan to write proposals
- Compose informal proposals
- Compose formal proposals

Terms

appendix, p. 382
executive summary, p. 370
letter of transmittal, p. 382
limitations, p. 375
memo of transmittal, p. 382
pagination, p. 383
prefatory material, p. 385
proposal, p. 369
RFP, p. 370
scope, p. 375
solicited proposal, p. 370
unsolicited proposal, p. 371

Write to Learn

Think of a time when you had a successful sales experience. Perhaps you persuaded a person or a group to buy a product or service or to agree to an idea such as a fundraiser or a community or family project. In a journal entry, write a narrative about that experience. Include ways in which you prepared to make the sale as well as a description of your audience.

FOCUS on Proposals

Read Figure 14.1 on the next page and answer these questions:

- Who might the head custodian have consulted about the proposed solution?
- What are some alternative solutions the custodians may have considered?
- Do you agree with the recommendation to hire a new custodian? Why or why not?
- What would you include in a list of the positive and negative supporting ideas for one alternative solution that you choose?

What If?

How would the model change if . . .

- Most of the events requiring special setup were scheduled in the summer when school was not in session?
- The school had a hiring freeze?
- The current custodians' hours and wages had been reduced because of budget problems?

TO: Dr. Martin Svoboda, Principal

FROM: Emmett Yackley, Head Custodian   EMY

DATE: July 14, 20—

SUBJECT: **Proposal for Additional Night Custodian**

Problem

The custodians who work the evening shift cannot complete all of the special setups required for meetings *and* clean the rooms efficiently. Hiring an additional custodian to work the midnight shift would help ensure that all of the work gets done.

Background

The workload for the night shift consists of cleaning the classrooms and offices, the halls, and the restrooms. When setups are required, custodians must move tables and assemble rows of chairs. In addition, the cleaning of these areas still must be done. The number of special setups has been increasing, as the following data shows.

	January	February	March	April	May	June	Half-Year Total
2014	7	12	18	21	21	19	98
2015	9	12	21	23	24	19	108
2016	11	17	24	26	31	25	134

Teachers, students, and visitors often comment that the building sometimes looks clean and sometimes appears dirty. Unfortunately, a dirty building does not make for good public relations.

Solution

An additional custodian working the midnight shift could dismantle the setups. This person would free the regular night custodians to clean. When no special setups are required, this person could help clean, wash and polish floors, and vacuum offices. The estimated cost to fill the position of a night shift custodian is $22,500–$27,000 a year.

Benefits

If the midnight shift workload was shared by an additional custodian, the problems described would be eliminated.

Conclusion

Staffing this new position will be costly, but I believe the benefits far outweigh the financial considerations. I hope you will pursue the hiring of a custodian for the night shift. Please let me know if I may post a position announcement through the district office.

Figure 14.1   Sample Proposal

Writing @Work

Courtesy of Meredith Beattie

CareerClusters®
PATHWAYS TO COLLEGE & CAREER READINESS
Government & Public Administration
Source: The Center to Advance CTE

Meredith Beattie is cofounder of The BEL Group, a company that works toward capacity building in the government and nonprofit sectors. She writes grant proposals for workforce development, public safety infrastructure, and K–12 educational and cultural programs.

"Competitive proposal development requires time up front to carefully consider the long-term effects of having a proposal accepted," says Meredith. "The difficulty is that an organization's staff may have little time to meet with you and want you to 'just write it.' This can lead to a proposal that wins the grant but is not feasible for the organization to implement. Getting organizations to spend planning time with you translates into a better working team and a realistic proposal."

The writing process is a complex endeavor that requires methodical attention to detail. "A proposal has many moving parts, so the absolute first thing one should do when beginning to write is to read, tear apart, and 'become one' with the entire proposal structure," advises Meredith. "The sections of a proposal are interrelated. If you do not have a thorough grasp of the complete picture, you can create a proposal that is full of contradictions."

In Meredith's experience, collaboration with the organization's stakeholders is key to a realistic proposal. "Reaching agreement on the overall goal, the resources available to meet the goal, and the benchmarks the organization will meet provides a clear framework for the writer. An accepted proposal becomes the foundation of the contract with the funder. Reminding your stakeholders of this may help them articulate reasonable and achievable goals."

A major difficulty in writing a persuasive proposal is that the writer does not know who his or her audience or competitors are. "Your writing needs to be able to carry any reader—expert or neophyte—to the inevitable conclusion that the applicant is best positioned to fulfill the intent and requirements stated in the application," says Meredith. "Your proposal may be the 200th one the reviewer reads, so make it as easy as possible to digest, avoid colloquialisms, and be compelling without being sensational."

Think Critically

1. Why is it important that Meredith work with the organization to plan the proposal? What may happen if she does not get enough input?

2. How would a writer make a proposal "as easy as possible to digest"?

Printed with permission of Meredith Beattie

Writing in Government and Public Administration

Writers for government and public administration often face the challenge of communicating with a broad general audience. For instance, writers for a federal agency, such as Social Security, who communicate service, benefit, and eligibility information to citizens must be aware that their readers range in age, education, interest, motivation, language skills, culture, religion, expectations, and more. Therefore, these writers must anticipate much: what readers will understand and what they are less likely to comprehend, what information they will need, what questions they have, what might offend or threaten them, and what media and methods will best reach them. Clear, precise, and direct communication is valuable in government and public administration.

14.1 WHAT IS A PROPOSAL?

A **proposal** is a persuasive document that offers a solution to an identified problem or need. Proposals attempt to sell an idea, a product or service, or a new concept or plan. Proposals may be brief or long. A one-page request for a room change written to a club adviser and a 2,000-page multivolume document selling a new type of amphibious tank to the Department of Defense are examples of proposals.

Proposal comes from the base word *propose*. Have you ever proposed an idea for a party to your friends? Do you know anyone who has proposed marriage? If you are thinking of the meaning "to suggest" or "to make an offer," you are beginning to understand the purpose of a proposal.

A proposal can be a request for support. For instance, the local Boys and Girls Club may send a proposal to the United Way requesting money to resurface the club's tennis court. Another proposal might offer a customer goods or services. If a school organization sells candy to raise money, the project probably began with a proposal from the candy supplier.

The successful proposal persuades an audience to accept the solution offered and to invest in the idea, product, plan, or service. Employees can use proposals to respond to problems rather than merely complain about them. The proposal provides a professional means of presenting the employees' ideas for change, which can be empowering.

As Figure 14.2 illustrates, proposals can be categorized in several ways relating to the audience: (1) internal or external; (2) formal or informal; (3) solicited or unsolicited; or (4) sales, research, grant, or planning.

What physical projects took place at your school during the past year (for example, repainting, repairs, new walkways, or new landscaping)? As you read this part of the chapter, list the types of proposals likely to have been written before this work could have been done.

Typical Reader

Any person (owner, manager, director, technician, or client/customer) who makes decisions.

Writer's Focus

Clearly and persuasively presenting information the reader needs in order to make an informed decision, anticipating questions and arguments, using an organizational plan that is logical and convincing, and developing appropriate visual aids to enhance the message.

PROPOSAL CATEGORY	DEFINITION OF CATEGORY
A. internal	directed to an audience within the organization
external	directed to an audience outside the organization
B. formal	contains parts used in formal reports
informal	omits elements of formal reports; is often brief
C. solicited	is written in response to a request
unsolicited	is written independently without a request
D. sales	attempts to sell a product or service
research	seeks approval for a research study
grant	asks for funding for a project
planning	attempts to persuade the audience to take a certain action

Figure 14.2 Types of Proposals

Internal and External

Readers of some proposals will be internal—that is, inside the writer's organization. Other readers will be external, or outside the writer's organization. Internal proposals usually attempt to sell an idea or a plan, such as how providing on-site day care can reduce the absentee rate at work, how merit raise funds should be distributed, and how eliminating classes the day before finals can ease stress and improve scores. External proposals frequently try to sell goods or services as well as ideas.

Informal and Formal

A proposal is informal or formal based on the degree to which the conventions of formal report writing are followed and how "dressed up" the document looks. Formal proposals contain more parts than informal proposals. Writers decide how formal a document should be based primarily on the audience and its needs.

Because informal proposals often address an internal audience that understands why the document was written, these proposals are typically brief, generally from one to ten pages. An informed audience eliminates the need for background information or an explanation of the problem. In addition, the report has a flexible organizational plan, uses less formal language, and is frequently presented as a letter or memo. Occasionally, however, a brief informal proposal may be written to an external audience when the subject matter and proposed solution are simple and require little explanation.

A proposal going to someone close (in the ranks of the organization) to the writer is usually informal. Likewise, a problem and solution that can be explained in a simple manner are presented in an informal report. The proposal writer would not invest the often lengthy preparation time involved in a formal proposal to suggest something as simple, for example, as changing lunch schedules to allow for a company-wide meeting.

Formal proposals, on the other hand, usually address an external and often unfamiliar audience. They are organized according to standard elements of formal researched reports, with a cover page, a letter of transmittal, a title page, a table of contents, a list of illustrations, an **executive summary** (a summary of the key information in each section of the proposal), body discussion divided by headings and subheadings, appendixes, a glossary of key terms, and a bibliography. (Not all formal reports will have all of these sections.)

Solicited and Unsolicited

A proposal is solicited or unsolicited depending on the audience's role in its initiation. A **solicited proposal** is a proposal that the reader asked the writer to prepare. A request may come from a manager at work who sees a problem. The manager asks an individual or a team to study solutions to the problem and present recommendations in a proposal. The request might also appear in an **RFP**, or request for proposal. RFPs may be published in journals or websites targeting the audience or sent directly to the potential audience. The RFP states exactly what the customer seeks. Proposal writers then prepare their documents to address the needs stated in the RFP. An **unsolicited proposal** begins when the writer discovers a problem, such as an inefficient production line or a lack of water fountains for employees who use wheelchairs. The writer independently identifies a problem, explains it, and offers solutions.

Sales, Research, Grant, and Planning Proposals

Based on function, or what the writer wants the audience to agree to do, proposals fall into one of four categories: sales, research, grant, and planning. Each category is explained below.

- The sales proposal tries to sell a product or service.

- The research proposal asks for approval to begin a study or an investigation. A marine biologist at a university, for instance, might request approval (and perhaps funding) to study the effect of acid rain on a particular fish species.

- The grant proposal seeks money from a government agency, foundation, or other funding source for a specified project, such as developing a horseback riding program for children with cerebral palsy.

- The planning proposal attempts to persuade an audience to take a particular action, as in a plan to improve food service at a restaurant's drive-through window by rearranging preparation tables for efficiency.

A single proposal may combine several of the categories mentioned here.

Formatting

The best format for a proposal is determined by the needs of the audience and the function or type of proposal. Writers who are submitting a formal proposal to a prospective client might want to prepare a bound book-like document for decision makers to read and review. The writers of an informal proposal that suggests ways to improve recycling efforts in a printing company could send their proposal to the manager as an e-mail attachment.

A company that installs fiber-optic cable in public buildings could post a proposal to a website for viewers' access. Some proposal writers take advantage of images and hyperlinks to persuade the audience by sending a DVD with sound and video and links to useful sites.

Decision makers throughout business and industry read proposals. Most of these people read only a portion of the proposal. They read those sections that deal with their area of interest and expertise. Thus, readers evaluate the proposal based on the data presented in the section or sections they review, passing their acceptance or rejection to the person or group making the final decision.

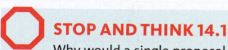
STOP AND THINK 14.1

Why would a single proposal be categorized in more than one way?

WARM UP

14.2 GETTING STARTED ON PROPOSALS

Now that you know about the different types of proposals, you are ready to plan for writing one. The proposal begins with a problem or need. The problem may be one that you discovered or one that someone pointed out to you, as in an RFP or in a memo or letter from another professional.

A problem-solving strategy such as the following can make your work as a proposal writer easier and can help you focus on the problem.

- Determine whether you have a problem or need.
- If you do, define the problem or need and your purpose.
- Conduct preliminary research.
- Determine the scope and limitations of your study.
- Identify the factors or subparts of the problem or need.
- Brainstorm possible solutions.
- Gather data to support the possible solutions.
- If possible, test and evaluate the solutions.

Once you have gone through the problem-solving process and are ready to write your proposal, you can use one of several strategies to help you appeal to your audience. Create a chart with a line drawn down the middle. On the left side of the chart, write everything you think the readers need or want from the solution. For instance, if you have an RFP, the criteria, as with a job advertisement, are probably noted there. If you do not have an RFP, make the list based on your research and insight into the problem and audience.

On the right side of the chart, list what your solution offers the reader in fulfilling his or her wants or needs. In other words, for every want or need in the left column, explain in the right column how your plan will satisfy that want or need. Thus, you will have persuasive tools ready to begin composing your proposal. Table 14.1 relates to a sales proposal for football helmets.

Table 14.1

Criterion	Response
Protects players	• 1" of solid tempered plastic covered with fiberglass for resistance • 3/4" foam padding from ear to ear • Adjustable liner for greater protection
Is economical	• $29.90 per unit, 10% less than the average football helmet • 10-year warranty/automatic replacements

Another technique that some proposal writers use when analyzing their audience is to imagine how the readers think and feel. Anticipating the readers' questions and concerns may help you understand the readers' points of view and anticipate their needs. You can also gather audience information relating to the issues in the proposal, as shown in Table 14.2.

Table 14.2

Problem	• Is the reader aware of the problem? • How much does the reader know about the problem? • What factors about the problem most concern the reader?
Solution	• What do the criteria (perhaps in an RFP) established by the audience tell you about the audience? • How would you prioritize the decision maker's concerns: personnel, money, time, production, public image, and ethics? • How open-minded or how critical will your audience be?

You can add other questions to this audience analysis as you consider the problem, solution, and benefits of the solution.

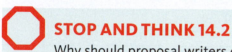

STOP AND THINK 14.2
Why should proposal writers define or state the problem?

14.3 COMPOSING INFORMAL PROPOSALS WARM UP

The organizational strategy of the informal proposal, like that of many technical reports, is designed for the busy decision maker. The proposal usually opens with the most important information. So writers give information about the problem and solution at the beginning of the report. The organization of the rest of the proposal is flexible to fit the different situations that writers are likely to encounter in their work. No matter how you organize your proposals, you must remember your audience throughout the writing process and ask yourself if you are responding to all of their questions and doubts.

Informal proposals begin with an executive summary, or abstract. Following the summary information, the proposals contain the same parts as any other written document: an introduction, a body, and a conclusion. The summary, or abstract, is a condensed version of the proposal. The introduction presents the problem and solution and whatever background information the reader needs. The body of the proposal is the main section. It covers the facts—the specific evidence to convince the reader that the plan is worthwhile.

The last section, the conclusion, wraps up the report and spurs the reader to action.

The specific information contained—and thus the headings used (with the exception of the Executive Summary, or Abstract)—in each section may vary. Depending on the problem and solution being proposed, the writer decides which subsections to include and which to omit. Possible headings used in each section are listed in Table 14.3.

Table 14.3

Section	Possible Headings
Introduction	Introduction Problem Addressed and Solution (could be two headings) Objectives of Proposed Plan Background Data Sources Scope and Limitations
Body	Methods Scheduling Capabilities and Qualifications of Personnel Materials and Equipment Expected Results Plan for Evaluating Results Feasibility Budget (usually in tabular form) Justification of Budget Items (where necessary)
Conclusion	Conclusion Summary of Key Points Request for Action

Drafting the Summary

The summary, or abstract, is designed with the busy decision maker in mind. In a short informal proposal, this section may appear on the title page or, typically, as the first paragraph in the report. It provides a brief overview of the essential ideas presented in the proposal. The summary should include a problem statement, the proposed work objectives, the project impact, and the work plan. Cost is not usually discussed in the summary because writers first want to present all of their evidence to persuade readers. They hope readers will not be "turned off" by the cost but will be convinced by the proposal to justify the expense.

Drafting the Introduction

The introduction answers the "why" in the reader's mind. It explains why the proposal was written. You must identify the problem up front. Another important element of the introduction is your proposed solution to the problem. This statement should be clear but brief. Later, in the body, you will provide further details and justify your proposal.

The introduction further explains your objectives, or what you hope to accomplish, and clarifies the value of the work and why it is worth the investment you seek. You also may need to include a brief background of the problem in this section.

For example, a proposal to college administrators that recommends doubling the number of bike racks on campus will be taken more seriously when the writer explains the problem leading to the proposal and the way the bike racks address the problem.

> Students' budgets are tighter than ever, and the cost of commuting adds to students' financial burden. The college raised the cost of a campus parking permit twice in the last two years, and the one-way fare on the most popular bus route to campus is currently $3.65. Secure bike racks placed around campus would encourage students to commute by bike.

An explanation of the background shows your reader that you have a grasp of the problem. In addition, the introduction may explain the need for a solution. Some readers may ask, "Why not simply leave things as they are?" For these readers, note the effects of ignoring the problem.

The introduction also explains how you or other personnel are qualified to solve the problem. In addition, you might describe where you will seek information to help you solve the problem. Data sources could be printed materials (for example, books, reports, or brochures), interviews, observations, or experiments. The introduction also might define the **scope**, or the extent to which you will search for solutions, as well as any **limitations**, or boundaries, of the project (for example, restrictions on time, space, equipment, money, or staff).

Drafting the Body

After you have described the problem and solution in the introduction, you use the body of the informal proposal to become more specific about your plan. The specific details—facts, figures, statistics, dates, locations, and costs—are the materials you use to persuade your audience. For this section, you address *only* the topics in Table 14.4 that you and your readers need.

Table 14.4

Methods	Explain your methodology—what your approach to the problem will be, what criteria (perhaps from the RFP) you will meet, and what outcome or product you will deliver at the date you specify. Justify your plan of work and any exceptions to the RFP as needed.
Scheduling	Present a calendar of the work planned and expected completion dates to assure your audience that you anticipate efficiency. Effectively illustrate scheduling as appropriate. Flowcharts or timelines are excellent for visual presentation of timetables. List numbers and qualifications of personnel. Describe facilities (both available and needed) to be used.
Capabilities	Assure your audience that you can deliver the work you propose by (1) noting the abilities of people involved and (2) describing your organization's successful track record.
Materials and Equipment	Review materials and equipment to be used. This section is particularly important in scientific and construction projects.
Expected Results	Explain what you think the result or outcome of your work will be.

(continues)

Table 14.4 *(Continued)*

Plan for Evaluating Results	Outline your plan for evaluating the success of the solution once it is implemented.
Feasibility	Explain how you find the solution reasonable to implement.
Budget	Present (typically in a table) the costs for the work, including salaries, equipment, materials, travel, communication, services, and other expenses.
Justification	Explain clearly and persuasively the reason for any expenses your audience may question.

Drafting the Conclusion

The conclusion should be straightforward and brief. It might include a summary of key points, such as those noted in the summary section, and it should call for the audience to take action. Make the call to action specific and clear, including dates, deadlines, and amounts.

Collaborate

As proposals are often read and evaluated by a number of people with expertise in different areas, proposals frequently are written by a team whose members possess different skills and experiences. These teams generally use software, such as Google Docs, that allows members to add and edit text at the same time, allowing others on the team to see all elements of the proposal develop. Effective communication among the team is essential for the proposal to come together as a logical and unified whole.

Explore the Composing Strategies with a Model

Consider a sample problem to illustrate the composing process: Chaya Sotelo, a graduate of Martinique College, has noticed that the online campus newsletter, *The Martinique,* contains little information about the careers and lives of alumni. Occasionally, the newsletter carries a brief report about a former student who has gone on to be quite successful, but she would like to see stories about the careers of "everyday" alumni too. You will follow Chaya through the process of writing a short informal proposal to the editor, in which she suggests a solution. Chaya decides to write the summary last, pulling ideas for the summary from the proposal.

To help the editor understand the problem, Chaya considers the "why" question. She writes a clear statement of the problem: *Except for occasional brief reports, no news about the careers and lives of Martinique College alumni appears in the online newsletter* The Martinique. Then she lists her goals, as follows:

- Include specific features on alumni and their chosen careers.

- Include general news about alumni.

- Report on alumni who deserve attention for their career achievements.

- Provide a forum for alumni.

- Encourage more alumni to read the college's website and newsletter.

Chaya brainstorms several solutions to meet these goals: (1) Develop a link on the website for alumni to submit personal and career information, (2) request that alumni be given space for contributions, and (3) ask *The Martinique* to cover alumni news in a more intentional and comprehensive manner.

Chaya moves from brainstorming to analysis. For each solution she developed, she lists positives and negatives. For example, for the first solution, developing links on the website, she lists the following:

Positive	Negative
Alumni would be able to highlight positive aspects of graduating from Martinique.	Would enough alumni be interested?
Alumni and students would be able to network.	Would alumni be willing to participate?
Alumni would read and support their website.	Would alumni read the website and support its sponsors?

Chaya realizes that her proposal is directed to an editor, Gina Hollinger, who is interested in the effects of Chaya's proposed action on Ms. Hollinger's work: profits, personnel, schedule, and image. Chaya knows that a solid plan with accurate facts and figures is necessary to convince her reader. After choosing the plan with the most "positives" and the least "negatives," she again brainstorms ideas to include in the body of her proposal.

Chaya decides that the best solution is to include an article in the quarterly online newsletter *The Martinique*. She must assure Ms. Hollinger of a sound plan for implementing this idea. Chaya explains the specifics of her idea and proposes how the work will be done. To make the work process clear, she develops a chart that shows each step in the development of the feature. The chart identifies who or what is responsible for each phase. Chaya uses this chart to check for steps she might have overlooked.

Chaya prepares to write her conclusion by reviewing her strongest selling points. She knows that her closing should include a summary of key points and make a call to action. Chaya presents the benefits of including a new alumni-generated column in *The Martinique* and asks Ms. Hollinger to consider adding the new feature to the quarterly online newsletter. Chaya also offers to volunteer if the proposal is accepted. In addition, she provides her contact information so that Ms. Hollinger may easily respond to the proposal. Read Chaya's final two-page draft in Figure 14.3.

P.O. Box 1423
Davenport, IA 52809-2128
October 23, 20—

Ms. Gina Hollinger, Editor
The Martinique
113 South Sperry Road
Hancock Hall, Room 101
Davenport, IA 52802-3108

Dear Ms. Hollinger:

As an alumna of Martinique College who has pursued a career in commercial art, I read your online newsletter regularly. I have been impressed with the innovative design and attractive page layout of your publication, and I admire its distinctive look. However, I have noticed one element that could be improved.

Problem

The problem is lack of news about Martinique College alumni. Your reporters cover the events of Martinique College very well, yet little mention is made of the lives and careers of graduates. I believe that current students would be interested in learning what other students did after graduating and that alumni would be interested in reading about former classmates. With the tough economic times, it also would be a way for alumni to share helpful information about the job market, careers, job openings, and specific job skills.

Solution

News about alumni could be obtained at no expense to *The Martinique*. Your webmaster could create an online questionnaire as a way for alumni to submit their personal and professional information. Using one of your top-notch editors to compile and edit the material, you could include an article about one alumnus or alumna in each quarterly newsletter. Of particular interest to readers would be "life after graduation"—travels, career moves, suggestions for soon-to-be graduates, and any personal information they would care to share. Readers also might be interested in knowing in what part of the country the alumni live and whether they have lived or are currently living abroad.

Objectives

Including news about alumni may have several effects. More students and alumni are likely to read the newsletter, and they may benefit by doing so. *The Martinique* will benefit by developing more readers, who, in turn, will support its sponsors. In fact, alumni may choose to advertise their businesses in the newsletter, benefiting themselves as well as *The Martinique*.

Figure 14.3 Informal Proposal for an External Audience *(continues)*

Ms. Gina Hollinger
Page 2
October 23, 20—

Methods and Scheduling

If you accept this proposal, your webmaster could likely create an online questionnaire in no more than one month. During that time, you could "spread the word" about the upcoming change to the newsletter, ask students and alumni to submit suggestions for the name of the column, and determine responsibilities of your staff and guidelines. In fact, I would be willing to volunteer my time in whatever capacity you need, as I live within a short drive of Martinque's campus.

The workflow, as illustrated in Figure 1 below, is designed so that all work will be done well and on time. Your in-house editorial board will review story ideas, select the best, assign writers and photographers, help with editing, and submit the final article to you for publication. The editorial board will approve all work before it is submitted to you.

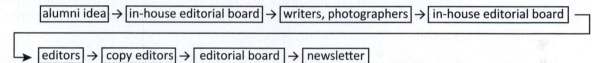

Figure 1: Workflow Process for Submitting Articles

Maintaining the Article

During summer break and school holidays, the column could be suspended. On the other hand, you could retain readers by continuing the column or perhaps reprinting a particularly popular article.

Conclusion

An alumni-generated column in *The Martinique* will be beneficial in many ways. It will create new readers and keep readers informed of alumni's successes after they leave college. It will not cost you any more in time or wages. It will bring alumni and students closer together and allow them to network. It might become a vehicle for current students to find mentors. Please consider making these things happen by allowing space for an alumni article in Martinique College's online newsletter. In addition, please call me at 261-555-0112 if you would like to accept my offer to serve as a volunteer for the newsletter.

Sincerely,

Chaya Sotelo

Chaya Sotelo

Figure 14.3 (continued) Informal Proposal for an External Audience

STOP AND THINK 14.3

In a large organization, different people are likely to read only the sections of a proposal relating to their area of expertise. Consider the sections the following employees might read: a chief executive officer (CEO), a technical expert, and a comptroller (financial officer).

Select three textbooks and examine them to determine the parts that make up each book. Make a list of the elements you find. For example, how does the book begin? Is the first element a title page or a note to the reader? What other parts do you find?

The preceding section of this chapter presented information about informal proposals. Informal and formal proposals are similar. Both are persuasive documents that offer the writers' answers to the readers' problems or needs. In both proposals, writers choose from the same optional subsections in the same order under the headings *Introduction, Body,* and *Conclusion.*

Formal proposals may differ from informal proposals in the following ways:

- Tone, such as the detached, professional voice writers might use with a high-level official

- Additional parts of the report, such as the glossary, appendixes, and transmittal correspondence

- Complexity of the outcome, such as the construction of a new building or the $2 billion purchase of jet airliners

Although formal proposals are not used as frequently as informal proposals, they are called for in many circumstances. The following examples are typical:

- A marine biologist, disturbed by the fish kills in a local estuarine system, wants to study the effect of municipal wastewater dumping on the fish. The biologist seeks funds from the State Department of Fish and Wildlife for a five-year study.

- The owner of a Montessori preschool receives an RFP from a local assisted-living center to open a branch of the preschool at the center.

- A mechanic in a ball-bearing plant is inspired to improve the precision of a robotic welding machine after studying similar machines at another facility. Having decided on the adjustments needed and the cost in work hours and materials, the mechanic requests approval from her manager.

As you read about formal proposals, look at the sample formal proposal in Figure 14.4, starting on page 386.

Prewriting

Prewriting techniques should help you plan to write a formal proposal. During the prewriting phase, you collect and organize data and determine your objectives. Because a formal proposal is often longer and more involved than other technical reports, prewriting is especially important.

Planning for Persuasion

The readers of formal proposals need to be convinced, as a salesperson convinces a customer. If you are to be a successful proposal writer, you must address your audience effectively and prevent any skepticism. Here are some guidelines for convincing your audience.

- Collect as many facts as you can to support your proposed plan.

- Be accurate. Plan to check your data. If your reader discovers a discrepancy, an exaggeration, or a mistake, you lose credibility.

A team of employees at Blue Vale Packing worked for two months on a sales proposal to a major national online retail company. The proposal offered to supply all foam packaging materials for the business. Because this proposal could represent a major portion of Blue Vale's business, the team worked diligently to develop and present the best plan possible. However, a serious problem arose the team had not anticipated. Most sales proposals must be approved and signed by someone in an executive position in the organization. The team scheduled time for researching, prewriting, composing, and editing before the submission deadline. What they did not anticipate was that the president of Blue Vale planned to leave on a three-week business trip ten days before the proposal's due date. Therefore, the president would not be available to approve or sign the proposal in time to meet the submission deadline.

Communication
Dilemma

Think Critically

What could the team do? Could they salvage the situation and meet the submission deadline? If so, how?

- Study your audience and the situation so you understand the reader's point of view. Planning with an understanding of the reader allows you to write a more convincing proposal.

- Be realistic in your planning. Do not propose to do a job in two weeks to make a sale when you honestly believe the work will take a month. You may suffer the consequences later because your proposal becomes a legal document when it is accepted.

Planning for Integration

Another goal of prewriting the formal proposal is planning for integration. The entire document must come together as a logical whole. The description of the problem, for example, will affect how the reader views the effectiveness of the solution. When different writers are composing different sections, a primary writer or editor should plan and edit the entire report for consistency and flow.

Planning for Graphics, Definitions, and Supplemental Materials

As you gather data, consider whether a graphic would help your audience understand the information. Then decide what type of graphic aid will most clearly depict the idea (for example, a pie graph, a diagram, or a bar graph). See Chapter 6, "Document Design and Graphics," for more aid.

Plan what terms you will use and whether your readers will need definitions for them. If the proposal needs definitions, decide whether you serve your audience better by placing the definitions in the report or in a glossary at the end of the report. If you need to provide only a few definitions, it may be easier for you to include them in the text. (Your reader will probably find that arrangement easier to use as well.) However, proposals that require numerous definitions should probably contain a glossary after the body of the report.

In addition to graphics and definitions, think about materials you might like your readers to have access to but do not want to include in the body of the proposal. Consider placing relevant but not essential materials in an **appendix** (material that you want readers to have access to but that is not a primary persuasive part of the proposal). For example, if you used the results of a questionnaire in your proposal, you may want to show interested readers how you gathered data by including the questionnaire as an appendix. You can read more about appendixes on page 385.

Parts of Formal Proposals

The format of formal proposals is designed to aid the readers. Each formal proposal follows the same basic plan so that readers and writers know what to expect and where to find the information they seek. Remember, many expert readers review only the one or two sections of a formal proposal that deal with their area(s) of expertise.

The parts listed below make up the formal proposal. Those parts with an asterisk (*) are used in informal proposals as well.

Letter or Memo of Transmittal	Body (or Discussion)*
Title Page	Conclusion (or Summary)*
Table of Contents	Glossary
List of Illustrations	Appendixes
Executive Summary (or Abstract)*	Works Cited (or References)
Introduction*	

Letter or Memo of Transmittal

The **letter** or **memo of transmittal** is similar to the cover letter that is mailed with a resume. It is an official greeting and an introduction of the document to the reader. Write a letter to accompany a proposal when you are addressing an external audience and a memo when you are addressing an internal audience. Key the letter or memo using acceptable formatting guidelines.

Because the message is usually good news for the audience, this letter or memo uses the direct strategy, as follows:

1. Begin with the purpose, the fact that you are submitting a proposal. Name the proposal topic and explain whether you are responding to an RFP, responding to a request, or initiating the proposal on your own.

2. Note areas of special interest to the reader.

3. Thank the audience for reviewing the proposal. You may offer to provide more information or answer questions.

The letter or memo of transmittal is usually written after the proposal.

Title Page

The title page of a formal proposal, like a book cover, gives the reader important information about the document. In designing the title page, use white space to make the page attractive. Be clear, accurate, complete, and precise in composing the title page. Provide the following:

- A descriptive title of the proposal

- The name of the company or companies involved

- The names of the writers

- The date the proposal is being submitted

As part of the title page, some internal proposals have a routing list of readers who will review the document.

Note that a precise title such as *Proposal to Develop a Policy Governing Substitute Staffing for Absentee Technicians in the Fiber Twist Area* or *Proposal to Purchase and Install the Evermorr Secure 3120 Security System in Glynndale Condominiums* is useful because it gives readers more information than a vague title such as *Proposal to Deal with Absent Workers* or *Proposal to Improve Security in Glynndale Condominiums.*

Table of Contents

The table of contents should be designed so that it is attractive, easy to read, and clear. The table of contents may appear alone on a page or on the same page with the list of illustrations, which appears at the bottom. The words *TABLE OF CONTENTS* in all capital letters should be boldfaced and centered at the top of the page. The list of contents should start at the left margin under the title and visually demonstrate relationships between ideas. Typically, section headings are flush with the left margin and subheadings are indented underneath.

Enter headings and subheadings on the left side of the page, **pagination** (the arrangement of page numbers) on the right side of the page, and leaders (periods) between each heading and its page number.

List of Illustrations   Begin with the words *List of Illustrations* (using initial caps and boldfaced type) at the left margin under the last entry in the table of contents. Under the title, provide the label, number, and descriptive title of the graphic on the left and the page on which the illustration is located on the right.

Communication
Technologies

Word processing software has features to aid in creating a formal proposal, such as a feature to create a table of contents and styles for each section of the proposal. If you are working on a group proposal, the writing team leader can create a master document as the template for the proposal. Team members can work within the template.

Think Critically

Create a document with heading styles (or add headings to an existing document) and generate a table of contents. Explore different ways to format the table of contents.

Executive Summary (or Abstract)

Centered at the top of the page, key the words *EXECUTIVE SUMMARY* or *ABSTRACT* (in all capital letters and boldfaced type). The executive summary is usually two to four paragraphs on a page by itself.

Write the executive summary after you finish the rest of the report. Keep the reader in mind while you compose it. This section, as the title *Executive Summary* implies, is designed with the administrator in mind. Busy executives want the story quickly and want only the essential information: the problem, the solution, and the benefits of the solution. Because these readers are concerned with the big picture, the overall health of the organization, they may not read the specific information in the body of the proposal, only the summary. However, proposal writers should plan the summary for all readers, not just executives.

Introduction, Body of Discussion, and Conclusion

In long reports (perhaps 20 pages or more), each major section heading may begin a new, separate part of the formal proposal. Each section starts on a new page with the heading name, such as *INTRODUCTION*, in all capital letters and boldfaced type centered at the top of the page. In shorter reports, the entire body may flow from one section to another without page breaks.

The Introduction The introduction is the framework that prepares readers for the body of the proposal. The introduction answers the questions *what* and *why*. No matter which subparts of the introduction you include in your document, clearly state for your readers the problem and a solution or alternative solutions. If you determine that the readers need background information, summarize the situation and the proposer's qualifications. Include information about your company and personnel that will enhance the credibility of your proposal, such as the number of years in business, staff and equipment resources, previous clients, and success with similar projects. Because any reader may read the introductory material, remember to communicate in a way that administrators, managers, technical experts, and financial managers can understand. Introductions should be strong and clear, in which case people are likely to read them. In addition, by coming at the beginning of the proposal, introductions make an important first impression.

The Body of Discussion If the introduction sets the framework of ideas, the body of a formal proposal is the crux of the argument, the specifics of persuasion. In the body, you explain how the technical data prove that your idea (solution) will work. Describe methods for carrying out the project, specific tasks, time schedules, personnel, facilities, and equipment. You could include an organizational chart of people working on the project so the reader will know who is responsible for particular areas. In addition to outlining what you will do, these specific details convince the reader that your approach is best for the situation. The project's budget should clearly show and perhaps justify the costs. The graphics you have planned should enhance the text of your proposal, not take the place of the text.

Furthermore, keep in mind that the body of the proposal is most often read by technical experts who have the skills and ability to understand the detailed technical information. These readers expect precise, accurate, and up-to-date information.

The Conclusion Be concise and direct when you write the conclusion of your formal proposal. You have already provided the information to sway your audience to your point of view. This is not the time to add to a sales pitch—or *any* new information that belongs in the body of the proposal. Instead, summarize your most convincing points regarding the importance of the project and the benefits of the solution. Then suggest a course of action.

Glossary

If you include a glossary, design it to be easy to read. In the text of the proposal, designate words appearing in the glossary using asterisks, italics, or another highlighting technique. Include a footnote or parenthetical note beside the first entry telling readers they can find definitions in the glossary.

At the top of the glossary page, center the title *GLOSSARY* (in all capital letters and boldfaced type). Make the entry word—the word being defined—stand out by using boldface or columns. When using columns, place the entry words on the left and definitions on the right. Alphabetize all words, acronyms, and symbols, as dictionaries do.

Consider the needs of your readers when you choose the words to define and determine the extent of the definitions. Do not define words the audience already understands. At the same time, if several people will read your proposal, define a term even if you think that only one reader will need the definition. Avoid overly technical definitions (unless you are writing a highly technical proposal for an audience generally familiar with the vocabulary used in the proposal). Use language the readers will understand and consider including graphic aids if they will help readers understand the concepts in the proposal.

Works Cited

If your proposal uses ideas or text from a source you need to credit, prepare works cited or references pages according to the guidelines of the appropriate style manual. Consult the style manual your organization or the RFP requires and follow it precisely.

Appendixes

An appendix is material you want readers to have access to but that is not a primary part of the proposal. In the body of the proposal, where the topic an appendix supports is mentioned, refer readers to the appendix, as in "See Appendix C." Each appendix is labeled with the word *Appendix* and given a letter or number and a descriptive title, similar to the system for identifying graphics. Put every document in a separate appendix.

Page Numbers

Assigning page numbers for formal proposals works the same as pagination in books. **Prefatory material,** or material placed before the actual report begins, is numbered with lowercase Roman numerals. Prefatory material includes a letter or memo of transmittal, a title page, and a table of contents.

The first two pages, the letter or memo of transmittal and the title page, are not numbered. The table of contents, the third prefatory page, is numbered iii. The first page, which usually begins with the executive summary, is not numbered. Place an Arabic number 2 on the next page. (In other words, 2 is the first Arabic page number because the first page of the body is not numbered.) Number the rest of the document with Arabic numerals in sequence. Center page numbers at the bottom or place them in the upper right corner of the page.

TO: Barkley Wolfe, Owner
Eastbrook Shopping Center

FROM: Delores C. Ondecko, Chief of Operations   *DCO*

DATE: 23 November 20—

SUBJECT: Proposal for Improving Exterior Lighting at Eastbrook

I am submitting for your review my department's proposal to upgrade the exterior lighting system at Eastbrook Shopping Center. This document responds to our 15 October 20— tenants' meeting and subsequent discussions with you regarding safety on the property.

Of special note are the following sections addressing questions you or our tenants brought up:

Thank you for reviewing our data and suggestions. We look forward to your response. If you decide to accept our proposal, we are eager to implement the needed changes.

Figure 14.4 Formal Proposal *(continues)*

PROPOSAL FOR IMPROVED EXTERIOR LIGHTING AT EASTBROOK SHOPPING CENTER

Prepared for

Barkley Wolfe, Owner

Eastbrook Shopping Center

Prepared by

Delores C. Ondecko, Chief of Operations

23 November 20—

Figure 14.4 (continued) Formal Proposal (*continues*)

TABLE OF CONTENTS

List of Illustrations

Figure 14.4 (continued) Formal Proposal *(continues)*

EXECUTIVE SUMMARY

Evidence from our security office, police records, and customer attitude survey proves that Eastbrook Shopping Center has a problem with inadequate and inefficient lighting outside the building at night.

To improve the lighting so that it meets recommendations of the Illuminating Engineering Society and other experts, we need to retrofit our existing pole fixtures and exchange our current metal halide lamps for 93-watt LED bulbs and install five new pole lights, six new wall-mount lamps, and a lighting control system.

The recommended changes will cost less than $2,900 and will improve our security level, liability rating, and public image, along with decreasing our energy costs.

Figure 14.4 (continued) Formal Proposal *(continues)*

2

INTRODUCTION

Problem

Inadequate illumination in Eastbrook Shopping Center's parking areas is a serious concern. Some parking areas have sufficient illumination while others do not, and we have had some complaints from the residential development on our northeast side related to light trespass. The residents say that illumination from our parking area is intruding and ruining their enjoyment of the night sky. Further, the contrast in low light and high light areas creates problems for pedestrians' vision and image quality for our video surveillance system. As good corporate citizens, we have a responsibility to the community to maintain a safe environment. As merchants, we recognize that shoppers and employees expect and have a right to a safe environment. However, it is evident from our research that poor lighting in our parking lots means safety is not ensured. Not only do our parking areas need greater quantity but also greater quality lighting. Uniformity of light will improve the images from our security cameras and will help with "safe vehicle and pedestrian interaction" (United States). We risk losing customers if Eastbrook does not maintain a secure, peaceful image. We also must watch expenses, and the old metal halide* bulbs we currently use are not efficient to operate. (Terms designated by an asterisk are defined in the glossary on page 8.)

Solution

Problems with lighting can be eliminated if we upgrade our exterior lighting system to meet recommendations of local law enforcement and utilities personnel and Illuminating Engineering Society (IES)* guidelines. To increase illumination sufficiently in all areas outside the building and improve uniformity of lighting, we must retrofit our lighting units to exchange the metal halide bulbs in use now for LED lights as well as add six wall-mount lights and five new poles in the parking areas. In addition, we should install a lighting control system to maximize efficiency and control costs.

Additional benefits of implementing this proposal are decreased light pollution and less hazardous waste. Metal halides waste a great deal of light from the top and sides of the lamp, often causing light trespass into areas where the light is not desired. However, the narrow beam angle and directional capabilities of LED lights promote efficiency and reduce night sky pollution (Pou). Also, while metal halide lamps contain hazardous mercury, LED is a much less environmentally damaging product ("Metal Halide").

Figure 14.4 (continued) Formal Proposal *(continues)*

3

Objectives

The purpose of this proposal is to improve the quality, uniformity, and energy efficiency of exterior lighting at Eastbrook Shopping Center so that customers, employees, and staff feel safe walking to and from the building and their vehicles and so that our parking area does not become the site of illegal activities and unnecessary accidents. In addition, the proposal, if implemented, will save the company money in utility bills, maintenance fees, and lamp/bulb replacement costs and make us better neighbors to the residents living nearby by reducing glare (BUG) ratings and light trespass (DiLaura 26.22).

Background

Our records for the last six months prove that we do, indeed, have a problem:

8 incidents of petty theft (unresolved)	3 purse/bag snatchings
1 vehicle-pedestrian accident	1 attempted kidnapping

Further, the police department rates the relative safety of Eastbrook to be low compared to other shopping centers in our region. (See Appendix A.)

In addition, the survey our marketing agency conducted last month showed that more than 50% of the 400 respondents feel some concern for their safety in entering or exiting our building after dark. Refer to Table 1 for the breakdown of the responses

Table 1. Attitudes Regarding Eastbrook's Exterior Environment at Night (by percentage)

Respondents by Age	Extremely Comfortable	Slightly Comfortable	Comfortable	Slightly Uncomfortable	Uncomfortable
18–20	5	31	15	42	7
21–35	15	19	39	15	12
36–50	5	14	22	23	36
over 50	1	9	13	28	49
TOTAL	26	73	89	108	104
PERCENTAGE	**7**	**18**	**22**	**27**	**26**

If this unsafe image continues in the public mind, we will begin to lose valuable customers and eventually will lose business occupants of our shopping center. Note particularly the high rate (49%) of people over 50 who are uncomfortable. With the "graying of America," this group includes a large number of customers we cannot afford to lose. Businesses will move to a location where they and their customers feel safe. Moreover, we risk a lawsuit if accidents or criminal incidents occur that we could have prevented.

Figure 14.4 (continued) Formal Proposal *(continues)*

4

Data Sources

The data used to create this proposal came from our security records; interviews with Edison Electric personnel, a local engineer, and public safety directors at other shopping centers; a customer survey we commissioned; data and recommendations from law enforcement and the Illuminating Engineering Society*, and an experiment conducted by our staff.

Scope and Limitations

In seeking solutions, we wanted to increase safety without creating the image of an armed fortress. The solution must appeal to the public and our business occupants. In addition, any changes we make should be visually attractive and not unpleasant for our commercial and residential neighbors. We also have considered cost and energy consumption.

DISCUSSION

Methods

To determine the amount of light currently being produced, we used a footcandle meter* at the base of each pole. An Edison Electric representative recommended an average of two footcandles* per square foot (Smith). Research revealed that *IES Lighting Handbook* supports this recommendation, suggesting 0.9 or more footcandles (Kaufman 20–26) although, according to a local engineer, most professionals now are designing for at least two footcandles per square foot in parking areas (Pou). Our results indicated that Eastbrook's lights are generally lower than the suggested illumination. The readings ranged from a high of 1.8 to a low of 0.4, as you can see in Figure 1 below.

Figure 1. Exterior Light Intensity and Proposed Fixture Additions

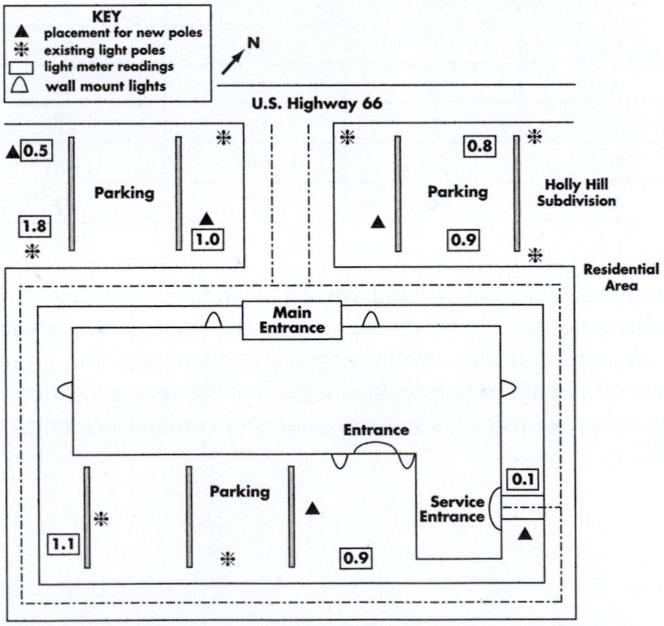

Figure 14.4 (continued) Formal Proposal *(continues)*

5

In addition, a video-recorded experiment revealed that in landscaped sections of our parking lots, a person could stand undetected beside a tree or large shrub until the observer was as close as 2 feet. Our research indicates that almost all parking and pedestrian walkway areas need increased lighting.

Given the video-recorded experiment and the footcandle meter readings we collected, an engineer at Edison Electric recommended placement of five new poles outside our building, as indicated on the map in Figure 1 above. Along with the new pole lights, the engineer said that six wall-mount lights installed on the building should bring illumination up to the standard recommendation levels. The six lights will be mounted as follows: one on each side of the main entrance and one on each side of the back entrance, with the remaining two placed on the northeast and the southwest walls (Smith).

Moreover, all old pole fixtures will be retrofitted by removing the old ballast and metal halide bulbs and replacing them with solid state LED lighting. The retrofit process takes about 20 minutes for each typical shoebox on a pole; the ballast is removed and replaced with an LED driver and then the lamp is installed (Neumann). LED lamps will be used in all new light fixtures as well. The LED lighting will be "shielded" to prevent light trespass in the direction of the northeast residential area and light pollution going up into the night sky.

In addition, the installation of lighting controls will ensure quality lighting while conserving energy. The controls will dim lights on bright, full moon nights and increase illumination on dark or overcast nights.

Scheduling

We would like to make the suggested improvements as soon as possible. Once equipment has been ordered and received, the project should take less than three weeks, as you can see in Figure 2.

Figure 2. Schedule for Improving Eastbrook's Exterior Lighting

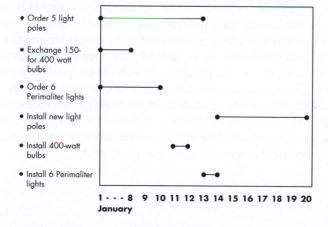

The installation of the five new poles according to IES guidelines will require an outside contractor. Edison Electric has the special equipment needed and can install the poles in one week. Because we do not have the bucket truck required to do the retrofit job, Edison also will handle that task. This effort should take

Figure 14.4 (continued) Formal Proposal *(continues)*

no more than one day. Three members of our maintenance staff can install the six wall-mount lights in less than one day. Once our staff has completed the wall-mounts, Edison will return to add the lighting controls to the system. The entire project should be complete and lighting improved within a month.

Materials and Equipment

We can purchase the 93-watt LED bulbs from our current supplier, Witherspoon Inc., for only $12 per unit more than we are paying now for the 400-watt metal halide bulbs. Moreover, Witherspoon offers a 10% discount on our first LED order.

Edison Electric will order the materials, including the lighting control panel and sensors, and erect the five new poles we need.

Cost

The adjustments necessary to retrofit and upgrade exterior lighting and implement IES guidelines will cost $2,823.75. The following budget details the expenses for this project.

Five 40-foot metal poles (shoebox)	5 @ $211.95	$1,059.75
Six wall-mount lights	6 @ $70.00	420.00
93-watt LED lamps for all fixtures (including shipping and 10% discount)	17 @ $22.00	374.00
Lighting control system		495.00
Edison Electric service fee		475.00
		$2,823.75

We will incur the one-time installation costs, and the purchase price of LED lamps is higher than that of metal halide lamps. However, decreasing service costs and operating costs will positively impact our budget if this proposal is implemented. Two reasons for the decrease are the longer life and the lower energy consumption of LED lamps. The metal halide lamps we currently use have an average rated life of 10,000–20,000 hours ("Metal Halide Lamps"), while LED lamps are likely to be good for 50–100,000 hours or 12 hours per day, every day for 10–20 years (Neumann). In addition, our current lights use 456 watts, including the ballast, while the LED will provide an equal or better quality luminance with 93 watts. Edison Electric experts suggest that we will see up to an 80% reduction in energy use with the LED lamps (Smith). Furthermore, maintenance charges will dramatically decline since we will not need to rent aerial lift bucket trucks for fixing failed ballasts or replacing bulbs every two years.

Figure 14.4 (continued) Formal Proposal *(continues)*

7

CONCLUSION

If Eastbrook's exterior lighting is not improved, future problems are likely to occur. We might face a decrease in the number of customers willing to shop with us during the evening and an increase in our insurance rates as a result of liability suits. This proposal is a corrective as well as preventive measure that increases the safety level for everyone on the property at night. Eastbrook will benefit from a stable environment both night and day and more economical operation.

We recommend that $2,823.75 be allocated in this quarter's operating budget for the installation of 5 new 40-foot metal light poles, 6 new wall-mount fixtures, and a new control system, along with the replacement of all metal halide lamps with 93-watt LED lamps. These changes will enhance our security and our image at a reasonable cost.

Figure 14.4 (continued) Formal Proposal *(continues)*

8

GLOSSARY

bulb   A synthetic light source operated with electricity.

footcandle   A unit of illuminance, the amount of light a candle or bulb produces one foot away.

footcandle meter   A meter that indicates the amount of light one candle will produce in one foot of space.

IES   Illuminating Engineering Society of North America, a professional organization founded in 1906 and dedicated to the theory and practice of illuminating engineering.

lamp   A synthetic light source operated with electricity.

metal halide lamps   Created in the 1960s, electric lamps that produce light by an electric arc through a gaseous mixture of vaporized mercury and metal halides compounds of metals with bromine or iodine. These high-intensity discharge (HID) gas discharge lamps are supposed to improve the efficiency and color rendition of the light over earlier design types.

Figure 14.4 (continued)   Formal Proposal (*continues*)

9

WORKS CITED

Abbott, Marvin, Chief of Security, Golden Crossing Mall. Personal interview. 5 Nov. 20—.

DiLaura, David L. et al, eds. *The Lighting Handbook: Tenth Edition: Reference and Application*. New York: The Illuminating Engineering Society, 2011. Print.

Kaufman, John E., ed. *IES Lighting Handbook: A Reference*. New York: Waverly Press, 1984. Print.

Langley, Leonard R., Chief of Security, Caruso's Crossing. Personal interview. 21 Nov. 20—.

"Metal Halide Lamps: An HID Light Source with Great Color Rendering." *Edison Tech Center*. Edison Tech Center, 2012. Web. 26 Feb. 2016. http://edisontechcenter.org/metalhalide.html

Neumann, Gary. "LED Parking Lot Light Retrofit." Online video clip. YouTube. YouTube, 26 Mar. 2013. Web. 2 Mar. 2016. Pou, Wilson, Engineer. Engineering Source of NC. Online interview. 17 Mar. 20—.

Smith, Jason, Chief Engineer, Edison Electric. Personal interview. 1 November 20—.

Sorcar, Prafulla C. *Energy Saving Lighting Systems*. New York: Van Norstrand Reinhold, 1982. Print.

United States. Dept. of Energy. Energy Efficiency and Renewable Energy. Federal Energy Management Program. *Guide to FEMP-Designated Parking Lot Lighting*. EERE Information Center, Mar. 2013. Web. 24 Jan. 2016.

Yates, Abigail, Chief of Security, South Dunbury Center. Personal interview. 14 Nov. 20—.

Figure 14.4 (continued) Formal Proposal *(continues)*

10

APPENDIX A
Police Security Ranking for
Shopping Centers and Malls

Metropolitan Police Quarterly Report
June 20— Security Ranking—Shopping Centers and Malls

1 = Most Secure Environment   5 = Least Secure Environment

Rankings are based on a formula including reported incidents, severity of crime, victims, and cost.

Monrovian Heights	1	Wrightly Way Mall	3
Riggan's Place	1	Anandana Plaza	3
Crossroads Mall	2	Caruso's Crossing	4
South Dunbury Center	2	Eastbrook Shopping Center	4
Newtown Shopping Center	2	Benton Shopping Center	5
Village Mall	2	Bargain Hunter's Way	5

Figure 14.4 (continued) Formal Proposal

⬢ STOP AND THINK 14.4

Who reads the executive summary, or abstract, of a formal proposal? Where should terms be defined in a formal proposal?

Focus on Ethics

It is possible for writers to use facts, accurate information, to mislead readers. However, intentionally misleading the audience of a proposal to get a positive answer can have severe and long-lasting consequences. For example, if a proposal to expand a business by adding a new division has used misleading tactics, the proposal writers are likely to be blamed if the new division fails, employees become unemployed, new buildings are left vacant, and more.

Think Critically

How would misleading proposal readers impact the credibility and work relationships of writers?

14 CHAPTER REVIEW

Summary

1. Proposals are persuasive documents that suggest a solution to a problem or a change.

2. Proposals are defined and categorized according to the audience and their needs: internal or external; informal or formal; solicited or unsolicited; sales, research, planning, or grant.

3. Proposals are in memo, letter, or manuscript format, the choice determined by the audience and the complexity of the proposal.

4. The introduction identifies the problem and offers a solution, along with any background information the audience might find helpful. The body uses facts, figures, statistics, graphics, and other evidence to convince readers to accept the solution or change. The conclusion restates key points and calls on the audience to take action.

5. Formal proposals contain many special parts that have unique formatting guidelines. These parts may include a letter or memo of transmittal, a title page, a table of contents, a list of illustrations, an executive summary (or abstract), an introduction, a body (or discussion), a conclusion (or summary), a glossary, appendixes, and a works cited section or bibliography.

Checklist

- Have I identified the problem I want to see resolved?

- Have I analyzed my audience and then listed the audience's needs?

- Have I brainstormed alternate solutions? Have I listed positives and negatives for each solution on my list?

- Have I thought about and listed my goals?

- Have I explained the problem clearly in the introduction?

- Does the body give readers enough information to make a decision?

- Have I provided enough evidence, such as facts, figures, and testimony?

- Does my conclusion contain the most important ideas from the proposal? Does it call for action from the readers?

- Have I made information easy to use with headings and subheadings?

- If I am writing a formal proposal, have I included all of the parts that are needed?

Build Your Foundation

1. Interview an employee about a particular problem as well as the solution for which he or she was responsible. Write a description of the problem, the methods the employee used to solve the problem, the effectiveness of the solution, and the employee's (and employer's) satisfaction with the work.

2. Use library research to learn more about a great problem solver or innovator (for example, Thomas Edison, Steve Jobs or Bill Gates, Mother Theresa, Albert Einstein, Eleanor Roosevelt, or Jonas Salk). Find out as much as you can about the methods the person used in seeking solutions. Give an oral presentation of your findings to your class.

3. Interview a proposal writer to find out how his or her company uses formal proposals, who else in the writer's organization writes proposals, and how successful the proposals have been. Ask what this writer thinks is essential in preparing an effective formal proposal.

4. Use the Internet, regional or state newspapers, or professional journals to search for requests for proposals.

   a. Copy the RFPs and bring them to class for discussion.
   b. From a careful reading of one RFP, identify the problem or need.
   c. Identify the audience the proposal writer needs to address.
   d. Brainstorm a list of ideas to include in the proposal's introduction.

5. Prepare a list of glossary terms for the RFP you read in item 4. If the RFP has a glossary, evaluate it for completeness. Identify any terms the writer omitted that are unfamiliar to you. Research and define the terms.

6. Choose two problems for which you would consider proposing a solution. Write one or two paragraphs describing the problem and the decision maker (audience) for each problem.

7. For item 6, list possible solutions to each problem or need you identified.

8. Using a problem whose solution has already been implemented, re-create the thinking process that the proposal writers might have used by:

   a. Developing a list of positive and negative aspects of the solution.
   b. Creating a list showing how the solution meets the needs of the audience or solves the problem.

9. Read or listen to the international news for one week. Pick an issue and write a statement of the problem. Brainstorm at least four solutions and list the positives and negatives of the two most realistic solutions.

10. Critique a proposal from business or industry. Analyze how the writers met (or did not meet) the needs of the audience. Review the proposal's formatting features. Determine its organizational patterns. Share the results of your critique orally or in an essay.

11. Have you heard the saying "Every problem used to be a solution"? Everyone involved in the U.S. health care debate acknowledges that the employer-based insurance system has its problems. Now others argue about the problems with insurance in the Affordable Care Act (or ObamaCare). Research the origins of the employer-based system and put yourself in the shoes of those decision makers from long ago. Use your imagination to list several alternatives they may have brainstormed. Then make a list of what you think they considered to be the positives and negatives of the system they eventually chose. Make sure you analyze the situation from the earlier point of view, when the current employer-based health insurance system was selected as the best choice. Alternately, consider the positives and negatives of the insurance system within the Affordable Care Act.

Your Turn

1. Write a proposal convincing your parents or guardians to take you (or to allow you to go with friends) on the vacation of your dreams. Identify the problem, explain the solution,

convince them of the reasonableness of your plan, and justify the cost by preparing a budget.

2. Imagine that you asked your parents or guardians for a car. They said, "Yes, but. . . ." Your responsibility will be to pay for insurance, gas, and maintenance if they buy this car for you. In an informal proposal:

   a. Explain the type of car you want and why you want it.

   b. Describe how you will pay for the car's expenses if you do not have money and your parents or guardians do not want you to work more than ten hours a week, as would be required at a restaurant, grocery store, or department store. Identify your problem and consider alternative solutions. Be creative. Think of ways you can earn money other than by holding a regular job. List as many options as you can.

   c. Write the solution you would propose to your parents or guardians.

3. With a group of classmates who share your interests, write a formal proposal to solve a specific problem. Identify a problem at school, at work, or in the community that must be dealt with by decision makers distant from you on the organizational ladder (for example, a superintendent, president, dean, or member of the board of trustees). Your proposal should require some research. Your internal formal proposal should include the following:

   a. Transmittal letter or memorandum

   b. Executive summary

   c. Introduction

   d. Body, including sufficient details for an informed decision, timeline or schedule, appropriate visuals, and a budget if costs are involved

   e. Conclusion, including a specific call to action

Here are examples of problems to solve.

School	Work	Community
new or improved equipment	equipment or work space	sidewalks and bike paths
access to the computer lab	wages or department budget	zoning or use of land
snack bar	improved working conditions	street/traffic signs
new club or sport	sponsorship of team sports	access for people with disabilities to neighborhood stores
needed programs	insurance and benefits	street and park lighting

4. Write an informal sales proposal to Karyn Grissom, owner of Mason Office Center. As owner of Green Thumb Planting, an indoor plant service, you are asking Ms. Grissom to become a new client. After visiting the office complex, you determine that the building could use 31 large and 14 medium-sized low-light plants. Your service provides plants and pots, weekly maintenance, and monthly replacement of sickly plants. If Ms. Grissom accepts your proposal, you can install the plantings within one week. For your service, she will pay a $350 installation fee and a $35 maintenance fee each month thereafter. Your proposal should persuade her to sign a service contract. Create and use any additional details or graphics you need to prepare an effective document.

Community Connection

1. Visit a nonprofit organization in your community to learn about the procedures and processes used there. Explain to your contact at the nonprofit that you are studying proposals for this class and ask if he or she can help you practice some of the prewriting steps for a proposal. Ask your contact to select an issue that he or she would like to apply for grant money to solve. Following the process that Chaya Sotelo used to prepare her proposal, starting on page 376, do the following:

   a. List the goals for the proposal (the things the organization would like to have happen as a result of getting the grant).

   b. Brainstorm different ways to meet these goals.

   c. Analyze each possible solution by listing its positives and negatives.

Offer to share your document with the organization and make sure you thank everyone with whom you worked for his or her time—while you are there and afterwards—by sending a written thank-you note.

2. Identify a local government agency whose work involves proposals. For example, your town or city government's Public Works Department might publish RFPs or RFBs (requests for bids) seeking proposals or bids for pending construction projects. Or the Health Department might issue RFPs to select the best contractor for providing substance abuse counseling in the community. Ask for copies of RFPs and, if possible, interview the writer(s).

   a. Write a brief narrative after your interview with the RFP writer(s) to explain to your instructor and classmates how the professional(s) develop RFPs. Explain who contributes information and how the final document is approved for publication.

   b. Share the RFPs with your class. Use them to identify criteria requested by the issuing agency in the proposal. In other words, what factors does the agency want to see covered in the proposals to solve the problem or fill the need?

3. Schedule an appointment to meet with a professional grant writer, perhaps at school or at a local nonprofit organization. Ask for permission to review a recently funded or approved grant. Using the guidelines in this chapter, explain in a brief essay the factors that led to the grant's success.

4. In teams of three to five class members, identify a local organization that could have a stronger presence on your campus. Perhaps a local ice cream shop could open a kiosk. Or a smoking cessation group might run a semester-long program. Develop a proposal addressed to the appropriate decision maker at your school in which you attempt to persuade him or her to approve your

plan. Remember to analyze your audience carefully, considering any reservations or negative history he or she might have regarding the plan.

EXPLORE THE NET

The National Science Foundation (NSF) presents an online guide for proposal writing. The U.S. government is one of the nation's largest providers of grant funding, and the NSF is an independent federal agency that oversees funding for a large number of scientific research projects. (A grant proposal, or grant, is a type of proposal that seeks money from a government agency, foundation, or other funding source for a specified project.) The mission of the NSF is "to promote the progress of science; to advance the national health, prosperity, and welfare; to secure the national defense. . . ." With an annual budget of $7.5 billion for 2016, the NSF funds approximately 24 percent of all federally supported basic research conducted by America's colleges and universities. The NSF provides "limited-term grants—currently about 12,000 new awards per year, with an average duration of three years—to fund specific research proposals that have been judged the most promising by a rigorous and objective merit-review system. Most of these awards go to individuals or small groups of investigators. Others provide funding for research centers, instruments, and facilities that allow scientists, engineers, and students to work at the outermost frontiers of knowledge" (http://www.nsf.gov/about/glance.jsp). Go to the National Science Foundation website and do a site search for the "guide for proposal writing." Once the pdf opens, scan the table of contents and read sections that interest you. In particular, read on page 20 "Little Things that Can Make a Difference." Create a PowerPoint® presentation about the key points of that section.

15 ETHICS IN THE WORKPLACE

Goals

- Explain what it means to act ethically
- Describe a culture of ethics
- Develop a plan for resolving an ethical dilemma
- Identify the barriers to ethical behavior
- Debate the ethical challenges of emerging technology

Terms

code of ethics, p. 412

corporate code of ethics, p. 412

dignity, p. 418

ethics, p. 407

personal code of ethics, p. 413

principles, p. 407

rights, p. 418

utility, p. 419

values, p. 407

whistle-blower, p. 421

Write to Learn

Think of someone you admire and respect, someone you want to be like—a parent, friend, teacher, or political or entertainment figure. What, in particular, has this person done to earn your respect? What values—for example, honesty, hard work, and courage—would this person say are important? Write a journal entry describing this person and list several accomplishments. Summarize by identifying which values are most important to this individual.

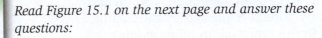 **FOCUS** **on the Ethics in the Workplace**

Read Figure 15.1 on the next page and answer these questions:

- Why does the Society for Technical Communication (STC) list the six core values in this order?
- What are five ways technical communicators can practice honesty?
- How can technical communicators maintain professionalism?
- Why do the principles include confidentiality?

What If?

How would the model change if. . .

- The principles were being explained to students considering a career as a technical communicator?
- Technical communicators needed STC guidelines for writing blogs and text for webpages?
- A banking or finance industry wanted to use similar principles?

Ethical Principles for Technical Communicators

As technical communicators, we observe the following ethical principles in our professional activities.

Legality

We observe the laws and regulations governing our profession. We meet the terms of contracts we undertake. We ensure that all terms are consistent with laws and regulations locally and globally, as applicable, and with STC ethical principles.

Honesty

We seek to promote the public good in our activities. To the best of our ability, we provide truthful and accurate communications. We also dedicate ourselves to conciseness, clarity, coherence, and creativity, striving to meet the needs of those who use our products and services. We alert our clients and employers when we believe that material is ambiguous. Before using another person's work, we obtain permission. We attribute authorship of material and ideas only to those who make an original and substantive contribution. We do not perform work outside our job scope during hours compensated by clients or employers, except with their permission; nor do we use their facilities, equipment, or supplies without their approval. When we advertise our services, we do so truthfully.

Confidentiality

We respect the confidentiality of our clients, employers, and professional organizations. We disclose business-sensitive information only with their consent or when legally required to do so. We obtain releases from clients and employers before including any business-sensitive materials in our portfolios or commercial demonstrations or before using such materials for another client or employer.

Quality

We endeavor to produce excellence in our communication products. We negotiate realistic agreements with clients and employers on schedules, budgets, and deliverables during project planning. Then we strive to fulfill our obligations in a timely, responsible manner.

Fairness

We respect cultural variety and other aspects of diversity in our clients, employers, development teams, and audiences. We serve the business interests of our clients and employers as long as they are consistent with the public good. Whenever possible, we avoid conflicts of interest in fulfilling our professional responsibilities and activities. If we discern a conflict of interests, we disclose it to those concerned and obtain their approval before proceeding.

Professionalism

We evaluate communication products and services constructively and tactfully, and seek definitive assessments of our own professional performance. We advance technical communication through our integrity and excellence in performing each task we undertake. Additionally, we assist other persons in our profession through mentoring, networking, and instruction. We also pursue professional self-improvement, especially through courses and conferences.

Adopted by the STC Board of Directors
September, 1998

Figure 15.1 Ethical Principles for Technical Communicators Reprinted with permission of STC

Writing @Work

Courtesy of Rick Leuner

CareerClusters®
PATHWAYS TO COLLEGE & CAREER READINESS
Transportation, Distribution & Logistics
Source: The Center to Advance CTE

Rick Leuner is a sales associate for NAI Realvest, a commercial real estate brokerage firm in Orlando, Florida. He helps companies find and purchase or lease large facilities to serve as offices, stores, and warehouses. He also looks for buyers or lessees for commercial spaces that are being built or have been vacated in his territory.

In general, Rick is bound by real estate ethics codes implemented at local, state, and national levels: "Members of the National Association of Realtors (NAR) are required to periodically pass a test on the NAR Code of Ethics, a document that spells out the ethical practices one must use with other realtors, clients, and the public. I also follow regulations and legal requirements set by Florida state regulators. These rules have the force of law for any person practicing real estate in Florida."

In Rick's field—and many others—ethical behavior draws more business opportunities. Therefore, it is beneficial to observe proper business decorum. "Our industry relies greatly on networking with fellow professionals to close deals. Referrals are an important source of business, and brokers frequently refer clients to their most respected colleagues when they know that all parties will benefit. This process of referral creates a web of goodwill between peers and encourages brokers to earn a positive reputation and share their business in the future."

In addition to helping his colleagues, Rick protects his clients' confidential information. "I need to understand their detailed business requirements to provide the best real estate service and advice," explains Rick. "Businesspeople do not readily reveal this proprietary information to outsiders, so I must earn my clients' trust and respect their desire for confidentiality. Whether this is guaranteed through nondisclosure agreements or with a handshake, the promise is the foundation for a respectful, successful business relationship."

Think Critically

1. In Rick's field, why does ethical behavior draw more business opportunities?

2. Think about two career fields with which you are familiar. Is networking as important in these fields as it is in commercial real estate? What are some of the confidentiality issues in these fields?

Printed with permission of Rick Leuner

Writing in Transportation, Distribution, and Logistics

The manufacturing side of a company produces the goods, but the transportation manager makes sure the goods are delivered to the customer. A trucking transportation manager oversees all aspects of this process including the drivers who haul the merchandise. She must be versatile, for she may be involved with budgeting, training, and scheduling as well as customer service.

Proposing a budget means figuring costs, writing explanations of routine expenses such as maintenance, and writing justifications for new expenditures, such as a new delivery vehicle. Setting up training sessions requires the manager to send out an agenda, prepare materials, and then conduct the session. Tailored to the audience, training brings drivers up to date on company policies and government regulations overseeing trucking operations. To schedule delivery dates and drivers, the manager enters data using transportation software. As a customer service representative, the transportation manager may write reports investigating complaints, particularly late deliveries, and consult others who can assist with solutions.

Because this individual works with people in different roles, a trucking transportation manager should have good communication and people skills.

15.1 WHAT IS ETHICS?

The principles and values that help people resolve questions of right and wrong constitute their **ethics**. A system of ethics, or morality, is based on **values**, the ideals that govern a person's actions. Many people have similar values—believing in honesty, justice, hard work, and equality, for example. Values help people set rules, or **principles**, to guide their behavior. When you make a decision to return a $10 bill to a stranger who unknowingly dropped it, you are making an ethical decision. Your honesty motivates you to return the money to its owner rather than keep it for yourself.

People's ethics come initially from their families and culture, where they may have learned the Golden Rule: Do unto others as you would have them do unto you. Also, the world's great religions contain moral systems of conduct by which people are encouraged to live: Do not kill, do not steal, and do not lie. As people mature, many of them reassess the moral code passed down to them, revising it according to their experiences. For example, a youngster taught not to kill may reassess that lesson if, as a young adult, this person is asked to defend her country.

Benefits of Ethical Decisions

Living ethically brings certain benefits—for instance, gaining the respect of others and having access to the privileges of society. Responsible and ethical people get to vote, borrow money, serve in public office, and travel freely. Acting ethically:

- Helps a person live amicably and responsibly with other human beings.

- Contributes to a clear conscience and peace of mind.

- Defines a person's character and what it means to be uniquely human.

Mitch is a pharmacy technician at Fullerton's. As he is organizing prescriptions for pickup, he sees one for naltrexone, a medication that helps alcoholics control the compulsion to drink. The prescription was filled for the high school principal, who suspended Mitch several years ago when, according to Mitch, he did not deserve it. Mitch is tempted to tell his wife about the prescription. He knows she can keep a secret.

That evening Mitch decides not to say anything to his wife. And coincidentally, the next day he runs into the principal quite by chance. Although Mitch feels somewhat self-conscious, he greets the man with a clear conscience. That afternoon Mitch goes to work, feeling good about himself. His discretion defines his character. He is not the type of person who has to spread a juicy story to get attention from others.

© Photographer's Choice/Getty Images

© Diego Cervo, 2009/Shutterstock

Typical Citizen, Customer, Client

Wants to be treated with fairness, honesty, respect, and consideration.

Writer's Focus

Developing codes of ethics that publicize intentions to behave ethically. Internalizing those codes so that ethical behavior becomes the norm.

Consequences of Unethical Behavior

When people do not behave ethically, they are subject to the pitfalls that result from their poor judgment—possible convictions, questionable reputations, and guilt. Unethical behavior affects not only an individual personally but also family members and members of society who must deal with the consequences.

At work one afternoon, Mitch thought about what could have happened if he had told his wife about the principal's prescription. First, he liked his job and knew he could be fired for a breach of confidentiality. Second, he considered the repercussions if prescriptions of other customers were revealed. Mitch's sister, who takes an antidepressant, would be embarrassed if anyone except her family knew. Third, he realized his motive—revenge against someone he thought had done him an injustice—was immature. If only more people like Mitch would stop to think through the consequences of their actions and examine their motives!

In the highly publicized 2015 "diesel dupe" scandal, Volkswagen (VW) deliberately deceived its customer base by installing a "defeat device" on its cars, software that misrepresented emissions testing results. This device somehow "knew" when the vehicle was being operated under controlled laboratory conditions, thus making the VW appear to comply with U.S. emissions standards. However, when on the road, the cars were actually emitting nitrogen oxide pollutants up to 40 times above what is admissible in the United States. The consequences of VW's lie and cover up—hazardous pollution levels, a sullied reputation, and severe economic troubles—were serious. In October 2015, VW posted its first quarterly loss in 15 years. The CEO, Martin Winterkorn, resigned with more resignations to follow along with a number of firings. VW lost some $25 million in market share and risked $18 billion in fines. Moreover, the public lost confidence in Volkswagon (Hotten).

What was the motive for falsifying financial emissions results on such a large scale? In retrospect, what would the leaders of VW say now that they have seen the full story of their collusion play out?

Like Mitch, everyone faces the temptation to do wrong, to take the easy way out, or to give in to a malicious impulse. Unlike Mitch, not everyone takes the time to reason through the implications of a choice. The Volkswagen "diesel dupe" illustrates that the fallout from illegal activity can be far reaching and long lasting, affecting many lives for years to come.

STOP AND THINK 15.1

Define ethics. What are the benefits of living an ethical life? What are the consequences of making poor ethical decisions?

15.2 CREATING A CULTURE OF ETHICS

The Ethical Resource Center's (ERC) *2013 National Business Ethics Survey* provides some disturbing news. Some 41 percent of employees questioned had seen someone involved in an ethical violation. The good news is this percentage is down from 55 percent in 2007. The bad news is most hesitated to report a violation because of fear of reprisals (ERC).

To encourage employees to act ethically, companies can create a culture of ethics, a healthy work environment that supports integrity, mutual respect, and fair-mindedness. In such a climate, everyone knows that values matter. To create such an ethical culture, leaders must set the example and actively promote ethical behavior.

Healthy Work Environment

A number of ethical issues can contribute to a toxic work environment, among them fraud, a discriminatory and inhospitable climate, and inappropriate use of online media.

Preventing Fraud

According to research from FTI Consulting, businesses lose 5 percent of their revenue each year to fraud. Raftery and Holder suggest companies look at their culture to reduce opportunities for fraud by screening applicants, implementing and evaluating codes of conduct, and employing systems of checks and balances such as a periodic review of expenditures. Most importantly, leaders must model integrity, for 26 percent of infractions are reportedly committed by upper-level managers.

Hospitable Environment

To meet goals for the organization, people must work together in a collegial atmosphere. To this end, showing respect for colleagues and customers is vital through common courtesy and timely completion of tasks. Work relations can be tense when there is a conflict, but tensions can be eased by displaying tolerance for others' opinions, arguing with evidence for differing views, and concentrating on common objectives. Gossiping and backbiting have no place at work, for such negativity undermines a comfortable working environment. Furthermore, failure to contribute to a positive work flow can show up on performance evaluations and reference checks.

Workplace conduct is further regulated by laws for fair treatment. Most importantly, Title VII of the Civil Rights Acts of 1964 (United States) outlaws discriminatory workplace behavior and protects victims from retaliation (see the EEOC website for more information):

> This law makes it illegal to discriminate against someone on the basis of race, color, religion, national origin, or sex. . . . [Later the law included other populations.] The law also requires that employers reasonably accommodate applicants' and employees' sincerely held religious practices. . . .

> The law also makes it illegal to retaliate against a person who complained of discrimination.

Moreover, harassment, prohibited until Title VII, is "unwelcome conduct based on race, color, religion, sex (including pregnancy), national origin, age (40 or older), disability or genetic information. . . ." If the "conduct create[s] a work environment that would be intimidating, hostile, or offensive to reasonable people," harassment becomes a form of discrimination.

Joking and teasing—while seemingly innocent to some—may constitute a hostile work environment for others. If you're not sure whether your good-natured teasing is offensive, ask and adjust your behavior accordingly. For example, a female supervisor repeatedly touched the shoulder of one of her male workers when she teased him about his martial arts ability. When he asked her to stop, she did. As this example shows, both parties are responsible for correcting a misunderstanding: the worker who brought it to the supervisor's attention and the supervisor who adjusted her behavior.

If you know of someone who is being harassed and do not report it to the proper authorities, you can be held financially liable. Talk over fair workplace practices with your human resources professional or someone you can trust if you have questions.

Responsible Online Behavior

Your employer has the right to monitor your online activity—including activity on your personal e-mail or social media accounts—if you access these accounts from work. Be aware of company policies and follow them.

Ethical Leaders

In 1982, someone found a way to lace Tylenol with cyanide. As a result of the tampering, seven people died. Even though the makers of Tylenol, Johnson & Johnson, did not cause the deaths, the public stopped purchasing Tylenol, resulting in Johnson & Johnson losing $1 billion of its market share (Baker).

In 1986, when Johnson & Johnson faced a similar threat of tampering, the company wasted no time in removing Tylenol from store shelves and did not restock Tylenol until it had produced a tamper-free cap. As a result, the public learned it could trust Johnson & Johnson to do the right thing. Within five months, the company had recovered most of its market share.

Johnson & Johnson's culture of ethics guided the company's decision to do what was best for its customers. When the question was posed—Do we recall our product?—there was no doubt the recall was the right thing to do. Figure 15.2 shows Johnson & Johnson's Credo of Values. Written in 1943, it made a commitment to the company's customers. Chairman James Burke's leadership during the Tylenol crisis reestablished that commitment.

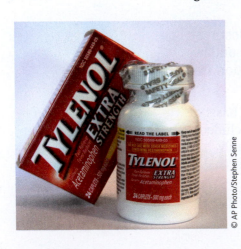
© AP Photo/Stephen Senne

The experience at Johnson & Johnson underscores one of the principal findings of the ERC's *Survey*: Leaders who model ethical behavior positively impact the ethical climates of the institutions they run. Employees who perceive their leaders as moral beings:

- Feel less pressure to compromise ethical standards.

- Observe less misconduct on the job.

- Are more satisfied with their organization overall.

- Feel more valued as employees.

Our Credo

We believe our first responsibility is to the doctors, nurses and patients,
to mothers and fathers and all others who use our products and services.
In meeting their needs everything we do must be of high quality.
We must constantly strive to reduce our costs
in order to maintain reasonable prices.
Customers' orders must be serviced promptly and accurately.
Our suppliers and distributors must have an opportunity
to make a fair profit.

We are responsible to our employees,
the men and women who work with us throughout the world.
Everyone must be considered as an individual.
We must respect their dignity and recognize their merit.
They must have a sense of security in their jobs.
Compensation must be fair and adequate,
and working conditions clean, orderly and safe.
We must be mindful of ways to help our employees fulfill
their family responsibilities.
Employees must feel free to make suggestions and complaints.
There must be equal opportunity for employment, development
and advancement for those qualified.
We must provide competent management,
and their actions must be just and ethical.

We are responsible to the communities in which we live and work
and to the world community as well.
We must be good citizens—support good works and charities
and bear our fair share of taxes.
We must encourage civic improvements and better health and education.
We must maintain in good order
the property we are privileged to use,
protecting the environment and natural resources.

Our final responsibility is to our stockholders.
Business must make a sound profit.
We must experiment with new ideas.
Research must be carried on, innovative problems developed
and mistakes paid for.
New equipment must be purchased, new facilities provided
and new products launched.
Reserves must be created to provide for adverse times.
When we operate according to these principles,
the stockholders should realize a fair return.

Figure 15.2 Johnson & Johnson's Credo of Values Reprinted with permission of Johnson & Johnson

Unfortunately, not all companies hold ethical conduct is such high regard. Complaints are often heard about major department stores selling inferior merchandise for less money, making it difficult for small businesses to thrive. Some think it unfair that fast-food chains do not offer employees more benefits or higher wages. Communities rally behind environmental concerns such as waste from livestock running into rivers and seeping into groundwater.

Since 2013, one organization, Oxfam, has orchestrated a Behind the Brands campaign to alert consumers about the ethical practices of the companies

© Digital Vision/Getty Images

producing the products they love. The goal, according to Rachel Wilshaw, is to use consumer behavior to influence the behavior of food and beverage companies. And it has worked. Several top companies, including Coca-Cola, PepsiCo, Unilever, and Nestle, "have committed to zero tolerance of land grabs." Others, Kellogg and General Mills, have agreed to reduce emissions, while Nestle and Mars plan to work toward gender equality.

Culture of Ethics

To create an ethical climate at work, one that fosters responsible behavior from employees and their leaders, the ERC encourages companies to hire ethics officers and set up ethical oversight committees. In addition, companies should commit publicly to ethical behavior. Leaders should evaluate and reward employees' ethical conduct, keep communication lines open, and—and most importantly—"walk the talk." A good place to begin is with a published **code of ethics**, a written pledge to make responsible, moral decisions.

A **corporate code of ethics** states a company's commitment to ethical behavior. Generally, organizational codes express similar core values deemed important to the company's operation—integrity, fairness, and respect for others. Most corporate codes also include rules that are specific to their discipline (for example, checking and double-checking sources in news reporting and maintaining confidentiality in counseling).

A corporate code aims to protect the public rather than the members of the organization. Ideally, the code is enforceable and includes penalties— reprimands, probation, termination, legal action, or extended leave without pay. For instance, a doctor who harms patients not only can be prosecuted but also can lose the license to practice.

Writing a Code of Ethics

In companies for which no code of ethics exists, you may be asked to help write one. Or you may start your own business, one that could benefit from a written code. Writing a code of ethics requires you to think about your personal values and to reflect on the values you want your employees to exhibit.

Personal Code

The process begins with your **personal code of ethics**, a statement of your values and standards. You can begin by taking a hard look at your own sense of values and ethical conduct.

Consider writing a personal creed or personal philosophy, as one nurse did in Figure 15.3. A presenter at a workshop asked participants to pretend they were flies on the wall at their own wake, listening to the stories people told about them after they had passed away.[1] What were they hoping to hear? After reflecting on this question, the nurse wrote down ideas that eventually made their way into this code. His code hangs on his office wall so he can refer to it when he has a difficult decision to make.

Personal Philosophy

I am here to help others. So important is this belief to me that I became a nurse—to help others heal so they can live healthy, productive, and happy lives. While I will use my skills and knowledge to promote good health practices, I accept that death comes to all. When the time comes, I will respect my patients' last wishes and let go, honored to be a witness to this sacred passage.

"To be rather than to seem" sums up my approach to life. I will stay true to myself and not obsess over what others think.

I will adapt to changing circumstances but will not sacrifice my integrity. I value truth, even when it is unpleasant.

I consciously and willfully choose to see the good in people and circumstances. "People, not things" is my motto. The pursuit of things will never come at the expense of people.

I will remember the wisdom of my grandmother whose 97 years were a testament to common sense, resourcefulness, simple values, and fundamental decency.

Figure 15.3 Personal Code of Ethics

You might begin a similar process of writing a creed that expresses your core values and conveys what is important to you. Find a quiet place where you can think without interruption and consider these questions:

- **What are your core values?** List values important to you, such as compassion, courage, and honor. Narrow your list to the few values that really speak to you.

- **What are you passionate about?** Think about your career goals or your hobbies. What do they tell you about your life's purpose or direction?

---

[1]See Stephen Covey's *The 7 Habits of Highly Effective People* for similar exercises and other aids to writing personal mission statements.

For example, if you like taking care of animals, perhaps you see yourself working as a zoologist or a veterinarian.

- **What lessons have you learned?** What lessons have you learned from the situations you have encountered? If you have recovered from a serious illness or accident, you may now appreciate the importance of family or of finding beauty in each day.

Now that you have some ideas for your personal code, organize those ideas and express them in complete sentences. Choose a title; then put the draft aside. Come back a few days later to revise and finalize your draft. When you are finished, you may want to frame it and keep it close at hand. From time to time, you can revise it as circumstances refine your philosophy.

Corporate Code

A corporate code is likely to be a collaborative effort involving several team members. The following suggestions may help generate ideas for a corporate code.

- **What are the company's values?** Start with a discussion of personal values. If your team members have written personal codes, share them. Look for similarities in your values. Brainstorm values important to your organization. Look for overlapping personal and corporate values to see which ones are most critical.

- **What kinds of ethical conflicts are typical of your organization?** Write statements dealing with the ethics of those conflicts. Do the conflicts revolve around personnel problems, pay issues, discrimination, customer fairness, plagiarism, or malpractice? What ethics underlie those issues—fairness, equality, honesty? In other words, when an ethical dilemma arises, what values drive the resolution of the conflict?

- **How does the company want to treat others—its employees as well as its customers or clients?** Consider asking for feedback from members of your organization. Perhaps you can conduct a focus group, a small meeting in which members respond to prompts. Now might be a good time to review the codes of other companies in your field to see how they are organized.

After putting your ideas together, rank your information in order of importance to your organization, employees, and clients. Ask one person in the group to write a draft of a code based on the input thus far. The group can read the draft and make suggestions. After putting the code aside for a while, come back to it for final revising and editing. Seek approval from the governing body of the organization before you publish the code.

When the company's philosophy is written down where employees can easily see it, it becomes more authentic. In times of crisis, the words can inspire and guide employees' decision-making processes.

Some corporate codes are long and include such sections as a Preamble, Responsibilities, and Consequences. Some are short, similar to the Ethical Principles for Technical Communicators on page 405 and the Firefighter Code of Ethics in Figure 15.4. Notice how the Firefighter Code addresses the specific concerns of the firefighter: "to safeguard . . . life and property against the elements of fire and disaster . . . and maintain proficiency in the art and science of fire engineering."

Code of Ethics

As a firefighter and member of the International Association of Fire Fighters, my fundamental duty is to serve humanity; to safeguard and preserve life and property against the elements of fire and disaster; and maintain a proficiency in the art and science of fire engineering.

I will uphold the standards of my profession, continually search for new and improved methods and disseminate and share my knowledge and skills with my contemporaries and descendants.

I will never allow personal feelings, nor danger to self to deter me from my responsibilities as a firefighter.

I will at all times, respect the property and rights of all men, the laws of my community and my country, and the chosen way of life of my fellow citizens.

I recognize the badge of my office as a symbol of public faith, and I accept it as a public trust to be held so long as I am true to the ethics of the fire service. I will constantly strive to achieve these objectives and ideals, dedicating myself before God to my chosen profession—saving of life, fire prevention and fire suppression.

As a member of the International Association of Fire Fighters, I accept this self-imposed and self-enforced obligation as my responsibility.

Figure 15.4 Firefighter Code of Ethics Reprinted with permission of the International Association of Fire Fighters

STOP AND THINK 15.2

What are some ways to create a culture of ethics? Tell the story of Johnson & Johnson and the Tylenol scare. How might you get started on a personal or corporate code of ethics?

15.3 WHAT DO YOU DO WHEN FACED WITH AN ETHICAL DILEMMA?

Think of the most difficult ethical decision you ever made. What standards did you use to make your decision? Are you happy with the choice you made? Would you do something different today? Explain.

The best approach is to prevent an ethical conflict in the first place by behaving responsibly, talking about decisions with people you trust, following your personal values, and knowing and following the values held by your company. Sometimes the first indication you are facing an ethical dilemma is a feeling of discomfort. Self-reflection may help clarify your feelings. More analysis is necessary when you are not sure what to do.

Clarify Your Position

You may need to clarify your position before you decide whether you have an ethical dilemma and what, if anything, you should do about it. In the following paragraph, read about the dilemma Pilar faced at work.

> Pilar's manager has asked her not to report the latest investment totals until next month, after the auditors have left. But Pilar knows the company is legally bound to report them by the 25th of each month. She could wait, as her supervisor requested, but reporting the figures late would not be legal. She feels conflicted. After all, her supervisor hired her and even covered for her when her child was in the hospital last month. Pilar values loyalty, yet she also values honesty and a work ethic of doing what she is supposed to do when she is supposed to do it. She has been at this job only a short time and is not sure how to proceed.

Pilar used the following questions to help clarify her position regarding the dilemma and to reach a solution.

Would my actions be legal? If you are not sure, ask a lawyer or read your company's code of ethics. If the answer is no, you risk engaging in unethical behavior.	Postponing the latest investment figures is clearly not legal, but Pilar wonders who would be responsible—she or her manager? Pilar does not know how to handle the request, but she does know that breaking the law is not an option.
Have I thought through the possible consequences of my actions? If not, you need to think about where this action will lead and what will happen if you do nothing.	Failing to report the totals on time could cause Pilar to lose her job if someone discovers what she did. She could risk losing the company as a reference for future jobs. How would she explain during an interview why she left the company? If caught, Pilar could be prosecuted. If she does nothing, her manager could still misrepresent the data on her own. Pilar does not like the direction her thoughts are taking.
How uncomfortable am I? Will you be able to sleep tonight? How would you feel if the situation was published in the newspaper? If you cannot sleep and would be embarrassed if others knew, your action may be the wrong one.	Pilar is waking up in the middle of the night with her manager's request on her mind. Pilar pictures her coworkers in the lounge discussing her unflattering mug shot in the local newspaper. She is anxious and cannot reason her anxiety away.

What central conflict am I facing? Continue to think about your dilemma until it is clear to you which values are in conflict.	Pilar's central conflict is whether to be loyal to her manager or to do what she knows is right.
Is there an obvious solution? Sometimes human beings overcomplicate matters when there may be a simple and direct way to handle things.	After a few days of worrying, Pilar tells her manager she is not comfortable altering the dates on the report. Pilar points out the risks to both of them and is relieved to hear her manager feels conflicted too. Together they figure out the best way to present the current data and predict more promising figures after fall sales. Pilar's solution actually improves her relationship with her manager.

Analyze Your Ethical Dilemma

Some situations may require more analysis—especially if a course of action does not present itself early in your thought process. Read Wilma Kwon's ethical dilemma and follow her line of thinking as she analyzes the dilemma and comes up with alternatives.

> Wilma Kwon is chair of the selection committee for the position of vice president of production for Valli Shirt Factory. One applicant, 54-year-old David Zeltzer, has 23 years of experience, looks impressive on paper, has good references, and does well in the interview. When Wilma recommends him for the job, the president hesitates, wanting to hire a younger man instead—someone just out of college with no work experience. Wilma protests, but the president is firm. Wilma is angry. Her committee screened 32 applicants and conducted four interviews in good faith that the president would accept its recommendation. She found a good candidate. The president's decision looks like age discrimination to her. Wilma is worried about the legal ramifications if David decides to sue.

Take time to think about what is happening. You have heard it before: Count to 10. Do not react impulsively.	Wilma decides to take the weekend to think things over and to calm down.
Examine the facts. Ask questions. Play detective. Rumor, innuendo, and excessive drama are not the same as facts. What really has happened?	On Monday, Wilma reviews the selection committee's minutes and determines that her committee followed all company policies and broke no laws. She examines the company's records on hiring and finds a troubling trend toward hiring younger candidates over well-qualified older ones. She recalls her conversation with the president and takes some notes.
Clarify your short-term and long-term goals. Sometimes it is important to meet a short-term goal. However, after weighing the consequences of a short-term goal against a long-term goal, you may find that pursuing a long-term goal is a wiser, more stable option.	Wilma's short-term goal is to hire someone as quickly as possible. The company is facing tough economic decisions and needs a person with experience and talent. Her long-term goal is to find someone who will bring innovation to the company so it is still thriving in 15 years.

(continues)

(Continued)

Talk to someone you can trust. Maybe you can talk to an employee who has been with the firm a long time. Or you could talk to a friend, relative, minister, or counselor.	Wilma shares her concerns with a committee member who has been with the company since it began. He reminds Wilma that the founder of the company was an older gentleman and encourages her to keep looking for a solution. Wilma also consults the human resources director, who says to gather more evidence and see if she can convince the president to hire David.
Review your company's code of ethics. Sometimes a review of your company's code of ethics will provide the answer you seek.	Wilma reviews the company's creed and finds the statement: "Valli Shirt Factory is an equal opportunity employer committed to diversity." She is reminded of the importance of diversity—for herself as a woman, as well as for others.
Talk to legal counsel. It never hurts to find out just where you and the company stand legally.	Wilma talks to the company's lawyer, who says it is difficult to prove discrimination. But if the two candidates' qualifications are that different—and with a prior record of hiring younger employees over older ones—the company could have a problem proving that it did not discriminate.
Listen to your conscience. Review your personal code of ethics to tune in with your values. What does your inner voice tell you to do?	Wilma recalls the statement in her own code about having the courage to stand up for what is right. Wilma believes David is the best candidate for the job, and she is not comfortable with any form of discrimination. She now feels compelled to speak out on his behalf.
Explore alternatives. Brainstorm alternatives. List the advantages and disadvantages of each.	Hiring the younger candidate would be the easiest course of action now, but what happens to the company if he cannot perform the job successfully? In addition, if David decides to sue, a lawsuit would be stressful, time-consuming, and expensive. Trying to convince the president to hire David also would take time and might strain Wilma's relationship with him. On the other hand, if Wilma can convince him to hire David, the company could hire a good employee and avoid a lawsuit.
Choose an alternative. After weighing the pros and cons, it is time to act on the alternative that is both ethical and logical.	Wilma makes an appointment with the president to present her findings. She asks the human resources director to join them. If the president still insists on hiring the younger candidate, at least he will be aware of the consequences.

Choose a Responsible Course of Action

Over the centuries, philosophers and religious leaders have given advice on how to select a responsible course of action. The following criteria are often touted as a way to judge the right thing to do:

- **Rights:** Will my actions infringe on the **rights** (personal freedoms) and **dignity** (self-respect) of others? If I drink and drive, I am taking away someone else's right to drive on a safe roadway. If I neglect to wash my nursing home patient's hair, I am depriving her of her dignity.

- **Justice:** Are my actions just or fair? Are the good or bad consequences to be uniformly divided among all members of the group? Deciding that all of my employees except my friend Cecelia must work on a holiday does

Nereza, a research assistant, taps lightly on her supervisor's door before walking into his office—as she has done many times before. Richard is sitting with a male employee. They are looking out the window and laughing. Richard calls Nereza over and makes a joke about Claire, an overweight coworker who is getting out of a car. Nereza says, "I like Claire. She does a good job. Besides, we all have our physical challenges" (as she looks at Richard's receding hairline). Nereza shoots Richard a "you should know better" look and leaves.

Think Critically

What do you think about Nereza's reaction?

Communication
Dilemma

not provide justice for all. Equality is when the same opportunities and consequences apply to everyone.

- **Utility:** Will my actions affect most people in the best way possible? In other words, **utility** is based on what action will do the most good and the least harm. If I vote for a tax increase for the middle class and do not vote to tax the upper class proportionately, I may be voting to tax the group that is least able to bear the burden financially. This practice fails to affect most people in the best way possible.

- **Care:** Do my actions show that I care about and am considerate of others? If I have an opportunity to show care and compassion for the machinist on my staff whose house just burned down and I do not act, I have failed not only my employee but also my community.

- **Empathy:** Do I have empathy for other people? Have I asked myself what it would feel like to be in another person's shoes? Before I decide whether to let an employee go because of poor sales, I could ask myself how would I like to be treated. I could give the person as much notice as possible, provide some kind of severance pay, or offer to rehire when business improves.

- **Consistency:** Is my decision consistent with my other policies? If my policy is to allow makeup tests for students who have legitimate reasons to miss a test and I do not allow Nora to make up a presentation she missed, I am not being consistent.

- **Values and principles:** Is my action consistent with the values and principles I follow? If I value honesty but do not tell the grocer he undercharged me $25 for the salmon I ordered, I am not honoring my values of honesty and fairness.

- **Universal consequences:** To envision universal consequences, think about what would happen if everyone did the same action. If everyone threw soda cans onto the highway, what would happen?

- **Extenuating circumstances:** Are there extenuating circumstances to take into account? If I am late to a job interview because my flight was delayed due to inclement weather, then it's fair for the employer to grant me an interview at another time since the circumstances surrounding the delayed flight were out of my control.

With any ethical dilemma, after you have chosen an alternative, evaluate what you did. How do you feel about your decision now? Are you satisfied you chose the right course? What, if anything, would you do differently next time? Your reevaluation may cause you to adjust your behavior if you encounter a similar dilemma.

When Do You Blow the Whistle?

In December 2014, Dr. Katherine Mitchell, was honored by the Department of Veterans Affairs with its Public Servant of the Year award for blowing the whistle on inadequate and negligent treatment of patients. Among her complaints were excessive wait times for veterans seeking appointments and inadequate training for emergency room triage. Mitchell is one of many Veterans Administration (VA) personnel who exposed these and other issues with patient care at the Carl T. Hayden Medical Center in Phoenix (Wagner).

Dr. Sam Foote, retired director of the Phoenix VA system, also came forward alleging appointment records had been falsified and some 40 veterans had died waiting for treatment from the Phoenix facility. Both Mitchell and Foote issued complaints to Congress, the VA Officer of Inspector General, and the news media (Wagner). It took investigative journalism from *The Arizona Republic* and CNN to bring congressional attention to the poor treatment of veterans at Phoenix.

After news of the Phoenix problems broke, more complaints about the treatment of veterans in other VA centers poured in. The VA's cover-up and scandalous behavior have caused veterans to suffer twice, once on the battlefield and again, ironically, in the supposed safe haven of their own country. Amid the revelations of misconduct under his leadership, VA Secretary Eric Shinseki resigned.

The whistle-blowers' journeys were fraught with difficulty. Many suffered retaliation in one form or another. Mitchell was investigated, transferred, and harassed. Foote was given more hours and higher case loads. Special Council Carolyn Lerner, whose office investigates retaliation complaints, says 38 percent of reprisal complaints coming into her office in 2015 came from VA personnel.

Lerner acknowledges the heroic role of whistle-blowers: "Whistleblower disclosures also can play a pivotal role in promoting accountability. These are important victories for employees who risked their professional lives to improve VA operations and the quality of care provided to veterans."

A **whistle-blower** is a person who publicly alleges an organization's wrongful practices. Mitchell and Foote are good examples, but there are many others—such as tobacco giant Brown & Williamson's Dr. Jeffrey Wigland, Enron's Sherron Watkins, and Firestone's Thomas A. Robertson. As you can see, whistle-blowing takes courage, persistence, and conviction. And although many companies welcome reports of misdeeds so they can correct them, some want only to cover up their misdeeds and continue business as usual.

Whistle-blowing can be risky. Laws protect whistle-blowers from retribution from their employers, but fighting for that protection can be a long, messy, and stressful process. As doctors, Mitchell and Foote took an ethical oath to "apply, for the benefit of the sick, all measures which are required." Improvements in patient care in VA centers as a result of their testimony will save lives and improve the quality of life for many. We can all be grateful their values and concern for patients prompted them to come forward.

How does someone decide whether to blow the whistle? For most people, whistle-blowing is a matter of strong conscience, something to be used as a last resort. If you are thinking about blowing the whistle on an organization, think through the situation. Try to find a way to work out your differences by talking to someone. If negotiation is not an option, most authorities suggest you thoroughly document the infractions and keep your notes in a safe place. Maintain good relationships with as many people in the company as you can, and talk over the situation with someone you trust. Most importantly, *seek the advice of an attorney who specializes in whistle-blowing in your field.*

STOP AND THINK 15.3

What questions can help you clarify an ethical dilemma? What criteria help you analyze a dilemma? How do you choose a responsible course of action?

15.4 WHY IS IT DIFFICULT TO BEHAVE ETHICALLY?

Why do some people have a difficult time doing the right thing? What are the obstacles to making good ethical choices?

When Jamie saw Tom being teased by a group of boys because he had worn the "wrong" team's sweatshirt that day, Jamie jumped to Tom's defense. It was the right thing to do. Sallie Mae, a social worker, argued for more funds for the foster kids in her care despite the system's prejudice. It was the right thing to do.

People don't always do the right thing, though. If asked, many of us could think of a time when we succumbed to peer pressure or looked the other way when someone committed a wrongdoing. Why do good people compromise their values? Ethics are more easily compromised under certain conditions, and people use defense mechanisms to avoid facing uncomfortable feelings of guilt.

Conditions

According to M. S. Baucus and J. P. Near, illegal activities are more likely to occur in larger companies than in smaller companies and when resources abound rather than when they are lacking. Furthermore, illegal activities take place during times of change and growth—before a company has a chance to examine its ethics—and in certain industries in which misconduct seems to generate a climate of complicity. For instance, politics gets a bad rap because people think it does not matter how a politician behaves as long as he gets elected. Managers agree most employees abide by a moral code, but the pressure to perform or achieve management objectives can lead otherwise ethical workers to behave unethically.

© Digital Vision/Getty Images

Another problem is a legal system that often lags behind current debates on ethics. In other words, *legal* is not the same as *ethical*. It might not be illegal to talk about your boss behind his back, but it is unethical. At one time, it was legal but not ethical to own slaves. When enlightened and passionate people stand up for just causes, laws catch up to the ethics.

Fear and uncertainty undermine choice. Workers fear reprisals if they report unethical activity—fear of being laid off, harassed, or demoted. With families to support, the financial repercussions affect not only the worker but the worker's family.

Finally, it can be difficult to figure out the proper course of action. It's natural to spend a period of time confused, partly in denial, while assessing the situation. Moral dilemmas do not always have easy, clear-cut solutions. Where it may be clear that taking money out of the tip jar at the sandwich shop is wrong, it's not as clear when your coworker uses the money from the tip jar to buy needed food for her three-year-old niece.

Defense Mechanisms

Because people like to see themselves in the best light possible, they often refuse to acknowledge their bad behavior for what it is. Perhaps you will recognize the following common defense mechanisms.

- **Bandwagon approach:** When students notice other students coming to class late, they can easily justify the bad habit: Everyone is doing it, the thinking goes. If they can do it, so can I.

- **Denial:** People deny that anything is wrong. The situation is not that bad, they say, or they look the other way because avoiding the situation is easier than dealing with the problem. Denial, though, usually makes matters worse, not better.

- **Rationalization:** People invent excuses for their behavior. A person may think, I have to look out for myself, or this is what I have to do right now. I'll do better—later. Rationalization is generally a way to avoid looking at the real issues.

- **False sense of security:** Who is going to know? People reason that no one will find out; but if someone does, their supervisor will be able to cover for them. Experience shows that the errors of a person's ways are eventually discovered. Besides, wrongdoers know what they have done and must live with the consequences.

- **Stress:** Stress clouds people's judgment. The pressure to make a sale, bring in money, or meet a deadline can push people to the edge. It may be best to deal with the stress and the moral dilemma separately, as they are two different issues.

- **Revenge:** People want to fight back against a perceived injustice. Some who think the government tax code is unfair may justify not claiming additional income from a part-time job on a tax return. However, two wrongs do not make a right.

- **Blame:** People sometimes believe they do not have to correct a problem they did not create. A wise person understands it is best for everyone to correct an ethical violation, regardless of who caused it.

Doing the right thing requires self-knowledge and courage. When individuals improve their ethical behavior, a more judicious and harmonious society emerges.

STOP AND THINK 15.4
Why do people behave unethically?

15.5 ETHICAL CHALLENGES OF EMERGING TECHNOLOGY

Technology is one of the greatest change agents in the world.

Emerging technologies such as zero emissions vehicles and recyclable plastics are eagerly anticipated (Meyerson). But other technologies—such as gene therapy, electronic surveillance, and artificial intelligence—are met with greater caution, for they can dramatically alter the way we live. To implement new technology responsibly, we must investigate each innovation and debate the possible consequences and implications.

Gene Therapy

Two types of gene therapy offer the potential to improve health: somatic gene therapy and germ-line cell therapy. In somatic gene therapy, a normal gene is delivered to a patient's cells to correct an abnormal gene responsible for disease. Germ-line or reproductive therapy repairs or enhances egg and sperm cells to prevent genetic disorders or enhance traits in the unborn. Reproductive cell therapy is more controversial since the genetic changes can be passed on to subsequent generations. It is not currently allowed in a number of countries and is carefully regulated in the Unites States. While somatic gene therapy has been successful in some cases (severe combined immunodeficiency disease, for example), it is still experimental and can cause adverse results in patients, including death.

Genetically modified organisms (GMOs) already increase crop yields and nutritional value in the United States and abroad. More GMO foods on the horizon offer needed hunger relief for communities; however, many are still worried about the long-range effects of GMOs.

All gene therapy raises important ethical questions: Do we have a moral obligation to prevent disease, cure malnutrition, and ensure good health for the next generation? Or are the risks of re-engineering worth the gain? Is this intervention playing God, as some have suggested? Is it OK to enhance genes to improve hair color or IQ, or should this technology be used for repair only? Genetic enhancement could discriminate—giving some people with a higher IQ an unfair advantage, for instance. If we have the opportunity to extend the human lifespan, should we? What if we could genetically modify humans to be rid of aggressive tendencies?

Electronic Surveillance

Today everything has an online presence, in a database, on social media, in the cloud. We are warned not to put personal data on Facebook. We are told our webcams become the eyes through which an unscrupulous hacker can spy on us. Companies such as Planet Labs or Skybox Imaging have launched satellites that can record events on Earth in real time with resolutions up to one foot (Baron).

Hackers wear both black and white hats. The latest breach by hackers at Target compromised 40 million credit cards during the 2013 holiday shopping season, leading to the theft of as many as 110 million people's personal information (Cooney and Kurane). What else is at risk? Will other personal information such as human medical and genetic information remain private? Some hackers engage in "hactivism" and use their skills for political purposes. Indeed, cyber warfare seems to be necessary for our national security but at some risk to our privacy.

Article 12 of the *Universal Declaration of Human Rights* (United Nations) declares privacy is a human right. We may all agree on the importance of privacy, but how do we decide what to monitor and how often? How do we weigh our safety and security against our right to privacy? Credit card transactions, PINS, and passwords—is all this data as secure as our institutions would have us believe?

Artificial Intelligence

Neuromorphic chip technology could create robots and computers that are as smart as humans (Baron). Currently, robots handle many routine assembly line tasks. What happens when a computer can learn more efficiently than a human? What are the implications for humans if autonomous computers and robots can react to a situation without prompting from their human owners? What happens when GPS and networking capabilities send robots into the world on their own? Could this technology run amuck?

The race of Cylons infiltrated human civilization in *Battlestar Galactica,* blurring the lines between humanity and machines, warning us, as does Shelley in *Frankenstein,* we are responsible for what we create. Yet the doctor's emergency medical holograph in *Voyager* illustrates a humanitarian use of artificial intelligence while also exploring the effects of prejudice and exploitation.

Unquestionably, technology has a role in remedying world-wide shortages of water, food, and energy and improving our quality of life, but it can also be used as a destructive force. Perhaps science fiction is one place to "try out" new technology before it becomes commonplace. Science fiction author Robert Sawyer believes his role is instructive. "Our job," he says, "is not to predict *the* future. Rather, it's to suggest all the possible futures—so that society can make informed decisions about where we want to go."

 STOP AND THINK 15.5
List the advantages and potential dangers of gene therapy, electronic surveillance, and artificial intelligence. Explain why these emerging technologies represent ethical dilemmas.

15 CHAPTER REVIEW

Summary

1. Ethics are the principles and values that help people resolve questions of right and wrong. Responsible ethical decisions provide peace of mind and allow people to live together amicably. Irresponsible choices bring negative consequences such as convictions, sullied reputations, and guilt.

2. A culture of ethics in the workplace promotes responsible, humane decision making. Leaders must actively promote values. Personal and corporate codes set up guidelines for proper behavior.

3. Working through an ethical dilemma requires careful thought to clarify and analyze the dilemma before selecting a responsible course of action. Whistle-blowing may be an option as a last resort.

4. Conditions in the workplace and defense mechanisms can contribute to unethical behavior.

5. It's important to think through the ethical challenges posed by emerging technologies to ensure positive and productive uses and guard against harm.

Checklist

- Do I know the benefits of ethical choices and the consequences of unethical choices?

- Can I provide suggestions for creating a culture of ethics?

- Have I made a list of my core values?

- Have I determined my life's purpose?

- Have I determined how I want to treat others?

- Do I use questions to help clarify my ethical position and come up with an alternative?

- Do I use questions to help analyze an ethical dilemma and select an alternative?

- Do I use criteria to help choose a responsible course of action?

- Am I aware of the defense mechanisms that I and others use to make poor ethical choices?

- What are ethical implications of emerging technologies?

Build Your Foundation

1. Rank the values below from 1 through 15 in order of their importance to you, with 1 being most important and 15 being least important. Then work with a few classmates to compare your rankings. Add the numbers for each value to see which values are important to the group. Discuss why people ranked the values as they did.

honesty	recognition	peace	freedom
justice	altruism	nature	family
equality	self-sufficiency	friendship	health
compassion	community	success	

2. What value is implied by each of the following well-known sayings? For instance, the proverb "Give a man a fish and you feed him for a day; teach a man to fish and he'll eat forever" advocates the value of education.

Different strokes for different folks.	Stop and smell the roses.
A penny saved is a penny earned.	Haste makes waste.
Where there's a will, there's a way.	Look before you leap.
What goes around comes around.	Pretty is as pretty does.

3. Discuss the values implied by these sayings from other cultures.[2]

Even a sheet of paper has two sides. (Japanese)	Shrouds are made without pockets. (Yiddish)
Bury the hatchet beneath the root of the tree. (Native American)	Unjustly got wealth is snow sprinkled with hot water. (Chinese)
One does evil enough when one does nothing good. (German)	One head cannot hold all wisdom. (Maasai)

4. Bring in examples of current ethical dilemmas from news sources such as newspapers, television, or the Internet. Discuss the examples in terms of the criteria under "Choose a Responsible Course of Action" beginning on page 418.

5. Reruns of television shows and movies present moral dilemmas that earlier generations faced. Share with the class an episode or a movie that presents a moral dilemma and explain different sides of the controversy. Or explain two sides of an ethical dilemma you have faced.

6. Select an industry or profession—maybe the tobacco industry, medical profession, food industry, or politics. Read a few news stories and discuss possible ethics violations.

7. Which of the defense mechanisms on page 423 have you or someone you know used? Share one example with your classmates.

Your Turn

1. Write a personal creed. Find a quiet place, and take notes about your values and their importance to you. Think about ethical decisions you have made and what those decisions say about you. Write your code as an essay, a poem, or a letter.

2. Write an ethics statement for the career you plan to enter. Then look up a code of ethics from a company in your field. The Center for the Study of Ethics in the Professions publishes codes from different fields. How does your code compare to one you find from an actual company?

3. In a small group or as a class project, write a code of ethics for your class. Consider those values that promote proper classroom behavior and optimal learning. Publish your code on the classroom bulletin board or on the school's Facebook page.

4. What value(s) or belief(s) motivate the people in the following scenarios? Are the people acting ethically? Explain.

   a. An amputee who served in Iraq said that despite his disability, he wants to return to Iraq to serve his country.

   b. An employee takes $25 from the petty cash fund to pay for a movie. The employee returns the money the next day.

---

[2]See http://wiseoldsayings.com for these and other aphorisms.

c. Norm shares an idea for an advertising slogan with another employee, who then passes it along to the supervisor as her own. Norm never reveals the idea was his originally and permits his coworker to take the credit.

d. Olga, a middle-aged mother of three, supervises a young crew of help desk personnel, five men and two women. When the men's jokes become a little racy, Olga simply but firmly reminds them, "Gentlemen, this is not a bar and ladies are present. Keep the language G-rated." The conversation then becomes more respectful.

5. Analyze the following ethical dilemmas using relevant questions and criteria from in the chapter. What advice do you have for Jayden and Susan? Discuss possible solutions and test them using the criteria beginning on page 423 under "Choose a Responsible Course of Action."

a. Jayden is a chemist at a pharmaceutical plant. Part of quality control is to check samples of each drug for purity and potency. Jayden notices that the person in charge of pulling the samples, Becca, does not test every drug, turning her attention to other tasks instead. When Jayden asks Becca about it, she replies, "What's your problem? I've got too much to do to keep up with all of them. We've never found a bad sample anyway." To complicate the matter, Jayden used to date Becca, having recently broken up with her. "Maybe Becca's right," he thinks. "We're all pretty careful." What should Jayden do?

b. It is December 10, and Susan Petrov has a big decision to make. She is the chief executive officer of Chesterson Refrigeration, a small company with U.S. and overseas locations that makes refrigerators and freezers. Because sales have dropped, the plant, which employs 786 workers, must lay off 240 employees if it is to remain open. Some employees are near retirement, a large number have worked for the company for ten years or more, some are college students, and some are legal immigrants. Susan is hoping that sales will pick up next summer. Limited funds are available to use as severance pay, and a few scholarships are available for retraining. How should Susan handle the situation? What is the most ethical way to decide who gets laid off? When should the layoffs begin? Is there anything Susan can do to make the situation better? When and how should she announce the layoffs?

6. Look for possible defense mechanisms at work in the following predicaments. What are the central conflicts in each case? What might happen if Gil and Cisco do nothing? Suggest possible solutions. Test those solutions using the criteria beginning on page 418 under "Choose a Responsible Course of Action."

a. Gil is a freshman at North Central State. He has been helping Tazim, a classmate who has been struggling in their calculus class. Tazim wants to sit next to Gil during the final exam so Tazim can check his answers against Gil's. Gil is not concerned, thinking he is not the one who is cheating; he is just taking the exam. What are the consequences if Gil lets Tazim check a few answers? What should Gil do?

b. Cisco and Val are medical assistants at Tremont Hospital. Cisco has noticed Val is often late to work. She also calls in sick more than she used to. She has a new boyfriend who has a reputation for drinking and using drugs. Cisco notices Val has lost weight, and she is not her usual bubbly self. One day Cisco sees her nervously eyeing the medicine cart. He walks the other way and thinks, "Her problems are not my concern. Maybe she is just working too hard." What might be going on? What should Cisco do?

7. Imagine you are part of a start-up company in manufacturing, bioengineering, construction, publishing, or some other endeavor. The company is located outside the United States—perhaps Mexico, India, or China. Write commitment statements to appear on the company web portal for three of these topics: treatment of employees, environmental concerns, safety, treatment of customers, confidentiality, conflict of interest, or equality.

Community Connection

1. Visit a local business, charity, hospital, or wellness center. Ask someone in a position of authority to describe the ethical climate there.

Write a short informative report on what you found. If the organization has a written creed or mission statement, ask if you can have a copy.

2. Ask five senior citizens to rank their values using the list in item 1 of "Build Your Foundation" on page 427. Ask them to explain their rankings. Then ask five people under the age of 20 to rank and explain their values. What differences do you see in the values the two generations provided? Prepare a short written report to present to your class.

EXPLORE THE NET

The Ethics Resource Center conducts independent research and publishes articles on its website for institutions interested in maintaining high standards of ethics. After browsing the Center's resources, read one resource and share three relevant pieces of information with your classmates.

Works Cited

Baker, Mallen. "Johnson & Johnson and Tylenol—Crisis Management Case Study." *Mallen Baker's Respectful Business Blog*. 8 Sept. 2008. mallenbaker.net/article/clear-reflection/johnson-johnson-and-tylenol-crisis-management-case-study. Accessed 5 May 2009.

Baron, Jessica. "John J. Reilly Center: Science, Technology, and Values Releases 2015 List of Emerging Ethical Dilemmas and Policy Issues in Science and Technology." University of Notre Dame. 8 Dec. 2014. reilly.nd.edu/news-and-events/news/the-reilly-center-for-science-technology-and-values-releases-2015-list-of-emerging-ethical-dilemmas-and-policy-issues-in-science-and-technology/. Accessed 16 Jan. 2016.

Baucus, Melissa S. and Janet P. Near. "Can Illegal Corporate Behavior Be Predicated? An Event History Analysis." *Academy of Management Journal* 34.1 (1991): 9–36.

Cooney, Peter and Supriya Kurane. "Target to Pay $10M in Settlement over Data Breach." *Las Vegas Review Journal*. Reuters. 19 Mar. 2015. www.reuters.com/article/us-target-settlement-idUSKBN0MF04K20150319. Accessed 15 Feb. 2016.

Ethics Resource Center (ERC). 2013 *National Business Ethics Survey*. 2013. www.ethics.org/ecihome/research/nbes. Accessed 11 Jan. 2016."Five Keys to Reducing Ethics and Compliance Risk." n.d. *Ethics Compliance Initiative* (ECI). www.ethics.org/resources/free-toolkit/code-of-conduct. Accessed 24 Feb. 2016.

Hotten, Russell. "Volkswagen: The Scandal Explained." Business. *BBC News*. 10 Dec. 2015. www.bbc.com/news/business-34324772. Accessed 11 Jan. 2015.

Lerner, Carolyn. "Improving VA Accountability: Examining First-Hand Accounts of Department of Veterans Affairs Whistleblowers." Testimony to U.S. Senate Committee on Homeland Security and Governmental Affairs. 22 Sept. 2015.

Meyerson, Bernard. "Top 10 Emerging Technologies of 2015." *Scientific American*. 4 Mar. 2015. www.scientificamerican.com/article/top-10-emerging-technologies-of-20151/. Accessed 8 Feb. 2016.

Raftery, Heather and Frank L. Holder. "Business Fraud: Culture Is the Culprit." *FTI Journal*. 23 Sept. 2014. ftijournal.com/article/business-fraud-culture-is-the-culprit. Accessed 11 Jan. 2016.

United Nations. *Universal Declaration of Human Rights*. Article 12. 10 Dec. 1948. Accessed 3 July 2017. www.un.org/en/universal-declaration-human-rights/.

United States. Equal Employment Opportunity Commission. "Laws Enforced by the EEOC." *Title VII of the Civil Rights Act of 1964*. n.d. www.eeoc.gov/laws/statutes/. Accessed 10 Feb. 2016.

Wagner, Dennis. "The Doctor Who Launched the VA Scandal." *The Republic*. 21 September 2015. www.azcentral.com/story/news/arizona/investigations/2014/05/31/va-scandal-whistleblower-sam-foote/9830057/. Accessed 11 Nov. 2015.

Wigland, Jeffrey. Interview. *60 Minutes*. CBS. New York. 4 Feb. 1996. Television.

Wilshaw, Rachel. "How the Behind the Brands Campaign Has Driven Change in Corporate Policy." *Oxfam Policy and Practice Blog*. 2 Nov. 2015. policy-practice.oxfam.org.uk/blog/2015/10/how-the-behind-the-brands-campaign-has-driven-change-in-corporate-policy. Accessed 12 Feb. 2016.

16 TECHNICAL READING

Goals

- Explain the difference between technical reading and literary reading
- Preview and anticipate material before you read
- Use strategies for reading technical passages

Terms

acronyms, p. 441
annotating, p. 438
anticipate, p. 433
background knowledge, p. 437
formal outline, p. 439
graphic organizers, p. 440
informal outline, p. 439
literary reading, p. 433
pace, p. 437
previewing, p. 433
technical reading, p. 433
technical vocabulary, p. 441

Write to Learn

How does a science or computer textbook differ from a work of literature? Do you read scientific or technical material differently from the way you read literature? If so, how? Do you like to read? Why or why not? How often do you read scientific or technical information? How do you remember what you read? Write a journal entry addressing these questions.

FOCUS on Technical Reading

Read Figure 16.1 on the next page and answer these questions:

- What features of technical writing do you recognize in the passage?
- What has the reader done to interact with and understand this passage?
- What kind of information has the reader noted?

What If?

How might the model change if . . .

- The passage included more technical vocabulary?
- The information in the passage was part of a presentation on satellites?
- The passage included a couple of graphics?

Satellites Have Become Important Tools in Ocean Exploration   *How?*

The National Aeronautics and Space Administration (NASA), organized in 1958, has become an important institutional contributor to marine science. For 4 months in 1978, NASA's *Seasat*, the first oceanographic satellite, beamed oceanographic data to Earth. More recent contributions have been made by satellites beaming radar signals off the sea surface to determine wave height, variations in sea-surface contour and temperature, and <u>other information</u> of interests to marine scientists.

Satellites IMPT tool

such as ?

① The first of a new generation of oceanographic satellites was launched in 1992 as a joint effort of NASA and the Centre National d'Études Spatiales (the French space agency). The centerpiece of *TOPEX/Poseidon,* as the project is known, is a satellite orbiting 1,336 kilometers (835 miles) above Earth in an orbit that allows coverage of 95% of the ice-free ocean every 10 days. The satellite's *TOPography EXperiment* uses a positioning device that allows researchers to determine its position to within 1 centimeter ($1/2$ inch) of Earth's center! The radars aboard can then determine the height of the sea surface with unprecedented accuracy. Other experiments in this 5-year program include sensing water vapor over the ocean, determining the precise location of <u>ocean currents</u>, and determining <u>wind speed</u> and <u>direction</u>.

② *Jason-1*, NASA's ambitious follow-on to *TOPEX/Poseidon,* was launched in December 2001. Now flying 1 minute and 370 kilometers (230 miles) ahead of *TOPEX/Poseidon* on an identical ground track, its primary task is to monitor <u>global climate interactions</u> between the sea and the atmosphere. Its 5-year mission has been extended.

③ *AQUA*, one of three of NASA's next generation of Earth-observing satellites, was launched into polar orbit on 4 May 2002. It is the centerpiece of a project named for the large amount of information that will be collected about Earth's water cycle, including <u>evaporation</u> from the oceans; <u>water vapor</u> in the atmosphere; phytoplankton and <u>dissolved organic matter</u> in the oceans; and air, land, and water temperatures. *AQUA* flies in formation with sister *TERRA, AURA, PARASOL*, and *CloudSat* to monitor Earth and air....

?

NASA's "A-Train," a string of satellites that orbit Earth one behind the other on the same track. They are spaced a few minutes apart so their collective observations may be used to <u>build three-dimensional images of Earth's atmosphere, ocean surface, and land topography</u>. *amazing !*

NASA

A satellite system you can use every day? The U.S. Department of Defense has built the <u>Global Positioning System (GPS)</u>, a constellation of 24 satellites (21 active and 3 spare) in orbit 17,000 kilometers (10,600 miles) above Earth. The satellites are spaced so that at least four of them are above the horizon from any point on Earth. Each satellite contains a computer, an atomic clock, and a radio transmitter. On the ground, every GPS receiver contains a computer that calculates its own geographical position using information from at least three of the satellites. The longitude and latitude it reports are <u>accurate to less than 1 meter (39.37 inches)</u>, depending on the type of equipment used. Handheld GPS receivers can be purchased for less than US$70—most "smartphones" contain this technology. The use of the GPS in marine navigation and positioning has revolutionized data collection at sea.

Figure 16.1 Sample of Technical Reading Source: From Essentials of *Oceanography* by Garrison, 2009. Reprinted with permission of Brooks/Cole, Cengage Learning.

Writing @Work

Courtesy of Stephen Freas

Architecture & Construction

CareerClusters®
PATHWAYS TO COLLEGE & CAREER READINESS

Source: The Center to Advance CTE

Stephen Freas is a construction subcontractor in Winston Salem, North Carolina. He is a supervisor on job sites and manages small crews to build projects based on drawings provided by the general contractor. He writes contracts, e-mails with clients, and often consults manuals and building codes.

The contracts Stephen writes are more than just fine print to be skimmed and signed. "A contract lets the client know exactly what we're going to do—what materials and processes will be necessary, what those will cost, and what the potential risks are," says Stephen. "A detailed contract also prevents us from doing costly work for free."

Stephen's job requires him to do a great deal of technical reading. "Reading construction plans and technical manuals requires a physical engagement with the writing," he says. "In these texts, an action usually follows each sentence or image. This makes for slow but 'action-packed' reading that helps you accomplish something you had no idea how to do previously."

Stephen often combines information gleaned from several different pieces of technical writing in order to make proper decisions. For example, "Once, we built a handicap ramp to the specifications written by the contractor. Upon inspection, the city told us that the ramp did not meet its building code standards. I refused to rebuild the ramp until I read the city code myself. The code listed specifics such as ramp thickness; railing height; and, most important, ramp slope. I calculated that in order to meet city code specifications, the ramp needed to be three times longer than the contractor's original plan and, coincidentally, the same slope as the existing sidewalk."

Stephen credits his technical reading dexterity to countless hours of following instruction manuals for his car, photography, climbing, and other hobbies.

Think Critically

1. Why does Stephen consider construction plans and technical manuals to be "action-packed"?

2. Think about the completed handicap ramp from the point of view of Stephen, the general contractor, and the building inspector. What solution would work for everyone?

Printed with permission of Stephen Freas

Writing in Architecture and Construction

Building contractors plan, coordinate, and supervise construction projects. Writing consists of evaluating the job site and scope of work; designing specifications with accompanying photos; and creating bid documents, change orders, and general correspondence. Evaluations assess the feasibility of the project considering such things as removal of asbestos for renovations or placement of sewer lines for new construction. The scope of work pinpoints the responsibilities of the contractor. For example, the contractor may or may not be responsible for landscaping, depending on the agreement reached.

Putting in writing the exact building specifications and accompanying costs is an essential task for a contractor. For example, the description of the wooden steps should be precise and clear to prevent misunderstandings later: "A new set of timber-framed steps with hand rails (meeting the SC Residential Building Code) will be added within the porch to access the porch from the front door (to replace existing concrete steps." Change orders revise the initial plan when a homeowner wants to add something, such as a half bath, or when a problem arises that neither the contractor nor homeowner foresaw. Once the project is underway, the contractor's ability to convey clear instructions to workers is critical.

Estimating costs may be the most difficult part of the contractor's job. Contractors research all current material costs and subcontractors' estimates. They need a realistic understanding of the time to complete the project. Whether calculating time and materials or a turn-key contract price, builders estimate costs carefully and include a sufficient profit margin—or risk losing money.

16.1 TECHNICAL READING

Technical reading is distinguished by technical subject matter, specialized vocabulary, use of graphics, and descriptions of mechanisms and processes. Reading a technical text is different from reading a work of literature. **Literary reading** requires the reader to draw inferences—to read between the lines and interpret symbolic language. Technical documents, though, require the reader to grasp the logic of text packed with detailed and precise information. Those able to digest technical information quickly stay on top of the latest developments in their fields.

16.2 BEFORE YOU READ

Technical readers develop habits to enable them to read efficiently. The first tactic is to employ pre-reading strategies. To aid their comprehension, proficient readers familiarize themselves with the text before they read by previewing the material and anticipating the line of reasoning.

Preview the Material

Previewing warms up the mind for reading, just as stretching warms up the body for exercise. After previewing, you read with greater efficiency and retention because you know what to expect.

When previewing, skim the introduction to determine the subject. Turn headings into questions, **anticipate** and foresee the information to follow, and notice where information is placed. In a manual, for example, thumb through the pages to see where the schematics and descriptions of parts are located.

The example on the next page shows how one student previewed the sample passage on page 431 by anticipating the subject and turning the headings into questions.

Subject: The title "Satellites Have Become Important Tools in Ocean Exploration" and the first sentence suggest that the passage will discuss how satellites are used to study the ocean.

Questions: How are satellites used to study the oceans? What kind of data do satellites provide? How useful is this data?

Anticipate the Line of Reasoning

Knowing the patterns of thinking typically seen in technical passages will help you anticipate and mentally prepare for their logic. Most technical passages focus on

- A process or procedure (instructions or how something works)
- A cause/effect relationship (what makes something happen)
- A mechanism (what something looks like and what it's supposed to do)

Figure 16.2 shows a process description of air flow in coastal regions. This process description, however, also includes several cause/effect relationships. One action (the sunlight) results in a second action (warming the land and sea). Soon a chain reaction ensues (heat transfer to air which expands) and the process develops further.

Land breezes and sea breezes are small, daily mini-monsoons. Morning sunlight falls on land and adjacent sea, warming both. The temperature of the water doesn't rise as much as the temperature of the land, however. The warmer inland rocks transfer heat to the air, which expands and rises, creating a zone of low atmospheric pressure over the land. Cooler air from over the sea then moves toward land; this is the **sea breeze** (Figure 8.20a) The situation reverses after sunset, with land losing heat to space and falling rapidly in temperature. After a while, the air over the still-warm ocean will be warmer than the air over the cooling land. This air will then rise, and the breeze direction will reverse, becoming a **land breeze** (Figure 8.20b). Land breezes and sea breezes are common and welcome occurrences in coastal areas.

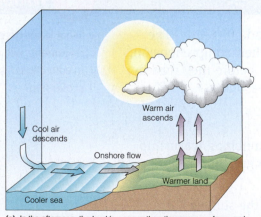
(a) In the afternoon, the land is warmer than the ocean surface, and warm air rising from the land is replaced by an onshore sea breeze.

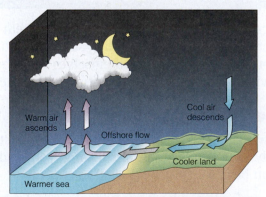
(b) At night, as the land cools, the air over the ocean is now warmer than the air over the land. The ocean air rises. Air flows offshore to replace it, generating an offshore flow (a land breeze).

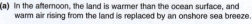
Figure 8.20: The flow of air in coastal regions during stable weather conditions.

Figure 16.2 Process Description Source: Tom Garrison and Robert Ellis, *Oceanography: An Invitation to Marine Science*, 9th ed. 2016.

Figure 16.3 shows another process: instructions for setting up and testing a network. The reasoning here is linear—a chronologically organized sequence of events. The steps are numbered to help the technician follow the sequence.

Do the following to set up and test the network:

1. Connect two computers using a crossover cable. Using the Network and Sharing Center, verify your network is up. What is the IP address of Computer A? of Computer B?
2. Join the two computers to the same home group. Then use Windows Explorer to view the files on the other computer shared with the home group.
3. Convert the TCP/IP configuration to static IP addressing. Assign a private IP address to each computer. What is the IP address of Computer A? of Computer B?
4. Verify you can still see files shared with the home group on each computer.

Figure 16.3 Step-by-Step Process Souce: *A+ Guide to Hardware: Managing, Maintaining, and Troubleshooting* by Jean Andrews, 6th ed. 2014.

Figure 16.4 shows cause-to-effect reasoning as the text explains how humans contribute to the extinction of species. Notice the use of words such as *cause, because,* and *as a result* to pinpoint the causes and effects.

Humans cause habitat loss, degradation of habitat, and habitat fragmentation, all of which can endanger a species. Humans also directly reduce populations and endanger species by overharvesting. Species introductions also cause declines of native species. In most cases, a species becomes endangered because of multiple factors. Sometimes, a decline in one species as a result of human activity leads to decline of another species.

Figure 16.4 Cause-to-Effect Relationships Source: From *Biology: The Unity and Diversity of Life* by Starr et al., Brooks/Cole, Cengage Learning, 2013.

Figure 16.5 shows a mechanism description that first names and then describes the function of each part of a light switch.

The most common type of switch used in residential wiring is called a single-pole switch. This switch type is used in 120-volt circuits to control a lighting outlet or outlets from only one location. An installation example would be in a bedroom where the single-pole switch is located next to the door and allows a person to turn on a lighting fixture when the person enters the room. Figure 2-40 shows the parts of a basic single-pole switch. The main parts include the following:

- Switch toggle: Used to place the switch in the ON or OFF position when moved up or down
- Screw terminals: Used to attach the lighting circuit wiring to the switch. On a single-pole switch, the two terminal screws are the same color, usually bronze
- Grounding screw terminal: Used to attach the circuit-grounding conductor to the switch. It is green in color
- Mounting ears: Used to secure the switch in a device box with two 6-32 size screws

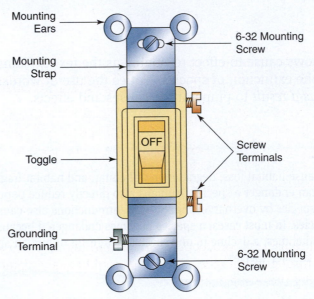

Figure 2.40: The parts of a single-pole switch.

Figure 16.5 Mechanism Description Source: Fletcher, Gregory. *Residential Construction Academy: Howe Wiring*, 4th ed. 2016, Delmar/Cengage Learning.

 STOP AND THINK 16.2

How do you preview a reading passage? What reasoning is typical of technical passages?

Discriminating readers use their critical-thinking skills to look out for information that is inaccurate, biased, sensationalized, or lacking in pertinent details.

When you use material from your reading, you have an ethical obligation to double-check its accuracy, looking for other sources that report the same findings. Publications that must be produced quickly—such as newspapers, magazines, and books on the latest technology—are prone to errors. Information published with few, if any, editorial guidelines—for example, some articles on the Internet and stories in tabloids—cannot be trusted.

The next time you find an Internet article that promises the fountain of youth or hands you a get-rich-quick scheme, be skeptical and remember: You cannot believe everything you read.

Think Critically

What might motivate people to publish articles that are not completely factual?

Communication
Dilemma

16.3 AS YOU READ

 **WARM UP**

What strategies do you currently use for reading and studying?

Because technical reading is different from other kinds of reading, you must approach technical reading with a plan. Good readers pace themselves and interact with the text by activating background knowledge, annotating the passage, repeating information aloud, understanding the vocabulary, paying attention to numbers, studying graphics, and adjusting to online media.

Pace Yourself

Runners **pace** themselves, proceeding slowly and regularly, to expend their energy evenly throughout a race. You, too, should pace yourself when you read by following these suggestions:

- Read slowly. Technical reading is packed with details. Make sure you take them all in.

- Read small amounts of information for short periods of time (perhaps 10 to 15 minutes). Then take a break, summarizing information and taking notes.

- Read the selection twice. During the second reading, you can see what you missed the first time. Also, a second reading allows you to see the transitions that denote how the parts of the passage fit together.

Activate Your Background Knowledge

Use the preview to activate your **background knowledge**, what you already know about the subject, to gain more meaning from the passage. The more you read in your technical subject, the better reader you will become in

Communication Technologies

Readability is a free app for your web browser and Android and iOS devices to create a more pleasant online reading experience. It can sync articles you come across online that you want to read later. It also turns a web page into a clean, simple, uncluttered view—without banners or ads to distract. The app gives you the option to archive and share articles as well as a way to change the settings to improve visibility.

Thinking Critically

How does a clean, uncluttered page enhance the reading experience?

that area. For example, if you regularly read auto mechanics magazines, you will comprehend a new article about a hybrid car better than someone who regularly reads computer magazines.

Knowledge of the subject and familiarity with vocabulary used in the subject gives you background knowledge on which to build a new understanding. You activate this knowledge when a concept or an example reminds you of something you already know.

As you read, allow your mind to form associations with knowledge you have already stored. When Adrienne previewed "Satellites Have Become Important Tools in Ocean Exploration," she immediately brought up images of a trip to SeaWorld and an exhibit on climate change. Plus her uncle works for NASA and had described the "A Train" to her when she was twelve. These associations piqued her interest in the subject.

Annotate the Reading Passage

Writing about what you read is important for retaining information. As you write, you activate different areas of the brain and, therefore, understand and retain more information. In this way, annotating jump-starts your learning.

Annotating a passage means taking your own notes and actively engaging with the text. When annotating a passage, use abbreviations, note what is significant, outline the passage, use graphic organizers, and/or answer questions.

Use Abbreviations

To help you write about what you read, devise or borrow a system of abbreviations for marking information. Here are a few examples:

IMPT or !	important information
EX or ex	example
∴	math symbol for therefore
b/c	because
?	questions; don't understand
① ② ③	items in a sequence

Note What Is Significant

Take notes on a technical passage by summarizing sections and writing the main ideas in your own words. Also note any specialized vocabulary, answers to questions you posed during the preview, descriptions of processes, and cause-and-effect reasoning. Mark segments you do not understand so you can reread, ask questions, and seek clarification.

If you own the book or article, you can mark important information with annotations, your handwritten notes, in the margins. If you prefer to take notes in a notebook, write the same information there. The opening sample on page 431 shows a technical passage with a student's annotations using short phrases, symbols, abbreviations, and underlining.

Consider an Outline

Figure 16.6 shows a **formal outline**, which is set with Roman numerals, numbers, and a system of letters, for the oceanography passage.

Satellites Have Become Important Tools in Ocean Exploration

I. Major NASA satellites in ocean exploration
  A. TOPEX/Poseidon 1992
    1. Accuracy to within 1 cm of Earth's center
    2. Data on sea height, water vapor, ocean currents, winds
  B. Jason-1 2001
  C. AQUA 2002
    1. Flies with sister satellites
    2. Measures Earth's water cycle
  D. GPS technology

Figure 16.6 Formal Outline

Figure 16.7 shows an **informal outline**, a less structured system, for the same material.

Satellites Have Become Important Tools in Ocean Exploration

NASA Satellites

TOPEX/Poseidon 1992
  – Satellite positioning within 1 cm of Earth's center
  – Data—height of sear surface, water vapor, oceans currents, winds
Jason-1 2001
  – Data—climate interaction
AQUA-2002
  – 1 of 4 satellites
  – Data—Earth's water cycle
GPS technology

Figure 16.7 Informal Outline

Both outlines help the reader see major divisions in the passage and serve as effective summaries.

Consider Graphic Organizers

Some students draw **graphic organizers** to map the relationships among ideas by using circles, blocks, and lines. A circle or block represents the central idea. Lines between circles or blocks show how other parts of the topic relate to the central idea. Figure 16.8 illustrates how one student presented topics visually.

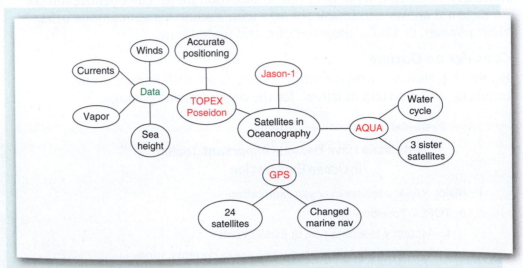

Figure 16.8 Graphic Organizer

Answer Questions

Answering questions can be a helpful note-taking tool. The questions can be your own preview or your instructor's study guide, or they may come from end-of-chapter exercises. Or the questions can come from a conversation you have with a classmate or friend as you discuss what you've read.

Figure 16.9 shows written answers to questions. One student answers the questions posed during the preview and then moves to the end-of-chapter questions.

Answers to questions in preview:

1. Satellites beam radar signals off the surface of the ocean. String of satellites spaced a few minutes apart build three-dimensional images of Earth.
2. Satellites provide information about ocean currents, water vapor, marine productivity, wind direction and speed, and sea height. GPS satellites provide information about location and position.
3. Satellites provide huge amounts of data that would be otherwise be difficult to gather and offer current information about our planet.

Answer to an end-of-chapter question:

How does the GPS work? Satellites (21 active; 3 spare) orbit 10,600 miles above Earth. At least 4 are above the horizon at any time from any place on Earth—each with a computer, an atomic clock, and a radio transmitter. Each GPS receiver on Earth has a computer to calculate its position (accurate to within 1 meter) from three satellites in longitude and latitude.

Figure 16.9 Answers to Questions

Repeat More Difficult Notes Aloud

Hearing what you have written and read in silence may help you retain difficult information. Try repeating the following notes aloud:

> Freud divided the personality into the id, the pleasure principle; the ego, the reality principle; and the superego, the morality principle. Freud divided the personality into the id, the pleasure principle; the ego, the reality principle; and the superego, the morality principle. Freud divided the personality into . . .

After reading and rereading this passage, a student can probably name the three parts of the personality and describe each one. If the student is still confused, talking to someone about Sigmund Freud's psychoanalytic theory of personality development might help her retain the concepts.

Understand the Vocabulary

Sometimes you can figure out **technical vocabulary**, specialized terms, from the context—from a description or an example. Other times the term is defined in the text—after a linking verb, in parentheses, or in an appositive.

Figure 16.10 shows examples of several terms defined in a text. Note that some words, such as *alley* and *husband,* do not mean the same thing for the production specialist or conservationist as they do for you. Even terms that are familiar may be used in different ways for the technical reader. In addition, notice the use of **acronyms** (letters that stand for a long or complicated term or series of terms).

A parasite lives in or on another living organism called its host, feeding on the host without killing or benefiting the host.

A market is a group of buyers and sellers interested in transacting business over a particular good or service. A competitive market is a market with sufficient buyers and sellers so that the market price is not significantly impacted.

The alley, or space between two columns of text, is too wide.

Environmentally conscious citizens are careful to husband our natural resources and protect those resources for future generations.

Childhood vaccines include the MMR (measles-mumps-rubella) vaccine and IPV (inactivated polio vaccine).

Figure 16.10   Vocabulary Defined in a Text

When you cannot determine the vocabulary from the context, use a dictionary or a glossary provided in the document to look up the term. Another option is to ask an expert to define a word for you.

Some definitions need more than a phrase or a sentence and extend to a paragraph or more. Figure 16.11 illustrates an extended definition of the term *desert*. The examples and description help the reader gain a more complete understanding of the term.

Deserts receive an average of less than 10 centimeters (4 inches) of rain per year. They cover about one-fifth of Earth's land surface and many are located at about 30° north and south latitude, where global air circulation patterns cause dry air to sink. Rain shadows also reduce rainfall. For example, Chile's Atacama Desert is on the leeward side of the Andes, and the Himalayas prevent rain from falling in China's Gobi desert.

Lack of rainfall keeps the humidity in deserts low. With little water vapor to block rays, intense sunlight reaches and heats the ground. At night, the lack of insulating water vapor in the air allows the temperature to fall fast. As a result, deserts tend to have larger daily temperature shifts than other biomes.

Desert soils have very little topsoil . . . , the layer most important for plant growth. The soils often are somewhat salty, because rain that falls usually evaporates before seeping into the ground. Rapid evaporation allows any salt in rainwater to accumulate at the soil surface.

Figure 16.11 Extended Definition Source: From *Biology: The Unity and Diversity of Life* by Starr et al., Brooks/Cole, Cengage Learning, 2013.

Learn to Read Graphics

Be prepared to think visually when you begin to read a technical passage. Draw a picture of what you are reading—on paper or in your mind. To read graphics included in the text, make sure you understand the purpose of each type of graphic. Then closely study the graphic as well as the author's explanation of it. How does the graphic support the author's message? What does the author want you to notice about the graphic?

Understand the Purpose of the Graphic

Become familiar with the purpose of each type of graphic. When you see a diagram, for example, know that the purpose is to help you see what an object looks like. You can then read the graphic with that purpose in mind. Recall the following graphics and their purpose:

- Tables organize numerical and verbal data in rows and columns.

- Pie graphs show how the whole is divided into parts.

- Bar graphs contrast sets of data.

- Line graphs show trends over time or relationships among data.

- Flowcharts present various processes, including decision-making processes or the hierarchy of an organization.

- Gantt charts present a timeline for a project.

- Diagrams and photos show what something looks like.

Read the Graphic Closely

After you have finished noting what kind of graphic you are reading and what its purpose is, read the graphic closely, noticing everything about it.

- Read the title to determine the subject matter of the graphic.

- Look for keys or legends to see what each part represents.

- Read the callouts to identify parts.

- Read the *x* axis and the *y* axis to see the relationship among the sets of data.

Next, relate the information in the graphic to the author's discussion of the graphic. What does the author want you to notice about the graphic? If you are asked to remember a diagram, you may want to draw the diagram yourself.

A number of the technical reading passages in this chapter illustrate the importance of graphics. Figure 16.2 uses a picture and arrows to represent the creation of land and sea breezes. Figure 16.5 includes a diagram of a light switch to make the description easy to follow. Each graphic presents technical information efficiently and clarifies the explanation with words.

Pay Attention to Numerical Data

Resist the temptation to read too quickly through discussions that contain numbers. Note the number $1,231.49, while only six digits long, actually stands for nine words—one thousand two hundred thirty-one dollars and forty-nine cents. Even though digits save space on the page, take time to process the digits mentally as words.

Focus on Ethics

When she received her new Trust Bank Credit Card, Elena reviewed the Terms and Conditions, written in 8-point type. She read the disclosures on page 1 carefully, which covered the interest rate and various fees. On page 2 she read about overdraft protection and payment calculation. By the end of page 2, she skipped notices to Ohio and Wisconsin residents—since she lived in Michigan. Elena was tired of reading but did see the bold-faced warning—that terms could be changed at any time by the credit card company. Page 4 had some good news: If her phone was stolen or damaged, her new credit card company would pay for a new one.

A few months later, Elena's phone was stolen. When she contacted Trust Bank about a new phone, she was told the company would not cover the cost, unless she had used the credit card to pay her phone bill. Elena argued with the representative who told her to review the Terms and Conditions— and there it was, on the last page in the middle of a long paragraph: "This protection is available only when cell phone bills are paid from your Trust Bank Credit Card." Elena was livid. She had refused replacement insurance from her cell phone provider because she thought she had coverage through Trust Bank.

Think Critically

Who is responsible for the misreading of the terms? What role did Elena play? Is Trust Bank to blame—at all?

Adjust to Online Media

Reading on devices is on the rise—on tablets, from 30 percent in 2012 to 41 percent in 2015, and on smart phones, from 20 percent in 2012 to 54 percent in 2015 (qtd. in Maloney). Reading on a device is a different reading experience from reading on paper. Some studies suggest reading comprehension drops when reading on a device, but more recent studies suggest there is not much difference, although people do seem to remember more of what they read in print (DuVall).

Modify Reading Strategies

People tend to read printed material sequentially with few distractions, from one page to the next. It's a tactile experience—turning pages, writing notes, flipping back to reread. With print media, people claim the page structure helps them remember information more easily by recalling where they read it (page in the middle of the book, top right, for instance). For these reasons, many prefer print media when comprehension and deep learning matters.

Reading online, on the other hand, is nonsequential. Readers jump from one hyperlink to another, from text to video or to another website. Interaction with the screen forces a reader to stop concentrating on the passage long enough to make decisions about where to go next. He can be easily thrown off track by a compelling headline enticing the reader but disappointing him once the link is opened. To lessen the disruption,

- Train yourself to read each page in the same way—top, left, down, and across, for instance

- Skim by noticing headlines and key words and *then* slow down for something of interest

- Resist the urge to jump to a hyperlink until you've thought about whether it is likely to lead to useful information.

There's little doubt that reading on devices is harder on the eyes. Kindle's electronic ink mimics print reading with its sharply defined lines and is easier to read. Other devices have a backlit LCD screen, similar to a computer monitor. Some express concern that light from these devices may, over time, harm the retina. More probably, the eyestrain from computer vision syndrome (CVS) is the bigger concern. To reduce eyestrain when reading on a screen,

- Follow the 20/20/20 rule: Every 20 minutes, look 20 feet away for 20 seconds.

- Sit 20–28 inches away from the monitor

- Adjust computer settings to reduce glare, change type size, or resolution

- Consider setting a lamp close by to lessen the contrast between the bright light from the screen and any darkness surrounding the screen

- Rest your eyes on the top 1/3 of your monitor to avoid crooking your neck downward.

Other forms of electronic reading include instructional video and audio files. If your preferred learning style is visual or auditory, you may benefit from "reading" instructions on YouTube or Audible. Visual learners can view a YouTube video on hanging sheetrock and have the process down. Auditory learners can listen to a lecture on tax exemptions and remember much of what was said. Sometimes written instructions accompany multimedia files, and readers can read them while viewing or listening.

Most electronic media give readers the option to rewind, reverse, replay, reread, or back track to assist recall or comprehension. To help you remember what you've read online, bookmark passages and continue to use the strategies mentioned in this chapter: take notes, re-read silently and aloud, understand new vocabulary, summarize information at regular intervals, or talk to someone about what you've learned.

Evaluate Online Information

Because it's easy to post anything online, information can be unreliable; therefore, it's important to evaluate a site for its credibility:

- **Author:** Do you know who the author is? Does this person have the credentials to write intelligently about the subject? Does this author's name appear in other publications? Did the author use a bibliography? *When the author's credibility is in doubt, the information cannot be trusted.*

- **Content:** Is the language clear and error-free? Is the content developed enough for your purposes? Does the content agree with other information you have found? If the content disagrees with other information, is it well supported? Is the tone objective or overly persuasive, one-sided, or emotionally charged? *Mistakes, incendiary language, and strong sales pitches are signs the information is problematic.*

- **Website:** Does the site look professional? Is it organized? Do the links work? Information constantly changes, so check to see if it is updated regularly. *Sites that look thrown together or are not regularly updated may not be reliable.*

Look at the domain extensions: Government and educational sites ending in .gov or .edu are bound to standards of accuracy and thoroughness. Judge a .com site more carefully. It could be a reputable news agency or reliable primary source information, *but sometimes these sites present a biased view.*

STOP AND THINK 16.3

What are the technical reading strategies? How do strategies for reading online differ from strategies for reading on paper? What questions help you evaluate the credibility of an online source?

16 CHAPTER REVIEW

Summary

1. Technical reading is different from literary reading in its subject matter and its emphasis on precision, specialized vocabulary, use of graphics, and descriptions of mechanisms and processes.

2. Before you read technical documents, preview the material and anticipate the line of reasoning.

3. As you read technical documents, pace yourself, activate your background knowledge, annotate the passage, repeat difficult notes aloud, make sure you understand the vocabulary, read the graphics, pay attention to numerical data, and adjust to online reading material. Evaluate online sources for credibility.

Checklist

- Have I previewed the material I am preparing to read?

- Have I anticipated the line of reasoning? Is the reasoning a process or procedure, a cause-and-effect relationship, or a mechanism?

- Have I paced myself?

- Have I activated my background knowledge?

- Have I annotated the reading passage with notes, an outline, a graphic organizer, and/or answers to questions?

- Have I considered repeating difficult notes aloud?

- Do I understand the vocabulary?

- Have I read the graphics?

- Have I paid close attention to numerical data?

- Have I adjusted strategies for an online medium and evaluated my source?

Build Your Foundation

1. How did you read technical passages before you read this chapter? Will you change anything about how you read technical passages now? Explain.

2. Compile a list of three terms in a technical field with which you are familiar. Ask your classmates if they understand the vocabulary.

3. Conduct a poll of twenty people to find out what kind of reading each person prefers—technical or literary. What kind of technical articles do they read? How do the results of your poll compare to your reading preferences?

4. Analyze your textbooks or technical magazines. Isolate one chapter or one article. How much of the vocabulary is new to you? How much technical vocabulary is in the passage? How many graphic aids are there? Do some of the passages use numbers? If so, how? Which parts would be clearer if you repeated them aloud? How would you organize this information if you had to learn it for a test?

5. Locate the technical word and the part of the sentence that defines that word in these sentences adapted from *A + Guide to Hardware* by Jean Andrews.

   a. If an easier path (one with less resistance) is available, the electricity follows that path. This can cause a short, a sudden increase in flow that can also create a sudden increase in temperature—enough to start a fire and injure both people and equipment.
   b. A rectifier is a device that converts alternating current to direct current.
   c. A multimeter is a more general-purpose tool that can measure several characteristics of electricity in a variety of devices.
   d. An extractor, a spring-loaded device that looks like a hypodermic needle, can be used to pick up a screw that has fallen into a place where hands and fingers can't reach.
   e. A SIM (Subscriber Identity Module) card is a small flash memory card that contains all the information you need to connect to a cellular network.
   f. A ground bracelet, also called an antistatic strap or ESD (electrostatic discharge) bracelet, is a strap you wear around your wrist that is attached to the computer case, ground mat, or another ground so that ESD is discharged from your body before you touch sensitive components inside a computer.
   g. Fiber-optic cables transmit signals as pulses of light over glass strands inside protected tubing.
   h. VoIP (Voice over Internet Protocol) is a TCP/IP protocol that manages voice communication over the Internet.

Your Turn

1. Read the excerpt on the next page from *Principles of Economics.* Pick out the technical reading elements.

   a. Do you see a description of a process? If so, where?
   b. Do you see cause-and-effect reasoning? If so, where?
   c. Do you see specialized vocabulary of the discipline? If so, which terms? Are the terms defined in the text so that you understand what they mean?
   d. Look at the graphic closely. Interpret the graphic and explain how you read it.

DEMAND

To an economist, the term demand—whether the demand for tickets or the demand for roses—has a very specific meaning. **Demand** is a relationship between two economic variables: (1) *the price of a particular good* and (2) *the quantity of that good that consumers are willing to buy at that price during a specific time period,* all other things being equal. For short, we call the first variable the **price** and the second variable the **quantity demanded**. The phrase *all other things being equal,* or *ceteris paribus,* is appended to the definition of demand because the quantity that consumers are willing to buy depends on many other things besides the price of the good; we want to hold these other things constant, or equal, while we examine the relationship between price and quantity demanded.

Demand can be represented by a numerical table or by a graph. In either case, demand describes how much of a good consumers will purchase at each price. Consider the demand for bicycles in a particular country, as presented in Table 1. Of course, there are many kind of bicycles—mountain bikes, racing bikes, children's bikes, and inexpensive one-speed bikes with cruiser brakes—so you need to simplify and think about this table as describing demand for an average, or typical, bike.

PRICE	QUANTITY DEMANDED	PRICE	QUANTITY DEMANDED
$140	18	$240	5
$160	14	$260	3
$180	11	$280	2
$200	9	$300	1
$200	7		

Table 1 Demand Schedule for Bicycles (millions of bicycles per year)

Observe that as the price rises, the quantity demanded by consumers goes down. If the price goes up from $180 to $200 per bicycle, for example, the quantity demanded goes down from 11 million to 9 million bicycles. On the other hand, if the price goes down, the quantity demanded goes up. If the price falls from $180 to $160, for example, the quantity demanded rises from 11 million to 14 million bicycles.

. . . The **law of demand** says that the higher the price, the lower the quantity demanded in the market; and the lower the price, the higher the quantity demanded in the market.

Source: Taylor and Weerapana, *Principles of Economics*, 2010, 53–54. Used with permission of Cengage Learning.

2. Take notes from the passage using on the following page suggestions from the chapter.

   a. Preview the passage, making annotations. Either photocopy the passage and write on it or take notes on a separate sheet of paper.
   b. Outline the passage (formally or informally) or draw a graphic organizer.
   c. Answer the questions posed during your preview and read them aloud.

3. Onlinenewspapers.com provides links to many newspapers, journals, and specialty publications from all over the world. Locate a newspaper from another state or country. Then find an article that you find interesting, and share highlights of the article with your class.

4. In small groups, discuss your experiences reading with tablets and smartphones. What does your group read on devices? How often? How does this experience compare to reading printed material? Is one preferred over the other? Pull up three websites on topics of interest. Evaluate them for reliable content using questions posed in the chapter.

Labor is the mental and physical capacity of workers to produce goods and services. The services of farmers, assembly-line workers, lawyers, professional football players, and economists are all *labor*. The labor resource is measured both by the number of people available for work and by the skills or quality of workers. One reason nations differ in their ability to produce is that human characteristics, such as the education, experience, health, and motivation of workers, differ among nations.

Entrepreneurship is a special type of labor. Entrepreneurship is the creative ability of individuals to seek profits by taking risks and combining resources to produce innovative products. An *entrepreneur* is a motivated person who seeks profits by undertaking such risky activities as starting new businesses, creating new products, or inventing new ways of accomplishing tasks. Entrepreneurship is a scarce human resource because relatively few people are willing or able to innovate and make decisions involving greater-than-normal chances for failure. An important benefit of entrepreneurship is that it creates a growing economy.

Entrepreneurs are the agents of change who bring material progress to society. The birth of the Levi Strauss Company is a classic entrepreneurial success story. In 1853, at the age of 24, Levi Strauss, who was born in Bavaria, sailed from New York to join the California Gold Rush. His intent was not to dig for gold but to sell cloth. By the time he arrived in San Francisco, he had sold most of his cloth to other people on the ship. The only cloth he had left was a roll of canvas for tents and covered wagons. On the dock, he met a miner who wanted sturdy pants that would last while digging for gold, so Levi made a pair from the canvas. Later, a customer gave Levi the idea of using little copper rivets to strengthen the seams. Presto! Strauss knew a good thing when he saw it, so he hired workers, built factories, and became one of the largest pants makers in the world. As a reward for taking business risks, organizing production, and introducing a product, the Levi Strauss Company earned profits, and Strauss became rich and famous.

Source: Tucker, Irvin B. *Economics for Today*, 9th ed. 2017, Cengage Learning.

Community Connection

1. Interview two people who work in technical fields. Find out how much they read on the job and what strategies help them understand and remember the information they read. Write your interview in question-and-answer format.

2. Find an article to read to a shut-in, a visually impaired person, or a group of school children. Annotate your text and become familiar with the vocabulary beforehand. Write a short trip report to summarize your experience.

EXPLORE THE NET

Time magazine's online publication (Time.com) is a reputable source for current news. Select an article online, accessing three hyperlinks within the article as you read. Jot down the key points in each article. Describe your experience. Were the hyperlinked articles and videos distracting or useful? What is your reaction to the sponsored advertisements? Did jotting down the key points help you remember what you read?

Works Cited

DuVall, Jeremey. "How to Improve Your Reading Retention on Any Device." *Crew Blog*. 07 August 2014. crew. co/blog/reading-retention/. Accessed 23 Feb. 2016.

Maloney, Jennifer. "The Rise of Phone Reading." *Wall Street Journal*. 14 Aug. 2015. www.wsj.com/articles/ the-rise-of-phone-reading-1439398395. Accessed 25 Feb. 2016.

TECH WRITING TIPS

THE INSIDE TRACK

YOU ATTITUDE

With the exception of the science lab report, most technical writing should be reader-centered rather than writer-centered. A reader-centered approach, or *you* attitude, attempts to look at situations from the reader's perspective instead of the writer's perspective. The *you* attitude points out advantages to the reader and makes him or her more likely to accept what the writer says.

Use the *you* attitude to persuade your audience to think or act in a certain way. For example, you might send an e-mail to your supervisor asking for time off, a letter to a newspaper editor opposing a proposed city curfew, or a message to a dry cleaner asking for a reduction in your bill because your clothes were not clean when you picked them up.

Notice the difference between the *I* or *we* attitude and the *you* attitude in the following example. The *you* attitude sounds friendlier and more positive. The *you* attitude stresses how a customer can benefit from buying a home from Mountain View Homes. Using the *you* approach is psychologically smart as a motivator, and it makes a good sales pitch.

Manufactured Home Dealer

I or *we* attitude:

Do we, at Mountain View Homes, have deals! Our 14 × 70 single-wides have been marked down 20%. And our 14 × 80s can be purchased with a rebate of $1,000!

You attitude:

You can find a real deal at Mountain View Homes. You can purchase our 14 × 70 single-wides at 20% off the regular price. And you can receive a rebate of $1,000 on a brand new 14 × 80.

To use the *you* attitude, simply consider the situation from your reader's viewpoint. What is the advantage to him or her? Then, where appropriate, add more *you*'s and *your*'s to your message and take out some of the *I*'s, *we*'s, or company names. Point out the benefit of your message to your reader.

THE INSIDE TRACK: *YOUR TURN*

1. Rewrite these sentences to reflect a stronger *you* attitude. Remember, you cannot eliminate uses of *I*, *we*, and company names, but you can slant the writing to be more reader-centered. Add any information that will help the reader see the advantages.

   a. We will ship the rest of your order next week.

   b. Powell Insurance Company is reliable. We have been in business at the same location for more than 50 years.

c. I want you to take the conversational Spanish classes for several reasons.

d. Your overdue account must be paid within 30 days. Otherwise, we will give you a poor credit rating and stop taking your orders.

e. We do not have your order in stock. We will notify you when we do.

f. I expect you to be in the office by 8 a.m. for several reasons.

g. I do not think you should choose clothes that are difficult and time-consuming to take care of.

h. We want all students to stay on school grounds during lunch so they will not be late for class.

i. We have marked down all furniture for our moving sale. We would rather sell the furniture than move it. Everything must go!

j. You are required to take 30 semester hours of general college courses.

2. Rewrite the following announcements to reflect a stronger *you* attitude.

a. Our Volunteer Club has many items for sale. Members are selling backpacks, DVDs, and club T-shirts that have never been worn. One member is bringing boxes of science-fiction novels. We are selling game cartridges and earrings. The earrings are handcrafted by one of our members. We have a set of golf clubs, a TV, and a chest of drawers. These items and many more can be seen at 2323 East Third Street on Saturday morning at 6 a.m. We hope to raise enough money to help victims of the recent flood in our area.

b. Mama's Kitchen, a hip new home-cooking restaurant, is proud to announce its grand opening at 2349 Michelin Circle on Saturday, January 31, 20—. Renowned chef and owner Daria O'Doole says that her restaurant will offer the best blue plate specials in town, and she wants everyone to come in and try her meatloaf, which is made from a recipe handed down to her and originating with her great-grandmother. Ms. O'Doole wants to keep her blue-plate specials under $10 because she says her mother taught her to be frugal.

TONE

Tone refers to the emotional overtones that words emit. Words not only provide information but also convey emotions. Because human beings are both rational and emotional creatures, tone can affect the way readers react to words.

Unlike the objective tone in technical reports, letters give writers an opportunity to show a range of emotions—from apathy to warmth, from enthusiasm to anger. While some unanswered complaint letters may appropriately display anger, most letters you write should convey a positive, upbeat, and reader-centered tone.

Read the following passage. Describe the tone. Which words contribute to that tone?

Chemical Processing Division Members:

Do not be late for the hazmat training on Tuesday, September 8. The session is scheduled for 8–11 A.M. The trainer has another appointment after our training. Arrive promptly at 8 A.M. or earlier. If you are not seated by 8 A.M. in Room TR2045, you will find the session closed to you. Then you will be required to earn your certification at a later session.

Here you see that the short, terse style creates a negative tone. The words *Arrive promptly* and *If you are not seated by 8 A.M.* may spark anger in some employees who perceive that they are being treated like children. The following version is improved.

Chemical Processing Division Members:

We are pleased you have registered for hazmat training on Tuesday, September 8, 8–11 A.M.

Please plan to arrive in Room TR2045 no later than 8 A.M. Our instructor must conduct the session on schedule so he can begin his afternoon training on time.

Thank you for your cooperation. If you have any questions, please contact . . .

A positive tone makes people more likely to cooperate. You can create a positive tone by using the following suggestions:

- **Avoid Negative Words.** A number of words carry such negative messages that you should try to avoid them. Words such as *never, failed, cannot,* and *regret* often can be replaced with more positive words.

- **Use Tact.** Choose your words carefully. Be sensitive to their impact. Instead of saying that you do not like a particular sweater, try saying that the sweater reflects a style different than your preferences.

- **Accentuate the Positive.** Be optimistic. Most people prefer to do what is right and best for all concerned. Remember that you can think of the cup being half full (accentuating the positive) instead of half empty (accentuating the negative).

- **Remember Your Manners.** Say *please* and *thank you.*

Note the differences in the following examples. What did the writer do to change a negative tone in the left column to a more positive tone in the right column?

Do not sign the evaluations.	Please keep the evaluations anonymous.
If you fail to sign the form, your return will be late.	Please sign the form to avoid unnecessary delays.
We insist that you include a deposit.	Please enclose a deposit.
We received your fax in which you claim that we sent you damaged goods.	Your faxed letter of July 5 indicates that you received damaged goods.
If you decide to visit our museum . . .	When you visit our museum . . .
Your essay is disorganized.	Concentrate on organizing your ideas.

THE INSIDE TRACK: *YOUR TURN*

Make the following statements more user-friendly by rephrasing them to sound more positive.

1. Your outfit is too loud for the commercial. Mr. Carlson will not like it. It will clash with the background.

2. We told you to be at work by 8 A.M. sharp!

3. You claim to have had a flat tire on the way to the Springfield warehouse.

4. We cannot allow you to make inappropriate comments.

5. You have had more than enough time to pay the small amount shown on the enclosed bill.

6. If you cannot attend the rehearsals on time, you cannot speak with the product development team.

7. Our sweatshirts will not shrink.

8. You will not encounter any problems with our software.

9. Do not walk on the grass. Stay on the sidewalks!

10. If you do not contact us before November 17, we will not have time to process your request.

11. You are working too fast to be accurate. You are making careless errors.

12. Our stores are never closed.

13. If you decide to contribute to the children's fund, your money will never be spent unwisely.

PARALLELISM

In writing, sets of words or phrases are parallel because they use the same grammatical structure. Your ability to recognize parallel structure depends on your ear and your knowledge of grammar. Words, phrases, and clauses joined by coordinating conjunctions and used in lists should be parallel.

Parallel Words, Phrases, and Clauses

Can you hear that these sets of words are not parallel?

1. I like running, biking, and to paint.

2. He told us to wash the developer pan and that we must sweep the floor.

3. I like to inventory the stock, list the overruns, and to read orders reports.

The grammatical structure of these sentences may help you see where the break in parallel structure occurs:

    S V   Gerund   Gerund   Infinitive

1. I like running, biking, and to paint.

In Sentence 1, the infinitive breaks the parallelism because the list started with *-ing* words, or gerunds.

    S   V Indirect object   Infinitive phrase   Dependent clause

2. He told us to wash the developer pan and that we must sweep the floor.

In Sentence 2, the dependent clause breaks the parallelism because the list started with an infinitive phrase.

    S V   *to* + verb/object   verb + object   *to* + verb/object

3. I like to inventory the stock, list the overruns, and to read orders reports.

In Sentence 3, *to* was not repeated in each part of the series, so the parallelism was broken.

Here are improved versions of the preceding sentences:

1. I like running, biking, and painting.
I like to run, bike, and paint.

2. He told us to wash the developer pan and to sweep the floor.
He told us to wash the developer pan and sweep the floor.
He told us that we must wash the developer pan and sweep the floor.

3. I like to inventory the stock, to list the overruns, and to read orders reports.
I like to inventory the stock, list the overruns, and read orders reports.

Parallel Lists

The itemized list below is not parallel. Which parts of the list are more alike than other parts?

At the next Spanish Club meeting, we will discuss these items:

- Next year's budget
- Which person to nominate for chair
- Implementing our attendance policy
- Whether to donate money to the senior class project
- Elections

The above list is not parallel because one item is a noun preceded by an adjective, two are listed as questions, one starts with an *-ing* word, and one is a simple noun. To make the list parallel, begin each part of the list the same way. Use all *-ing* beginnings, all questions, all nouns, or all nouns preceded by adjectives.

The following list makes the entire group parallel with the first item by repeating the adjective(s) + noun structure.

- Next year's budget
- Chair nominations
- Attendance policy
- Senior class project donations
- Upcoming elections

Parallel Order

Using the same order of information also makes parts of a resume parallel.

For example, if you present the employment experience of Position 1 as Name (of business), City/State (of business), Dates (of work), and Job Title, you must present the experience of Position 2 in the same order. Do not put dates first, name second, address third, and so on.

The following example shows three job descriptions that use correct parallel order.

Taylor Computer Manufacturing; Erie, PA; July 2009–Present; Project Manager

Hix Landscaping Service; Pittsburgh, PA; May 2008–June 2009; Assistant Landscape Technician

BookWorld Publishing Services and Discount Books; Pittsburgh, PA; October 2005–March 2008; Salesclerk

THE INSIDE TRACK: *YOUR TURN*

1. Refer to the unparallel list at the top of the previous page . Make the list parallel to the second item, "Which person to nominate for chair." Then make the list parallel to the third item, "Implementing our attendance policy." Which of those two lists do you prefer? Why?

2. Make a list of your morning routine. Set up your list with this statement: *Every morning I follow the same routine.*

3. Make the activities in the following list parallel:

   - Chairperson of Booster Club
   - Delivered Meals on Wheels to shut-ins
   - United Way: accepted pledges
   - Recorder for Debate Team

4. Fill in the blank with an appropriate word or phrase to improve parallelism for each sentence.

   a. The fitness instructor ran a marathon, _____, and won a weight-lifting contest.

   b. The following people will be receiving computer upgrades this year: Leo Vasquez, Chief of Operations; Carla Willoughby, Quality Assurance Director; and Lucy Alva, _____.

   c. Shoe cobblers liked stiletto heels because the tips needed frequent repair, doctors warned against stiletto heels because they caused sprained or broken ankles, and _____.

5. Correct these sentences for faulty parallelism.

   a. The letter directed us to preview the contracts, sign them, and to return them promptly.

   b. The rules were fair but that they could not be enforced.

   c. Margarita and Jerome were told to be at the office at 2 P.M. and that they had to refill the rental car with gasoline.

   d. She had trouble explaining her position and which decision to make.

   e. The new product line is noted for its durability, its attractiveness, and it is reliable.

6. Revise the following sets of job descriptions to correct the faulty parallelism.

   a. Baylor Industries, Huntington, WV. June 2007 to February 2010—. Sales Representative: called on customers and kept accounts.

   b. Sales Director. January 1999 to August 2009. United Sales Corporation, Beckley, West Virginia. Duties included supervising sales personnel, training new personnel, and calling on customers.

   c. Cookeville, TN, May 2002 to September 2008 Murphy's Art Supply, Salesclerk, ordered art supplies, created company newsletter, arranged displays, and wrote proposal to acquire funds to open a coffee shop in the store.

   d. Branyon Fine Arts Group, taught piano and voice lessons, Cookeville, TN, October 2006 to present, served as music teacher.

ECONOMY

Good technical writing is economical. As good food is rich in nutrition and low in fat and sugar, good technical documents are rich in meaning and low in unneeded words and phrases. Technical writers who think of their readers try to write clearly and concisely so that documents take less time and trouble to read. As a writer, you also save production time and costs when your writing is economical. The following tips will help you cut unnecessary words and phrases:

- *Avoid* **There is/There are, Here is/Here are,** *and* **It is** *Sentence Openings*. Revise sentences starting with *There is* or *There are* to give the sentence a subject at the beginning, where it will get more attention, followed by an action verb. *There is* and *There are* sentences are not wrong, but they are weak sentences that waste words. Getting directly to the point of the sentence is better. Look at the following examples:

WEAK:	There are some vegetarians who eat dairy products and eggs but not meat, fish, or poultry.
IMPROVED:	Some vegetarians eat dairy products and eggs but not meat, fish, or poultry.
WEAK	Here are the sketches for your sun room in the attached portfolio
	IMPROVED The sketches for your sun room are in the attached portfolio..
WEAK:	There are nine candidates applying for the position of Office Manager .
IMPROVED:	Nine candidates applied for the position of Office Manager.

To revise these sentences, (1) cross out the *There is/There are, Here is/Here are,* or *It is* opening. (2) Move the subject of the sentence to the opening position. (3) Create an action verb, sometimes from a word that follows the subject.

Likewise, sentences should not start with *it* unless the *it* refers to a specific person, place, or thing already mentioned. Revise the sentence to give a stronger meaning without the unnecessary *it*. Refer to the following examples:

WEAK:	It gives me great pleasure to introduce our new quality assurance officer, Rebecca Beckett.
IMPROVED:	I am pleased to introduce our new quality assurance officer, Rebecca Beckett.
WEAK:	It is the thermostat that received an electrical surge.
IMPROVED:	The thermostat received an electrical surge.

- **Delete Unnecessary Modifiers.** In the following examples, the modifier placed before each word is unnecessary. These words do not need modification. For instance, can something be very essential? No, something is either essential or not essential. Here are other common examples of unnecessary modifiers:

highly satisfactory	extremely competent
very rare	slightly expensive
barely visible	perfectly clear

- **Avoid Redundancy.** Redundancy is needless repetition. Redundancy adds words but does not add meaning. Omit unnecessary repetition. You can probably think of other redundant expressions to add to the following list.

refer back	advance warning	cancel out
blue in color	large in size	the state of Nevada
the month of June	basic fundamentals	3 A.M. in the morning

- **Reduce Needless Phrases, Clichés, and Overused Expressions.** Writers sometimes pad their writing, intentionally or unintentionally, with unnecessary phrases. Do not use an entire phrase when a single word will do. Each phrase listed below would be better replaced by its single-word equivalent after the equal sign.

due to the fact that = because	prior to = before
in the event that = if	at a later date = later
be aware of the fact that = know	at a rapid rate = rapidly
in this modern day and age = today	in many cases = often, frequently

Many of the overused expressions listed below may sound familiar to you because you have read or heard them often. Although these clichés may be easy to write because they jump from your memory, they are not exciting to read. Each of the following clichés is followed by a possible replacement.

every effort will be made—we will try   attached herewith is—attached

as per your request—as you asked   upon receipt of—having received

as a general rule—generally   under separate cover—separately

I will be most grateful if—Please   afford an opportunity—allow

for the reason that—because   based on the fact that—because of

- **Replace *-ion* Nouns with Stronger Action Verbs.** Use of *-ion* nouns often adds words without advancing meaning. These nouns can usually be omitted, making the sentence shorter and stronger.

  Notice in the improved sentences that the *-ion* nouns have been turned into action verbs.

WEAK:	The Food and Drug Administration, under public pressure, took into consideration the adoption of several new Alzheimer's medications.
IMPROVED:	The Food and Drug Administration, under public pressure, considered adopting several new Alzheimer's medications.
WEAK:	Heidi came to the conclusion that the report was a summation of court procedure.
IMPROVED:	Heidi concluded that the report summarized court procedure.

- **Avoid Strings of Prepositional Phrases.** Some prepositional phrases may be necessary to join ideas, but too many of them can be distracting. Whenever possible, revise sentences to remove excessive prepositional phrases.

WEAK:	The drop in deposits by students in their accounts at the bank is of great concern for management.
IMPROVED:	Decreasing student bank deposits concerns management.
WEAK:	The EPA office in Anchorage plans to send out warnings to residents about possible contamination from lead in the water.
IMPROVED:	The Anchorage EPA office will warn residents about possible lead-contaminated water.

- **Remove Unneeded *That*.** In many sentences with a relative clause beginning with *that,* writers can omit *that* without changing the meaning.

With that:	The camera operator thought that the set was too dark.
Without that:	The camera operator thought the set was too dark.

  Read the sentence aloud without *that*. If the sentence makes sense and the meaning does not change, you can omit *that*.

THE INSIDE TRACK: *YOUR TURN*

1. Revise the following sentences to omit the *There is/There are* and *It* openings.

   a. There are ten cases of welding rods on order.

   b. It is certain that the cable to connect the CD-ROM to the computer is missing.

   c. There is a solution that strips the silver from the film to create the photographic contrast.

   d. It is phosphate that encourages growth of algae in the river.

   e. It gives me great anxiety knowing that the federal inspectors may come any day.

2. Revise the following sentences to eliminate unnecessary modifiers, redundancies, and needless phrases.

   a. The new packaging, which is oval in shape, has proven quite satisfactory in tests in the northeast market.

   b. The CAD software is 5% faster than it was prior to the upgrade.

   c. Designers should be aware of the fact that hidden cameras record their production process.

   d. In this modern day and age, we expect companies to actively support green initiatives.

   e. As a general rule, the attorney general ensures victims that every effort will be made to protect their privacy.

3. Revise these sentences to replace the *-ion* nouns with stronger action verbs.

   a. The bulletin provides a description of a closed electrical circuit.

   b. The committee took our amendment into consideration.

   c. The continuation of Naoko's project depends on the financial support of UpStart.

   d. The Research Division presented a recommendation that all toxic wastes be disposed of through Standard Corporation.

   e. The synthetic fibers make an action like natural filament.

4. Revise the following sentences to omit clichés and unnecessary prepositional phrases.

   a. As per your request, I am sending through FedEx ground the multi directional HDTV antenna you ordered.

   b. The combinations of fragrance seem to sell well in areas of large metropolitan population in the United States.

   c. The toner cartridge for the printer needs to be replaced with care.

   d. With precision and swiftness, the photographer loaded the film into the camera.

   e. I will be most grateful if you can afford me an opportunity to interview for the vacant position in your accounting area.

5. Revise the following paragraphs, using the skills you learned in this section to make the writing economical and easier to comprehend.

   a. There are more than 2,600 automatic external defibrillators being recalled by Good Heart Inc. It has been learned that the United States Food and Drug Administration (FDA) has received reports of electrical problems of the machine in the electrode pads for placement on the chest. Although very rare, this problem could make the use of the device dangerous.

   b. Defibrillators are used by emergency responders, amateur and professional, to treat sudden, unexpected, and unforeseen cardiac arrest. Good Heart Inc. representatives said every effort will be made to locate customers and replace defective units. Purchasers may refer back to their invoices; if the model number is BC 4039–BC 5011, in many cases, these machines are included in the recall. These units were manufactured from January in the year of 2010 through August in the year of 2011.

   c. While the recall is voluntary, the FDA is considering further investigation and a mandatory recall at a later date. It is not known how many people have been adversely affected by malfunctions of automatic external defibrillators from Good Heart Inc. `

USING NUMBERS

The following rules are generally accepted as guidelines to help you decide when to write numbers as figures and when to write numbers as words in technical documents.

1. Generally, use figures for numbers 10 and above. Use words for numbers one through nine.

> Oleander Community College presented 22 partial scholarships and 15 full scholarships to first-year students.
>
> Two computers and four of the operators were relocated to Operations.

2. Use figures when a series contains numbers above and below 10.

The client's estate included 498 acres of land, 173 paintings, 3 mansions, and 15 thoroughbreds.

3. Use figures when several numbers (including fractions) are presented in a single sentence or in several related sentences.

The delivery is lacking 2 metric tons of steel I-beams, 3/4 case of stainless steel bolts, 1/8 of the paint needed, and 1 spool of electrical wire.

4. Use figures for units of measurement. Note that the unit of measurement may be expressed as a word, an abbreviation, or a symbol.

18 meters	5 1/3 cups	4.25 liters	55 mph
5.5 centimeters	66 2/3 feet	75 MHz	35 mm film
0.05 margin of error	14.4 K baud	32"	8" × 10"

5. Use figures for fractions and decimals presented with whole numbers.

5 1/3   66 2/3   72.6   10.25

6. Use figures to express exact amounts of money.

$181.95   8¢ $0.95

7. Use figures for data presented in tables and illustrations.

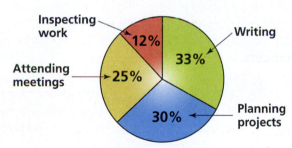

Figure 1 Time Spent on Tasks

8. Use figures for addresses and dates.

Route 5 Box 182   103 East Maple Street   January 3, 1865

9. Use figures to express age.

3 years old   a man in his 20s   an 18-year-old woman

10. Use figures for identification numbers.

The correct number is 378-18-3555.

The engine number is JEMH00347WE99678.

11. Use figures for one of two numbers written next to each other.

     two 42-cent stamps   16 two-liter bottles

12. Use figures to indicate time not expressed with o'clock.

     8 A.M.   12:10 P.M.

13. Use figures for statistics and scores.

     The odds were 3 to 1 in the district attorney's favor.

     The Cavaliers won the game, 96–89.

14. Use figures for page and volume numbers.

     Turn to page 45 in volume 2 of your manual.

15. Use figures and words for very large numbers (over 6 digits).

     $6 trillion   4 million people   5.3 billion years

16. Use words at the beginning of a sentence. Rewrite awkward sentences so that the numbers are written as figures within the sentence.

     Nine thousand seven hundred and sixty-six citizens signed the petition.

     The petition contained 9,766 signatures.

17. Use words for indefinite or approximate numbers.

     More than one hundred scientists attended the symposium.

     Approximately 50 frogs were examined for the parasite.

18. Use words for fractions not connected to whole numbers.

     Approximately three-fourths of the nurses have been vaccinated.

19. Use words for ordinals below 10. Use figures and last letters for ordinals over 10.

     third base   ninth inning   10th person   21st birthday

THE INSIDE TRACK: *YOUR TURN*

1. In each pair of sentences [(a) and (b), (c) and (d), and so on], choose the sentence that illustrates the best use of numbers and figures.

    a. The credit union is offering 8.25% interest for CDs.

    b. The credit union is offering eight and a quarter percent interest for CDs.

    c. AG Goldsmiths reported the theft of eighteen diamonds over two carats each.

    d. AG Goldsmiths reported the theft of 18 diamonds over two carats each.

    e. 5,031 people reside within the city limits.

    f. Five thousand thirty-one people reside within the city limits.

    g. The bus departs at three in the afternoon.

    h. The bus departs at 3 P.M.

    i. Over 1/2 of the laboratory rats were infected.

    j. Over one-half of the laboratory rats were infected.

2. Using the guidelines from this section, rewrite the following passages to use numbers and figures appropriately.

    a. *Penguin* is the common name for fifteen species of flightless marine birds. They live on four continents in the Southern Hemisphere. One penguin, the Galapagos, lives within six degrees of the equator. Penguins can swim through the water at speeds of up to twenty-five miles per hour. The largest species, the emperor penguin, ranges from three to four feet tall. The smallest, the Adelie, stands about two feet tall.

    b. On the twenty-third of February in the year two thousand and seven, one hundred forty-two mallards were tagged off the coast of Florida. For five years, researchers tracked approximately seventy of the mallards over three hundred and ninety-seven miles. The ducks survived in temperatures as low as minus ten degrees Celsius. A report was distributed to twenty-seven agencies in seven states. The research cost six thousand forty-five dollars and fifty-six cents. It is estimated that seven and one half million mallards inhabit the southeastern area of the United States. Biologists estimate that ninety percent of the mallards follow predictable patterns of migration.

CLARITY

Good technical writing is clear. To make your writing clear, follow these suggestions:

1. Use traditional *S-V-MODIFERS, S-V-OBJECT,* or *S-V-COMPLEMENT* word order.

    - *Adequate:* Behind Tray 2 and beside Bin 3 is where the blockage occurred.
    - *Improved:* The blockage occurred behind Tray 2 and beside Bin 3.
    - *Adequate:* The production order she wrote.
    - *Improved:* She wrote the production order.
    - *Adequate:* Hectic was the ambassador's schedule.
    - *Improved:* The ambassador's schedule was hectic.

2. Write moderately short sentences (12–24 words).

- *Adequate:* The registration procedure begins with the student making an appointment with his or her adviser, at which time the adviser and student will discuss the student's career goals, placement test scores, and transcripts to determine a schedule of classes that the adviser will enter into the computer and that the student will pay for before the registration period ends—that is, unless the computers are down, in which case the student must come back another time.

- *Improved:* The registration procedure begins with the student making an appointment with his or her adviser. At this time, the adviser and student will discuss career goals, placement test scores, and transcripts to determine a schedule of classes. Next, the adviser will enter the schedule into the computer. The student will pay for the classes by the end of the registration period. If the computers are down, the student must come back.

3. Place the main idea (the subject or topic) first.

- *Adequate:* The board of directors agreed to open three new staff positions as well as fill five vacant slots. The board also voted last week to invest the money awarded in the lawsuit in facility upgrades. Now the board is considering a motion to halt dividends for the next two years. The board of directors favors company growth over dividends.

- *Improved:* The board of directors favors company growth over dividends. The board also voted last week to invest the money awarded in the lawsuit in facility upgrades. The board of directors agreed to open three new staff positions as well as fill five vacant slots. Now the board is considering a motion to halt dividends for the next two years.

4. Use active voice—unless you have a good reason to use passive voice.

- *Adequate:* The new computers were purchased by the school board.
- *Improved:* The school board purchased the new computers.

(Also see The Inside Track: Active Voice and Passive Voice on pages 463–466.)

5. Use parallel structure.

- *Adequate:* Orientation consisted of the following activities:
  - Meeting our adviser
  - Tour the campus
  - Placement tests

- *Improved:* Orientation consisted of the following activities:
  - Meeting our adviser
  - Touring the campus
  - Taking placement tests

(Also see The Inside Track: Parallelism on pages 453–454.)

6. Use first person (*I* or *we*) whenever possible.
- *Adequate:* The defective parts were returned to the AM Machining Company.
- *Improved:* We returned the defective parts to the AM Machining Company.

7. Choose precise nouns and verbs.
- *Adequate:* Last night the security guard sounded an alarm.
- *Improved:* On Wednesday, October 16, 20—, at 8:53 P.M., Juwan Minnifield, the security guard on duty at the southeast entrance of Whitley Laboratory, reported smoke coming from under the Electronic Control Room door.

THE INSIDE TRACK: *YOUR TURN*

1. The following sentences lack clarity. Revise these sentences to make the meaning clearer.

    a. The speed limit is somewhere between 50 and 60 mph.

    b. The tickets are to be distributed sometime next week by the committee.

    c. In came my father to tell me the good news.

    d. Maintain good health by exercising regularly, eating a balanced diet, and for goodness sake, keep a positive attitude.

2. Using the suggestions from this section, rewrite the following paragraph to make the sentences and the message clearer.

    First, he hoed a small area until the dirt was broken up. Then he raked out the clumps of grass, pulling up those stubborn weeds. The fertilizer was applied lightly and worked into the ground with a hoe. Next, plastic stuff was placed all over the plot of land and stuck to the ground at intervals of 3 feet to keep the grass from growing and to allow the rain to drain through and bring needed moisture to the roots. Then holes were cut in the plastic stuff, not too far apart. François planted some flowers through the plastic stuff into the ground. Then over the plastic stuff and around the plants pebble rocks were placed to hold down the plastic and so the area would look neat. François made planting a garden look easy.

ACTIVE AND PASSIVE VOICE

Which of these sentences do you prefer? Why?

Active Voice: Mariah hit the ball during Saturday's game.
Passive Voice: The ball was hit during Saturday's game by Mariah.

Most people prefer the first sentence because it is direct, clear, and interesting. As a result, it is easier to read than the second sentence.

Look at the verbs in each sentence. The active voice sentence uses only one verb. The passive voice sentence uses two verbs: the verb *to be* + the past participle of another verb. (The verb *to be* includes *is, am, are, was, were, to be, been,* and *being.*) The past participle is simply the past tense form of the verb that uses a helping verb.

Look at the subject in each sentence. In the active voice sentence, the subject is the doer of the action. In other words, Mariah performs the action: She hits the ball. In the passive voice sentence, the subject is being acted upon. In other words, the ball was acted upon (was hit) by Mariah.

Use active voice when you want to emphasize an action. Because active voice sentences are more direct, you should write in active voice unless you have a good reason for writing in passive voice. Sometimes there are good reasons to use passive voice, as the following rules explain.

1. If you do not know the doer of the action, passive voice gives you the opportunity to leave out the doer.

    Passive: The money was taken.
    Active: The thief took the money.

2. Maybe you know who the doer is but do not want to say. Sometimes passive voice can help you be diplomatic or polite.

Passive:	Your blueprints have been delayed.
Active:	We lost the blueprints.
Passive:	The microscope was broken.
Active:	You broke the microscope.

3. Scientific writing calls for an objective tone, which is hampered when the doer of the action is included in the sentence. Scientific writing focuses on the process, not the person.

Passive: The fluid volume was increased 20% with the addition of sodium.

Active: The fluid volume increased 20% with the addition of sodium.

Active: The researcher increased the fluid volume 20% by adding sodium.

4. Sometimes the receiver of the action is more important than the doer. You can emphasize the receiver by using passive voice. Ads, in particular, like to stress *you* as the receiver of services that companies can offer.

Passive: Ted Kennedy was elected to the U.S. Senate for nine terms.

Active: The people of Massachusetts elected Ted Kennedy senator for nine terms.

Passive: You are kept up-to-date with Newsweek.

Active: Newsweek keeps you up to date.

- **Changing Voice: Passive to Active.** Look for two-word passive voice verbs—the verb *to be* and the past participle. If you see that a report contains too many passive voice sentences, convert the passive verbs to one-word active verbs by (1) placing the doer as the subject of the sentence, (2) adding a doer that is not included in the sentence, or (3) turning the simple subject of the verb into a direct object.

Passive: The car was repaired by the mechanic.

Active: The mechanic repaired the car.

Passive: The window was replaced last month.

Active: Calvin replaced the window last month.

- **Changing Voice: Active to Passive.** If your science report calls for more passive voice construction, decide what process, material, or mechanism you want to emphasize and place that item in the subject position. Make sure your verb includes *to be* + the past participle. Or if you would prefer not to point an accusing finger at a particular person, focus the sentence on the object that received the action.

Try changing the direct object of the verb into the simple subject of the passive voice verb.

Active: The scientist added a cooling agent to the compound.

Passive: A cooling agent was added to the compound.

Active: Phillipa completed the company's annual report yesterday.

Passive: The company's annual report was completed yesterday.

THE INSIDE TRACK: *YOUR TURN*

1. Find the passive voice verbs in the following sentences. Then change these passive voice sentences to active voice.

   a. The accident report is submitted by the manufacturing engineer.

   b. The minutes for Wednesday's meeting were lost on the computer.

   c. The computerized key to my office has been deactivated.

   d. The Area VI Tennis Classic is being sponsored by the Alpha Deltas in May.

   e. The blueberry bushes were ordered by my assistant, who is managing the landscaping project.

   f. According to our parents, my brother and I are needed to run errands for the family business this Saturday.

   g. Jerry McGinty has been placed on inactive status by the coach.

   h. All plastics are required to be placed in recycling bins by order of the City Council.

   i. Thanksgiving dinner is being served at the shelter on Wednesday.

   j. With six weeks of consecutive shopping orders, coupons for free gas are offered by Lambert Food Stores.

2. Find the active voice verbs. Then change these active voice sentences to passive voice.

   a. John Hinkley shot President Reagan.

   b. The chemist introduced sulfuric acid to the mixture.

   c. Shelly Malone, your teacher's aide, sent three difficult students to the office last week.

   d. An unknown person robbed Mr. Miller's convenient mart last Thursday evening.

   e. Onyx Computer provides you with complete support.

   f. You waste fuel when you idle your car at stop signs.

   g. Balducci's invites you to shop the big sale.

   h. The technician in framing spilled glue on your portrait.

   i. Jensen Furniture's quality assurance staff thoroughly tested the lounge chair's durability.

   j. Helen finished the wedding cake two hours before the ceremony began.

3. Read the following memo. Consider the content and identify the audience. Decide which verbs should be active and which should be passive and revise accordingly.

TO: Salvadore Alvarez, Public Relations Director

FROM: Elenore Lucia, Crew Chief, Graphics

DATE: October 31, 20—

SUBJECT: Production Delay for Employee Appreciation Project

The artwork you requested for the Employee Appreciation display will not be ready for the November 15, 20—, deadline. While the graphics professionals usually are aware of scheduling, this time my assistant, Frank Stanwych, overlooked two other major projects.

Despite our problems, some of your requests will be completed on schedule. The two lighted stars can be hung from the skylight. The posters covered with employees' photographs may be printed. In addition, Erin Taft and Vince Delgado will produce the traditional Employees of the Year Awards booklet. The booklet will be available to visitors and staff beginning December 1.

GENDER-UNBIASED LANGUAGE

Technical writers should be sensitive to diversity in the workplace. One way to begin is to use gender-unbiased language.

1. Avoid biased language by choosing words that include both genders.

Use	Rather Than	Use	Rather Than
representative	Congressman	synthetic	manmade
firefighter	fireman	polite	ladylike
police officer	policeman	doctor	woman doctor
mail carrier	mailman or postman	nurse	male nurse
chair/presiding officer	chairman	people/humanity/human beings	mankind
supervisor/manager	foreman	synthetic	manmade

2. Avoid biased language by using pronoun references that include both genders.

The following sentence implies that all scientists are men:

Each scientist files his laboratory's OSHA report after completing his quarterly review.

Two ways to solve this problem are to (1) reword the sentence to omit any reference to gender and (2) include both genders.

   a. Each scientist files the laboratory OSHA report after completing the quarterly review.
   b. All scientists file their laboratories' OSHA reports after completing their quarterly review.
   c. Each scientist files his or her laboratory's OSHA report after completing the quarterly review. (Using *his or her* can be awkward when it is repeated in a number of sentences.)

3. Avoid biased language by referring to men and women in the same way when using courtesy titles in similar situations. The preferred title for women (unless you know the woman's preference) is *Ms.*

Use This	Not This
Darnell Griggs and Erica Stokes	Darnell Griggs and Erica
Mr. Barnes and Ms. Pedroza	Peter Barnes and Ms. Pedroza
Austin and Kara Peterson	Mr. and Mrs. Austin Peterson
Caroline and Anthony Russo	Caroline Russo and her husband

4. Avoid biased language in letter salutations by including both sexes. Of course, you should use the receiver's name if possible. When you cannot determine the receiver's name, these options may be used:

   a. Use a job title such as Dear Personnel Officer.
   b. Omit the salutation and complimentary close (simplified letter style).
   c. As a last choice, use either of the following: Dear Sir or Madam or Dear Madam or Sir (alphabetical).

THE INSIDE TRACK: *YOUR TURN*

1. In each pair of sentences [(a) and (b), (c) and (d), and (e) and (f)], select the sentence that uses gender most appropriately.

   a. The Human Resources Officer is responsible for notifying candidates of their interview day and time.

   b. The man in charge of the Human Resources Department is responsible for notifying each candidate of his interview day and time.

   c. The mailman is late, and I'm hoping for a response from Lucas Marthey and Julianna.

   d. The mail carrier is late, and I'm hoping for a response from Lucas and Julianna Marthey.

   e. A female pastor conducted the funeral service.

   f. An Episcopal pastor conducted the funeral service.

2. Revise the following sentences to eliminate biased language.

   a. Each of the paratroopers was trained to his maximum ability.
   b. Miss Maxine Faulkner, Fausto Diaz, and Kha'n Vu are listed as having senior security clearance.
   c. The woman doctor should begin her letter to the Swiss hospital administrator with *Dear Sir* because she does not know the administrator.
   d. Any businessman needs to be aware of his educational options.
   e. The nurse must record her observations on the patients' charts.
   f. All mankind is responsible for making the earth a cleaner, safer place to live.
   g. Mrs. Michelle Obama, Supreme Court Justice Sonia Sotomayor, and Al Gore appeared in the photograph.
   h. The foremen will file their reports with the CPD director each Friday.
   i. Did you ever want to be a fireman or a policeman when you were young?

3. Revise the following paragraph to avoid gender-biased language.

   To Whom It May Concern: Dr. Patrice Harbaugh has been an excellent female dentist for more than 20 years. Each of her colleagues sends his best wishes, and patients at Mirabelle Center will miss her. Her team members—Dr. Castillo, Miss Alice Lazar, and Theo and Melinda Baines—offer congratulations on her retirement.

EFFECTIVE TRANSITIONS

Like any good writing, technical documents need logical connections between ideas. These connections make writing smooth and improve readers' comprehension. The following four techniques help a writer achieve these logical relationships between ideas and between sentences and paragraphs:

- Repeated keywords
- Pronouns
- Parallel structures
- Transitional terms

Repeated Keywords

Repeated keywords often refer to the topic or important information in a document. They remind readers of what is significant in the discussion or what the document is trying to achieve. For example, if you were writing about lumber cut for housing construction, you might begin with the word *lumber* and later repeat that word or use synonyms such as *boards, logs, planks,* or *timber.*

Pronouns

While repeating keywords can improve coherence, using the same word over and over can become boring. Therefore, writers also use pronouns to tie ideas together. Read the following partial instructions to see how the pronouns connect ideas and improve coherence.

> When you are planning to paddle down a river, get an accurate large-scale map and mark the rapids on it. Study it and keep it handy. Rapids are caused by a drop in the riverbed, so remember that you might not see them when you approach.

The pronoun *it* refers to map, and the pronoun *them* refers to rapids. The difference in the singular *it* (*map* is singular) and the plural *them* (*rapids* is plural) keeps readers from becoming confused.

Parallel Structures

Writers also use parallel structures to link content within and between sentences. Like parallel lines, parallel structures in writing are aligned, meaning that words, phrases, and sentences are grammatically similar, as shown in the next pair of examples.

> Survey respondents preferred ice fishing, skiing, snowboarding, and skating.
>
> *not*
>
> Survey respondents preferred ice fishing, skiing, snowboarding, and to skate.

> As a parent, I care about the safety of my children. As a police officer, I care about the rights of individuals. And as a citizen, I care about getting criminals off the streets.
>
> *not*
>
> As a parent, I care about the safety of my children. The rights of individuals is important to me in my role as a police officer. Because I am a concerned citizen, I want to get criminals off the streets.

The repeated grammatical structure helps to connect ideas.

Transitional Terms

Transitional terms (or transitions), the fourth technique for improving coherence, are words or phrases that highlight the relationships between ideas.

Below is a list of some transitional terms you might use. The column on the left indicates the relationship the term implies in its connection.

Meaning	Transitional Terms
Addition	*also, in addition, moreover, furthermore, and, as well as, besides*
Contrast	*but, however, yet, nevertheless, on the contrary, on the other hand*
Time	*before, after, currently, afterward, during, later, now, recently, then, meanwhile, while, at the same time*
Emphasis	*in fact, of course, indeed, truly*
Example	*for instance, for example, to illustrate*
Sequence	*first, second, third, and so on; next; finally; last*
Cause and effect	*therefore, consequently, thus*
Similarity	*likewise, similarly, also, in the same way*

The following paragraph shows how transitional terms can be used to improve coherence.

This past summer I had guests from Sweden who told me about cooking in bed. <u>At first</u>, I thought my friend sat in bed while preparing vegetables. <u>No</u>, she told me that she literally cooks her food in bed <u>while she goes to the beach</u>. <u>For example</u>, she starts potatoes on the stove and <u>once the water is boiling</u>, removes the pot from the stove, places it in the bed, and surrounds it with blankets. The potatoes are done <u>when she returns a few hours later</u>. <u>However</u>, I would be concerned about bacteria growing during this kind of low-temperature slow cooking.

THE INSIDE TRACK: *YOUR TURN*

1. Identify transitional elements in the following passages.

   a. A thunderstorm is a process. It begins with warm air rising. The storm then feeds on moisture and heat. As the rising air becomes cooler, water drops form from the condensing vapor. A picture of the air currents inside a thunderhead could look like a nest of writhing snakes.

   b. In 1940, Comity's hired its first female employee. In 1948, Comity's made that employee the company president.

   c. The PTO shaft was slightly bent in the crash. Consequently, I cannot operate the conveyor belt.

2. Revise the following sentences to create parallel structure.

   a. With the new Najik, enjoy scanning that is faster, works more precisely, and that can be more economical than ever before.

b. First is the group that reacts to the trend by selling every energy stock in the portfolio. As a result of the trend, the second group responds with a threat to sell every energy stock in the portfolio.

c. First, select a single or double mat for the print, and then the picture will need a frame, and finally you must choose whether to use nonglare or
plain glass.

d. Security officers will be stationed in the following locations:
- In the entrance foyer
- The computing center
- The president's office will be heavily guarded
- Two officers will be on the roof of the manufacturing building.

e. According to some users, the Turbo 040 is the superior product; others say the best machine is the ChipStar.

3. Combine each of the following groups of short, choppy sentences into a single sentence by using transition strategies.

a. The veterinarian prescribed an anesthetic. The anesthetic was for the dog. The pharmacy could not fill the prescription.

b. Sound waves that hit a plain wall bounce back to distort the sound. Sonex-covered walls absorb sound waves that hit the walls. Absorbing these waves enhances the sound.

c. The problem with the collating machine is worn gears. The mirrors on the collating machine are scratched and are part of the problem. The collating machine's levers, which are bent, are a problem.

d. To apply for the position, job candidates must fill out an application form. They must fill out the form completely. The candidates must submit a resume. They must supply a list of three references.

GLOSSARY

A

abstracts short, concise versions of longer pieces of communication; include only the most important general information

academic writing the expository and persuasive writing done in academic circles; examples include personal essays, research papers, analyses, and arguments

accommodate to adjust; to change circumstances so that others will be more comfortable or more at ease

acronyms letters that stand for a long or complicated term or series of terms

adrenaline a stimulant; something that excites and creates extra energy

ambiguous more than one interpretation is possible; describes writing that means different things to different people

anecdote a humorous story

animation text or graphics that move

annotating handwritten notes, often placed in the margins of a document being read

anticipate to guess or predict before actually reading a passage what kind of reasoning it might present

appendix (plural, *appendixes*) usually the last element or special part of a formal report; a place to include documents, data, or graphics not necessary to the discussion in the report but perhaps helpful or interesting to the audience

archives collections or repositories of documents

artifact can be a document, video, tool, painting, sculpture, or any item representing a message created by and for human beings

asynchronous events occurring at different times in different locations

auditory related to the sense of hearing or perceived through the sense of hearing

B

background knowledge knowledge and vocabulary that a reader has already learned and then calls upon to better understand new information

bar cluster a bar graph with more than one bar for each measurement

bar graph a graph using a horizontal axis and a vertical axis to compare numerical data presented in rectangular bars

block letter style the letter style that aligns the return address, dateline, and closing at the left margin

blog a website with periodic news or commentary posted in reverse chronological order; short for *weblog*

buffer something positive written to soften bad news to come

C

callouts names of specific parts of a diagram that are connected to the diagram or drawing with lines

cautions statements designed to keep a person from harming the mechanism with which he or she is working

chart a drawing with boxes, words, and lines to show a process or an organizational structure

chronological resume a traditional resume that provides a history of employment and education in reverse chronological order

citations written indications of the sources for borrowed materials

close-ended questions questions that restrict the number of possible answers

co-authoring software allow several writers to author and edit a text synchronously (at the same time) or asynchronously (at different times in different locations)

code of ethics a written pledge to make responsible, moral decisions

collaborative writing writing with others in a group

conclusion the logical, inductive leap made after all of the details of an experiment are considered; what is learned from an experiment

concurrent testing determining the usefulness of a product or an activity by observing someone's performance while he or she is using the product or engaging in the activity

copyediting proofreading a document for correctness in spelling, grammar, and mechanics

corporate code of ethics a document stating a company's commitment to ethical behavior; includes core values, rules specific to the industry, and often penalties for violations

cover letter a letter accompanying a resume that highlights the applicant's strengths

criteria the plural form of *criterion;* the factors on which a decision is made; things to consider when making a decision

culture the special beliefs, customs, or values that are specific to a particular group of people or a particular region

D

dateline the feature of a press release that identifies the location of a story

decision flowchart a type of flowchart that uses symbols to indicate the critical steps in making a decision

deductive reasoning reasoning from the general to the particular

demographics defining characteristics of an audience; information about a group such as the age, sex, income, and educational level of its members

design elements considerations in writing a document that affect page layout; the way a document looks

diagram a line drawing

dignity a person's sense of self-respect

direct approach a presentation strategy in which the main idea is stated first, then the idea is explained and supported with details

direct quotation the use of borrowed ideas, words, phrases, and sentences exactly as they appear in the original source

discussion forum a website where users can discuss items of interest or get specific questions answered

divided column graph is a type of bar graph that shows how all the parts in each column relate to a total quantity

documentation a system of giving credit for borrowed ideas and words

draft an early version of a document that is subject to change

drafting the stage after planning when the writer actually writes a first, second, or third (or later) version of the document

E

electronic resume a chronological or functional resume that is formatted so that it can be sent electronically as an e-mail resume, an ASCII Text resume, a scannable resume, or an online resume

embargo to withhold or delay publication of a story

employment ePortfolio You can improve your chances of getting hired by creating an employment ePortfolio and registering with select social media and job posting sites

ethics a system of moral standards and rules that guides human behavior

ethos appeal to ethics; use of the speaker's or writer's credibility and good character

executive summary a short synopsis of the content of a proposal that is written to meet the needs of a busy decision maker; it is located after the table of contents in a formal proposal

explanation information coming after a step that provides additional data to clarify the step

exploding pie graph pie graph that separates, or "explodes," one wedge from the graph, drawing attention to that piece of the pie

expository writing to explain or inform

external audience receivers outside the sender's organization; listeners outside an organization

F

FAQ an acronym for *Frequently Asked Questions;* a document posted on the Internet containing answers to common questions about a topic

feedback the verbal and nonverbal response to a communication process or product

field research research done in the field, especially through surveys and interviews

field-test to check instructions with a small sample of people to see whether the instructions are clear

fiscal year an organization's operating year

flowchart a drawing with lines and arrows to show a process or series of steps

follow-up letter a letter thanking a prospective employer for an interview

forensic reports investigative reports that analyze evidence for legal purposes

formal outline a listing of main ideas and subtopics arranged in a traditional format of Roman numerals, capital letters, numbers, and lowercase letters

formal presentations presentations that are planned in advance, carefully prepared and rehearsed, and often accompanied by visual aids

formal table numerical information set up in rows and columns and drawn with rules; used to present figures

format the details of a document's arrangement: the type of document, its length, the preferred style manual, and its organization; the layout of a publication; standard elements of a document's presentation

freewriting writing freely to discover an idea; can be open (no topic yet), focused (on a topic), or looping (stopping, summarizing, and continuing)

functional resume a nontraditional resume that organizes information around a person's unique skills in order to highlight his or her special abilities or experience

G

Gantt chart a type of bar graph used to schedule the major tasks of a complex project; it uses bars to depict the length of time needed to complete each task

goodwill a feeling of friendship; the value of doing things that create mutual admiration and respect

graphic organizers the use of circles, rectangles, and connecting lines in notes to show the relative importance of one piece of information to another

graphics information presented in a visual form, such as tables, graphs, and diagrams

groupthink the tendency of group members to conform to the wishes of the group without thinking through an issue individually

H

hierarchical order the order in which names are listed from the top to the bottom of an organizational chart

histogram is a type of bar graph. Instead of specific numbers, however, this graph uses ranges of numbers derived from the data collected rather than separate categories. A histogram is appropriate for depicting the frequency of an occurrence

home page the first page of a website

hook in a news story, opening elements whose purpose is to engage the reader, grab his or her attention, and lead into the subject; attention-getters; words or sentences designed to engage the reader or to create interest in an idea

hyperlink a word, phrase, or graphic used to allow readers of a web page to move easily to another page; also called a *link*

I

icon a simple, easily recognizable picture or drawing that represents an idea or a concept; often used as a signal for recurring ideas or themes in a document

imaginative writing writing such as novels, short stories, drama, and poetry whose situations grow out of fantasy or imagination; events and people are fictional although the themes may reveal universal truths

imperative mood the form of a verb that signals a command or an instruction; the subject is "you" or understood "you"

incident reports reports that objectively relate the details of unusual events, such as accidents or equipment malfunctions

indirect approach a presentation strategy in which the main idea is not presented up front; the speaker builds evidence to convince the audience of his or her point

inductive reasoning reasoning from the particular to the general

inferences judgments about a reading that the author does not make for the reader

informal outline a listing of main ideas and subtopics arranged in a less traditional format of single headings and indented notes

informal presentations presentations that occur without preparation or rehearsal

informal table a graphic that uses rows and columns drawn without rules or stubs

information graphic To combine text and graphics to present factual information quickly, There is a finds this information graphic (also infographic) from the CDC

instructions a sequence of steps explaining how to complete a task

interactive refers to any document, such as a website, that responds to user input

internal audience receivers inside the sender's organization; listeners within an organization

Internet a global system of networks connecting computers through the World Wide Web, e-mail, instant messaging, and other protocols

J

jargon the highly specialized language of a discipline or technical field

K

kairos appeal to the opportune moment, the best time to deliver a message

keywords important words, especially nouns, that indicate subject areas in a web document; words in a scannable resume that match the employer's list of key qualifications

L

letter of transmittal a letter formally or officially conveying a formal report from the writers to the external audience

limitations factors or situations that prevent problem solving

line graph a graph using a horizontal axis and a vertical axis to show a trend or relationship among numbers

literary reading reading literature such as short stories, essays, poetry, and novels

logos appeal to logic; use of evidence and a well-reasoned argument

M

mechanism description a description of the main parts of a device or machine; includes the purpose of the device and an overall description, a description of the parts, and the function of each part

media systems or means of mass communication

medium a means by which information is conveyed, such as a newspaper article, a television commercial, or a speech before a live audience

memo of transmittal a memo formally or officially conveying a formal report from the writers to the internal audience

modified block letter the letter style in which the dateline and closing begin at the center of the page

multiple audience an audience that includes readers whose points of view differ

multiple bar graph a graph using horizontal and vertical axes to compare data, drawn with more than one bar for each measurement

multiple line graph a graph using more than one line to compare data

O

objectivity an attitude signifying that no personal bias or opinion has distorted or slanted a researcher's thinking

online instructions instructions using computer technology as the medium; include help menus, CD-ROMs, and web-based instructions

online resume a type of electronic resume posted on a website

open-ended questions questions that encourage the respondent to provide any answer he or she likes; the questions give no suggested answers

organizational chart a drawing with boxes, words, and lines to show how an organization is structured

P

pace to read efficiently; to read at a rate that is slow enough to allow the mind to absorb information but fast enough to complete the reading assignment

pagination the assignment of sequential page numbers within a document

parallel structure use of the same grammatical structure of a phrase or sentence

paraphrase to present someone else's ideas in your own words, phrases, and sentence structure

passive voice the verb *to be* plus the past participle of the verb; used in scientific writing to focus on the process instead of the performer

pathos appeal to emotion; identification with or sympathy for an audience or cause

periodic reports reports that explain the accomplishments for all projects of a work group or of an entire organization during the reporting period

periodicals materials published at specified intervals of time, such as magazines, journals, newsletters, and newspapers

personal code of ethics a personal creed or philosophy that expresses an individual's core values

persuasive writing writing to convince others

pictograph a type of bar graph that uses pictures instead of bars to represent data

pie graph a circular graph showing how parts relate to the whole, which equals 100 percent

plagiarism the act of using another person's words and/or ideas without properly documenting their source or giving credit

planning the first stage of the writing process, during which a writer thinks of an idea and plans how to develop and research it

point-by-point organization a comparison/contrast structure that covers two or three items under one criterion

population the group from whom you want to gather data

prefatory material parts or elements of a report (letter or memo of transmittal, title page, and table of contents) that come before the main text

previewing looking over a reading assignment before reading it; determining the subject matter and any questions about the material before reading it

primary audience the readers or listeners to whom you are responsible first; often the readers(s) who requested or authorized the document

primary sources direct or firsthand reports of facts or observations, such as an eyewitness account or a diary

principles rules that guide behavior

priority order the organization of a resume that presents information from most important to least important

process description usually explain events that happen through time without the reader's taking action, such as photosynthesis, yeast growth in bread production, or the election of a U.S. president

progress reports reports that describe the work that has been completed during a specified time on only one project

proposal a persuasive document that offers a solution to an identified problem or need

PSAs an acronym for *public service announcements;* news published for the benefit of the public

public relations plans or actions taken by an individual or an organization to create a positive relationship with the public

publishing sending a document to the person who requested it

purpose a specific end or outcome to be obtained; what you want your reader to do after reading your document

R

rank the relative importance of one criterion to another; usually ranked from most important to least important

receptive audience readers who are open to ideas or suggestions in a recommendation report

recommendation report a report that responds to a need that arises in the workplace; it suggests the best solution to a problem or need, helping the readers to make a choice

recursive a circular or back-and-forth motion; describes the movement of the writing process back and forth between predictable stages

reliable data data that provide results that can be duplicated under similar circumstances

reporting period the time span covered by a report

resignation letter a letter written to an employer or a supervisor stating the writer's intention to resign his or her position with the company

respondents people chosen to answer questions

result an observable effect of an experiment

resume a one- or two-page summary of a person's job qualifications; uses elements of page design to highlight the applicant's most impressive qualifications

retrospective testing checking the usefulness of a product or an activity after someone has used the product or performed the activity

reverse chronological order the organization of a resume that presents information backward in time

revising reading a document and making changes in content, organization, and word choice

RFP an acronym for *request for proposal*; an advertisement seeking proposals to solve a problem or fill a need and often listing criteria for the solution

rhetorical act A rhetorical act, or communication process designed to influence another's point of view, requires a speaker or writer to think through the rhetorical situation

rhetorical question a question designed to provoke thought; a question for which the speaker expects no answer

rhetorical sensitivity adapting a message to the audience's needs and wants and framing it within a relevant context

rhetorical situation the real-life event prompting the need for some kind of response

rights personal freedoms that must be respected

role the function or job someone performs at work

RSS an acronym for *Really Simple Syndication;* standardized web feed formats that allow blog posts to be sent directly to readers

S

sample a subgroup with the same characteristics as the entire population

satisficing a term coined by Herbert Simon to describe the tendency of a consumer to choose a quick solution that is good enough rather than invest time in figuring out the best solution

scannable refers to text for the Web that allows readers to locate important words and phrases quickly, using short paragraphs and sentences, headings, lists, and keywords

scannable resumes resumes written to be scanned for keywords by an optical scanner

scientific method the use of both inductive and deductive reasoning and a system of controls to objectively explore natural phenomena

scope the extent of treatment, activity, or influence; what is included and what is not included; what you examine in your efforts to solve a particular problem

secondary audience the reader(s) to whom you are responsible after you have met the needs of the primary audience

secondary sources indirect or secondhand reports of information, such as the description of an event the writer or speaker did not witness

shaping a step early in the writing process during which a writer narrows a topic, determines a direction for a topic, generates subtopics, and organizes the subtopics

social media is web-based software that allows users to share content with others in an online community.

solicited refers to a document, such as a report, in which readers ask for several alternatives

solicited letter a letter of application written for an advertised position

solicited proposal a proposal that is written in response to an RFP or upon the request of a supervisor or manager

spatial order refers to mechanism descriptions that explain the parts from left to right, right to left, top to bottom, or bottom to top or in another logical pattern

specific audience a single person or group whose point of view is the same

standard a means of defining and limiting a criterion

standard conventions expectations for content, organization, and design—which have evolved over Facebook's short life span

step one action in a set of instructions

style the way an author uses words and sentences

subcriteria smaller categories under a category that help to define each criterion

summarize to condense longer material, keeping essential or main ideas and omitting unnecessary parts such as examples and illustrations

summary a condensed version of a piece of communication; includes general information and may include a few important details

synchronous events occurring at the same time

T

target audience the audience for which a message is written; the audience with whom the writer seeks to communicate

technical communication communication done in the workplace; the subject is usually technical; the purpose and audience are specific; the approach is straightforward

technical reading reading science, business, or technology publications

technical vocabulary specialized words used in specific ways unique to a particular discipline

technical writing writing done in the workplace; the subject is usually technical, written carefully for a specific audience; the organization is predictable and apparent; the style is concise; the tone is objective and businesslike; special features include visual elements

tentative outline an informal, changeable plan for organizing topics and subtopics

testimonials personal stories or people's statements (often from famous people) that endorse a product or service

text file an ASCII plain text fi le that can be opened by most word processing programs

tone emotional overtones; the way words make readers feel

trip reports reports that tell what was accomplished during a trip and what was learned from the trip

U

unreceptive audience readers who are not open to ideas or suggestions

unsolicited refers to a document, such as a report, that has not been asked for; the audience is not expecting the recommendations

unsolicited letter a letter of application written for an unadvertised position

unsolicited proposal a proposal in which the writer identifies a problem or need that he or she discovered, explains it, and offers solutions

usability the ease with which an audience can access and use a website

utility a means of evaluating actions based on what will do the most good and the least harm

V

valid data data that provide an accurate measurement of what an individual intends to measure

values ideals that govern a person's or an organization's actions

verbal tables tables that use words instead of numbers and the information is given in rows and columns

video resume Sent or posted electronically and useful especially for the performing arts or careers relying on presentation skills such as teaching or sales

warnings statements designed to keep a person from being harmed

Web Accessibility Initiative (WAI) a program intended to make web content available to users with a wide range of disabilities; websites should follow the program's Web Content Accessibility Guidelines 2.0

whistle-blower a person who publicly alleges an organization's wrongful practices

wiki a website that allows users to author web pages collaboratively

World Wide Web a collection of online resources such as websites

writing process the stages a writer goes through to write a document; includes planning (prewriting, shaping, researching), drafting and revising, and copyediting